Aggrieved Taxpayers Versus Tax Authorities

Aggrieved Taxpayers Versus Tax Authorities

Naoki Matsuda

Wolters Kluwer

Published by:
Kluwer Law International B.V.
PO Box 316
2400 AH Alphen aan den Rijn
The Netherlands
E-mail: lrs-sales@wolterskluwer.com
Website: www.wolterskluwer.com/en/solutions/kluwerlawinternational

Sold and distributed by:
Wolters Kluwer Legal & Regulatory U.S.
920 Links Avenue
Landisville, PA 17538
United States of America
E-mail: customer.service@wolterskluwer.com

ISBN 978-94-035-2208-1

e-Book: ISBN 978-94-035-2218-0
web-PDF: ISBN 978-94-035-2228-9

Table of Contents

List of Abbreviations

AAT	Administrative Appeals Tribunal
AATA	Australian Appeals Tribunal Act
ABN	Australian Business Number
ACCC	Aarhus Convention Compliance Committee
AD (JR)	Administrative Decision (Judicial Review)
ADA	Americans with Disabilities Act
ADJRA	Administrative Decisions (Judicial Review) Act 1977
ADML	Administrative Law Manual
ADR	Alternative/Administrative Dispute Resolution
AG	(NTA's) Administrative Guideline
AGRNT	Act on General Rules for National Taxes
ALRC	Australian Law Review Commission
APA	Advance Pricing Agreement
ARs	(NTA's) Administrative Rulings
ARTG	Appeals Reviews and Tax Tribunals Guidance
AR 6	Clause 6 of (NTA's) Administrative Rulings on Assets Valuation
AR ex 24-4	Ex Clause 24-4 of (NTA's) Administrative Rulings on Assets Valuation
ATO	Australian Taxation Office
BC	British Columbia
C&AG	Ireland's Office of the Comptroller and Auditor General
CDP	Collection Due Process
CFR	Code of Federal Regulations/Register
CH	Compliance Handbook
CIR	Commissioner of Inland Revenue
Cir.	Circuit Court

CIT(A)	Corporate Income Tax (Act)
CJIP	convention judiciaire d'intérêt public (Public Interest Judicial Convention)
Collection Act	National Taxes Collection Act
CP	Collection Process/Collection Procedure
CPA	Civil Procedure Act
CPR	Civil Procedure Rules
CRCA	Commissioners for Revenue and Customs Act
CT(A)	Consumption Tax (Act)
CTD	Collection of Tax Tribunal decisions
DRU	Disputes Review Unit
ECHR	European Court of Human Rights/European Convention on Human Rights
ECJ	Court of Justice of the European Union
EEC EIA	Environmental Impact Assessment
et al.	Et alia (and others)
FBAR	Reports of Foreign Financial Accounts
FCT	Federal Commissioner of Taxation
Fed. CL	US Court of Federal Claims
FTM	Fast Track Mediation
FTP	Failure to Pay Penalty
FTS	Fast Track Settlement
FTT	First-Tier Tribunal
FY	fiscal year
GAO	United States General Accounting Office
GST	Goods and Services Tax
GTA	General Tax Act (Algemene wet inzake rijksbelastingen)
HL	House of Lords
HMRC	Her Majesty's Revenue & Customs
HMRC TAC	Tax Assurance Commissioner
HR	Hoge Raad
H.R.	House of Representatives
IASP	Independent Assurance of Settlement Program
ICTA	Income and Corporation Taxes Act
IGT(A)	Inheritance/Gift Tax Act or Inspector General of Taxation
IR(D)	Ireland's Inland Revenue (Department)
IRC	Inland Revenue Code/Inland Revenue Commissioners
IRM	Inland Revenue Manual
IRS	Inland Revenue Service
IS	Information Statement
IT(A)	Income Tax (Act)

ITAA	Income Tax Assessment Act
JCT	Joint Committee of Taxation
JSIC	Japan's Standard Industry Classification
LAPSO Act	Legal Aid, Sentencing and Punishment of Offenders Act 2002
LITC	Low Income Taxpayer Clinic
LJ	Lord Justice
LRC	Law Reform Commission
NAO	Australian National Audit Office
NL	Netherlands
NOPA	Notice of Proposed Adjustment
NOR	Notice of Response
NSW	New South Wales
NTA	(Japan's) National Tax Agency
NZ	New Zealand
OAC	Office of the Appeals Commissioners
P	a person
PL/P.L./Pub.L.	Public Law
PS LA	Law Administration Practice Statement
Ref.	References (in the end pages of the book)
Rev.	Revenue
Rev. Rul.	Revenue Ruling
S	Senate
SAM	Self-Assessment Manual
SB/SE	Small Business/Small Enterprise
SCCO	Senior Courts Costs Office
SDGs	Sustainable Development Goals
SOR	Statutory Orders and Regulations
SPC	Special Commissioner
SPS	Standard Practice Statement
STML	Special Taxation Measures Law
T(TARM) Act 2011	Taxation (Tax Administration and Remedial Matters) Act 2011
TAA	Australia's Taxation Administration Act or NZ's Tax Administration Act
TABOR	Taxpayer Bill of Rights
TAC (Ireland)	Tax Appeals Commission
TAS	Office of the Taxpayer Advocate Service
Tax Tribunal	National Tax (Appeals) Tribunal
TC/T.C.	Tax Court
TCE Act	Tax Tribunals, Courts and Enforcement Act 2007
TDRB	Tax Disputes Resolution Board

TFEU	Treaty on the Functioning of the European Union
TMA	Tax Management Act
TP	Transfer Pricing
TR	Taxation Ruling
TRA	NZ's Taxation Review Authority
U.S.C.	United States Code
USPR	Uniform Civil Procedures Rule
VAT(A)	Value Added Tax (Act)
WT	Withholding Tax

Prologue

The number of tax disputes in Japan is less than that in other major countries.[1] This is desirable from the standpoint of realizing speedy resolution of tax disputes and of reducing the burden of courts and the National Tax Tribunal (hereinafter referred to as the "Tax Tribunal"), which is the administrative body that handles aggrieved taxpayers' objections (review requests) on the tax re/assessments made on them. However, the relatively small number of tax disputes does not necessarily mean that there are no problems or challenges to be addressed.[2] For example, the Judicial System Reform Council's opinion dated 6/12/2001 proposed the establishment of such a judicial system that would enable people to have easy access to the judiciary and obtain substantial, prompt, and effective judicial remedies that meet their diverse needs, and it pointed out the need for reforms to realize such judicial system. Lying under such a proposal, there must be a recognition that the relatively small number of administrative case litigations as a whole in Japan is not an absolute blessing but contains issues and rules to be discussed and reformed as well. The judicial system applicable currently to tax disputes in Japan may not be an exception to such a call for discussions and reforms.

In this connection, it is worth noting that the Sustainable Development Goals (SDGs) lists, in the 2030 Agenda for Sustainable Development, Goal 16 (Peace, justice, and strong institutions), whose main objectives include the assurance of "equal access to justice" for all. As for the level of Japan's attainment of this Goal, the SDGs Media Compact, which was established in 2018 with the aim of raising awareness of the "Sustainable Development Goals," reported that challenges remain in the case of Japan in 2017, while in 2021, it reported that Japan is "on track or maintaining SDG's achievement." It might be open to question whether such an evaluation in the 2021

1. In this book, aggrieved taxpayers' objections to tax authorities and tax litigations at court over the disputed tax re/assessments, etc., are collectively referred to as tax disputes, and here tax disputes mean only those disputes over national taxes or federal taxes.
2. The fact that there is a relatively small number of tax disputes may, depending on the causes for it, not be absolute blessing even for the tax authority. The analysis in this book confirms this point. *See* the paragraph just below Figure 1.9 and Epilogue in Chapter 6.

report is appropriate or not. Even if it is appropriate, there is no question that there is room for improvement in the current system, as suggested by the abovementioned Judicial System Reform Council's 2001 opinion. Particularly in light of such opinion and SDG's Goal 16, it might be that the relatively small number of tax disputes in Japan also has some negative aspects, which may include a possibility that there are some administrative/judicial systems or practices that are functioning in such a way that they restrict aggrieved taxpayers' access to justice in one way or another.

Doubtlessly, there should be various reasons and factors responsible for Japan's relatively small number of tax disputes. It is generally said that Japanese people do not like conflicts, and their legal compliance level is also high. These reasons may be partially responsible for the small number of administrative appeals and litigations as a whole. Furthermore, in the context of taxation, the relationship between the tax authorities and taxpayers is relatively good, and tax re/assessments are generally solid and made rather cautiously. Even so, some point out that other reasons and causes are exerting a strong influence on the number of litigations on administrative cases. Some of them also assert that includable in them are the cost of time and money needed for the litigations, imbalance of power between people/claimants and the government, courts' judicial deference, and so forth. Those reasons and causes could, in some cases, give people a sense that, coupled with the current low ratio of court rulings in favor of the appellants, litigations on administrative cases against government agencies are not worthwhile.[3] It might be that those reasons and causes are also at work considerably in the case of taxpayers who are aggrieved over the tax re/assessments on them.

It is also true that, in addition to those mentioned above, there should be other reasons, factors, and systems that also exert a strong influence on the number of tax disputes. For instance, tax structure, wordings of tax law, the number of taxpayers subject to taxation, the annual number of tax audits, the ratio of revocation of the disputed re/assessments by the organs in charge of reviewing them, variations in their ways of resolving tax disputes and so forth must affect the number of tax disputes as well. Indeed, the status and realities of those factors and systems should vary from one country to another, and some countries may also have a few factors or attributes that are rather peculiar to them and function as strong inducers of tax disputes. In this book, attempts are made to look into and analyze those factors, systems, and so forth in various countries that have a lot to do with the number of tax disputes in those countries. Such analysis would help shed a brighter light on the reasons for the small number of tax disputes in Japan and give some insights on what options are worth discussing for addressing problems and challenges that lie beneath the fact of tax disputes in Japan being small in number.

Meanwhile, in line with the recent global trend of increasing taxpayers' awareness of their rights, every country has lately been facing two fundamental challenges: (i) realizing speedier resolution of tax disputes and (ii) improving taxpayers' access to justice. Progress in realizing both of those two challenges is basically beneficial for taxpayers, but efforts to address the above (i) challenge often defeat those efforts to

3. *See* Yasutaka Abe, Bibliography (1) p. 28.

address the above (ii) challenge because improved access to justice would increase the number of tax disputes, making it more difficult to deal with the above (i) challenge.[4] Therefore, usually, the need for addressing those two challenges should be weighed out, and a balance needs to be struck between those two efforts. It must be interesting to look into how such balance has been attained in some major countries and what kind of relevant reforms have been lately implemented to fine-tune such balance. The countries this book highlights to make comparisons with and draw insights from include, in particular, the U.S., the UK, some Commonwealth countries (Australia and NZ), and EU countries (Ireland and the Netherlands). Those countries are equipped with some systems and practices not available in Japan, which could greatly affect the number of tax disputes, and some of them have gone through significant reforms lately.

The author is no expert in foreign countries' tax affairs and tax litigations, so this book is only for general information purposes. Moreover, in drafting this book, the author encountered some problems that are mostly attributable to the limited publication of data on the details of tax objections and review results in foreign countries. Despite such problems and limitations, as well as the above nature/purpose of this book, the author hopes that the book has succeeded to some extent not only in extracting the key factors that affect the number of tax disputes but also in attempting to make cross-country comparison of how those factors could be at work in various countries. Also, the author hopes that this book's rough general illustrations of the rules and practices on tax disputes, their realities and their resolutions in those countries will assist the readers to have a bird's-eye view of them and interest them to look further into some of them.[5] The author concludes this Prologue by expressing much gratitude to several tax authorities and review organs that provided the author in 2019 and 2020 with some relevant information and knowledge.[6]

4. Zuckerman states that all countries have long tried to reduce the delays and costs of litigation, but few have had even moderate success in reaching a sensible balance. *See* Andrian Zuckerman, Justice in Crisis: Comparative Dimensions of Civil Procedure, *Civil Justice in Crisis: Comparative Perspectives of Civil Procedure,* Oxford University Press (1999) p. 51.
5. The issues covered in this book and some more also appear in the author's book "*Sozeifunso*" written in Japanese that is published by *Zaikeishohosha* in 2024.
6. They include the IRS's Office of Appeals, the U.S. Tax Court, NZ's Inland Revenue and the Taxation Review Authority, Ireland's Revenue and the Tax Appeals Commission, the tax authority in the Netherlands. Also, Dr. Vishakha Singh (Indian Revenue Service) kindly did some editing for the book, but the views expressed in the book are of the author only.

Executive Summary

The number of tax disputes (taxpayers' objections/appeals to the Tax Tribunal and courts concerning the NTA's re/assessments on their national taxes, administrative (civil) penalties, and collection actions, etc.) in Japan is much smaller than that in other major countries. This is bound to raise such questions as: ① What are the main causes for that? ② It must be wonderful for the tax authority, but is it good for taxpayers? The possible answer to the above question ② is generally in the affirmative in that they can expect speedy decisions/rulings on their objections/appeals, while there are also some negative sides to it, making it worthwhile to discuss possible reform options to mitigate some of them. This book aims to come up with answers to the above question ①, and, as for question ② that might receive both positive and negative answers, searches for some reform options that could make the latter less negative through the analysis and extraction of lessons from some other major countries' rules, practices and facts that exert not a little influence on the number of tax disputes and their resolutions.

In Chapter 1 (Status in Japan), Section 1 narrates major rules, facts, issues and data concerning taxpayers' objections raised and handled by the assessors (in most cases, tax offices) and the Tax Tribunal. The Tax Tribunal is a semi-independent review organ with the mission of securing taxpayers' rights as well as sound tax administration. The majority of its reviewers are officials dispatched and seconded for a fixed term (usually for a couple of years) from the NTA, while its decisions bind the NTA only. Among the overviews shown in the section, especially notable is the fact that the decisions of the tax assessors and the Tax Tribunal are given without much delay, while the ratio of decisions canceling the disputed re/assessments has not been so high (lately, around 10%). It is also observable that, due to the 2014 reform of the Act on General Rules for National Taxes (AGRNT), the number of objections brought directly to the Tax Tribunal without going through the stage of objections to the assessors has been on the rise since then, placing a heavier burden on the Tax Tribunal in attaining its proclaimed goal of processing more than 95% of the objections within one year that has mostly been attained so far.

Sections 2 to 3 extract "highly disputed (tax) themes" and look for those attributes contained in them that work as inducements for some tax provisions to be disputed more frequently than others. In this book, the decision of which themes or tax provisions are highly disputed ones is made in accordance with the number of the Tax Tribunal decisions made public on its HP (*see* Attachment), while there is a possibility and limitation that in some cases, such number does not reflect well the actual level of frequency of those themes being disputed because not all of its decisions are disclosed on its HP. Despite such possible limitations, the analysis of those "highly disputed themes" should help reveal a couple of distinguishing attributes in some tax provisions that work as strong inducements for taxpayers to dispute the legality/adequacy of the re/assessments that pivot on those themes and tax provisions. In fact, the analysis has led the author to conclude that such attributes contained in those tax provisions include, in particular: (i) uncertainty in the scope of their application, (ii) allowance of exceptions/salvation, and (iii) grant of preferential treatments.

In Section 4, the author has confirmed that tax provisions with the above (ii) and (iii) attributes often induce taxpayers' inappropriate attempts to avail exceptions and preferential treatments allowed under those provisions. Identifying those attributes and their effects is certainly important for willowing out the main causes for tax disputes, but it does not lead us to concrete reform options that would directly mitigate some negative aspects of the current systems and rules related to tax disputes. Therefore, some propose such direct reform options as follows: (i) detaching the Tax Tribunal completely from the NTA and transferring it under the control of the Cabinet Minister, (ii) replacing the Tax Tribunal with a Tax Court, (iii) granting the NTA a power to enter into agreements on tax disputes with aggrieved taxpayers in some cases, (iv) granting some aggrieved taxpayers an option of having its case reviewed and decided by a neutral body prior to the re/assessments as in the case of Korea, and (v) enabling successful nationals in litigations against the government to recover their attorney's fees.

In Chapter 2 (Status in the U.S.), Section 1 portrays the main characteristics of tax objection procedures adopted by the Office of Appeals in the Inland Revenue Service (IRS). As its mission states, the Office of Appeals aims, whenever appropriate, to settle tax disputes without litigation. To carry out its mission, it weighs litigation risk and very frequently enters into a flexible settlement with an aggrieved taxpayer before a "90-day letter" (a Notice of Deficiency) is issued to the taxpayer. About 85% to 90% of the disputes brought to the Office of Appeals are resolved without ending up in court. Some of the major limitations imposed on the Office of Appeals' power to resolve tax disputes flexibly include the prohibition of ex parte communication, nuisance value settlements, and using penalty as a bargaining chip for maintaining the disputed re/assessments. Lately, Alternative/Administrative Dispute Resolution (ADR), including Fast Track Settlement, has also been used as one method of flexible settlement, but the National Taxpayer Advocate has frequently pointed out that it has still been underutilized.

Section 2 explains the function of the Tax Court. Despite the Tax Court's tradition of not looking behind a Notice of Deficiency and its not-so-high ratio of upholding the appeal (lately, about 20% on average), the majority of aggrieved taxpayers opt for the Tax Court rather than the District Courts or Court of Federal Claims mainly because: (i) the Tax Court allows litigation without prepayment of the disputed tax amount, (ii) the

Tax Court has special trial judges in charge of small cases to realize speedy decision-making with no right of the disputants for further appeal, (iii) a Notice of Deficiency mentions only the Tax Court. The majority of tax disputes (78% on average during 2012-2021) at the Tax Court are also resolved by agreements between the parties in disputes. A high percentage (lately about 90% in the case of Small Claim cases and 50% in the other cases) of plaintiffs at the Tax Court are pro se litigants, and it is reported that the ratio of the Tax Court decisions favorable for them is 10% to 20% lower than that for litigants with representatives.

Section 3 explores the "American rule" or the party/party rule as it applies as the costs rule on the parties in administrative and judicial proceedings and its metamorphosis/evolution. The "American rule" does not let the prevailing party in the judicial proceedings recover its attorney's fee from the other party. But it has evolved in such a way that the purport of the Civil Right Attorney Fees Act of 1976 of allowing the court's discretion in shifting the burden of the prevailing party's reasonable attorney's fee to the other party was adopted in many legislations (Educational Laws, Environmental Laws, etc.). Likewise, U.S. Code Title 28 §2412, which was revised by the Equal Access to Justice Act of 1980, set a rule to allow the prevailing party (other than the United States) meeting the net worth requirements to recover its reasonable attorney's fee unless the U.S. government's position in the proceeding is substantially justified or special circumstances exist, and such rule was legislated as it is or with some modifications in various Acts (IRC §7430, Consumer Protection Law, etc.).

Section 4 sheds light on highly litigated tax cases/issues. Those cases ranked in the most litigated ten issues almost every year at the Tax Court are penalty issues, Collection Due Process issues, innocent spouse relief issues, gross income issues, and trade or business expenses issues. The reasons for them to be ranked high in the list of most litigated cases vary from one to another, but they tend to have attributes similar to those (in particular, uncertainty in the scope of application and allowance of exceptions) found in the tax provisions that are highly disputed at Japan's Tax Tribunal. For example, in the case of an innocent spouse relief clause, its scope of application is by no means clear, and it also has the attribute of temping a taxpayer to claim that there are private circumstances of the taxpayer that the IRS is not aware of and they are claimed to indicate the fact that the taxpayer had no reason to know the causes for the under-reporting of its spouse's income on the joint return so that the taxpayer should be relieved from his joint and several liabilities on it.

In Chapter 3 (Status in the UK), Section 1 describes the outline of tax dispute procedures adopted before and after the introduction of the 2007 Act (the Tribunals, Courts and Enforcement Act) and the issue of Treasury Order No. 56 (The Transfer of Tribunal Functions and Revenue and Customs Appeal Order 2009). Under the old tax dispute procedures, there were General/Special Commissioners appointed by the Chancellor of the Exchequer (Lord Chancellor after 1986), as well as various types of tribunals. There were many tax disputes (in particular penalty cases) brought to those review organs. More than 90% of them were settled by agreements between taxpayers and the tax authority, which could be justified by the care and management function of the Commissioner. Even so, as pointed out in the 2002 Report of Lord Chancellor's Department, the old tax dispute procedures had some rules and practices that could be amended to provide aggrieved taxpayers with a higher level of convenience and more independent review of their cases.

As Section 2 expounds, under the current tax dispute procedures, the door of statutory reviews offered by the Solicitor's Office and Legal Services of the tax authority (HMRC) has been opened more widely, and lately, the ratio of disputed re/assessments canceled at the stage of the HMRC's statutory reviews is about 50% to 60%. Moreover, the HMRC has been willing to utilize ADR at any stage of disputes whenever it is appropriate, and the recent ratio of succeeding in resolving disputes in the case of ADR has been as high as 80% to 90%. The width of the Commissioner's care and management function is also observable from the fact that its exercise is not subject to judicial review unless it is deemed quite unreasonable ("Wednesbury unreasonableness"). Nevertheless, it is notable that, to secure a higher level of trust in tax administration, the Tax Assurance Commissioner and some other inner review groups were appointed and set up in the HMRC in 2012, and they monitor settlements with taxpayers on big/complex tax dispute cases.

Section 3 enquires into the function of Tribunals. Lately, the First-tier Tribunal annually receives 4,000 to 7,000 cases of tax objections, and its ratio of revoking wholly or partially the disputed re/assessments is about 20% to 50%. Those cases are to be classified at the First-tier Tribunal into four categories, and the procedures and rules on them differ depending on the category they come under. Usually, relatively simple cases are handled speedily as Default Paper Cases and some Basic Cases may not require hearings. As for Complex Cases, they take a longer time before decisions are handed down and the decisions usually contain orders for costs because the "English rule" (or "Costs follow the event") is applicable and the HMRC does not apply the "Sheldon practice" (HMRC's practice of not asking costs recovery) to unsuccessful taxpayers with Complex Cases as well as those at the Upper Tribunal and courts while the "Rees practice" (which is applicable when the Tribunal decision favorable to a taxpayer is overturned by court's ruling) is observed by the HMRC.

Section 4 delineates the metamorphosis/evolution of the "English rule." The "English rule" or the "Costs follow the event" rule has merit in discouraging unworthy disputes from entering into the litigation stage. But it may also discourage meritorious ones from appearing on a litigation stage. Recent increases in the accumulation of the number of tax objections at the First-tier Tribunal could make this negative effect more conspicuous. While the "English rule" has metamorphosed itself in such a way that it allows its exceptions in some cases. One example is the Litigant in Person (Costs and Expenses) Act 1975 §1, which allows some recovery of costs of a successful litigant in person that are incurred in connection with the proceedings. Also, there are methods and services, such as "McKenzie friend," conditional fee agreements, after-the-event insurance premiums, etc., that could be utilized by some taxpayers with limited financial means to reduce the risk and burden involved in the litigation.

Section 5 probes into the reasons why a penalty case is a much-disputed one in the UK. Reasons for penalty cases to be highly disputed lie in the fact that there are a large number of impositions of automatically assessed penalties as well as behavioral penalties, and they could be mitigated, exempted, or suspended under the collection and management function of the Commissioner, by the discretion of authorized HMRC officials and reasonable excuse exceptions and so forth. Particularly, in the case of shortfall penalties, their rates vary depending on the behavior (reasons for under-reporting, level of disclosure and cooperation, etc.) of the taxpayers and thus have uncertainty and flexibility in their application, resulting in disputes frequently brought to the First-tier Tribunal. In reality, objections to penalty impositions brought to the HMRC's statutory review and the First-tier Tribunal are quite large in number, and they are abated quite often by their decisions (lately 50% to 80% in the case of a statutory review).

In Chapter 4 (Status in Australia and NZ), Section 1 gives an overview of Australia's tax dispute procedures and their main features. The number of taxpayers' objections to taxation decisions or statements of audit position (in the case of large business taxpayers) brought to the tax authority (ATO) has been relatively large, and the ratio of them being canceled fully or partially often exceeded 50%. Some pointed out that the ATO used to be not so willing to settle disputes by agreements with taxpayers, but the ATO's stance over agreements has gradually changed, as manifested in the introduction in 2014 of ADR ("in-house facilitation"), which could be employed at any stage of disputes and the recent increase, particularly in the number of agreements with taxpayers relatively in the early stages of the disputes. Moreover, the variance or the ratio of reduction from the reassessed tax amount after its review has been publicly disclosed to enhance the level of transparency on the agreements and, since 2016, its disclosure includes the agreements reached on big cases, tax avoidance cases, etc., which are subject to the Independent Assurance Program review.

Those taxpayers who did not reach agreements with the ATO or are dissatisfied with the ATO's decisions on the objections tend to choose or opt for the Administrative Appeals Tribunal (AAT) rather than the courts as the next stage of dispute resolution. One of the main reasons for such a choice, even though there has not been much difference in the ratio (lately 40% to 80%) of their decisions/rulings in favor of the aggrieved taxpayers, should be found in the fact that in contrast to the court's judicial review, the AAT could not only vary the ATO's decisions but also, standing in the shoes of the Commissioner, review the appropriateness of the Commissioner's discretion from the perspective of relevant legislations and administrative policies, and, in actuality, frequently makes decisions of setting them aside or substituting them with its own. Another main reason may lie in the fact that shifting of attorney's fees of the successful party to the unsuccessful party in accordance with the "costs follow the event" rule, which is basically applicable in court, does not apply at the stage of the AAT.

Truly, the "costs follow the event" rule adopted in litigations in Australian courts has metamorphosed just as in the UK, but its metamorphosis seems to be less conspicuous as it can be seen in some courts' negative views on the Chorley exception applicable in the UK to a successful solicitor litigating in person. The ATO implements a test case litigation program in which the ATO fully or partially finances taxpayers with several meritorious or important cases when the ATO tries to challenge at court the AAT's decisions on them. They have a similar effect to the UK's "Rees practice" in that both of them could enable taxpayers to avoid the risk of the financial burden that remains under the strict application of the "costs follow the event" rule. Similarity to the UK is also observable in the fact that penalty cases (in particular behavioral penalty cases) and those cases involving the issue of Commissioner's discretion (particularly on provisions subject to extension of time) have been highly disputed.

Section 2 illustrates the main features of tax disputes and relevant rules in NZ. In NZ, the 1994 Richardson Committee Report pointed out that the tax objection procedure at that time took a long time to resolve disputes partially because new issues and pieces of evidence were often submitted at a later stage of the disputes. The current procedure adopted in 1996 is structured to address such problems. As the current procedure is often called a "ritual dance," the disputant and the tax authority (Inland Revenue) are required to follow the strict timeline and should "disclose all the cards on the table," which in principle prohibits new claims from being made at the subsequent dispute stage ("evidence exclusion rule"). It has resulted in the reduction of the number of tax cases brought to the Taxation Review Authority and courts. Some observed that such a result might be partially attributable to the fact that the current objection procedure places a heavy burden on the disputants at the objection stage, and it could burn them out. Moreover, the ratio of decisions of the Disputes Review Unit of the Inland Revenue that are favorable to the disputing taxpayers has been relatively low (lately 4% to 18%).

In light of such observations and situations mentioned above, the "evidence exclusion rule" has been relaxed lately, and the view that the Commissioner can settle tax disputes by agreements has become more dominant. Even so, the overall changes to the conventional rules on tax dispute settlements have not become so conspicuous as in the UK and Australia. For example, ADR has hardly been used to solve tax disputes in NZ, and the "English rule" adopted in NZ is the "primary rule" (sitting somewhere between the "English rule" and the "American rule") by which pro se taxpayers successful at court can recover disbursements but not costs. Moreover, the Tax Administration Act (TAA) §109, which serves as the ouster provision, and the Act §113 (Commissioner may at any time amend assessments) widens the scope of the Commissioner's discretion so much that some cases are outside of the scope of court's judicial review, and a taxpayer's request ("TAA §113 request") for tax refund could be practically denied depending on the resources required to review the related evidence submitted by the taxpayer.

In Chapter 5 (Status in Ireland and Netherlands), Section 1 depicts the outline and main features of Ireland's tax dispute procedures and related facts. It used to be pointed out that the procedures governing Irish tax objections to Inland Revenue (Revenue) and the Office of Appeal Commissioners (OAC) had such challenges and problems as: (i) the OAC's independence was not high enough, (ii) its decisions were not publicly disclosed, (iii) there was the Revenue's intervention in bringing a taxpayer's objection to the OAC, and (iv) accumulation of cases delayed the OAC's decisions. The current tax dispute procedures adopted in March 2016 have solved most of the abovementioned problems. In particular, the availability of a taxpayer's choice of direct submission of a notice of appeal to the Tax Appeals Commission (TAC, which replaced OAC) and publication of the TAC decisions have solved the above (i), (ii), and (iii) problems. Attempts to solve the above (iv) problem have been facilitated by the sharp decline in the number of cases brought to the TAC as well as the recent increase in financial and human resources allocated to the TAC.

As for the rules and practices relating to tax dispute settlement, Ireland is similar to the UK in that, even if the Commissioner's scope of discretion based on the care and management function is not as wide in Ireland as that in the UK, the ratio of settlement by agreements in Ireland is also very high while ADR as a method of tax dispute settlement has still been underutilized in Ireland. Also common to both countries is the large number of civil penalties imposed and the high frequency of disputes on behavioral penalties, while Ireland has the Taxes Consolidation Act §1065, which provides for the discretion of the Commissioner to mitigate a behavioral penalty up to 50%. Although the UK exited the EU in 2019, the impact of EU law is strongly observable in both countries. In the context of penalties and the "English rule," Article 6 of the European Convention on Human Rights and Council directives on the Aarhus Convention impose restrictions on the mode of their application, and the European Commission found that some of their relevant rules and application in UK and Ireland contravened EU Law.

Section 2 highlights some characteristics of tax dispute procedures and related facts in the Netherlands. The Netherlands differs from the abovementioned foreign countries in that it has neither a Tax Tribunal nor a Tax Court. It is also different from them in that it is a civil law country. Despite such differences, they are similar in that, in the Netherlands, many tax disputes are also resolved using agreements with taxpayers, and ADR (particularly mediation) plays a very active role in the flexible resolution of tax disputes. The legal background of flexible resolution of tax disputes in the Netherlands is found in Article 7:900 of civil law (Burgerlijk Wetboek) and the principle of legitimate expectations, which has its origin in the German principle of Vertrauensshtz and has become one of the overriding EU principles through rulings of the European Court of Justice (ECJ). Thus, the principle of legitimate expectations overrides the principle of taxation by law, which is stipulated under Article 104 of the Netherlands' Constitution.

EU law has exerted a profound influence on EU countries' modes of tax dispute settlements. One example is various Council directives on ADR. Another example is Article 107 of the Treaty on the Functioning of the European Union (TFEU), which prohibits State aid from distorting or threatening to distort competition in the EU internal market. The impact of Article 107 of the TFEU on flexible tax dispute settlements has been strong because the European Commission often determined that some agreements with taxpayers in some Member countries, including the Netherlands, were in contravention of the article, and the ECJ ruled in favor of the Commission even in those cases where the Commission turned to "an arm's length principle particular to EU law." Once some agreements with taxpayers are determined or ruled to be State aid, the concerned Member countries are obliged to recover the State aid, and the ECJ ruled in some cases that the principle of legitimate expectations cannot, in principle, be relied upon in justifying their failure to fulfill such obligation.

In Chapter 6 (cross-country comparison and Japan's options for reform), Sections 1 and 2 recount how the following eight *Factors* (①～⑧), which should exert much influence on the number of tax objections/litigations, are at work in the countries covered in the preceding chapters. The author has deduced those *Factors* mainly through the analysis of highly disputed tax issues as well as the scrutiny of relevant systems, rules, and practices on tax dispute settlements in those countries. Those eight *Factors* are: ①*tax structure* (level of tax burden, complexity of tax system, nature/attributes of taxes, scope of tax authority's discretionary power, etc.), ②*tax audit* (audit ratio, ratio/volume of re/assessments, etc.), ③*compliance*, ④*dispute resolution methods* (availability/frequency of flexible dispute resolution, etc.), ⑤*level of disputing taxpayers' burden*, ⑥*structure and performance of the reviewing bodies* (ratio of revocation of disputed re/assessments, etc.), ⑦*complementary (administrative/legal) measures favorable for taxpayers*, and ⑧*requirement for and effect of filing tax objections/litigations*.

Naturally, there are variations in how the effects of the above *Factors* (①～⑧) are like in those foreign countries, but the analysis in Section 1 reveals that as for *Factor* ④*(dispute resolution methods)*, its impact on the number of tax disputes is quite strong because the availability of a flexible tax dispute settlement has an effect of incentivizing some taxpayer's attempt to gain concessions from the tax authorities while the level of its effect varies among those countries depending on how widely they are applicable and how actively agreements with taxpayers are pursued. The effect of *Factor* ⑤*(level of disputing taxpayers' burden)* on the number of tax disputes is also significant because taxpayers' risk and burden in terms of money and time greatly affects taxpayers' decision of whether they initiate administrative objections/litigations. In this sense, it follows that the "English rule" is generally more inhibitive in increasing tax litigations than the "American rule." *Factor* ⑥*(structure and performance of the reviewing bodies)* could also impact such taxpayers' decisions because the ratio of tax objections upheld by the review organs could affect taxpayers' sense of expectation on their cases.

In Section 2, it is stressed that, in Japan, *Factor* ④*(dispute resolution methods)* does not work strongly toward increasing the number of tax disputes because it does not allow flexible settlements once re/assessments are made. In addition, in connection with *Factor* ①*(tax structure) and Factor* ②*(tax audit)*, it could be said that the level of complexity of tax law may not be so conspicuous, and the ratio of audits has been on the decline. As for *Factor* ③*(compliance)*, it is generally high, and taxpayers' trust in tax administration is also fairly high. On *Factor* ⑧*(requirement for and effect of filing tax objections/litigations)*, a filing of an objection to the Tax Tribunal in Japan does not, in principle, suspend tax collection action (except for the procedure of selling seized property by public auction, etc.), so it encourages tax delinquents to raise objections less than otherwise. Those main facts may constitute the primary reasons for the relatively small number of tax objections/litigations in Japan, while the effect of main facts regarding the other *Factors* on the number of tax disputes should be rather neutral because they contain both inducements and deterrents.

The Proposal of transferring the control of the Tax Tribunal to the Cabinet Minister and the Proposal of establishing a Tax Court in Japan referred to in Chapter 1 are particularly relevant to *Factors* ⑤*(level of disputing taxpayers' burden)* and ⑥*(structure and performance of the reviewing bodies)*, and they might also increase the number of tax disputes. However, the author concludes in Section 3 that they might not lessen taxpayers' burden mainly because they should entail the grant to the NTA the right to appeal their decisions to court. The Proposal of introducing in Japan such a tax dispute pre-review system similar to that in Korea has a similar problem of depriving the tax authority of its absolute power on the re/assessment. Therefore, in Section 4, the author makes a few proposals, which include, in connection with *Factor ②(tax audit)*, more resources for the NTA to deter the declining trend of its audit ratio and also, in connection with *Factor ⑤*, adopting a rule that allows a successful taxpayer (with limited means) on a nontax-avoidance case to recover its reasonable litigation costs solely in a case where the tax authority loses on its appeal against the preceding court's ruling favorable to the taxpayer.

CHAPTER 1
Status in Japan

SECTION 1 OVERVIEW OF TAX OBJECTIONS AND TAX TRIBUNAL

1 Tax Tribunal's Structural Change and Its Function

Nearly 54% of Japan's national revenue in the FY2021 budget was revenue from national taxes.[1] For the same year, the revenue from national taxes represents about 60% of all tax revenue, and tax bases of many major local taxes (except for such taxes as fixed assets tax imposed by municipal governments) are practically piggy-backed on those of such main national taxes as IT, CIT and CT.[2] Therefore, in most cases, taxpayers' primary tax concerns are about the amount of national taxes they have to pay. In cases where they are unsatisfied with the re/assessments made on them,[3] they must follow the tax objection procedures under Chapter 8 (Articles 75-116) of the Act of General Rules on National Taxes (AGRNT). As Figure 1.1 shows, prior to the 2014 revision of AGRNT, aggrieved taxpayers, before they appeal to court, had to file an objection (or make a request for review) to the assessor (tax offices or Regional Tax Bureau, in most cases the former) of the NTA first and then they could appeal further to the Tax Tribunal.[4] The Tax Tribunal was established in 1970 as the NTA's special

1. For details, *see* NTA's Report 2021.
2. For details, *see* 2021 White Paper on Local Finance by MIC (Ministry of Internal Affairs and Communications). Those primary local taxes are inhabitant's tax on individuals and corporations, corporate enterprise tax and local consumption tax.
3. Taxpayers could file objections with the Tax Tribunal on the NTA's determination of refusing requested tax refunds, administrative penalty impositions, tax collection action on them, etc.
4. Prior to this revision, under para. 4 of Article 75 of AGRNT, only blue return filers could opt out of objections to the local tax offices. Tax law provides some preferential treatments to blue return filers who are required to keep books and records properly to maintain its blue return filers' status. See footnote 42. Article 115 provides that, in principle, unless there is a justifiable reason, an objection to the Tax Tribunal must precede an appeal to a court while the appeal can be made once three months have passed after the objection is filed. Article 77 stipulates that no objection

agency for handling national tax disputes,[5] and its mission is to secure taxpayers' legitimate rights and maintain equitable tax administration by correct and speedy handling of disputed cases.

Figure 1.1 Tax Dispute Resolution Procedure

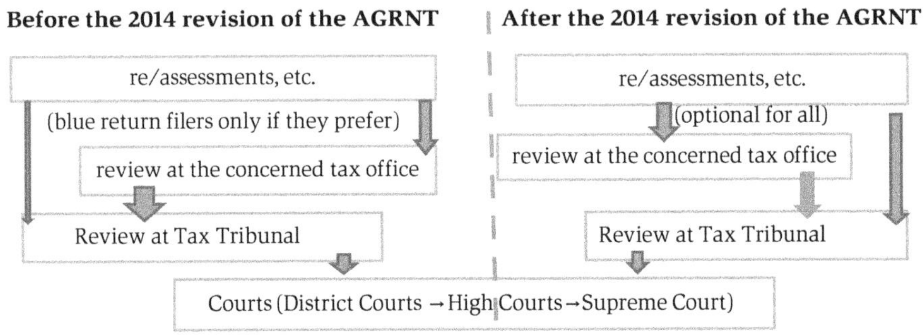

The Headquarters of the Tax Tribunal and the NTA are located in Kasumigaseki, Tokyo. They both have twelve branches (or Regional Tax Bureaus) in the same prefectures, while the Tax Tribunal has an extra seven sub-branches in major urban areas as well. Chapter 8 of AGRNT contains various provisions on the Tax Tribunal. Article 113 of AGRNT dictates that the decision-making authority of the Commissioner General of the Tax Tribunal Headquarters may be delegated to Commissioners of the branches. Actually, in principle, a tax objection is processed by the Tax Tribunal branch that has jurisdiction over the district in which a tax office or a Regional Taxation Bureau has made the disputed re/assessment. Even so, from the perspective of the need to ensure consistency in the Tax Tribunal decisions, there is a certain degree of coordination between the branches and the headquarters in their processing of tax objections.[6] In addition, whenever there is a difference between the Tax Tribunal and the NTA on the interpretation of a relevant provision of Tax Law or NTA's AR that could set a precedent, Article 99 of AGRNT stipulates that the Tax Tribunal decision is to be made based on the conclusion of the National Tax Council which is consisted of tax specialists and knowledgeable members from various professional sectors.

Thus, even if the reviews of the Tax Tribunal are conducted from the perspective of a third party, its level of independence and neutrality in terms of its organizational structure and personnel may not be as high as many aggrieved taxpayers may wish. However, AGRNT does have some provisions and rules on the Tax Tribunal that are

---

to the Tax Tribunal can be made after one year has passed after the receipt of a notice of assessment unless there is a justifiable reason.

5. Article 22(1) of the Act for Establishment of the Treasury stipulates that the Tax Tribunal is established under NTA.
6. For details, *see* Rie Nagata, Bibliography (2) pp. 35-37.

particularly favorable for them. For example: (i) Article 98 of AGRNT forbids the Tax Tribunal from handing down a decision that changes the disputed re/assessment worse for the applicant;[7] (ii) Article 155 of AGRNT does not necessarily require an aggrieved taxpayer to receive the Tax Tribunal decision before he files a suit to court (*see* footnote 4); (iii) Article 102(1) of AGRNT provides that the Tax Tribunal decision binds the NTA so that the NTA, in contrast to the applicant, cannot dispute the validity of the decision in court even if the NTA disagrees with the decision; (iv) Article 102(2) of AGRNT stipulates that the Tax Tribunal can decide on whether the disputed re/assessment is administratively appropriate or not, and if it finds it inappropriate/ unjust, it could be substituted by its decision. In the case of court, it may do the same only when it is unlawful or there is an abuse of the NTA's discretion/digression from its discretionary power.[8]

Nevertheless, there have been some who maintain that there is room for improvement in the structure and the function of the Tax Tribunal so that it becomes more independent and could enhance the level of convenience on the part of aggrieved taxpayers. For example, the Tax Commission (Advisory body to Prime Minister), in its 9/14/2010 report, gave credit to the Tax Tribunal for the fact that about 90% of the disputes brought to the concerned tax offices and to the Tax Tribunal have been resolved without going to court and the Tax Tribunal has contributed much to sorting out points of contentions of the disputed cases, while it also pointed out that further discussions about the structure of the Tax Tribunal, its procedures for making objections, and so forth are needed. A similar view was expressed in the Outline of 2010 Tax Reform, which particularly problematized the fact that not only those staff handling administrative affairs but also those reviewers in charge at the Tax Tribunal were composed of tax officials seconded/dispatched on a fixed term from the NTA and objectors/applicants were not even allowed to photocopy materials and pieces of evidence collected and submitted by the concerned tax offices and those collected by the Tax Tribunal.[9]

In response to the views expressed in the above Tax Commission's 2010 report and similar opinions, some procedures on the tax objections and the Tax Tribunal's structure have been reformed. Particularly notable is the fact that, under the current

7. While review organs such as the IRS Office of Appeals in U.S., UK Tribunals, etc., could increase the disputed tax amount in some cases. *See* 2 in Section 1 of Chapter 2 and footnote 79 in Chapter 3.
8. *See* Article 30 of the Administrative Litigation Act. A similar difference in the authority of Tribunals and courts is found in the UK where the principle of "Wednesbury unreasonableness" is adopted and in Australia where the merit review system is adopted. *See* the third para. in 1 in Section 2 of Chapter 3 and footnotes 43 and 62 in Chapter 4. In Japan, the Tax Tribunal substituted the disputed reassessments for its decisions particularly in the case of taxation by estimation. *See* 1(3) in Section 2 of Chapter 1.
9. Article 97 of AGRNT empowers reviewers in charge at the Tax Tribunal to go out whenever necessary to collect information and evidence that supplement those submitted by the concerned parties while it is not to be done for supporting the concerned re/assessment.

structure, not only the head Commissioner and several reviewers at the Tax Tribunal branches are either judges dispatched from the Ministry of Justice or public prosecutors but also approximately half of the reviewers (not including assistant reviewers) are lawyers, certified public accountants and tax accountants recruited on a fixed term from the public sectors. Moreover, the abovementioned 2014 revision of AGRNT has realized such reforms as follows: (i) aggrieved taxpayers can opt to make a direct objection to the Tax Tribunal (*see* Figure 1.1), (ii) the Tax Tribunal decisions made public on its HP has accumulated to 2,594 as of December 2021 (*see* Attachment), (iii) opportunities are given to the applicants to pose via the reviewers in charge of the case oral questions to the assessors (⑥ in Figure 1.2), (iv) the applicants can make a request to have access to and photocopy the materials and evidence collected and submitted by the assessors and those collected by Tax Tribunal (⑤ in Figure 1.2).

Figure 1.2 Tax Objection Proceedings

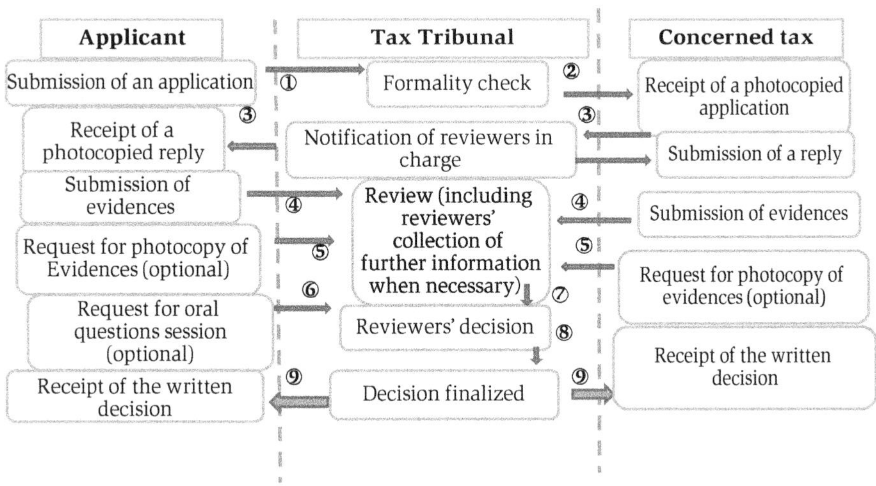

Source: Created based on Tax Tribunal HP/website "Procedures for requesting a review at Tax Tribunal (general flow of proceedings)."

As for the above (ii) reform, it is to be noted that the Tax Commission mentioned in its 1968 Report that Tax Tribunal decisions were not made public in principle at that time, and there should be discussions on ways to make public such Tax Tribunal decisions that could serve as precedents or the General Commissioner considers important. Since the Report was released, there has been an accumulation of the Tax Tribunal decisions made public on its HP (*see* Attachment). Figure 1.3 shows the recent annual number of publicized Tax Tribunal decisions. Now that the annual number of the Tax Tribunal decisions is not made open, the ratio of publicized decisions against the total number of its decisions cannot be ascertained.[10] It seems certain that, until recently, the ratio of the publicized Tax Tribunal decisions was not so high. In fact, the Report released in 2000 by the Administrative Inspection Bureau of the Management and Coordination Agency specifies that the ratio of the Tax Tribunal's published decisions between FY1995 and FY1998 was 3.9% to 5.8%. But the ratio started to rise after the Tax Tribunal made it a rule lately to publicize, particularly those decisions that cancel the disputed re/assessments as well as those that serve as precedents.

Figure 1.3 Changes in the Annual Number of Publicized Tax Tribunal Decisions

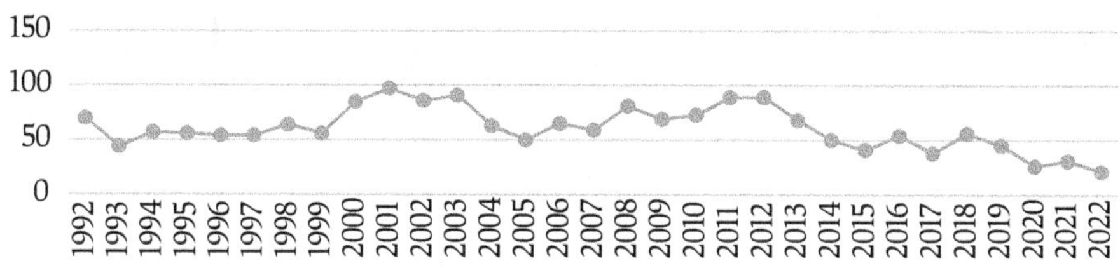

Source: Annual Number of decisions published on Tax Tribunal website.

It is conjectured that the number of objections to the Tax Tribunal counted on the basis of the applicants must be about one-fifth of the number of objections counted on a cumulative basis in Figure 1.4 so that the annual number of applicants filing objections with the Tax Tribunal should be about 600 to 700 lately and the ratio of its publicized decisions against the total number of its decisions should be about 10% to 15%.[11] If this conjecture is not out of the mark, there has lately been an increase in the ratio of the Tax Tribunal's publicized decisions. Figure 1.3 also reveals that the annual number of the Tax Tribunal's publicized decisions during the periods of FY2000 to FY2003 almost doubled from the periods of FY1993 to FY1999. Despite such an increase, some maintain that the ratio of the Tax Tribunal's publicized decisions is not high enough yet, and, indeed, it generally started to decline from 2012 onwards. But this decline should not be due to the decline in the ratio of the annually publicized number of its decisions but mostly due to the recent general declining trend in the number of objections filed with the Tax Tribunal (*see* Figure 1.4). In particular, the change in the annual number of the Tax Tribunal's publicized decisions from 2017 to 2021 mirrors the change in the number of objections filed with it during this period.

10. The government's Reference Document dated 5/132010 ("Small committee on *Nouzeisha Kankyouseibi*") informs on p. 5 that, during 2005 to 2008, the average number of objections on ITA-related and IGTA-related themes to the Tax Tribunal counted on the basis of the applicants was 585, and it was about 5% of about 11,000 to 12,000 re/assessments and about half of the number of objections with the assessors.
11. *See* Takemi Fujimagari, Bibliography (3) p. 259.

Figure 1.4 Recent Trends in the Number (Counted Cumulatively) of Tax Objections to Tax Tribunal and Their Breakdown by Tax Items

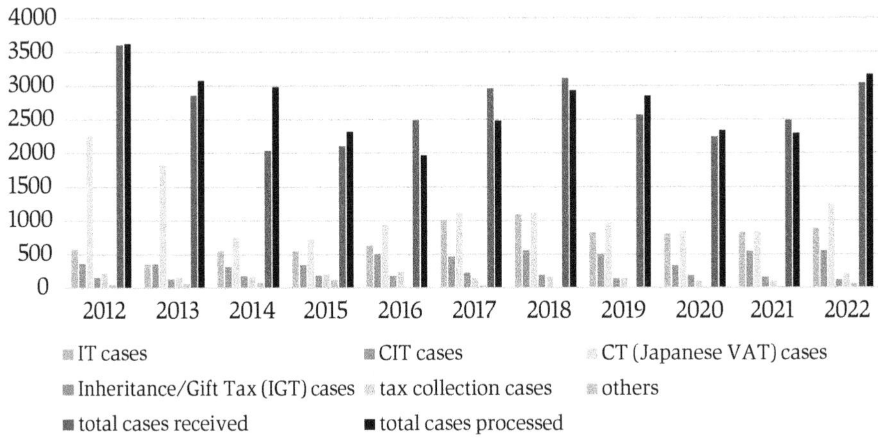

Source: Tax Tribunal "Summary of Review Requests (2018 edition and 2022 edition, etc.)."

But, more influential on how many of the Tax Tribunal's decisions are to be publicized should be the annual number of cancellations of the disputed re/assessments by the Tax Tribunal because the majority of the Tax Tribunal's publicized decisions are those canceling fully or partially the disputed re/assessments. Figures 1.4 and 1.5 do confirm that the annual number of the publicized decisions of the Tax Tribunal is generally small in a year when its annual ratio of the canceled re/assessments is small, as this is conspicuous particularly from FY2013 to FY2015. Therefore, the recent decline in the number of objections filed with the Tax Tribunal, as well as the recent annual ratio of the canceled re/assessment, which shows a trend of small decline, must be the main reasons for the recent decline in its annual number of publicized decisions. Some may regard this declining trend as a problem, but it may not be such a serious one now that not only anybody could request the Tax Tribunal for a copy of its unpublished decisions for a small fee but also many of them (including reviews on some of them) are posted/stored on various private websites/databases.

Figure 1.5 Percentage of Cases Processed by Tax Tribunal Within One Year and Canceled Re/assessments, Etc.

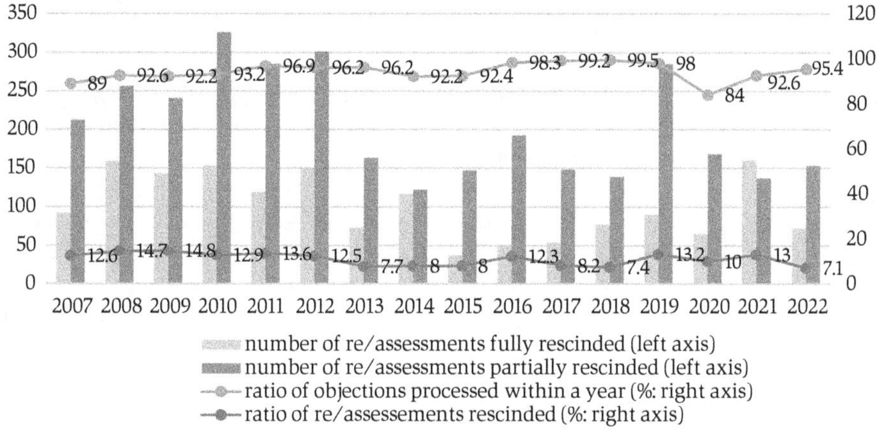

Source: Tax Tribunal "Summary of Review Requests (2018 edition and 2022 edition, etc.)."

2 Data Analysis and Facts on Review at Tax Tribunal and Assessors

Figure 1.4 displays the recent annual number of tax objections received at the Tax Tribunal and their breakdown by types of national taxes. The number of objections to the Tax Tribunal and that to the assessors in Figures 1.4 and 1.6 is counted cumulatively (i.e., counted not by the number of applicants but by aggregating the number of re/assessments in different years disputed by each applicant),[12] and their breakdown by tax types is also based on cumulative numbers. Figure 1.4 reveals that in FY2021, as for the ratio of respective taxes against the total number of objections (2,458) received at the Tax Tribunal, it is 33% for IT cases, about 22% for CIT cases, about 6% for IGT cases, about 34% for CT (Japanese VAT) cases, about 4% for collection cases, and about 1% for the others. In many cases, disputes over the amount of IT payable or CIT payable often pivot on the amount of business sales amount of the applicants, so such cases usually give rise to disputes over the amount of CT payable simultaneously. That is why the number of disputes on CT cases tends to become larger than that on other taxes. However, the number or the ratio of IGT cases disputed at the Tax Tribunal is relatively high compared with its tax revenue ratio and the number of audits on it (*see* Figures 1.12 and 1.13).

12. Therefore, for example, if objections are filed by an applicant regarding the reassessments on IT and CT payable for three years, the number of the objections are counted to be six.

The Tax Tribunal's proclaimed administrative goals include the attainment of processing more than 95 % of the disputes within a year, and Figure 1.5 shows that this goal has been attained lately in most of the years. This fact should facilitate aggrieved taxpayers' decisions to file objections with the Tax Tribunal. Moreover, it is not required for the applicant to pay any fee to make a request for the Tax Tribunal's review, and the applicant does not have to appoint a representative to dispute its case at the Tax Tribunal so that, in actuality, the majority of the applicants either dispute their cases on their own (pro se disputants) or let their certified tax accountants on a retainer represent them at the Tax Tribunal.[13] After the 2016 revision of AGRNT, aggrieved taxpayers could also economize their time in some cases if they choose to skip requesting for review at the assessor and make a direct request for review at the Tax Tribunal. As Figures 1.4 and 1.6 show, there were times when the number of objections to the assessors was more than 1.5 times that to the Tax Tribunal, but now the table is turned, and there are more aggrieved taxpayers filing objections with the Tax Tribunal than those filing objections with the assessors.

The assessors' review, which is concluded within ninety days in principle by those in the assessor's office who did not engage in the audit of the aggrieved taxpayer, should be functioning as a screen to winnow out many of those re/assessments that do not stand on solid grounds. Nevertheless, Figures 1.5 and 1.6 reveal that from 2013 to 2022, the average ratio of cancelations at the Tax Tribunal was 9.5 % and a little higher than 9.3 % at the assessors. Moreover, during this period, the ratio of full cancelations to that of partial cancelations has been 4 % to 29 % at the assessors and 10 % to 53 % at the Tax Tribunal. These figures indicate that the relief granted to the applicants by the Tax Tribunal's favorable decisions has been more significant than the ratios of revocation of the re/assessments at the Tax Tribunal, as suggested in Figure 1.5. Even so, irrespective of which tax disputing stage an aggrieved taxpayer is in, filing tax objections/appeals does not suspend the collection action on the disputed tax in principle,[14] and the assessor's substitution of the legal ground for the re/assessments may be possible in cases where such substitution practically would not undermine the taxpayers' defense of their claims.[15]

13. In the U.S., there are many pro se litigants at the Tax Court and some view the relatively low success rate of those unrepresented taxpayers at the Tax Court as a problem to be addressed. *See* the paragraph just below Figure 2.6 in Chapter 2.
14. The exceptions to this principle, as prescribed under Article 105, include: (i) public sale of the seized asset of the delinquent taxpayer, (ii) cases where the NTA or the Tax Tribunal finds the suspension necessary, etc. *See* 3(4) of Section 3 for further details.
15. For relevant court cases on this issue, *see* 2(4) in Section 3. As for the post-re/assessment substitution of reasons and legal grounds, it seems to have become more difficult ever since a notice of re/assessment to be issued for a non-blue return filer that does not file a return/an amended return in accordance with the audit result should also have written reasons on it from 2012. *See* footnote 19 and 2(4) in Section 3 for details. On this issue in US, *see* 2 in Section 1 of Chapter 2.

Figure 1.6 Number (counted cumulatively) of Tax Objections to Assessors and Assessors' Ratios of Cancellation of Disputed Re/Assessments, Etc.

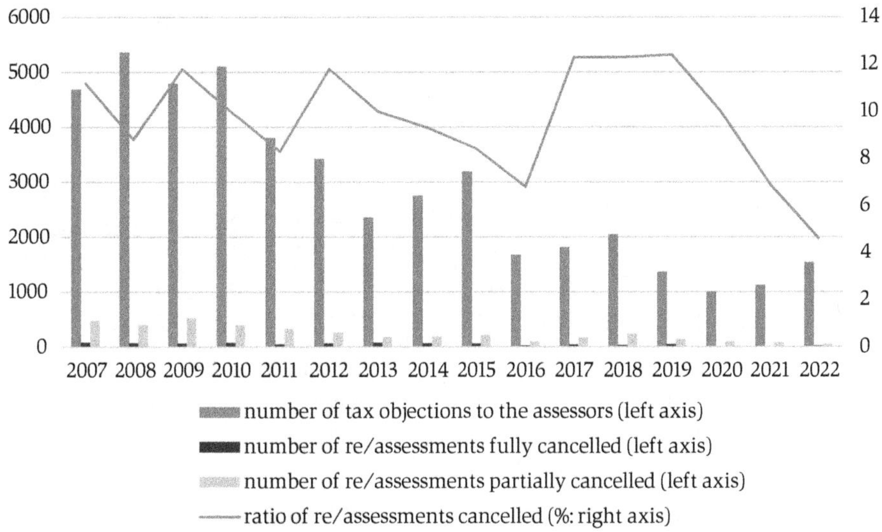

Source: NTA "Summary of tax objections to the assessors (2018 edition and 2022 edition, etc.)."

3 Data Analysis and Facts on Review at Court

Where an aggrieved taxpayer wants to dispute the Tax Tribunal decision, he must file a lawsuit. Figure 1.7 shows the annual number of tax lawsuits (counted by the number of cases/suits) received at court and their breakdown by types of taxes. It unveils a big difference in the number of CT cases disputed at the Tax Tribunal and the courts. This difference should be accounted for mainly by the fact that CTA is relatively simple and does not contain as many provisions and issues as direct taxes (*see* Attachment) that are contentious as to be disputed so frequently in court. On the other hand, IGT cases represent a fairly large ratio not only at the Tax Tribunal but also at court, and its ratio has been increasing lately. There must be several reasons for this, and they include: (i) the top IGT rate is as high as 55%, (ii) IGT is a nonrecurring tax on inheritors of assets that used to be managed and controlled by the inheritees, (iii) IGT often involves property appraisal issues which could have a certain range on their value,[16] (iv) 2013 revision of IGTA (implemented from 2015) has lowered the nontaxable threshold (or decreased the amount deductible in calculating the amount of taxable net inherited assets) of Inheritance Tax.[17]

16. Also notable is the fact that the statute of limitation for re/assessments on gift tax is six years (in principle, five years for other taxes) under para. 1 of Article 36 of IGTA.
17. The amount deductible in calculating the amount of taxable net inherited assets was, before 2015, JPY 50 million + (JPY 10 million × number of statutory heirs) while it is now JPY 30

Figure 1.7 Number of Tax Lawsuits by Tax Item

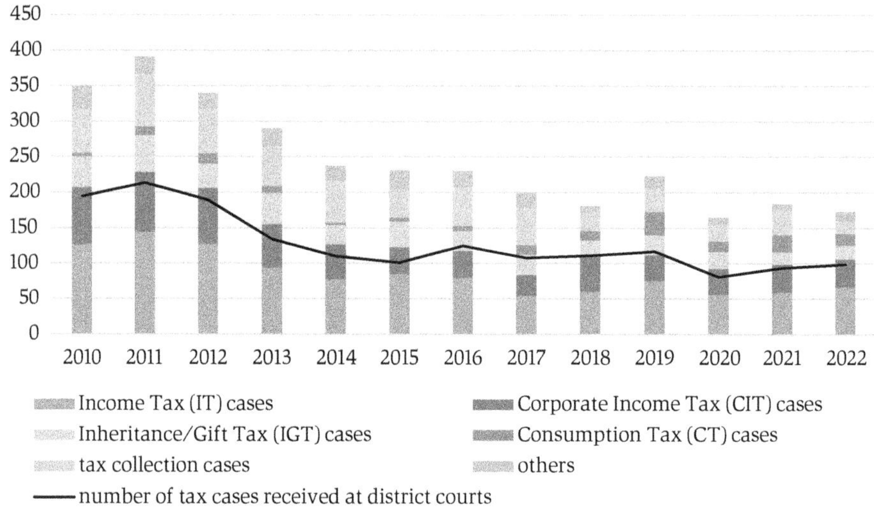

Source: NTA "Summary of Lawsuits (FY2018 edition and FY2022 edition)."

Figure 1.8 divulges the recent annual number and ratio of courts' judgments revoking the disputed re/assessments fully or partially. Comparison of Figures 1.7 and 1.8 exposes the fact that the annual number of tax lawsuits received and those resolved at court are almost the same, so the problem of accumulation of unresolved cases at court is not grave. It can be said that, at the Tax Tribunal, a considerable amount of efforts is made to sort out the issues of contention and clarify the claims of the parties to the dispute, with the result that those cases contested at court are mostly those which aggrieved taxpayers consider being worthy of disputing. Their decisions on whether their cases are worthy of lawsuits may be affected somewhat by the fact that, as Figure 1.8 shows, from FY2002 to FY2022, the percentage of taxpayers who won all or part of tax lawsuits at court ranged from 3.4% to 13.4 % (7.46 % on average) which is lower than the average (10.3%) at the Tax Tribunal during the same years, while, at courts, in contrast to the case at the assessors and the Tax Tribunal, the ratio of full revocation of the disputed re/assessments, etc., is usually higher than that of partial revocation of them.

million + (JPY 6 million × number of statutory heirs). The number of statutory heirs differs depending on the number of the bereaved family members and so forth. In the most typical case of a married couple with two children, statutory heirs are the spouse of the deceased and the two children.

Figure 1.8 Number of Court Rulings on Tax Cases and the Ratio of Rulings Revoking the Disputed Tax Re/assessments, Etc.

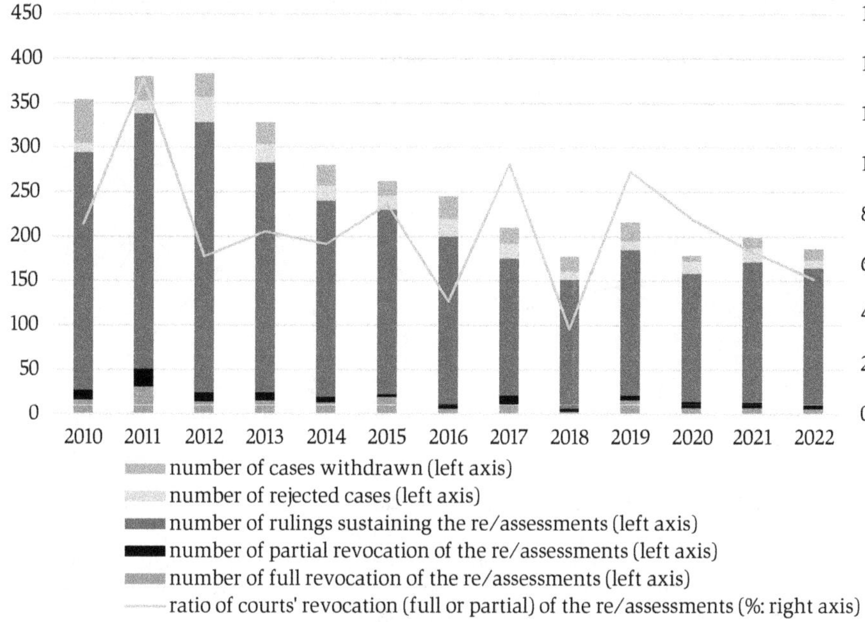

Source: NTA "Summary of Lawsuits (FY2018 edition and FY2022 edition)."

4 Relationship Between On-Site Audits and the Number of Objections/Lawsuits Filed

Figure 1.9 is a comparison at a glance of the ratio of revocation of the disputed re/assessments, etc., at the respective stage of the review and aggregation of a recent number of tax objections to the assessors and the Tax Tribunal (counted on the cumulative number basis) as well as that of tax litigations (counted by the number of cases/suits). Although there has been no significant change in the ratio of revocation of the disputed re/assessments at the respective stages from FY2010 to FY2022, the number of tax disputes has generally been on the decline. There must be various causes for this, and one of them is a decrease in the number of national tax officials from 57,202 in 1997 to 56,263 in 2011 and 55,766 in 2016, while there is an increasing trend in the number of tax returns, the complexity of tax laws, and the globalization of transactions. This has given rise to the general decline in the ratios of tax officials' on-site audits, as is collaborated in Figure 1.10 for field audits of individuals and corporations,[18] and this declining trend has been accelerated by the 2011 revision of AGRNT which made it necessary for the tax auditors to provide in writing the audited taxpayers with the reasons and legal ground for the re/assessments in cases where they do not file amended returns voluntarily even if they are not blue return filers.[19]

Figure 1.9 Number of Tax Objections/Lawsuits and the Ratio of Revocation of the Disputed Re/assessments, Etc.

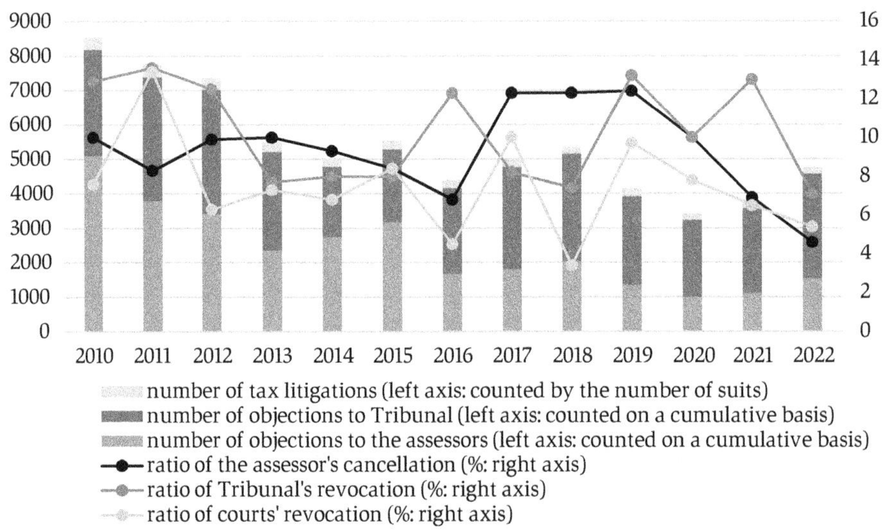

Sources: NTA "Summary of Objections to the Assessors (2022 edition, etc.)," "Summary of Tax Litigation (2022 edition, etc.)," and Tax Tribunal "Summary of Objections (2022 edition," etc.).

In principle, the fact that the number of tax disputes is small is a welcome situation for the NTA, but if it is partially due to the low rate or decline in the rate of on-site tax audits, it may not be so for the NTA. It is positive that (i) the decline in the number of on-site audits is partly responsible for (ii) the recent declining trend in the number of objections to the Tax Tribunal), and Figures 1.6 and 1.10 also indicate that these (i) and (ii) trends are well synchronized.[20] Lately, there has been the active

18. For example, the number of corporations increased from about 2.35 million in 1989 to about 3.08 million in 2017. For details, *see* NTA's "Current Status and Issues of Tax Administration" (1/24/2018), pp. 3-4. These respective ratios represent the number of on-site audits of corporations against the total number of corporations and the number of on-site audits against the total number of individual taxpayers with tax liability.
19. *See* Article 74-14 of AGRNT. Prior to the revision, the assessor's requirement of presentation of the reasons and legal grounds for the re/assessments in writing was one of the privileges of the blue return filers who fulfill the obligation of maintaining proper bookkeeping and records. This revision has given rise to some disputes over whether those reasons are appropriate and sufficient. *See* 2(4) in Section 3.
20. Also, in U.S., the change in the number of "90-day letter" issued is synchronized much with that in the number of cases brought to the Tax Court. *See* Figure 2.5 in Chapter 2.

implementation of "simple contacts" (such as tax offices' requests for taxpayers' voluntary review of their returns through written or telephone contacts and interviews by requesting a visit to the office), so the NTA's problem of tax revenue decrease caused by the recent decline in the number of on-site audits has been mitigated by the recent increase in the additional tax revenue collected through "simple contacts."[21] But the recent declining trend of the number of tax disputes attributable partly to the recent decreasing trend of the tax audit ratio could not be mitigated much by the increase in the number of "simple contacts" because the issues pointed out through "simple contacts" are usually not complex enough to give rise to tax audits and disputes.[22]

Figure 1.10 Number and Ratio of On-Site Audits on Individual and Corporate Taxpayers

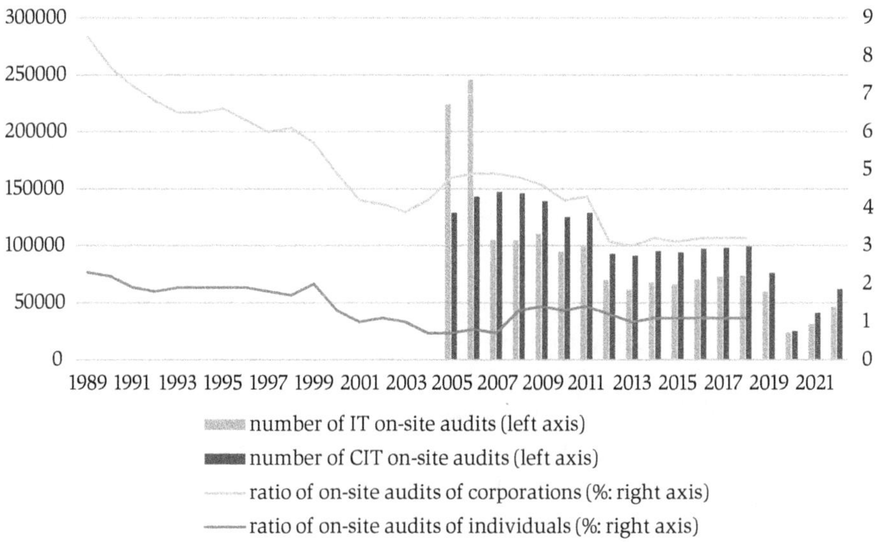

Sources: NTA "Current Status and Issues of Tax Administration," NTA "Status of IT and CT Audits in FY2022," and NTA "Summary of CIT Audit Results in FY2022," etc.

However, it should be possible to put a brake on the decline in the number of tax disputes, which is partly attributable to the decrease in the number of on-site tax audits if the rate of re/assessments (or detection rate of tax deficiencies) and the average additional tax collected by the on-site tax audit goes up. Figure 1.11 shows the recent increasing trend of the rate of detection of tax deficiencies and the average additional

21. In the case of IT, the number of " simple contacts" in the FY2006-FY2020 was 350,000 to 850,000 cases every year. The number of on-site tax audits for capital gains tax was about 90,000 in FY2019 and about 30,000 in FY2020. *See* sources of Figures 1.10 and 1.12.
22. In the case of IT, the number of "simple contacts" in FY2022 is about 591,000 and it is more than ten times of the number of on-site audits (46,000), while in the case of CT, the difference has not been so conspicuous (the former is about 66,000 (67,000) and the latter is 62,000 (41,000) for FY2022 (2021)). For details, *see* source of Figures 1.10 and 1.12.

tax collected by the on-site tax audits. Therefore, it is quite likely that the recent declining trend in the number of tax disputes caused much by the declining trend of the number of on-site tax audits is counteracted by the recent increasing trend of the rate of detection of tax deficiencies and the average additional tax amount collected by the on-site tax audits, and Figure 1.11 insinuates that such counteraction should be strong, especially around the years after 2018. Even so, as the data in Figures 1.9, 1.10 and 1.11 suggest, it seems that such counteraction could not become strong enough to halt the declining trend of the number of tax disputes, which must be accelerated significantly by the declining trend of the number of on-site tax audits.

Figure 1.11 Ratio of Deficiencies Detected and Amount of Tax Collected by On-Site Audits

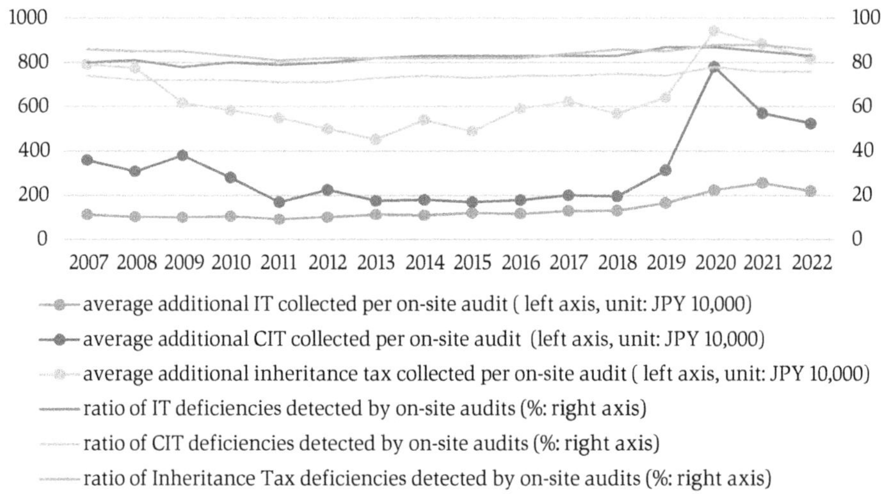

Source: Data from Source on Figures 1.10 and 1.12.

As Figure 1.12 illustrates, there has been a fairly large number of "simple contacts" lately in the case of Inheritance Tax as well.[23] Moreover, Inheritance Tax revenue decrease under the declining trend in the number of its on-site audits has been reversed by the significant increase in the number of taxable inheritees (the number of inheritees appearing in the submitted inheritance tax returns) and the taxable ratio of Inheritance Tax (the number of taxable inheritees divided by the total number of inheritees) made possible by the lowering of the nontaxable threshold of Inheritance Tax by the aforementioned 2013 revision of IGTA which has been implemented since 2015.[24] Figure 1.12 does show the significant increase since 2015 in the number of

23. It was after 2016 that the number of "simple contacts" in the case of Inheritance Tax was made public. The number of on-site audits for gift tax was 5,671 in 2011, but declined to 3,383 in 2019 and 1,867 in 2020. For details, *see* p. 5 of NTA's "Inheritance Tax audit status in 2020."
24. *See* footnote 17.

inheritees giving rise to Inheritance Tax and its ratio has risen as high as 10% in 2022. Moreover, in the case of Inheritance Tax, the ratio of a strict penalty imposition (the number of strict penalty impositions divided by the number of deficiencies in the returns) should also be usually higher, as Figure 1.11 implies, and it was indeed as high as 17% in FY2019 and 16.1% in FY2020.

Figure 1.12 Number of On-Site Audits/"Simple Contact" on Taxpayers of Inheritance Tax, number of Taxable Inheritees, and Taxable Ratio

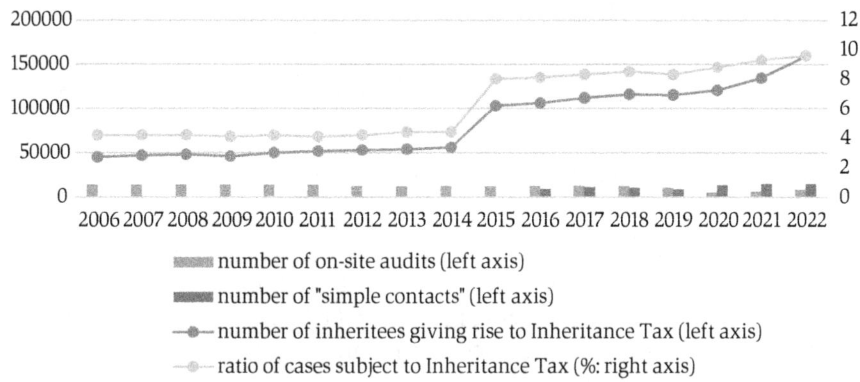

Source: Created from the 2003 edition of NTA's Statistical Annual Report, NTA's "Inheritance tax investigation status" and "Inheritance tax filing results" in 2020, 2024, etc."

Obviously, the higher ratio of detection of deficiencies and the larger amount of additional tax collected by on-site audits should have an effect of increasing the ratio of tax disputes or tax objections against the total number of audited cases. Even so, as mentioned above, this effect is not strong enough to prevent a decrease in the number of tax disputes, which should be caused much by the decline in the number of on-site tax audits. Likewise, the increase in the number of "simple contacts," which are mostly targeted at clear cases of tax deficiencies, is not likely to do much in increasing the number of tax disputes. Indeed, as Figure 1.4 shows, the recent decline in the number of tax disputes over IGT seems not to be as conspicuous as that over other taxes, but the comparison of Figures 1.11 and 1.13 intimates that the above effect should also be at work in the case of Inheritance Tax because the increase in the average amount of additional tax collected by on-site audits from 2019 to 2022 is much greater in the case of Inheritance Tax than IT while the increase in the ratio of the number of objections to the Tax Tribunal against the total number of on-site tax audits during this period is greater in the case of IT than Inheritance Tax.[25]

25. Source on Figures 1.10 and 1.12 also reveal that the number of on-site audits increased from 2020 to 2022 at a higher rate for IT (from 23,804 to 46,306) than that for Inheritance Tax (from about 5,106 to 8,196).

Figure 1.13 Ratio of the Number of Objections to the Tax Tribunal Against the Number of On-Site Audits Concerning IT, CIT and IGT

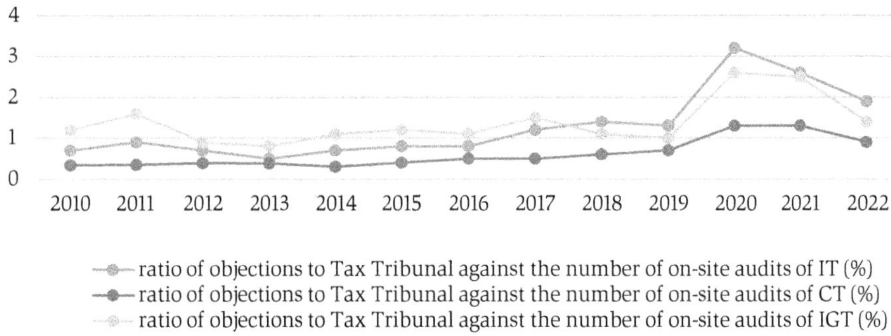

Source: Created from materials and data in Source on Figures 1.4 and 1.11.

The analysis made so far should give a rough idea of some main factors impacting the number of tax disputes in Japan. In the following Sections, the Attachment (A condensed English-translated version of the Tax Tribunal's list of publicized decisions shown on its website) which appears at the end of the Book) is analyzed to find those factors in the tax provisions that possess strong inducements to tax disputes. In the Attachment, the Tax Tribunal has made public, as of December 2021, 2,594 decisions (IT 26% (33%),[26] CIT 17% (20%), IGT 15% (16%), CT 5%, tax collection 7%, and others (mostly AGRNT) 18%(20%)),[27] and it sorts them out in accordance with their disputed themes or points of dispute.[28] Now that not all of the Tax Tribunal decisions are made public, themes with a large number of publicized decisions may not necessarily be highly disputed ones at the Tax Tribunal, but generally, they are quite likely to be disputed more frequently than those with a smaller number of publicized decisions. Therefore, in this book, those themes with a large number of publicized decisions at the Attachment are deemed ≪highly disputed themes≫, and attempts are to be made to ascertain the attributes or inducements they possess that prompt taxpayers to dispute them more frequently than others.

26. The number in the bracket shows the percentage of cases of the respective taxes when it is calculated by including respectively in them those relevant themes (282 cases in total) contained in the Special Taxation Measures Act (STMA).
27. TAINS, a data base of the Federation of Tax Accountants, which contains some unpublished ones lists, as of 8/15/2022, 5,734 Tax Tribunals decisions (2,204 (38%) on IT, 1,630 (28%) on CIT, 1,187 (21%) on IGT, 474 (8%) on CT and 239 on others (5%)) as well as 12,105 court rulings on tax cases (52% on IT, 28% on CIT, 13% on IGT, 3% on CT and 4% on others).
28. In this book, themes appearing in the Attachment in block letters are bracketed by【 】, those headed by the numerical number are bracketed by 『 』, those headed by a capital letter of the alphabet is bracketed by [ ], and those headed by a small letter of the alphabet is bracketed by 〔 〕.

SECTION 2 ≪HIGHLY DISPUTED THEMES≫ OF DIRECT TAXES AT TAX TRIBUNAL

1 Characteristics of ≪Highly Disputed Themes≫ of Income Tax Act (ITA)

The number of the Tax Tribunal decisions listed/publicized in the Attachment on IT-related themes is 681 (848, including those on the IT-related provisions contained in STMA). Among those IT decisions/themes bracketed by 【 】, 【Necessary expenses】 (167 cases) accounts for the most. Its breakdown shows that 『Business income』 represents about one-third of it. The next largest in number among those bracketed by 【 】is 【Categories of income】, but it does not have any one theme that is particularly large in number. As for those bracketed by 『 』, 『Calculation of gross income』 has 45 cases, 『Salary, etc.』 under 【withholding tax】 has 34 cases, 『Re/assessment by estimation』 has 22 cases, 『Income sourced in Japan』 has 16 cases, 『Denial of a family company's actions or calculations』 has 15 cases. Among those IT themes contained in STMA, the largest in number is [Special credit for capital gains from the transfer of a resided property], which has 46 cases, and it is followed by 『Special credit for housing loans』 which has 24 cases. In the following subsections (1) to (6), an analysis is to be made of the abovementioned underlined themes as they were disputed in the Tax Tribunal and courts in the hope that it would unveil the attributes that make them ≪highly disputed themes≫.

(1) 【*Necessary expenses*】

As mentioned above, 【Necessary expenses】 is most frequently disputed in relation to 『business income』.[29] Article 37 of ITA stipulates that the amount to be included in necessary expenses is the amount of expenses directly incurred for the acquisition of revenue, such as costs of goods sold as well as other expenses incurred to generate income.[30] In addition, Article 45 of ITA and Article 96 of ITA Enforcement Order spells out the standards and scope of deductible household-related expenses. They stipulate that household-related expenses are deductible provided that their main part is necessary for carrying out activities that generate business income and that the main part can be separated. There are also some related tax provisions and ARs that give further details on what could constitute necessary expenses. Even so, these are not by any means sufficient nor clear enough in some cases to decide whether some expenses

29. In the U.S., IRC §162 (Trade or business expenses) is also one of the most litigated issues at Tax Court. While the criterion for the deductibility may be stricter because it is "ordinary and necessary" and the term "necessary" is interpreted narrowly enough to exclude, in sharp contrast to ITA, entertainment expenses of a business proprietor in the majority of case. *See* 5(2) in Section 4 of Chapter 2.
30. AR 45-1 and 45-2 on IT specifies that the parts of household-related expenses deductible as necessary expenses are to be decided by taking into account various relevant facts, but in principle, the main part, if it is not separable, should exceed 50% of the expenditure if the expenditure is to be deductible as a necessary expense.

are deductible as necessary expenses.[31] Moreover, there are arguments and contradicting court judgments on the question of whether an individual business proprietor's expenses are deductible even if they are inordinary or are not directly related to his business.[32]

In particular, the Tax Tribunal's 10/27/2003 decision is one of those cases which could incur the above arguments. In this case, at issue was whether the applicant/lawyer could deduct from his business revenue those expenses laid out as tuition to the graduate school and a donation to the U.S. university from which he graduated. He claimed that they are deductible because the rules of the Association of Lawyers provide for the need for continuous training and the university alumni often make a request to him to do some work for them. However, the Tax Tribunal ruled that some classes at the graduate school certainly have some relevance to his business, but it does not mean that the tuition is an expense directly related to his business and ordinary, and the same is true for the donation to the US university. A similar view was expressed by the Aomori District Court 11/5/1985(1984(GyoU)3) judgment in which the Court ruled that in order for expenses to be deductible as business expenses, they must have, viewed objectively, a direct relation to the activities of the business and they must be normally necessary for the execution of the business. The Tokyo District Court 8/9/2011(2009(GyoU)454) judgment was also one of those that ruled in favor of the assessor by adopting a similar view on necessary expenses.

Whereas, the above Tokyo District Court 8/9/2011 judgment was overturned by the Tokyo High Court 9/19/2012 (2011(GyoU)454) judgment. In this Tokyo High Court judgment, at issue was the deductibility of a banquet participation fee as a business expense of the appellant/lawyer which was paid in relation to his status as director of the Association of Lawyers. In this case, the Court ruled that if some expenses are necessary for executing the business, they have relevance to the business, and there is no legal ground for demanding their direct relation to the business as the precondition for them to be deducted. The Court must have a view that even if the expense is incurred as director of the Association of Lawyers, which is an identity different from a lawyer in pursuit of gaining business income, such expense is deductible if it is an expense necessary in carrying out activities of director of the Association of Lawyers. The NTA's appeal to the Supreme Court on this case was not entertained, while the Tax Tribunal, in its 3/6/2014 decision (even after this High Court judgment was handed down), denying the deductibility of the accountant's Rotary Club enrollment fee,[33] took

31. Such requirements for business expenses deduction are similar to those in Australia and NZ referred to in Chapter 4 and they are theoretically broader in scope than UK's 2005 ITA §34 referred to in 2 in Section 5 of Chapter 3 and Ireland's 1997 Tax Consolidation Act §81(2) (and §114 mentioned in footnote 126 of Chapter 5) which only allow deduction of those expenses "wholly and exclusively" incurred for the taxpayer's business.
32. Some maintain that Article 37 does not contain the term "ordinary," so that, unlike IRC §162, expenses that are necessary but not ordinary for business should also be deductible. *See* Hiroshi Kaneko, Bibliography (4) p. 264.
33. While AR 9-7-15-2 on CIT treats Rotary Club enrollment fee as a corporate entertainment expense which may be deductible in some cases. *See* 2 (2) in Section 2 for details on corporate entertainment expenses.

a position that a deductible expense must be necessary for business and it must be directly related to the activities that generate business income.[34]

(2) 『Salary, Etc.』 under 【Withholding Tax】

The Attachment denotes that more than 50% of fifty-one cases that are under the theme 【Withholding tax】 concern themselves with 『Salary, etc.』. Article 183 of ITA provides for the payer's withholding obligation at the time of its "payment" of a salary, etc. However, withholding obligation may arise even in cases where a payer is not quite aware of it. For example, economic benefit to a corporate executive of his family company could be "deemed bonus" which is subject to withholding tax even in cases where the family company may not have an intention of giving such economic benefit. Such a wide definition of bonuses and wide coverage of withholding tax obligation are the main reasons for 『Salary, etc.』 to be a ≪highly disputed theme≫. In fact, the Osaka High Court ruled in 8/27/2003(2002 (GyoKo) 85) judgment that even if the president of the social welfare corporation (which is exempt from CIT and not a family company) drew money illegally from the corporation, the corporation owes the withholding obligation on it so long as it is to be deemed a bonus to the embezzler who practically controls the corporation because it is irrelevant whether the fulfillment of the withholding obligation is difficult or not. A similar view was also expressed by the Sendai High Court 3/12/2004 (2003 (GyoKo)15) judgment.[35]

The listed Tax Tribunal decisions in the Attachment also include a case where the assessor's claim that the corporation failed to fulfill its tax withholding obligation timely of its deemed payment of bonus to its director was voided by the Tax Tribunal 9/11/1974 decision, intimating the difficulty even on the part of the NTA to determine correctly whether there has arisen tax withholding obligation in some cases.[36] Such difficulty is also implied by the Supreme Court 10/8/2015 judgment (2014(GyoHi)167). In this case, the Hiroshima High Court ruled in the 1/30/2014 judgment that the taxpayer/corporation does not owe an obligation of withholding tax on the amount of debt forgiven vis-à-vis its director because it was due to the insolvent director's inability to repay and dismissed the appellant's primary assertion of the corporation's failure to withhold tax on this debt forgiveness as well as its preliminary argument that

34. For example, in the case of U.S., Rotary club dues may not come under IRC §274(a)(3) (Denial of deduction for club dues) and be deductible as business expenses. *See* 5(2) in Section 4 of Chapter 2 and https://www.churchlawandtax.com/understand-taxes/expenses/qa-how-should-we-handle-our-pastors-club-dues/.
35. While in the case of a regular corporation that is subject to CIT, an employee's embezzlement of its money could give rise to a question of whether it subjects the corporation to a strict penalty whose standard rate is 35% rather than a penalty with a regular rate of 10% for the underreporting of CIT on account of such embezzlement. The answer was affirmative in the Tax Tribunal 4/16/2018 decision where such embezzlement could be deemed to be an act of the corporation because the corporation failed to supervise and manage properly the embezzler even if the embezzler was not a director but a staff in the accounting section.
36. Another example is the Tax Tribunal 5/7/2018 decision which canceled the assessment of imposing the withholding tax obligation on the corporation/applicant because the embezzler was its director who was found not to be in control of the management of the corporation in practice.

the corporation failed to withhold tax on the part that the director's assets exceed his liabilities after the concerned debt is forgiven. But the above Supreme Court judgment voided this High Court judgment and remanded the case to it. The remand trial by the Hiroshima High Court 2/8/2017 judgment sustained the above NTA's preliminary assertion and the imposition of withholding tax.[37]

The abovementioned problems of the withholding tax obligation ((i) the difficulty of either becoming aware of the fact that withholding tax obligation has arisen or determining whether it has arisen, (ii) unclarity on the scope of withholding obligation) may manifest themselves in cases of payment of salary, bonus and retirement money as well as cases of other payments. Moreover, the above problem (i) also gives rise to the question of whether such difficulty could be a reason for the exemption of the withholding tax obligation and the penalty for failing to withhold tax timely. The abovementioned Osaka High Court 8/27/2003 judgment dictates that such difficulty may not become a reason for the exemption of withholding tax obligation as well as the penalty (*see also* footnotes 37 and 94). However, in the Tokyo District Court 5/19/2016 judgment referred to in 2(2) in Section 3, the penalty for the failure to fulfill the withholding obligation in time was exempted at the stage of tax audit, and the Court did not dismiss the plaintiff/payor's claim for exemption from the withholding tax obligations outright. Instead, the Court dismissed the plaintiff's claim for the exemption of the withholding tax obligation after having determined that the plaintiff failed to exercise due care in fulfilling its withholding obligation on the foreigner for his income sourced in Japan.

Even so, in reality, there have been no reported cases where the withholding tax obligation was exempted for the reason that the person with tax withholding obligation exercised due care vis-à-vis the withholding obligation. As for the exemption of a penalty on a person with the withholding obligation, the case disputed in the above Tokyo District Court judgment is not the only one in which a penalty was not applied. Article 67 of AGRNT provides for the exemption of a penalty on the failure to withhold tax in time in cases where there is a justifiable reason and the NTA's guideline dated 7/3/2000 on an administrative penalty for the failure to comply with the withholding tax obligation in time mentions that a penalty could be exempted in cases where there are truly unavoidable causes such as natural disasters, stoppage of traffic or telecommunication, etc., that prevented those with a withholding tax obligation from complying with this obligation timely.[38] Such being the case, the abovementioned problems (i) and (ii) have often become a cause for tax disputes not only for taxpayers claiming the exemption from the withholding tax obligation or the inapplicability of a strict penalty

37. AR 36-17 on IT, before it was abolished by Article 44-2 of IT introduced in 2014 which may set a higher hurdle for the insolvency requirement, prescribed that the amount of debt forgiven due to the debtor's insolvency is not includable in the debtor's income. This remand trial by the Hiroshima High Court brushed off the taxpayer's claim of the difficulty in fulfilling the withholding obligation, and the subsequent Supreme Court 9/25/2018 judgment (2017(GyoHi)209) held that this High Court judgment was correct in its conclusion.
38. As for the issue of a penalty exemption based on a justifiable reason, *see* footnote 96 and 2(2) in Section 3.

but also for those claiming the exemption from a penalty on the failure to withhold tax in time.

(3) 『Re/assessment by Estimation』

Where a tax auditor cannot confirm whether the returns filed by a taxpayer are correct or not because the taxpayer did not keep proper books and records or refuses to present them to the auditor at the time of the audit, the tax auditor has to employ the method of re/assessment by estimation as Article 156 of ITA and 131 of CITA dictate. As the Attachment unveils, there is a fairly large number of published Tax Tribunal decisions on this theme, which include fifteen cases canceling the disputed re/assessments. The main reasons for this theme to be a ≪highly disputed theme≫ should include the following: (i) re/assessment by estimation means for a blue return filer, the loss of a blue return status/privileges; (ii) a taxpayer could contest the appropriateness of either a method employed to come up with the estimated tax amount for the taxpayer or the way its method is applied, (iii) a taxpayer could challenge the appropriateness of the estimated tax amount by claiming the allegedly real tax amount payable, (iv) a taxpayer could expect that the Tax Tribunal might substitute the tax estimation method employed in the re/assessment for another method if it considers the latter to be a more rational method than the one employed in the former while there is a question of whether the court could or should do the same.

The Tax Tribunal 6/17/2011 decision is an example of the above (ii) because it actually substituted the method of estimating the taxpayer's annual sales amount employed in the reassessment on IT and CT (estimation made basically on the change in the number of disposal chopsticks used by the taxpayer's customers) for the method of estimating the amount of his annual sales by the ratio of utility bills against the amount of revenue in the case of businesses of a similar size in the same business and handed down a decision to revoke a part of the re/assessment to the taxpayer's favor.[39] One example of the above (iii) is the Tokyo District Court judgment of 9/13/1993 (1990(GyoU)176) in which the Court ruled that, as for the amount of expenses on items specific to his business, the taxpayer's claim which should reflect the actual amount must be accepted and revoked as part of the disputed reassessment made by the income estimation. The Tokyo High Court 4/7/1961 judgment (1956(Ne)1514) is an example of the above (iv) because it ruled that the income estimation by the annual change in the net assets of the taxpayer adopted by the appellant should be substituted by another method based on the amount of consumption of the essential ingredient of the food/commodity now that the latter is more appropriate while the substitution does not amount to the negation of the appropriateness of the re/assessments.

Whereas, the Kyoto District Court 6/16/1995(1990(GyoU)1) judgment seems not to have followed the footstep of the above Tokyo High Court ruling of 4/7/1961

39. CTA differs from IT and CIT in that it does not have an explicit provision allowing the NTA to employ taxation by estimation while courts, as in the case of the Kumamoto District Court 2/18/2015(2011(GyoU)19) judgment, have ruled that taxation by estimation is inherent in the tax law which has adopted a self-assessment method.

because it expressed a view that it is sufficient for a result of taxation by estimation to be an approximation of the real amount of income and even if there is an estimation method which is more reasonable than the method employed by the assessor, the assessor's estimation method is lawful so long as it has a certain degree of rationality, so the taxpayer/plaintiff's claim of which estimation method is preferable is out of the mark. The validity and lawfulness of such a view and the re/assessment were also confirmed by the Osaka High Court 10/30/1996 judgment (1995(GyoKo)47) that upheld the above Kyoto District Court judgment. This difference between the Tax Tribunal and courts with respect to their stance on the issue of substituting an estimation method employed by the assessor with the more rational method is mostly attributable to Article 97 of AGRNT, which provides for the Tax Tribunal's authority of auditing related parties of the taxpayer/applicant and to Article 102 of AGRNT which stipulates its ability to determine the appropriateness of the re/assessment as well as its lawfulness.[40]

As the above (i) indicates, re/assessment by estimation is particularly a big issue for a blue return filer because it is the action resulting from the tax auditor's finding of the audited business proprietor/corporation's failure to fulfill its obligation as the blue return filer of keeping proper books and records.[41] The deprivation of the blue return status goes back to the business year in which such failure occurred so that the blue return privileges such as the carryover of business net loss to succeeding years, deduction of reasonable amount of salaries paid to his full-time family employees in his business, tax credit for the blue return filers, etc., become inapplicable retroactively to incur additional tax that he could have been avoided only if he had fulfilled the obligations.[42] There is no such privilege in the case of white return filers, and it is one of the main reasons for the larger number of reassessments by estimation on them. But the 2022 tax reform may decrease the number of re/assessments by estimation and disputes over them because it has introduced a penalty rate increase on undeclared/underreported IT, CIT and CT in cases where books and records are not presented to a tax auditor or less than half of sales are not recorded on books (rate increase by 10%, while rate increase by 5% when unrecorded sales on books are less than two-thirds).

40. Such difference between Tax Tribunal and courts on their power to substitute the assessor's decision on the re/assessment is particularly conspicuous in Australia where AAT has an authority of merit review. *See* footnote 43 and 3 in Section 1 of Chapter 4. As for Article 97 and 102 of AGRNT, see footnotes 8 and 9.
41. The privileges for a blue return filer vary to some extent depending on whether the filer is an individual or corporation, which bookkeeping method (double-entry or a simpler one) is adopted, and so forth. Lately, about 60% to 70% of the business proprietors and more than 90% of corporations are blue return filers.
42. Blue return privilege/status may also be retroactively canceled in such cases where a strict penalty is applied, a return is not filed in time more than once, or directions of a local tax director are not abided by.

(4) 『Income Sourced in Japan』

The reasons for this theme to be a ≪highly disputed theme≫ could be found in such facts as: (i) recent acceleration in the globalization of transactions and mobility of taxpayers have made it all the more difficult in some cases for an assessor and an assessee to have timely and sufficient access to those facts which determine the nature or source of income, (ii) some taxpayers attempt to take advantage of the differences in tax treatment on source rules under various tax treaties, (iii) tax treatment of income sourced in Japan differs depending on whether a receiver of such income is a resident in Japan or a nonresident that has/has not a PE in Japan. In connection with the above fact (i), the Tokyo High Court 12/15/1998 (1992(GyoKo)133) judgment annulled the Tokyo District Court 5/13/1984 judgment (1981(Wa)3126) by ruling that the taxpayer/respondent's payment to the US corporation for the right to use the patent certainly has dual aspects of it being for its production of commodities in Japan and for their sale in the U.S. but its main part is in the latter, so it is sourced in the U.S. and not to be subject to tax in Japan in accordance with Article 6(3) of the Japan-U.S. tax treaty which at that time allocated right of taxation of such income to the country where it is used.

Another case related to the above fact (i) is found in the Tax Tribunal 3/29/1995 decision (CTD No. 49-374). In this case, at issue was whether or not the buyer/applicant of the land in Japan failed to fulfill its obligation of withholding tax on the payment made to the seller of the land, who was abroad at that time. The assessor claimed that the seller was a nonresident at the time of the transaction because the power of attorney the seller entrusted to his representative carried his address in a foreign country, and he left Japan with his family and with no professional duty to be fulfilled in Japan. While the Tax Tribunal mentioned that the address written by the seller on the power of attorney does not necessarily represent the center of his living at that time, it also referred to the fact that the domestic workers in the seller's house in Japan confessed that they thought that the seller's departure from Japan was temporary and the seller would come back to Japan. Accommodating the above, the Tax Tribunal determined that the seller was not a nonresident of Japan at the time of the transaction, and therefore, the assessment of the withholding tax obligation on the applicant must be voided.

The Tokyo High Court 6/28/2007 (2005(GyoKo)278) judgment relates to the above fact (ii). In this case, the subsidiary in Japan made a payment to the subsidiary in the Netherlands (both are subsidiaries of the same U.S. corporate group). The assessor claimed that the subsidiary in the Netherlands/applicant had a PE in Japan and the contract in accordance with which the concerned payment was made was a partnership contract in essence, so the payment received is subject to tax in Japan under Article 8 (business income) of the Japan-Netherlands tax treaty that was in effect at that time. Since the Tax Tribunal confirmed that the concerned contract was a silent partnership ("tokumei-kumiai") contract and the applicant did not have a PE in Japan, the payment received is other income stipulated under Article 23 of the tax treaty, and it does not allocate taxation right on it to Japan. The Tax Tribunal 11/25/2011 decision relating to the above fact (iii) upheld the assessment which determined the apartment and the storage of the nonresident applicant to be PE in Japan because they are not just for the storage and delivery of the goods sold by the Internet in light of the fact that they added extra value in the form of attaching instruction manuals written in Japanese to the goods sold in Japan and so forth.[43]

(5) 『Denial of a Family Company's Actions or Calculations』

Japan has some semi-comprehensive anti-avoidance rules, and they include Article 157 of ITA, Article 132 of CITA, and Article 64 of IGTA providing for the denial of a family company's actions or calculations.[44] These provisions apply to cases where the transaction in question is entered into by a taxpayer and its family company, and it reduces the tax burden of the taxpayer inappropriately. Just like GAAR (General Anti-Avoidance Rule), there is ambiguity about the applicable scope of those provisions as their application criteria of "inappropriate reduction of the taxpayer's tax burden" does not provide a clear demarcation on it while a series of court rulings serve as guidance on the demarcation. According to them, those provisions generally apply to such cases where a transaction in question involving a family company is not an act that is normally carried out by independent parties or a transaction in question is an act that is irrational or unnatural to a prudent business person. But a question remains on whether those provisions are to be applied to a transaction involving a family company in a case where it digresses from a regular transaction and has a tax reduction effect while it may have some rational business purpose.

For instance, in a case where the assessor applied Article 157 of ITA to the interest-free loan made by the family company's main shareholder to the family company and deemed the accrual of miscellaneous income by recharacterizing it as a regular interest-carrying transaction, the Tokyo District Court 4/25/1997 (1995(GyoU)27) judgment upheld the assessment. Indeed, the Court spelled out that the question of whether Article 157 of ITA is applicable or not is to be determined by looking at relevant facts objectively, and its application is not premised on a taxpayer's awareness of the transaction's tax reduction effect. However, the Court also pointed out that Article 157 of ITA does not apply to cases where it is appropriate in light of the social norms to reduce the main shareholder's economic benefit for the sake of increasing the economic benefit of the family company. Likewise, the Tokyo District Court, in its 6/27/2019 (2014(GyoU)468, 2016(GyoU)503 and 2018(GyoU)444) judgment, stated that a decision of whether Article 132 of CITA is applicable or not should be made by finding out whether the transaction in question has an economic benefit

43. The relevant tax treaty provides in Article 7 that the profits of an enterprise of a Contracting State shall be taxable only in that Contracting State unless the enterprise carries on business in the other Contracting State through a permanent establishment situated therein and in Article 5(4) that the term "permanent establishment" shall not be deemed to include the use of facilities solely for the purpose of storage, display or delivery of goods or merchandise belonging to the enterprise.
44. Section 1(10) of Article 2 of CITA defines a family company to be one whose 50% or more of its shares are held by not more than three separate major holders and those in a special relationship with them.

other than that derived from the reduction of CIT and rescinded the assessment that applied Article 132 of CITA to the transaction in question.

Japan does not have GAAR, and the transfer pricing (TP) rule stipulated in Article 66-4 of STMA could be applied only to a domestic corporation's cross-border transactions with its foreign affiliate. Therefore, those semi-comprehensive anti-avoidance rules, as mentioned above, are important to fill the vacuum in the realm of countermeasures against tax avoidance and tax strategies. As the above Tokyo District Court 6/27/2019 judgment suggests, there is an ambiguity about the application scope of those Articles providing for the denial of a family company's actions or calculations, but such ambiguity is more or less inherent in many other semi-comprehensive countermeasures such as Article 22-2 (Calculation of income for the respective business year) and Article 37 (Deduction of corporate contribution) of CITA. Moreover, they are also among those ≪highly disputed themes≫ and are discussed in 2(3) of this section. The applicability of many of those countermeasures pivots on the question of whether the transactions in question deviate from those transactions between independent parties, and even if they do, rational economic reasons that they may have could rationalize such deviation and make them be out of the application scope of those countermeasures.

Another ambiguity often found in the case of anti-avoidance rules of a general nature is the interrelationship among them because, in some cases, more than one such anti-avoidance rule, as mentioned, could be applicable. Such a case often arises in a situation where a family company's transaction with its foreign affiliate, whose no less than 50% of shares are held by the family company, deviates from an arm's length transaction. The answer to the question of which of those articles mentioned above should apply to such a case seems to differ depending on the nature/content of the transaction. The possible difference in tax treatment depending on which one of these articles should be applied is mitigated by the 1986 introduction in Article 66-4(3) of STMA, which, to attain consistency in tax treatment with the TP rule, does not allow any deduction of the corporate contribution made by a domestic corporation to its foreign affiliate while corporate contribution to a domestic affiliate is deductible up to a threshold amount which is determined by its amount of capital and income for the business year.[45]

(6) [Special Credit for Capital Gains from the Transfer of a Resided Property]/『Special Credit for Housing Loans』

A lack of clarity on the application scope is a main attribute that accounts for the primary reason for the above (1) to (5)themes to be ≪highly disputed themes≫.

45. Article 66-4(3) of STMA provides for an exceptional treatment of corporate contribution because it practically makes a change to the nature of (general) corporate contribution which is deductible up to the threshold amount for CIT purposes for the reason that its relationship with a corporate business is ambiguous. The concept of corporate contribution contrasts in particular with the "wholly and exclusively" standard adopted in the UK, etc., which is based on the idea that corporation's expenses are either deductible or nondeductible at all. For this standard, *see* 2 in Section 5 of Chapter 3.

However, in the case of Articles 35 (Special credit for capital gains from the transfer of a resided property) and Article 41 (Special credit for housing loan) of STMA), a different attribute is at work as a primary cause for making them ≪highly disputed themes≫ because they, just like Article 69-4 (special calculation case for a small housing lot for Inheritance Tax purposes) of STMA which is also a ≪highly disputed theme≫ under 【Special rules on IGTA】, grant special tax treatments to the taxpayers who meet certain requirements. In actuality, tax disputes on those themes usually arise mainly for the following reasons: (i) taxpayers claim for the application of these special treatments based on their misunderstanding of the applicable scope of these provisions, (ii) taxpayers whose eligibility for those provisions are denied by the NTA claim that there are excusable circumstances that should salvage them to become eligible for them, (iii) some taxpayers inappropriately try to earn these special treatments.

The Tax Tribunal 4/30/1998 decision was on the case which seems to have arisen for the above reason (i). In this case, at issue was whether Article 35 of STMA is applicable to the applicant who was living in a house with his father before it was burned down in Oct. 1993 and moved to a different residence. After the applicant's father, who was the owner of the land and the house, passed away in January 1994, the applicant sold this land in April 1994 and claimed the application of Article 35 of STMA to the part of the capital gains that corresponded to the residential area of the land sold. The assessor denied in its reassessment the application of the provision to this case and the Tax Tribunal upheld the reassessment. The Tax Tribunal pointed out that for Article 35 of STMA to be applicable, it is necessary for a taxpayer to have owned and lived on the sold property, while in this case, the house was burned down before the death of his father, and the applicant never lived in the house as its owner.[46] Therefore, the Tax Tribunal determined that the applicant did not fulfill the requirements necessary for Article 35 of STMA to be applicable. Instead, the Tax Tribunal sustained the assessor's claim of applying Article 31 (special credit for long-term capital gains) (4) of STMA to this case.

The Tax Tribunal's 1/28/2014 decision was on the case, which seems to have arisen for the above reason (ii). In this case, the assessor denied the application of Article 41 of STMA to the applicant because the applicant's IT return filed in time did have some of the materials (such as detailed statements on the calculation of the creditable amount for the housing loan and a certificate of the applicant's registered address) necessary for claiming its application but they are insufficient because they specified neither the date of acquiring the house nor the price paid for the house. Moreover, the assessor requested the applicant to submit additional materials that could specify them, but he only turned them in after he filed a request for review of the case with the Tax Tribunal. In light of such facts, the Tax Tribunal stated that paragraph 18 (currently 28) of Article 41 of STMA prescribing the application of the

46. Article 35 of STMA stipulates in clauses (3) and (4) that special treatments also apply to a case where an inheritor sells land (which was resided in by the inheritee just before the day of inheritance) inherited from an inheritee prior to the last day of the third year from the day of the inheritance, provided that its sales price is no more than JPY 100,000,000. While, in this case, the sold land was not resided by the inheritee at the time of the inheritance.

special credit for housing loans in exceptional cases (cases where there are excusable circumstances) does not apply to the applicant. The Tax Tribunal also mentioned that paragraph 4 of Article 65 of AGRNT, which exempts an administrative penalty for underreporting of tax in a case where there is a justifiable reason, is also not applicable to the applicant.

The Tax Tribunal 11/10/2000 decision was on the case which seems to have arisen for the above reason (iii). In this case, the assessor denied the applicant's return, which applied Article 35 of STMA to the capital gains realized in February 1997 from the sale of the land and house that the applicant inherited in April 1993 and imposed a strict penalty stipulated under Article 68 of AGRNT. The applicant claimed that she moved to the sold house in February 1994, but the Tax Tribunal confirmed that her registered address during the periods of September 1985 to June 1996 was different from that of the sold house and the volume of utility bills of the apartment with that address hardly changed over those periods. Moreover, the Tax Tribunal pointed out that the address of the applicant written on its IT returns of 1994 and 1995 was not that of the sold house but that of the apartment, and she suddenly changed its registered address to that of the sold house in September 1996. In light of those facts, the Tax Tribunal concluded that the applicant's base and center of living was at the address of the apartment when the real estate was sold, and she falsely changed its registered address to apply the special credit to the capital gains, so the concerned reassessment and the imposition of the strict penalty should be upheld.

2 Characteristics of ≪Highly Disputed Themes≫ of Corporate Income Tax Act (CITA)

The Attachment reveals that, among those publicized CIT themes bracketed by 【 】, 【Calculation of income amount】 represents the majority of them. A breakdown of this theme divulges that among those themes bracketed by 『 』, 『Scope and calculation of deductible expenses』 is the largest in number (228 cases), and its breakdown reveals that: (i) [*Directors' remunerations, bonus, and retirement money*] is the largest in number (58 cases), followed by (ii) [Depreciation of depreciable assets] (35 cases) and (iii) [Corporate contribution] (29 cases). A breakdown of the above (i) unveils that 〔Director's bonus〕 has the largest number (25 cases) while in the case of the above (iii), it is <u>〔Gratis transfer of economic benefits〕</u> (15 cases). Among those themes bracketed by 『 』, the second largest in number is <u>『Attributable business years of taxable profits』</u>(46 cases), followed by <u>『Attributable business years of deductible expenses』</u> (28 cases). Among CIT themes contained in STMA, the largest number of published cases is <u>『Entertainment expenses, etc.』</u> (19 cases), and it is most disputed under the theme [Distinction from other expenses] (17 cases). These underlined themes are analyzed below to explore the reasons for them to be highly disputed.

(1) [Directors' Remunerations, Bonus, and Retirement Money]

As for the corporate director's bonus, it is currently deductible for CIT purposes so long as it meets the requirements (reasonable in amount, predetermined or pre-notified to the tax office, etc.) prescribed in Article 34 of ITA. But, prior to the 2006 revision of ITA, corporate director's bonus, which is distinguishable from its salary, was not deductible at all for ITA purposes because it was considered to be the appropriation of corporate profit, so there was a corporate incentive to reward its directors in other ways. Such a reward to a corporate director may be given in the form of remunerations or an economic benefit to him in an attempt to reduce the tax burden of the corporation and the director, while in some cases, such a grant of reward may not be intended for tax avoidance. Irrespective of whether such intention on the part of a corporation existed or not, once such reward was deemed to be the director's bonus, the corporation faced practically the double penalty (the penalty for underreporting of its CIT and the penalty for its failure to withhold tax on the bonus). Obviously, corporations wanted to avoid such disastrous consequences, so there was little wonder that 〔Director's bonus, etc.〕 was one of the ≪highly disputed themes≫.

In reality, there are many Tax Tribunal decisions on cases in which it is difficult to wipe out a doubt that the applicants/corporations (especially family companies) intended to provide unreasonable financial benefit to their directors (usually main shareholders as well) at the expense of the corporations. For example, the Tax Tribunal's 6/19/1973 decision (CTD No. 6-p. 38) was on the case in which the applicant paid a fairly large amount of salary to its directors (the president's wife who hardly worked for the applicant in reality, and his son who was a college student). Another example is the Tax Tribunal 12/4/1985 decision (CTD No. 32-p. 220) on the case where the applicant paid the expenses incurred in connection with the trip in which only the directors of the applicant and the trading partners participated. Similarly, the Tax Tribunal's 11/27/1980 decision (CTD No. 21-p. 127) and 8/9/1989 decision (CTD No. 38-p. 188) were on the cases where the applicants sold their land to their directors at prices far lower than their market prices, and the Tax Tribunal upheld the reassessments which regarded such economic benefit given to the applicants' directors in the form of the difference between their transactional prices and the market prices as bonus to them and denied its deduction for CIT purposes.

Whereas, some bona fide payments to corporate directors may face unintended negative tax consequences because the payments that constitute "inappropriately high" parts are not deductible for CIT purposes, while it is difficult to see the monetary threshold of being "inappropriately high" because a director's contribution, etc., to the corporation varies from one to another. This point is often disputed in the case of a corporation's payment of retirement money to its director. The NTA usually determines this monetary threshold based on the average amount of retirement money paid by a couple of corporations that are quite similar to a taxpayer in question in terms of the type of business, sales turnover, geographical location, etc., and the concerned taxpayer's payment exceeding this average amount is often deemed as being "inappropriately high."[47] However, the taxpayer has practically no access to the NTA's confidential data on the payments made to the directors by those allegedly comparable corporations, so it can neither determine in advance whether the payment could be "inappropriately high" nor confirm after the reassessments are made on it, the validity of the NTA's claim on the comparability of the corporations/their directors with the taxpayer/its director.

As mentioned above, the 2006 revision of CITA somewhat changed the scene. In particular, the revised Article 34 of CITA has discarded the difference in CIT treatments on the bonus and remunerations paid to corporate directors, and they are deductible for CIT purposes so long as they are included in the amount of pre-registered reasonable amount of salary that is classified as: (i) fixed amount of salary paid monthly, (ii) registered pre-confirmed amount of salary other than (i), or (iii) salary amount proportional to the achievements, and so forth.[48] This revision has not only expanded practically the scope of deductible payments to corporate directors but also narrowed the scope of manipulation of payment forms for the purpose of reducing the tax burden of the corporation so that it should work towards reducing the number of tax disputes on this theme. Actually, those cases disputing the application of the revised Article 34 of CITA are mostly about whether payments to directors made in a form that deviates from the procedures under the Article could nevertheless receive the tax treatment under the Article as in the case of the Tax Tribunal's 5/24/2010 decision that denied it because of the concerned payment's failure to fulfill the above requirement (ii) of being fixed in amount and notified in advance.[49]

(2) 『Entertainment Expenses, Etc.』

The deduction of expenses of a corporation could be restricted if they are regarded as entertainment expenses, etc., for CIT purposes.[50] Therefore, it could be a serious issue for a corporation whether or not some of its expenses fall under entertainment expenses, etc., stipulated under Article 61-4 of STMA. Actually, the majority of disputes over entertainment expenses, etc., revolve around the point of whether a corporation's concerned expense is to be regarded as an entertainment expense, etc., or other

47. Some claim that only such parts exceeding the largest amount (instead of the average amount) of the retirement money paid to the directors by the comparable corporations should be deemed "inappropriately high," and there are actually a few court rulings that seem to have adopted this claim. *See* Tokyo District Court 4/22/2016 judgment.
48. The change brought about by this revision may be relatively limited in effect in the case of tax treatment of retirement money to a corporate director.
49. Likewise, the Tokyo High Court 3/14/2013 (2012(GyoKo)424) judgment sustained the reassessment of negating the appellant/corporation's deduction for CIT purposes its director's salary whose amount was less than the registered amount and it did not notify the assessor of the change within the deadline.
50. The amount of entertainment expenses, etc., deductible for CITA purposes differs depending on: (i) the amount of capital of a corporation, (ii) the nature of the entertainment expenses (i.e., expenses for food and drinks or the others). The concept of entertainment expenses, etc., prescribed in STMA is broader than that of entertainment expenses in general terms. *See* footnote 52.

expense such as corporate contribution, welfare expense, sales promotion expense, advertisement expense, etc. In some cases, it is not so easy to determine whether a certain corporate expense is an entertainment expense, etc., or not, while a series of court decisions have established some criteria for the determination.[51] According to them, an expense is an entertainment expense, etc., if: (i) it is expended for those who are related to the business,[52] (ii) it is expended for the purpose of entertaining them, providing service or other similar benefits to them (or it is expended for the purpose of facilitating a transactional relationship with them by becoming better acquainted), (iii) it is expended in a form of action that is similar to entertainment, gift, provision of service or similar benefit, and so forth.

The above (i) and (ii) criteria were relied on by the Tokyo High Court 11/30/1977 (1975(GyoU)43) judgment, and the Court ruled that the tips given by the appellant/owner of a roadside shop to the bus drivers every time they parked their sightseeing buses in the appellant's parking lot just in front of the shop were entertainment expenses, etc., because they meet both of those criteria. Usually, the above (iii) criterion should be useful in helping confirm the determination of whether or not a concerned corporate expense is an entertainment expense, etc., based on the above criteria (i) and (ii) while it might compound the difficulty in making such a confirmation in such cases where the determination based on the criterion (iii) does not accord with that based on the criteria (i) and (ii).[53] The case handled by the Tokyo High Court 9/9/2003 (1975(GyoKo)242) judgment intimates that there might arise such a difficulty. In this case, the appellant/pharmaceutical corporation received a request for the translation of medical research papers written by a team of young doctors and trainees of the hospital, which had business transactions with the appellant. The appellant often received similar requests from others, but the appellant's charges on them were much higher.

In the above case, the respondent deemed that the difference between the regular prices and the lower price for the translation for the concerned medical research papers was an entertainment expense, etc., for CIT purposes, but the above Tokyo High Court, without making any reference to the appellant's claim of it being a corporate contribution, dismissed the respondent's claim by pointing out that the expense in question is not an entertainment expense, etc., because: (i) the medical team's relation with the appellant's business was not so strong because it was mostly composed of young

51. For instance, the Tax Tribunal's 1/26/1996 decision sustained the reassessment that the cost of the employees' trips that was borne by the corporation was excessive in amount and constitute salaries to them.
52. IT-related AR 61-4(1)-22 on STMA provides that for the purposes of Article 61-4(4) of STMA, those who are related to a corporation's business include its employees and shareholders. While some assert that a corporation's grant of economic benefits to its employees as a whole could not be entertainment expenses but either welfare expenses or salaries to them. *See* Satoshi Matsuzawa, Bibliography (5) p. 329.
53. The author believes that if the purpose of an expense is to entertain business associates, the mode of expenditure shall take a form of entertainment and so forth, so that criteria (i) and (ii) may be sufficient to determine whether or not an expenditure is an entertainment expense, etc., and the criterion (iii) might make such determination more difficult in cases where an expenditure intended for entertainment, etc., is made in a way where a form differs from its substance.

doctors and trainees, (ii) the expense borne by the appellant was not so much in amount, and the team was not aware of the benefits because the appellant's bearing of the difference in costs between the regular prices and the lower price for the translation of the concerned papers was not made known to them. In other words, the court's determination was that the expense in question was not something like a gift or economic benefit that could win their favors but something with a strong tint of academic encouragement, then it overturned the preceding Tokyo District Court 9/13/2002 (1999(GyoU)20) judgment by ruling that, in light of the criteria (i), (ii) and (iii), it is not an entertainment expense, etc.[54]

In addition to the above (i) to (iii) criteria, there is also a question of whether the amount of expenses could be a factor to be considered in determining whether they are entertainment expenses, etc., for CIT purposes. On this point, it is at least clear that the amount of expenses could matter much in determining whether the expenses in question are welfare expenses, entertainment expenses, etc.[55] In the above Tokyo High Court 11/30/1977 judgment, the Court dismissed the appellant's claim that a question of whether an expense is high in amount or extravagant in nature should also be an independent criterion in determining whether the concerned expenses (tips for the bus drivers) are entertainment expenses, etc. Likewise, in the 12/20/1978 decision, the Tax Tribunal specified that not only the relevant Article of STMA stipulates that corporate expenses spent for entertaining business associates, etc., constitute entertainment expenses, etc., unless they are either corporate contributions, sales discounts, rebates, advertisement expense, welfare expense, or salaries, but also those expenses to be excluded from entertainment expenses, etc., are explicitly prescribed in the Implementation Order of STMA, so the question of whether or not expenses in question are entertainment expenses, etc., shall not be contingent on their amount.

(3) 〔*Gratuitous Transfer of Economic Benefits*〕

There are corporate expenses whose relevance to the corporation's business is not so clear. Therefore, Japan's CITA treats such expenses as a corporate contribution whose deductibility could be limited for CIT purposes unless they are designated contributions to public-interest corporations, etc. Therefore, when a corporation makes a gratuitous transfer of economic benefits to another body, Article 22(2) of CITA dictates that the transferor is deemed to have received arm's length amount of payment while the same amount is deemed to be contributed to the transferee under Article 37 of ITA unless such economic benefits are entertainment expenses, welfare expenses, etc. The

54. The Tokyo District Court took a position that it is irrelevant whether or not the recipients of the benefits were aware of the benefits given to them in regarding the concerned granted benefits as entertainment expenses, etc., for CIT purposes. Certainly, some must view negatively the determination of the nature of a corporation's expense or provision of economic benefits for CIT purposes based on the recipients' subjective sense or their level of awareness of those benefits.
55. The NTA's Tax Answer No. 2603 explains that one of the criteria for determining whether a corporate expense is a welfare expense is its amount. Many court rulings including Fukuoka District Court 4/25/2017 (2015 (GyoU)15) judgment confirm this when dividing lines between welfare expenses and entertainment expenses, etc., are not clear enough.

result of such treatment is taxable corporate income on its transferor to the extent that the amount of such benefits constituting corporate contribution exceeds the threshold of the deductible amount, which is to be determined by the amount of capital and income of the transferor for the relevant business year. Similarly, Article 37(8) of CITA stipulates that, in a case where a corporation transfers an asset at a price lower than its market price, the gifted part (usually the difference between the asset's transfer price and the market price) is deemed to be corporate contribution.

But, there is an ambiguity on the scope of corporate contribution. For instance, in a case where a parent company/respondent made an interest-free loan to its subsidiary and the appellant made the reassessment deeming the respondent's receipt of the arm's length interest, the Osaka High Court in its 3/30/1978 (1972(GyoKo)42) judgment mentioned that gratuitous transfer of an asset is, even if it is necessary for generating corporate revenue, to be deemed corporate contribution, and it ruled that the reassessment was to be upheld while the arm's length interest rate should be 6% instead of 10%. Nevertheless, the Court stated that if there were rational economic reasons for giving up an arm's length amount of interest, there is no deemed revenue nor corporate contribution for CIT purposes. The NTA's AR 9-4-1 and 9-4-2 on CIT also confirm that interest-free loans and debt waivers do not constitute corporate contributions in cases where they have rational economic reasons. The hurdles set by those AR provisions are rather high, but there are some cases, such as the Tax Tribunal 6/22/1982 decision (CTD No. 24-110), in which it was found that there was a rational economic reason for the applicant's debt waiver on the loan it made to its related corporation and therefore it was not to be deemed corporate contribution.[56]

What constitutes a rational economic reason is not so clear, and that compounds the problem of ambiguity in the scope of corporate contribution. For example, in a case where the assessor made a reassessment in which the plaintiff's payment to its related corporation was deemed excessive in amount and the excessive part constituted corporate contribution, the Tokyo District Court remarked in its 2/3/2000 (1995(GyoU)262) judgment that the question of whether or not the payment in question constitutes corporate contribution should be decided from the perspective of whether the payment in question digresses conspicuously from the arm's length payment and is recognized as a manipulation for tax avoidance purpose by the related parties. Then, the Court ruled that, in this case, there was no evidence showing that the part of the payment in question was a manipulation, so the reassessment should be voided.[57] Whereas, in the 2/28/1994 (1993(Gyoo)3) judgment, the Miyazaki branch of Fukuoka High Court affirmed the Miyazaki District Court's 9/17/1993 (1992(GyoU)2 and 3) ruling of dismissing the taxpayer's claim that the application of Article 37 of CITA should be limited to tax avoidance cases or those cases where the transaction in question is unnatural and lacks economic rationality.

56. For further analysis on this point, *see* footnotes 139 and 140.
57. There is a view that this court ruling possibly serves as a clarification of what rational economic reason means in relation to Article 37 of CITA. For such view, *see* Suetada Ito, Bibliography (6) p. 32.

The above court rulings showing different views on the applicable scope of Article 37 of CITA illustrate that it is not clear enough. What is clear is the fact that over the years, there seems to have been some metamorphosis in the nature of corporate contribution prescribed under Article 37 of CITA in such a way that its scope of application has become narrower since the above Osaka High Court 3/30/1978 was rendered.[58] As mentioned in 2(2) of Section 2, there is also some ambiguity on the lines dividing corporate contribution from some other expenses, including entertainment expenses, etc. The Tax Tribunal's 7/18/1991 decision (CTD No. 42, p. 128) may be one example of such ambiguity. In this case, the respondent made a reassessment based on the view that the plaintiff bore more expenses than its share for the trip participated in by the employees of the applicant and some business partners, and the excess part of the expenses constitutes corporate contribution to the latter. But the Tax Tribunal voided the reassessment by stating that the ratio of expenses to be borne respectively among the participating corporations does not have to be arithmetically proportional if there is a rational reason for that, and in this case, the expenses borne by the applicant are not so large in amount that they should constitute welfare expenses.[59]

(4) 『Attributable Business Years of Taxable Profits/Deductible Expenses』

Taxable profits and deductible expenses for CIT purposes are often disputed not only in terms of their scope but also in terms of the years to which they should belong.[60] A corporation tends to have an incentive for deferring the appropriation of taxable profits and moving up deductible expenses for CIT purposes. AR 2-2-1 on CIT specifies that, as for the costs of goods sold whose prices are not determined by the end of a business year, they should, under the principle of matching cost and revenue, estimate the costs properly and appropriate them as deductible expenses in the relevant business year.[61] As for the period expenses such as selling costs, general and administrative expenses, etc. (excluding amortization expenses), such estimation is not possible, and they must be, in accordance with the principle of fixed debts, fixed as debts by the end of the business year in order for them to be deductible for the year. For such debts to be fixed, AR 2-2-12 on CIT requires that by the end of the business year, (i) such debts are established, (ii) there should exist facts which cause such debts to be paid, and (iii)

58. This metamorphosis may be in line with the application of the TP rule in and out of country now that OECD's final BEPS Report also mentions in paras. 1.123-1.124 of Actions 8-10, "The non-recognition of a transaction that possesses the commercial rationality of an arm's length arrangement is not an appropriate application of the arm's length principle." The metamorphosis of the nature of corporate contribution is also observable in the adoption of para. 3 of Article 66-4 of STMA under which the amount of a corporation's expense for its foreign affiliate that is deemed a corporate contribution is *not deductible at all* for CIT purposes. *See* footnote 45.
59. *See* footnote 55 for the NTA's Tax Answer No. 2603 on welfare expenses.
60. A taxpayer's failure to attribute profits and losses properly to the concerned year incurs the imposition of underreporting penalty while chances for its remission in such a case seem to be high in Australia. *See* 5(1) in Section 1 and footnote 137 of Chapter 4.
61. While, in the case of individual proprietors, AR 37-1 on IT prescribes that cost of sales and other expenses directly incurred for gaining the total amount of revenue is, unless otherwise specified, limited to those fixed as debts for the year.

their amounts could be rationally calculated. Similar requirements for costs to be fixed also apply in the case of individual proprietors for IT purposes as it is prescribed under AR 37-2 on IT.

Despite the above guidelines, there are cases where it is not so easy to determine which business year taxable profits and deductible expenses for CIT purposes should be allocated to. For example, in the Supreme Court 10/29/2004 (2000(A)1714) judgment, at issue was whether the assessor's reassessment, which denied the corporation/appellant's estimated appropriation of construction-related cost to the concerned business year in accordance with the principle of matching cost and revenue was lawful or not. In the original Tokyo High Court 10/20/2000 (1999(U)1196) judgment, the Court upheld the reassessment by concluding that the payment obligation of the concerned construction-related cost was not specific enough to be estimated at the end of the concerned business year. The Supreme Court voided this High Court's ruling by determining that even if the debt in question was not fixed by the end of the concerned business year, it could be expected with a substantial degree of likelihood that the debt would be paid shortly and the amount of the debt could be estimated properly at that time just like the concerned construction-related cost, it could be appropriated to the concerned business year as the deductible cost of sales for CIT purposes.

The question of how AR 2-2-12 on CIT applies to the appropriation of the period expenses could also be difficult. Such difficulty manifested in the Supreme Court 12/24/2004 (2002(GyoHi)147) judgment. In this judgment, the disputed point was whether or not the reassessment of the appellant/financial institution's deduction of its nonperforming loan for the concerned business year was lawful. The assessor/respondent claimed that the nonperforming loan could not be deemed uncollectible at the end of the concerned year now that the waiver of the debt was subject to cancelation. However, the Supreme Court stated that the question of whether the debt is uncollectible or not is to be answered by taking the social norm collectively into consideration, i.e., the debtor's circumstances as well as the debt collector's circumstances, which include the efforts needed to collect it, a possible collision with the other creditors by attempting to collect it forcefully, surrounding economic circumstances and so forth. Then, it ruled that it had already been objectively evident at the end of the concerned business year that the nonperforming loan in question was uncollectible, so the original/preceding Tokyo High Court 3/14/2002 (2001(GyoKo)94) judgment should be voided.[62]

Now that AR 9-6-2 on CIT sets forth that a bad debt should be appropriated in the year when it has become clear that it could not be collected in its entirety in light of the debtor's assets, payment capability, etc., there might remain a subtle difference between this AR and the above Supreme Court's standpoint. Moreover, the uncertainty

62. It is generally said that this Supreme Court judgment is remarkable in pointing out the need of taking into consideration the circumstances of the collector's side as well in determining whether the nonperforming loan is uncollectible or not. This judgment is also said to be socially significant enough to work toward encouraging corporations to filing tax suits in the future. *See* Minoru Nakazato, Bibliography (7) p. 107.

about which business year earnings and expenses should be allocated to has the problem of posing a risk that, if a corporation fails to deduct it timely, it might lose its chance of deducting it or be deemed to have made a corporate contribution to the debtor for CIT purposes. Actually, in the 6/26/2008 decision (CTD No. 75-314), the Tax Tribunal upheld the reassessment, which denied the applicant's deduction of the trade receivable against the business partner in 2006 when the applicant claimed it to have become unrecoverable. The Tax Tribunal reasoned that the business year in which the concerned trade receivable must be deducted should not be 2006 when the applicant's board of directors determined it to be uncollectible, but be 1999, when a court finalized the business partner's bankruptcy procedure and its bankruptcy was notified in the official gazette, so its deduction in 2006 is not in line with the principle of fair and adequate accounting treatment and could not be allowed.

3 Characteristics of ≪Highly Disputed Themes≫ of Inheritance/Gift Tax Act (IGTA)

The Attachment lists published 372 cases on IGT (395 cases, including IGT-related provisions under STMA). In terms of the number of themes bracketed by 【 】, approximately 45% of those 395 cases are under 【Property appraisal】(167 cases)followed by 【Scope of property subject to Inheritance Tax】 (55 cases), 【Calculation of taxable amount of inherited property】 (53 cases), 【Scope of taxable gifts】 (37 cases) and 【Special rules on IGTA】 (23 cases). A breakdown of the most disputed theme (【Property appraisal】) divulges that 『Rights and surface rights on land』 has the largest number of cases (96 cases) followed by 『Principles of appraisal』(27 cases). Breakdown of 【Scope of property subject to Inheritance Tax】 exposes that 『Deposits』 (12 cases) is the most highly disputed theme, while the breakdown of 【Calculation of taxable amount of inherited property】 and 【Special rules on IGTA】 reveals that, among them, 『Deductible debt』 (29 cases) and 『Special rules on calculation of taxable price of small resided property for Inheritance Tax purposes』 (16 cases) respectively have the largest number of the publicized cases.[63] In the following, the underlined themes are looked into to explore the attributes that make them ≪highly disputed themes≫.

(1) 『Principles of Appraisal』

The principal reason for 『Principles of appraisal』 to be a ≪high-disputed theme≫ lies in the fact that Article 22 of IGTA stipulates that the price of inherited property is, unless prescribed otherwise in the Act, its market price at the time of its acquisition, and the market price is understood to be an objective exchange value of the property, but this objective exchange value is not so clear. This problem of ambiguity is

63. As for 『Special rules on calculation of taxable price of small resided property for Inheritance Tax purposes』, the primary reason or the attribute for it to be a ≪highly disputed theme≫ should be basically the same as that for [special credit for capital gains from the transfer of a resided property]/『Special credit for housing loan』, so *see* 1(6) of Section 2 and 1(3) in Section 4 for its attribute.

conspicuous, particularly in the case of inherited land and unlisted shares, but the NTA's annual publication of roadside land prices on a nationwide scale and its AR on Property Appraisal mitigate this problem very much. The NTA does the conservative appraisal of land for IGT purposes by setting roadside land prices at approximately 80% of the standard transactional prices on various points announced yearly by the Ministry of Land, Infrastructure, Transport, and Tourism, mostly due to the possible change of land prices between the date of their publication and the time by which the inheritor/donee must file its tax return. An inheritor/a donee or his tax agent is expected to use a publicized proper roadside land price as a reference in calculating the price of the inherited/gifted land and the methods enumerated in ARs for calculating the prices of other inherited/gifted property for IGT purposes.

The reason for the NTA's AR on Property Appraisal being followed as if they were legal provisions lies in the fact that, if it were not for it, various appraisal methods would be employed for various properties, and it would hinder the speedy handling of cases that come up on a recurrent and large-scale basis, while standardized appraisal methods are more rational from the viewpoint of fairness among taxpayers, reduction in administrative burden and taxpayers' convenience. It was also pointed out in the Osaka High Court 5/31/2005 (2004(GyoKo)95) judgment that the standardized appraisal methods prescribed under the NTA's AR on Property Appraisal should be relied upon in relation to every taxpayer and applying an appraisal method other than the one laid down under the AR to a particular taxpayer should, even if it gives the property price which is within the rational range of the market price which is referred to by Article 22 of IGTA as the price of an inherited property, not to be accepted. As an exception, the AR on Property Appraisal has a clause 6 (hereinafter called "AR 6") prescribing that in cases where there are special circumstances that would lead the application of the AR's appraisal methods to produce an inappropriate price, its appraisal should be done in accordance with the NTA Commissioner's direction.

The Tokyo High Court 3/15/1993(1992(GyoKo)93) judgment is a case where the AR 6 was applied to the case of tax avoidance. In this case, in 1986, a hospitalized elderly person/inheritee borrowed JPY 1.8 billion and purchased land at the price of JPY 1.6 billion, and in 1987, the inheritors filed inheritance tax returns in which the land was valued at approximately JPY 100 million, and a large amount of the loan was deducted as debt. Right after the land was inherited, it was sold at the price of JPY 1.8 billion. The assessor/respondent did not dispute the fact that the price of the land becomes around JPY 100 million in accordance with the applicable roadside land price but claimed it to be equivalent to the acquisition price by applying the AR 6 to this case.[64] The court upheld the assessor's claim by ruling as follows: (i) in cases where land prices abnormally soared and such change in land price cannot timely be reflected in the AR on Property Appraisal, the prices calculated in accordance with a relevant provision of the AR is not the market price laid down under Article 22 of IGTA, (ii) the primary reason for the acquisition of this land in question was not assets management

64. The total amount of inheritance tax was about JPY 800 million if the AR 6 was applicable while it was about JPY 50 million if it was not applicable. Japan's land price soared immensely until it fell down dramatically in 1991 with the collapse of bubble economy.

but tax avoidance which is unacceptable from the perspective of fairness of tax burden between those who can utilize it and those who cannot.[65]

The AR 6 could also be applicable in a case where a divergence from the price calculated in accordance with the AR on Property Appraisal has been caused by reasons other than the tax saving/avoidance of a taxpayer. For example, in the Tokyo District Court 2/26/2003 (2000(GyoU)221) judgment, at issue was whether the appraised price of JPY 260 million claimed by the plaintiff for IGT purposes for one of the inherited lands without resorting to the AR on Property Appraisal but relying on the certified real estate appraiser was rational or not. The respondent also did not rely on the AR on Property Appraisal but relied on the AR 6 and appraised it as cleared land of JPY 300 million. The Court agreed that, since the standard transactional price of the land close to this land announced by the Ministry of Land, Infrastructure, Transport, and Tourism declined by 32.9% within one year during which this inheritance occurred, there is doubt about the appropriateness of the price (JPY 360 million) calculated in accordance with the AR. Then, the Court ruled that there are special circumstances that justify appraising the price of this land without relying on the AR on Property Appraisal and its price appraised as the cleared land should be JPY 271 million.

The Supreme Court 4/19/2022 (2020(Gyou-hi)283) judgment may have further compounded the ambiguity of the application scope of the AR 6. In this case, the inheritee borrowed much to purchase a high-floor room in a skyscraper whose market price is usually much higher than that of a low-floor room, while there is not much difference between them in terms of their prices calculated pursuant to roadside land prices and relevant provisions in the AR for IGT purposes. The assessor claimed the application of the AR 6 in determining the price of this room inherited by the appellant, whereas the Court ruled as follows: (i) unless there is a rational reason, it is against the principle of fairness and unlawful for the assessor to apply a higher price to an inherited property of a particular taxpayer than that applicable under the AR even if that higher price does not exceed the market price of the property; (ii) in this case, the inheritee and the appellant knew that the loan and the purchase of the concerned room would reduce the future inheritance tax burden; (iii) the application of the relevant provisions of the AR to this case would cause significant unfairness between the appellant and those who do not do the same.[66] Then, the Court concluded that, in this case, there is a rational reason for the AR 6 to become applicable.

65. As a measure to counteract such tax avoidance, the 1987 amendment of STMA introduced Article 69-4 which dictates that the price of a real estate for IGTA purposes which is acquired within three years before its inheritance is the price of its acquisition, but it is now only applicable to a case where a corporation is an acquirer.
66. While the Tokyo High Court stated in the 6/24/2020 (2019(GyoKo)239) judgment which precedes this judgment on this case that even if there were a property in a similar situation whose price is appraised in accordance with the AR's relevant provisions in spite of the fact that there is as much difference as this case between the price given by them and that given by the professional real estate valuators, it does not necessarily follow that such appraised price of that property without applying the AR 6 would become unlawful on account of its alleged violation of the principle of equality in taxation.

The Supreme Court also expressed in the above judgment a view that the mere fact of a large gap existing between the price appraised in accordance with the relevant provisions in the AR and that given by the certified real estate appraiser is not enough for the AR 6 to become applicable. This Supreme Court's view practically negates an opinion/criticism that, in coming up with the price of inherited property for inheritance tax purposes and considering whether or not the AR 6 is applicable, subjective factors such as tax avoidance motive should not be taken into account,[67] and it also raises a question of how it should be reconciled with such lower court judgments as the above Tokyo District Court 2/26/2003 in which the AR 6 was applied in the case where there was no taxpayer's attempt to reduce tax.[68] Moreover, this Supreme Court's view not only leaves a question of how grave such tax avoidance should be for the AR 6 to become applicable but also compounds an issue of whether a penalty for the non/underreporting of IGT could be exempted in an ambiguous case where the AR 6 could apply but there is a reason for the non/underreporting.[69] While, in reality, there are practically no cases where the Tax Tribunal or courts accepted the taxpayer's claim based on a justifiable reason for the exemption of the penalty when the AR 6 was applied.

(2) 『Rights and Surface Rights on Land』

『Rights and surface rights on land』 is the most ≪highly disputed theme≫ among those themes under 【Property appraisal】, and the reason for that is attributable to the fact that 〔Adjustments based on various influential factors〕 under 『Rights and surface rights on land』 has as many published cases as twenty-seven cases. Among the themes under 〔Adjustments based on various influential factors〕, the most frequently disputed theme is AR 24-4 (Appraisal of "the specific spacious land") on Property Appraisal (hereinafter called "AR ex 24-4") before it was abolished and replaced in 2017 by the AR 20-2 (Appraisal of a spacious residential site) on Property Appraisal. "The specific spacious land" to which the AR ex 24-4 was applicable had to meet the requirements shown in the following flowchart in Figure 1.14, and once it meets them, the price of the land for IGT purposes is reduced significantly because the price of "the specific spacious land" is calculated in accordance with the formula (rate of the road adjacent to the land) × (0.6-0.05 × square meters of the land/1,000 square meters) × square meters of the land. In fact, in some cases, the price of spacious land for IGT purposes could be almost halved if it is "the specific spacious land" by meeting the above requirements.

---

67. For such opinion, *see* Sadao Kishida, Bibliography (8) p. 213 and Masahiro Midorikawa, Bibliography (9) pp. 21-22.
68. The Tokyo High Court 1/28/1981 (1978(GyoKo)75) judgment is another example of such lower court judgments.
69. Also *see* footnote 66 on the court's view on what the principle of equity in taxation among taxpayers in similar situations means. As for the analysis of the reasons that exempt penalties, *see* 2(2) in Section 3.

Figure 1.14 Flowchart for Determining Whether or Not A Spacious Land Is "the Specific Spacious Land"

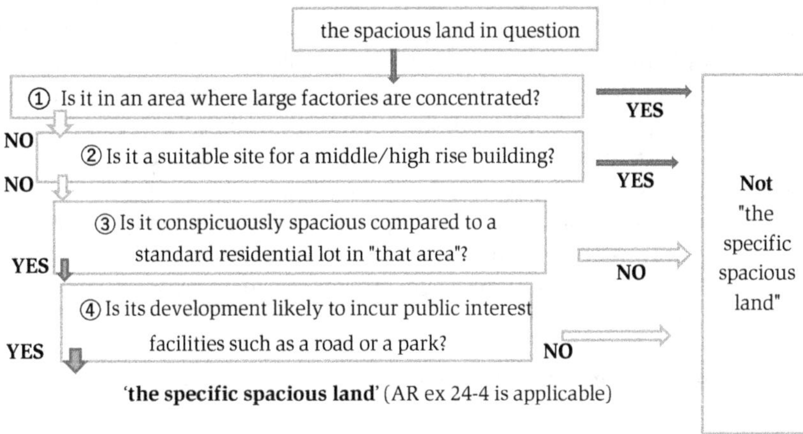

This significant reduction in the value of land for IGT purposes was a principal reason for the AR ex 24-4 to be a ≪highly disputed theme≫. Another principal reason was the difficulty in some cases in determining whether or not the requirements for its application are fulfilled. The rationale for the price of "the specific spacious land" to be reduced significantly for IGT purposes is found in the fact that the development of "the specific spacious land" usually requires the construction of a road passage or a semi-public space for the subdivided residential sites of the land, which not only reduces the size of the residential lot as a whole but also sets a restriction on its development plan. In many cases, a critical point regarding the question ③ in Figure 1.14 is where "that area" is. Depending on how widely or narrowly "that area" encompassing a spacious land in question is defined or claimed to cover, it may or may not be "the specific spacious land." A critical point regarding the question ④ in Figure 1.14 is whether it is more rational for the spacious land in question to be developed in such a way that it is subdivided into residential sites without constructing a road passage or a semi-public space in the land. In reality, the views of the taxpayers and the assessors differ very often on those critical points.[70]

Such difference in views appeared in the Tax Tribunal 7/9/2007 case/decision (CTD No. 74-326). In this case, the applicant requested the application of AR ex 24-4 to the land he inherited, but the assessor dismissed the request. The Tax Tribunal stated that, in determining whether or not the AR ex 24-4 is applicable to the case, it should

70. Whereas, the Tax Tribunal 7/9/2007 decision (CTD No. 74-342) is one example in which at issue was whether or not the concerned spacious land is a suitable site for a middle/high rise building and it was affirmative on this issue.

be ascertained whether constructing a road passage, etc., is more economically rational in light of the following: (i) Would the division of the concerned land without constructing a road create residential sites whose respective size is about the standard size of a residential lot common to "that area?" (ii) Would it not violate relevant law (such as City Planning Act)? (iii) Would it be economically advantageous in light of the local area's ratio of floor areas against the size of the building and the land? (iv) What is a generally adopted development method in and around "that area"?[71] Then, it concluded that developing the land in question without constructing a road passage is economically the most rational way. However, the Tokyo High Court 3/28/2006 (2005(GyoKo)320) judgment may be harder to swallow for the taxpayer because it supported the assessor's development plan (Figure 1.15) of the land in question for the reason that it accords with the above (iii) and also provides different types of residential sites which could accommodate differences in purchasers' purchasing powers and preferences.

Figure 1.15 Assessor's Development Plan Presented at Tokyo High Court 3/28/2006 Case

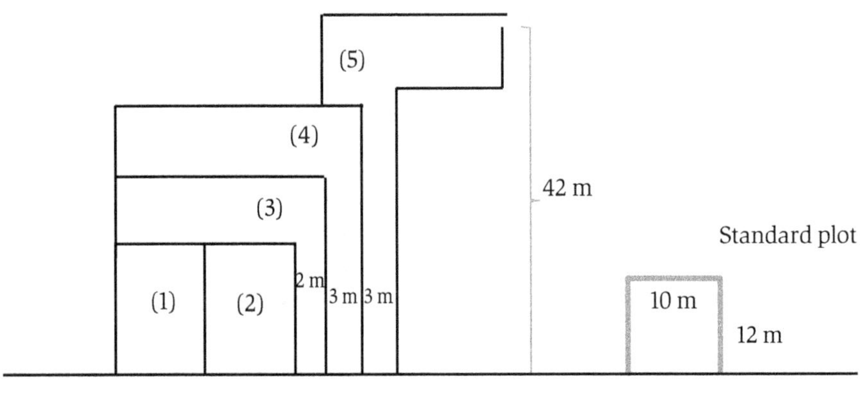

Source: Keiko Iizawa, Ref. 1(10) p. 205.

As for the Tokyo District Court 2/10/2006 (2005(GyoU)108) judgment that favored the assessor's development plan in Figure 1.17 rather than the plaintiff's development plan in Figure 1.16 for the reason that the former is more economically advantageous than the latter, it may be less difficult to swallow for the plaintiff as well

71. Tax Tribunal also confirmed that "that area" is to be decided by taking into account such factors: (a) natural divisions of areas, (b) administrative jurisdictions, (c) applicable administrative rules, (d) such dividers as roads, rivers, and railroads, etc., (e) which area has characteristics and features that are common or quite similar to the land in question.

as taxpayers in general while there still remained some who questioned whether there was a contradiction between the City Planning Act's objective of building cities with order and finding economic rationality in developing irregular shapes of residential sites. They even asserted that a development plan of spacious land without constructing a road passage should be limited to such a case where, at the time of the taxpayer's Inheritance Tax return filing, there is a high chance of such a development plan being actually adopted and implemented in the future.[72] Now that the AR ex 24-4 was replaced by the AR 20-2 in 2017, there is no more need to determine how appropriate and valid such a question and assertions are. Furthermore, a spacious land does not have to clear the strict test shown in Figure 1.14 for the application of AR 20-2, but the ratio of reduction in the value of a spacious residential land under AR 20-2 is much less,[73] so disputes over its application have not arisen as often as those under the AR ex 24-4.

Figure 1.16 Land Development Plan of the Plaintiff in Tokyo District Court 2/10/2006 Judgment

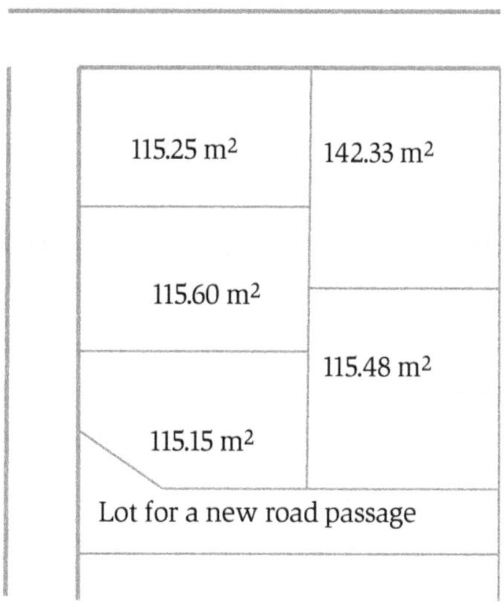

72. For such opinion, *see* Keiko Iizawa, Bibliography (10) p. 206.
73. Under the AR 20-2, the value of a spacious residential site for IGT purpose is to be calculated in accordance with the following formula: amount of applicable road rating × applicable various adjustment rates for the configuration × applicable adjustment rate for the size × square meters of the land. These adjustment rates under the AR 20-2 accommodate, in coming up with a price of a spacious land, such differences in the land's configuration, location, square meters, and so forth much more than the AR ex 24-4. Moreover, the AR 20-2 is not applicable to land situated in an area designated by the local governments as "small and medium enterprise area."

Figure 1.17 Land Development Plan of the Assessor in Tokyo District Court 2/10/2006 Judgment

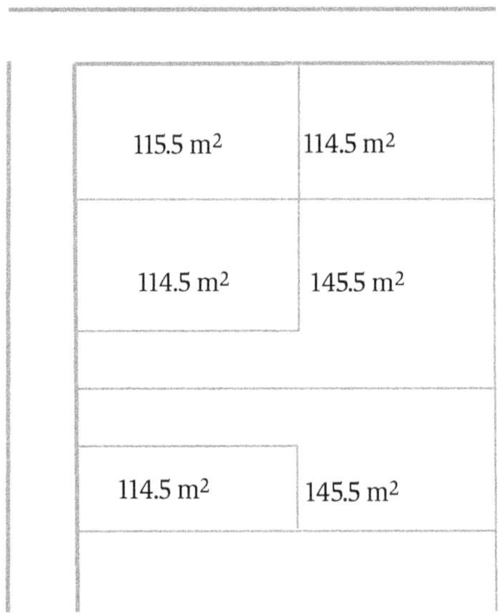

(3) **【*Scope of Property Subject to Inheritance Tax*】**

【Scope of property subject to Inheritance Tax】is a "highly disputed theme" for reasons such as:(i) inheritors may not have a good grip of what taxable assets and creditable liabilities the deceased had; (ii) it may sometimes be legally or practically difficult to determine which properties and debts are includable in taxable assets and creditable liabilities due to uncertainties about their nature and attribution under IGTA;[74] (iii) attempts were made to transfer assets without paying gift tax before the inheritee passed away, while it is not certain at the time of inheritance whether such attempts were successful while the statute of limitation on gift tax is six years (seven years in a case of "deceit or other fraudulent acts"). Also, some inheritors (particularly those under the above (i) or (ii) cases) may claim a justifiable reason for exempting the penalty on their non/underreporting (usually 15%/10% respectively) of Inheritance Tax. As for the above (iii) cases, if attempts for inter vivo transfer of assets without paying gift tax were not successful, there might be some cases where a strict penalty on the non/underreporting (usually 40%/35% respectively) of Inheritance Tax is applicable if the attempts were regarded as acts of tax evasion or concealment/falsification of relevant facts on their obligation of filing inheritance tax returns.[75]

74. As for the standard or condition for a debt to be deductible for inheritance tax purposes, *see* 3(4) in Section 2.
75. As for the analysis of the disputes on the application of a strict penalty, *see* 2(3) in Section 3.

In connection with the above (ii), Article 896 of the Civil Law dictates that an exclusive right of an inheritee is not inherited property, but uncertainty remains on what constitutes an exclusive right of an inheritee. The Tokyo High Court did not support in its 9/17/1963 (1963(Ne)1010) judgment the respondent's assertion that the appellant's claim against the offender for damage in connection with his brother's death in the traffic accident should, due to its nature of not being an exclusive right, constitute a taxable asset for inheritance tax purposes, irrespective of whether or not the deceased brother had the will to claim it. This judgment was in line with the Supreme Court 5/17/1938 judgment. But the Supreme Court 11/1/1967 (1963(O)1408) judgment practically turned the table around by stating that damage of both property and nonproperty rights gives rise to the victims' claims for damage and, unless there are special circumstances which indicate the relinquishment of them by the victims of such claims, such claims should be deemed to be inherited by the inheritors. However, the NTA's Tax Answer No. 4111 mentions that damage compensation assured to be received but not received by the victim in the traffic accident while he was alive is includable in taxable inherited property while the part of the claim for his life is, irrespective of whether it belongs to the deceased or the bereaved families, not includable in taxable property for IGT purposes.

The Tax Tribunal's 6/20/2005 decision was also related to the above (ii) because it was on the case where there was a question of whether there was a justifiable reason on the part of the inheritor for not including in taxable property the inheritee's claim for a tax refund which was not certain to be secured at the time of inheritance. In this case, the applicant/inheritor succeeded the inheritee's lawsuit over the lawfulness of the reassessment on him and won the court's final judgment of canceling the reassessment. Acting on this judgment, the assessor refunded the tax but it claimed it to be the inheritor's taxable property. The applicant's counterclaim was that it should not be includable in the taxable inherited property because this litigation status was his exclusive right. The Tax Tribunal dismissed such claim of the applicant by mentioning that the litigation status in question was a claim for refund and it constitutes a taxable inherited property. As for the imposition of the underreporting penalty, the Tax Tribunal canceled it by stating that at the time of inheritance, it was not possible on the part of the applicant to come up with the right amount of the refund, and the assessor who claimed the nonexistence of the refund had not been in a position to expect the refund to be included in the inherited property.

The Tax Tribunal's 5/30/1994 decision was on the case falling under the above (iii). In this case, the applicant/inheritor claimed that in 1989, a tax accountant bought, to provide full-fledged support to the corporation the applicant was running, some of the corporation's shares held by the inheritee at the price of JPY 5 million, and the accountant included in his income tax returns dividend from the shares, so those shares should not be includable in the taxable property of the inheritee who died in 1990. However, the Tax Tribunal dismissed such claim and concluded that the disputed reassessment of Inheritance Tax and imposition of a strict penalty on the applicant was lawful by pointing out the following: ① the transactional price on the shares in the contract was lower than their market price at that time, and the fact of the accountant not paying gift tax on it indicates that he was aware of the fictitious nature of this sale, ② there is no rational economic reason for the accountant to become the head shareholder of the corporation to provide support, ③ there was no endorsement of this transaction by the board of directors of the corporation, ④ this was a fictitious transaction colluded by the accountant, the inheritor, and the inheritee to reduce the amount of Inheritance Tax significantly.

(4) 『Deductible Debt』

【Deductible debt】 is similar to the above 【Scope of property subject to Inheritance Tax】 in that the main reason for them to a "highly disputed theme" lies in difficulty in some cases in finding out whether or not there is an inheritee's debt and its debt is deductible for Inheritance Tax purposes. Article 14 of IGTA prescribes that an inheritee's debt deductible in calculating the amount of Inheritance Tax should be "certain." The NTA's AR 14-1 on IGTA also mentions that the existence of written evidence is not a prerequisite for determining whether there is a deductible debt, and, even if the amount of debt is not determined, it is deductible to the extent that there exists a debt that is certain in light of the circumstances at the time of inheritance. In contrast, Article 37 of ITA spells out that, among the expenses incurred in generating business income, real estate income and miscellaneous income, sales costs, general and administrative expenses (excluding depreciation costs), etc., that are not fixed or "determined" at the end of the year to be debts are to be excluded from necessary expenses in calculating the amount of IT payable for the year. Practically, the same requirement must be met under Article 22(3) of CITA for those expenses to be deductible.[76]

Therefore, it could be said that the hurdle to clear for debts to be deductible for Inheritance Tax purposes is lower than that for sales costs and general and administrative expenses to be deductible for IT and CIT purposes. However, it does not necessarily mean that the determination of deductibility is easier to make in the former than in the latter. For example, in the Tokyo District Court 4/26/1984 (1981(GyoU)44) judgment, at issue was whether or not the loan claim of the inheritee against his family company was unrecoverable at the time of inheritance and the inheritee's debt guarantee for the family company's debt to a financial institution was deductible in calculating the inheritor's Inheritance Tax. The Court observed that the concerned family company was not in a state of insolvency at the time of inheritance, so it held that the inheritee's loan claim against it had asset value to be included in the taxable assets of the inheritor. The Court also ruled that if the inheritee had paid the debt for the concerned company, such loss of the inheritee could have been compensated by the inheritee's exercise of its right to indemnification, so this debt guarantee is not a debt that is deemed to be certain and deductible under Article 14 of IGTA.

A series of court rulings and Tax Tribunal decisions have confirmed that the standard for the debt guarantee to be deductible shown in the above Tokyo District

76. While the NTA's AR 2-2-1 CIT lays down the principle of matching cost with revenue for the cost of goods sold by a corporation, *see* 2(4) in Section 2.

Court 4/26/1984 judgment is basically applicable in determining whether an inheritee's joint liability is deductible for IGT purposes while its hurdle may become higher in some cases because its deductibility also depends on a main debtor. For example, in the 9/24/2013 decision, the Tax Tribunal stated that an inheritee's joint liability does not, in principle, constitute a "certain" debt, but an exception applies in a case where an inheritee was in a position to pay the debt because the main debtor could not pay the debt and the inheritee could not expect the reimbursement for its payment. Then, the Tax Tribunal concluded that in this case, as for the inheritee's joint liability for the borrower of the loan, the borrower was not insolvent, and there is no evidence showing that the inheritee had ever been demanded to pay for the loan on account of his joint liability, so the inheritee's joint liability is not "certain" debt and does not constitute a deductible debt for IGT purposes. As for the inheritee's loan claims against corporation A, the Tax Tribunal concluded that one of them does not constitute a taxable property because it was irrecoverable at the time of inheritance.

As the above cases intimate, taxpayers sometimes face two difficult challenges with respect to Inheritance Tax. The first challenge is the difficulty of grasping correctly the assets and liabilities of the inheritee, and the other is the difficulty of assessing them correctly for inheritance tax purposes. These difficulties are the main reasons for 【Scope of property subject to Inheritance Tax】 and 『Deductible debt』 to be one of the "highly disputed themes." In some cases, the first challenge might involve the question of whether *inter vivo* gift of the inheritee's assets is realized for IGT purposes. If it is not realized, such assets might constitute taxable assets of the inheritor for inheritance tax purposes.[77] The second challenge might arise from the fact that the scope of the taxable assets and deductible debts should be determined by taking into consideration all relevant legal facts and their economic substance. Moreover, there is a range of value on such inherited property as land and shares, and the AR on Property Appraisal may not serve as a reliable guideline in cases where inherited property contains special circumstances to be taken into account for determining its price for inheritance tax purposes, or attempts are made, prior to the inheritance, to reduce Inheritance Tax in connection with that property.

SECTION 3 《HIGHLY DISPUTED THEMES》 OF CONSUMPTION TAX ACT (CTA), AGRNT, AND COLLECTION ACT

1 Characteristics of 《Highly Disputed Themes》 Related to CTA

CT (Japanese VAT) was introduced in 1989, so it has a relatively short history, and its system design is simpler than other major tax items. In addition, disputes over CTA are often linked to or incidental to disputes over the amount of IT or CIT because if the amount of business sales is disputed in connection with the latter, it is often to be disputed in connection with the former as well. Nevertheless, there are not a small

77. For some relevant examples and court judgments, *see* Naoki Matsuda, Tax Strategies VS. Countermeasures, Xlibris (2015)pp. 32-34.

number of cases in which those problems unique to CT are the main points of contention. According to the Attachment, among the 141 published decisions on CTA cases, the most highly disputed issue is 【Tax credits, etc.】 (70 cases). The next one is 【Taxable scope】 (39 cases). Breakdowns of the theme 【Tax credits, etc.】 unveil that among those bracketed by 『 』 and [ ] under this theme, 『Input tax credit』 (69 cases) and [*Simplified taxation method*] (26 cases) are the largest in number. Among the theme 【Taxable scope】, 『Taxable transactions』, 『Tax-exempt transactions』, and 『Nontaxable transactions』 has more than ten cases, respectively. In the following, attempts are made to look into possible causes for the underlined themes to be ≪highly -disputed themes≫.

(1) 『Input Tax Credit』

Article 30(7) of CTA stipulates that if a business operator does not keep books and records on creditable input tax, it does not allow an input tax credit for that. Thus, Japan's VAT (or its input tax credit) is based on the so-called account method rather than invoice method. There are many cases where it is disputed whether or not the requirements set forth in this provision for input tax credit are met. For example, in the Supreme Court 12/16/2004 (2001(GyoHi)116) judgment, despite the tax auditor's request, the appellant did not present him with books and receipts (except for those related to entertainment expenses, etc.), so the auditor estimated the amount of his IT and CT based on the ratio of peers' turnovers in the same industry. In doing so, he deducted estimated expenses for IT purposes but did not apply the input tax credit laid down in Article 30(7) of CTA. In this judgment, the Supreme Court affirmed the lawfulness of the reassessment based on this estimated taxation and stated that input tax credit is not applicable to businesses in cases where relevant books and records were not kept in such a way that they could be presented to the tax auditor at the time of the audit unless they prove that they were unable to present them due to a disaster or other unavoidable circumstances.[78]

Judgments similar to the above were also rendered in the Supreme Court 12/20/2004 (2004(GyoHi) 37) judgment, but Judge Takii expressed his dissenting opinion. He asserted that considering the purpose of the CT system that the amount of input tax to be credited against should be credited without fail, there should not be any reason for interpreting the term "keeping books and records" adopted in Article 30(7) of CTA in such a way that it goes beyond its normal meaning and includes in the term their presentation at the time of tax audit. In fact, the Osaka District Court 8/10/1998 (1995(GyoU)25) judgment and the Tokyo District Court 9/30/1998 (1996(GyoU)232) judgment, which were rendered on the cases where the taxpayers' books and records on input tax credits were not presented to the auditors, were in line with the above Judge Takii's dissenting opinion. But those two judgments differ in their conclusion. In the former, the Osaka District Court allowed the crediting of some input tax for CT

78. For example, the Tsu District Court mentioned in 9/10/1998(1994(GyoU)9) judgment that even if a business/plaintiff had not presented books or records but did so for the first time in the dispute proceedings, input tax credit would not be allowed.

purposes, while in the latter, the Tokyo District Court, while admitting the term "presenting" not being included in the term "keeping," did not allow input tax credits at all because the taxpayer's failure to present books and records at the time of the tax audit without a justifiable reason should be regarded as his failure in keeping them as Article 30(7) of CTA requires.

As for input tax credit, there is another question of whether it is applicable or possible in cases where the suppliers listed in the taxpayer's books and records are incorrect or unauthentic. In the Tokyo District Court 8/28/1997 (1995(GyoU)232) judgment, the Court specified that such books as they are referred to in Article 30(7) of CTA must be those that have items enumerated in Article 30(8), i.e., names of the suppliers, dates of purchase and so forth, and naturally they must be true and correct. The Court admitted that there are exceptions to this because certain categories of businesses are legally permitted to omit names of the suppliers because of the inherent nature of their transactions with an indefinite number of suppliers,[79] while in this case, where the plaintiff was aware that there were some suppliers who were engaging in transactions under false names and there were no such circumstances that made it difficult for the plaintiff to identify true and correct names of those suppliers. In light of the above, the court concluded that the assessor's denial of the input tax credit in question was lawful, and this conclusion was supported by the Tokyo High Court 9/30/1998 (1997(GyoKo)128) judgment on this case.

What the above Tokyo District Court 8/28/1997 judgment did not make clear enough was whether or not input tax credit is possible in a case where a taxpayer/purchaser is not to be blamed for the incorrect names of the suppliers written on his books and records. The answer to this could be found in the Tax Tribunal 4/3/2002 decision in which the applicant maintained that in cash transactions, even if the suppliers do not provide correct identities, those incorrect identities on the receipts are to be taken as correct ones, and there are rational reasons for such treatment. Indeed, the Tax Tribunal mentioned that in a case where a taxpayer/purchaser can prove that the reason for the taxpayer to have failed to keep books and records that meet the requirements laid down under Article 30(7) of CTA was attributable to the fact that the purchaser rationally believed that the incorrect names on the receipts were true, input tax credit is possible. But, in this case, the Tax Tribunal concluded that, in spite of the fact that there were doubts about the correctness of the identities of the suppliers, the applicant engaged in the transactions with them without confirming their identities, so there were no rational reasons for the applicant's failure to keep books and records in line with Article 30(7) of CTA.

(2) [Simplified Taxation Method]

As can be seen from (1) above, the requirements for input tax credits are strict. On the other hand, under CTA, there are some systems or measures adopted mainly for

79. Such exceptions to wholesalers of recyclable resources and certain categories of retailers are stipulated under Article 49(2) of Administrative Order of CTA and Article 30(9) of CTA.

reducing the administrative burden of small-scale businesses but in most cases, these measures have made it possible for them to reduce their CT burden as well. Such systems include, in particular: ① the simplified taxation method available for those businesses whose taxable sales in the "base (business) period" (in principle, two years before the ongoing business year) was JPY 50 million or less, ② the CT exemption available for businesses whose taxable sales in the "base period" is JPY 10 million or less, and ③ CT exemption in the year of establishment of a corporation whose capital is JPY 10 million or less.[80] As for businesses that are allowed to apply the abovementioned ① (simplified taxation method), they can, instead of calculating the payable amount of CT by crediting input tax against CT on taxable sales, calculate the amount of CT payable by the formula (A − A × a deemed purchase rate) in which A represents the amount of CT on taxable sales and the fixed deemed purchase ratio varies depending on which business category a taxpayer's business falls under.[81]

As the Attachment shows, almost all of the disputes on the simplified taxation method are either about (i) whether a taxpayer seeking the application of this method is eligible for it and has fulfilled the relevant administrative requirements properly (13 cases) or about (ii) which deemed purchase rate should apply to the applicants (13 cases). For example, the Tax Tribunal 9/26/1994 decision (CTD No. 48, p. 405) was on the above (i). In this case, the applicant had submitted documents needed for opting for the simplified taxation method and actually paid the amount of CT that was calculated in accordance with the abovementioned formula for the business period of 4/1/1991 to 3/31/1992 but later requested for refund of some of the amount by claiming that the simplified taxation method should not apply to the business now that the submission of the application for the simplified taxation method was due to a mistake. The Tax Tribunal upheld the assessor's refusal of the refund payment by specifying that a mistake in opting for the simplified taxation method is only invalid in a case where such a mistake is objectively clear and significant, while in this case, even if there were a mistake, it would not be clear and significant.

The Nagoya High Court 2/9/2006 (2005(GyoKo)45) judgment is an example of disputes over the above (ii).[82] In this case, the respondent trading in the dental technology industry calculated the amount of payable CT by applying the deemed purchase rate of 70% applicable to producers, while the appellant/assessor claimed that it should be 50%, which applies to service providers. The Court ruled that Japan's Standard Industry Classification (JSIC) is the most prevalent and rational industrial classification, and the AR 13-2-4 on CTA, which is based on JSIC, specifies that this business in question comes under medical care/welfare (business of service provision), so the original Nagoya District Court 6/29/2005 (2004(GyoU)56) judgment which ruled in favor of the respondent by taking into account the nature of this business and various views including the definition of production put forward by the

80. The damage compensation claim of the plaintiff/consumer for the alleged unconstitutionality of ① and ② was dismissed by the Tokyo High Court 3/26/1990 (1991(Wa)5194) judgment.
81. A deemed purchase rate is 90% for wholesalers, 80% for retailers, 70% for producers, 50% for service providers, 40% for real estate dealers and 60% for others.
82. The Tax Tribunal 6/30/2001 decision which sustained the assessor's denial of the applicant's application of the highest deemed purchase rate is another example.

Supreme Court 6/24/1982 (1981(GyoTsu)177) judgment must be voided.[83] It is also to be noted that the AR 13-2-4 on CTA cautions that as for those businesses engaged in selling commodities purchased from others without changing their nature and form, they should, even if they come under production business, service providers' business or real estate business by JSIC, come under wholesalers or retailers for CT purposes.

(3) 『Tax-Exempt Transactions』

Controversies often arise as to whether the transactions in question meet the procedural and substantive requirements for tax-exempt transactions. For example, in the Tokyo District Court 11/9/2006(2004(GyoU)392) judgment, at issue was whether or not the plaintiff's business was tax-exempt for CT purposes. The plaintiff was selling old cars to foreigners temporarily staying in Japan on the premise that they would take them abroad, but the respondent/assessor made an assessment that the plaintiff's sales in question did not fall under tax-exempt transactions. The Court pointed out that payments by the foreigners to the plaintiff were made at the time of the sales contract when they came under the possession of the buyers, and they could be sold in Japan, so it is not objectively clear that those old cars would be taken out of the country immediately and the plaintiff took care of the customs clearance and export of those cars in the place of the purchasers. Also, the court added that this case is different from that in which passengers drop in and purchase goods at satellite shops at the airport just before they board international flights, so it concluded that the AR 7-2-21 on CTA does not apply to this case and the assessor's assessment should be upheld.[84]

There are also cases where a taxpayer's application for tax exemption is obviously ill-natured. One such example is the case in which the Osaka High Court handed down the 9/29/2004 (2003(GyoKo)66) judgment. In this case, the respondent/taxpayer received a refund of CT in connection with the export transactions while the applicant/assessor claimed that the concerned transactions were fictitious and imposed a strict penalty on the respondent. The Court pointed out that the president of the third-party company colluded with the respondent and did not include those sales from the concerned transactions in the company's profit but faked them as if they were carried out by the respondent. Moreover, the Court noted that the respondent had opted to give up its exempt business for CT purposes, so he became a taxable business whose tax liability arose as a result of the reassessment, which reduced the amount of the refund claimable by the respondent. Then, the Court voided the original Kyoto District Court 7/10/2003 judgment (2001(GyoU)19) that was skeptical about the legal ground for deeming the respondent as the taxpayer of CT and

83. In this judgment, the Supreme Court expressed a view that production as it is termed in Article 3(2) of the Commodity Tax Act is, in accordance with the general concept, to be interpreted as an action of producing a new commodity by making a physical and chemical change to a material or making an addition to it.
84. The AR 7-2-21 on CTA is about export tax exemption when a person who has a permit for a bonded warehouse transfers taxable assets to people travelling abroad.

sustained the reassessment as well as the imposition of the strict penalty on the respondent.

As it is clear from the above, there are disputes over those points or themes that are specific to CT, while it is nevertheless true that, compared to Acts related to direct taxes, the problem of unclearness and ambiguity in the provisions of CTA is not so conspicuous. In reality, many disputes over CTA are, aside from those on input tax credits, etc., not about how the relevant provisions are to be interpreted but about whether the requirements for the application of relevant systems are met or not. This is also related much to the fact that CTA provides for various preferential systems from the perspective of reducing the administrative burden on small businesses. At the same time, these preferential systems are also the causes for disputes because they attract not only those who are not so sure about their qualification but also those who seek their application despite their obvious lack of qualifications.[85] On the other hand, there will be some changes in disputed points and themes on CT because, from Oct. 2023, Japan's CT system is to move gradually from the present "account method" to the "invoice method," which is expected to drive many exempt businesses to opt for taxable business status that is a precondition for issuing qualified invoices that are necessary for the purchasers' input tax credit.[86]

2 Characteristics of ≪Highly Disputed Themes≫ Related to AGRNT

The Attachment shows the Tax Tribunal's published 2,594 decisions, and among them, those related to AGRNT are 433 (16.7%). The most ≪highly disputed theme≫ among those bracketed by 【 】 is 【Penalties】. Breakdowns of 【Penalties】 show that 『Strict penalty』 on a taxpayer's concealment or fabrication of facts relevant to the bases for calculating the amount of tax due (152 cases) is the most ≪highly disputed theme≫ while among those bracketed by [ ] under 【Penalties】, [*Justifiable reason*] for penalty exemption is most frequently disputed. The second largest in the number of published Tax Tribunal decisions on AGRNT cases among those bracketed by 【 】 is 【Confirmation of tax payment obligation】 under which 『Refund request』 (57 cases)and 『Reassessments or assessments』 (20 cases) are most frequently disputed among those bracketed by 『』. Majority of themes categorized under 『Reassessments or assessments』 are related to *tax audit procedures*. Cases disputing over the lawfulness or appropriateness of tax audits are also included in the other themes of AGRNT and

85. Such an aspect is expected to become more conspicuous with the expected increase in coming years in CT rate, CT avoidance or illegal receipt of CT refund as the recent incidents abusing CT exemption for exports and the situation in EU suggest. *See* the ECJ judgment of 1/12/2006 (C-484/03) in the *Bond House Systems Ltd v. Commissioner of Customs & Excise* case (C-484/03) and ECJ 2/21/2006 (C-255/02) judgment *in Halifax Plc, Leeds Permanent Development Services Ltd, County Wide Property. Investments Ltd v. Customs & Excise.*

86. Up to September 30, 2026, there will remain an exception to the invoice method so that the "account method" remains valid for the input tax credit on transactions of less than JPY 10,000 goods, and also available is the reduction in the administrative burden and the amount of CT payment of small businesses changing their status from nontaxable to taxable businesses for CT purposes.

other Tax Acts while they are often disputed in connection with substantive themes.[87] In the following, an analysis is to be made of the characteristics of the above-underlined themes and causes for them to be highly disputed.

(1) 『Refund Request』

There could be various reasons why the payable amount of tax declared by a taxpayer in its original return turns out to be excessive. Filing a tax return with an excessive amount of tax payable could be due to a taxpayer's mistake, misunderstanding, events that happened after the filing of the return, and so forth. In this connection, Article 23 of AGRNT provides in paragraph 1 that a refund request can be made only if the amount of tax payable became excessive due to the mistake in calculating the tax amount or the content of the return filed did not follow the rules of tax law, and in paragraph 2 that a refund request could be made in cases where, as in a case of the finalized court ruling, the occurrence of events after the filing of the return rendered the amount of tax payable declared in the original return excessive. Thus, this article does not give blanket approval of requests for refund in cases where the amount of tax payable in the original return turned out to be excessive, while it is sometimes difficult to determine whether a request for refund meets the requirements laid down in the Article. This difficulty in ascertaining precisely the applicable scope of Article 23 of AGRNT should be one of the main reasons for this theme being one of the most frequently disputed themes.

The Tax Tribunal 11/25/1994 decision (CTD No. 48-100) may serve as one of those cases which intimate the abovementioned difficulty. In this case, the taxpayer/applicant requested a partial refund of the amount of IT paid because the finalized court ruling canceled the sales contract of his land on account of the fraudulent act of the purchaser. At the time of the filing of the return on income having arisen from this sale of the land, the applicant was not aware that the purchaser of the land was fraudulent, but the Tax Tribunal pointed out that the land in question had already been resold to a third party and the court's ruling allowed the applicant's claim for damage compensation which could be deemed to be the partial payment for the concerned land sold, so it follows that the applicant's request for refund should not be allowed. On the other hand, the Tax Tribunal found that the purchaser of the concerned land does not have the financial capacity to pay the applicant for the damage, and the applicant could not expect to recoup fully the amount of the damage. In light of such circumstances, the Tax Tribunal decided that the assessor's disposition of refusing the applicant's request for a refund of the overpaid IT should be partially voided.

It is also to be noted that, as Article 51(2) of IT and the AR 2-2-16 on CIT specify, in the case of IT of business proprietors and CIT of corporations, income adjustments

87. Disputes over tax audit procedures are also contained in the Tax Tribunal decisions that are categorized under【Investigation】(AGRNT-related theme), 【Investigation procedures】(IT-related theme), 【Reassessments and assessments】and【Blue return】(CIT-related themes), etc., of the Attachment.

in the ongoing business period rather than a refund request is a norm even if such events as unpaid debts, return of goods sold, etc., happened after the filing of a return relate to the amount of income in the preceding business period. This could add more difficulty and confusion on the part of taxpayers as to which cases enable them to make requests for refunds. The Tax Tribunal 8/22/2013 decision illustrates another example of such difficulty and limitation inherent in a refund request. In this case, after the inheritance tax return was filed by the applicant/inheritor, one of the other inheritors won a finalized court ruling that denied the existence of the inheritee's loan claim. Acting on this ruling, the applicant requested for refund of some of the inheritance tax paid, but the Tax Tribunal pointed out that a court ruling referred to in Article 23(2) of AGRNT should be interpreted to include only those to which a taxpayer making a refund request is a party because the effect of the court ruling is limited to the parties in litigation, and concluded that the assessor's disposition of refusing the applicant's request for refund is lawful.

Another difficulty and limitation concerning this theme are found in the principle that a regretted choice over the options of various tax treatments specified in Tax Acts does not entitle a taxpayer to request a refund. For instance, in the Supreme Court 11/10/1987(1985(GyoTsu)81) judgment, the Court ruled that a doctor who chose the formula-based calculation method of business expenses laid down under Article 26 of STMA in filing his original IT return cannot request a refund after he became aware of the fact that the calculation of business expenses based on their actual amount could reduce his payable amount of IT. Similarly, the Fukuoka District Court ruled in the 5/27/1997 (1996(GyoU)4) judgment that a taxpayer cannot change the choice of legally available calculation methods on the amount of creditable input tax after its CT return is filed. It is confirmed in the Supreme Court 6/5/1990 (1987(GyoTsu)152) judgment that it should be allowed for the doctor to choose, in his submission of the rectified IT return, the business expenses calculation method other than the one chosen at the time of filing his original return. This 1990 Supreme Court judgment practically allowed the taxpayer's withdrawal of his original choice at the time of filing the return while it was not on a refund request case but a rectified return case.[88]

(2) [Justifiable Reason] for Penalty Exemption

In a case where a tax auditor finds that a taxpayer with an obligation to file a tax return and pay tax fails to fulfill such obligation properly in time, he is subject to a

88. Such difference in tax treatment on the regretted choice must be due to the distinction that a rectified return is filed to increase payable tax amount from that of the original return while a refund request is made to decrease payable tax amount from that of the original return. The refund request is more widely accepted in the UK, while it often depends on the tax authority's discretion in NZ. *See* the UK's 2009 Finance Act Schedule 52 and 3(2) of Section 2 of Chapter 4. As for cases for refund request and income adjustments in the ongoing business period in NZ, *see* 3(2) in Section 2 and footnote 200 of Chapter 4.

(administrative/civil) penalty for the non/underreporting of tax.[89] The penalty rates vary, but the standard rates are 10% (or 15%) for underreporting and 15% (or 20%) for non-reporting unless such failure is subject to a strict penalty as a result of a taxpayer's concealment or fabrication of relevant facts on its filing obligation, etc.[90] Those penalties with the standard rates are waived in a case where there is a justifiable reason for such failure.[91] Various reasons could constitute a justifiable reason that exempts a penalty. But a series of court decisions hint that a hurdle to clear for the exemption of a penalty based on a justifiable reason is quite high and its applicable scope is quite limited. First of all, it is well established that ignorance of tax law does not constitute a justifiable reason. Moreover, a tax agent's mistake or misunderstanding of tax law provisions does not exempt the imposition of a penalty on the taxpayer who asked him to prepare his return. This is so irrespective of whether or not a tax law provision in question is quite technical, and it is practical for the taxpayer to seek damage compensation from the tax agent who is responsible for the non/underreporting.[92]

The NTA's revised 2016 notice on penalties mentions that there is a justifiable reason for the failure to file a return in time in a case where there is truly an unavoidable circumstance, such as natural disaster, disruption of traffic and telecommunication, etc., that accounts for such failure. Moreover, the Supreme Court 4/20/2006 (2005(GyoHi)9) judgment spells out that there is a justifiable reason for exempting a penalty for underreporting of payable tax amount in a case where there is an objective situation that is not attributable to a taxpayer and makes it improper or cruel to impose a penalty on the taxpayer. Despite those principles and guidance, there remain uncertainties on what could constitute a justifiable reason.[93] The height of the hurdle set by a justifiable reason may be intimated by the fact that poor health condition does not, in principle, constitute a justifiable reason as the Tax Tribunal 6/8/2004 decision (CTD No. 67, p. 46) turned down the applicant's claim for exempting the penalty on his delayed filing of an Inheritance Tax return because the applicant could have asked a daughter living with him or a tax accountant to file the

89. For example, from FY2005 to FY2008, the annual number of penalties was 235,000 to 308,000 which was about twenty to thirty times of the annual number of corrections made during those years. *See* p. 5 of the government's Reference Document referred to in footnote 10.
90. The bracketed higher standard rates are applicable when the non/underreported tax amount exceeds the larger of JPY 500,000 or the originally reported tax amount unless a penalty is on a withholding agent. The standard strict penalty is 35% in the case of underreporting and 40% in the case of non-reporting. There are some cases where applicable rates of standard and strict penalties are reduced or increased in order to encourage compliance with assets disclosure rules, prevent digitized falsification of books/records, their refusal of presentation at tax audit as well as a large volume of unreported sales on them.
91. *See* Articles 65 to 67 of AGRNT. Those Articles also have provisions that exempt or reduce an administrative penalty in a case where a taxpayer files a return (or an amended return) without anticipating the assessor's re/assessment. *See* footnote 51 in Chapter 5.
92. *See* Tax Tribunal 1/20/2014 decision. While in some countries, such as the U.S. and the UK, ignorance of law (or tax agent's mistake on technical issues) could be a reason for the exemption of civil penalty for non/underreporting of tax. *See* 2(2) in Section 4 in Chapter 2 and 1(2)/1(3) in Section 5 in Chapter 3.
93. It is possible that the hurdle for the exemption of penalties is practically lower in some cases at the audit stage or the stage of review of objections by the assessor.

return in time now that the applicant's claim of him being deprived of mental capacity or ability to make a judgment at the time of filing an Inheritance Tax return cannot be sustained.

Nevertheless, there are certainly a few typical cases that could constitute a justifiable reason. Particularly, a wrong answer given by a tax officer with whom a taxpayer consulted could be one of those provided that there is nothing to be blamed on the taxpayer in filing his return based on the answer provided by the officer, and the taxpayer could prove that such wrong answer was given to him. Usually, the difficulty for a taxpayer to become aware that a withholding obligation has arisen does not constitute a justifiable reason, as the aforementioned Osaka High Court judgment (2003) confirms,[94] but there are some exceptions. For example, a penalty on a taxpayer's failure to withhold tax on the payment to a nonresident is waived by the Tax Tribunal 5/21/2013 decision on the case of a tenant/applicant paying monthly business rents to the nonresident who departed from Japan without notifying the tenant timely.[95] While in the case of a real estate dealer paying for the land purchased from a nonresident whose residency status or withholding obligation was not notified timely to the purchaser, a penalty was exempted in the case of the Tokyo District Court 5/19/2016 (2014 (GyoU)114) judgment,[96] but not in the case of the Tokyo District Court 3/4/2011 (2009(GyoU)121) judgment.

Another typical category of a justifiable reason for exempting a penalty, which the NTA lists in its guidance, is where a taxpayer's non/underreporting of tax is due to the *ex post* change of the NTA's interpretation or treatment on a relevant tax provision. For example, in the Supreme Court 10/24/2006 (2005(GyoHi)20) judgment, the Court ruled in favor of the appellant taxpayer who claimed the exemption of the underreporting penalty based on the justifiable reason that his reporting of the income accrued from the exercise of the right of the stock options granted by the parent of the employer company was temporal income instead of salary income because the NTA's general guidance at the filing consultations at that time instructed it to be reported as temporal income. Also, in the Supreme Court 6/12/2015 (2012(GyoHi)408) judgment, the imposition of an underreporting penalty by the assessor was voided by the court's determination that the taxpayer's underreporting of the income in question was due to the NTA's delayed official change in the categorization of such income (change from real estate income to miscellaneous income) that is received by the partners in Japan from a silent partnership formed abroad that was engaged in the business of leasing aircraft.

94. This judgment is faithful to the so-called principle of "automatic confirmation nature of withholding tax obligation." *See* 1(2) in Section 2 and footnote 96.
95. While Article 328(2) of the ITA Administrative Order provides that no withholding of tax is required in a case where the payment of a rent is made by an individual tenant who utilizes the nonresident owner's real estate for his or his relatives' residence.
96. In this case, the NTA allowed the exemption of the penalty for the failure to collect and pay withholding tax timely on account of a justifiable reason while the Court upheld the NTA's notice of failure to collect withholding tax timely issued on the taxpayer by determining that the taxpayer failed in its fulfilment of duly ascertaining the residential status of the seller. This approach may digress from the so-called principle of "automatic confirmation nature of withholding tax obligation" (*see* footnote 94 and 1(2) in Section 2).

The Tax Tribunal's 2/2/2006 decision (CTD No. 71-118) may be compared with the above Supreme Court 6/12/2015 judgment as a showcase of the high hurdle of a justifiable reason. In this case, the applicant claimed that the loss attributed to him based on the contract with a limited partnership (LPS) in country A is negative real estate income that could be set off against other positive income for the years 1999 to 2001 while the assessor regarded it as dividend and made a reassessment of denying such setoff. At that time, there were some litigations disputing which criteria are to be relied on in determining for IT purposes the nature of income received by a taxpayer from foreign (transparent) business entities.[97] In the midst of such uncertainty, the Tax Tribunal determined that, in this case, the concerned LPS has attributes that make it neither a partnership nor a corporation under relevant Japanese laws, so the income in question is miscellaneous income. This determination has led to the partial cancellation of the reassessment while the Tax Tribunal decided that there was no explicit tax office's authorized expression in the preceding audits of the taxpayer about the nature of this concerned income, so there is no justifiable reason for exempting the penalty for the underreporting.

(3) 『Strict Penalty』 on Concealment or Fabrication of Relevant Facts

In a case where a taxpayer's delayed filing of a tax return or his underreporting in a tax return involves his concealment or fabrication of relevant facts that constitute proof of tax evasion, a strict (administrative/civil) penalty rate (40% in the former and 35% in the latter) applies as Article 68 of AGRNT stipulates. This criterion is practically identical to the criterion of a taxpayer's deceit or other fraudulent acts adopted in various tax provisions that could subject the taxpayer to a criminal penalty for tax evasion while the NTA's criminal investigation and court's upholding of the prosecution of the tax evader by the Office of Prosecutors is necessary for the imposition of a criminal penalty.[98] Previously, the hurdle to clear for the NTA to apply this strict administrative/civil penalty used to be quite high as it was implied by the Supreme Court 7/9/1949 (1949(Re)893) judgment in which the Court specified that a penalty application on deceit or other fraudulent acts is only possible in cases where such deceit or fraudulent acts are employed actively, and if there is a need for penalizing tax evasion by non-filing of a tax return, such need is to be addressed by legislative

97. ITA has ten categories of income whose tax calculation methods vary. Different criteria relied on by different courts led to conflicting rulings on the category of income received from foreign entities but such differences were ironed out by the Supreme Court 7/17/2015 2013(GyoTsu)309 judgment that determined the disputed income to be dividend and the Court maintained that the nature of income from a foreign entity should be determined in accordance with such factors as whether it is given a corporate body in that foreign country and whether it is an entity to which its rights and obligations belong. Nevertheless, practically such determination may not be so easy because various types of entities exist abroad.

98. Therefore, in noncriminal cases, the criterion of deceit or other fraudulent acts adopted in Article 70(4) of AGRNT is relied on by the NTA only to extend the statute of limitation for re/assessment. *See* footnote 101.

measures.[99] This judgment was on a criminal penalty but it seems that a similar view or an identical criterion was also adopted around that time on a strict penalty.

Thenceforth, some court rulings came out to give an impression that the hurdle for the application of a strict penalty on the concealment or fabrication of relevant facts seems to have been lowered. In particular, the Supreme Court took a view in its 3/20/1973 (1971(A)1901) judgment that a taxpayer's act of filing a tax return which inordinarily underreports the amount of his income tax payable coupled with his intent of tax evasion is not simply inaction of the taxpayer but is tantamount to deceit or other fraudulent acts. This view was interpreted in such a way that the existence of a taxpayer's physical action of concealing or fabricating relevant facts is not necessarily a prerequisite for the application of a criminal penalty or a strict penalty. Another notable court ruling in this connection was the Supreme Court 4/28/1995(1998(GyoTsu)215) judgment in which the Court stated that a penalty for the concealment or fabrication of relevant facts does not require a taxpayer's such concrete action as using a fictitious bank account or concealment of relevant documents as a precondition for its application; instead, it is also applicable in a case where a taxpayer had the intent to evade tax and "such intent was manifested in his behavior which is observable from outside."

In the above 1995 case, the Supreme Court specified in particular that the taxpayer's negative replies to the tax agent's repeated questions on possible income from his transactions of shares were indicative of his intention to evade IT on it. Indeed, there is an opacity on what kind of a taxpayer's behavior constitutes the manifestation of his intent to evade tax that is observable from outside, but, thenceforth, the NTA relies on this expression or standard frequently as a rationale for imposing a strict penalty where it fails to grasp more concrete evidence for the fabrication or the concealment of facts relevant to the taxpayer's filing of a tax return.[100] The recent lowering of the hurdle for the application of a strict penalty means a lot to the NTA because, in a case where there is a taxpayer's concealment or fabrication of relevant facts that could constitute his deceit or other fraudulent acts, the statute of limitation for re/assessment is as Article 70(4) of AGRNT prescribes, seven years instead of standard five years.[101] Moreover, the 2016 tax reform amended Articles 66 and 68 of AGRNT to increase the penalty rates by 10% (i.e., 25% or 45% (50%), respectively) for

99. In view of such cases where a large amount of gains from foreign exchange transactions were not reported at all by some taxpayers, the 2011 tax reform introduced Article 238(3) of ITA, Article 159(3) of CIT, Article 68(3) of IGTA, and Article 64(5) of CT to lower a hurdle for imposing a criminal penalty for tax evasion on a non-filer of a return.

100. This Supreme Court case was on the strict penalty for the underreporting of tax but the NTA applied the same criterion in the case of the strict penalty on a non-filing of a return and such application has been upheld in some cases by the Tax Tribunal. *See* Tax Tribunal 6/3/2011 decision. While some court rulings such as the Fukuoka District Court 3/29/1975 (1970(GyoU)44) judgment stress the difference in the criterion for acknowledging the deceit and other fraudulent acts (or the imposition of a strict penalty) for the non-filing of a return and that for the underreporting of tax.

101. Recently, there is also a new twist of imposing underreporting penalties instead of strict penalties in cases where reassessments going back seven years are made based on the deceit or other fraudulent acts. *See,* the Tokyo District Court 2/12/2004 (2001(GyoU)313, etc.) judgment, the Tokyo District Court 4/19/2004 (2001(GyoU)407) judgment, and the Tax Tribunal's

the delayed filing of a return or filing of a (delayed) return on account of the concealment or fabrication of relevant facts, provided that the taxpayer was subjected to either one of those penalties in the past five (business) years.[102]

A strict penalty has taken another twist lately in such a way that works favorably for taxpayers. In principle, taxpayers cannot avoid strict penalties by blaming the falsification or concealment of relevant facts regarding their tax returns on their preparers/tax agents.[103] For example, in the 2/25/1997 (1996(GyoHi)20) judgment, the Osaka High Court ruled that the strict penalty applies to the taxpayer unless he was not negligent in the selection and supervision of the preparer of his return.[104] While, in the aforementioned 4/20/2006 judgment (*see* 2(2) of this Section), the Supreme Court did confirm the principle that falsification or concealment of relevant facts by the tax agent should be deemed to have been done by the taxpayer, but it stated that the taxpayer's negligence in the selection and supervision of the tax agent may not be sufficient for applying the strict penalty on him and in this case the taxpayer was deceived and his tax money embezzled by the tax agent.[105] In conclusion, the Court ruled that the strict penalty must be voided and replaced by the underreporting penalty, for which there is no justifiable reason in this case.[106] This recent twist and developments mentioned above on the application of a strict penalty are likely to work toward increasing further the number of disputes over it.

(4) Tax Audit Procedures

Taxpayers may argue over the unlawfulness or inappropriateness of not only the re/assessment on them but also that of tax audit procedures that resulted in the

1/24/2012 decision (in footnote 145). They should be based on the view that the concept of the deceit or other fraudulent act is wider in scope than that of the fabrication or concealment of the relevant facts on the returns.

102. This reform as well as those mentioned in footnote 90 shows the recent increase in complexity of the penalty structure which used to be quite simple.
103. This is partially based on the idea that, if a taxpayer's financial damage has resulted from the auditor's detection of his incorrect or false return and it could be blamed on the preparer, the taxpayer should/could file a damage suit against the preparer. *See* footnote 147 for an example of such damage suit.
104. Likewise, in the 3/23/1992 (1985(GyoU)40) judgment, the Kyoto District Court ruled that, when the preparer filed a false return for the taxpayer and it was caused by the taxpayer's failure to supervise him and check the return, the taxpayer cannot avoid the strict penalty unless there is a special circumstance.
105. A similar view was expressed by the 1/18/2006 (2005(GyoKo)25) judgment of the Tokyo High Court to which the case was remanded by the Supreme Court 1/17/2005 (2002(GyoHi)103) judgment to deliberate on whether or not there was a collusion between the taxpayer and the preparer of his tax return.
106. While an underreporting penalty was exempted in the Supreme Court's 4/25/2006 judgment (2004(GyoHi)86) in which the tax official as well as the tax agent were involved in the false return of the taxpayer. The hurdle to clear for the waiver of a fraud penalty on account of "reasonable cause" in the U.S. seems to be lower. *See* 2(2) in Section 4 of Chapter 2.

re/assessments.[107] Such arguments are often made particularly in cases disputing over "re/assessment by estimation," "input tax credit," and themes related to the Collection Act. However, it is not common for the re/assessments to be voided on account of the auditor's failure to follow the audit procedures properly. For example, in the 6/6/1991 (1989(GyoKo)164) judgment, the Tokyo High Court stated that a mere flaw in the audit procedure does not affect the reassessment while the reassessment may have a cause for being canceled once the audit violated criminal acts and regulations, resulting in the violation of public order and morals,[108] because, in such a case, the reassessment becomes tainted with significant illegality making it something to be regarded practically as the reassessment made without the audit. In this case, however, the Court concluded that the auditor did not tell the reasons for the audit, and he requested the taxpayer to show him books and records without specifying their scope, but they did not become a cause for voiding the reassessment. The view shown in this Court judgment has been followed by many, including the Tax Tribunal's 6/22/2017 decision.

While Article 155(2) of ITA and Article 130(2) of CITA provide for the assessor's obligation of showing in a notice of re/assessment to the audited blue return filer the reasons for it,[109] and there are more cases where re/assessments were canceled on account of deficiencies in those reasons. For example, the Supreme Court spelled out in 4/25/1974 (1970(GyoTsu)36) judgment that, in this case, the mere specification of the relevant provision in writing as the reason for the reassessment is not enough because the purport of the assessor's obligation of showing in writing reasons for the re/assessment is akin to that of other nontax administrative dispositions and it is not only for securing the assessor's prudence but also for providing the taxpayer with convenience for appeals. Then, the Court concluded that the reason shown in the concerned notice of reassessment fails to attain this purpose, so the concerned reassessment should be voided. The court also added that written reasons in a notice of re/assessment should include the assessor's explanations of how the relevant tax provisions apply to the facts and circumstances of the audited taxpayers, and such explanations made later at the stage of administrative/judicial stage would not cure the deficiencies in the audit procedure.[110]

107. Whereas, the U.S. Tax Court has the "rule of not looking behind a notice of deficiency." *See* 2 in Section 2 of Chapter 2.
108. The Kyoto District Court 2/25/2000 (1995(GyoU)4) judgment is one of those rare cases where the administrative disposition of revoking the blue return filer's status was revoked for the reason that there was on the part of the auditor a momentous illegal action that exceeds the limit of a noncompulsory tax audit.
109. As for the blue return system only applicable for IT and CIT purposes in Japan, *see* footnotes 41 and 42. Even if deficiencies in the returns are found by tax audits, in the majority of cases, taxpayers agree on them and file amended returns accordingly, making it unnecessary for tax auditors to show in writing reasons for the re/assessments.
110. This requirement on the assessor to present the audited taxpayers with clear and sufficient reasons for the re/assessments contrasts with the IRS's issue of a notice of deficiency which does not necessarily require strict accuracy for the reassessment. *See* 2 in Section 2 of Chapter 2.

Moreover, in the 11/26/1980 (1979(GyoKo)61) judgment, the Osaka High Court revoked the reassessment on account of the insufficiency of the reason written in the notice of reassessment because it was as follows: the assessor looked into whether or not the taxpayer's application of the accelerated depreciation method to the newly acquired air-conditioning facility is appropriate, and determined that it is the auxiliary equipment to which the accelerated depreciation method is not applicable. Indeed, this judgment was overturned by the Supreme Court 4/23/1985 judgment (1981(GyoTsu)36), but the hurdle intimated by the Supreme Court for the assessor to clear for fulfilling the conditions required for the written reasons for re/assessments to be appropriate seems to be fairly high because the Court mentioned that the reasons to be written in the notice of re/assessment should be informative enough to enable the taxpayer to do a point-by-point verification of the determination process of the assessor. The tide turned favorably further for the taxpayers now that Article 74-14 of AGRNT, revised in 2011, has expanded the assessor's requirement of presenting in writing the reasons for the re/assessments so that it should also apply to such cases where the audited non-blue (regular white) return filers do not file (amended) returns accordingly.

The recent favorable tide for the taxpayers on the issue of the reasons for re/assessments to be presented to the audited taxpayers did lead to their triumph in the Osaka High Court 1/18/2013 judgment (2012(Gyou-ko)32). In this case, the reassessment was made to include in the taxable income of the public interest corporation income from its profit-making activities, and the reasons presented in the notice of reassessment to the taxpayer referred only to the fact that the concerned income is taxable income. The respondent/assessor asserted that the reference to the conclusion of the tax audit is all that is needed to show the reason for the reassessment. But the Court ruled that the reason presented in writing to the taxpayer only shows the result of the reassessment and it lacks the assessor's deliberation process on the relationship among the related tax provisions and the relevant AR as well as how the assessor, based on the deliberation, reached the conclusion. Then, the Court concluded that the reason presented in the notice of reassessment does not enable the taxpayer to do a point-by-point verification of the determination process of the assessor, so the reassessment should be voided.[111] The respondent did not appeal this case to the Supreme Court, so this Osaka High Court's judgment was finalized.

The recent trend of requiring sufficient explanations to be made in a notice of reassessment has also been observable at the Tax Tribunal. One example is the Tax Tribunal 4/9/2012 decision. In this case, the respondent showed a list of the assets of

111. The High Court admitted that there are cases where showing in a notice of re/assessment only the conclusion of the re/assessment could be enough but, as it was mentioned by the Supreme Court 12/27/1963 (1962(O)1015) judgment, the level or content of written reasons for re/assessments should not vary depending on whether or not the audited taxpayers could speculate those reasons.

the applicant and identified among them some building's facilities whose depreciations are not deductible for CIT purposes for the reason that they do not exist. Then, the respondent claimed that it is a sufficient explanation in writing for the reassessment because the applicant could recognize which assets are identified as fictitious ones. But the Tax Tribunal revoked the reassessment as well as the imposition of underreporting and strict penalties by stating that the respondent neither provided any material that shows the rational ground for the reassessment nor showed in writing concrete explanations of the process by which it came to a conclusion. Another example is the Tax Tribunal 11/18/2014 decision in which it determined that the reasons shown in the notice of reassessment failed to specify which reason out of more than a few possible ones the assessor relied on in denying the deduction for inheritance tax purposes of the payment obligation of the debt which the inheritee owed as an unlimited liability partner of the corporation.[112]

Another point related to the issue of the reasons in the notice of reassessment is whether the NTA can substitute them for new reasons later at the stage of administrative/judicial review.[113] As mentioned in the above Supreme Court 4/25/1974 judgment, explanations made later at the disputing stage would not cure the deficiencies in the audit procedure. However, in the 7/14/1981 (1977(GyoTsu)62) judgment, the Supreme Court allowed the assessor's change at the litigation stage of the amount of the acquisition price (from JPY 6 million to JPY 6.7 million) of the transferred real estate written in the notice of reassessment. The Court explained that now that the sales price of the real estate was JPY 9.5 million rather than JPY 7 million which was claimed by the appellant, such change by the assessor, even if it is allowed, would neither disadvantage the appellant at the litigation nor undermine the purport of the Supreme Court 12/5/1972 judgment (1972(GyoTsu)61) which expressed the same view that was shown in the above Supreme Court 4/25/1974 judgment.[114] Even so, in reality, there should be cases where taxpayers and the NTA wonder how much is required for the reasons in the notice of reassessment to be good enough and when the delayed substitution of the original reasons for the reassessments for new ones is possible.

112. Other examples include the Tax Tribunal's decisions made on 9/1/2014 (CTD No. 96-40) and 12/10/2014 (CTD No. 97-1).

113. In some countries, some tax dispute review organs not only allow the substitution of the original reasons for re/assessment with new ones but also allow the assessor to increase the reassessed tax amount. For example, *see* 2 in Section 1 of Chapter 2, 2 in Section 1 and 2 in in Section 2 of Chapter 5.

114. *See* footnote 110. Likewise, in the 11/29/1996 judgment (1994(GyoU)300), the Tokyo District Court allowed the change of the reason/legal ground for the reassessment from the denial of crediting the corporate director's excessive remuneration (ex-Article 34(1) of CITA) to the denial of a family company's actions or calculations (Article 132 of CITA). It may be open to debate if these judgments still stand under the recent trend of generally requiring the reasons in the notice of re/assessment to be precise and sufficient. *See* footnote 15.

3 Attributes of ≪Highly Disputed Themes≫ of Collection Act

The Attachment divulges that, as for themes on the Collection Act, ≪highly disputed themes≫ among those bracketed by 【 】, the largest in number is the 【Secondary tax payment obligation】 (66 cases) followed by 【Seizure】 (47 cases). As for the former, 『Secondary tax payment obligation for receiving the defaulter's property with no/low costs』 is the largest in number (46 cases) among those bracketed by 『 』, while, for the latter, [Attribution of seized property] is the largest in number (21 cases) among those bracketed by [ ]. It is little wonder that many delinquent taxpayers question the validity/appropriateness of the seizure, seek the suspension of collection action, or even transfer their property to close acquaintances in an attempt to avoid its seizure. As for the NTA, the hurdle to clear to collect tax from a secondary taxpayer is much lower than that for collection of tax from a taxpayer who allegedly received the delinquent taxpayer's property by his prejudicial acts. Those themes mentioned above are often disputed from the perspective of the *scope of administrative disposition, benefits of appeals/standing to sue*, or *suspension, etc., of collection action*. Therefore, in the following, they are analyzed mainly from the underlined perspectives.

(1) Scope of Administrative Disposition

Figure 1.18 shows a standard procedure for delinquent tax collection under the Collection Act. Questions may arise on which collection procedure constitutes administrative disposition against which a delinquent taxpayer can make an appeal to the assessor, the Tax Tribunal, and the court.[115] The tax collection steps ②, ③, ⑥ and ⑧ are administrative dispositions, while there were some uncertainties on which other steps constitute administrative dispositions against which a delinquent taxpayer can appeal. As for ①, the Tokyo High Court concluded in 7/14/1992 (1992(GyoKo)20) judgment that neither the assessor's appropriation of the appellant's refund to delinquent Inheritance Tax nor the assessor's request for payment of the appellant's delinquent IT is administrative disposition so that the appellant cannot appeal against those assessor's actions.[116] Such High Court's view was, however, denied by the Supreme Court's 10/8/1993 (1992(GyoTsu)183) judgment in which it specified that those assessor's actions in question are both administrative dispositions based on Tax Acts with an effect on the taxpayer's legal status while the appellant's claim for the unlawfulness of them do not have a leg to stand on so that the wrong view of the above High Court's judgment does not affect the conclusion on this case.

115. While, in the U.S., prior to the 1998 IRS Reform, the IRS's collection action was not subject to the review at the Office of Appeals. *See* Section 1 of Chapter 2.
116. Article 57 of AGRNT provides that, in a case where there is tax refundable to a taxpayer, the NTA should appropriate it to the taxpayer's unpaid tax instead of refunding it to the taxpayer.

Figure 1.18 Tax Collection Procedures for Delinquent Taxes

① Request for payment of delinquent tax (Article 37 of AGRNT)

↓

② Seizure of property (Articles 47-78 of the Collection Act)

↓

③ Public notice on auction of seized property (Article 95 of the Colletion Act)

↓

④ Public notice of estimated sales price of seized property on auction (Article 99 of the Collection Act)

↓

⑤ Public tender (Article 101 of the Collection Act)

↓

⑥ Determination of the purchaser (Articles 111 and 113 of the Collection Act)

↓

⑦ Money receipt from the purchaser and transfer of the title (Articles 115-127 of the Collection Act)

↓

⑧ Distribution of money paid by the purchaser (Articles 128-135 of the Collection Act)

It may be desirable from the perspective of speedy remedy of taxpayers' rights to interpret widely the scope of administrative dispositions, while such interpretation might aggravate the problem that some delinquent taxpayers make objections or appeals against them at multiple stages of tax collection procedures for identical reasons or irrational grounds.[117] Certainly, aggravation of this problem is prevented by the fact that a taxpayer's objection to the assessor and the Tax Tribunal, as well as appeals to the court, do not suspend the collection action on him in principle while there are some legally/administratively prescribed exceptions (*see* 3(4) of this section and footnotes 14, 123, 124). Some collection actions of the NTA have been confirmed not to constitute administrative dispositions. For example, in the 11/24/2004 decision (CTD No. 68, p. 285), the Tax Tribunal stated that a notice to the delinquent taxpayer of the public tender of its seized property, which is sent pursuant to Article 96 of the Collection Act, is not an administrative disposition because it is only intended to give the taxpayer the last chance to pay the delinquent tax and inform him of what is to be included in the public notice so that it would not for itself affect the taxpayer's rights and obligations.

Another example is the Tokyo District Court 7/17/2015 (2014(GyoU)134) judgment. In this case, the Court reaffirmed that low price estimation in the public notice of the assets of the tax delinquent to be auctioned publicly does not constitute a cause for the unlawfulness of ④ (Public notice of estimated sales prices of assets on auction) because this notice is not legally intended to create directly people's rights and

117. For example, in U.S., filing of suits on collection cases based on unreasonable grounds is restrained by giving the courts the authority to impose penalties on it. *See* 3 in Section 4 of Chapter 2, IRC §6673 and IRC §6702 for details.

obligations so that it does not constitute an administrative disposition.[118] It is also to be noted that, in principle, a taxpayer cannot claim the unlawfulness of collection action on him on account of the alleged unlawfulness of the relevant re/assessment on him. This is in line with the principle shown by the Supreme Court 10/29/1964 (1962(O)296) judgment in which the Court assured that, even if an administrative disposition is unlawful, it carries a presumption of legality unless it is voided by an authorized agency.[119] Nevertheless, as it is confirmed by the Tax Tribunal's 3/24/2003 decision (CTD No. 65-993) etc., the above principle does not apply in such cases where a deficiency of the re/assessment is serious and obvious, or there are special circumstances where the application of such principle would damage the taxpayer significantly.

(2) Benefits of Appeals/Standing to Sue

Even if there is an administrative disposition that could be appealed to the Tax Tribunal and court, such appeals would not be valid unless they are raised by persons with the right to file objections/lawsuits and could reap personal benefits by doing so. This is evident from the Supreme Court 3/14/1978 (1974 (GyoTsu)99) judgment. In this judgment, a point of contention was whether or not the appellant, who was just a consumer in general, would be allowed to file an appeal against the Fair Trade Commission's disposition by an appeal procedure prescribed under Article 10(6) of Act against Unjustifiable Premiums and Misleading Representations. In rejecting the allegation of the appellant, the Supreme Court made it clear that ensuring the proper operation of the public administration is only an indirect effect achieved through the salvation of the rights and interests of the people who could make appeals to administrative review organs and courts. Thenceforth, the Supreme Court declared that, unless otherwise provided for by law, those who can make such appeals are limited to those whose rights or legally protected interests are damaged or are sure to be damaged as a result of administrative dispositions and consequently have legal benefits to be recoverable in cases where such dispositions are revoked.[120]

Thus, on the part of a taxpayer wishing to dispute the collection action, there is an issue of standing to sue as well as the issue mentioned in the above (1). Obviously, this issue could also arise in the case of a taxpayer with secondary tax payment obligation. As for a taxpayer with secondary tax payment obligation, Article 39 of the Collection Act provides that, in a case where delinquent tax cannot be fully recoverable from an original delinquent taxpayer for the reason that he transferred his property free

118. This judgment is sustained by the Tokyo High Court 1/14/2016 (2015(GyoKo)293) judgment on this case.
119. The Tax Tribunal 10/20/2000 decision (CTD No. 60, p. 605) was also based on this principle and concluded that the tax delinquent's assertion on the unlawfulness of the relevant reassessment on his inheritance tax liability is pointless now that he failed to make a request for review of the reassessment within the legally prescribed timeframe.
120. Tax Tribunal's 12/5/2002 decision (CTD No. 64-114) also confirms that, if the seized assets do not belong to the applicant as he claims, it follows that he does not have benefits of appeal, and his application for review is not lawful.

of charge or at a significantly low price, exempted debt of another person, or provided economic benefits to him in other ways within the timeframe of one year before the statutory due date of his payment of tax, the transferee or such person owes secondary tax payment obligation for the unrecovered tax to the extent that economic benefit received from such transfer, etc., still remains (in the case of the transferee in a special relationship with the transferor, to the extent that he received economic benefit). Such being the case, a question could arise more often on the part of a transferee with secondary tax payment obligation as to whether it is possible for him to dispute at administrative/judicial review stages the lawfulness of the re/assessment made on the original delinquent taxpayer.

Negative answers were given on the above question by the Supreme Court 8/27/1975 (1973(GyoTsu)112) judgment and the Tokyo High Court 6/15/2004 (2004(GyoKo)58) judgment because they ruled that a person served with a notice of secondary tax payment obligation can claim neither the unlawfulness of the re/assessment on the original tax delinquent nor the incorrectness of the tax amount owed by the original delinquent. But the Supreme Court 1/19/2006 (2004(GyoHi)275) judgment overruled the above Tokyo High Court 6/15/2004 judgment by specifying that a person served with a notice of secondary tax payment obligation has benefits of appeals and recoverable legal interests in asserting in its objection to the notice of secondary tax obligation the unlawfulness of the relevant re/assessment on the original tax delinquent because its partial or full cancellation impacts on his obligation. Moreover, in this Supreme Court judgment, Judge Izumi expressed his opinion that the abovementioned Supreme Court 8/27/1975 judgment should be revoked now that it was neither mindful of the independent nature of a person served with a notice of secondary tax payment obligation nor the fact that secondary tax payment obligation goes into effect with a notice of secondary tax obligation being served.

As mentioned above, one of the reasons for the 【Secondary tax payment obligation】 to be one of the ≪highly disputed themes≫ of the Collection Act lies in the fact that there are some taxpayers with secondary tax liability to question the validity of the re/assessments on the original delinquent taxpayer, but probably the more common reason is found in the fact that many taxpayers to whom the property of the original delinquent taxpayer was transferred consider that the transfer does not meet the condition prescribed under the above Article 39 of the Collection Act. One example of such a case is the Tax Tribunal 5/31/2000 decision in which at issue was whether or not the applicant who received land of the original delinquent taxpayer at a significantly low price. AR 39-7 on the Collection Act stipulates that the question of whether or not the property is transferred at a significantly low price is to be answered by comparing the price of the transfer with its normal transactional price and being higher than half of it does not always save the transferee from becoming a taxpayer with secondary tax obligation, but the Tax Tribunal decided that the price of the transferred land was more than half of its market price in this case is enough for the applicant not to become a taxpayer with the secondary tax payment obligation.

(3) [Seizure]

As can be confirmed from the Attachment, when delinquent taxpayers point out the problems with the seizure of their property, they are often concerned with Article 153 of the Collection Act, which lays down the conditions for suspension of tax collection, or/and Article 48 of the Act which prohibits the excessive or useless seizure of the tax delinquent's property.[121] As stipulated in Article 48(1) of the Collection Act, the prohibition of excessive seizure means that any property other than that necessary for collecting delinquent taxes cannot be seized. As for what useless seizure means, Article 48(2) of the Act indicates that it is a case in which the value of property to be seized cannot be expected to exceed the aggregated amount of collection costs, other claims with collection priority over delinquent tax, etc. However, Article 63 of the Act states that when a collection official seizes a delinquent taxpayer's legal claim, it must seize its entire amount, while a partial seizure is also allowed when it is appropriate. These provisions describe the fundamental principles on what kind of seizure is allowed/prohibited, but there is also some discretion on the part of those who seize the property so that the seizure could be disputed not only from the perspective of whether it is lawful but also from that of whether it is appropriate exercise of the NTA's discretion.

In the Tax Tribunal's 4/7/2003 decision (CTD No. 65, p. 1095), the applicant/delinquent taxpayer claimed that he owns land other than the seized land on which his house is built, and the value of the former land corresponds to the amount of delinquent tax, so such seizure is against Article 48 as well as the AR 17 on Article 47 of the Collection Act which grants a tax collector discretion on the selection of property to be seized but directs him to give a priority on such property that affects least the tax delinquent's life and business. In this decision, the Tax Tribunal referred to some guiding principles in determining whether the seizure of the property in question meets the requirements of the above Article 63 and Article 48 of the Collection Act. Those principles are: (i) the question of whether or not the concerned seizure is excessive should be decided by taking into account the fact that the seized property is deemed a casualty property whose value decreases accordingly; (ii) even if the expected sales price of the seized property exceeds the amount of delinquent tax, it is not an excessive seizure unless there are such special circumstances as there is a tax delinquent's other property with which he could pay the tax liability and the tax collector exceeded the limit of reasonable discretion. In light of those principles, the Tax Tribunal concluded that the applicant's claim does not stand.

Likewise, in the Tax Tribunal 12/17/2007 decision (CTD No. 74, p. 478), the applicant claimed that the seizure in question was unlawful because it was not only an excessive and useless seizure but also a wrong selection of the property to be seized. In particular, the applicant asserted that the tax collector abused its discretion by not only failing to notice that the applicant has other property (claims on rent and loans) but also seized the concerned property without consulting beforehand with the applicant.

121. As for Article 153 of the Collection Act, *see* footnote 123 and 3(4) in Section 3.

However, the Tax Tribunal assured that the Collection Act and other relevant legislations neither contain any provisions that set any restrictions on the categories and the order to be respected in the selection of the property to be seized nor require a tax collector to have a good grasp of all the property of the concerned delinquent taxpayer, so that selection of property to be seized is left to rational discretion of a tax collector. Then, the Tax Tribunal dismissed the applicant's claims by concluding that in the process of the tax collector's seizure of the concerned property, there are no observable facts that indicate the tax collector's abuse of discretion, and there is nothing irrational about the estimated price of the seized property which was calculated by the tax collector.

(4) Suspension, Etc., of Collection Action

Article 25 of the Administrative Case Litigation Law, which was amended in 2005, provides for the principle of non-suspension of execution of administrative actions in paragraph 1. Also, Article 105(1) of AGRNT provides for the non-suspension of the collection action even if the lawfulness or appropriateness of the concerned re/assessment or the executed collection action is contested at the administrative/judicial review stage.[122] But, Article 25 of the Administrative Case Litigation Law states in paragraphs 2 and 3 that the exception to this principle applies in a case where the execution results in serious damage, and paragraph 1(2) of Article 153 of the Collection Act dictates that collection action is to be suspended when it runs a risk of making the tax delinquent's life extremely difficult.[123] Moreover, Article 105(2) of AGRNT provides that collection action could be canceled, deferred, or suspended in such cases where the NTA Commissioner or Tax Tribunal finds it necessary.[124] Therefore, some tax delinquents assert that the collection action should be suspended. However, the hurdle to clear for its suspension is high, and the NTA Commissioner's discretion on it is not carte blanche discretion but legal discretion,[125] so the number of publicized cases disputing this issue is quite small compared with that disputing the theme 【seizure】.

The height of the hurdle for the suspension of collection action is implied by the Osaka District Court's 3/5/2012 judgment. In this case, the plaintiff/corporate taxpayer claimed that the collection action on the plaintiff should be suspended until a court ruling in another case on the lawfulness of the reassessment is handed down because, once the seized land and the building on the land which was used as the main office of

122. There are many countries that have adopted a rule that in principle a taxpayer's filing of an objection or lawsuit suspends the collection action. For example, *see* 3 in Section 4 of Chapter 2 and 1 in Section 1 of Chapter 5, etc.
123. As for details, *see* AR on Article 153 of the Collection Act and the NTA's AG dated 6/30/2000 on "Suspension of Tax Collection."
124. Moreover, the NTA's AG on the conversion of seized property dated 13/6/2008 prescribes: (i) In principle, the NTA treats an objection to the assessor/Tax Tribunal filed before the stage ③, ⑥, or ⑦ in Figure 1.17 as a cause for suspending the collection action before it proceeds to the next stage, respectively.
125. *See* 2(1) in Section 4. While, in some countries, the tax authority's discretion is much wider. *See*, for instance, the case of Australia in 5(2) in Section 1 of Chapter 4.

the corporation is sold by a public auction, it would deprive the plaintiff of the governmental agency's permit of the business as well as the trust of the business partners, making it difficult for it to reopen the business. But the Court did not accept such claim of the plaintiff by mentioning that non-suspension of the collection action would not cause on the part of the plaintiff such serious damage as it is prescribed under Article 25(2) of the Administrative Case Litigation Law because additional costs which would arise on the part of the plaintiff by relocating its main office and securing places for keeping the applicant's books and records could be covered by monetary compensation and there would not be significant difficulties on the part of the plaintiff in going through the administrative procedures to reopen its business.

The Yokohama District Court 4/25/2007 (2004 (GyoU)41) judgment is one of those rare cases where the collection action was ruled to be suspended. In this case, the plaintiff asserted that one of the sized properties is a house in which the plaintiff lived for a long time, and once it is sold by a public auction, it would be hard to be compensated fully by money, so suspension of the collection action/the procedure of selling the concerned house would be necessary to prevent possible serious damage from being caused. At the same time, he was disputing the re/assessment on him in another case by alleging that the re/assessment on him was unlawful because the NTA wrongly determined that the income earned by the name of the corporation was to be attributed to the plaintiff. The Court acknowledged that at least some of the seized property is managed under the name of the corporation, so this is not a case without any merits as it is prescribed under Article 25(4) of the Administrative Case Litigation Law as the reason for not allowing the suspension. The Court also pointed out that the Article also provides that the suspension of the collection action is not allowed where it would exert serious damage on public welfare either, but the respondent did not make any reference to this connection, so it accepted the plaintiff's appeal.

As the analysis of the above (1) to(4)themes reveals, they do contain attributes that make them highly disputed at the Tax Tribunal and court. Those attributes could be multidimensional. Some tax delinquents wonder if their seized properties are proper ones or if the estimated price of them on public auction is too low. There must also be cases where a taxpayer who is served with a notice of secondary tax payment obligation wonders why he is obligated to pay the original tax delinquent's tax, especially when he is not aware of the fact that his business partner was a tax delinquent. Moreover, there must be many tax delinquents who just want to gain time before the collection action on their property proceeds to the next collection stage.[126] However, there are a few facts that strongly work towards putting a brake on the increase in the number of tax delinquents' requests for reviews and lawsuits. They include the principle that the filing of objections and lawsuits does not suspend the collection action on the appellants and that the NTA's Commissioner's discretion is legal discretion so that it grants little room for its flexible exercise while the scope of its discretion may be a little wider practically concerning its collection action.

---

126. Also in U.S., there are a large number of appeals concerning the collection action and some of them are frivolous. *See* 3 in Section 4 of Chapter 2.

SECTION 4 MAIN TRIGGERS FOR TAX DISPUTES AND SOME REFORM PROPOSALS

1 Main Attributes of ≪Highly Disputed Themes≫

(1) Opacity in the Scope of Application

The causes and attributes that make the themes analyzed in Sections 2 and 3 the ≪highly disputed themes≫ are diverse, so it would be difficult to enumerate them all. But it would be possible to list a few major ones. One of them is the lack of transparency in their application scope. Typical examples of provisions with such attributes are comprehensive anti-abuse provisions such as Article 132 of CITA and Article 157 of ITA (【Denial of a family company's actions or calculations】) as analyzed in 1(5) of Section 1, Article 22(2) of CITA (〔Gratuitous transfer of economic benefits〕) as analyzed in 2(3) of Section 1, the AR 6 on Property Appraisal discussed in 3(1) of Section 1 on the theme 『Principles of appraisal』 and a 『Strict penalty』 analyzed in 2(3) of Section 1.[127] A strict penalty differs from the others mentioned above in that it has another strong attribute of entailing a disgrace of tax evasion as well as an extra fiscal burden that incentivizes many taxpayers with cases sitting on the border to dispute them.[128] Also, a strict penalty has many publicized Tax Tribunal decisions in favor of the cancellation of its application (68 cases in contrast to 59 cases sustaining it), providing evidence that it is certainly a highly disputed theme and its application scope is not clear enough.[129]

[Special exemption for capital gains from resided property] discussed in 1(6) of Section 2, the AR ex 24-4 on 『Property Appraisal』 analyzed in 3(2) of Section 2 and [Justifiable reason] looked into in 2(2) of Section 3 are the ≪highly disputed themes≫ that also have an attribute of opacity in their scope of application. But these themes or provisions have, just like the theme 『strict penalty』, another major attribute that makes them ≪highly disputed themes≫, and it is an attribute of providing taxpayers with a favorable tax treatment or an exception to the regular tax treatment. Moreover, some of these provisions have appeasement clauses or allow room for the NTA's discretion that is not carte blanche discretion but contains opacity. These attributes also incentivize many taxpayers to dispute whether they apply to their cases.[130] In the following (2) and (3), an analysis is to be made of such attributes mainly from the

127. Major foreign countries also have comprehensive anti-avoidance provisions (e.g., U.S. IRC §7701(o), the UK's 2013 Finance Act §206, Australia's Part IVA, Canada's ITA §260, and Ireland's "Tax Consolidation Act" §811C, etc.), but the criteria for and the scope of its application comprise considerable opacity. For details, *see* Matsuda, *supra* "Tax Strategies VS. Countermeasures" (especially at Section 1 in Chapter 1 and Section 1 in Chapter 2).
128. Penalties are also highly disputed in many other countries as well. *See* 2 in Section 4 of Chapter 2, Section 5 of Chapter 3, 5 in Section 1 of Chapter 4 and 4 in Section 1 of Chapter 5.
129. While almost all of the published decisions of the Tax Tribunal regarding Article 157 of ITA and the AR 6 on Property Appraisal applied to cases involving tax avoidance are in favor of the assessor/respondent. As for its published decisions on the application of Article 22(2) of CITA, four out of fifteen are in favor of the applicants.
130. In the U.S., a typical provision which is a highly litigated tax theme on account of such attribute is IRC §6013(e) (Spouse relieved of liability in certain cases). *See* 4 in Section 4 of Chapter 2.

following perspectives: (i) how differences in the phrases adopted as the conditions to be met for those exceptions/salvation to apply could potentially impact on the number of disputes over them, and (ii) how preferential treatments/incentives and their application rules could influence the number of related disputes and taxpayers' actions.

(2) Exceptions and Salvation

(2-1) Exceptions/Salvation Based on Comprehensive Criteria

Analysis in Sections 2 and 3 intimates that some taxpayers' requests for review come mainly from their belief that the NTA should take into account their personal circumstances in applying tax provisions. There are certainly some appeasement clauses and provisions that explicitly allow exceptions. There are some variations among the phrases of those clauses and provisions, but in most cases, they have adopted a comprehensive term or criterion, so there are uncertainties about its application scope. For example, Articles 65 to 67 of AGRNT adopts [Justifiable reason] whose hurdle is set fairly high as it is analyzed in 2 in this Section, while Article 23 of AGRNT, which provides for 『Refund request』 allows exceptions for "unavoidable reasons" or "substantial reasons." Provisions such as Article 30(7) of CTA, which stipulates an "Input tax credit," Article 35(12) of STMA, which provides for [Special deduction for capital gains on residential properties], and Article 41(20) of STMA providing for 『Special credit for housing loans』 allow exceptions due to "unavoidable circumstances." Differences among those phrases and terms are subtle in some cases,[131] but such differences could make differences in the application of the exceptions.

It is pointed out that the breadth of application scope of some common phrases or terms adopted in appeasement clauses and exceptions in the ascending order should be as follows: "unavoidable circumstances" > "substantial reasons" > "justifiable reasons." Certainly, many of the appeasement clauses that use the term "unavoidable circumstances" stipulate that they are to be applied based on the tax office director's judgment, so it can be interpreted to have room for the tax office director's discretion, and it is not unreasonable to think that the scope of "unavoidable circumstances" is wider than that of "justifiable reasons" as well as that of "substantial reasons" that require a high level of rationality and objectivity.[132] Indeed, in the 5/21/1997 (1996(GyoKo)154) judgment, the Tokyo High Court mentioned that a justifiable reason

131. In particular, the difference among "unavoidable circumstances," "special circumstances" and "substantial reasons" is subtle in some cases. For instance, Article 46(5) (Requirements for tax payment deferment, etc.) of AGRNT uses the phrase "special circumstances" while Article 23 (Refund request)(5) of AGRNT prescribes that, even if a refund request is made, collection is not to be postponed, but it is if the director of the tax office recognizes that there is a "substantial reason."

132. The hurdles to clear for the exemption of penalties for non-reporting or underreporting of tax in many other countries are generally lower and the phrases adopted in connection with them are also less restrictive than "justifiable reasons" and closer to "substantial reasons" adopted in

means that there is a *truly* unavoidable reason as in such a case where the tax amount originally reported in a tax return to be lower than that to be legally payable was caused by an objective obstruction for which the taxpayer could not be blamed.[133] Following the view of this court judgment, the breadth of the terms or criteria adopted for the exceptions in the ascending order should be as follows: "justifiable reasons" = "truly unavoidable reasons" < "unavoidable reasons."[134]

On the one hand, there are cases where the application scope of "unavoidable circumstances" is interpreted rather restrictively. For example, in the Tax Tribunal 6/27/2001 decision (CTD No. 61, p. 427), at issue was whether the applicant's claim for the application of the "unavoidable circumstances" laid down in 65-2(5) of STMA (Special credit for income in the case of expropriated land) whose applicability is to be determined at the discretion of the director of the tax office was to be accepted or not.[135] In this case, the applicant did not apply for the special credit in its CIT return for the 1997 business year and claimed that there were "unavoidable circumstances" for it, but the Tax Tribunal mentioned that the "unavoidable circumstances" referred to in the concerned provision were objective circumstances such as natural disasters that are not attributable to taxpayers while the circumstances the applicant claimed for its failure to apply the special credit were no other than personal or subjective circumstances. Then, the Tax Tribunal upheld the assessor's disposition of not accepting the applicant's claim for the application of this special credit in his amended/rectified return.

On the other hand, when a taxpayer fails to follow in time the procedural requirements under paragraphs 4 and 5 of Article 9 of CTA to opt for or opt out of an exempt business for CT purposes, clause 9 of the Article allows their application provided that there were "unavoidable circumstances" and the AR 1-4-16 on CTA mentions further that those circumstances that are recognized by a director of a tax office to be equivalent to the "unavoidable circumstances" are also to be included in the "unavoidable circumstances" prescribed under Article 9(9). Consequently, it must follow that the scope of "unavoidable circumstances" laid down under the above paragraphs 4 and 5 of Article 9 of CTA is practically wider than otherwise. All in all, it should be pertinent to mention that many appeasement provisions use the phrase "unavoidable circumstances," but their scope of application may vary depending on

Japan. *See* 2(1) in Section 4 of Chapter 2, 2(2) in Section 5 of Chapter 3, 5(1) in Section 1 of Chapter 4, 1 in Section 2 of Chapter 6.

133. Also, in the Tokyo High Court 7/15/2010 (2009(GyoKo)372) judgment, the request for downward correction on the plaintiff's return which did not apply the special credit for capital gains from the transfer of a resided property on account of the consulted tax officer's guidance was allowed on the grounds that there were unavoidable circumstances stipulated in Article 35(12) of STMA.

134. It is also stated in the Tax Tribunal's 2/28/2003 decision (CTD No. 65, p. 26) that, "if there is a justifiable reason, it is the filing of the under-reported return due to a *truly unavoidable reason*, and this means that it would be unfair or cruel to impose a penalty on the underreported taxpayer."

135. This paragraph states that "if there are unavoidable circumstances for a CIT return being filed without the descriptions or attachments set forth in the preceding para, a director of tax office could apply the special credit laid down in para 1 or para 2 of this Article, provided that the necessary documents are submitted later on."

which provision it is incorporated in or whether it provides for preferential treatment (as in the case of the Tokyo High Court 7/15/2010 judgment in footnote 133). This opacity in appeasement/exception clauses should add momentum to the taxpayers' inclination to dispute the unlawfulness or inappropriateness of the assessor's determination of not accepting the application of the exceptions.

(2-2) Exceptions/Salvation Based on Specific or Judicially Developed Criteria

Some tax provisions allow salvation and exceptions based on more specific criteria. For example, Article 153 (Requirements for suspension of the collection action) of the Collection Act, which is often relied on in requesting for review at the Tax Tribunal by a taxpayer disputing over the theme [seizure], provides in paragraph 1(2) that director of a tax office could suspend the collection action when there is a risk of significant financial hardship to be caused by its execution. Likewise, paragraph 2(5) of Article 46 of AGRNT prescribes that the director of a tax office could defer payment of tax in such cases where a taxpayer has incurred a significant loss in his business. Certainly, the criteria adopted in those provisions are more specific than those adopted in the provisions referred to in the above (2-1), but judgments based on those criteria could also be difficult depending on the circumstances of the taxpayers. Such difficulty, coupled with the allure of those provisions allowing exceptions, is likely to give rise to many tax disputes and, actually, according to the Attachment, there are thirteen published decisions that dealt with 『deferment of tax payment』, which is a point of contention under the abovementioned paragraph 2(5) of Article 46 of AGRNT.

For example, in the Tokyo District Court 12/15/2015 (2015(GyoU)372) judgment, the plaintiff claimed that, even though the respondent could naturally foresee that the plaintiff's life would get extremely impoverished due to the execution of the collection action, the respondent did not apply the Article 153 of the Collection Act to this case and seized its property, so that it digresses from its proper exercise of discretion or constitutes its abuse.[136] While the Court determined that even if the seized property is sold by tender, the plaintiff would not suffer serious damage. Moreover, the Court stated that the conditions for seizing the property of the delinquent taxpayers are stipulated in Articles 47 to 78 of the Collection Act, and these provisions do not stipulate that the property of the delinquent cannot be seized in such cases where there are facts that come under Article 153(1) of the Collection Act. Based on this observation, the court concluded that, even if the plaintiff's life would be severely distressed due to the execution of the collection action, it would not make the seizure unlawful. The Court seems to be based on a view that, in principle, courts should give deference to the way the NTA's discretion is exercised unless there is a specific tax provision that puts an overriding restriction on how it is to be exercised.[137]

---

136. It is pointed out in the Tokyo District Court 12/21/2016 (2016 (GyoU)194) judgment that a failure of a local tax office's director to suspend collection action could also constitute such abuse in some cases.
137. Also, in the 9/8/2006 decision, the Tax Tribunal determined that the suspension of tax delinquency procedures stipulated in Article 153(1) of the Collection Act is allowed at the

Whereas, in the Tax Tribunal 6/1/2015 case, the applicant claimed that the assessor did not take into consideration his difficult living condition in reviewing his request for tax payment in installments and seized his claim against third-party debtors even though such action of the assessor was contrary to the tax administration policy, which is basically supportive of such treatments as the grace of tax payments when taxpayers are in need. The Tax Tribunal decided that if there is an abuse of discretion or digression from its scope on the part of a tax collector concerning the seizure, it becomes unlawful, but it did not recognize any facts showing that the concerned seizure was illegal or unjust. Nevertheless, the Tax Tribunal stated that, even if there is no such illegality, the judgment of a tax collector regarding the seizure could be irrational in light of the purport of the relevant provisions of the Collection Act, etc., and seizure of the tax delinquent's property could be unjust.[138] Actually, in some cases, the Tax Tribunal canceled the NTA's dispositions because they were inappropriate exercise of its discretion. The number of such cases is not large, but they are most likely to be found in the collection cases.

Furthermore, there are some cases where courts granted to taxpayers in special circumstances unprescribed exceptions to the tax treatments under some provisions. For example, in connection with the theme [Gratuitous transfer of monetary or economic benefits], Article 22(2) and Article 37 of ITA recognize corporate contribution on the part of a corporation for providing such benefits mostly to a related company, and it gives rise to corporate income if some of that corporate contribution exceeds its threshold deductible amount while the aforementioned Osaka High Court 3/30/1978 judgment allowed an exception to this treatment even if it is not prescribed in relevant provisions,[139] provided that such benefits are given to related parties in the form of debt exemption, interest-free loan, etc. to prevent their bankruptcy and has a rational economic purpose. This exception is now adopted in the AR 9-4-1 and 9-4-2 on CIT.[140] Likewise, the Tax Tribunal allowed in the 4/3/2002 decision an input tax credit for CT purposes, even if the names of the suppliers on the taxpayers' account books and receipts were false, provided that there were unavoidable circumstances on the part of the taxpayer to believe that they are authentic.[141]

(3) *Preferential Treatments/Tax Incentives*

Just as tax provisions with appeasement clauses or exceptions tend to become ≪highly disputed themes≫ because they provide taxpayers with favorable tax treatments and

discretion of the director of a tax office or the director of the Regional Taxation Bureau, and appeals against their failure to do so should be dismissed as not falling within the jurisdiction of the Tax Tribunal.

138. This is in line with Article 102(2) of AGRNT. *See* 1 in Section 1 and footnote 8.
139. *See* 2(3) of Section 2. While some do not see the validity of such unprescribed exceptions.
140. The Transfer Pricing AG 3-20 also states that, if a corporation sets or changes the transaction price of a foreign-related transaction for the purpose of providing financial support, etc., to a foreign-related party, Article 66-4(3) of STMA prescribing the TP rule does not apply when there are "substantial reasons" as in the case of the AR 9-4-2 on CIT. Also, *see* footnote 58.
141. *See* 1(1) in Section 3.

often involve NTA's legal discretion, tax provisions granting preferential treatments/tax incentives also tend to become ≪highly disputed themes≫. Moreover, they are not granted on an exceptional basis but are widely granted so long as certain requirements in such tax provisions are met. Such being the case, there are many disputes over some of those provisions granting preferential treatment. 『Revocation of blue return status』 stipulated in Article 150 of ITA and Article 127 of CITA, which is one of the ≪highly disputed themes≫, is one example of them, while the requirements for revoking blue return status are specified in laws and administrative guidelines and the number of the Tax Tribunal's decisions canceling the assessor's determination of rescinding the blue return filer's status is small. These facts suggest that the main cause for such disputes lies in the great merit that the blue return privilege provides, just as such merit is one of the main causes for the AR ex 24-4 on Property Appraisal referred to 3(2) in Section 2 to be a ≪highly disputed theme≫.

Furthermore, in the case of preferential treatments, taxpayers' incentive to seek its application sometimes becomes too strong and induces inordinary attempts to gain their applications and ends up in disputes over whether such attempts constitute tax avoidance or tax evasion that usually incurs the application of a strict penalty. For example, while there may be arguments over whether or not the foreign tax credit system stipulated in Article 69 of ITA is preferential treatment,[142] the Supreme Court, in the 12/19/2005 (1998(GyoTsu)149) judgment, pointed out that the taxpayer's inappropriate attempt to utilize foreign tax credit system for the reduction of its tax burden was an abuse of the system while it was not subjected to a strict penalty. But [special credit for capital gains from the transfer of resided property] prescribed under Article 35 of STMA often tempted some taxpayers' inappropriate attempts on which a strict penalty is imposed because such attempts are usually made in such a way that a nonprimary residence is registered as a taxpayer's primary residence just before its transfer in an attempt to avail this special credit.[143] Other cases involve some taxpayers' fake export of goods in an attempt to become applicable to export exemption prescribed under Article 7 of CTA.[144]

Article 25 (Special provision for taxation of agricultural income from the sale of beef cattle) of STMA is another provision whose preferential treatment could induce a taxpayer's inappropriate attempt to seek its application. For this provision to be applicable, a taxpayer's sale of beef cattle must be entrusted to agricultural cooperatives, etc. In the Tax Tribunal 1/24/2012 decision, at issue was whether Article 25 of STMA applies to the applicant's sale of beef cattle from the years 2003 to 2007 and

142. The Osaka High Court in 6/14/2002(2001(GyoKo)47) judgment considers the foreign tax credit system as a preferential or tax reduction/exemption provision. However, some argue that the foreign tax credit system is not a policy-based tax exemption measure. *See* Tadatsune Mizuno, Bibliography (11) p. 23.

143. *See* Tax Tribunal 11/10/2000 decision shown in 1(6) in Section 2.

144. *See* the Osaka High Court 9/29/2004 judgment shown in 1(3) in Section 3. Asahi Newspaper dated 12/28/2022 informs that NTA imposed additional JPY 14,000 million CT on a corporation by certifying that its commodities sold in exceptionally large number to foreign visitors to Japan are intended to be resold by intermediaries abroad.

2009, which formally involved an agricultural cooperative. The Tax Tribunal determined that the cooperative's involvement was superficial and in substance they were negotiated transactions between the applicant and its business partners. The Tax Tribunal also found that the sales certificates were not attached to the applicant's tax returns and that many of the cash sales from the transactions were deposited into a bank account without being recorded in the applicant's accounting journal. Moreover, these transactions were not disclosed to the applicant's tax accountant. Based on these findings, it determined that these applicants' actions fall under the deceit or other fraudulent acts prescribed in Article 70(5) of AGRNT and upheld the reassessment as well as the imposition of underreporting penalties for the concerned years.[145]

Moreover, in cases where provisions granting special treatments have exceptions/salvation clauses, they add further spur to the number of their applications as well as disputes over them.[146] Nevertheless, the majority of salvation clauses concern themselves with taxpayers' failures to follow formalities for unavoidable circumstances, so many disputes over whether or not a provision granting preferential treatment is applicable do not pivot on the substantive issue but on the nonsubstantive issue. In this connection, it is to be noted that it has been confirmed by judicial precedents that a taxpayer cannot request to substitute a method of tax calculation in a tax law that he preferred at the time of his filing of a return with another one after the filing deadline is passed.[147] The Supreme Court 11/10/1987 judgment mentioned in 2(1) in Section 3 is one example in which the Court ruled that, once the filing deadline is passed, the taxpayer/doctor cannot claim the deduction of the amount of expenses he actually incurred in the relevant year because, in his original return, he opted for the application of Article 26 of STMA which allows for IT purposes deduction of an approximate amount of social insurance medical expenses.[148]

The above rule that does not allow the *ex post* request for substitution of the original choice of a particular treatment for another one also applies in such a case where a taxpayer's original choice must be made before a tax return is filed, as in the case of Article 9 and Article 36 of CTA which requires an eligible small business to notify the NTA well in advance (one or two business years ahead) of the applicable

145. For other cases where the taxpayer's actions fell under the deceit or other fraudulent acts and a regular underreporting penalty rather than a strict penalty was imposed on them, *see* footnote 101.

146. The Attachment lists fairly large number of disputed cases on tax incentives with appeasement clauses such as Article 69-4 (Special rule for calculating the taxable value of IT for small-scale resided land, etc.) of STMA and Article 41 (Special credit for housing loans) of STMA and Article 32 (Special rule for refund request) of IGTA.

147. If an error in the return is attributable to the taxpayer's agent, a claim for damages may be filed against the tax accountant. However, for example, in the Tokyo District Court 10/26/1999 (1996 (Wa) 23902) judgment, such claim was dismissed because the breach of duty of due care by the tax accountant was not recognized (while it was partially accepted by the Tokyo High Court 7/11/2001 judgment).

148. As mentioned in 2(1) in Section 3 and footnote 88, the Supreme Court 6/5/1990 judgment has confirmed that the *ex post* opting out of the original choice is possible in the case of an amended return rather than a refund request. While in NZ, there is a High Court judgment that implies the possibility of granting a relief to a taxpayer's regretted choice. *See* footnote 201 of Chapter 4.

business year of its choice of opting in/out of tax-exempt business status and the simplified taxation method respectively. However, disputes over those articles arise more often because they do have salvation clauses, and it is quite likely that an eligible business's choice may be the best for it when it was made, but depending on the circumstances of the succeeding business years, it may not turn out to be the best for the applicable business year. In such cases, some of them regret their original choices and may claim the invalidity of their requests for the application of the originally preferred treatment. But such a claim usually fails, as in the case of the Tax Tribunal 9/26/1994 decision referred to in 1(2) of Section 3 in which the taxpayer's request for refund of his CT was not allowed even if he claimed that the submission of his request for the application of the simplified taxation method was due to his error and therefore invalid.

2 Reform Proposals for Tax Dispute System and Procedures

(1) Drastic Reform Proposal of Tax Tribunal and "Proposal of Flexible Dispute Resolution"

Analysis in the above 1 confirms that ≪highly disputed themes≫ have certain attributes that trigger tax disputes. The main attributes with strong triggering power are opacity in the scope of application, exceptions/salvation, and preferential treatments/tax incentives. Reforms to reduce the number of tax provisions that have such attributes would work towards reducing the number of tax disputes. Particularly, reforms to mitigate the problem of opacity of the application scope of some tax provisions and reduce the number of exceptions/preferential treatments should be effective in this sense, but the former should be very difficult to realize and might not be so beneficial for taxpayers while the latter would definitely not be beneficial for taxpayers. Therefore, it should be more realistic to confine reform options to those that are targeted at the procedures and rules on tax disputes as well as the review organs. Moreover, such reform options could be beneficial for taxpayers in general because they should have the merit of having direct effects not only on the ways of handling tax disputes but also on the power imbalance between the NTA and the aggrieved taxpayers, which are claimed by some to be corrected.

The most frequently discussed reform option is the restructuring of the Tax Tribunal in a way to enhance its independence and neutrality. That is probably the most realistic reform option, and so far, the reforms have been made that way since the establishment of the Tax Tribunal. There are still voices calling for further reforms to enhance the independence and neutrality of the Tax Tribunal, and some propose drastic reform of it. One such proposal is to detach the Tax Tribunal from the Treasury and the NTA to transfer it to the Cabinet Office (hereinafter called "Proposal of transferring Tax Tribunal to Cabinet Office").[149] Another one is to dissolve the Tax Tribunal into the Tax Court (hereinafter called "Proposal for establishing Tax Court") and this proposal incorporates the following mechanisms: (i) a Tax Court adopts the "Proposal of Flexible Dispute Resolution," (ii) a single judge may decide a simple case and a case in which a disputed tax amount is small, (iii) the Tax Court judges are granted with investigation power just like the Tax Tribunal reviewers, (iv) when the disputed parties at the Tax Court wish to dispute its judgment, they can appeal to the High Court,[150] (v) the Tax Court judges are consisted of reviewers at the dissolved Tax Tribunal, lawyers, college professors specializing in tax law, and so forth.[151]

As for the "Proposal of Flexible Dispute Settlement" incorporated in the above "Proposal for establishment Tax Court," some find merits in it irrespective of whether a Tax Court exists or not. But Article 84 of the Japanese Constitution provides for taxation by the law, and it is generally accepted that a flexible settlement of potential tax disputes between a taxpayer and a tax auditor could be done in practice only before the re/assessment is made on the taxpayer.[152] As for flexible settlement of tax disputes after re/assessments are made, quite predominant are cons arguments against it, and they are based on the view that even in cases where provisions of tax acts grant discretion to the director of a tax office, the scope of such discretion is by no means wide so that such discretion cannot be exercised to reach an agreement with taxpayers.[153] These arguments are in line with the fact that in other administrative disputes, flexible dispute resolution is generally not allowed. Moreover, in 2007, the Legislation for Fostering the Utilization of ADR was introduced, but utilization of ADR has been quite limited as a means to settle administrative disputes, and it is not applicable at all in the context of tax disputes.[154]

(2) "Proposal of Review at Pre-Assessment Stage"

In light of the Constitutional restriction on flexible settlement of tax disputes in Japan, those proponents of active utilization of flexible settlements may look for reforms at a

149. Such reform option was also presented, for example, in September 14, 2010, by the Expert Committee of the Tax Research Commission ("Summary of Issues Concerning Improvement of the Environment for Tax Payment").
150. On April 1, 2005, based on Law No. 119 of 2004, the Intellectual Property High Court was established as a special branch of the Tokyo High Court to specialize in intellectual property-related cases.
151. Fumihiro Komamiya, Bibliography (12) pp. 224-225.
152. *See* 3(4) in Section 3. In reality, there are a few exceptional cases. For example, an out of court settlement was reached between the Tokyo Metropolitan government and some financial institutions on the amount of local enterprise tax payable by them after the government lost at the Tokyo High Court 1/30/2003 (2002(GyoKo)94, 245 to 261) judgment.
153. The Tokyo District Court 11/30/1970 (1968(Gyo)No. 38-1) states that taxation must be based on legal grounds and it is clear that exemption from tax claims based on a contract between the tax authority and the taxpayer is not permissible. However, in practice, it seems that several cases of lawsuits related to tax collection cases are flexibly settled each year, intimating the NTA's wider discretion with respect to collection cases. *See* pp. 342-346 of the 143rd NTA Statistical Yearbook 2017.
154. Some Japan's tax treaties have ADR as a method of relieving international double taxation. *See* footnote 133 in Chapter 5.

pre-assessment stage. In fact, in some countries, persons with some neutrality are relied on to resolve potential tax disputes at a pre-assessment stage,[155] and there is a "Proposal for Review at Pre-Assessment Stage," which is similar to that employed in Korea.[156] In Korea, the adoption in 1997 of the Taxpayers Charter introduced the pre-assessment review system in Article 81(15) of the Basic Act of National Taxes.[157] This system enables a taxpayer to request a review committee to decide on an audit result report sent to the taxpayer before the reassessment is made in a case where the disputed tax amount exceeds a certain amount (KRW 5 million at the time of its introduction but currently KRW 1 billion), or it involves a possibility of change in the way of interpreting a tax provision. The review committee is composed of the director of the concerned tax office (chairman with no voting rights for the decision), four tax specialists from the public sector appointed by him as well as three directors of the non-audit sections. The committee's decision binds the tax authority and the decision is notified to the taxpayer within thirty days after the request for review is made.[158]

According to the Korean tax authority's statistics report, the ratio of the committee's decision in favor of the taxpayers during the period 2003 ~ 2005 was around 35% to 37%, and the ratio is not much different from those ratios of decisions of the assessors and the Tax Tribunal which were favorable to the aggrieved taxpayers,[159] but this Korean pre-assessment review system has great merit for the aggrieved taxpayers because it could realize a speedy resolution of a potential tax dispute. This pre-assessment review system places a heavy restriction on the tax authority's power of reassessment, but the adoption of Article 8 of the Taxpayers' Charter has made it possible for such a system to be introduced. This Article stipulates that taxpayers have the right to receive legal and speedy relief before they are subjected to reassessments that might undermine their rights and interests on account of their unlawfulness or inappropriateness. Therefore, the abovementioned "Proposal for Review at Pre-Assessment Stage" is made in conjunction with the adoption in Japan of such Taxpayers' Charter, which has a provision similar to Article 8 of the Taxpayers' Charter in Korea.

155. One example is "pre-assessment ADR" employed by the IRS. *See* Section 1 in Chapter 2.
156. Hiroshi Hasegawa, Bibliography (13) pp. 22-23 and 59-60.
157. For several years before the introduction of this system, it was implemented based on the tax authority's directives.
158. If the decision is not notified within such time limit, 50% of the increased burden resulting from the delay will be reduced. For more information, *see* "Current Status of Tax Investigations in South Korea" (https://www.tains.org/wp-content/uploads/2018/12/%E7%AC%AC11%E5%9B%9E%EF%BC%882015%EF%BC%89%EF%BC%88%E6%97%A5%E6%9C%AC%E8%AA%9E%EF%BC%89.pdf).
159. *See* Hasegawa, *supra* Bibliography (13) p. 62 and Bibliography (14) p. 77. According to the tax authority's statistics, between 2005 and 2008, there were about annual 5,000 to 6,500 cases that were subjected to the pre-assessment review system, and the ratio of decisions favorable to the taxpayers was about 30% to 38%.

3 "Proposal of Adopting Costs Shifting Rule"

This book's Prologue and Section 1 of this chapter confirm that the number of tax objections/lawsuits in Japan is not so large, and one of the main reasons for this seems to be the low rate of revocation of the disputed re/assessments. Figures 1.8 and 1.19 show that this rate in courts is small, even from an international perspective.[160] There might be room for debate as to whether or not this is a cause for concern, and even if it is a cause for concern, it is not what could be dealt with easily. On the other hand, if one of the reasons for the relatively small number of tax disputes in Japan is found in the taxpayer's burden in terms of time and money to be incurred by litigations, there must be some measures to lessen it. Some attribute the low number of administrative suits in Japan to various negative causes, such as the imbalance in fiscal resources between the government and the plaintiff, judicial passivism, and much emphasis placed on judicial precedents, etc., and propose that the stamp duty required for litigations on the part of the plaintiff should be made free of charge and that if the plaintiff wins the case, a system should be established to provide the plaintiff with a financial reward now that the plaintiff has worked hard to rectify the illegal administration.[161]

Figure 1.19 Percentage of Court Rulings in Favor of Tax Authorities (2015)

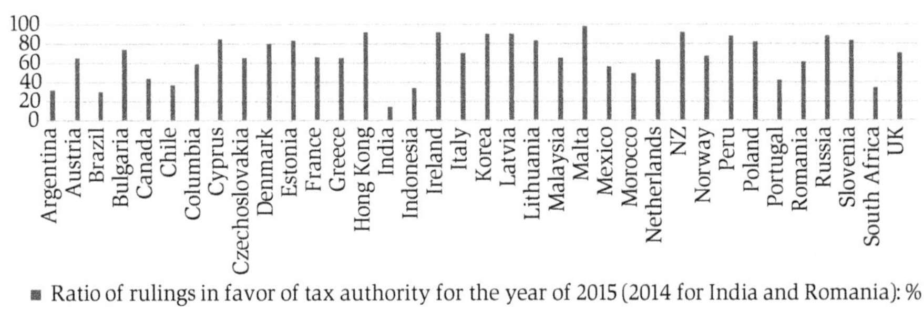

Source: Tax Administration 2017—Comparative information on OECD and Other Advanced and Emerging Economies, Figure 6.23 p. 115 at https://www.oecd-ilibrary.org/taxation/tax-administration-2017_tax_admin-2017-en.

Obviously, the above proposal of granting financial rewards to winning plaintiffs at administrative litigations does not exclude winning taxpayers at tax suits, and it certainly has a good point. However, the objective and the effect this opinion intends could also be attained by expanding the scope of the winning plaintiff's litigation-related costs that could be reimbursed. In this connection, it is to be noted that Article

160. Recently, the percentage of judgments favorable to the tax authorities in Japan ranges from 88% to 96%, as shown in Figure 1.8, while the average for the countries listed in Figure 1.19 is around 65%.
161. *See* Abe, *supra* Bibliography (1) p. 29.

61 of the Civil Procedure Code (Principle of the burden of court costs) stipulates that the litigation-related expenses shall be borne by the losing party,[162] while such expenses do not include attorney's fees, which usually account for most of the lawsuit-related expenses of the plaintiff. As for the relationship between civil and administrative lawsuits, Article 7 of the Administrative Case Litigation Act prescribes that, regarding administrative lawsuits, those matters not stipulated in this law shall be governed by the examples of civil lawsuits, and there are some exceptions to the above costs rule. In particular, Article 709 of the Civil Code (Compensation for damages due to tort) dictates that a person who intentionally or negligently infringes the rights of others or the legally protected interests shall compensate for the damage caused thereby.

There is also an established judicial precedent that includes in the plaintiff's claim for damages an amount equivalent to the reasonable amount of the attorney's fees payable by the plaintiff. For example, in the 2/27/1969(1966(O)280) judgment, the Supreme Court ruled that the respondent suffered damage from the appellant's illegal action because the respondent was obliged to file a lawsuit against the appellant to stop public sale of the real estate that was petitioned by the appellant. Then, the Court stated that our country has not adopted the principle of compulsory representation by an attorney in litigation, and the attorney's fee is not included in the litigation expenses, while a person in general usually would not carry out litigating activities sufficiently without an attorney. Now that normally an attorney acts as a representative in carrying out such activities, the Court declared that there should be a causal relationship between the damage inflicted by the illegal action and the attorney's fee to the extent that it is proper in the amount in light of the difficulties of the case, the amount of damage claimed and relevant circumstances. In conclusion, the Court determined that the start-up fee paid by the respondent to the attorney for entrusting him with this litigation is damage arisen normally as a result of the appellant's illegal action.

A view similar to the above shown in the above Supreme Court 2/27/1969 judgment is also expressed in the Supreme Court 12/17/2004 (2004(Jyu)633) judgment on the administrative case litigation. In this case, the respondent (metropolitan tax office in Tokyo) imposed fixed asset tax and city planning tax on the appellant for the year 2000, and the appellant sought, based on Article 1(1) of the National Redress Law, for damage compensation on account of the illegal administration of the office. After this lawsuit was filed, the respondent canceled its disposition of imposing these taxes on the appellant and refunded to the appellant those taxes with interest, but the appellant claimed the reimbursement of its attorney's fee and a solatium. In this judgment, the Court pointed out that the appellant's filing of this lawsuit led to the cancellation of the respondent's concerned disposition so that, among the appellant's attorney's fee incurred in connection with this lawsuit, such reasonable part of it should be damage that has a causal relationship with the concerned disposition.

162. The expenses that can be recovered by the successful party are usually limited to small amounts, such as the fees to be paid to the court, travel and accommodation costs for witnesses, and costs related to the preparation of translated documents.

Thenceforth, the Court concluded that the Tokyo High Court 1/21/2004 (2003(Ne)5457) judgment on this case was wrong in failing to affirm such a causal relationship, and it remanded the case back to the High Court.[163]

Moreover, recently, although limited in number, some judicial precedents allow partial recovery of attorney's fees even in cases other than torts.[164] In particular, the Osaka High Court 2/17/2011(2020(Ne)2028) judgment rejected the recovery of attorney's fees while accepting the worker's claim for damages based on default on the grounds of the employer's violation of the obligation to maintain safety, but this original judgment was not fully sustained by the Supreme Court 2/24/2012 (2011(Jyu)1039) judgment. Interestingly enough, the Supreme Court pointed out that the facts to be proved in this case are almost the same as those for claiming damages based on tort, and it is difficult to carry out sufficient litigation activities unless the right to claim damages is entrusted to an attorney. Based on such a view, the Supreme Court ruled that a part of the appellant's attorney fee is damage to the extent that it has, in light of the difficulties of the case, the amount of damage claimed and relevant circumstances, a causal relationship with the respondent's violation of its obligation to maintain safety, and remanded the case back to the High Court to deliberate on the amount of the attorney's fee to be recoverable by the appellant.

As mentioned above, judicial precedents confirm that it would be possible to recover the amount equivalent to attorney's fees as a claim for damages in tort or a similar claim to the extent deemed appropriate. However, irrespective of whether an amount equivalent to attorney's fees is included in litigation-related expenses to be recoverable by a person who wins a lawsuit, the recoverable amount is not automatically determined by the trial. Instead, as Article 71 of the Civil Procedure Code prescribes, it is determined by the clerk of the court of first instance on the petition after its payment has become enforceable after the judgment is made. Thus, the procedure for determining recoverable litigation-related expenses is cumbersome, and the amount that can be recovered is usually small.[165] Such being the case, such a petition is made roughly in one out of a hundred cases and the aforementioned Judicial System Reform Council pointed out in 2001 the need for simplifying the procedures. In

163. Article 242-2 of the Local Autonomy Act also stipulates in para. 1 that residents of ordinary local governments may request a "resident audit," and in para. 12 that the person who filed the lawsuit under the provisions of para. 1 wins (including partial wins) and in the case of doing so, when a fee is to be paid to a lawyer or a legal corporation, the ordinary local public entity can be requested to pay an amount that is considered to be appropriate within the scope of the fee.

164. For example, in the 3/26/2019 judgment, the Osaka District Court specified that the right to claim damages based on the breach of the obligation to collect and provide information recognized in this judgment is the right to claim damages based on default, but, now that it is based on the principle of good faith (Article 1(2) of the Civil Code), it could be constructed as a claim for damages based on tort. Then, the court held that it is appropriate to recognize that the amount of damages as attorney's fees in this case should be JPY 30,000 for each of the plaintiffs.

165. Moreover, the amount of attorney's fees that can be recovered as having a substantial causal relationship with the tort is calculated based on the allowable amount of the claim for damages, not the actual amount paid. Consequently, for instance, in many cases of traffic accidents, it is about 10% of the allowable amount.

response, an amendment to the Court Law was made in 2003 for the Reform of the Judicial System so that the amount of expenses for civil litigation should be calculated as much as possible based on the facts that are clear in the records and the submission of explanatory materials is required no more. But it is only a partial solution.

In light of the current situation, some opinions expressed in the 2001 Justice System Reform Council Report are in favor of the adoption of an attorney's fee shifting by the "Loser pays rule," while some others are in favor of the one-way "Loser pays rule" (under this rule, shifting of a winner's attorney's fee is done only in a case where a citizen wins against the government) over the two-way "Loser pays rule." Such a one-way "Loser pays rule" should be particularly appropriate in administrative case litigations and national reparation litigations in which the winning ratio of a citizen against the government is low and there usually exists a power imbalance as well as an imbalance of financial resources. Also, it should be more effective in enhancing citizens' access to justice.[166] On the other hand, such a one-way "Loser pays rule" might have some negative effects, such as an increase in the number of administrative case litigations, which may also contain some unworthy ones. With those positive and negative effects of shifting a winner's attorney's fee to the loser in litigation, there is a question of whether the rule is appropriate in the case of tax litigation and, if it is, in what circumstances, shifting of the attorney's fee should be allowed.

As for the amount of attorney's fees usually charged to a disputant/litigant, the Bar Association used to have set standards, as shown in Table 1.1. However, it was abolished by the 2003 revision of the Attorney Act, which liberalized the amount of chargeable attorney's fees after April 2004, and this has lately resulted in the general trend of the ratio of attorney's fees rising in a litigant's total litigation expenses.[167] Some apprehend that such a trend, in combination with the principle of self-payment of attorney's fees in litigation, may work as a factor that discourages those claiming to have suffered damage or loss by administrative dispositions and actions from resorting to court proceedings while, in some foreign countries, a one-way "Loser pays rule" is adopted, and it often has led to the achievement of their nationals' higher level of access to justice. Such being the case, despite the abovementioned negative aspects of the one-way "Loser pays rule," some opinions expressed in the above Justice System Reform Council stress the need for looking into the possibility of adopting the loser payment rule from the perspective of which categories of cases are appropriate for the rule to be introduced into and, if it is adopted in some categories of cases, how much of a winner's attorney's fee should be recovered.[168]

166. The abovementioned Japan Bar Association's opinion pointed out that in the case of Japan, the amount of legal aid borne by the government is particularly small, and the hurdle for it is also quite high.
167. Currently the remuneration provisions of the Bar Association simply state in Article 2 that the remuneration for attorneys must be appropriate in light of economic benefits, the difficulty of the case, time and labor, and other circumstances.
168. The Japan Bar Association's opinion dated 8/22/2003 on the "Treatment of Lawyer's Fees to be Paid by the Unsuccessful" also concluded that the scope of lawsuits for which the unilateral payment rule should be introduced must be examined as soon as possible.

Table 1.1 Former Remuneration Standards for Attorneys Set by Federation of Bar Association

1. Litigation cases (with some exceptions), administrative cases, etc.	**Amount of economic benefit from the case**	**Amount of expenses (Minimum amount of the start-up fee is JPY 100,000; start-up fee and compensation can be increased or decreased within 30% of the following amount depending on the content of the case)**
	JPY 3 million or less	Start-up fee: 8% of economic benefit Compensation: 16% of economic benefit
	Over JPY 3 million to JPY 30 million	Start-up fee: 5% + JPY 90,000 Compensation: 10% + JPY 180,000
	Over JPY 30 million to JPY 300 million	Start-up fee: 3% + JPY 690,000 Compensation: 6% + JPY 1.38 million
	Over JPY 300 million	Start-up fee: 2% + JPY 3.69 million Compensation: 4% + JPY 7.38 million
2. Administrative objections, requests for administrative review, etc.		Start-up fee: two-thirds of the remuneration amount in 1 above, and the minimum amount is JPY 100,000. Compensation: one-half of the remuneration amount in 1 above. However, the start-up fee and the remuneration after going through an interrogation or an oral hearing shall be the amount equivalent to 1 above.

Source: Created based on the Former Federation of Bar Association Remuneration Standards.

With the results of the analysis made in this chapter in mind, in the following chapters, a focus is to be shifted to some other countries with particularly noteworthy systems and practices on tax disputes and their resolution. Then, an analysis is to be made, especially of those points in those countries that are relevant to the main issues covered in this chapter, to make a cross-country comparison and draw some lessons for Japan. In concrete, an analysis from a cross-country comparative perspective is to be made mainly on the following issues in those countries: (i) tax objection procedures and their notable points as well as their recent reform directions, (ii) functional features and performance of the objections review organs, (iii) attributes and triggers of highly disputed tax themes, (iv) availability and level of usage of flexible tax settlement methods such as ADR and agreements between taxpayers and the tax authority as well as their limitation, (v) attorney's fee payment rules in tax litigation and administrative litigation in general as well as their historical metamorphosis, (vi) other issues and rules with significant influence on the number of tax disputes and taxpayers' access to justice, (vii) problems and challenges regarding the resolution of tax disputes.

CHAPTER 2

Status in the United States

SECTION 1 TAX OBJECTIONS TO OFFICE OF APPEALS

1 Standard Objections Procedures and Office of Appeals' Function

If a taxpayer's underreporting of income tax (IT) is discovered by an audit carried out by the U.S. Inland Revenue Service (IRS) and no agreement is reached between the taxpayer and the office in charge of the audit,[1] the standard procedure is that the taxpayer shall be issued a "30-day letter" which is consisted of Letter 525 (examination report), Form 4549 (IT examination changes) and so forth.[2] A "30-day letter" contains (i) audit results and amount of payable tax, (ii) reasons for re/assessments and calculation process of the payable tax amount, (iii) interest and penalties (if applicable), and (iv) a notice informing the taxpayer to file an objection/(appeal) with the Office of Appeals if he does not consent to the audit results. If he consents to them, he is to pay the tax (often after he has sent back to IRS Form 4549, which he signed), while the dissenting taxpayer, as Figure 2.1 shows, has to notify the IRS within thirty days after the issue date of the "30-day letter" of his intention of filing an objection to the Office of Appeals (the IRS' independent review organ),[3] and prepare documents showing reasons for the appeals and justifications for his claim.[4]

1. IRM 4.10.7.5.3.1 states, "Examination personnel have the authority and responsibility to reach a definite conclusion based on a balanced and impartial evaluation of all the evidence ... . This authority does not extend to consideration of hazards of litigation."
2. A "thirty-day non-filer report" may be issued to a non-filer of IT return.
3. There is also the option of paying the tax and then make a request for refund.
4. If the amount of tax (total amount including interest, etc.) to which a taxpayer makes an objection at the Office of Appeals is no more than USD 25,000, it is " small case request" that enables him to make an objection orally. *See* Publication 5 (Your Appeals Rights and How to Prepare a Protest If You don't Agree).

Figure 2.1 Standard Tax Objections Procedures

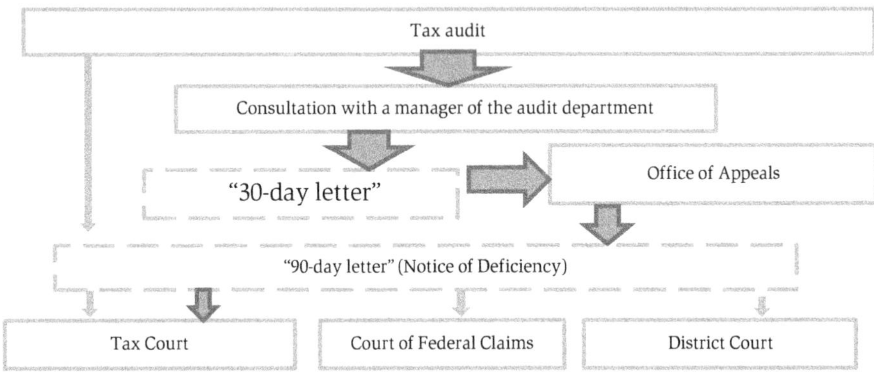

As exhibited in Figure 2.2, the Office of Appeals has recently received approximately 100,000 objections per year. The 1998 enactment of the IRS Restructuring and Reform Act (PL 105-206: IRS Restructuring and Reform Act of 1998, hereinafter called "the 1998 IRS Reform Act") had a major impact on the number of objections received by the Office of Appeals. Due to the enactment of this Act, the IRS was forced to reduce the number of its personnel and tax audits,[5] and it resulted in a temporary decrease in the number of appeals filed to the Office of Appeals. Whereas, before the 1998 IRS Reform Act, the IRS could take collection actions without the involvement of the Office of Appeals or the courts, but the Act introduced the Collection Due Process (CDP) in IRC §6320 (Notice and opportunity for hearing upon filing of a notice of lien), IRC §6330 (Notice and opportunity for hearing before levy), etc. that allow tax delinquents to be heard by the Office of Appeals before the completion of the collection action.[6] Acting on these provisions, many tax delinquents have started to make objections to the Office of Appeals by asserting the unlawfulness/inappropriateness of the collection action, requesting its suspension, etc., and it increased the number of objections to the Office of Appeals again until it hit its peak in 2011.

5. According to Table 32 of the 2021 IRS Data Book, in FY2021, there were 80,411 IRS employees (94,346 in FY2010) and 934 Appeals officers (902 in FY2010) while the GAO Report ("Tax Administration: Opportunities Exist to Improve Monitoring and Transparency of Appeal Resolution Timeliness," GAO-18-659) p. 22 shows that the number of staff in the Office of Appeals was 2,172 in FY2010 and 1,345 in FY2017.
6. Before 1998, tax delinquents who wanted to dispute the lawfulness of collection procedures had the limited option of filing a tax refund suit or a damage suit to court. IRC §6320 states in para. (a) (Requirement of notice) (1) that the Secretary shall notify in writing the person of the filing of a notice of lien, and para. (b) (Right to fair hearings) (1) that if the person requests a hearing in writing under subsection (a)(3)(B) and states the grounds for the requested hearing, such hearing shall be held by the IRS Independent Office of Appeals. IRC §6330 also provides likewise in paras. (a) and (b). As for IRC §6330(e)(Suspension of collection and statute of limitation), *see* footnote 165. IRS notifies it by sending a Letter 3172 (Notice of Federal Tax Lien Filing and You Right to a Hearing under IRC §6320) to a tax delinquent. Also, the 1998 IRS Reform Act introduced IRC §6334(e)(1) that requires the IRS to obtain prior court approval before a delinquent taxpayer's principal residence is seized.

Figure 2.2 Number of Objections Received by the Office of Appeals and Cumulative Number of Unprocessed Cases

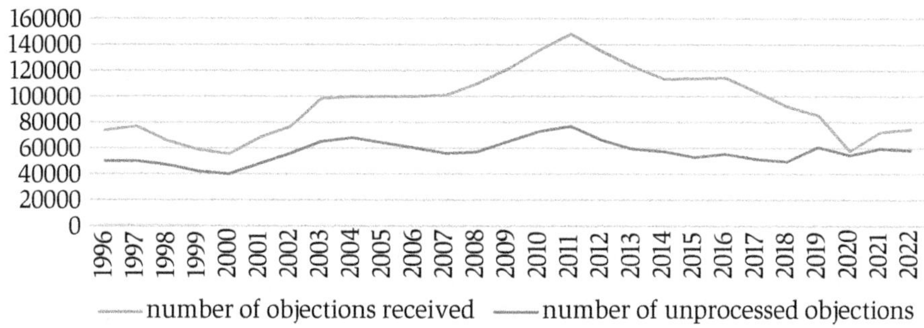

Source: 1996-2022 IRS Data Book Table: Appeals Workload, by Type of Case, etc.

Personal IT and social security taxes typically account for more than 80% of the federal government's revenue,[7] while, as Figure 2.3 shows, CDP cases generally account for the largest portion (about 30%-35% of the total) of the cases recently appealed to the Office of Appeals.[8] For example, in 2002, less than 10% of all the objections were filed regarding an "offer-in-compromise," which grants a reduction or exemption on the tax amount payable under certain conditions to delinquent taxpayers who are found to be in financial difficulties while since 2003, it has accounted for 17% or more. The largest proportion of objections next to CDP cases is on "examination cases" ("deficiency cases"), accounting for about 28% to 32% of the total. Among them, the number of objections against audits of small-scale business cases, which have a particularly large number of investigations, is quite large.[9] There are also many objections related to penalty issues, accounting recently for about 13% to 17% of the total. Objections on cases pivoting on IRC §6015 (Relief from joint and several liability on joint return), which allows a spouse's exemption from his joint and several liability based on his innocent ignorance of the other spouse's error in the married couple's joint income tax return, are lately around 5% of the total.[10]

7. In FY2021, about 51% of federal government revenue came from personal IT, about 32% from social security taxes, and about 9% from corporate IT. *See* Historical Tables, Office of Management and Budget, Table 2.1.
8. The recent decline in the number of objections (particularly "collection issues") received by the Office of Appeals is, as the Figure 2.5 intimates, partly due to the decline in the number of issue of "90-day letters," liens and levies.
9. About 95% of the "investigated" cases are individual federal IT and estate tax cases, and the majority of the remaining 5% or so are corporate federal IT cases ("industry cases").
10. *See* 4 in Section 4 for details on IRC §6015.

Figure 2.3 Breakdown by Themes of the Objections at the Office of Appeals

Source: 2002-2022 IRS Data Book Table: Appeals Workload, by Type of Case, etc.

Figure 2.2 reveals that the number of accumulated unprocessed cases at the Office of Appeals has generally been on the decline since 2011, so aggrieved taxpayers can now expect speedier resolution of their objections at the Office of Appeals. The number of days needed for processing the objections also depends on the content of the objections (type, classification, and complexity of the disputed cases). It is reported that from FY2014 to FY2017, the average number of days required by the Office of Appeals to process "large examination cases" was 529 days, 232 days for "other examination cases," 219 days for "innocent spouse" cases, 193 days for CDP cases, and 179 days for "Offer-in-Compromise" cases, 120 days for penalty issues, and 62 days for other cases.[11] Figure 2.3 reveals that the sharp decline since 2011 in the number of objections received and unprocessed at the Office of Appeals is attributable much to the declining trend of the number of objections coming under "examination" cases and CDP cases, which usually take a longer time to be processed. As for the issue of what other major factors could affect the number of days needed for processing objections at the Office of Appeals, it is necessary to look into the Office of Appeals' organization, function, performance, and so forth.[12]

A major organizational feature of the Office of Appeals is that it was established in 1927 as a department of the IRS, and its independence has been strengthened by the 1998 IRS Reform Act that gave a legal basis to its independence.[13] The independence of

11. For details, *see* the abovementioned "GAO-18-659" pp. 35-36.
12. Treasury Inspector General 2007 Report ("The Office of Appeals Needs to Improve the Monitoring of Its Campus Operations Quality," Ref. No: 2007-10-071) and the aforementioned GAO-18-659 point out the feasibility and necessity of more expeditious processing of objections by the Office of Appeals.
13. Once an IRS employee is assigned to the Appeals Division, he is basically not transferred back to the Investigation Division after that.

the Office of Appeals is, *inter alia,* secured by the prohibition of "ex parte communications" between its staff and other IRS staff.[14] This rule basically does not allow Appeals officers to discuss with other IRS officials the facts of the objections and the application of laws and regulations to them without requesting the participation of the appellants/(objectors) or their representatives. Certainly, this rule is not applied as rigorously as in judicial proceedings and they also have exceptions. For example, Revenue Procedure 2000-43 mentions on page 407 that, under IRC §7803 (Commissioner of Internal Revenue), the Commissioner and those officials who have overall supervisory responsibility for the IRS operations may communicate with Appeals about specific cases or issues and may direct that other IRS officials participate in meetings or discussions about such cases or issues without providing the taxpayer or representative with an opportunity to participate.[15] Actually, some argue that the Office of Appeals' independence is not sufficient, with numerous exceptions to this rule.[16]

For example, the National Taxpayer Advocate, the head of the Office of the Taxpayer Advocate Service (TAS) which was established in 1996 by replacing the Office of the Taxpayer Ombudsman that was set up in 1988 by IRC §7811 (Taxpayer Assistance Orders), is one of those that problematized some of those exceptions. The TAS not only supports taxpayers in difficult circumstances who file Form 911 (Request for Taxpayer Advocate Service Assistance) but also proposes measures to protect taxpayer rights by submitting annual reports to Congress (hereinafter referred to as "TAS Report"). In particular, the TAS Reports of 2004 and 2006 identified the issue of independence of the Office of Appeals as one of the most serious problems and pointed out that: (i) there are some cases where compliance with the rule prohibiting "ex parte communications" between its staff and other IRS staff should be viewed as problematic, (ii) there seems to be a tendency at the Office of Appeals to prioritize efficient handling of cases over its independence vis-à-vis the increase in the number of appeal cases,[17] (iii) recent opinions of taxpayers and courts support the idea that the independence of the Office of Appeals remains questionable.[18]

However, in the first place, it should be noted that there are legal restrictions on the independence of the Office of Appeals, which was confirmed by the Tax Court judgment on *Fonticiella v. Commissioner* (TC Memo 2019-74) and so forth. In this judgment, the plaintiff maintained that the Appeals settlement officer is not appointed as an "Officer of the United States" pursuant to §2(2) of Article II of the U.S. Constitution, which is referred to as the "Appointments Clause," so it violates the separation of powers. Then, he argued that he should be granted an opportunity for a hearing by an Appeals officer who is appointed in a way that does not violate the

14. *See* PL 105-206§1001(a).
15. For example, when the issue is a matter unrelated to the essence of the appeal case, or when the dispute is resolved by a certain ADR (FTS, etc., mentioned below), this rule does not apply either.
16. Gerald A Kafka, Rita A. Cavanagh and Sean M. Akins, Do IRS Appeals' Office Ex Parte Prohibitions Need Strengthening?, *Tax Notes*, March 30 (2009) pp. 1591-1601.
17. Refer to pp. 264 to 289 of the 2004 TAS Report.
18. Refer to p. 280 of the 2006 TAS Report.

separation of powers.[19] But the Court, citing Columbia District Circuit Court of Appeals judgment on *Tucker v. Commissioner* ([2012] F 3d 1129), ruled that the 1998 IRS Reform Act explicitly provides for the independent appeals function within the IRS, and although Congress established an independent function within the IRS and prescribed procedures for Appeals, the use of the term "independent" to describe Appeals' function does not automatically make Appeals an independent agency.[20]

It is not only the degree of independence and neutrality that taxpayers are concerned about vis-à-vis the Office of Appeals. For example, delays in the processing of appeals could result in more interest to be paid by the appellant if he had not paid the amount of tax in dispute, so the time needed for their appeals to be processed is a concern to many appellants. Figures 2.2 and 2.3 suggest that it is better now than before, but the number of IRS staff has decreased after the 1998 IRS Reform Act was enacted, and the Office of Appeals was no exception.[21] So, there is a certain limit in the Office of Appeals' speedy handling of objections.[22] Nevertheless, as described in 2 below, in many cases, the Appeals officers' handling of appeals is aimed at a flexible resolution by agreement of the disputing parties rather than a black-or-white resolution of the dispute, and this has resulted in the majority of disputes being resolved without litigation. On the other hand, now that flexible dispute resolution makes it possible in many cases to reduce the tax amount indicated in the "30-day letter," it also has an aspect of increasing the number of objections to the Office of Appeals by those taxpayers in anticipation of the reduction in the disputed tax amount by agreements.

2 Flexible Dispute Resolution

The mission and major functions of the Office of Appeals are expressed in IRM 8.6.4.2 (Fair and Impartial Settlements per Appeals Mission). It states that the Appeals mission is to resolve tax controversies without litigation on a basis that is fair and impartial to both the Government and the taxpayer, and a fair and impartial resolution is one which reflects, on an issue-by-issue basis, the probable result in the event of litigation or one which reflects mutual concessions for the purpose of settlement based on the relative strength of the opposing positions where there is substantial uncertainty of the result in the event of litigation. Likewise, the IRS Policy Statement 8-47 (Consideration to be given to offers of settlement) mentions that Appeals is the only administrative function of the Service with authority to consider settlements of tax controversies, and Appeals will ordinarily give serious consideration to an offer to settle a tax controversy on a

19. For example, Chief of the Taxpayer Advocacy Service who owes an obligation of directly reporting to Congress is, like the Chief Counsel, appointed in accordance with §2(2) of Article II of the U.S. Constitution. Therefore, it can be said that their independence is higher, but the "Taxpayer First Act" enacted in 2019 stipulates that the head of the Office of Appeals will also be appointed in accordance with this provision.
20. *See* PL 105-206 §1001(a)(4).
21. *See* footnote 5.
22. While most of the consultations (about 80% to 90%) by the Appeals officers are implemented over the phone rather than face-to-face with the appellants. For more information, *see* Andrew Strelka and Sean Morrison, IRS and America's Longest Running ADR Program, The *Federal Lawyer* (October/November 2016) pp. 29-30.

basis which fairly reflects the relative merits of the opposing views in the light of the hazards which would exist if the case were litigated. In reality, about 85% to 90% of cases appealed to the Office of Appeals are resolved without ending up in courts.[23]

Parties who have reached an agreement may sign Form 870 (Waiver of Restrictions on Assessment and Collection of Deficiency in Tax and Acceptance of Overassessment), Form 870-AD (Offer to Waive Restrictions on Assessment and Collection of Deficiency in Tax and Acceptance of Overassessment) or "final agreement" as defined in IRC §7121 (Closing Agreements),[24] while the legal effect varies slightly depending on which document is signed. Once the "final agreement" is signed, the agreed case may be reviewed only in cases of fraud, tort, or misrepresentation. In contrast, signing Form 870 does not preclude the possibility of the taxpayer's subsequent filing of a refund claim or being re-corrected by the IRS. The signing of Form 870-AD, which is the most commonly used form in practice, may also result in the taxpayer's subsequent filing of a lawsuit for refund or the re-correction by the IRS, but such possibility is more limited compared to the case where Form 870 is signed.[25] Even if an agreement is reached by the parties to the dispute, the contents of that agreement do not necessarily serve as precedents for other disputes nor set the direction for how those disputes should be resolved.[26]

Treasury Regulations §601.106 (Appeals functions) (f) (Conference and practice requirements) (2) (Rule II) also stipulates that the Office of Appeals may take "hazards of litigation" into consideration in processing appeals. "Hazards of litigation" is a factor that incorporates the possibility of the IRS losing in the event of a case being litigated at court, litigation costs, and so forth.[27] In concrete, in determining how many "hazards of litigation" the case in question has, the Office of Appeals has pointed out that it takes into consideration the following: (i) the relevant facts; (ii) the effect of the testimony expected to be given in court; (iii) the interpretation a court would be expected to give, given the past rulings, on the relevant laws and regulations; (iv) the administrative cost of continuing litigation; and (v) the impact of the outcome of the litigation on the IRS.[28] In cases where parties of the dispute consider that there is substantial uncertainty in the event of litigation as to how the courts would interpret and apply the law or as to what facts the courts would find, a settlement through mutual concession is considered appropriate for the disposition of such cases.[29]

---

23. *See* Thomas Carter Louthan and Steven C. Wrappe, Building a Better Resolution: Adapting IRS Procedures to Fit the Dispute, *Tax Notes International* (1996) p. 361.
24. Treasury Regulations §361.7121-1(a) states, "A closing agreement may be entered into in any case in which there appears to be an advantage in having the case permanently and conclusively closed."
25. Regarding the lack of uniform court views on the legal effect of signing Form 870-AD, *see* https://www.bragertaxlaw.com/what-to-do-when-IRS-says-noadministrative-remedies.htmls.
26. For example, IRM 35.5.5.8 (Agreement to mediate, 12-14-2010) states, "The agreement should provide that a settlement reached by the parties through mediation shall not serve as an estoppel in any other proceeding; and such settlement ... may not be used as precedent."
27. *See* Treasury Regulations §601.106(f)(2) and IRM1.2.1.9.6(Policy Statement 8-47, Consideration to be given to offers of settlement, 04-06-1987).
28. For more information, visit http://www.robinsontaxlawcom/Tax-practice/Tax-Audit-Exams-And-Appeals/Tax-Appeals.
29. *See* IRM 8.6.4.2.1(Mutual-Concession Settlements, 10-26-2007).

In some cases, as IRM 8.6.4.2.2 (Split-Issue Settlements, 06-16-2020) mentions, it is possible to have the settlement for a percentage or a stipulated amount of the tax even in the controversy that, if litigated, would result in a decision completely for the Government or the taxpayer. Also, IRM 8.6.4.2.3 (Specific Dollar Settlements, 06-16-2020) mentions that it is possible to have the settlement of a case for a percentage or stipulated amount of the tax in the controversy that approximates the amount that would have been reached by computing the tax.[30] The Office of Appeals could neither exact a concession nor grant a concession solely to relieve either party of such inconvenience or cost, as IRM 8.6.4.2.4 (Nuisance value settlements, 10-26-2007) specifies. Policy Statement 8–47 also states that no settlement will be made if it is based on nuisance value to either party, and nuisance value is any concession made solely to eliminate the inconvenience or cost of further negotiations or litigation and is unrelated to the merits of the issues.[31] In addition, it is not permitted to use the penalty as a "bargaining chip" to amend other matters (correction amount, etc.) or reach an agreement.[32]

It is true that, in the past, penalties were sometimes utilized as "bargaining chips" for reaching agreements with taxpayers, so the 1998 IRS Reform Act introduced IRC §6751 (Procedural requirements) (b) (Approval of assessment) which requires the written approval of the investigator's supervisor for the imposition of penalties,[33] except those that are automatically imposed.[34] However, even after IRC §6751 was implemented, it was not fully complied with. For example, in *Chai v. Commissioner of Internal Revenue* ([2017] No. 15-1653), the Second Circuit Court of Appeals revoked the accuracy-related penalty because the Commissioner of the IRS failed to fulfill its burden of proving sufficient compliance with IRC §6751 in this case. In *Clay v. Commissioner* ([2019] 152 TC No. 13), the Tax Court vacated the imposition of penalties for negligence and substantial understatement for the tax year 2006 by ruling that IRC §6751 requires the auditor to obtain the supervisor's written approval for the

30. IRM 8.6.4.1.2(1)(10-26-2007), before it was revised, stated as follows, "Policy Statement 8-48 states Appeals may enter into settlements based on a percentage or stipulated amount of the tax in controversy, but such settlement, identified as split-issue settlement, is only used when no other method of settlement is appropriate." IRM 8.6.4.2.3 specifies that specific dollar settlements are appropriate when the case is a small tax case, a nonrecurring issue, a single taxpayer issue, etc. While "splitting the difference" is not employed by the UK's tax authority. *See* footnote 52 in Chapter 3.
31. The term "nuisance value settlement" refers to an amount in the range of 10% to 15% or less of the amount in dispute, according to Steven C. Salch, Administrative Procedures: Representation Before IRS Appeals Office (May 2007) p. 15 at http://www.lexisnexis.com/documents/pdf/20080507043030large.rft.
32. IRM 8.6.4.2(5) dictates as follows: "Penalty issues are not traded in Appeals. Penalties are settled, but the settlement is based on the merits and hazards surrounding each penalty issue standing alone."
33. The 1998 Senate Report (S. Rep. 105-174, p. 65) also cited the primary reason for introducing IRC §6751 to prevent penalties being used as "bargaining chips."
34. IRC §6751(1)(b) states, "No penalty under this title shall be assessed unless the initial determination of such assessment is personally approved (in writing) by the immediate supervisor of the individual making such determination or such higher level official as the Secretary designated."

imposition of penalties before the issue of the "30-day letter" (accompanying the Revenue Agent Report), but in this case, this requirement was not met in time.

Despite some restrictions on flexible settlements of tax disputes as mentioned above at the Office of Appeals, IRM 8.6.4.1(3) states that the majority of objections filed with the Office of Appeals are resolved in a manner that can be agreed upon by the taxpayers and the IRS, so it could be assumed that there are many cases in which the objections succeeded in reducing the amount of tax payable.[35] However, it is to be noted that the Office of Appeals might do the following: (i) inform the collections staff of those points that are deemed necessary for investigation or confirmation and have them look into them, and (ii) correct calculation errors that affect the tax amount. Moreover, the Office of Appeals, in handling objections, does not, in principle, bring up "new issues" that have not been taken up in the "30-day letter" or working papers, but there are some exceptions.[36] As for the auditor, he might bring up "new issues" (especially in a refund case),[37] and the amount shown in the "30-day letter" and penalty could be increased.[38] In worst cases, the appellant could be charged with penalties under IRC §7206 (Fraud and false statements) (1) (Declaration under penalties of perjury).

3 Recent New Developments at Office of Appeals

(1) Utilization of ADR and Challenges

In recent years, the flexible dispute resolution methods used by the Office of Appeals include not only mutual concessions by the disputing parties through negotiation but also what is called ADR (Alternative/Administrative Dispute Resolution). The background to the use of ADR is the enactment of the "Administrative Dispute Resolution Act of 1990" (ADR Act, P.L. 320), which pushed the IRS to expand programs that led to the expansion of ADR use. The ADR utilized by the Office of Appeals includes not

35. Although the data is not published by the IRS, it is presumed that the portion where the tax amount (original disposal amount) is maintained ("sustention rate") is about 25% to 50% on average. *See*, John Klotsche, Jousting with the Tax Man: ADR at IRS, Part II, *Tax Notes*, July 27 (2009) p. 362.
36. The exception is where there is a substantial change in the amount of tax that, if litigated, is certain to be sustained by courts.
37. At court, the acceptability of bringing up "new issues" not indicated in the "90-day letter" or the written answer depends on whether or not the plaintiff suffers a disadvantage in preparing for litigation. For details, *see* IRM 35.2.2.1.4 (Filing amended answers) and *Pagel, Inc. v. Commissioner* (91 TC. 200(1988)). As the Tax Court judgment in *Wegbreit v. Commissioner* (T.C. Memo. 2019-82) which granted a 70% rate penalty for alleged fraud under IRC §6663 rather than the 20% rate civil penalty under IRC §6662 shown in the 90-day letter shows, courts usually accept IRS's claim to bring in a "new matter." This is in contrast with Japan's Tax Tribunal's treatment under Article 98(3) of AGRNT (see footnote 7 in Chapter 1).
38. In practice, taxpayer representatives often do not participate in meetings offered by the Appeals Board because of the possibility that "new matters" may be raised, *see* Tax Adviser, May 1 (2008) (also at https://www.thetaxadviser.com/issues/2008/may/thequalifiedffoerthe taxpayers90dayletter.html). In the case of a refund claim, the Supreme Court judgment on *Lewis v. Reynolds* ([1932] 284 U.S. 281) confirms that the increase in tax due to the discovery of new matters will not exceed the amount of refund sought.

only "post-appeals ADR" (mediation, arbitration, etc.) but also "pre-appeals ADR" such as FTS (Fast Track Settlement), FTM (Fast Track Mediation), and Early Referral. As for "post-appeals ADR," trained Appeals officers serve as mediators (in some cases, with the consent of the Office of Appeals, qualified specialists chosen by the appellants could be co-mediators) or arbitrators, and it basically covers both legal interpretations and factual disputes where no agreement has been reached by the disputing parties despite negotiations by the Office of Appeals.[39] The potential scope of their application is also wide, but they had some problems that include, in particular, the low rate of utilization by the Office of Appeals.[40]

As for "pre-appeals ADR," it started to be offered in the wake of the 1998 IRS Reform Act implementing IRC §7123 (Appeals dispute resolution procedures).[41] Early Referral is based on the belief that early resolution of a key issue may encourage taxpayers and the IRS to agree on other issues in the case. Although Early Referral generally covers most of the examination and collection issues, the IRS mentions that it is particularly useful in the following cases: (i) facts and points related to the issue on which a referral is made are sufficiently clear and fully developed, and (ii) the issue to be made a referral on is part of a case where the remaining issues are not expected to be completed before the referral case is resolved.[42] As for FTM, it is basically limited to investigation and collection issues on "Small Business/Self-Employed (SB/SE),"[43] but it covers a wide range of issues that are not docketed in any court, and the time required for its processing is targeted to be about thirty to forty days which is quicker than two months usually needed in the case of post-appeals mediation. A major FTM's limit may lie in the fact that an FTM mediator's settlement proposal must strictly be based on the legal merits of the case and might not take into consideration the costs of litigation or the likelihood of success.[44]

Admittedly, the introduction of Early Referrals and FTM has alleviated some of the problems associated with mediation and arbitration or "post-appeals ADR," but it is FTS, which has been available since 2006, that has facilitated most of the use of ADR by the Office of Appeals. FTS applies to both legal interpretation and factual disputes faced by SB/SE and Large Businesses, etc.[45] As exposed in Figure 2.4, FTS is the most

39. A major case in which disputes have been resolved through mediation is the 1996 case (*EI Dupont de Nemours* case), in which income shifting (a case concerning the application of IRC §482) was at issue. For details, *see* Dupont Mediates Case Through IRS Program, *Alternatives to High Cost Litigation*, Vol. 14, Issue 4 (1996) at https://onlinelibrary.wiley.com/action/doSearch?AllField=Vol.14%2C+Issue+4+1996&SeriesKey=15494381.
40. It is pointed out that there are some taxpayers apprehending that disclosure of information at the ADR stage might work against them at litigation in spite of the fact that Revenue Procedures 2002-44 (Bulletin No. 2002-26)§5 (Mediation Process)10 prohibits its use at litigation. David Parsly, The Internal Revenue Service and Alternative Dispute Resolution: Moving from Infancy to Legitimacy, *Cardozo Journal of Conflict See Resolution*, Vol. 8:677 (2007) pp. 700-701.
41. Publication 4167 (Rev. 7-2012) shows the details of "pre-appeals ADR" utilized by IRS.
42. For more information, *see* IRS Publication 4167 (Rev. 7-2021) and Revenue Procedures 99-28.
43. For more information on cases covered by the FTM, *see* Revenue Procedures 2003-41 (Bulletin No. 2003-25).
44. *See* Section 2.02 in Revenue Procedure 2003-41 and Parsly, *supra* "The Internal Revenue Service and Alternative Dispute Resolution" p. 696.
45. "Large Businesses" includes Large Businesses and International (LB&I) as well as Tax Exempt and Government Entities (TE/GE).

widely used among various ADR methods.[46] In FTS, the trained Appeals officer usually acts as an intermediary, explaining to the taxpayer and the tax examiner team the "hazards of litigation" that both parties have and then adjusting the correction amount to realize an agreement.[47] The IRS points out the following as the major advantages of FTS: (i) application can be made with a simple form (Form 14017: Application for Fast Track Settlement), (ii) dispute resolution is usually realized within 120 days (90 days for sole proprietors, etc.), (iii) "Hazards of litigation" is taken into account in carrying out FTS, (iv) FTS application can be withdrawn in the middle, (v) no need to give up normal appeal procedures, (vi)no application of the high-interest rate ("hot interest") specified by IRC §6621(c).[48] Owing to FTS, which has such merits as mentioned above, the usage rate of ADR showed some increase from 2006 to 2014.[49]

Figure 2.4 Recent Status of ADR Use

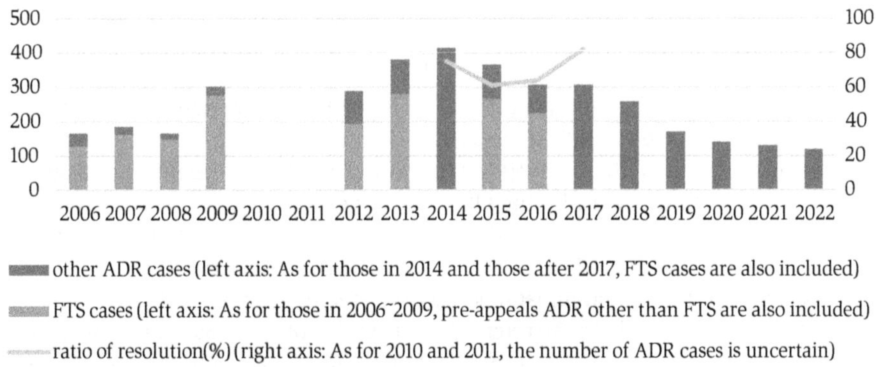

Source: 2016 TAS Report 216 pp., Tax Notes March 9 (2009) p. 1244/July 27 (2009) p. 358, GAO-23-105552, Fast Track and IRS Appeals Developments at https://www.crowell.com/files/20160930-Fast-Track-Settlements-Fisher-jiang-pdf.

Nevertheless, it has long been pointed out that the start and progress of the use of ADR in the IRS has been slow compared to those in many other administrative agencies and courts.[50] The Tax Court judge Parr also said in 2009 that the IRS's

46. For details on cases where FTS cannot be used, *see* Revenue Procedures 2017-25.
47. *See* Revenue Procedures 2003-40, Publication 4539 (Rev. 5-2012), IRM 4514 and IRM 8.26.2 for further details.
48. IRC §6621(Determination of rate of interest)(a)(General rule)(2)(Underpayment rate) states that interest on underpayments is the federal short-term interest rate plus 3%, but, for underpayments of more than USD 100,000, IRC §6621(c)(Increase in underpayment rate for large corporate underpayments) substitutes 5% for this 3% as a "hot interest."
49. *See* Amy Elliott, ADR Options for *IRS* Debated at Tax Analysts Conference, *Tax Notes*, June 29 (2009) p. 1511. Moreover, recently the rate of disputes being resolved is generally higher for FTS cases than for other ADR cases. *See* p. 216 of the 2016 TAS Report.
50. The 2004 TAS Report points out in p. 291 that many other U.S. administrative agencies have confirmed the usefulness (high dispute resolution rate, large cost reduction, etc.) of ADR.

"post-appeals ADR" was broken.[51] "Pre-appeals ADR" could be a means to overcome such a situation, but in practice, despite the provisions of IRC §7123(a), there are not a few limits to "pre-appeals ADR" that disqualify some taxpayers in various circumstances from using some types of ADR.[52] Also, some point out that in the field of tax disputes, measures should be taken so that the main precondition for the success of ADR in the non-administrative field could be met, and such main precondition is the existence of a neutral forum where neither party to the dispute feels that he is disadvantaged. There is also a view that no significant improvement can be expected unless measures are taken to increase the independence of the Office of Appeals or establish an ADR center that is detached from the Office of Appeals.[53] Likewise, the TAS Reports often pointed out that the IRS is not very active in the use of ADR and recommended that disputes be resolved more quickly through more active use of ADR.[54]

(2) "Taxpayer First Act" and Expanded Support Measures for Low-Income Disputants

Just as ADR is not available to all tax disputes, the Office of Appeals is not open to all disputes. This is because the IRS Reform Act certainly guaranteed tax delinquents the right to be heard by the Office of Appeals, but it did not fully guarantee all aggrieved taxpayers the right to be heard by the Office of Appeals. In fact, Revenue Procedures 2016-22 states in section 3(3) that the IRS's Office of Chief Counsel will not refer to the Office of Appeals any docketed case or issue that has been designated for litigation by the Counsel and, in limited circumstances, a docketed case or issue that has not been designated for litigation will not be referred to the Office of Appeals if Division Counsel or a higher level Counsel official determines that referral is not in the interest of sound tax administration. In this connection, it is to be noted that IRM 33.3.6 (Designating a case for litigation) explains that the reasons and merits of designating a case for litigation lie in the early setting of judicial precedents for tax shelters and other cases involving many taxpayers to reduce resources and litigation costs of taxpayers and the IRS.

It has been pointed out that the number of cases designated for litigation has been increasing recently.[55] However, it is not entirely clear what kinds of cases are designated as litigation cases or excluded from review by the Office of Appeals for the reason that they are not in line with the interest of sound tax administration. In fact, the

51. Carolyn Miller Parr, Why Postappeal Mediation Isn't Working and How to Fix It, *TAX.COM* (September 16, 2009) at http://www.tax.com/taxcom/features.nsf/Articles/11704085C68E8F 7885 2576330002C150.
52. Refer to IRS Publication 4167 (Rev. 7-2012) and IRM 4.51.4.4, etc. for details of reasons for the unavailability of ADR in some cases.
53. *See* Stephen Folan, Even ADR Must Pay Its Dues: An Analysis of the Evolution of the Internal Revenue Service's ADR Programs and Where They Still Need to Grow, *Pepperdine Dispute Resolution Law Journal*, Article 3 (2013) pp. 12-17.
54. *See*, for example, p. 144 of the 2016 TAS Report, and pp. 308-310 of the 2004 TAS Report.
55. Such increasing trend is conspicuous among TP cases. *See* Marie Sapirie, The Increase in Cases Designated for Litigation, *Tax Notes*, March 14 (2016) p. 1223.

IRS made it a rule not to disclose to the taxpayers the reasons why their cases are excluded from review by the Office of Appeals while the Counsel notifies the taxpayers of such treatment. It is just that section 3.3 of Revenue Procedures 2016-22 gives some ideas by mentioning that Counsel may decide not to refer a docketed case to Appeals in cases involving a significant issue common to other cases in litigation for which it is important that the IRS maintains a consistent position or in cases related to a case over which the Department of Justice has jurisdiction. It seems that typical examples of such cases include a case of tax avoidance using standardized tax shelter products.[56] It is also explained in the above section 3(3) of the Revenue Procedures 2016-22 that in such cases, even if the case is once pending before Tax Court, it does not exercise the Counsel's authority to transfer the case to the Office of Appeals.

The treatment under the above section 3(3) of the Revenue Procedures 2016-22 was, just like the level of independence and neutrality of the Office of Appeals, deemed as the main challenges and problems confronting taxpayers' appeals. But the Taxpayer First Act of 2019, enacted in 2019, improved the independence of the Office of Appeals and strengthened taxpayer rights. In particular, under the newly introduced IRC §7803 (Commissioner of Internal Revenue; other officials) (e) (Independent Office of Appeals), the Office of Appeals is renamed to Independent Office of Appeals. Also, IRC §7803(e)(5) (Limitation on designation cases as not eligible for referral to Independent Office of Appeals) (A) (In General) stipulates that, in the event of a refusal to be heard by the independent Office of Appeals, the Commissioner of the IRS shall provide the taxpayer with a written statement outlining the facts involved, the basis and detailed reasons for the refusal as well as the explanations of the procedures for disputing the refusal. In addition, IRC §7803(e)(5) (B) (Report to Congress) dictates the IRS's obligation to report to Congress in writing the annual number of refusals of taxpayers' requests for review by the Independent Office of Appeals and the reasons therefor.

Whereas, as for those taxpayers who have been issued a "30-day letter" but did not file an appeal with the Office of Appeals within the deadline even though they are eligible for it, they are likely to be issued with a "90-day letter" (CP 3219A or Letter 3219, etc.) in accordance with IRC §6212 (Notice of deficiency) (a) (In general), just as the taxpayers whose disputed cases were not resolved at the Office of Appeals.[57] These days, as Figure 2.5 reveals, the IRS issues about 2.6 million to 3.8 million "90-day letters" annually.[58] A "90-day letter" contains: (i) the amount of tax underpayment and penalties, (ii) the calculation methods for them, (iii) the address and telephone number of the Taxpayer Advocate Service officer, and (iv) the time limit for filing an appeal to the Tax Court, and so forth. If a taxpayer served with a "90-day letter" does not intend to contest it in court, he shall pay the amounts due within ninety days from the date of its issuance, or an arrangement is to be made with the IRS on its payment methods. Otherwise, the IRS would be able to initiate collection procedures for the amounts due.

56. In fact, cases falling under the so-called Son-of-Boss scheme used by many taxpayers were designated as litigation cases.
57. IRC §6212(a) stipulates, "If the Secretary determines that there is a deficiency in respect of any tax imposed by subtitles A or B or chapter 41, 42, 43, or 44 he is authorized to send notice of such deficiency to the taxpayer by certified mail or registered mail."
58. For details, *see* Figure 2.5 and p. 202 of the 2019 TAS Report.

If he has problems with that and prefers to contest the legality of the "90-day letter" issued to him, the next stage for the contestation is the courts.

SECTION 2 TAX LITIGATION IN COURT

1 Implications of Selecting Tax Court as a Litigation Forum

As presented in Figure 2.1, if a taxpayer who received the "90-day letter" wants to challenge its legality, he usually has an option of making an appeal to the Tax Court, the Federal District Courts, or the Court of Federal Claims.[59] This point is basically the same when tax delinquents challenge the legality of a "Notice of Determination" issued by the Office of Appeals after going through a hearing under CDP. Depending on the type of tax or matter that is the subject of the dispute at court, a taxpayer may not have a choice as to courts.[60] If a point of dispute is mainly on the issue of interpretation of a tax provision, a taxpayer may choose the Tax Court, while a Federal District Court with a jury may be his preference if he intends to dispute the re/assessment from the point of fairness and equality. Whereas, the Federal Court of Claims might be a taxpayer's choice if he attaches importance to the difference in judicial precedents of those courts in various jurisdictions on cases similar to his. But the reality is that many taxpayers choose to make appeals to the Tax Court, mainly because (i) they do not need to pay the full amount of disputed tax and penalties;[61] (ii), as it is pointed out, a "90-day letter" specifically mentions (*see* the last paragraph in Section 1) that it is possible to appeal to the Tax Court to dispute the lawfulness of the re/assessments on them.[62]

In addition, in the case of the Tax Court, nineteen judges appointed by the President preside over cases, but IRC §7463 (Disputes involving USD 50,000 or less) (a) (In general) dictates that in the case of the disputed yearly amount of tax (including the amount of penalties, etc.) being USD 50,000 or less, the appellant can in principle choose its case to be handled in "a small case division" where a special trial judge appointed by the chief judge of the Tax Court can speed up its trial process by following a simplified procedure and issuing a summary opinion.[63] Moreover, IRC §7463 (b) (Finality of decisions) states that the decisions of the special trial judges are distinct

59. There are small number of tax cases appealed to the Bankruptcy Court.
60. For details, *see* Choice of Forum in Federal Civil Tax Litigation (Part I), *The Practical Tax Lawyer* (Winter 2011) pp. 55-64 (also at https:/iwww.papers.ssrn.com/sol3/papers.cfm?abstract_id=1633111).
61. This is why the Tax Court is referred to as "prepayment jurisdiction," and the Federal District Court and Federal Court of Claims are referred to as "refund jurisdiction." In the former, the federal government is represented by a qualified IRS lawyer, and in the latter by a qualified lawyer from the Ministry of Justice. However, in some cases, a lawsuit for refund may be filed with the Tax Court.
62. Peter J. Panuthos, Procedural Issues of Human Rights and Taxation, Access to Justice, *Bulletin for International Taxation* (July 2017) p. 392.
63. Even in small claim cases, if they are important issues, issues common to other cases, or matters establishing legal principles important to other cases, they may, in response to the allegation of the disputants or by the judgment of the Tax Court, be classified as an ordinary case outside the

from those judgments (TC opinions and Memo opinions) of the Tax Court in that, as IRC §7463(b) states, a decision entered in any case in which the proceedings are conducted under this section shall not be reviewed in any other court and shall not be treated as a precedent for any other case. This could be a significant advantage, especially for taxpayers who attach great importance to a speedy resolution of their disputes and a reduction in litigation-related expenses. It has also been confirmed in *Koprowski v. Commissioner* (138 TC 54 (2012)) that the judgment of the special trial judge has res judicata from January 2001.

As mentioned above, for those aggrieved taxpayers with relatively low income, the non-requirement of advance payment of the disputed tax amount and the existence of a small case division in the Tax Court could particularly be important points in choosing a court to file an appeal to. The reason why the Tax Court differs from other courts in terms of whether or not full payment of the tax amount in dispute is a precondition for filing an appeal could be found in the Supreme Court judgment on *Flora v. United States* (362. U.S. 145 (1960)). In this judgment, at issue was whether the Federal District Court could accept a petition for a refund of the partially paid additional tax amount by a taxpayer who had received a correction order to collect the additional tax amount. As a relevant provision on this matter, IRC §1346 (United States as defendant) (a) states, "The District Courts shall have original jurisdiction, concurrent with the United States Court of Federal Claims, of (1) any civil action against the United States for the recovery of any internal revenue tax alleged to have been erroneously or illegally assessed or collected, or any penalty claimed to have been collected without authority or any sum alleged to have been excessive or in any manner wrongfully collected under internal revenue laws."

In the above Supreme Court judgment, an important point pivots on whether "any internal revenue tax" or any penalty for which the recovery is sought under IRC §1346(a)(1) above is, just as the plaintiff/taxpayer claims, to be construed to include the payment of a portion of the disputed tax or penalty.[64] The Supreme Court stated that "any internal revenue tax" is to be construed to refer to payment of the entire amount of an assessment, and it is in line with the Third Circuit Court of Appeals judgment on *Suhr v. United States* (18 F.2d 81 (1927)) in which the court stated that the payment of a part does not confer jurisdiction upon the courts and there is no provision for the refund to the taxpayer of any excess payment of any installment or part of his tax if the whole tax for the year has not been paid. Then, the Supreme Court dismissed

---

scope of the special trial judge. *See* Harold Dubroff and Brian J. Hellwig, *The United States Tax Court—An Historical Analysis*, pp. 891-893 (https://www.U.S.taxcourt.gov/resources/book/Dubroff_Hellwig.pdf).

64. On this point, the government has positioned the Tax Court as a court for rulings on the amount of tax underpayment, and the District Courts and Federal Court of Claims as courts for rulings on refunds. It argues, among other things, that obscuring such a distinction would distort the interpretation of IRC 1346(a).

the petitioner/taxpayer's claim by concluding that the Government has a substantial interest in protecting the public purse, an interest which would be substantially impaired if a taxpayer could sue in a District Court without paying his tax in full, so that IRC §1346(a)(1), correctly construed, requires full payment of the assessment before an income tax refund suit can be filed in a Federal District Court.

Whereas, filing a lawsuit with the Tax Court is not without its risks because IRC §6214 (Determinations by Tax Court) (a) (Jurisdiction as to increase of deficiency, additional amounts, or additions to the tax) provides that the Tax Court (and other federal courts) shall have jurisdiction to re-determine the correct amount of the deficiency even if the amount so re-determined is greater than the amount of the deficiency, notice of which has been mailed to the taxpayer. Also, IRC §6512 (Limitations in case of petition to Tax Court) (b) (Overpayment determined by Tax Court) dictates that such re-determination by the Tax Court is possible in the case of a refund suit.[65] While IRC §7463 (Disputes involving USD 50,000 or less) (c) (Limitation of jurisdiction) stipulates that no decision shall be entered re-determining the amount of a deficiency or determining an overpayment, except with respect to amounts placed in dispute within limits described in subsection (a) and with respect to amounts conceded by the parties, so that the amount to be re-determined by a special trial judge with respect to the amount of the deficiency placed in the dispute or the amount of any claimed overpayment in a small case division could not exceed the larger of USD 50,000 or the amounts conceded by the parties.

2 "Rule of Not Looking Behind a Notice of Deficiency" and Nature of "90-Day Letter"

Moreover, The Tax Court has adopted the "rule of not looking behind a notice of deficiency" so that taxpayers generally cannot expect the disputed re/assessment to be voided by the unlawful audit procedure. For example, in *Greenberg's Express, Inc. v. Commissioner* judgment ([1974] 62 TC 324), the plaintiff argued that the "90-day letter" issued without following the defendant's established investigative procedures was invalid. However, the Tax Court stated, "As a general rule, this Court will not look behind a deficiency notice to examine the evidence used or the propriety of respondent's motives or of the administrative policy or procedure involved in making his determinations and the underlying rationale for this rule lies in the fact that a trial before Tax Court is a proceeding de novo." The Court did admit that on occasion, it recognized an exception to this rule when there is substantial evidence of unconstitutional conduct on the respondent's part and the integrity of the judicial process would

65. For an actual example of it, *see* The Tax Court judgment on *Wegbreit* case (2019) listed in footnote 37.

be impugned if it were to let the respondent benefit from such conduct, but in such limited situations it has refused to declare the deficiency notice null and void. Then, the Court added that the broad sweep of the power to enforce revenue laws has repeatedly been recognized and dismissed the plaintiff's claim.[66]

As intimated by the above Greenberg's Express judgment, the "rule of not looking behind a notice of deficiency" is deeply related to the nature of the "90-day letter." In the first place, even if the amount of tax indicated in the "90-day letter" is incorrect, unless it is proved that the IRS Commissioner was dogmatic, capricious, or unreasonable in determining the amount, it is not invalid because of the presumption of correctness at work.[67] Actually, in *Olsen v. Helvering* ([1937] 88 F 2d 650), the Second Circuit Court of Appeals confirmed that a notice of deficiency is only to advise the person who is to pay the deficiency that the Commissioner means to assess him and anything that does this unequivocally is good enough.[68] Also, in *CIR v. Stewart* ([1951] 186 F 2d 239), the Sixth Circuit Court of Appeals stated that a notice of deficiency is not invalid without any explanation or details regarding the amount of the tax underpayment. Furthermore, in the *City Line Candy & Tobacco Corp v. Commissioner* ([2013] 141 TC No. 13), the Tax Court held that it appears that the respondent made mistakes in adjusting petitioner's inventory in the notice of deficiency, and he appears to have conceded as much, but it is not sufficient to support a finding that his determinations were arbitrary, capricious or unreasonable.

The abovementioned nature of the "90-day letter" has not changed even after the introduction in 2015 of IRC §7803(a)(3) (Execution of duties in accord with taxpayer rights), which embodies the purport of the Taxpayer Bill of Rights (TABOR) by specifying the ten rights of taxpayers.[69] This could be confirmed by *Maria Ivon Moya v. Commissioner* ([2019] 152 TC No. 11). In this case, the plaintiff contacted and requested the IRS to conduct an examination and interviews regarding IT returns for the years 2011 to 2013 in the area where she moved to after the examination began, but

66. The Tax Court's rules of practice and procedure 142(Burden of proof) also dictates: "The burden of proof shall be upon the petitioner, except as otherwise provided by statute or determined by the Court; and except that, in respect of any new matter, increases in deficiency, and affirmative defenses, pleaded in the answer, it shall be upon the respondent."

67. In *Welch v. Helvering* ([1933] 290 U.S. 111), the Supreme Court confirmed that IRS decisions set out in the "90-day letter" has the support of a presumption of correctness and the taxpayers have the burden of proving them to be wrong. Also, *see* Sheila A. Murphy, *Reports of the United States Tax Court*, Vol. 41, U.S. Government Printing Office (2013) p. 420.

68. This nature of a "90-day letter" contrasts with that of a notice of re/assessment in Japan that requires a higher level of correctness. *See* footnote 110 and 2(4) in Section 3 of Chapter 1.

69. *See* 4 in Section 2 and footnote 98 for the Taxpayer Bill of Rights. IRC §7803(a)(3) provides: (a) the right to be informed, (b) the right to quality service, (c) the right to pay no more than the correct amount of tax, (d) the right to challenge the position of IRS and be heard, (e) the right to appeal a decision of IRS in an independent forum, (f) the right to finality, (g) the right to privacy, (h) the right to confidentiality, (i) the right to retain representation, and (j) the right to a fair and just tax system.

received almost no response before she was served with the "90-day letter." The plaintiff did not allege error regarding the "90-day letter" but claimed that the IRS violated "the right to be informed" and "the right to challenge the position of IRS and be heard" under IRC §7803.[70] The Court accepted the plaintiff's claim of the IRS's violation of TABOR but did not dismiss the respondent's claim that TBOR does not embody constitutional rights and therefore a violation of the TBOR does not provide an exception to the principle expressed in the *Greenberg's Express* case (1974). In its judgment, the Court upheld the "90-day letter" by ruling that the plaintiff did not fulfill its burden of proving that the IRS's determinations of deficiencies shown in it were in error.

However, it has also been confirmed that a "90-day letter" is invalid if it does not meet the minimum requirements. For example, In *Commissioner v. Chelsea Products, Inc.* ([1952] 197 F.2d 620), the Third Circuit Court of Appeals held that it was fraudulent to rely on justifying the reassessment on IRC §45 and IRC §129, which are not mentioned in the "90-day letter."[71] Also, in the Ninth Circuit Court of Appeals judgment on *Weimerskirch v. Commissioner* ([1979] 596 F 2d 358), the Court pointed out that in order to give effect to the presumption on which the Commissioner relies, some evidence must appear which would support an inference of the taxpayer's involvement in activities that give rise to income while the IRS Commissioner offered no evidence linking the appellant to the sale of narcotics nor any records to substantiate the computation made by the IRS, so the Commissioner merely chose to rely upon the naked assertion that the appellant made such income. Then, the Court concluded that, now that a deficiency determination which is not supported by the proper foundation of substantive evidence is clearly arbitrary and erroneous, the Tax Court judgment ([1977] 67 TC 672) on this case erred in finding that the presumption of correctness is attached to the deficiency determination.[72]

Certainly, in *Scar v. Commissioner* ([1983] 81, TC 855, 860-61), the Tax Court ruled in favor of the IRS Commissioner by stating that going behind the statutory notice is a policy consideration on which its jurisdiction is not dependent, and the requirements of section 6212(a) are met now that the notice of deficiency sets forth the amount of the deficiency and the amount of the year concerned. But this ruling was reversed by the Ninth Circuit Court of Appeals judgment ([1987] 814 F.2d 1363) in which the Court found that the concerned notice of deficiency referred to a tax shelter that had no connection with the taxpayers or their return. Thenceforth, the Court concluded that the above deficiencies in the concerned notice of deficiency indicate that it did not meet the substantial requirements of IRC §6212(a), and the failure to comply with the

70. Also, IRS's Publication 1 (Your rights as a taxpayer) states, "Taxpayers have the right to raise objections ... to expect that IRS will consider their timely objections and documentation promptly and fairly, and to receive a response if IRS does not agree with their positions."
71. But the Circuit Court did not specifically mention that the "90-day letter" was invalid because the appellant could not sustain it even by relying on those provisions.
72. Other examples with similar views include the Third Circuit judgment on *Gerado v. CIR* ([1977] 552 F.2d 549, 552) and the Fifth Circuit judgment on *Carson v. United States* ([1977] 560 F.2d 693, 696-698).

statutory requirements renders the concerned "90-day letter null and void.[73] Judge Hall dissented by stating that the majority ignores the rule that a deficiency notice needs not contain any explanation whatsoever, and he warned that requiring the Commissioner to prove the basis of his determination before the Tax Court can assert jurisdiction would not only unduly burden him and the Tax Court but also go against the notice of deficiency's purpose of early notice to the taxpayer.[74]

3 Characteristics of Dispute Resolution by Tax Court

As mentioned above, there are a few rules of the Tax Court that might work unfavorably for the appellants, but the majority of tax suits are filed with the Tax Court rather than other courts.[75] In fact, as shown in Figure 2.5, the number of cases brought to the Tax Court has increased steadily since around 2000(two years after the enactment of the 1998 IRS Reform Act,[76] but then it started to show a declining trend until it went up to about 30,000 in 2021.[77] As is clear from Figure 2.3 and Figure 2.5, there is basically a synchronization among the number of appeals filed with the Office of Appeals, the number of 90-day letters issued, the number of seizures (levies), and the number of appeals filed with the Tax Court.[78] The breakdown of the number of disputes at the Tax Court reveals that the majority of them are on "deficiency cases" (or "examination cases") in which a point of contention concerns the lawfulness/correctness of the amount of tax payable indicated in the "90-day letter." As for the number of disputes on CDP cases, they represent a substantial ratio (30% to 35% of all the disputed cases) at the Office of Appeals, but they represent only about 3% to 6% of the total at the Tax Court.

---

73. For IRC §6212(a), *see* footnote 57.
74. Judge Hall also mentioned that the majority eagerly expands jurisdictional requirements while discarding the carefully honed and expedient jurisdictional rules that exist and the precedent holding that the validity of the deficiency notice is to be determined on its face was effective in furthering policy goals which benefit the taxpayer and the public.
75. For FY2007, for example, 29,040, 219 and 96 tax cases were filed with the Tax Court, the District Court and the Federal Claims Court, respectively. For details, *see supra* "Choice of Forum" p. 60. Recently, Tax Court has not disclosed the number of cases it received on its website.
76. Between 1971 and 1974, 8,300 to 9,600 cases were pending before tax courts, 10% to 20% of which were "small tax cases." *See* Christopher J. Badum, The Small Tax Case Procedure: How it Works—Does It Work?, *Fordham Urban Law Journal*, Vol. 44, No. 2 (1976) p. 395.
77. Figure 2.5 suggests that about 2.7 million 90-day letters were issued in FY2017, and that less than one-tenth of the taxpayers who received them filed suits with Tax Court. TAS rates this figure as low. *See* 2019 TAS Report, p. 199.
78. As shown in Figure 3.10 of 2021 TAS Report, the number of both seizures and liens has lately been on the decline. IRS issues a notice of Federal tax lien pursuant to IRC §6323 (Validity and priority against certain persons), and it is customary for delinquent taxpayers to file an appeal after being notified of its issue. IRC §6323 states that the lien imposed by section 6321 shall not be valid as against any purchaser, until notice thereof which meets the requirements of subsection (f) has been filed by the Secretary.

Figure 2.5 Number of "90-Day Letters" Issued and Number/Breakdown of Lawsuits Filed with Tax Court

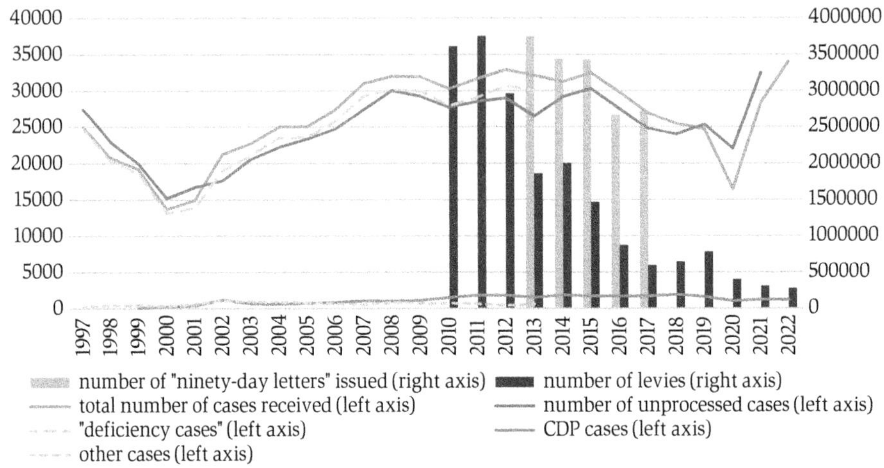

Source: 2018 TAS report Figure 1.13.1, 2020 TAS Report Figure 2.0.5, 2021 TAS Report Figure 3.6 and Figure 3.10, 2022 TAS Report Figure 3.5/3.17, Dubroff and Hellwig, *United States Tax Court—An Historical Analysis* p. 909.

As is clear from the comparison of Figures 2.3 and 2.5, the number of taxpayers disputing their cases at courts is small compared with that at the administrative appeal stage. However, it seems that the size of the disputed amount is not necessarily a decisive factor for a taxpayer to determine whether or not he files a lawsuit as it is intimated by the following fact shown in the 2018 TAS Report: (i) more than 2.7 million "90-day letters" were issued in FY2017 and more than 70% of those who received them had an annual income of less than USD 100,000, (ii) less than one-tenth of those who received 2.7 million "90-day letters" issued in FY2017 filed suits with the Tax Court, and their breakdown shows that 20.5% of the litigants at the Tax Court are those with an annual income of less than USD 25,000, and the ratio was 16.3% (25.1%) for those with annual income range of above USD 25,000 below USD 50,000 (above USD 50,000 below USD 100,000).[79] The Report suggests that at the Tax Court, there are more cases in which the disputed tax amount is not so large, and a plaintiff is a pro se litigant mainly due to his financial situation. In fact, from 2006 to 2013, 48% to 52% of the appeals to the Tax Court were small claim cases, and in 2012, the total ratio of pro se litigants was 68%.[80]

79. The Report reveals further in pp. 198-203 that, as for FY2017, the litigants at the Tax Court with an annual income above USD 50,000 below USD 100,000: 25.1%, above USD 100,000 below USD 250,000: 25.7%, above USD 250,000 below USD 500,000: 5.8%, above USD 500,000 below USD 1,000,000: 3.0%, and USD 1 million or more: 3.5%.
80. *See* Dunbroff and Hellwig, *supra "The United States Tax Court"* pp. 883-888.

Fortunately, litigation in court is no exception to the resolution by the disputing parties' agreement. The "Settlement Reference Manual" released by the Tax Department of the Ministry of Justice in 2012 mentions that settlements by agreement might be preferred particularly in the following cases: (i) a case is mainly on facts, and legal principles are well established, (ii) a case is legally and/or factually complex, (iii) a case needs prompt resolution, (iv) a case leads to greater future compliance if a consensual resolution is realized, (v) a case is solely a matter of collectability, (vi) a case poses substantial litigation hazards for both parties, (vii) litigation costs outweigh benefits of winning a case. However, the Manual does confirm that the Tax Department usually does not enter into "nuisance value settlement" nor agrees on settling disputes in such a way that less than 20% of the amount of correction is conceded on account of litigation risk because it would otherwise give rise to litigations aimed at such settlements. Also, the Manual informs that cases disfavoring settlements include the following: (a) a case in need of a legal precedent, (b) a case clearly with no merit, and (c) a case involving significant legal issues.[81]

In reality, many litigation cases are settled by the agreement of the disputing parties. For example, in FY2012-2021, on average, 78% of cases brought to the Tax Court were settled by agreement, 20.5% were dismissed, and 1.4% were decided. In particular, the proportion of cases on which the Tax Court handed down judgments exceeded 2% of the number of cases processed in some years until FY2014, but since then, it has been less than 2% of the number of cases processed. In FY2021, approximately 28,400 cases were received by the Tax Court, and only about 18,200 cases were processed. The rate of settlement by agreement was about 82%, while the number of cases in which judgments were rendered was 1.1%.[82] While, as shown in Figure 2.6, the declining trend in the success rate for unrepresented taxpayers in the Tax Court has slowed down somewhat recently. The main cause for this trend may be found in the fact that, as described in 4 below, there has been an increase in procedural and financial support for lawsuits (especially lawsuits at tax courts) filed by pro se taxpayers who are, in most cases, low-income earners.[83] Even so, litigations generally require much time and costs, and it is pointed out that generally, less than 5% of the cases on which the Tax Court handed down judgments have been appealed against at higher courts.[84]

4 Protection of Litigation Rights of Taxpayers with Limited Means

As mentioned above, many lawsuits at the Tax Court are filed by those with low-income and pro se litigants. For example, from FY2008 to FY2017, there were

81. For details, refer to the Manual, pp. 10-11.
82. *See* 2022 TAS Report, p. 183.
83. In particular, in FY2020/FY2021, the Office of the Chief Litigator of the IRS held an event (Settlement Days) in major cities in collaboration with public interest groups and lawyers' associations, and settled disputes by agreement with 280/148 pro se litigants at the Tax Court. For details, *see* 2021 TAS Report, pp. 196-197.
84. Keith Fogg, The United States Tax Court: A Court for All Parties, *Bulletin for International Taxation*, January/February (2016) p. 76 DOI: 10.59403/10rvxp3.

annually approximately 4,700 to 6,900 lawsuits filed with the Tax Court by taxpayers with representation, compared with approximately 22,000 to 27,000 lawsuits filed by pro se litigants annually.[85] Moreover, the ratio of pro se litigants at the Tax Court has lately been on the rise. For instance, in 2012, the proportion was 78%, but since then, it has exceeded 80%, and it accounts for 86% in 2021.[86] As for small claim cases, under the Tax Court Rule 200 (Admission to practice and periodic registration fee) (3) (Other Applicants), a person who has passed the court's written examination and is not qualified as a legal professional can also represent the claimant, but the proportion of pro se litigants in the case of small claims cases at the Tax Court has also been on the rising trend, and lately it has reached over 90%, while it is about 50% in the other cases.[87] In particular, in FY2017, among approximately 27,000 cases filed with the Tax Court, about 83% of them were filed by pro se litigants, and in the case of small claim cases, the proportion of pro se litigants stands for about 94%.[88]

The above situation must be one of the causes for the fact that taxpayers' winning rate at the Tax Court is generally lower than that in other courts.[89] Each year, the TAS Report lists the top ten "most litigated issues" on which the Tax Court handed down its judgments.[90] Figure 2.6 exposes the recent number of Tax Court judgments on the top ten "most litigated issues" and the plaintiff's winning rate (percentage of judgments fully or partially in favor of the taxpayers). Lately, about 60% to 75% of the Tax Court's judgments are on pro se litigants/taxpayers, and Figure 2.6 reveals that the winning rate of those taxpayers with representatives is about 20% to 30%, while the winning rate of pro se litigants is around 10% to 15%. Moreover, for example, the 2017 (June 2016 to May 2017) TAS Report divulges the fact that the percentage of the Tax Court dismissing a lawsuit filed by a pro se litigant/taxpayer is 28%, which is about two and a half times higher than the 9% rate of dismissal for a case filed by a taxpayer with a representative.[91] The above 2017 TAS Report also reveals that, as for disputes over CDP at the Tax Court, their resolution ratio is 58%, and their dismissal ratio is 37% in the case of taxpayers with representatives, while the former ratio is 39% and the latter ratio is 53% in the case of pro se litigants.

85. *See* 2018 TAS report, p. 300.
86. *See* 2021 TAS Report Figure 3.11 for details.
87. Panuthos, *supra* "Procedural Issues" p. 392.
88. *See* p. 299 of the 2018 TAS Report. The ratio of taxpayers with no representative should be much higher at Tax Court than that (probably less than 30%) at the Tax Tribunal in Japan.
89. It is pointed out that around 1980, the IRS won about 80% of cases at the Federal District Court, about 70% at the Supreme Court, and about 90% in the Tax Court, *see* Howard Matthew, *Judicial Decision Making, IRS Policy and Taxpayer Litigation, Interdependence and Democratic Control*, UMI Dissertation Services (1998) pp. 50-54. Table 3.1.3 and Appendix 3 of the 2005 TAS Report also show that the Tax Court judgments favorable to taxpayers account for around 10%.
90. *See* Figures 2.6 and 2.8 for recent trends in the number of the Tax Court judgments related to the top ten "most litigated issues." For example, in FY2021, the number of such judgments is 246 while their number in terms of the number of cases to be processed by the Tax Court is 22,768. *See* the 2021 TAS Report Figures 3.1 and 3.2.
91. For details, *see* pp. 298-301 of the 2018 TAS Report.

Figure 2.6 Number of Judgments on the Top Ten "Most Litigated Issues" and Taxpayers' Winning Rate on Them at Tax Court

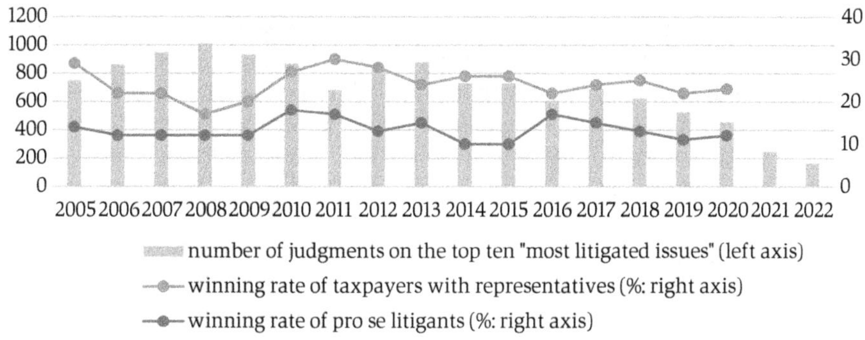

Source: Aggregated coefficients for Most Litigated Issues: Introduction in 2005 to 2022 TAS Reports.

The recent TAS Reports consider the situation shown in Figure 2.6 to be indicative of the problems and challenges that pro se litigants and taxpayers with small annual incomes have been confronted with. But those problems and challenges would have been more serious if it were not for various measures that the Tax Court has implemented or been involved in to assist those taxpayers.[92] Such measures include, in particular, the "Calendar Call Program," which refers to the date and time when the parties to the litigation are requested to attend prior to the start of the litigation to hear the current status of the litigated issue and to determine the trial schedule, etc., and low-income pro se litigants could obtain free legal assistance from lawyers' associations.[93] Also notable is the "Low-Income Taxpayer Clinic (LITC) Program," which was institutionalized by IRC §7526 (low-income taxpayer clinics), which the 1998 IRS Reform Act introduced. Based on this provision, qualified low-income taxpayers could not only receive financial support from the government[94] but also be assisted at clinics nationwide for a small fee on their appeals to the IRS and courts by tax experts who meet certain requirements and students who specialize in law and accounting.[95]

Behind the implementation and expansion of assistance measures for low-income pro se litigants/taxpayers, there are such concerns and moves as follows: (i) More than half of those who received the "90-day letter" (approximately 60% in FY2017) have annual income of less than USD 50,000,[96] and many of those who have

92. *See* Donbroff and Hellwig, *supra "The United States Tax Court"* pp. 897-899.
93. *See* IRM 35.61(Calendar Calls) for details. For example, the American Bar Association (ABA)'s Model Rules of Professional Conduct 6.1 requires its members to render a minimum of fifty hours of public service per year without compensation and it is recommended that most of it is to be rendered for those who are especially incapable of paying attorney's fees.
94. IRC §7526(a)(In General) provides: "The Secretary may, subject to the availability of appropriate funds, make grants to provide matching funds for the development, expansion, or continuation of qualified low-income taxpayer clinics."
95. *See* Low-Income Taxpayer Clinics Program Report 2018 for details.
96. Between 2013 and 2017, 2.66 million to 3.74 million "90-day letters" were issued each year. For details, *see* pp. 202-203 of 2018 TAS Report.

not filed lawsuits with the Tax Court (75% in FY2018) also have annual income of less than USD 50,000, (ii) the number of pro se litigants has lately been on the increase,[97] (iii) "Charter of Taxpayers' Rights" (TABOR I), which was adopted in 1988, has been expanded through several revisions.[98] In relation to the above (iii), the IRS states in its publication that, in connection with IRC §7803 (Commissioner of Internal Revenue; other officials) (3) (Execution of duties in accord with taxpayer rights) (1) (the right to retain representation),[99] taxpayers with income below a certain level could ask a LITC which is funded by the IRS but its employees and volunteers are independent of the IRS to represent them in their dispute before the IRS or a federal court for free of charge or for a minimal fee and many such Clinics could offer services in languages other than English.[100]

SECTION 3 RULES ON COSTS

1 The Traditional "American Rule" and Its Metamorphosis

From the perspective of solidifying the protection of taxpayers' rights and enhancing their access to justice further, measures other than those analyzed in the above in Sections 1 and 2, which help reduce taxpayers' litigation-related expenses, may also be pursued further. In the U.S., the traditional rule on costs order is that each party bears its own costs regardless of the outcome of the lawsuit, and it is called the "American rule," which is contrasted with the "English rule" described in Chapter 3 under which the losing party bears the costs of the winning party.[101] The Supreme Court judgment on *Arcambel v. Wiseman* ([1796] 3 U.S. 3 Dall. 306) was the first to recognize the existence of the "American rule." The judgment of the District of Rhode Island Circuit Court, which was the original trial of this case, ordered the losing party to be liable for damages and the burden of attorney's fees of USD 1,600 for the winning party. However, the Supreme Court voided such shifting of the burden of attorney's fees by ruling that the U.S. general practice on costs is in opposition to it, and even if that practice were not strictly correct in principle, it is entitled to the respect of the Court, till it is changed or modified by statute. Such practice or the "American rule" confirmed by this Supreme Court judgment has been respected in subsequent courts.

97. It is pointed out that the ratio of pro-se litigants was about 62% in 1988 but it increased to 74% in 1992. *See* Matthew, *supra "Judicial Decision Making"* p. 60.
98. In 1996, TABOR II (PL 104-168) established Taxpayer Advocates and in 1998 TABOR III (S.1747-105th Congress) was adopted. In 2008, "Taxpayer Rights Charter Act" (S.3215-111th Congress) was enacted to incorporate in IRC §7529 (Statement of taxpayer rights and obligations) ten rights similar to those (*see* footnote 69) in IRC §7803(3).
99. *See* https://www.irs.gov/newsroom/taxpayer-bill-of-rights-9-the-right-to-retain-representation-1.
100. Tax Court also states in its Administrative Order No. 2019-01 that it will proceed with the development of litigation procedures that would contribute to those support measures for low-income litigants.
101. The "American rule" is also called the "Party/party rule," and the "English rule" which is the "Loser pays rule" is also called the "Cost indemnity rule" (or "Costs follow the event rule").

The rationales for the "American rule" in the U.S. are, as confirmed in a series of judgments,[102] basically as follows: (i) the "English rule" acts in a way that constrains the filing of lawsuits by those who are financially disadvantaged; (ii) the outcome of the lawsuit is unclear, so it would be excessive to shift the burden of attorneys' fees to the loser; otherwise, the lawsuit would be a means of revenge; and (iii) calculation of the attorneys' fees to be recovered is by no means easy. In addition, the "American rule" was consistent with the "sovereign immunity doctrine." For example, in the Supreme Court judgment on *United States v. Mitchell* ([1980] 445 U.S. 535, 538), at issue was whether or not the government is accountable for money damages for its alleged breaches of trust in connection with its management of forest resources on allotted lands of the Indian Reservation, and the Court set aside the original Court of Federal Claims judgment that found the government's liability for damages and remanded it by ruling that the 1877 Indian General Allotment Act (28 U.S.C 1505) cannot be construed to have entrusted a fiduciary responsibility on the resource in question to the government and it is elementary that the U.S., as sovereign, is immune from suit save as it consents to be sued and in the absence of clear congressional consent, there is no jurisdiction in courts to entertain suits against the U.S.[103]

However, some statutes adopted a number of exceptions to the "American rule," and the rule has also undergone numerous revisions. The main judicial principle that allows exceptions to the "American rule" is the "common fund (or common interest/benefit) principle."[104] This principle was relied on, for example, by some corporate shareholders at the Supreme Court judgment on *Boeing Co. v. Van Gemert* ([1980] 444 U.S. 472). In this judgment, the Court stated that, in accordance with the "common benefit principle" confirmed by the Supreme Court judgments on *Trustees v. Greenough* ([1882] 105 U.S. 527) and *Central Railroad & Banking Co. v. Pettus* ([1885] 113 U.S. 116), etc., the other shareholders' right to share the harvest of the suit is a benefit in the fund created by the efforts of the class representatives and their counsel, and unless absentees contribute to the payment of attorney's fees incurred on their behalves, they will pay nothing for the creation of the fund, so the other shareholders who have not participated in the lawsuit should bear part of the appellees' attorney's fees. This principle has often been relied upon in connection with class action litigation, in which the winning party or its attorneys recover reasonable attorney's fees not directly from the losing party but indirectly from those (which may include insurance companies, etc.) that are to benefit unjustly from the litigation.

102. These series of judgments include the Second Circuit Court of Appeals judgment on *Conte v. Flota Mercante Del Estado* ([1960] 277 F.2d 664, 672), the Supreme Court judgment on *Oelrichs v. Spain* ([1872] 82 U.S. 211), the Second Circuit Court of Appeals judgment on *Farmer v. Arabian Am. Oil Co* ([1963] 324 F.2d 359, 370). *See* Peter N. Cubita, Jeffrey S. Lichtman and Daniel D. Rubino, Awards of Attorney's Fees in the Federal Courts, *St. John's Law Review*, Vol. 56, No. 2 (1982) p. 279.

103. However, the Federal Court of Claims judgment ([1981] 229 Ct. Cl. 1, 664 F.2d 265) again recognized the state's liability for damages, and in the subsequent Supreme Court judgment ([1983] 463 U.S. 206), it was ruled that related laws and regulations other than the 1877 Act recognize the existence of fiduciary duty of the government and it is liable for damages on account of its breach of that duty.

104. "Substantial benefit doctrine" is also a similar principle.

Another major judicial doctrine that allows exceptions to the "American rule" is the "private attorney-general theory."[105] The idea behind this theory is that a person who wins a lawsuit in the public interest should be entitled to recover attorneys' fees in respect of that lawsuit, as he functions similarly to a "private attorney-general" who files a lawsuit in the public interest. This theory intends to encourage lawsuits of high social importance where there is not much incentive to do so at the individual level. In fact, some states have adopted provisions in their laws that embody the "private attorney-general theory."[106] Whereas the court's view of the "private attorney-general principle" in the absence of any statute to be relied on is not necessarily positive. In particular, in the Supreme Court judgment on *Alyeska Pipeline Co. v. Wilderness Society* ([1975] No. 73-1977), the Court held that Congressional utilization of the private attorney-general concept can in no sense be construed as a grant of authority to the Judiciary to jettison the traditional rule to award attorneys' fees whenever the courts deem appropriate so that the judgment of the Court of Appeals for the District of Columbia ([1974] 161 U.S. App. DC 495 F.2d 1026) granting recovery of attorneys' fees, etc. to the appellee who opposed to the government agency's permission of the concerned pipeline construction is to be voided.

Certainly, the U.S.C. Title 28 (Judiciary and Judicial Procedure) §2412 (Costs and fees) is based on the traditional "American rule" in that it does not permit the shift of attorney's fees, etc., to the losing party, except as specifically provided for by law.[107] The table was turned around by the creation of the Civil Rights Attorney Fees Act of 1976 (42 U.S.C)§1988 (Proceedings in vindication of civil rights). In particular, paragraph (b) (Attorney's fees) of this section prescribes that in any action or proceeding to enforce a provision of sections 1981, etc., and Title VI of the Civil Rights Act of 1964, the court, in its discretion, may allow the prevailing party, other than the U.S., a reasonable attorney's fee as part of the costs.[108] After the enactment of this law,

105. Another major judicial doctrine is the "bad faith doctrine," which permits the transfer of costs to those who make frivolous claims. Judgments that have relied on the "exception in cases of bad faith" include the Supreme Court judgment on *Hall v. Cole* ([1973] 412 U.S. 1). For details, refer to the provisional version of the Jackson Report (Review of Civil Litigation Costs Preliminary Report), Vol. 2 (2009) p. 618.
106. For example, California's Civil Procedure Code §1021.5(Attorney fees in cases resulting in public benefit) stipulates, "Upon motion, a court may award attorneys' fees to a successful party...in any action which has resulted in the enforcement of an important right affecting the public interest if: (a) a significant benefit, ...has been conferred on the general public or a large class of persons."
107. This provision states, "(1) Except as otherwise specifically provided by statute, a judgment for costs, as enumerated in section 1920 of this title but not including the fees and expenses of attorneys may be awarded to the prevailing party in any civil action brought by or against the United States."
108. U.S.C. Title 28§1920 (Taxation of costs) stipulates, "*Any court* of the United States may tax as costs the following: (1) Fees of the clerk and marshal; (2) Fees for printed or electronically recorded transcripts; (3) Fees and disbursements for printing and witnesses; (4) Fees for exemplification and the costs of making copies of any materials where the copies are necessarily obtained for use in the case; (5) Docket; (6) Compensation of court appointed experts, compensation of interpreters, and salaries, fees, expenses, and costs of special interpretation services." Here, the definition of "costs," unlike in the UK (*see* 1 in Section 4 of Chapter 3), does not include attorney fees, primarily because the district court is best suited to make an order on them. For details, *see supra* "The Jackson Report (Provisional)" p. 615.

legislative amendments were made to allow for reasonable attorney's fee recovery with respect to those laws (e.g., Clean Air Act 307 (Administrative proceedings and judicial review) (f) (Costs), Fair Housing Act §3612(p) (Attorneys' fees), Resource Conservation and Recovery Act §7002(e) and the like) under which lawsuits by citizens play an important role for the protection of civil rights and other Constitutionally protected rights.

Indeed, even if a litigant other than the U.S. government becomes a "prevailing party" as stipulated in the Civil Rights Attorney Fees Act §1988, there was a problem of much uncertainty about whether he would recover his attorney's fees and generally, courts would not approve the recovery especially when he had sufficient means, and the other party in the lawsuit is the U.S. government to which the "sovereign immunity doctrine" applies.[109] But, the Equal Access to Justice Act(34 CFR §21.1) was enacted in 1980 to mitigate this problem, and it amended the aforementioned U.S.C. Title 28§2412, which provided for the traditional "American Rule." The amended §2412(b) provides, "a court may award reasonable fees and expenses of attorneys, ... to the prevailing party in any civil action brought by or against the United States." The amended §2412(d)(1)(A) stipulates, "a court shall award to a prevailing party other than the United States fees and other expenses, ... to prevailing party in any civil action (other than cases sounding in tort), ... unless the court finds that the position of the United States was substantially justified or that special circumstances make an award unjust." However, as mentioned below, the prevailing party who could recover the attorney's fee clears the net worth requirement prescribed under IRC §2412(d)(2)(B).

2 Differences/Similarities Between Civil Rights Attorney Fees Act and Equal Access to Justice Act

Provisions with a similar purport and treatment under the Equal Access to Justice Act have also been adopted in various Acts, including the U.S. Consumer Protection Statutes.[110] This, in conjunction with the Civil Rights Attorney Fees Act, means that the traditional "American rule" has been revised to the extent that it has practically become a hybrid with the "English rule." The question of how much the "American rule" has been revised depends partly on the definition and application scope of the "prevailing parties." It is understood that Congress intended to include the "catalyst theory" in defining and delimiting the scope of the "prevailing party" adopted in §1988(b) of the

109. *See* H.A. Zionts, The Civil Rights Attorney's Fees Awards Act of 1976: A View from the Second Circuit, *Buffalo Law Review* Vol. 29, No. 3 (1980) p. 570. Actually, in *the National Council of Community Mental Health Centers, Inc. v. Mathews* ([1976] 546 F.2d 1003) case, the U.S. Court of Appeals (District of Columbia Circuit) stated, "If we find that the unexpected grant funds belong to the United States rather than to the grantees and we cannot find a specific statute providing for the award of attorney's fees against the United States in this situation, the district court's fee award cannot be upheld."

110. There are well over fifty statutes that provide for the recovery of attorneys' fees for the "prevailing parties." *See* Kyle A. Loring, The Catalyst Theory Meets the Supreme Court—Common Sense Takes a Vacation, *Boston College Law Review*, Vol. 43, No. 4 (2002) p. 977.

Civil Rights Attorney Fees Act.[111] As for the notion of the "catalyst theory," it could be deduced from *Parham v. Southwestern Bell Telephone Co.* judgment([1970] 433 F.2d 421) in which the Eighth Circuit Court of Appeals did not issue an injunction against the appellee's unlawful employment discrimination for the alleged violation of the Equal Employment Opportunity Act but held that the appellant should be entitled to a reasonable amount of attorney's fee recovery because the filling of this suit was a catalyst for prompting the appellee to take action for the implementation of fair employment policies.

In fact, many courts have adopted the definition and application scope of "the prevailing party" based on the "catalyst theory." In particular, the Supreme Court judgment on *New York Gaslight Club, Inc. v. Carey* ([1980] 447 U.S. 54) ordered the recovery of attorneys' fees incurred at the administrative proceeding by the "prevailing party" who alleged employment discrimination based on race while the relevant statute at issue was the Civil Rights Act 1964 §706 (Prevention of unlawful employment practices) (k) which stipulates, "In any action or proceeding under this title, the court in its discretion, may allow the prevailing party, other than the Commission or the United States, a reasonable attorney's fee as part of the costs." While the Supreme Court judgment on *Webb v. Board of Education of Dyer County, Tennessee, et al.* ([1985] 471 U.S. 234) may have a point in dismissing the appellant/prevailing party's claim based on the Civil Rights Attorney Fees Act §1988 for the recovery of attorney's fees, etc., at the administrative stage beyond those incurred in the course of the trial on the grounds that, in contrast to the *New York Gaslight* case, it is not a requirement for the administrative stage to be gone through.

However, the validity of the widely accepted "catalyst theory" was challenged by the Supreme Court judgment on *Buckhannon Board & Care Home, Inc. v. West Virginia Department of Health & Human Resources* (532 U.S. 598(2001)). In this case, the petitioners filed a lawsuit on account of the alleged violation by the defendant/State agencies of the Americans with Disabilities Act of 1990 (ADA) and the Fair Housing Amendments Act of 1988 (FHAA), and the defendants withdrew the related regulatory action, so the petitioners claimed the recovery of its attorney's fee.[112] But the Supreme Court dismissed such claim by ruling that the use of "prevailing party" in the federal law should be interpreted to mean a party that has received a remedy from the court and relying on vague suggestions in the legislative history of the "catalyst theory" is not sufficient to alter the clear meaning of "prevailing party" in the fee-shifting statutes, so the defendant's voluntary change in conduct, although perhaps accomplishing what the petitioners sought to achieve by the lawsuit, lacks the necessary judicial *imprimatur* on the change in the parties' legal relationship.[113]

There is a question of whether the above negative view of the "catalyst theory" expressed by the Supreme Court judgment on Buckhannon also applies to those cases

111. *See* HR Rep. No. 94-1558(1976) and S. Rep. No. 94-1011(1976).
112. ADA §12205 (Attorney's fee) reads, "In any action or administrative proceedings commenced pursuant to this chapter, the court or agency, in its discretion, may allow the prevailing party, other than the United States, a reasonable attorney's fee."
113. For more information, *see* Loring, *supra* "The Catalyst Theory Meets the Supreme Court" pp. 973-1008.

where the relevant statute is the Equal Access to Justice Act of 1980, etc. In *Brickwood Contractors v. United States* judgment ([2001] 49 Fed. Cl. 148), even if the plaintiff was not given the judicial imprimatur, the Court of Federal Claims ordered the recovery of the attorney fees incurred at the administrative dispute stage of the "prevailing party" for the reason that the relevant Act, in this case, is different from that in *Buckhannon* case in terms of the phrases adopted in those Acts on the courts' authority to order the costs.[114] Such interpretation of the Court has a point because, in the case of the Equal Access to Justice Act, etc., the recovery of the attorney's fees by a "prevailing party" (who clears the net worth requirement) is only possible where the government cannot substantially justify its position or there are no special circumstances that make the award unjust, and it is apprehended that negation of such interpretation might prompt the government that considers it difficult to substantially justify its position to settle the dispute before it goes to court to avoid the payment of the other party's attorney's fee.[115]

But the above interpretation in the Court of Federal Claims judgment on the *Brickwood* case was not followed by the subsequent Federal Circuit Court of Appeals judgment ([2002] 288 F.3d 1371, 1379), so there remains a cause for the apprehension mentioned above. Some statutes set lower hurdles by explicitly granting wide discretion to courts in deciding whether the recovery of the attorney's fee is to be ordered. For instance, the Endangered Species Act of 2000(16 U.S.C) §1540(g)(4) states, "The court, ... may award costs of litigation (including reasonable attorney and expert witness fees) to any party, whenever the court determines such award is appropriate." Also, there are statutes that allow the prevailing party the recovery of its attorney's fees even at the administrative dispute stages. One such example is U.S.C. Title 5 §504 (Costs and fees of parties)(a)(1), which provides, "An agency that conducts an adversary adjudication shall award, to a prevailing party other than the United States, fees and other expenses incurred by that party in connection with that proceeding...(d) Fees and other expenses awarded under this section shall be paid by any agency over which the party prevails from any funds made available to the agency by appropriation or otherwise."

Differences between the Civil Rights Attorney Fees Act and the Equal Access to Justice Act are also observable in the recoverable amount of the attorney's fee by the "prevailing party." For instance, in the Court of Appeals for the Fifth Circuit in *Johnson v. Georgia Highway Express, Inc.* judgment ([1974] 488 F 2d 714), at issue, was whether or not there was a violation of the Civil Rights Act of 1964 Title 7§706,[116] and the Court pointed out twelve factors to be taken into consideration to come up with a reasonable amount of recoverable attorney's fees, and they were as follows: (i) the time and labor required; (ii) the novelty and difficulty of the questions; (iii) the skill requisite to perform the legal service properly; (iv) the preclusion of other employment by the

114. Indeed, U.S.C. Title 28 §2412(d) (as amended by the Equal Access to Justice Act, *see* last paragraph in 1 in this section) and U.S.C. Title 5 §504 (*see* next paragraph in the text) uses the phrase "shall award," whereas U.S.C. Title 42§12205 (*see* footnote 112) and the aforementioned Civil Rights Act §706(k) adopts the phrase "may allow."
115. *See* Loring, *supra* "The Catalyst Theory Meets the Supreme Court" p. 1004.
116. As for Title VII of the Civil Rights Act §706(k), *see* second paragraph of 2 in Section 3.

attorney due to acceptance of the case; (v) the customary fee; (vi) whether the fee is fixed or contingent; (vii) the limitations imposed by the client or the circumstances; (viii) the amount involved and the results obtained; (ix) the experience, reputation, and ability of the attorneys; (x) the undesirability of the case; (xi) the nature and length of the professional relationship with the client; (xii) awards in similar cases.

Many courts followed the calculation method presented by the abovementioned Court of Appeals judgment on Johnson while there were some criticisms against many subjective elements in the method that allow wide discretion of the district court.[117] Then, two other methods have also come to be relied upon. The first, known as the "Lodestar method," was presented by the Third Circuit Court of Appeals judgment on *Lindy Bros. Builders, Inc. of Philadelphia v. American Radiator & Standard Sanitary Corp.* ([1973] 487 F.2d 161, 168). Under the "Lodestar method," the recoverable amount of reasonable attorney's fees is based on the amount of reasonable attorney's fees per hour multiplied by the amount of reasonable time spent, and adjustments are made to it in light of the complexity of the case, the number of days and the amount of money in dispute. The other is the " percentage method," under which a certain percentage (usually 20% to 30%) of the amount recovered in a lawsuit is the recoverable attorney's fee. The "percentage method" might be preferable because under the "Lodestar method," there is an incentive to prolong the litigation and avoid settlement by agreement in order to increase the recoverable attorney's fee, while even under the "percentage method," the factors presented by the Court of Appeals judgment on Johnson are usually taken into consideration.[118]

Whereas, under the Equal Access to Justice Act, U.S.C. Title 28§2412(d)(2) stipulates, "(A)...a court shall award to a prevailing party other than the United States fees and other expenses,...(iii) attorney fees shall not be awarded in excess of $125 per hour unless the court determines that an increase in the cost of living or a special factor, such as the limited availability of qualified attorneys for the proceedings involved, justifies a higher fee,...(B) "party" means (i) an individual whose net worth did not exceed $2,000,000 at the time the civil action was filed, or (ii) any owner of an unincorporated business, or any partnership, corporation, association, unit of local government, or organization, the net worth of which did not exceed $7,000,000 at the time the civil action was filed, and which had not more than 500 employees at the time the civil action was filed;" Thus, recovery of fees and expenses is not granted to successful litigants that do not come under "prevailing party" because their net worth is high. As for the question of whether or not a pro se litigant can recover an attorney's fee, the Supreme Court judgment on *Kay v. Ehrler* (499 U.S. 432(1991)) confirmed that at least a pro se litigant who is also a lawyer may not be awarded attorney's fees under U.S.C. Title 42§1988 (Proceedings in vindication of civil rights).

117. For example, in *City of Riverside v. Rivera* ([1986] 477 U.S. 561), at issue was how much attorney fees can be recovered in this case in which there was a violation of the Civil Rights Attorney Fees Act §1988. The Supreme Court held that the recoverable amount of the attorney's fee is not proportional to the amount of damages actually obtained by the "prevailing party."

118. For more information, *see* Attorney's' Fee Awards in Federal Class Actions at http://www.reedsmith.com/en/perspectives/2001/08/attorneys-fee-awards-in-federal-class-actions.

Moreover, U.S.C Title 28 §68 (Offer of judgment), from the perspective of seeking to resolve disputes by agreement rather than judgments of courts, provides for exceptions to the principle that the "prevailing party" can recover litigation-related costs. Under this section, the defendant is allowed to present to the plaintiff an "offer of judgment" regarding the amount of damages, cost sharing, etc., within fourteen days before the commencement of the trial. If the plaintiff does not accept the "offer of judgment," and the outcome of the trial is more unfavorable to the plaintiff than the "offer of judgment," the plaintiff must bear the costs of the defendant incurred after the presentation of the "offer of judgment." This "offer of judgment" could, in some cases, prompt disputing parties to opt for it to avoid possible worse results or judgments courts might render on them, but an "offer of judgment" does not usually include an amount for attorney's fees, so the amount included therein is considerably less than the amount of an attorney's fee. In addition, the date of the presentation of an "offer of judgment" is near the date of the trial, so the amount of costs to be paid by the plaintiff is relatively small. Such being the case, in reality, an "offer of judgment" has not been actively utilized.[119]

3 Transformation of "American Rule" in Tax Disputes

The Tax Equity and Fiscal Responsibility Act of 1982 (PL 97-248) §292 (Awarding of costs and certain fees), which is similar to the above U.S.C. Title 28 §2412(d), stipulates that the Equal Access to Justice Act does not apply to tax disputes, so IRC §7430 (Awarding of costs and certain fees) was created. IRC §7430 has become, after revisions made in 1986, etc., very similar in structure to U.S.C. Title 5§504 and U.S.C. Title 28 §2412. However, IRC §7430 is more favorable to taxpayers in many respects now that under IRC §7430(c) (Definitions) (4) (Prevailing party), the definition of "prevailing party" includes not only the party who succeeded fully but also succeeded on main points of contention in the administrative or the litigation stage as well as the party who settled their case by agreement with the IRS. Moreover, IRC §7430 does not have the phrase "in special circumstances," which is incorporated in U.S.C. Title 5§504 as one of the conditions for disqualifying the recovery of an attorney's fee, and the maximum amount of recoverable attorney's fee under IRC §7430 is USD 200 per hour as of 2018 compared to USD 125 in the case of U.S.C. Title 28§2412, while those recoverable amounts could become higher if there are special circumstances.[120]

Particularly noteworthy among the treatments favorable to taxpayers under IRC §7430 is realized by its amendment by the Tax Reform Act of 1986 and the Technical

119. *See* Lionel M. Lavenue and Forrest A. Jones, Rule 68 Offer of Judgment: A Neglected Tool for Patent Infringement Defendants, *Westlaw Journal Intellectual Property,* March 1 (2017) also at https://www.finnegan.com/en/insights/articles/rule-68-offer-of-judgment-a-neglected-tool-for-patent.html.
120. *See* Rev. Proc. 2017-58, Treasury Regulation §301.7430-4(b)(2) for details.

and Miscellaneous Revenue Act of 1988 as IRC §7430 incorporates the "catalyst theory." IRC§7430(a) (In general) dictates, "In any administrative or court proceeding which is brought by or against the United States, the prevailing party may be awarded a judgment or a settlement of (1) reasonable administrative costs, and (2) reasonable litigation costs," and reasonable administrative and litigation costs could be recovered even in cases other than court judgments are handed down as IRC §7430(c)(4)(C) (Determination as to prevailing party) states, "Any determination … as to whether a party is a prevailing party shall be made by agreement of the parties or—(i) in the case where the final determination with respect to the tax, interest, or penalty is made at the administrative level, by the Internal Revenue Service, or (ii) in the case where such final determination is made by a court, the court."[121] IRC §7430(3) (Attorneys' fees) (A) (In general) must also be good news for some because it stipulates, "Fees for the services of an individual (whether or not an attorney) who is authorized to practice before Tax Court or before the Internal Revenue Service shall be treated as fees for the services of an attorney.

While it holds true that, as IRC §7430(c)(4)(D)(Special rules for applying net worth requirement) prescribes, in order for a "prevailing party" to recover reasonable administrative/litigation costs, the taxpayer must, as in other cases where the "Equal Access to Justice Act" etc. are at issue, clear the net worth requirement established under IRC §2412(d)(2)(B).[122] In addition, IRC §7430(c)(4)(B) (Exception if the United States establishes that its position was substantially justified) (i) (General rule) dictates that those costs are not recoverable in a case where the position of the U.S. in the proceeding is substantially justified.[123] As for the recovery of administrative costs, taxpayers are also required to apply for their reimbursement within 91 days of the IRS's final determination pursuant to IRC §7430(b) (Limitations) (4) (Period for applying to IRS for administrative costs) while the IRS's final decision on the application can be challenged in a tax court pursuant to IRC §7430(f) (Right of appeal) (2) (Administrative proceedings). To recover "reasonable litigation costs," it is also necessary that: (i) the taxpayer has exhausted all available administrative remedies in relation to the IRS (IRC §7430(b)(1)), and (ii) the taxpayer has not acted unreasonably to delay the proceedings (IRC §7430(b)(3)).

Among the various requirements or preconditions for the recovery of administrative/litigation costs above, particularly problematic is to determine whether

121. Under IRC §7430, prior to the 1986 amendments to the Act, "reasonable litigation costs" were limited to an aggregate limit of USD 25,000. After the amendment, recoverable attorney's fee was basically set at USD 75 per hour, and market rates and other factors were considered for other related expenses. After the 1988 revision, the recoverable hourly attorney's fee has been raised to USD 125, unless a special factor justifies a higher rate. *See* IRC §7430(c)(1)(B)(iii).

122. Prior to the 1986 amendments to IRC §7430, the size of the taxpayer's net worth was not a factor in determining whether reasonable administrative/litigation costs are recoverable or not.

123. Under IRC §7430, before the 1986 Act Amendment, it was enough for the government to establish that its position was not "unreasonable." *See also* the following Tax Court judgment on the *Phillips* case (1987).

the requirement under IRC §7430(c)(4)(B) is met or not. In this connection, it is stated in IRC §7430(c)(4)(B)(ii) that the position of the U.S. shall be presumed not to be substantially justified if the IRS did not follow its applicable published guidance in the administrative proceeding.[124] Certainly, in *Phillips v. Commissioner* (88 TC. 529(1987)), the Tax Court ordered the recovery of the plaintiff/taxpayer's reasonable litigation costs that are attributable to the respondent's "unreasonable" positions by ruling that the IRS should not, without going through necessary procedures for withdrawal or modification, deviate from the Revenue Ruling 72-539, etc., that allows a taxpayer who has not filed a return to opt for a joint return filing even after the limitation period for its selection is passed because it has been followed for a long time, even if the reason for issuing to the taxpayer the "90-day letter" whose content was not in line with the Ruling was due to the considerations given to the judgment of Seventh Circuit Court of Appeals judgment on *Durovic v. Commissioner* ([1973] 487 F.2d 36), etc. that practically invalidated the Ruling by stating that a joint return cannot be filed once a notice of deficiency applying a tax rate applicable in the case of a separate return is issued.[125]

Whereas, *Mearkle v. Commissioner* ([1986] 87 TC 527) presents an interesting contrast. In this case, the IRS issued to the plaintiff the "90-day letter," which relied on the proposed IT regulations §1.280A-2(i)(2)(ii) on IRC §280A (Disallowance of certain expenses in connection with business use of home, rental of vacation homes, etc.).[126] The regulations were restrictive in the scope of deductible expenses because it deemed gross income derived from the use of a unit to mean gross income from the business activity in the unit reduced by expenditures required for the activity but not allocable to the use of the unit itself, such as expenditures for supplies and compensation paid to other persons. Soon after the issue of the "90-day letter," the Tax Court held in *Scott v. Commissioner* ([1985] 84 TC 683) that the regulations were not in accord with IRC §280A, and it made the IRS acknowledge that there was no tax deficiency on the plaintiff. So, there arose a question of whether the reasonable litigation cost should be recovered by the plaintiff, but the Tax Court did not order its recovery by ruling that, although the Court needs not to accord the same deference to proposed regulations as to final regulations, the respondent cannot be held responsible for adhering to proposed regulations at least until they are judicially disapproved.

124. IRC §7430(c)(4)(B)(iii) provides, "In determining ... whether the position of the United States was substantially justified, the court shall take into account whether the United States has lost in courts of appeal for other circuits on substantially similar issues.
125. In the Phillips case, some judges expressed dissenting opinions by mentioning that normally substantial authority is not given to Revenue Rulings and the Tax Court has respected the Circuit Court of Appeals judgment on the *Durovic* case for sixteen years. In fact, the majority's opinion in the *Phillips* case was voided by its subsequent judgment ((851 F.2d 1492(D.C.Cir. 1988).
126. IRC §280A(c)(5) stipulates, "the deductions allowed under this chapter ... shall not exceed the excess of—(A) the gross income derived from such use ... over (B) the deductions allocable to such use ... whether or not such unit was so used," and at issue was how the phrase "gross income derived from such use" should be interpreted.

As for the recovery of reasonable litigation costs, a "prevailing party" should also meet the requirement under the abovementioned IRC §7430(b)(1) of having exhausted all available administrative remedies in relation to the IRS as well as the requirement under the abovementioned IRC §7430(b)(3) of not having unreasonably delayed the litigation proceedings. Examples of cases where the recovery of the reasonable attorney's fee by a "prevailing party" is denied on account of his failure to fulfill the former requirement include *McGowan v. Commissioner* (TC Memo 2005-80). In this case, now that the court's judgment on a separate case (*McGowan v. Commissioner* (TC Memo. 2004-146)) was in favor of the plaintiff denying his tax evasion, at issue was whether or not the plaintiff's request for recovery of reasonable litigation costs should be allowed. On this issue, the Tax Court pointed out that the government's position on the petitioner's alleged tax evasion was substantially justified, and the petitioner did not respond to the "30-day letter" informing him of his right to participate in the "Appeals conference" offered by the Office of Appeals and did not participate in it. In conclusion, the Court dismissed the plaintiff's claim for the recovery of his reasonable litigation costs by ruling that the petitioner has not exhausted all administrative remedies provided for under IRC §7430(b)(1).

4 Further Developments on the "American Rule" in Tax Disputes

The potential usefulness of IRC §7430 for taxpayers is certainly high, but the hurdles to be cleared for the recovery of the taxpayers' attorney's fees are not low as it could be ascertained by the fairly small number of cases where the courts ordered it. Even so, a taxpayer's likelihood of recovering reasonable attorney fees could be enhanced through the use of IRC §7430(g) (Qualified offer), which was introduced by §3101(e) of the 1998 IRS Reform Act. Under IRC §7430(g), a taxpayer who meets the aforementioned "net worth requirement" and has exhausted his administrative remedies can, within a qualified offer period,[127] specify to the IRS the offered amount of the taxpayer's liability and, in a case where the IRS does not accept it within ninety days and the taxpayer's liability pursuant to a judgment in a court proceeding is equal to or less than the liability of the taxpayer would have incurred if the IRS had accepted the offer, he may recover reasonable administrative/litigation costs irrespective of whether the position of the government in the proceeding is substantially justified.[128] In addition, a "qualified offer" also works for speedier resolution of disputes when the IRS accepts the qualified offer. Figure 2.7 below is a yes/no flow chart that determines whether or not a taxpayer can recover reasonable administrative appeals/litigation costs.

127. "Qualified offer period" means the period from the date of sending the tax shortfall notice to thirty days prior to the date of the first trial.
128. *See* Notice CC-2010-007 for details on "qualified offer."

Figure 2.7 Simplified Flow Chart for Judging Whether or Not Taxpayers Can Recover Reasonable Administrative/Litigation Costs (Yes: ⬇), (No: ⇩)

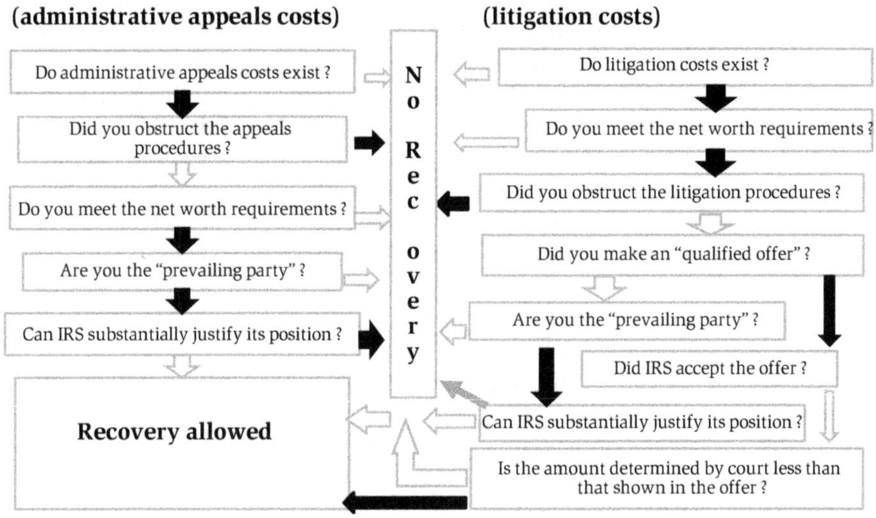

Source: Simplified version of the chart from Harris Bonnette, IRS Absolutely, Positively Not Pay Your Attorneys' Fees (Or Will They?), *Florida Bar Journal*, Vol. 84, No. 5 (2010) at https://www.floridabar.org/the-florida-bar-journal/the-irs-will-absolutely-positively-not-pay-your-attorneys-fees-or-will-they/

There are actually some cases where taxpayers recovered reasonable administrative appeals/litigation costs by utilizing a "qualified offer." For example, in the Tax Court judgment on *the Estate of Lippitz v. Commissioner* (TC Memo 2007-293), the petitioner made a "qualified offer" in which the amount of tax payable was USD 100 based on his claim that the "90-day letter" sent to him and his spouse was not correct because IRC §6015 (Relief from joint and several liability on joint return) (b) (procedures for relief from liability to all joint filers), whose application scope is also analyzed in 4 in Section 4, is applicable to him. The IRS did not accept the offer, but later, at the litigation stage, it conceded the petitioner's claim, so the issue was whether the petitioner could recover reasonable litigation costs. In this case, the Tax Court stated that neither the IRS's position on the "90-day letter" is substantially justifiable nor the IRS's "concession" in this case is a "settlement" to which no qualified offer is applicable in accordance with IRC §7430(c)(4)(E)(ii) (Exceptions), and it ruled that now that the plaintiff's additional amount of tax payable determined by the Court is less than that shown in the qualified offer, reasonable litigation costs of the plaintiff must be recovered.

Whereas, IRC §6673 (Sanctions and costs awarded by courts) amended by the Omnibus Budget Reconciliation Act of 1989 has clarified that the transformed "American rule" in the context of tax disputes could also work against the disputing taxpayers in some exceptional cases. Specifically, IRC §6673(a) (Tax court proceedings) provides in paragraph (1) (Proceedings instituted primarily for delay, etc.), "Whenever it appears to the Tax Court that—(A) proceedings before it have been instituted or maintained by the taxpayer primarily for delay, (B) the taxpayer's position in such proceeding is frivolous or groundless, or (C) the taxpayer unreasonably failed to pursue available administrative remedies, the Tax Court, in its decision, may require the taxpayer to pay to the United States a penalty not in excess of USD 25,000," and stipulates in paragraph (2) (Counsel's liability for excessive costs) that taxpayers who are parties to litigation and attorneys, as well as registered agents who are representatives of the government and have acted to multiply the proceedings in any case unreasonably and vexatiously may be ordered by the Tax Court to bear the costs incurred as a result of such action. Thus, this provision allows the Tax Court to order the government or the taxpayers to bear costs, while such orders are usually given to taxpayers.

Indeed, courts order penalties and costs on such actions that misuse legal proceedings even in cases where litigated cases pivot on the provisions of the Civil Rights Attorney Fees Act or the Equal Access to Justice Act, but it is not the transformation of the "American rule" that has enabled the courts to make such orders. This is evident from the Supreme Court judgment on *Christiansburg Garment Co. v. EEOC* ([1978] 434 U.S. 412). In this case, the prevailing defendant claimed the recovery of the attorney's fee based on Title VII of the Civil Rights Act §706 by asserting that the right of the plaintiff/Equal Employment Opportunity Commission to sue on behalf of the individual who asserted the defendant's alleged violation of Title VII of the Civil Rights Act was exercised in bad faith,[129] but the Supreme Court affirmed the District Court's judgment that dismissed such claim by finding no such action of the plaintiff. Nevertheless, the Court specified, "no statutory provision would have been necessary had an award of attorney's fees to a prevailing defendant been based only on the plaintiff's bad faith in bringing the action, for even under the American common rule (...), such fees can be awarded against a party who has proceeded in bad faith."

As mentioned above, the Civil Rights Attorney Fees Act and the Equal Access to Justice Act do not differ greatly in their core ideas, but variations in their institutional designs and the degree of modifications to the traditional "American rule" have manifested in such respects as the scope and amount of the recoverable attorney's fee. As for IRC §7430, it has basically adopted the institutional design relied on by the Equal Access to Justice Act, but there are some notable differences between them. For example, in the case of an "offer of judgment" stipulated under U.S.C. Title 28§68, it could enable the respondent to recover some expenses (not attorney's fee) from the plaintiff. In contrast, a "qualified offer" under IRC §7430(g) makes it possible for a taxpayer who has become the "prevailing party" to recover his reasonable attorney's fee. Moreover, even if a "qualified offer" is not availed, the hurdle for the "prevailing

129. As for Title VII of the Civil Rights Act §706(k), *see* second paragraph of 2 in Section 3.

party" to recover the reasonable attorney's fee is lower, and the recoverable amount could be larger, so it could be said that the metamorphosis of the traditional "American rule" is generally more conspicuous in the context of tax litigation than litigations centering around the Equal Access to Justice Act, etc.

SECTION 4 ATTRIBUTES OF MOST LITIGATED TAX ISSUES

1 Regulars on the Top Ten "Most Litigated Issues"

As presented in Figure 2.3, at the stage of administrative appeals, highly disputed issues are "CDP cases" and "examination cases." While, at the Tax Court, as Figure 2.5 shows, the majority of disputes are on "deficiency cases" or examination cases while the number of litigations on "CDP cases" is not so large. But the breakdown of "deficiency cases" reveals, as shown in Figure 2.8, that "gross income issues," "trade or business expenses issues," and "penalty issues" (in particular, FTF/FTP penalties:failure-to-file penalty, failure-to-pay penalty and failure-to-pay estimated tax penalties), "CDP issues," "innocent spouse issues" are regulars on the top ten list of the "most litigated issues."[130] Those issues that are on the top 10 list on and off are "accuracy-related penalty issues,"[131] "fraud penalty issues," "summons enforcement issues," "collection issues" (other than "CDP issues") that revolve around the application of IRC §7403 (Action to enforce lien or to subject property to payment of tax), IRC §6673 (Sanctions and costs awarded by courts), "Charitable (contribution) deduction issues" that pivots on the application of IRC §170 (Charitable, etc., contributions and gifts),[132] "family status issues" that are in most cases on the applicability of IRC §24 (Child tax credit), IRC §32 (earned income), IRC §151 (allowance of deductions for personal exemptions), etc.

130. Determining what constitutes the top 10 "most litigated issues" comes from the annual TAS Reports. The number of those issues is based on their number reviewed/ruled at the Tax Court (and other federal courts). As for the top 10 "most litigated issues" for business year 2021 (June 1, 2020 to May 31, 2021) counted on a basis of receipt by the Tax Court, they were 22,768 ("gross income issues": 13,558, "business expenses issues": 2,255, "family status. issues": 1,838, "CDP issues": 1,191, "charitable contribution deduction issues": 736, "delinquency penalties issues": 173, the other 4 cases: 3,017). Figures 3.3 and 3.4 of TAS 2022 Report tells that in FY2022 the number of "gross income issues" petitioned to Tax Court by individual taxpayers and sole proprietors were 21,215 (top on the list) and 1,223 respectively while the number of "trade or business expenses issues" petitioned to Tax Court by sole proprietors was 2,834. While it is pointed out that the Tax Court has not recently published the number of judgments, etc., and there are some cases which TAS has not counted in, *see* Carlton Smith, Tax Court Orders: The Unpublished Litigation, *Tax Notes*, August. *See* 22(2016) p. 1163.

131. "Accuracy-related penalty issues" are sometimes not on the list because they are not standalone disputes while in FY2021 the number of Tax Court rulings on them was 72 and the number of petitions on them to Tax Court was 875. *See* pp. 183-188 of the 2021 TAS Report.

132. Figures 3.2 and 3.4 of TAS 2002 Report show that the number of "charitable contribution issues" petitioned to Tax Court and ruled on in FY2022 by business taxpayers was on the top 10 list and it was 41 and 8 respectively.

Figure 2.8 Number of Tax Court (and Other Federal Courts) Judgments on the Regulars Appearing on the Top Ten List of "Most Litigated Issues"

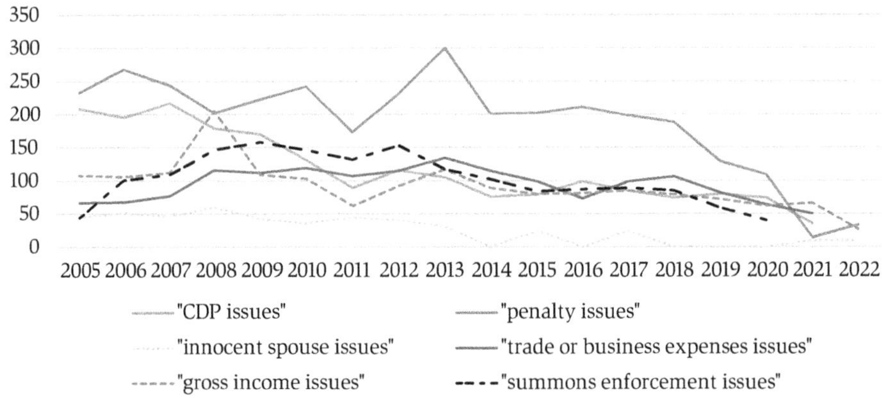

Source: Figures listed in the top ten Most Litigated Issues of each TAS report from 2005 to 2022.

As for penalties, there are also issues on accuracy-related penalties, laid down under IRC §6662 (Imposition of accuracy-related penalty) and issues on frivolous penalties prescribed under IRC §6673 (Frivolous issues penalty) that showed up on and off on the top ten list of the "most litigated issues."[133] These penalty issues are not included in the abovementioned "penalty issues" (FTF/FTP penalties imposed by IRC §6651 (Addition to the tax) (a)(1),[134] IRC §6651(a)(2), and IRC §6654(Failure by an individual to pay estimated income tax)).[135] Moreover, there are other penalties, such as those imposed on failures to submit information returns and more serious cases of underreporting, and some of them are disputed frequently. Therefore, when it comes to the analysis of the main reasons for penalties being highly disputed, it would be better not to confine it solely to the above delinquency penalties but rather expand it by redefining "penalty issues" so that they become more comprehensive to include issues on some other penalties. After having applied this redefinition to "penalty issues," in the following 2 to 5, an analysis is to be made of the attributes of those regular top ten

133. *See* footnote 130 and the 2021 TAS Report, p. 188. IRC §6673 is imposed by court on a taxpayer who disputes lawfulness of the re/assessment or other penalties on him fails to utilize available administrative remedies without reasonable grounds, or makes frivolous allegations in court. *See* 3 in this section as well.
134. IRC §6651(a) dictates, "In case of failure—(1) to file any return ..., on the date prescribed therefor (...), there shall be added to the amount required to be shown as tax on such return 5 percent of the amount of such tax if the failure is for not more than 1 month, with an additional 5 percent for each additional month or fraction thereof during which such failure continues, not exceeding 25 percent in the aggregate; (2) to pay the amount shown as tax on any return ..., there shall be added to the amount shown as tax on such return 0.5 percent of the amount of such tax ... ."
135. IRC §6654 is to be imposed on a person who earns income whose tax is not withheld at source properly but fails to pay quarterly on time in accordance with the "Pay As You Go (PAYG)" principle.
on the failure to prepay tax as required via withholding or estimated tax payments.

"most litigated issues" (except for "summons enforcement issues," which have little implications for Japan).

2 Disputes on Penalty Issues

(1) Recent Status of Penalty Issues

Underneath the fact that "penalty issues" are highly disputed, there are such reasons: (i) quite a large number of taxpayers are required to file tax returns/information returns and failures to do so are large in number,[136] (ii) some penalty rates are quite high,[137] (iii) there are various kinds of penalties that exceed 150 in number, (iv) a taxpayer may face multiple penalties.[138] *Dynamo Holdings Ltd. Partnership v. Commissioner* (T.C. Memo. 2018-61)is one example of the above (iv). In this case, there was cross-border transfer of property among the plaintiffs and the related entities and one of the plaintiffs was subjected to a penalty laid down under IRC §6651 (Failure to file tax return or to pay tax) for the failure to timely file Form 1042 (Annual Withholding Tax Return for U.S. Source Income of Foreign Persons) in accordance with IRC §1442 (Withholding of tax on foreign corporations) and a penalty under IRC §6656 (Failure to make deposit of taxes) for each year of 2005 and 2006.[139] In this case, the plaintiff claimed that it had reasonable cause for its failure to timely file and timely deposit because it did not believe that any distribution had occurred, but the Tax Court did not find that the plaintiff acted with reasonable cause and not willful neglect, so it dismissed the plaintiff's claim of exemption from those penalties.

While in actuality, there are many penalty abatements and it also constitutes another main reason for the large number of disputes over penalties. For instance, in 2021, approximately 11% (4,621,826 cases) of the number of civil penalties imposed (40,914,975 cases) were either exempted or reduced in amount. The number of civil penalties related to personal IT imposed in 2021 was 33,393,194.[140] Among them, the failure-to-pay penalty accounts for about 51%, the failure-to-pay estimated tax penalty represents approximately 31%, and the failure-to-file tax takes up about 10%, but approximately 9% of them are either exempted or reduced in amount.[141] In fact, these

136. This reason is also conspicuous in UK where taxpayers whose earnings are below the personal allowance amount are required to file IT returns and many penalties are imposed on their failures to do so. *See* 1(3) in Section 5 and Figure 3.11 of Chapter 3.
137. For example, if the failure to file is "fraudulent," the applicable penalty rate under IRC §6651(f) (Increase in penalty for fraudulent failure to file) ranges from 15% to 75%.
138. A taxpayers faces multiple penalties particularly in a case where a court imposes him a penalty under IRC §6673. For example, in *Cabirac v. Commissioner* ([2003] 120 T.C. 163, 170), the plaintiff was subjected to penalties under IRC §6651 and IRC §6673.
139. As for IRC §6651(a), *see* footnote 134. For this case, *see* 5(1) in this section and footnote 187. *Ellwest Stereo Theatres of Memphis, Inc. v. Commissioner* (T.C. Memo 1995) has confirmed that Form 1042 constitutes a return for the purpose of this section. IRC §1442 states, "In the case of foreign corporations subject to taxation under this subtitle, there shall be deducted and withheld at the source ... a tax equal to 30 percent thereof." Under IRC §6656, a penalty of 2% to 10% is applicable to tax underpayment depending on the delay length of tax deposit.
140. *See* 2021 URS Data Book Table 26.
141. For IRC §6654, see footnote 135.

penalties have become one of the top ten "most litigated issues" each year, either singly or jointly. As for the accuracy-related penalties, they are also frequently disputed and sometimes singly rank among the top ten "most litigated issues." But, as Figure 2.9 exposes, the number of accuracy-related penalties imposed is small compared to that of other penalties, and the ratio of its abatement is also only 5%. Accuracy-related penalties under IRC §6662 include penalties for negligence, substantial understatement of income tax, substantial valuation misstatement, substantial understatement of liabilities, and substantial estate or gift tax valuation understatement.[142]

Figure 2.9 Percentage of Civil Penalties Related to Personal IT in 2001 in Terms of Their Number of Impositions (and Ratios of Abatement)

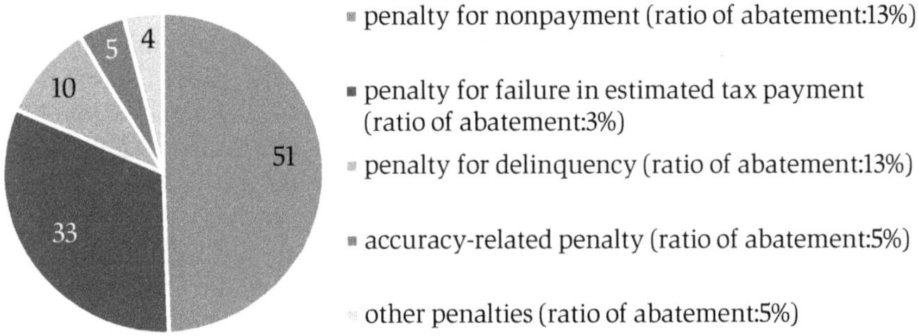

Source: Calculated from 2021 IRS Data Book Table 26.

The major reason why the number of penalties imposed and the ratio of penalty abatements varies greatly depending on the type of penalty is that the imposition procedures, applicable amounts/ratios, requirements for abatements, etc., are different. There are many impositions of penalty for nonpayment and penalty for delinquency stipulated in IRC §6651, and their ratio of abatement is also high because: (i) they are automatically imposed "systemically assessable penalties" so that they do not take into account the individual circumstances of taxpayers;[143] (ii) from 2001 and onward, as IRM 20.1.1.3.3.2.1(10-19-2020) states, "First Time Abate" (FTA) is applicable if a taxpayer who is subjected to those penalties under IRC §6651 meets the requirements that he has timely filed or filed a valid extension for all required returns currently due, and paid or arranged to pay any tax currently due and he was not subjected to any penalties in the past three years; (iii) it is possible to apply for FTA simply by telephone.[144] Whereas, the imposition, as well as the abatement of an

142. IRC §6662(a)(Imposition of penalty) provides, "If this section applies to any portion of an underpayment of tax required to be shown on a return, there shall be added to the tax an amount equal to 20 percent of the portion of the underpayment to which this section applies."
143. As for the "non-automatic" penalties, they are listed in IRC Chapter 68 Section B (Assessable penalties).
144. The 2012 Report ("Penalty Abatement Procedures Should be Applied Consistently to All Taxpayers and Should Encourage Voluntary Compliance," Report No. 2012-40-113) of the Treasury Inspector General for Tax Administration points out that in 2010 the number of

accuracy-related penalty, is usually done after tax audits or the issuance of the "90-day letter," and FTA is not applicable to it, so it entails a heavier burden on the IRS, and the hurdle for it to be abated becomes generally higher.[145]

However, the high ratios of abatement of mechanically and automatically imposed penalties are not limited to penalties covered by FTA. For example, IRC §6038A (Information with respect to foreign-owned corporations) (d) (Penalty for failure to furnish information or maintain records) is one of those penalties that are automatically applied. This penalty used to be imposed after it has become clear at the time of tax audit that there is no counterevidence against it, but currently, there are some impositions of this penalty (USD 25,000) in cases where Form 5472 is not submitted within a deadline irrespective of whether or not it carries such information that could affect the amount of the taxpayer's tax liability.[146] This change of practice has led to the high ratio of abatement of this penalty for such reasons as a taxpayer's ignorance of the submission requirement of Form 5472. For example, the ratio of abatement of this penalty from 2014 to 2018 was 55% to 72% in a case where it was applied automatically, and it was 17% to 39% in a case where it was not applied automatically.[147] In light of this, the TAS 2020 Report recommends that the automatic application of the penalty under IRC 6038A, which is not expressly permitted by law, should cease and instead be taken care of by a "90-day letter."[148]

Whereas, the relatively small number of accuracy-related penalty imposition should have a lot to do with IRC §7491 (Burden of proof) (c) (Penalties), which requires the IRS to have the burden of production in any court proceeding with respect to the liability of any individual for any penalty, addition to tax, or additional amount imposed by this title,[149] and this burden may become quite heavy with respect to an accuracy-related penalty in some cases. The IRS's perception of this burden does affect its stance on the imposition of accuracy-related penalties and the number of its impositions. For example, as Figure 2.10 shows, a negligence penalty under IRC §1662(b) (1) (negligence or disregard of rules or regulations), which is subsumed in the "accuracy-related penalties" and is to be imposed after the issue of a "90-day letter,"[150]

---

taxpayers who could avail themselves of FTA were about 250,000 in the case of a penalty for delinquency and approximately 1.2 million in the case of a penalty for nonpayment, but more than 90% of them did not receive FTA because most of them or their representatives did not know about FTA and there was not much action to make it known.

145. *See* footnote 147. FTA is also not applicable in the case of a penalty for underpayment of estimated tax.

146. Roughly the same practice is adopted in relation to IRC §6038 (Information reporting with respect to certain foreign corporations and partnerships) which establishes the obligation to file Form 5471.

147. *See* Figures 1.8.1 and 1.8.2 of the 2020 TAS report.

148. *See* pp. 119-131 of the 2020 TAS Report.

149. The burden of proof is basically on the taxpayer who is close to the documentary evidence. But, IRC §7941(a) provides that burden of proof shifts to IRS where a taxpayer produces credible evidence.

150. IRC §6662(c)(Negligence) states, "For purpose of this section, the term 'negligence' includes any failure to make a reasonable attempt to comply with the provisions of this title, and the term 'disregard' includes any careless, reckless, or intentional disregard." It has been confirmed in *Emmons v. Commissioner* ([1989] 92 T.C. 342) etc. that failure to file timely tax returns constitutes prima facie evidence of negligence.

declined in number significantly especially around 1997 to 1999, and it is pointed out that this decline intimates the high possibility that, although courts endorse the IRS's decisions to impose penalties in many cases, the IRS's claims for their application are sporadic, and the IRS's claims on the penalties are often withdrawn when taxpayers object to them. It is presumed that behind this, there must be the IRS's perception that persistence in the imposition of penalties can become an obstacle to the resolution of disputes over the reassessments.[151]

As is evident from the above, disputes over penalties arise for various reasons. At the litigation stage, quite highly litigated is the issue of abatement of penalties imposed on individuals,[152] and many of them claim reasonable cause prescribed in many penalty provisions as the reason for exempting the penalties.[153] For example, IRC §6651(a) provides for abatement of penalties imposed at the normal rate of 5% to 25% for non-filing and those imposed at the normal rate of 0.5% to 25% for nonpayment, provided that there is a "reasonable cause" for them and it can also be proven that it was not due to wilful neglect. [154] IRC §6664 (Definitions and special rules) (c) (reasonable cause exception for underpayments) (1) (In general) also provides, "No penalty shall be imposed under section 6662 or 6663 with respect to any portion of an underpayment if it is shown that there was reasonable cause for such portion that the taxpayer acted in good faith with respect to such portion." So, the exemption of a penalty on account of the requirements identical to the above IRC §6664(c)(1) is also applicable in the case of IRC §6663 (Imposition of fraud penalty), whose penalty rate is 75% on any part of underpayment of tax to be shown on a return being due to fraud.

Indeed, accuracy-related penalties are abated quite often on account of reasonable cause, etc. Figure 2.10 reveals that in the case of a negligence penalty, which constitutes one of the accuracy-related penalties and the number of its applications is larger than that of the others among them, there are some years (1998 and 1999 in particular) when there is not much difference in the number of it being imposed on individual taxpayers and the number of it abated later. While the introduction of IRC §6751 by the 1998 IRS Reform Act basically denied the IRS's use of penalties as bargaining chips for realizing settlement of disputes by agreement with taxpayers,[155] the IRS's stance on penalties has lately become more stringent. Against such background, there has lately arisen a general trend of decline in the number and percentage of cases where penalties are abated on account of reasonable cause, etc. Next, in (2),

151. *See* Richard Stark, A Principled Approach to Collection and Accuracy Related Penalties, *Tax Notes*, Apr. 2 (2001) p. 138.
152. *See* the 2005 TAS Report, p. 499. As for penalties other than IRC §6651, IRC §6654, and IRC §6662, disputes often arise as to whether prior written approval of a superior as required by IRC §6751(Procedural requirements) has been obtained in a timely manner and the approved rate of penalty is appropriate.
153. Penalties are also abated in the following cases: (i) IRS makes a mistake, (ii) the collection cost is not met, (iii) cases where the IRS approves payment of only a portion of the penalty. *See* 2020 IRS Data Book p. 61 for details.
154. *See* footnote 134 for IRC §6651(a). Having a "reasonable cause" usually means being not willfully negligent and acted in good faith, so here the focus is on the application scope of a "reasonable cause."
155. *See* 2 in Section 1 and footnote 33.

an analysis is to be made of the application scope of reasonable cause because it affects the number of abatement of penalties. In fact, the lack of clarity on this scope and the benefit of relief from the penalties (or applications of exceptions) constitute the main reasons for the large number of taxpayers claiming abatement of various kinds of penalties on account of reasonable cause.[156]

Figure 2.10 Number of Cases of Application/Abatement of Accuracy-Related Penalties (or a Negligence Penalty in particular) Related to Personal IT

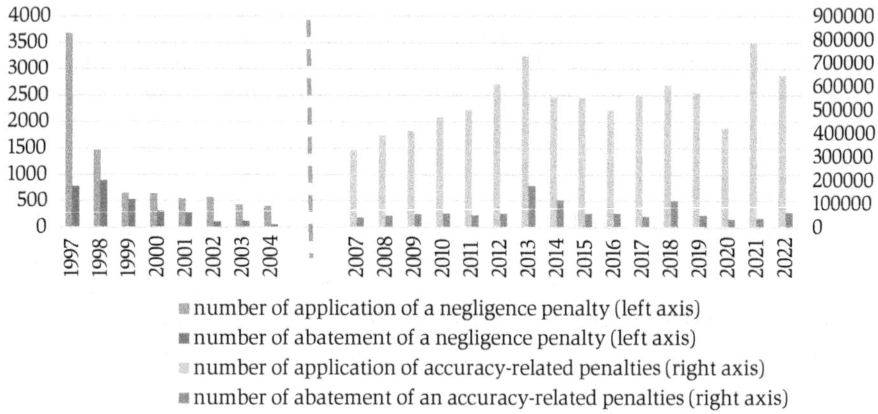

Source: 1997 ~ 2022 IRS Data Book: Table (Civil Penalties Assessed and Abated, by Tax and Type of Penalty).

(2) Reasonable Cause and Its Scope of Application

As for the application scope of reasonable cause, Treasury Regulations §1.6664-4 (Reasonable cause and good faith exception to section 6662 penalties) stipulates, "Generally, the most important factor is the extent of the taxpayer's effort to assess the taxpayer's proper tax liability. Circumstances that may indicate reasonable cause and good faith include an honest misunderstanding of fact or law that is reasonable in light of all of the facts and circumstances, including the experience, knowledge, and education of the taxpayer. An isolated computational or transcriptional error generally is not inconsistent with reasonable cause and good faith." Also, IRM 20.1.1.3.2.1 mentions, "Any reason that establishes a taxpayer exercised ordinary business care and prudence but nevertheless failed to comply with the tax law may be considered for

156. While such rules as IRC §1445 (Withholding of tax on dispositions of United States real property interests)(b)(Exemptions) and Treasury Regulations §1445-2(b)(Transferor not a foreign person)(2)(Transferor's certification of non-foreign status) are effective in curbing the potential disputes over penalties for the failure to timely withhold tax on the payment of domestic source income to a nonresident. *See* 2(2) in Section 3/footnote 95 of Chapter 1 for comparison with the status in Japan.

penalty relief." Then, IRM 20.1.1.3.2.2 (Ordinary business care and prudence) specifies, "a taxpayer may establish reasonable cause by providing facts and circumstances showing that they exercised ordinary business care and prudence," and the determination of whether the taxpayer exercised ordinary business care and prudence is made by reviewing such things as "taxpayer's reason," "compliance history," "length of time," "circumstances beyond the taxpayer's control," etc.

More specifically, for example, IRC §6404 (Abatements) (f) (Abatement of any penalty or addition to tax attributable to erroneous written advice by the Internal Revenue Service) provides, "In General—The Secretary shall abate any portion of any penalty or addition to tax attributable to erroneous advice furnished to the taxpayer in writing by an officer or employee of the Internal Revenue Service, acting in such officer's or employee's capacity." IRM also lists, as possible facts constituting reasonable cause, "Death, Serious Illness, or Unavoidable Absence," including a death or serious illness in the taxpayer's immediate family (IRM 1.1.3.2.2.1, 25/11/2011), "Fire, Casualty, Natural Disaster, or Other Disturbance" (IRM 20.1.1.3.2.2.2, 19/10/2020), "Unable to Obtain Records" (IRM 20.1.1.3.2.2.3, 11/12/2009), "Mistake Was Made" (IRM 20.1.1.3.2.2.4, 11/12/2009), "Erroneous Advice or Reliance" (IRM 20.1.1.3.3.4, 21/11/2017), "Ignorance of the Law" (IRM 20.1.1.3.2.2.6, 25/11/2011), "Forgetfulness" (IRM 5/8/2014), "Inaccessible Notices" (IRM 20.1.1.3.2.2.8, 29/3/2023), "Undue Hardship" (IRM 20.1.1.3.3.3, 5/8/2014), "Written Advice From the IRS" (IRM 20.1.1.3.3.4.1, 25/11/2011), "Oral Advice From the IRS" (IRM 20.1.1.3.3.4.2, 11/12/2009), etc.

It is pointed out that "reasonable cause" claimed by taxpayers could be generally categorized under (i) mental illness, (ii) difficulty in obtaining books and records, (iii) advice from tax experts, (iv) responsibility of the spouse and other representatives, (v) ignorance of the law,[157] or (vi) "zero return" filing.[158] In many cases, the above (i), (ii) and (vi) are asserted to avoid the application of penalties for non-reporting and late filing, the above (iv) is to avoid penalties for underreporting, and the above (iii) and (v) are relied on in both. Now that, as Figure 2.10 divulges, lately, there are some years when the ratio of abatement of accuracy-related penalties is pretty high, there must be many cases where the taxpayers' assertion of a penalty abatement on account of reasonable cause based on the above (i) to (vi) was accepted.[159] While there must also

157. Treasury Regulations §1.6664-4(c)(Reliance on opinion or advice) prescribes, "For example, the taxpayer's education, sophistication and business experience will be relevant in determining whether the taxpayer's reliance on tax advice was reasonable and made in good faith. In *Simonsen v. Commissioner* ([2018] 150 TC No. 8), the Tax Court ruled that it would not penalize taxpayers for mistakes of law in a complicated subject area that lacks clear guidance and granted waivers of 6662 penalties while the taxpayer's educational level was high.

158. *See* the 2005 TAS Report, pp. 499-500. A "zero return filing" is the filing of a nearly blank return to avoid the imposition of penalties for non-reporting under IRC §6651. As it is evident from the aforementioned Tax Court judgment on the *Cabirac* case (*see* footnote 138), etc., it is not considered a return for federal IT purposes, and it could be subjected to the penalty under IRC §6673 for its frivolous nature. *See* the 2005 TAS Report, pp. 511-513 for details.

159. For example, from June 2018 to May 2019, the taxpayers' success rate (full or partial cancellation rate) in lawsuits over "accuracy-related penalties" was about 34% (30% for 2019 June to May 2020 and June 2017 to May 2018). For details, *see* the 2017 TAS Report, p. 430; the 2019 TAS Report, p. 110; and the 2020 TAS Report, p. 168.

be cases in which it is difficult to determine whether an accuracy-related penalty is to be abated. Especially in cases falling under the above (iii) (advice from tax experts), there might arise on and off a question of what criteria are to be relied on in determining whether or not the taxpayer's assertion of "reasonable cause" based on erroneous advice from a tax expert is to be accepted.

The Supreme Court judgment on *Boyle v. United States* ([1985] 469 U.S. 241) may shed some light on what the above criteria are like. In this case, the appellee had submitted the necessary documents related to the federal estate tax return to the attorney-at-law and received a reply that the return would be submitted within the filing deadline. But the appellee was penalized under IRC §6651(a) for filing the return after the deadline, so the appellee argued that the late filing was caused by the agent who failed to check the submission deadline and that it falls under the reasonable cause stipulated in the proviso of this paragraph. The Supreme Court was well aware of many court judgments in favor of those taxpayers who asserted the application of the reasonable cause on account of erroneous advice from lawyers regarding legal issues.[160] However, the Court dismissed the appellee's assertion and overturned the preceding Seventh Circuit Court of Appeals judgment ([1983] 710 F.2d 1251) by ruling that this case differs from those cases in that it was about the filing deadline and does not concern itself with a question of law so that the appellee neither need to be a tax expert to know that there is a deadline for a tax return filing nor need special training to make an effort to confirm that the filing of the return is made within the deadline.

Some may find further clarification on the above view expressed in the *Boyle* case in the judgment of the Third Circuit Court of Appeals judgment on *the Estate of John RH Thouron v. United States* ([2014] No. 13-1603) in which the Court divided the issue of reliance on an expert's advice into three categories: (i) a taxpayer relies on an agent for the ministerial task of filing or paying, (ii) a taxpayer, in reliance on the advice of his accountant or attorney, files a return after the actual due date but within the time the adviser erroneously told him, (iii) an accountant or attorney advises a taxpayer on a matter of tax law. Then, the Court specified that the *Boyle* case fits into the above (i) category and cases coming under the above (ii) or (iii) are outside of its purview. In fact, the District Court for the Middle District of Pennsylvania on *the Estate of Esther Hake et al. v. United States* ([2017] Civil No. 1.15-CV-13823) relied on this categorization. In this case, a penalty based on IRC §6651(a) was imposed on the plaintiff who filed a federal estate tax return late on account of his attorney's misunderstanding that its filing deadline was extended, and the Court held that this case comes under the category (ii) and therefore the plaintiff's claim for the exemption of the penalty on account of reasonable cause should be accepted.

While some others, including the Ninth Circuit Court of Appeals judgment on *Knappe v. United States* ([2013] 713 F 3d 1164), did not follow suit. In this case, the accountant submitted Form 4786 (Application for extension of time to file a return and/or pay U.S. estate (and generation-skipping transfer) tax) at the request of the executor/appellant and was granted the extension, but the accountant misunderstood

160. The Court cites, as one of those cases in which such judgments were handed down, the Supreme Court judgment on *Lane-Wells Co. v. Commissioner* ([1944] 321 U.S. 219).

the extended filing deadline to be one year (in fact it was six months) and misled the appellant to file after the extended deadline passed.[161] The appellant claimed reasonable cause for the waiver of the penalty imposed in accordance with IRC §6651(a)(1), and this case should, in accordance with the *Thouron* case, be categorized under (ii) (a taxpayer, in reliance on the advice of his accountant or attorney, files a return after the actual due date but within the time the adviser erroneously told him). But the Court dismissed the appellant's claim by mentioning that an executor may only reasonably rely on an agent's advice about substantive tax matters and ascertaining a deadline is within the ambit of the executor's non-delegable duties because a deadline is a nonsubstantive matter,[162] and any other result would incentivize an agent to claim that he gave erroneous advice to the executor whether or not he did so.

As mentioned above, there remains uncertainty on how the view shown by the Supreme Court on the *Boyle* case should be interpreted, but it seems to be at least clear that a taxpayer's reliance on the erroneous advice of a tax agent on a substantive matter of tax law could be reasonable cause for the exemption of a penalty. Moreover, the aforementioned Treasury Regulations §1.6664-4 indicates that there are many other cases where "reasonable cause" could be asserted to win the waiver of the penalties. Therefore, the hurdle to clear for the abatement of penalties based on "reasonable cause" is by no means so high as "justifiable reason" laid down under Japan's AGRNT §65, etc., and this difference must be one of the main reasons for making "accuracy-related penalties" one of the top ten "most litigated issues" on and off. Another related point standing in contrast to a strict penalty in Japan is the application of reasonable cause based on 6664(C)(1) in the case of fraud penalty, which is to be applied pursuant to IRC §6663 at the rate of 75% of the portion of the underpayment which is attributable to fraud on the taxpayer.[163] This heavy penalty with such treatment might also work toward inducing taxpayers to dispute the application of this penalty much more strongly than a strict penalty in Japan, which cannot be exempted by a "justifiable reason."

161. IRC §6081(Extension of time for filing returns)(a)(General rule) states, "The Secretary may grant a reasonable extension of time for filing any return, declaration, statement, or other document required by this tittle or by regulations. Except in the case of taxpayers who are abroad, no such extension shall be for more than 6 months."
162. Indeed, on the *Boyle* case, the Supreme Court stated, "Most taxpayers are not competent to discern error in the substantive advice of an accountant or attorney. To require the taxpayer to challenge the attorney... would nullify the very purpose of seeking the advice of a presumed expert in the first place."
163. *See* 2(1) of Section 4 for IRC §6663 and IRC §6664(C)(1). In Japan, as mentioned in 2(3) in Section 3 and footnotes 104 to 106 of Chapter 1, even if the tax agent is to be blamed for fraud (or falsification or concealment of relevant facts on the tax return), the strict penalty on the taxpayer cannot be exempted unless the taxpayer is totally unaware of fraud, and even if he was totally unaware of it, an underreporting penalty on it cannot be exempted on account of justifiable reason unless a tax official is also involved in the fraud.

3 Disputes on Collection Issues

IRC §6331 (Levy and distraint) (a) (Authority of Secretary) provides, "If any person liable to pay any tax neglects or refuses to pay the same within 10 days after notice and demand, it shall be lawful for the Secretary to collect such tax (...) by levy upon all property and rights to property (...) belonging to such person or on which there is a lien provided in this chapter for the payment of such tax.[164] "Moreover, before the 1998 IRS Reform Act introduced IRC §6320 and IRC §6330, which provide for the taxpayers' rights for CDP hearings at the Office of Appeals,[165] the Secretary could go through this tax collection procedure without being interrupted by any administrative appeals, as the Supreme Court, in *Murry's Lessee v. Hoboken Land and Improvement Co.* ([1956] 59 U.S. 272), held that a distress warrant issued by the Solicitor of the Treasury was an exercise of executive, and not of judicial power and it is not inconsistent with that part of the Constitution which prohibits a citizen from being deprived of his liberty or property without due process of law. Therefore, before 1998, tax delinquents who wanted to dispute the lawfulness of collection procedures on them had to file a tax refund suit or a damage suit to court, and the number of cases disputing collection cases remained relatively small for some time even after 1998 as the analysis in 1 in Section 1 and Figure 2.5 show.

Certainly, even before 1998, there were some in favor of the idea of allowing administrative appeals against collection action. For example, in *Ryskamp v. Commissioner* ([2015] No. 14-1042), the Court of Appeals for the District of Columbia stated, "Post-payment review is almost certainly too late to redress a taxpayer's objections to the collection process. Requiring a taxpayer to pay his tax liability in full before he can obtain review of his claims about payment process or terms—such as that he would suffer economic hardship without an installment plan or offer-in-compromise—effectively nullifies the utility of such review." However, once CDP hearings were introduced, some have come to show concerns about negative aspects of CDP hearings at the Office of Appeals because some tax delinquents requested CDP hearings based on frivolous arguments. In fact, the above *Ryskamp* case was one of such cases, and the above Court of Appeals ruled that the IRS did not abuse its discretion in failing to respond substantively to Ryskamp's arguments and also referred to the Appeals office's correspondence with Ryskamp in which the Appeals Office specifically identified his argument as one that reflected a desire to delay or impede federal tax administration.

CDP requests possessing such merits and demerits mentioned above have, as IRC§6330(e) dictates, an effect of suspending collection action until the review by the Office of Appeals is over, so some tax delinquents did make CDP requests primarily for the sake of buying time. This resulted in an increase in the IRS's burden of dealing with

164. IRC §6331(b)(Seizure and sale of property) stipulates, "The term, 'levy' as used in this title includes the power of distraint and seizure by any means."
165. *See* footnote 6 for the rules of IRC §6320(a). IRC §6330(e) states, "if a hearing is requested ..., the levy actions which are the subject of the requested hearing and the running of any period of limitations ... shall be suspended for the period during which such hearing, and appeals therein, are pending."

requests for CDP hearings. This situation was compounded further by the increasing trend in the number of CDP requests[166] until this trend was gradually halted by some legislative and administrative/judicial actions. Those actions include, in particular, the Tax Court's active application of the aforementioned IRC §6673(a)(1) which authorizes the Tax Court to order the payment of a penalty not in excess of USD 25,000 in the case of procedures instituted primarily for delay, etc., and the adoption of IRC §6702 (Frivolous tax submissions) (b) (Civil penalty for specified frivolous submissions) (1) (imposition of penalty) which authorizes the IRS Commissioner to impose a USD 5,000 penalty on anyone who submits "a specified frivolous submission" and IRC §6330(g) (Frivolous requests for hearing, etc.) which authorizes the IRS Commissioner to treat "a specified frivolous submission" as if it were never submitted and it shall not be subject to any further administrative or judicial review.[167]

However, as for the treatment under the latter part of IRC §6330(g) above, it has practically been denied by some recent court decisions. For example, in the above-mentioned *Ryskamp* case (2015), the Court of Appeals agreed with the IRS and concluded that his CDP request was frivolous, but it nevertheless ruled that the denial of a petition for a hearing under IRC §6330(g) is subject to judicial review because, if no judicial review whatsoever were available, taxpayers would be without recourse when the IRS incorrectly concludes that their requests for hearings are entirely frivolous and such result is not what Congress cannot have intended.[168] Then, the Court affirmed the Tax Court's conclusion that the IRS abused its discretion in rejecting Ryskamp's request for a hearing without first articulating the grounds for determining its frivolousness. Judge Brown expressed his dissenting opinion, and the IRS's Office of the Chief Counsel issued a notice (CC-2016 -008) expressing the IRS's intention that it does not necessarily raise objections to the Tax Court's authority to examine the issue of whether or not a hearing opportunity was unfairly deprived but seek for the Office of Appeals to explain fully the reasons for not granting a hearing opportunity whenever it is appropriate to do so.

IRC §6330(g) contains such a difficult question as mentioned above, and how it should be interpreted and applied in practice would certainly affect the number of disputes and litigations on "collection issues." As for "offer-in-compromise," which has also been a highly disputed issue among "collection issues," the main reason for it being highly disputed must lie in the benefit IRC §7122 (Compromises) grants to the taxpayers whose requests for reduction in payable tax amount might be accepted by

166. Joint Committee of Taxation (JCT) pointed out that only about 5% of those who requested for CDP hearings make frivolous allegations, but the resulting burden on the IRS has become disproportionately heavy. *See* the Report of the Joint Committee on Taxation Relating to the Internal Revenue Service As Required by IRS Reform and Restructuring Act of 1998 (JCX-53-03) Appendix (p. 22).

167. As noted in 1 of Section 4, IRC §6673 constitutes an issue that often ranks among the top 10 "most litigated issues." IRC §6702(b)(2)(A) defines "a specified frivolous submission" to be one which is based on a position which the Secretary has identified as frivolous under subsection (c), or reflects a desire to delay or impede the administration of Federal tax laws.

168. Judgments similar in content to that of the Court of Appeal judgment in the *Ryskamp* case are also found in the *Buczek v. Commissioner* ([2014] 143 TC. 301) and *Thornberry v. Commissioner* (136 TC 356 (2011)).

the IRS.[169] As IRM 5.8.4.2 (Effective Tax Administration (ETA) and Doubt as to Collectability with Special Circumstances (DATCSC)) and IRM 5.8.11 (Effective Tax Administration) indicate, in investigating any offer-in-compromise, the IRS gives consideration to such factors as economic hardship of the taxpayer, public policy or equity, etc. and it is granted in cases where compromise would not undermine compliance with tax laws and a fairly large number of requests for "offer-in-compromise" have been accepted.[170] This merit of "offer-in-compromise" for delinquent taxpayers should be attractive enough for some of them to challenge the IRS's negative determination on their requests for offer-in-compromise, at least at the administrative review stage, where the costs for the challenges remain comparatively low.

4 Disputes on Innocent Spouse Issues

IRC §6013 (Joint returns of income tax by husband and wife) provides the option of filing a joint income tax return, but a joint IT return gives rise to "joint and several liability."[171] It is, in most cases, preferable, in terms of the combined amount of IT payable, to opt for a joint return filing, but "joint and several liability" may compound the risk and burden in a case where a joint return is an understatement of income tax. However, IRC §6015 (Relief from joint and several liability on joint return) (b) (1) stipulates that if the other individual filing the joint return establishes that in signing the return, he or she did not know or had no reason to know, that there was such understatement, and taking into account all the facts and circumstances, it is inequitable to hold the other individual liable for the deficiency in tax for such taxable year attributable to such understatement, then the other individual shall be relieved of liability for tax (including interest, penalties, and other amounts) for such taxable year to the extent such liability is attributable to such understatement. Therefore, for a taxpayer who claims having been unaware of his spouse's underreporting of income, it becomes critical whether IRC §6015 is applicable to him.[172]

Before 1971, there was no exception to the "joint and several liability" rule for those who file a joint IT return, so there were court rulings like *Scudder v. Commissioner* ([1967] 48 T.C. 36) in which Tax Court sympathized with the taxpayer who had

169. IRC §7122 prescribes, "The Secretary may compromise any civil or criminal case arising under the internal revenue laws prior to reference to the Department of Justice for prosecution or defense; and the Attorney General or his delegate may compromise any such case after reference to the Department of Justice for prosecution or defense."

170. This implies a broad discretion of the IRS on "offer-in-compromise." IRS Data Book 2020 p. 57 shows that since 2011, as high as 30% to 42% of the requests for offer-in-compromise submitted in the Form 656 (Offer-in-Compromise) have been accepted. It is explained that such high level of acceptance is due mostly to the fact that taxpayers can easily check their eligibility for making requests for it by following the checklist (Offer-in-Compromise Pre-Qualifier) provided by IRS.

171. IRC §6013(d)(Special rules) states, "If a joint return is made, the tax shall be computed on the aggregate income and the liability with respect to the tax shall be joint and several."

172. Moreover, "innocent spouse" relief could also be applicable partially in a case where the other spouse is only unaware of a portion of the erroneous item. *See* Publication 971 (Innocent spouse relief).

to suffer from the consequence of the irresponsible action of her spouse.[173] Cases of such sufferings were reduced by the introduction in 1971 of IRC §6013(e) (Spouse relieved of liability in certain cases). Then, the 1984 Tax Reform Act (PL. No. 98-369) §424 (Innocent spouse relieved of liability in certain cases) and 1998 IRS Reform Act §3201 (Relief from joint and several liability on joint return) led to the introduction of the abovementioned IRC §6015. IRC §6015 replaced the above IRC §6013(e), and the hurdle for exemption from "joint and several liability" has also become lower because it also abolished one of the preconditions to be met for the application of "innocent spouse relief" (i.e., a joint return had to be filed from which there was an omission from gross income attributable to one spouse amounting to more than twenty-five percent of the total gross income stated on the return) laid down under IRC §6013(e).

But, the precondition of the spouse having no reason to know the omission of income of the other spouse to be met for the application of "innocent spouse relief" under IRC §6013(e) remained under IRC §6015(b)(1)(C), and the uncertainty surrounding this phrase is one of the main reasons for the increase in the number of disputes over "innocent spouse issues." Such ambiguity seems to have manifested in not a few cases, including *Estate of Vella v. Commissioner* ([1982] 51 TCM). In this case, the Tax Court acknowledged that most of the husband's assets were owned before the marriage and that there were some extravagant expenditures compared to the reported amount, but such expenditures were not so much as to make his wife/plaintiff doubtful about the correctness of the reported amount. The Tax Court also noted that there is no evidence that the plaintiff, who left financial matters to her husband and accountant, knew the amount of money her husband made from the sale of the business. Then, the Tax Court ruled that, although she had some knowledge of her family's finances and her husband's investments, the extent of her knowledge was not sufficient to enable her to realize that there was an undeclared income so that she fulfilled the burden of proof that she had no reason to know the existence of the undeclared income.

While Court of Appeals for the Sixth Circuit judgment on *Sally A. Shea v. Commissioner* ([1986] 780. F.2d 561, 566) suggests that the hurdle to clear to fulfill the burden of proof on "no reason to know" is by no means low. In this case, the Court acknowledged that a standard to be applied in determining whether a taxpayer had reason to know of omissions is whether a reasonable person under the circumstances of the taxpayer at the time of signing the return could be expected to know of the omissions, and in this case, she knew of her husband's drinking problem and deteriorating physical/mental condition during the concerned years and had reason to suspect his inability to properly handle financial matters. The Court also pointed out that, under these circumstances, a prudent taxpayer would at least have inquired into her spouse's personal financial and tax situation, thereby discovering the omissions, but she did not make such efforts. Furthermore, the Court noted that the petitioner was an officer of the husband's company, and the participation in a spouse's business

173. In this case, the Tax Court ruled in favor of the IRS that taxed the undeclared embezzled income and imposed a fraud penalty (50% at that time) while the wife had no knowledge of her husband's embezzlement and had not profited from it.

affairs has commonly been held in some court rulings to negate an innocent spouse claim.[174] In conclusion, the Court ruled that the petitioner did not satisfy the "no reason to know" requirement.

IRC §6015(b)(1)(D), which provides for another precondition to be fulfilled for the application of "innocent spouse" relief, also has a problem of lack of transparency and predictability because the question of its fulfillment is determined whether it is inequitable, by taking into account all the facts and circumstances, to hold the other individual liable for the deficiency in tax for such taxable year attributable to such understatement. The IRS's determination on this is to be made by considering various factors, including the following: (i) marital status, (ii) economic hardship, (iii) knowledge or reason to know, (iv) legal obligation, (v) significant benefit, (vii) compliance with income tax laws, (viii) mental or physical health,[175] but the determination of equitability based on these factors may not be easy in some cases. For example, on the above factor (v), in the Circuit Court of Appeals judgment on *Clevenger v. Commissioner* ([1987] 826 F.2d 1379), the Court ruled that in this case not only improvements were made to the properties owned by the corporations whose total interests were equally held by the appellant and his spouse and they formed the basis for the tax deficiencies but also the appellant knew or should have known that his spouse received significant benefit from this, so the innocent spouse relief is not applicable to the appellant.

Whereas in the case of the *Estate of Cardulla v. Commissioner* ([1986] 51 T.C.M. 1511), it is pointed out that the benefit gained by the plaintiff was larger than that in the abovementioned Clevenger case,[176] but the Tax Court ruled in favor of the plaintiff. In this case, the Court found the following: (i) the plaintiff's involvement (e.g., as a sales clerk) in her husband's business was limited, (ii) the plaintiff's standard of living during the concerned periods did not increase in such a way that she would have been effectively on notice that the income earned by her husband was greatly in excess of that which her spouse reported on their federal IT returns, (iii) some assets were jointly held by the plaintiff and her spouse, but the plaintiff did not benefit significantly from her ownership in them, (iv) the benefits received by the plaintiff as a result of the unreported income were in the nature of ordinary family support, which is not a sufficient basis to support a finding of significant benefit as it is so ruled by *Terzian v. Commissioner* ([Dec. 36,348], 72 T.C. 1164, 1172, 1173 (1979)), etc.[177] So, the Court concluded that the plaintiff has sustained her burden of proving her entitlement to the benefits afforded to an innocent spouse pursuant to IRC §6013(e).

---

174. This Court cited, as examples of such rulings, *Quinn v. Commissioner* ([1974] 62 T.C. 223) and *Sonnenborn v. Commissioner* ([1971] 57 T.C. 373).
175. As for details on these factors, *see supra* Publication 971 and irs.gov/businesses/small-business-self-employed/innocent-spouse-relief.
176. Michael F. Lax, The Innocent Spouse Provision under Section 6013(e) of the Internal Revenue Code: Relief or Refuse, *University of Arkansas at Little Rock Law Review*, Vol. 12, No. 1 (1989) p. 50.
177. In the *Terzian* case, the plaintiff, who was 53 years old at the time of the trial, had received USD 155,000 as an alimony from her spouse who evaded IT, but the Tax Court ruled that the innocent spouse relief was applicable to her because it was normal support and not enough for her to live the rest of her life.

As is evident from above, there are demerits of opting for a joint return filing, and its demerits become particularly acute in such a case where a taxpayer does not have information and evidence to support his innocence on the omission of income by his spouse.[178] As for the IRS, joint return filings also entail a demerit of the administrative burden caused by taxpayers who claim the applicability of the "innocent spouse" relief. But, joint return filings also have some merits for the IRS as well because the joint and several liability applies not only to the tax liability shown on the return but also to any additional tax liability the IRS determines to be due (even if the additional tax is due to income, deductions, or credits of the other spouse or former spouse), and the IRS can still collect them from either of the joint return filers (even if they later divorce and their divorce decree states that either one of them will be solely responsible for the tax).[179] It is not clear how many taxpayers find merit in the lack of certainty on the application scope of IRC §6015, while it is positive that such uncertainty has worked in not a few cases toward incentivizing taxpayers (including those who knew or should have known the omission of income in their joint returns) to assert the application of the provision.

5 Disputes on Gross Income Issues and Trade or Business Expenses Issues

(1) Gross Income Issues

Gross income issues are consistently among the top ten "most litigated issues" mainly because, under IRC §61(a) (General definitions),[180] there sometimes arise such questions: (i) Is economic profit in question taxable income?; (ii) Is income in question attributable to the taxpayer?[181] For example, the latter question (ii) often arose on a contingent fee to be paid to an attorney for his client/taxpayer's successful litigation, and in such cases, some courts answered the question negatively for such reasons: (A) some state laws recognize attorneys' full property rights to the attorney's contingent fees; (B) a contingency fee does not practically belong to the taxpayer; (C) if a contingency fee is taxable income of a taxpayer, the taxpayer who opts for itemized deduction may not deduct it fully in some cases.[182] But the validity of such answer was negated by the Supreme Court judgment on *Banks v. Commissioner* ([2005] 543 U.S. 426) in which the Court ruled that, as held by the Supreme Court judgment on *Lucas v.*

178. Richard Beck, The Innocent Spouse Problem: Joint and Several Liability for Income Taxes Should Be Repeated, *Vanderbilt Law Review*, Vol. 43:317(1990), p. 363.
179. *See* IRS Publication 971 (10/2014, Innocent Spouse Relief).
180. IRC §61(a) states, "gross income means all income from whatever source derived, including (but not limited to) the following items": and lists fourteen income types.
181. Identical questions on gross income frequently arise in Japan as well while, in Japan, questions on the scope of taxable inherited assets and deductible debts are also frequently disputed. *See*, 3(3)-(4) of Section 2 in Chapter 1.
182. For example, in the Circuit Court judgment on *Banaitis v. Commissioner* (340 F.3d 1074, 9th Cir. 2003), the Court recognized attorneys' proprietary rights to the contingency fee in accordance with the Oregon State Law at that time and ruled in favor of the taxpayer not including in his gross income the fees directly paid to the attorney.

Earl ([1930] 281 U.S.), under the "anticipatory assignment of income doctrine," a taxpayer cannot exclude an economic gain from gross income by assigning the gain in advance to another party because gains should be taxed to those who earn them.[183]

The "anticipatory assignment of income doctrine" referred to in the above Supreme Court judgment on *Banks* case is a derivative of the "Fruits and tree doctrine," and it comes from the above *Lucas* case (1930) in which the Supreme Court judgment held, "the tax could not be escaped by anticipatory arrangements and contracts, however skillfully devised, to prevent the salary when paid from vesting even for a second in the man who earned it....no distinction can be taken according to the motives belonging to the arrangement by which the fruits are attributed to a different tree from that on which they grew." While, as the Supreme Court referred to in the above *Banks* case, the 2004 American Jobs Creation Act amended IRC, and currently IRC §62 (Adjusted gross income) (a) provides, "the term "adjusted gross income" means, in the case of an individual, gross income minus the following deductions:...(20) Any deduction allowable under this chapter for attorney fees and courts costs paid by, or on behalf of, the taxpayer in connection with any action involving a claim of unlawful discrimination...or a claim made under section 1862(b)(3)(A) of the Social Security Act."

As for the abovementioned question (i), it often arose in connection with IRC §104 (Compensation for injuries or sickness) and IRC §105 (Amounts received under accident and health plans) (b) (Amounts expended for medical care). Those provisions exclude economic benefits derived from injury or illness from taxable income, but their scope of application is not so clear. Consequently, such insufficient clarity gave rise to some litigations at the Tax Court, including *Threlkeld v. Commissioner, Inc.* ([1986] 87 TC 1294).[184] In this case, at issue was whether the plaintiff's agreed-upon damage compensation from the other should be excluded from his gross income. The Tax Court, after emphasizing that IRC §104(a)(2) states, "gross income does not include – (1)...(2) the amount of any damages (other than punitive damages) received (whether by suit or agreement and whether as lump sums or as periodic payments) on account of personal physical injuries or physical sickness," acknowledged that it presents a conceptual challenge in terms of its interpretation, but ruled that exclusion under IRC §104 will be appropriate if compensatory damages are received on account of any invasion of the rights that an individual possesses, so the compensatory damages received by the petitioner are excludable from his gross income.

Whereas, in *Vincent v. Commissioner* (TC Memo. 2005-95), the plaintiff filed a lawsuit against the employer, settled the lawsuit by agreement, received the settlement money, paid a portion of it to the attorney under a contingency fee agreement, and claimed that the settlement money should be excluded from gross income because it falls under IRC §104 (a)(2) as compensation for physical and mental damages. But the Tax Court cited *Robinson v. Commissioner* ([1994] 102 TC 116), in which the agreement between the parties was not taken at face value by the Court for determining

183. The Court also specified that the "anticipatory assignment of income doctrine" is not limited to instances where the precise dollar value of the assigned income is known in advance.
184. *See* the 2005 TAS Report, pp. 488-497, for further details.

its true nature because the settlement was "uncontested, nonadversarial, and entirely tax motivated"[185] and confirmed that the non-arm's length pretense reflected in the settlement agreement in this case does not reflect the reality of the underlying lawsuit, which was submitted to the jury as a discrimination action rather than as one arising from "personal physical injuries" to the petitioner. Then, the Court ruled that 63% of the settlement money constitutes gross income because they do not fall within the reach of section 104(a)(2).

Another theme on gross income is economic benefits granted by a corporation to its shareholders, which is often disputed from the perspective of whether or not they are constructive dividends under IRC §301 (Dividend received).[186] In *Dynamo Holdings* (2018) case referred to in 2(1) in this Section, the Tax Court applied the two-prong test to determine whether the difference between the undervalued price of the asset transferred from the entity/plaintiff in the U.S. to the shareholder in Canada and its fair market value constitutes constructive dividend,[187] and it found that both of the subjective and objective prongs are satisfied because such transfer allowed the shareholder to exercise control over such funds or property either directly or indirectly through some instrumentality other than the transferor corporation and the transfer occurred primarily for the common shareholder's personal benefit rather than for a valid business purpose. The Court also upheld the IRS's imposition of penalties under IRC §6651(a) (Addition to tax) (1) and IRC §6656(a) (Underpayment of deposits) by dismissing the plaintiff's claim that the plaintiff had reasonable cause for failure to timely file and timely deposit.

(2) Trade or Business Expenses Issues

The reason why trade or business expenses have often been one of the top 10 "most litigated issues" lies in the difficulty of determining in some cases whether some expenses of individual business proprietors and corporations are trade or business expenses. In order for expenses to be deductible under IRC §162 (Trade or business expenses), generally (i) they must accrue from profit-making activities as required under IRC §183(Activities not engaged in for profit),[188] (ii) they must be "ordinary and

185. In the *Robinson* case, the Tax Court ruled that the part of the settlement amount paid to plaintiffs for tort falls under IRC §104(a)(2) while the other part paid for the breach of the contract constitutes gross income but the Court of Appeals for the Fifth Circuit judgment ([1995] No. 94-41023) partially reversed the Tax Court judgment by denying the punitive damage received by the taxpayer to be included in the former.
186. According to the 2005 TAS Report, other frequently disputed issues on gross income include unreported income, disability and social security benefits and tax-advantaged retirement accounts.
187. 26 CFR §1.301-1 (Rules applicable with respect to distributions of money and other property)(j)(Transfer for less than fair market value) stipulates, "If property is transferred by a corporation to a shareholder which is not a corporation for an amount less than its fair market value in a sale or exchange, such shareholder shall be treated as having received a distribution to which section 301 applies."
188. IRC §280A(c)(5), whose interpretation became a problem in *Scott* case (1985) referred to in 3 of Section 3, has expenses deduction requirement similar to that in IRC §183(b)(2), so this case

necessary" expenses in carrying on any trade or business,[189] so some types of expenses are not deductible under IRC §274 (Disallowance of certain entertainment, etc., expense) (a) (Entertainment, amusement, recreation, or qualified transportation fringes),[190] (iii) taxpayers might be required to keep and submit books, records, etc. in accordance with IRC §6001 (Notice or regulations requiring records, statements, and special returns) to substantiate that the concerned expenses are deductible.[191] However, it may be difficult in some cases to determine whether or not some expenses fall under which categories of expenses or meet these requirements, and such difficulty has most frequently manifested regarding the above requirement (ii) ("ordinary and necessary" expenses).[192]

A prominent case that provides a useful guideline for determining whether the above (i) condition is met is the Supreme Court judgment on *Commissioner v. Groetzinger* ([1987] 480 U.S. 23). In this case, the IRS found the respondent's 1978 undeclared profit and loss arisen from his betting activities and claimed that those activities are not engaged in for profit, so a portion of the respondent's gambling-loss deduction was, under IRC as it existed in 1978, subject to a minimum tax under §56(a) of the Code because the gambling-loss deduction to which he was entitled was an item of tax preference that could be lessened by certain deductions that were attributable to a trade or business carried on by the taxpayer. But the Court dismissed the IRS's claim by ruling that if one's gambling activity is pursued full-time, in good faith, and with regularity, to the production of income for a livelihood and is not a mere hobby,[193] it is a trade or business. The Court also acknowledged that the difficulty rests in the Code's wide utilization in various contexts of the term "trade or business," but, in the absence of an all-purpose definition by statute or regulation, an attempt judicially to formulate and impose a test for all situations would be counterproductive.[194]

The difficulty of determining whether or not the above (ii) condition ("ordinary and necessary expenses") is fulfilled manifested in the Supreme Court judgment on *Deputy v. Du Pont* ([1940] 308 U.S. 488, 489). In this case, at issue was whether the

also serves as a guideline for interpreting this provision (calculation of amount of expenses deductible under this provision).

189. Japan's Article 37 of IT does not have in words the requirement of being ordinary for a business proprietor's expenses to be deductible while some claim that it could be a requirement. *See* 1(1) of Section 2 in Chapter 1.

190. While in Japan, entertainment expenses of a business proprietor are generally deductible for ITA purposes. *See* 1(1) in Section 2 of Chapter 1.

191. IRC §6001 states, "Whenever in the judgment of the Secretary it is necessary, he may require any person, by notice served upon such person or by regulations, to make such returns, render such statements, or keep such records, as the Secretary deems sufficient to show whether or not such person is liable to tax under this title."

192. *See* the 2005 TAS Report Table 3.4.1. These reasons are also more or less the causes for 【necessary expenses】 in Japan to be one of the < <highly disputed themes> >.

193. IRC §183(d)(presumption) prescribes, "If the gross income derived from an activity for 3 or more of the taxable years in the period of 5 consecutive taxable years which ends with the taxable year exceeds the deductions attributable to such activity (...), then, unless the Secretary establishes to the contrary, such activity shall be presumed...to be an activity engaged in for profit."

194. This judgment contains dissenting opinions of a few judges and the Equity and Fiscal Responsibility Act of 1982 made gambling not a trade or business.

amount the appellee paid in accordance with the loan agreement concluded to improve the efficiency of the business of the corporation in which the appellee was a shareholder was an ordinary and necessary expense for the business of the appellee who was involved in various investments. In this judgment, references were made not only to the Supreme Court's judgment on *Welch v. Helvering* ([1933] 290 U.S. 111), in which it was stated that an obligation to pay has arisen is not sufficient and what is crucial and controlling is the kind of transaction out of which the obligation arose and its normalcy in the particular business,[195] but also to the Supreme Court judgment on *Burnet v. Clark* ([1932] 287 U.S. 419) in which it was confirmed that "ordinary and necessary expenses" are limited to those directly connected with the taxpayer's business.[196] Then, the Supreme Court held that even assuming that the respondent's activity of increasing his property constitutes a business, the payment of this amount does not constitute a deductible "ordinary and necessary expense."

In fact, CFR, Title 26, Chapter 1 (Internal Revenue Service, Department of the Treasury) §1.162-1 (Business expenses) (a) (In general) also states, "Business expenses deductible from gross income include the ordinary and necessary expenditures directly connected with or pertaining to the taxpayer's trade or business." In addition, *Commissioner v. Tellier* ([1966] 383 U.S. 687) presents an interesting point. In this case, at issue was whether the respondent, who was a securities dealer and found to be guilty of violating securities laws, etc., could deduct as ordinary and necessary expense the attorney's fee for his criminal trial. In this judgment, the Supreme Court confirmed that the origin and character of the claim with respect to which an expense was incurred is the controlling basic test of whether the expense was "business" or "personal," and it has consistently construed the term "necessary" as imposing only the minimal requirement that the expense be "appropriate and helpful for the development of the taxpayer's business. Then, the Court held that, so long as the attorney fee in question is "ordinary" and "necessary" expenses within the meaning of §162(a), its deductibility cannot be denied on the ground of public policy in principle.[197]

While it is also necessary that, in principle, in order for "ordinary and necessary expenses" to be deductible, the aforementioned requirement (iii) (books, records, etc., to be kept and its deductibility to be substantiated) should be met. But the Second Circuit Court of Appeals judgment on *Cohan v. Commissioner* ([1930] 39 F.2d 540) made a notable change to this requirement. The Board of Appeals decision ([1928] 11B.TA 743),[198] which preceded this Court of Appeals judgment, sustained the

195. In this *Welch* case, the nature of a "90-day letter" was also at issue, as mentioned in footnote 67.
196. While the *Tellier* case (1966) below suggests that the hurdle for a business proprietor's expense to be deductible under IRC§162 is not so high as that implied by this *Burnet* case. Such opacity is also observable in the case of Japan's ITA §37. *See* the analysis in 1(1) in Section 2 of Chapter 1.
197. In Japan, AR 36-1 on IT provides that illegal income constitutes taxable income, and it should follow that an expense for the acquisition of illegal income is in principle deductible for IT purposes while the Supreme Court denied in the 9/16/1994 judgment (1989(a)28) the deduction of the corporation's payment of money to those who cooperated in hiding its income.
198. The Board of Appeals created in 1924 was replaced by the Tax Court in 1942, which was then transformed from an administrative court to a judicial court by the Tax Reform Act of 1969.

assessment of denying the deductibility of all of those expenses for the relevant years that the taxpayer did not keep adequate records on. However, the Court of Appeals stated, "Absolute certainty in such matters is usually impossible and is not necessary; the Board should make as close an approximation as it can, bearing heavily if it chooses upon the taxpayer whose inexactitude is of his own making, but to allow nothing at all appears to us inconsistent with saying that something was spent." Then, the Court remanded the case to the Board of Tax Appeals with instructions to make some estimate of the taxpayer's deductible entertainment expenses in light of the Board's express finding that Cohan had spent "considerable sums" and that such were allowable expenses.

The abovementioned Court of Appeals' opinion is called the "Cohan rule" and has been frequently cited and followed in subsequent court cases. But in 1962, as for IRC §274, mentioned in the above (ii), clause (d) (Substantiation required), which is called the "anti-Cohan rule," was introduced, and the rule was revised further by the 2017 Act (Tax Cuts and Jobs Act) etc. As a result, travel expenses, food and beverage expenses, gift expenses, and "listed property" stipulated in IRC §280F(Limitation on depreciation for luxury automobiles; limitation where certain property used for personal purposes) have become out of the scope of the above Cohan rule. Therefore, as far as those expenses are concerned, taxpayers are required, in order to prove their deductibility, to be capable of providing appropriate records and evidence of their amount, date, place, purpose, etc.[199] Certainly, the Treasury and the IRS have issued notices (Notice 2018-76, 2018-42, etc.) regarding the treatments under IRC §274, but there remains opacity about the scope of expenses deductible for Federal IT purposes. Such opacity must be at work in not only prompting taxpayers to dispute the IRS's denial of deductibility of some of their alleged trade and business expenses but also augmenting some of their hope for gaining some concessions from the IRS.

SECTION 5 SUMMARY AND ANALYSIS

The number of appeals received annually by the Office of Appeals is, as Figure 2.2 shows, approximately 100,000. This number is about two hundred times the number of cases (about 500 based on the premise that it may be about one-fifth of the reported number of about 2,500 cases counted on a cumulative basis) received by the Tax Tribunal in Japan,[200] and this difference is striking in light of the fact that the recent population in the U.S. is approximately three times of that in Japan.[201]Such being the case, taxpayers, the IRS and courts expect the Office of Appeals' effective and efficient

199. IRC §274(d) states, "No deduction or credit shall be allowed—(1) under section 162 or 212 for any traveling expense (including meals and lodging while away from home), (2) for any expense for gifts, or (3) with respect to any listed property (as defined in section 280F(d)(4))."

200. *See* 3 of Section 1 in Chapter 1 and Figure 2.3.

201. In FY2019, the IRS processed more than 250 million returns and conducted approximately 770,000 examinations (about a quarter of which were field examinations). The ratio of examinations is less than 0.25% (approximately 1% in 2010). For details, *see* IRS Data Book 2019, pp. 11-34. While in Japan the ratio of on-site audits of individuals/corporations is about 1%/3% lately (*see* Figure 1.10 in Chapter 1).

handling of tax disputes, and the Office has responded to such expectation by actively utilizing settlements by agreement. Flexible settlements also have an aspect of increasing the number of objections to the Office of Appeals raised by those taxpayers who hope to gain some concessions from the IRS. Thus, the availability of flexible settlement of disputes is a two-edged sword, and even if the ratio of settling disputes by the Office of Appeals is as high as around 90%, the recent annual number of appeals received by the Tax Court (about 25,000 which is about one-quarter of the number received by the Office of Appeals) stand around one hundred times of that (about 250 tax dispute cases) received by courts in Japan.

The Tax Court also has some rules and practices that help reduce its burden. They include the "rule of not looking behind a notice of deficiency" and the much higher ratio of settlements of disputes by agreements without handing down judgments. Moreover, a special trial judge who could settle small claims cases speedily without allowing further appeals is a merit not only for the Tax Court but also for the majority of appellants. On the other hand, the metamorphosis of the "American rule" into a hybrid of the "party/party rule" and the "English rule" may have worked toward increasing the number of appeals to courts even if the hurdle for the recovery of an appellant's attorney's fee is fairly high because it is only possible for those "prevailing party" that clears the net worth requirement, and in the majority of disputed cases, the government/IRS can prove that its position in the proceeding is substantially justified. Furthermore, the chance of recovery could be increased by the use of a "qualified offer" because it could realize the recovery in a case where the liability of the taxpayer pursuant to the judgment is equal to or less than the liability of the taxpayer, which would have been so determined if the IRS had accepted the qualified offer irrespective of whether the IRS can substantially justify its position, and a "qualified offer" could be effective even in cases where the IRS accepted it or conceded over the dispute.

Naturally, the number of tax disputes and the days needed for resolving them also depend on which issue is in dispute and some issues are disputed more frequently than others because they contain strong triggers. Regulars on the list of the "most litigated issues" at the Tax Court (and other federal courts) are collection issues, penalty issues, "innocent spouse" issues, gross income issues and trade or business expense issues. Collection issues are highly disputed because many tax delinquents desire the suspension of collection action on them or seek some favorable payment arrangements by "offer-in-compromise," etc. As for penalty issues, a strong trigger is the possibility of a penalty abatement on account of "reasonable cause," whose hurdle for its application is not extremely high. Triggers for gross income issues, as well as trade and business expense issues, are basically the same as those in Japan,[202] but the scope of deductible expenses may be wider in Japan if it does not require them to be ordinary as one of the legal requirements for their deductibility.[203] On the other hand, in the case of the U.S., some expenses that are not accounted for by records or evidence

202. *See* Section 2(1) in Chapter 1.
203. In particular, as mentioned in 5(2) in Section 4 and footnote 199, IRC §274 generally sets a higher hurdle than Japan's Article 37 of IT for the deductibility of entertainment expenses for IT purposes.

could be deducted in accordance with the "Cohen rule" even if IRC §274 excludes from them several types of expenses, including "listed property" under IRC §280F.

Among the above "most litigated issues," an "innocent spouse" issue is a very good example of how a tax structure impacts the number of tax disputes, and it possesses a very strong trigger for increasing it. The Tax Court's traditional "rule of not looking behind a notice of deficiency" should help put a brake on the increase in the number of tax disputes at the Court. Judge Hall, who gave a dissenting opinion on the *Scar* case (1983), was also in favor of the traditional view of the "rule of not looking behind a notice of deficiency" and the nature of a "90-day letter" because they work toward lessening the burden of the IRS and the Tax Court, and argued, "If the Commissioner discloses his theory at this stage, the majority's rule invites every taxpayer to litigate whether the Commissioner has made a determination before litigating the merits." However, at least as far as the "90-day letter" is concerned, as Japan's Article 74-14 of AGRNT requires a high level of accuracy in the reasons shown in the notice of deficiency has worked toward decreasing the number of re/assessments and tax disputes,[204] so the traditional view of not demanding a high level of accuracy in the "90-day letter" might, in not a few cases, raise taxpayers' doubts about their validity and prompt them to dispute them.

As mentioned above, there are many rules and systems in the U.S. that work toward increasing the number of tax disputes. Moreover, the majority of recent reforms include, in particular, expanded anti-tax avoidance/evasion rules, diversified/ strengthened penalties, as well as those that enhance taxpayers' rights and the independence of the Office of Appeals, such as the adoption of the Taxpayers Bill of Rights, the "Taxpayer First Act," etc. All of these reforms should work in the direction of intensifying tax disputes. Such being the case, the expectation of the IRS, taxpayers and courts toward the Office of Appeals in fulfilling its mission effectively should rise further, and there may arise discussions on what could be done to enhance its function of settling disputes more efficiently. In fact, there are some opinions and proposals exploring further changes in the ways to resolve tax disputes in the U.S. They include more active utilization of ADR by the Office of Appeals, the establishment of a department in charge of ADR independently of the IRS and the Office of Appeals, and so forth.[205] There seems to lie underneath these proposals a commonly held idea that there should be more merits than demerits in more active and varied use of flexible settlement of disputes, especially before they are brought to court.

204. *See* 2(4) of Section 3 in Chapter 1.

205. *See* Committee on Ways and Means U.S. House of Representatives (Serial No. 115-OS07), *Reforming How IRS Resolves Taxpayer Disputes* (2017) pp. 83-84. The GAO Report (aforementioned GAO-18-659, pp. 55-56) also points out that there is room for various measures to be taken to shorten the time required to process appeals. The IRS generally supports taking measures to realize it.

CHAPTER 3
Status in the United Kingdom

SECTION 1 TAX OBJECTION PROCEDURES

1 Tax Objection Procedures Before 2009 Reform

Under the tax objection procedures before they were abolished in 2009, a taxpayer who was aggrieved over a notice of assessment, a closure notice, etc., issued to him by a caseworker should file, as Figure 3.1 shows, an objection or a request for review with the Inland Revenue (after its merger in 2005 with Her Majesty's Customs and Excise (HMCE), Her Majesty's Revenue and Customs (HMRC)) or the Tribunals depending on a type of tax,[1] his preference and so forth in accordance with the Tax Management Act (TMA) §31(Right of appeal), etc.[2] When a taxpayer's objection did not result either in an agreement between the taxpayer and the tax authority or a decision in favor of the taxpayer at this stage, the next stage for the taxpayer before litigating his case in court was an appeal to the General/Special Commissioners in the case of a dispute on a direct tax (IT, CIT, capital gains tax, social securities tax, inheritance tax, etc.) which had not

1. The tax revenue recorded by HMRC was approximately GBP 608.8 billion for FY2020-2021, of which approximately 32% was IT revenue, 23% was social security tax revenue, 20% was VAT revenue, 9% was CIT revenue, and other tax revenue was about 16%. *See* HMRC Annual Reports and Accounts, Figure 3.
2. TMA §31 states, "(1) An appeal may be brought against an assessment to tax by a notice of appeal in writing given within thirty days after the date of the notice of assessment...(2) The notice of appeal shall be given to the inspector or other officer of the Board by whom the notice of assessment was given." Corporation Tax Act also had Schedule 18(Company tax returns, assessments and related tax matters)§34(Amendment of return after enquiry) that prescribed, "Notice of appeal must be given—(a) ... (c) to the officer of the Board by whom the partial or final closure notice was given." As for appeals procedure for penalties, in particular, since 1986, there is TMA §100B (Appeals against penalty determinations) with respect to penalties under TMA §100. As for the current TMA §100, *see* 1(1) of Section 5.

been reviewed at the Tribunals,[3] and to the VAT and Duties Tribunal while a request for internal review by the tax authority could precede it if it was preferred.

Figure 3.1 Standard Tax Appeals Procedures Before 2009 Reform

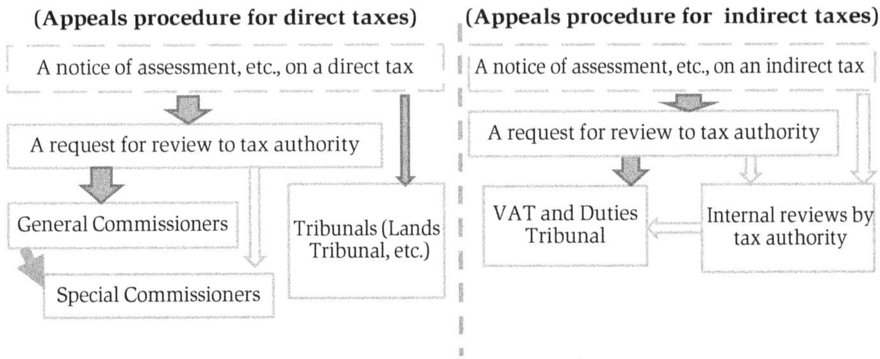

Source: HMRC's Consultation Document October 2007: Tax Appeals against decisions made by HMRC, VAT Guide (VAT Notice 700),https://www.lexology.com/library/detail.aspx?g=7e9715d5-8484-4e9b-aae4-4aba903f0c3e, etc.

The majority of objections on a direct tax case that had not been resolved by the tax authority's review were, as shown in Figure 3.1, submitted through the tax authority to the General Commissioners, who were expected to make decisions quickly and inexpensively,[4] but there were also those appeals that were subjected to the other appeals procedures, and they included those which were transferred to the Special Commissioners on account of their highly specialized nature.[5] Both the General Commissioners and the Special Commissioners were established by ITAs of 1803 and 1805. They gained legal status as the Tribunal by 1942 ITA, and their jurisdiction was expanded to cover other subsequently introduced direct taxes. They generally employed adversary proceedings, but relatively simple cases were often handled in writing without hearings. Both Commissioners, ever since their establishment, have

3. There was such Tribunals as the 2007 ITA §704 Tribunal which took over the functions of the 1988 ITA §706 Tribunal since 2007. It specialized in reviewing objections against the denial of tax avoidance through securities transactions stipulated in Article 704 of Chapter 1 (Transactions in securities) of Title 13 (Tax Avoidance) of ITA. Other Tribunals included the Social Security and Child Support Appeals Tribunal, which handled appeals against dispositions relating to social security benefits.
4. There were some who questioned the independence of such procedure from the perspective that the timing of the objections to the Commissioners were to be controlled by the tax authority. *See* Stephen Oliver, The Role of the Tax Tribunal, Striking the Balance: Tax Administration, Enforcement and Compliance in the 1990, *The Institute for Fiscal Studies Sixth Residential Conference 16-17* (April 1993, at www.econstor.eu › obitstream › 720456991_ocr) pp. 191-194.
5. For example, TMA §47 (Special jurisdiction relating to tax on chargeable gains) originally stipulated that appeals related to the valuation of securities, etc. not handled on the UK stock exchange are to be reviewed by the General Commissioners while disputes on double taxation relief under the old TMA §46C (General and Special Commissioners) (3)(e) were reviewed by the Special Commissioners.

been organs of the tax authority and were originally appointed by the Chancellor of Exchequer, but since 1986, the Lord Chancellor has appointed knowledgeable persons (legal qualification is not a precondition for the appointment) in various regions as the General Commissioners and legal experts (usually legally qualified) as the Special Commissioners.[6]

In 1986, the authority to establish various regulations concerning the General Commissioners and the Special Commissioners was also transferred to the Lord Chancellor, but there remained the tax authority's involvement in drafting those regulations, including the General Commissioners (Jurisdiction and Procedure) Regulations of 1994 and the Special Commissioners (Jurisdiction and Procedure) Regulations of 1994.[7] Nevertheless, there have been some notable legislative changes since then. In particular, the 1992 Finance (No. 2) Act (Schedule 16) introduced sections 46A (Regulations about jurisdiction) and 56B (Regulations about practice and procedure) of the Financial Management Act 1970. They led to the adoption of paragraph 13 (Hearings to be in private) of the General Commissioners Regulations and paragraph 15 (Hearings in public or in private) of the Special Commissioners Regulations. Consequently, in contrast to the "General Commissioners" hearings, those of the Special Commissioners became open to the public in principle. Moreover, decisions of the Special Commissioners were also made open in accordance with paragraph 20 (Publication of decisions in principle or final determination) of the Special Commissioners Regulations.

The General Commissioners consisted of 1,500 to 3,500 volunteers spread across more than 400 regions, making them geographically convenient for taxpayers. The number of appeals they received per year used to exceed 100,000 in some years, but in recent years, as shown in Table 3.1, their numbers and the number of hearings have fallen to less than half of the peak.[8] For example, in 2004, 18,314 cases were accepted, and 2,403 cases were heard.[9] Even the number of hearings by the Special Commissioners showed a decrease; it was about 1,500 in 1863, while it went down to below 100

6. During the periods when the Chancellor of Exchequer appointed the Special Commissioners, about half of them were appointed from tax officials (including many who were not qualified as legal professionals). It is pointed out that this fact was behind the change in the appointer of the Commissioners. *See* Lord Nolan, Some Historical Recollections of Tax Practice and of the Special Commissioners, *British Tax Review*, No. 1 (2005) pp. 34-35.
7. A similar fact was recognized in relation to the "Value Added Tax and Customs Tribunal" regulations, and this fact was pointed out by some to be against the spirit of the Taxpayer Charter and the spirit of Article 6 (Right to a fair trial) of the ECHR that stipulate the right to appeal to an independent tribunal, *see* Nolan, *supra*, "Some Historical Recollections," p. 33 and Oliver, *supra*, "The Role of the Tax Tribunals," pp. 193-194. As for Article 6 of the ECHR, *see* 1(4) of Section 5.
8. Table 3.1 reveals that, although the data is incomplete, compared to tax revenue, the number of objections relating to VAT is particularly small while the number of objections relating to corporation tax is fairly large.
9. For details, *see* Oliver, *supra* "The Role of the Tax Tribunal" p. 188, and Koji Ishimura, Drastic Reform of the British Tax Tribunal System (also at https://ci.nii.ac.jp/naid/110007344024).

in recent years. It is also pointed out that the number of decisions by the Special Commissioners was 77 in 2005, and recently, about two-thirds of their decisions were in favor of the tax authority after their hearings were held annually on 75 cases or so.[10] Taxpayers and the tax authority that were dissatisfied with the decisions of the Special Commissioners (or the General Commissioners in some cases)could, pursuant to TMA §56 (Statement of the case for the opinion of the High Court), which reflects the common law doctrine that juries are the best and final arbiter of facts,[11] make an appeal to the High Court by way of case stated on a point of law.[12]

Table 3.1 Number of Tax Appeals Filed in 2006-2007

Receiving Agency / *Classification of Cases*	*Tax Authority*	*General Commissioners*		*Special Commis-sioners' Hearings*	*VAT Customs Tribunal*		*Section 706/Social Security Tribunal*
		Received	*Hearings*		*Received*	*Hearings*	
Late IT Return Penalty	141,400	20,200	5,350	25	—	-	-
IT	43,300		3,200		-	-	-
employer tax	2,000		450		-	-	-
CIT	29,000	1,100	1,000	30	-	-	5
VAT	7,375				2,650	750	-
Customs duty and excise tax	3,800			70	275	100	-
Trial procedure	-		2,100		-	-	-
Others	455	205	100				
Capital gains tax			150		-	-	-

10. Stephen Oliver, Twenty-Five Years of the VAT Tribunals: A View from the President, *British Tax Review,* No. 6 (1998) p. 556 and John F. Avery Jones, The Reform of the Tax Tribunals: A Story of Uncompleted Business, *British Tax Review*, No. 3 (2006) p. 29.
11. As a rationale for such a common law doctrine, in the Court of Exchequer judgment on *Allen v. Sharp* ([1848] 154 ER 529), Judge Parke stated, "What a flood of litigation would follow, if every subject of the Crown, who was dissatisfied with the judgment of the assessors, had a right to dispute the propriety of their assessment ... juries would have to decide on facts without end, ... when the exigencies of the state required a speedy determination."
12. TMA §56 stipulates, "(1) Immediately after the determination of an appeal by the Commissioners, the appellant or the inspector or other officer of the Board, if dissatisfied with the determination as being erroneous in point of law may declare his dissatisfaction to the Commissioners who heard the appeal. (2) The appellant or the inspector or the officer of the Board, as the case may be ..., require the Commissioners to state and sign a case for the opinion of the High Court thereon."

Receiving Agency	*Tax Authority*	*General Commissioners*		*Special Commissioners' Hearings*	*VAT Customs Tribunal*		*Section 706/Social Security Tribunal*
Classification of Cases		*Received*	*Hearings*		*Received*	*Hearings*	
Social security tax	23,000				–	–	2,400
Total	227,330	21,505	12,350 (#)	125	2,925	850	2,405

Source: Explanatory Memorandum to The Transfer of Tribunal Function and Revenue Customs Appeal Order 2009 No. 56 Annex A and HMRC Consultation Document Oct. 2007: Tax Appeals against Decisions made by HMRC, p. 28. # indicating partially unknown.

As for aggrieved taxpayers on the re/assessments related to indirect taxes (VAT, commodity tax, customs duty, etc.), they could file an appeal with the tax authority as shown in Table 3.1, but they also had an option of requesting an "internal review" or "local reconsideration" by a tax official who was not involved in the audit. However, most of the aggrieved taxpayers preferred, pursuant to the VATA §83 (Appeals), an appeal to the VAT Tribunal, which was created under the Finance Act 1972 (after 1995, the VAT and Duties Tribunal), rather than an "internal review."[13] At the VAT and Duties Tribunal, judges (lawyers, private citizens, etc.) appointed by the tax authority and a chairman appointed by the Lord Chancellor reviewed the cases, and its review and decision were open to the public in principle. The number of appeals filed with the VAT and Duties Tribunal was less than 2,000 in 1987, but with the increase in the number of VAT penalty cases, the number of appeals filed with the VAT and Duties Tribunal exceeded 15,000 around 1998, and then gradually decreased in 2005 to 596 (273 cases related to VAT, 216 cases related to VAT penalty, 90 cases related to commodity tax, 17 cases related to customs duty).[14]

From the taxpayer's point of view, the cost of filing an appeal could also be a problem. In contrast to the appeals to the General/Special Commissioners, appeals to the VAT and Duties Tribunal required advance payment of the disputed tax amount in principle.[15] As for the transfer of litigation costs, the General Commissioners and

13. VATA §83 prescribed, "an appeal shall lie to the tribunal with respect to any of the following matters—(a) ... (b) the VAT chargeable on the supply of any goods or services ... (c) the amount of any input tax which may be credited to a person."
14. John F. Avery Jones, Tax Treaties: The Perspectives of Common Law Countries, *Courts and Tax Treaty Law*, IBFD (2007) pp. 31-80; Guglielmo Maisto, Courts and Tax Treaty Law, *EC and International Tax Law Series*, Vol. 3, IBFD (2007) p. 33, Oliver, *supra* "The Role of the Tax Tribunal" p. 188.
15. VATA §84 (Further provisions relating to appeals)(3) originally stated, "Where the appeal is against a decision with respect to any of the matters ..., it shall not be entertained unless the amount which the Commissioners have determined to be payable as VAT has been paid or deposited with them. Whereas, in the case of an appeal to the General/Special Commissioners, TMA §55 (Recovery of tax not in dispute)(2) originally prescribed, "Notwithstanding that the appeal is pending—(a) such part of the tax assessed as appears to the Commissioner not to be in dispute shall be collected and paid in all respects as if it were tax charged by an assessment in respect of which no appeal was pending."

Section 704 Tribunal of the ITA 2007 did not have the authority to order them, but the Special Commissioners had, as paragraph 21 (Order for costs) of the SC Rules prescribes, the authority of ordering some costs incurred in connection with the hearings procedure of one party to be paid by the other party only if he acted irrationally at the hearings.[16] Further, in the case of the VAT and Duties Tribunal, paragraph 29 (Awards and directions as to costs) (1) of the 1986 VAT Rules 1986 (No. 590) stipulated, "A tribunal may direct that a party or claimant shall pay to the other party to the appeal or application – (a) within such period as it may specify such sum as it may determine on account of the costs of such other party of and incidental to and consequent upon the appeal or application." However, in practice, even if the VAT and Duties Tribunal decides in favor of the tax authority, it is customary not to seek the taxpayer to bear the litigation costs of the tax authority.

The above customary practice is called "Sheldon practice," and it originated in the July 1987 statement made at the Parliament by Robert Sheldon, Financial Secretary to the Treasury at that time. He stated as follows, "the Commissioners [i.e., HM Customs & Excise] have concluded that, as a general rule, they should continue their policy of not seeking costs against unsuccessful appellants; however, they will ask for costs in certain cases to provide protection for public funds and the general body of taxpayers. For instance, they will seek costs at those exceptional tribunal hearings of substantial and complex cases where large sums are involved and which are comparable with High Court cases, unless the appeal involves an important point of law requiring clarification." He also mentioned that the Commissioner will also seek costs if the petitioner abuses the tribunal procedure, for example, if the petitioner fails to attend a mutually arranged hearing without full explanation. This is a case where public funds could have been saved if the relevant evidence had been disclosed at an early stage without missing the timing.[17] However, as will be explained later in 2 of Section 3, HMRC's stance regarding this practice has changed somewhat with the abolishment of the old tax appeal system.

2 Tax Objection Procedures After 2009 Reform

Before 2009, there existed various tribunals to process administrative appeals, and the same was true in the case of tax appeals, as shown above. However, a study group headed by Mr. Andrew Legatt prepared a Report ("Tribunals for users —One System, One Service," also known as "Legatt Committee Report") for the Lord Chancellor's Department in 2001. The Report pointed out that the old administrative appeals systems had problems, particularly in terms of the independence of the tribunals from

16. Some pointed out that the fact that the Special Commissioners decided in favor of the taxpayer but no recovery of his attorney's fees, etc., was not possible in principle should constitute a major impediment to filing an appeal. *See* Oliver, *supra* "The Role of the Tax Tribunal" pp. 194-195.
17. This statement is cited in para. 109 of the Upper Tribunal's decision on *Julian Massey* case (2015) to be referred to in the subsequent 2 in Section 3.

administrative organs and the convenience of taxpayers,[18] and proposed that a drastic reform was necessary.[19] Such a proposal was incorporated in the 2004 white paper (Transforming Public Services: Complaints, Redress and Tribunals, Cm. 6243) and culminated in the recommendation to create a two-tier tribunal. Acting on this recommendation, the "Tribunals, Courts and Enforcement Act" (hereinafter referred to as the "TCE Act") was adopted in 2007, and a new tribunal system was created. The former tax appeal system has also been fundamentally reformed by the 2009 No. 56 Order (the Transfer of Tribunal Functions and Revenue and Customs Appeal Order 2009) issued by the Lord Chancellor and the Treasury under the authority set forth in the TCE Act.

In response to the above Order No. 56 of 2009, the HMRC has also changed its tax appeals procedures. As illustrated in Figure 3.2, under the revised appeals procedures, a taxpayer who is dissatisfied with a notice of assessment on him issued by the HMRC may, as TMA §31 (Right of appeal) (1) prescribes, bring an appeal against it in writing within thirty days after the date of the notice of assessment.[20] In the case of an appeal against a notice of assessment on direct taxes, it usually triggers the HMRC's review and consultation with the appellant. If the consultation does not result in an agreement, or if the appellant is unsatisfied with the HMRC's decision on the appeal, the taxpayer's next step is, as shown in Figure 3.2, to follow the procedures under TMA §49A (Appeal: HMRC review or determination by tribunal) which provides the taxpayer with two options: (i) HMRC's statutory review which is either proposed by a caseworker via a "review process letter" or requested by the taxpayer,[21] (ii) an appeal to the First-tier Tribunal.[22] While, in the case of an appeal against a notice of assessment on indirect taxes, the taxpayer/appellant can choose from scratch the HMRC's statutory review or an appeal to the First-tier Tribunal.

18. On the problems associated with the convenience of taxpayers, the Report pointed out that (i) many of the chairs of the "VAT and Duties Tribunal" are not full-time, (ii) their adjudication centers eventually became three nationwide, and (iii) Its goal of processing appeals within three months from the receipt of the "Notice of Appeal" has not been achieved at a high rate. For example, in 1992, about 5,400 appeals were accepted, but about 2,000 decisions were handed down in the same year. *See* Oliver, *supra* "The Role of the Tax Tribunal" pp. 188-196 and Oliver, *supra* "Twenty-Five Years of the VAT tribunals" pp. 552-553.
19. As for details of the problems pointed out and the reforms proposed, *see* Jones, *supra* "The Reform of the Tax Tribunals" pp. 282-285.
20. As for details of the matters described in a notice of assessment, refer to ARTG (Appeals Reviews and Tribunals Guidance) 3050 (Review and appeals for indirect taxes: appealing against a decision or assessment: telling the customer of the decision).
21. A petition for a "statutory hearing" by an appellant may be filed without waiting for the results of consultations with the HMRC or the HMRC's decision, but a "statutory hearing" is not available in the case of "jeopardy amendment."
22. *See* the tax authority's Notice 700 in para. 28.3 (if you disagree with HMRC's decision about VAT). While separate procedures ("condemnation proceedings") apply to appeals relating to seizure or seized assets.

Figure 3.2 Current Tax Appeals Procedures

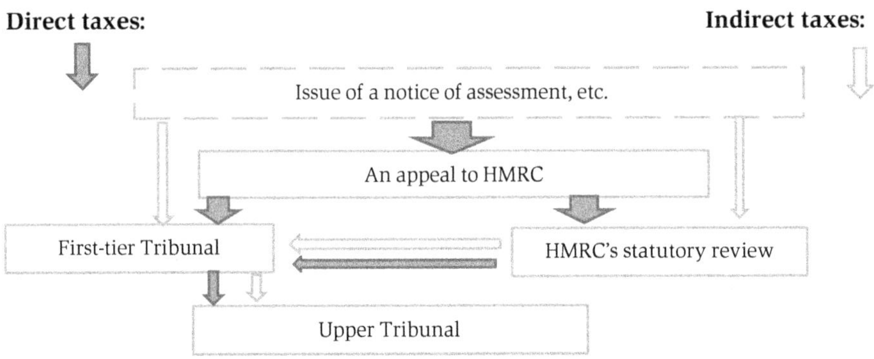

Source: Figure drawn based on the following: https://www.gov.uk/tax-appeals, https://www.litrg.org.uk/tax-nic/tax-checks-and-disputes/appealing-tax-decision, etc.

In a case where a caseworker proposes a statutory review as in (i) above, the taxpayer has thirty days to accept the proposal or should file an appeal with the First-tier Tribunal. If any of these is not done within the time limit, in principle, the taxpayer will not be able to contest the validity of the notice of assessment.[23] To apply for a statutory review, a taxpayer should, in principle, unless the appeal is against a notice of assessment related to indirect taxes or penalties, pay the disputed tax amount in advance, but he might be allowed to postpone the payment in some cases until the statutory review is over.[24] This statutory review is basically the same as an "internal review" that was applied to appeals against re/assessments on indirect taxes before Order No. 56 of 2009 was issued, and it is conducted by the HMRC's legal personnel (members of the Review Team within the Solicitor's Office and Legal Services Division) who are not involved in the disputed assessment.[25] The result of the statutory review shall be notified to the appellant within a certain period (in a case where a taxpayer requests a statutory review, it is within forty-five days after the day of its acceptance) by a "review conclusion letter" that shows relevant fact, reasons and legal grounds for the conclusion.[26]

23. This thirty-day rule may be extended if there is a "reasonable excuse" or an approval from the HMRC or the Tribunals is obtained. *See* https://www.gov.the UK/tax-appeals for details. What constitutes a reasonable excuse is determined based on the same standards as in the case of penalties for filing after the due date. *See* 1(3) in Section 5 for detailed criteria.
24. *See* Publications at https://www.gov.the UK/tax-appeals.
25. HMRC personnel who conduct a statutory review do not normally discuss disputed cases with the caseworkers, but may contact them to further their understanding of the "notice of assessment." For details, *see* HMRC, Agent Update, Issue 75 (December 2019-January 2020) pp. 3-4.
26. *See supra* HMRC's "Agent update" p. 4. While failure to notify the appellant of the outcome of the review within forty-five days or a mutually agreed upon deadline may be deemed a

As Figure 3.3 exhibits, the number of statutory reviews was on a declining trend recently before it showed its increase from 2021-2022, and there has not been much difference in the annual number of their receipt and that of their finalized processing. As for the ratio of the re/assessment canceled by statutory reviews, it has remained in the high 40% to low 50 % range for a long time since 2011-2012, but in 2020-2021, it has reached as high as 65%. Moreover, the number of full cancellations of the re/assessments by statutory reviews is five to ten times larger than the number of partial cancellations. For example, in 2019-2020 and 2020-2021, the number of partial cancellations by statutory reviews was 3,516 and 1,340, respectively, while the number of full cancellations was 20,478 and 11,762, respectively. It is not always clear what the yearly breakdown of petitioners requesting or accepting a statutory review is like, but in 2011-2012, the total number of statutory reviews was 56,228, and its breakdown shows that about 54% of them were corporations, 39% were individuals, and the rest was partnerships.[27] In the case of statutory reviews of re/assessments on individuals, the ratio of them having a representative was about 15% to 30%.

Figure 3.3 Number of Statutory Reviews, Their Ratio of Cancellations, The Ratio of Taxpayers Without a Representative in Statutory Reviews

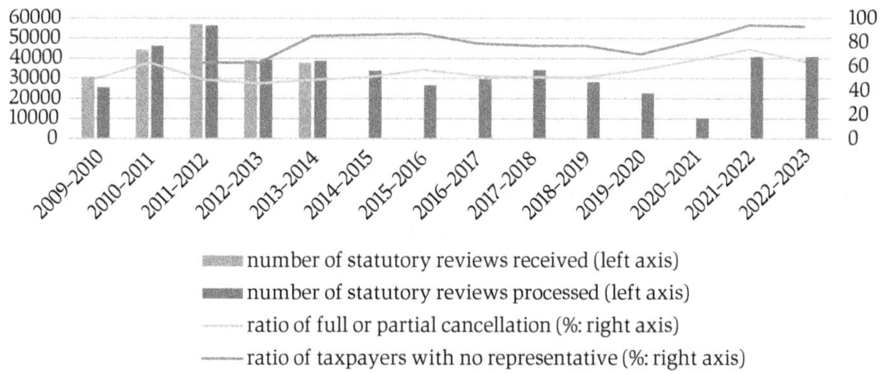

Source: Collected from data in TAC Reports for 2012-2023, Table: Summary of dispute outcomes at review and appeal, Annex: Review outcome coefficient and HMRC's Review and Appeals —2013-2014.

confirmation of the validity of the disputed assessment under TMA §49E(8) or VATA §83F(8) and the appellant could make an appeal to the Tribunals.

27. *See* Annex 2 of the 2012 TAC Report.

SECTION 2 FLEXIBLE TAX DISPUTE RESOLUTION

1 Basis and Scope of HMRC's Discretion for Flexible Dispute Resolution

It is pointed out that under the old tax appeals system, more than 90% of direct tax disputes were resolved without appeals to the General/Special Commissioners.[28] Even under the current appeals system, the HMRC explains that the majority of tax disputes are resolved by an "agreement" or "settlement" between the parties.[29] Behind this is the fact that the HMRC has broad discretionary powers regarding flexible dispute resolution. The rationale for such powers is found in TMA §1 (Taxes under care and management of the Board), which prescribed, before the 2005 revision, as follows, "Income tax, corporation tax, and capital gains tax shall be under the care and management of the Commissioners of Inland Revenue." The 2005 revision replaced the term "care and control" with the term "collection and management," and now it stipulates, "The Commissioner for HMRC shall be responsible for the collection and management of—(a) income tax, (b) corporation tax, (c) capital gains tax."[30] Commissioners for Revenue and Customs Act (CRCA) §51 (Interpretation) (3) explains, "Responsibility for collection and management has the same meaning as references to responsibility for care and management of revenue in enactments passed before this Act."[31]

The Supreme Court judgment *on IRC v. National Federation of Self-Employed and Small Business, Ltd* ([1982] AC 617) is a good example, having confirmed this wide discretionary power of the Commissioner. In this case, the appellee argued that the Tax Board's agreement with the tax evaders, owing to the difficulty of taxation and collection on them, was unfairly advantageous to them compared to the tax burden imposed on the appellees in the same occupation as those tax evaders so that the Tax Board does not have powers to enter into such an agreement and the agreement is invalid. But Lord Diplock stated that the Tax Board is conferred by law on behalf of the Queen tax collection and management functions, and in the exercise of these functions, it has a wide managerial discretion as to the best means of obtaining for the national exchequer from the taxes committed to their charge the highest net return that is

28. *See* Tribunal reform: General and Special Commissioners-RIP at https://www.lexology.com/library/detail.aspx?g=7e9715d5-8484-4e9b-aae4-4aba903f0c3e.
29. *See* the 2014 TAC Report, p. 6.
30. Regarding the tax authority's discretion in imposing penalties, TMA §102 (Mitigation of penalties) currently states, "The Board may in their discretion mitigate any penalty, or stay or compound any proceedings for a penalty, and may also, after judgment, further mitigate or entirely remit the penalty." HMRC's Enquiry Manual 5310 (Penalties: Mitigation) states that there is no appeal against HMRC's decision on TMA §102 mitigation and a taxpayer wishing to litigate would need to seek judicial review.
31. CRCA §5 (Commissioners' initial functions)(1)(a) is also similar to TMA §1 but is not identical because the former stipulates, "The Commissioner shall be responsible for—(a) the collection and management of *revenue* for which the Commissioners of Inland Revenue were responsible before the commencement of this section." Thus, CRCA §5 employs the term *revenue* and CRCA §5(4) states, "In this Act 'revenue' includes taxes, duties and national insurance contributions."

practicable having regard to the staff available to them and the cost of the collection."[32] Lord Diplock also pointed out that the exercise of this discretion is only subject to judicial review when it is either "ultra vires" or unlawful conduct of public authorities or their officials,[33] and dismissed the appellees' claim by ruling that they have not established that this HMRC's action was outside its powers or it was unlawful.

There is a question of what kind of cases constitute administrative agencies' "ultra vires" and become unlawful.[34] On this question, the Court of Appeal judgment on *Associated Provincial Picture Houses Ltd. v. Wednesbury Corporation* ([1948] 1.K.B. 223) provides a useful guideline. In this case, the appellant claimed that the defendant's condition imposed on the appellant's request for the operating days of its cinema was outside of its discretionary power authorized by the relevant law. The Court held that it has no power to quash the decision of the defendant simply because it disagrees with it, while it would adopt remedies against the decisions of public bodies when their decisions were made in the following ways: (i) in making their decisions, they failed to call their attention to the matters which they are bound to consider, (ii) They did not exclude, in their decision-making, from their consideration matters which are irrelevant to what they have to consider, (iii) there may be something so absurd with their decision that no sensible person could ever dream that it lay within their powers. Particularly, the above (iii) test/criterion has been cited by many subsequent court judgments as "Wednesbury unreasonableness" to determine whether decisions of the public bodies are subject to judicial review.

The tax authority's broad scope of discretion could also be confirmed by the Court of Appeal judgment on *IRC v. Nuttall* ([1990] BTC 107). In this case, the appellee agreed to pay a certain amount of tax on the condition that the tax authority would not file a lawsuit but subsequently claimed the agreement was invalid because it also concerned the year of no assessment nor appeals being made and for its noncompliance with TMA §54 (Settling of appeals by agreement) and TMA §102 (Mitigation of penalties), etc.[35] In this judgment, Bingham LJ concurred that those legislations do not expressly authorize the Revenue to compromise claims for back duty save where an

32. In 1995, NZ enacted §6A (Commissioner's duty of care and management)(2) of the 1994 Tax Administration Act with reference to these interpretations. *See* 3(1) in Section 2 of Chapter 4.
33. In this judgment, Lord Fraser mentioned that a case containing "exceptionally grave and widespread illegality" could also be subject to judicial review.
34. ADML3200 (Collection and Management: Legal Background) mentions, "The circumstances in which the Commissioners can exercise their discretion under their powers of collection and management are set out in case law and are tightly defined...There is no right of appeal against HMRC's decision to exercise discretion or not to exercise discretion, however the decision may be challenged by judicial review." Also, *see* footnote 30. Compare this with footnote 43/87 in Chapter 4 and footnote 137 in Chapter 1.
35. TMA §54, prior to its 2009 revision, stated; "Where ... the Crown and the appellant come to an agreement...that the assessment or decision under appeal should be treated as upheld without variation, or as varied in a particular manner ..., the like consequences shall ensue for all purposes as would have ensued if, at the time when the agreement was come to, the Commissioners had determined the appeal and had upheld the assessment or decision without variation, ... as the case may be." Prior to the 1989 amendment, TMA §102 stated, "The Board may mitigate any penalty, or stay or compound *any proceedings for recovery thereof.*" Compare it with the current version in footnote 30.

assessment has been made and appealed against,[36] but he preferred to accept this legislative omission as no anomaly and stated, "The power to make agreements with taxpayers for the payment of back duty, even in the absence of assessment and appeal, is in my view a power necessary for carrying into execution the legislation relating to Revenue within the meaning of s 1 of the 1890 Act. ...But if, in an appropriate case, the Revenue reasonably considers that the public interest in collecting taxes will be better served by informal compromise with the taxpayer than by exercising the full rigor of its coercive powers, such compromise seems to me to fall well within the wide managerial discretion of the body to whose care and management the collection of tax is committed."

The House of Lords Judgment on *R. v. Inland Revenue Commissioners, Ex parte Preston* ([1985] BTC 208) also dismissed the taxpayer/appellant's claim because he failed to prove that the tax authority abused its discretionary power by raising further assessments on him despite the agreement that the tax authority would refrain from them if the taxpayer agrees to give up certain claims for tax relief. Nevertheless, the Court stated that if there was a Commissioner's conduct that is equivalent to a breach of contract or a breach of representation, it would, just like a case containing "exceptionally grave and widespread illegality" mentioned in *the National Federation* case,[37] fall within the ambit of an abuse of power for which judicial review is the sole remedy,[38] intimating that the scope of judicial review implied in this judgment is broader than that intimated by the "Wednesbury unreasonableness" test. Moreover, after the enactment of the Human Rights Act of 1998, courts seem to have come to resile from the "Wednesbury unreasonableness" test and interpret more widely the scope of judicial review of the administrative agencies' discretionary actions. Coincidentally, the Court of Session judgment on *Al Fayed v. Advocate General for Scotland* ([2004] STC 1703) specified that the HMRC's "forward tax agreement" constitutes ultra vires.

The tax authority's limit in its discretionary power also manifested in the House of Lords judgment on *R (on the application of Wilkinson) v. CIR* ([2006] STC 270). In this case, the appellant/widower relied on TMA §1 to claim that the tax authority should exercise its authority of "extra-statutory concessions" so that the deduction applicable to a widow under the Income and Corporation Tax Act 1998 §262 (Construction of references to living together) applies to him. In fact, such authority was practically exercised in such a way that the deduction was applied to a widower who initiated proceedings in the ECJ. But, the House of Lords, in dismissing the appellant's claim, pointed out that the tax authority's discretion enables the Commissioners to

36. Whereas, prior to 2003 revision, TMA §105 (Evidence in cases of fraud or willful default)(1)(a) stipulated, "in relation to tax, the Board may accept pecuniary settlements instead of instituting proceedings," and the Court respected its tradition of being applied even in cases where there is no appeals while admitting that TMA §54 may have an anomality and "locus poenitentiae."
37. *See* footnote 33.
38. As for the view that then it should follow that such cases where the doctrine of estoppel is breached or a legitimate expectation is betrayed could be subject to judicial review, *see* Judith Freedman and Johan Vella, HMRC's Management of the UK: Tax System—The Boundaries of Legitimate Discretion, *Legal Research Paper Series* (Paper No. 73/2012) pp. 102-103.

formulate policy in the interstices of the tax legislation, dealing pragmatically with minor or transitory anomalies while TMA §1 does not justify construing the tax authority's power so widely as to enable the Commissioners to concede, by extra-statutory concession, an allowance which Parliament could have granted but did not grant, and on grounds not of pragmatism in the collection of tax but of general equity between men and women. The impact of this judgment on the tax authority must have been significant now that, since then, it has come to employ "extra-statutory concessions" as well as "equitable liability" less often.[39]

The relationship between the HMRC's exercise of discretion and equality/fairness is also an issue in the Upper Tribunal's decision on *HMRC v. Southern Cross Employment Agency Ltd* ([2015] UKUT 0122 (TCC)). In this case, the appellee claimed that its business of dispatching nurses to dentists is exempt from VAT, and it consulted with the HMRC to seek a refund of the VAT paid between 1998 and 2001. The HMRC initially proposed to pay half of the refund amount, but in the end, an agreement to let the appellee receive 74% of the refund amount plus interest was made. However, after that, the validity of the re/assessment of not exempting the taxpayer engaged in a similar business from VAT was sustained by the Upper Tribunal's decision on *Moher v. R&C Commissioners* ([2012] UKUT 260 (TCC)),[40] so the HMRC claimed that, indeed, VATA §85 provides for the binding nature of the settlement by agreement between the HMRC and the appellant,[41] but the agreement with the appellant is void because it was ultra vires on account of the VATA §80 (Credit for, or repayment of overstated or overpaid VAT) (7) which provides that the Commissioner shall not be liable to credit or repay any amount accounted for or paid to them by way of VAT that was not VAT due to them.

In the above Southern Cross case, the Upper Tribunal referred to the following points; (i) the *Nuttall* case (1990) shows that the HMRC can enter into binding agreements relating to direct taxes otherwise than under TMA §54, which corresponds to VATA §85, and much as Bingham LJ thought that it would be "extraordinary and also regrettable," if the HMRC lacked such a power, it should be preferable that the HMRC should be able, if they so choose, to dispose of claims under section 80 of the VATA on a final basis, and a "better view would be that, where no appeal is pending, HMRC's liabilities can similarly be fixed for the purposes of VATA §80(1) and (4A) by means of a contractual agreement outside VATA §85"; (ii) an agreement which is ultra vires is void, but, prior to the *Moher* case, it could not be known with certainty that supplies of dental nurses were not exempt, so "HMRC cannot be criticized for failing to treat the Moher decision as a foregone conclusion"; (iii) the agreement between the HMRC and the

39. For more information on this point and what is meant by "equable liability," *see* HMRC Manual (Self Assessment Claims Manual 12210—Overpayment relief: Equitable liability replaced by special relief), ADML4000 (Extra-statutory concessions: Contents), ADML3400 (Collection and Management: Tests to apply) and the abovementioned ADML3200.

40. In the *Moher* case, the Upper Tribunal decided that the appellant's nurses were practically employees under the control of the dentists/clients and what the appellant provided were persons and not a medical service which is exempt from VAT.

41. VATA §85 (Settling appeals by agreement)(1) stipulates, "before the appeal is determined by a tribunal, HMRC and the appellant come to an agreement (whether in writing or otherwise) ... the like consequence shall ensue for all purposes as would have ensued if ... a tribunal had determined the appeal in accordance with the terms of the agreement."

appellee was formed in light of the matters to be assessed on an objective basis even if they see things differently. Then, the Upper Tribunal dismissed the appeal made by the HMRC.

2 Internal Controls for Flexible Dispute Resolution

As mentioned above, although there are certain restrictions on the exercise of the HMRC's discretionary powers, its scope is fairly wide,[42] and many tax disputes have been resolved through its active exercise. However, due to its breadth and active use, it was pointed out by the Commons Public Accounts Committee's 2011 Report (HM Revenue and Customs 2010-11 Accounts: Tax Disputes, Session 2010-12, HC 1531, 20 December 2011) and the National Audit Office's 2011 Report (Comptroller and Auditor General, HM RC 2010-11 Accounts: Session 2010-2012, HC 981, July 2011) that there were some cases in which the HMRC might have exercised its discretionary powers inconsistently with its Litigation and Settlement Strategy. In response to those Reports, a third-party investigation was conducted, but it only confirmed some problems with the dispute settlement procedures.[43] The High Court judgment on the UK Uncut Legal Action Ltd and Commissioners of HMRC ([2013] EWHC 1283 (Admin)), which was filed by the public body, was also to the effect that the disputed agreement between HMRC and Goldman Sacks had some problems in terms of compliance with the dispute settlement procedures but there was nothing that raises the issue of illegality.

Nevertheless, such incidents as mentioned above made HMRC recognize strongly the need to revise dispute settlement procedures, and it implemented some reforms, including the appointment in 2012 of the Tax Assurance Commissioner (hereinafter referred to as "HMRC TAC"), the establishment of the Tax Disputes Resolution Board (TDRB), and the revision of the Code of Governance for resolving tax disputes (hereinafter referred to as the "Code of Governance."[44] In particular, under the Code of Governance 2 (Governance of decisions on resolving tax disputes), if an appeal case is a complex case, a high-value case, a tax avoidance case, a transfer pricing case, etc., instead of a caseworker reviewing and deciding by following the opinion of his superior, a review and decision-making are to be made by the so-called Governance Boards consisting of officials from multiple HMRC departments overseen by the TDRB. Included in those departments are the Customer Compliance Group (CCB), the Dispute Resolution Board (DRB), the Anti-Avoidance Board, etc.[45] Those cases are to be referred to or practically dealt with by 3 HMRC high-ranking officials ("Three

42. In this connection, section 9 (Ancillary powers) of the Commissioners for Revenue and Customs Act (CRCA) also states, "(1) The Commissioners may do anything which they think—(a) necessary or expedient in connection with the exercise of their functions, or (b) incidental or conducive to the exercise of their functions."
43. For details, *see* National Audit Office, Report by the Comptroller and Auditor General HC 188 Session 2012-13, June 14, 2012, Settling Large Tax Disputes, pp. 36-44.
44. For more information on these reforms, *see* Chapter 1 (Introduction and background) of the 2012-2013 TAC Report.
45. For details of the other Boards that make up the "Governance Boards", *see* the 2014 HMRC TAC Report, pp. 10-13.

Commissioners," one of whom is HMRC TAC) instead if they come under a difficult case or a case where the amount in dispute exceeds GBP 100 million.[46]

The HMRC TAC is a post appointed to assess the fairness and appropriateness of tax dispute resolution proposals to ensure the confidence of Congress and the public in the HMRC. The function of the HMRC TAC includes checks on the Internal Audit team's post facto reviews of the cases deliberated by the above various boards and groups, etc., submission of reports on the number of review cases and those that contained problems, proposals of measures for improvement. To carry out such function effectively, those cases reviewed by the "Governance Boards" are often referred to as the TDRB or the "Three Commissioners" with their comments and opinions attached to those cases.[47] Figure 3.4 shows the recent annual number of cases examined by the TDRB and the annual number of decisions made by the "Three Commissioners." It reveals that from 2012-2013 to 2020-2021, the ratio of acceptance of the taxpayers' proposals in the decisions made by the "Three Commissioners" ranged from 40% to 65%. Moreover, the ratio of settlements of disputes by the "Three Commissioners" is by far higher in the cases in which the taxpayers' proposals were fully accepted than in the cases in which the taxpayers' proposals were accepted with some conditions attached to them.

Figure 3.4 Dispute Resolutions by the "Three Commissioners," Etc.

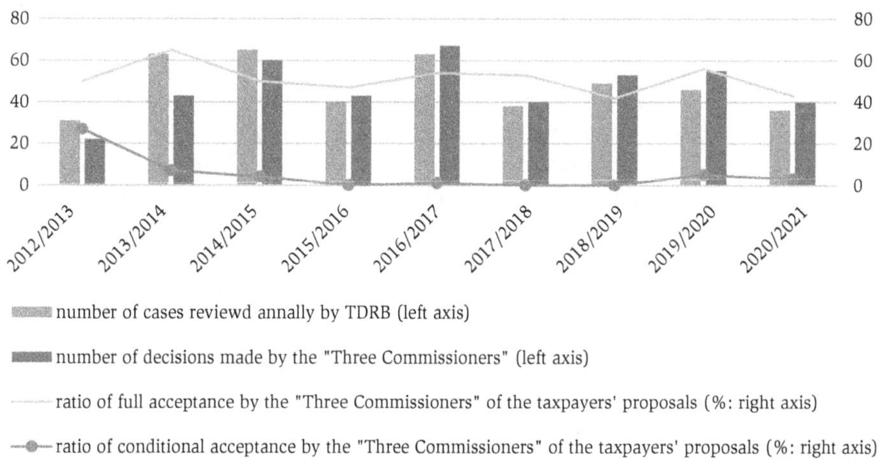

Source: Compiled from data in Annex 2, "Commissioners' Case Decisions" and "Tax Disputes Resolution Board" of HMRC TAC Reports for 2013-2023.

Through the reforms described above, internal control over the HMRC's flexible dispute resolution has been strengthened,[48] but there has not been much change in the

46. For details, *see* HMRC TAC Report 2019, p. 105.
47. For details, *see* 2017 Governance Policy's Annex C (Tax Disputes Resolution Board—terms of reference).
48. Some argue that the independent external audit process should be strengthened in response to calls for the independence of the HMRC TAC and the limitations of audits by the Board of Audit

conventional criteria for judging cases subject to flexible dispute resolution.[49] The HMRC's 2017 publication (Resolving tax disputes–Commentary on the litigation and settlement strategy, hereinafter called "HMRC L&S Strategy") states that tax disputes must, in all cases, be resolved in accordance with the law, but where discretion is properly exercised under the HMRC's legal powers of collection and management not to pursue an amount of tax, then the outcome is consistent with the law.[50] It also mentions that the HMRC will neither reach an out-of-court settlement for less than 100% of the tax, interest, and penalties (where appropriate) at stake[51] nor attempt to "split the difference" between its own and the customer's view of tax, etc., which does not give a result consistent with the law[52] if it believes it is likely to succeed in litigation and that litigation would be both effective and efficient.[53] As for ADR, the HMRC L&S Strategy explains that facilitation or mediation is not about "splitting the difference" or compromising but about supporting the parties in reaching an agreement that is in accordance with the law.

3 Background and Procedures for Proactive Use of ADR

The above explanation of ADR by the HMRC L&S Strategy intimates the HMRC's positive stance on ADR. ADR should also help many taxpayers in disputes reduce their attorneys' fees, which could be quite high in the UK. The active use of ADR is also recommended by the European Commission's various orders regarding ADR. In particular, Directive 2008/52/EC of the European Parliament and of the Council of 21 May 2008 on certain aspects of mediation in civil and commercial matters (hereinafter referred to as the "mediation order") states in paragraph 1 in Article 5 (Recourse to mediation), "A court before which an action is brought may, when appropriate and having regard to all the circumstances of the case, invite the parties to use mediation to settle the dispute."[54] In response to this, the UK's 1998 Civil Procedures Rules were amended in 2011, and in Title 1 (Overriding objective) 1.4 (Court's duty to manage cases) (2)(e) it now states: "(1) The court must further the overriding objective by actively managing cases. (2) Active case management includes – ... (e) encouraging the parties to use an alternative dispute resolution procedure if the court considers that appropriate and facilitating the use of such procedure."

---

and others. *See* Judith Freedman, The UK Institution for Tax Governance: Reviewing Tax Settlements, *British Tax Review*, Issue 1 (2016).

49. Whereas, some apprehended that HMRC's strengthened internal control might lead to its stricter interpretation of the standard for flexible dispute resolution. *See* Chris Davidson, Examining the Tax Assurance Commissioner's Latest Report, Tax *Journal*, August 5 (2016) pp. 8-9.
50. *See* HMRC L&S Strategy, pp. 6 and 40.
51. HMRC L&S expounds in p. 41 that this means that HMRC will not be able to compromise on a genuinely "all or nothing" dispute.
52. *See* HMRC L&S Strategy, p. 7. While the IRS's Office of Appeals may enter into "splitting the difference." *See* footnote 30 of Chapter 2 and IRS Policy Statement 8-48.
53. HMRC L&S Strategy states in p. 40, "An assessment of HMRC's prospects of success in litigation should in all cases be taken in consultation with Solicitors Office and Legal Services. This assessment will take account of not only the respective strengths of each party's position, but also the risks inherent in taking a case to court (litigation risk)."
54. In 2011, Cross-Border Mediation (EU Directive) Regulations were also issued.

Furthermore, now that Directive 2013/11/EU of the European Parliament and of the Council of 21 May 2013 on alternative dispute resolution of consumer disputes and amending Regulation (EC) No. 2006/2004 and Directive 2009/22(Directive on Consumer ADR)pointed out the usefulness of ADR and the need for its development, various measures for the use of mediation as a means of settling domestic disputes have been taken in the UK.[55] In the context of tax disputes, the Dispute Resolution Unit (DRU) was established within the HMRC in 2010, and a pilot program using ADR as a dispute resolution measure started in 2011. After its successful implementation,[56] it has been available to individuals and corporations in both direct and indirect tax disputes since 2013. Both taxpayers and caseworkers can propose to use ADR. Currently, ADR (albeit only through mediation) is provided at no charge by the HMRC's personnel who have received internal training for that purpose. In addition, since 2004, ADR is also provided by an expert from external bodies (the Center for Effective Dispute Resolution, etc.) whose costs for the mediation are to be shared by the parties.

The aforementioned HMRC's view that in contrast to ADR, some flexible tax dispute resolution methods, such as "splitting the difference," give rise to a result inconsistent with the law must also be spurring active use of ADR rather than other flexible resolution methods. Also, as the merits of ADR, the HMRC's 2013 Publication (Resolving Tax Disputes— Practical Guidance for HMRC Staff on the Use of Alternative Dispute Resolution in Large or Complex Cases) 4 (Benefits of using ADR) lists the following: (i) both parties retain ownership of the decision and can withdraw from the process at any time; (ii) a mediator could change the dynamics of a dispute and brings a fresh perspective; (iii) even if there is no settlement, ADR can enable a better understanding of why litigation is the appropriate way to resolve the dispute and help both parties better prepare for litigation; (iv) because both parties own the decision, any settlement will be seen by both sides as an outcome preferable to litigation; there is little downside to the process as all work and preparation involved is likely to be of direct relevance to and use in litigation in the event of ADR not resolving the issue; (v) ADR does not affect the taxpayer's right to make a request for a statutory review.

In particular, the HMRC's 2019 revised version of the ADR Guidance (Use of Alternative Dispute Resolution to settle a tax dispute) mentions that ADR could be useful and effective in such cases: (i) communications have broken down between a taxpayer and the HMRC, (ii) there are disputes about the facts, (iii) a dispute appears to be the result of a misunderstanding, (iv) a taxpayer is not clear on what information the HMRC has used, and he thinks that the HMRC may have made wrong assumptions. The HMRC's Publication(Compliance Checks: Alternative Dispute Resolution—CC/FS21)also acknowledges that ADR could also be useful even in cases where the dispute concerns a technical point or a point of law because ADR should help the taxpayer to be heard and have a better understanding of the caseworker's view. The ADR Guidance lists the following inappropriate cases for ADR: ① cases which are

55. Those measures include the enactment in 2015 of the Alternative Dispute Resolution for Consumer Disputes.

56. Evaluation of this program is shown in HMRC's 2012 publication (Alternative Dispute Resolution for the Mass Market—Pilot Evaluation Report 2).

categorized as "paper" or "basic" by the First-tier Tribunal,[57] ② debt recovery or payment issues, ③ disputes over default surcharges, ④ automatic late payment or late filing penalties, ⑤ extra-statutory concessions, ⑥ tax avoidance cases (in particular, those subjected to accelerated payments and follower notices), ⑦ civil evasion penalties, ⑧ forfeiture, etc.[58]

As mentioned above, the range of tax cases in which ADR can be used is not narrow, and as shown in Figure 3.5, the number of cases of ADR utilization and the ratio of tax dispute resolution by ADR has reached a considerable level. For example, the number of ADR applications was 499 (of which 398 were accepted and 95% of them were resolved) in FY2014-2015, 1,265 cases (of which 750 cases were accepted and 79% of them were resolved) in FY2016-2017, and 1,411 (of which 744 cases were accepted and 82% of them were resolved) in FY2017-2018. Moreover, the HMRC survey results show that the majority of taxpayers and agents who have experienced ADR are highly satisfied with ADR. In contrast, there are some cases where risks associated with ADR manifested. For instance, in the *Sussex Cars* case (2015) mentioned in 2 in Section 3, the First-tier Tribunal ordered the HMRC to pay the taxpayer's costs for ADR on account of the appointment of the inappropriate mediator. Also, in the *Serpentine Trust v. HMRC* ([2018] THE UKFTT 0535(TC), the First-tier Tribunal voided the resolution gained through ADR because it was ultra vires for the HMRC to have a resolution that contained future tax liabilities.[59]

Figure 3.5 Number of Cases of ADR Utilization and Ratio of Tax Dispute Resolution in the Case of ADR, Etc.

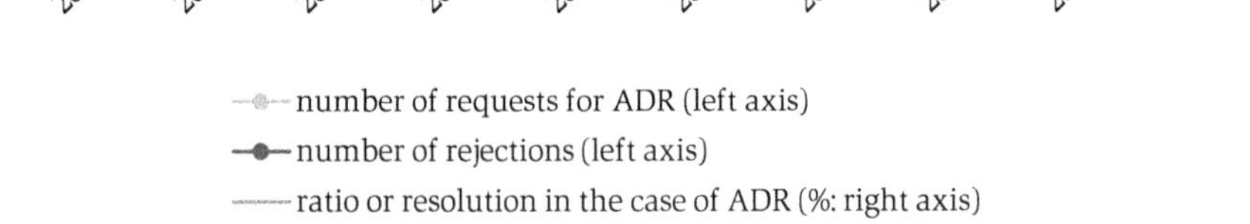

Source: Alternative Dispute Resolution Referrals in 2015-2021 HMRC TAC Reports.

57. For details on those categories, *see* 1 in Section 3.
58. Accelerated payments and follower notices were introduced by the sections 219 and 204 of the 2014 Finance Act as countermeasures against tax avoidance.
59. In this case, the HMRC claimed that the concerned ADR is invalid because a series of judgments mentioned in 2 of Section 1 (House of Lords judgment on Preston (1985), Court of Session on Al-Fayed (2004), House of Lords judgment on Wilkinson (2006), etc.) denied the HMRC to enter into an agreement on future tax payments.

Certainly, ADR has both merits and demerits. Also, it has a lot to do with the scope of the HMRC's discretionary powers. Tribunals and courts place much emphasis on ADR's merits and potential usefulness rather than its demerits. For example, in the Court of Appeal judgment on *Dunnet v. Railtrack plc* ([2002] EWCA Civ 303), the winning party refused to settle the dispute by ADR and demanded payment of its litigation costs by the losing party, and the Court warned in paragraph 15, "it is to be hoped that any publicity given to this part of the judgment of the court will draw the attention of lawyers to their duties to further the overriding objective in the way that is set out in Part 1 of the Rules and to the possibility that, if they tum down out of hand the chance of alternative dispute resolution when suggested by the court, as happened on this occasion, they may have to face uncomfortable costs consequences." Similarly, in the judgment in *Halsey v. Milton Keynes General NHS Trust* ([2004] EWCA Civ 576), the Court of Appeal ruled in paragraph 17, "Even the most ardent supporters of ADR acknowledge that the subject matter of some disputes renders them intrinsically unsuitable for ADR....other examples falling within this category are cases where a party wants the court to resolve a point of law ... But in our view, most cases are not by their very nature unsuitable for ADR."

SECTION 3 FUNCTIONS OF THE TRIBUNALS

1 Classification of Appeal Cases

After 2007, when the TCE Act was enacted, the next standard step for an aggrieved taxpayer who could not obtain relief through his objection to the HMRC, is to file through the HMRC an appeal with the First-tier Tribunal.[60] TMA §55 (Recovery of tax not postponed) (2) requires that an appeal to the Tribunal, in principle, requires payment of the disputed tax amount.[61] As Figure 3.6 shows, over the last ten years, the First-tier Tribunal received and processed an average of 5,000 to 6,000 tax appeals annually, and the comparison of Figures 3.3 and 3.6 reveals that the number of Tribunal decisions is between 4% and 19% (on average about 11%) of the number of the HMRC decisions on the statutory reviews. For example, in 2013-2014, the First-tier Tribunal closed (settled either by a formal hearing or by agreement before the hearing) 6,626 tax appeals, of which 1,631 (about 25%) had undergone statutory reviews.[62] In light of the statutory reviews' merits for taxpayers ((i) they are offered free of charge, (ii) a time limit is set on the duration of statutory reviews, (iii) as Figure 3.3 shows, statutory reviews have lately resulted in about 50% cancellation of the disputed

60. TMA §49A (Appeal: HMRC review or determination by tribunal) and §49D (Notifying appeal to the tribunal) provide that "(1) This section applies if notice of appeal has been given to HMRC." They indicate that the issue pointed out in the footnote 4 has not been resolved.
61. TMA §55(2) dictates that "the tax charged—(a) by the amendment or assessment, or (b) where the appeal is against a conclusion stated by a closure notice, as a result of that conclusion, shall be due and payable as if there had been no appeal."
62. *See supra* "HMRC's REVIEWS AND APPEALS—2013-2014" p. 5.

re/assessments, etc.),[63] some may wonder why more taxpayers do not utilize statutory reviews.[64]

Figure 3.6 Number of Appeals Received, Processed, Ratio to Disputed Re/assessments Cancelled, Etc., by First-Tier Tribunal

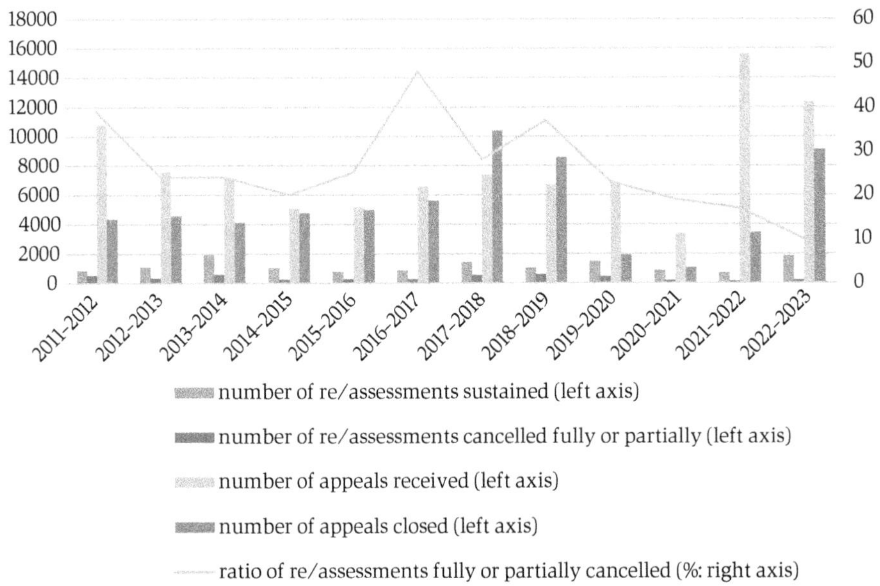

Source: Table: Overview of dispute outcomes at review and appeal and Annex: Review outcome in TAC Reports for 2012-2023.

Clues to the reasons and causes for the relatively low ratio of utilization of the statutory reviews might be found in the HMRC's 2014 Research Report: Statutory Review Process—Quantitative Research to Understand Customer's Experience and Perception of the Statutory Review Process, hereinafter called "HMRC 2014 Report"). According to the Report, about half of those who filed appeals directly to the Tribunals without going through statutory reviews did so because they either did not know about statutory reviews or did not receive proposals for statutory reviews. In addition, the main reason why those taxpayers whose claims had not been accepted at statutory reviews did not appeal to the Tribunals was the high financial cost (16%), time cost (14%), little prospect for the cancellation of the re/assessment (14%). Then, the Report concludes that the number of appeals to the First-tier Tribunal after having gone through statutory reviews would increase if progress is made, especially on such

63. As displayed in Figure 3.9, the ratio of cancellation of the re/assessments, etc. by statutory reviews is particularly high (50% to 80%) in appeal cases related to VAT penalties.
64. Paragraph 111 of the 2018 Report of the Parliament's Economic Affairs Committee ("The Powers of HMRC: Treating Taxpayers Fairly") also regrets the low level of use of statutory reviews which have a high ratio of dispute resolution.

challenges facing statutory reviews as: (i) shortening the time required for statutory reviews, (ii) improving communication and relationship between the claimants and those in charge of statutory reviews, (iii) enhancement in flexibility and impartiality of statutory reviews.[65]

There must also be some rules and procedures on appeals to the Tribunals that affect aggrieved taxpayers' decisions on how they appeal their cases. Such rules and procedures must include the treatment under the aforementioned TMA §55(2), which requires, in principle, the payment of the disputed tax amount for making appeals to the Tribunals.[66] Certainly, the financial difficulty caused by this provision could be mitigated in some cases by TMA §55(3), which allows a taxpayer to request HMRC and the First-tier Tribunal for its postponement,[67] but in the case of an appeal to the Upper Tribunal, the part of the tax amount (in some cases, interest as well) shown in the notice of assessment that is sustained by the First-Tier Tribunal must be paid.[68] In addition, as will be described later, at the First-tier Tribunal, it usually takes twelve to eighteen months to process tax appeals amid the accumulation of outstanding cases,[69] and the ratio of the disputed re/assessments being sustained by the First-tier Tribunal is, as Figure 3.6 shows, higher (50% to 80%). Therefore, a claimant's financial and time costs could be considerable even if the First-tier Tribunal's decision is favorable to the appellant.[70]

Nonetheless, there are some reasons for preferring an appeal to the First-tier Tribunal to statutory reviews. For example, Figure 3.6 shows that there is a significant gap between the number of appeals received and processed by the First-tier Tribunal and the number of its decisions, suggesting that negotiations are frequently entered into between the claimants and the HMRC even after their cases are pending, while there may also be withdraws of some their cases. For example, 5,400 cases (approximately 2.8 times the number of decisions) in FY2019-2020 and 3,826 cases (approximately 3.6 times the number of decisions) in FY2020-2021 were resolved by agreements. The high percentage of disputes at the First-tier Tribunal being resolved through such agreements may constitute a good reason, especially for those taxpayers who prioritize speedy resolution of their cases, not to go through statutory reviews. Many of

65. *See* HMRC 2014 Report, pp. 9-14. Actually, there are increases in the number of statutory reviews since 2021-2022 as shown in Figure 3.3.
66. *See* footnote 61 for TMA §55(2).
67. TMA §55(3) states, "If the appellant has grounds for believing that the amendment or assessment overcharges the appellant to tax, ... the appellant may—(a) first apply by notice in writing to HMRC ... the amount of tax of the payment of which should be postponed."
68. VAT §85B (Payment of tax where there is a further appeal) (4) does allow an exception to the prepayment on the grounds of financial difficulty, but its application is denied in some cases including the Upper Tribunal decision on *Snow Factor Ltd v. CRC* ([2019] THE UKUT 0077).
69. Among the outstanding cases, there are "stood over cases" which are agreed by the disputants to await a decision or trial that should serve as a precedent and their number is 15,250 in 2020-2021 (15,500 in 2019/2020). For details, *see* p. 116 of the 2019 HMRC TAC Report and p. 153 of the 2020 HMRC TAC Report.
70. For example, in 2011-2012 (2012/2013), 10,828 (7,660) appeals were filed, but 4,354 (4,564) were processed. For details, *see* "HMRC's REVIEWS AND APPEALS" (for FY2013-FY2014) p. 4. Also, there were unprocessed cases of 25,520 in FY2016-FY2017 and 28,800 cases in FY2017/2018 (*see Taxation*, March 21(2019) p. 5).

the taxpayers who file an appeal with the First-tier Tribunal without going through a statutory review have a large tax amount in dispute or have an attorney with them (about 2 to 2.5 times that in the case of statutory reviews),[71] and it is also pointed out that some of them have lawsuits in mind from the beginning and opt out of statutory reviews to reduce time and costs.[72]

Moreover, even if a case at the First-tier Tribunal is a type of tax dispute that is unlikely to be resolved by agreement with the HMRC, the Taxation Division of the Tribunal and the Tax and Chancery Chamber of the Upper Tribunal are composed of persons with legal professional qualifications such as judges, lawyers, and tax experts (charted public accountants, accountants, etc.), so their independence, neutrality, and expertise are high. Indeed, as shown in Figure 3.6, the recent ratio of revocation (in whole or in part) of the disputed re/assessments by the First-tier Tribunal has remained at around 20%-40%, which is lower than that by statutory reviews, and it has shown a downward trend lately. But, in some years, such as FY2016-2017, it rose to nearly 50%. Moreover, as in the case of the Special Commissioners and VAT & Duties Tribunal, the proceedings and decisions of the Tribunals are, in principle, open to the public, and the number of publicized decisions has been accumulating. Therefore, those who are considering an appeal could analyze past decisions of the Tribunals and might be able to obtain some clues as to the prospect of success of their cases as well as possible approaches they could take to increase their chance of winning favorable decisions.[73]

In addition to the above, there are other factors that have a considerable influence on the taxpayers' willingness to appeal to the First-tier Tribunal. Among them, a particularly important factor is the procedures applicable to the appeal to the First-tier Tribunal. The HMRC's internal manual (ARTG 8360—Appeals reviews and tribunals guidance) indicates that after a notice of appeal submitted by a taxpayer to the HMRC is sent to the First-tier Tribunal, the Tribunal will, as appropriate, inform the parties to the dispute of any additional documents to be submitted and designate the day and time of the hearings to be held. At the same time, on the Tribunal's receipt of the notice of appeal, the appealed case is, following paragraph 23 (Allocation of cases to categories) (2) of the Tribunal Procedure (First-tier Tribunal) (Tax Chamber) Rules 2009 (S.1.2009/273(L1)), to be categorized into: ① Default Paper cases, ② Basic cases, ③ Standard cases, ④ Complex cases, and different review procedures or treatments apply depending on which category the appealed case falls into. These differences in treatments, depending on the category of an appealed case, could make a difference in the time and costs that bear on the appellants.

The appeals, which are usually categorized into the above ① (Default Paper cases), include appeals against penalties of less than GBP 20,000. Among them, there

71. In 2012/2013, 32% of claimants were with representatives before the First-tier Tribunal, and 34% in 2013/2014. For details, *see* the HMRC TAC Report (Alternative Dispute Resolution Referrals) for the relevant years.
72. Malcolm Gammie, Tax Appeals and Reviews: The New Landscape, *British Tax Review*, No. 6 (2010) p. 668.
73. *See* 3(1) in Section 1 of Chapter 4 for a comparison with the Australia's Administrative Appeals Tribunal which has a "small business taxation department."

are many appeals on penalties stipulated under TMA §93 (Failure to make a return for income tax and capital gains tax). In principle, proceedings of appeal cases classified into this category will be conducted only on paper, but if the claimant or the HMRC requests a hearing, the rules and proceeding under the above category ② (Basic cases) generally apply.[74] The appeals to be categorized into ② (Basic cases) include those on penalties for underreporting and those on reduction of penalties. There are many appeals against penalties for underreporting/payment under paragraph 15 (appeal) in Schedule 24 (Penalties for errors) of the Finance Act 2007. Appeals, which are categorized into "Basic cases," are subject to hearings in principle, but the claimant and the HMRC may request a review only on paper instead if they consider it preferable. Even if hearings are to be conducted for "Basic cases," the materials required for preparing for the hearings are minimal, so they are also called "turn up and talk" cases.

The appeals to be categorized into the above ③ (Standard cases) are those that do not come under the other categories of cases. As for the appeals coming under the above ④ (Complex cases), they are those on: (i) complex matters, (ii) cases that require long hearings, or (iii) cases in which a disputed tax amount is large. A disputing party may request their case, which is categorized into "Standard cases," to be reclassified into "Complex cases," and a request for reclassification in the opposite direction is also possible. There is not much difference in the procedures to be followed by the disputing parties whose cases are categorized into either "Standard cases" or "Complex cases," but "Complex cases" may require case management hearings in order to clarify the points of contention or reorganize the parties' arguments. Also, in the case of an appeal coming under "Complex cases," the First-tier Tribunal may, after having considered various relevant circumstances and with the approval of the claimant and the HMRC, approach the head of the Tax Chamber and he could, with the consent of the Tax and Chancery Chamber of the Upper Tribunal, refer the case to the Upper Tribunal for its review of the case.

The abovementioned categorization of appeals into four in accordance with their content and applying different procedures to them should be effective in realizing efficient handling of appeals, but the reality is that the days needed for the First-tier Tribunal to process appeals are getting longer, and accordingly, as shown in Figure 3.7, the cumulative number of outstanding cases is also increasing. For example, in 2019-2020 and 2020-2021, the average number of days from the receipt of an appeal to its processing was 14 days and 22 days for "Default Paper cases," 33 days and 37 days for the "Basic cases," 60 days and 73 days for the "Standard cases" (lower category cases), 84 days and 110 days for the "Standard cases" (higher category cases), and 142 cases and 135 cases for the "Complex cases."[75] Such delays are caused by a variety of factors, and not all of them are attributable to the Tribunal, but one of the main reasons for this is the increasing number of cases in which the number of days spent from the

74. *See* ARTG8350 (First-tier and Upper Tribunals: preparing for tribunal: categories of tribunal case) and ARTG8370 (Default Paper cases) for details.
75. *See* The Tax Law Review Committee 2021 Report (The Tax Tribunals: The Next 10 Years) pp. 17-18 and Table 4.1.

day of the Tribunal's hearings to the day of its decision is quite long. For example, between 2000 and 2006, almost no cases took more than 200 days from the hearing to the decision, but after 2011, there were 10 cases to 32 cases that took more than 200 days from the hearing to the decision.[76]

Figure 3.7 Annual Number of First-Tier Tribunal's Delayed Processing of Published Cases

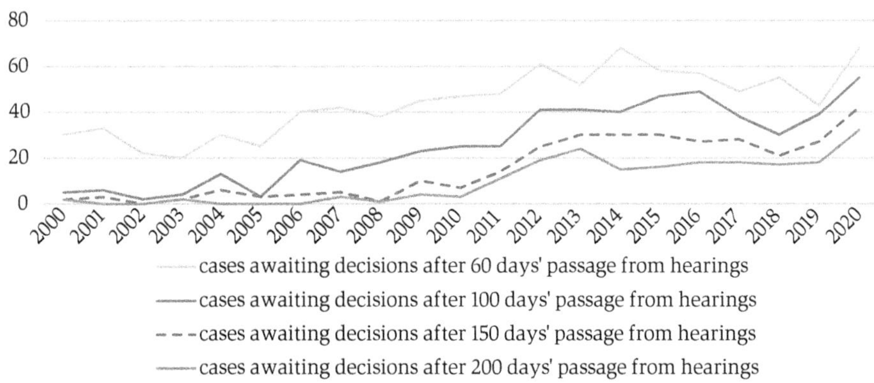

Source: Compiled from Table 4.2 of Tax Law Review Commission's The Tax Tribunals: the next 10 years.

Of course, the majority of cases that take many days before the First-tier Tribunal's decisions are made fall under the "Standard cases" (higher category) or "Complex cases," but the other categories also pose challenges because the availability of ADR is limited for those cases. This limit is also confirmed in the aforementioned HMRC publication (CC/FS21) and ADR Guidance, which state that those cases categorized by the First-tier Tribunal into "Default Paper cases" or "Basic cases" are not fit for ADR. The HMRC's practice follows this statement and has confined the use of ADR to those cases falling under "Standard cases" or "Complex cases."[77] Such practice gives rise to many decisions of the First-tier Tribunal, and for a party that is dissatisfied with them, the next step for further contestation is, in principle, as provided for in paragraph 39 (Application for permission to appeal) of the First Stage Tribunal Rules of Procedure, to request for admission to contest the decision within 56 days of the mailing date of the decision, but an appeal to the Upper Tribunal is allowed only on the point of law. If the First-tier Tribunal grants further appeal, it forwards its findings and decision to the Upper Tribunal.[78]

76. *See supra* "Tax Law Review Committee 2021 Report" Table 4.2.
77. However, tax avoidance scheme cases, which are often categorized into "Complex cases," are usually not subject to ADR.
78. If the First-tier Tribunal does not grant the appeal, a request for permission to appeal to the Upper Tribunal in accordance with para. 21 (application to the Upper Tribunal for permission to appeal) of the Tribunal Procedure (Amendment) Rules 2009 can be made.

2 Rules on Costs Recovery at Administrative Stages

As TMA §50 (Procedure) dictates, the burden of proof is, in principle, on the disputing taxpayer, and in a case where the Tribunals find such facts that should increase the tax amount in dispute, they should do so.[79] Certainly, the costs incurred in connection with the dispute at the administrative stage before the First-tier Tribunal are basically borne by the parties to the dispute. However, the Tribunal Procedure (First-tier Tribunal) (Tax Chamber) Rules 2009 (No. 273(L.1), hereinafter called "FTT Rule") 10 (Order for costs) (1) stipulates that the Tribunal may make an order for costs in such cases: (a) "wasted costs" under TCE Act §29(4) arose; (b) one party or its representative has acted unreasonably in conducting proceedings; (c) if the proceedings have been categorized as a "Complex case" and the taxpayer did not make a written request that the proceedings should be excluded from the potential liability of costs.[80] TCE Act§29(5) defines "wasted costs" under the above TCE Act§29(4) to be any costs incurred by a party as a result of any improper, unreasonable, or negligent act or omission on the part of any legal or other representative or which, in light of any such act or omission occurring after they were incurred, the Tribunal considers it is unreasonable to expect that party to pay.[81]

The First-Tier Tribunal's decision on Sussex Cars Association and the Commissioners for Her Majesty's Revenue and Customs (Appeal No: TC/2015/04250) is one example of the application of paragraph (1)(b) of the above FTT Rule 10. In this case, the HMRC sent a notice of assessment to impose VAT on the claimant's supply of goods to the third party, and then the claimant submitted a Notice of Appeal to the First-tier Tribunal and applied for ADR as well on the same day. After ADR did not lead to the resolution of the dispute, the HMRC withdrew its defense of the Appeal on this case at the First-Tier Tribunal, so at issue was whether the claimant could base itself on this paragraph/provision to request the HMRC to bear the costs of the claimant. In deciding on this issue, the First-Tier Tribunal relied on the following three criteria set out in the Upper Tribunal decision ([2014] UKUT 0362(TCC)) in Shahjahan Tarafdar (t/a Sha Indian Cuisine): (i) the reason for a party's withdrawal from a disputing case, (ii) whether or not the withdrawal from the proceedings could have been made at an earlier stage in light of the reasons for the withdrawal, and (iii) whether or not it was reasonable not to withdraw from the proceedings at an earlier stage.

79. The Court of Appeal ruled in *Brady v. Group Lotus* ([1987] STC), "Where the assessments are made in time, ... the burden lies on the taxpayer from the start to displace the assessment." TMA §50 provides in para. (7), "If, on an appeal notified to the tribunal, the tribunal decides—(a) that the appellant is undercharged to tax ... (b) ... (c) ..., the assessment or amounts shall be increased accordingly." Japan's Article 98 (3) of AGRNT provides that the Tax Tribunal's decision cannot change the dispute re/assessment worse for the claimant. *See* 1 in Section 1 of Chapter 1.

80. Most taxpayers, including large corporations, tend to request their cases not to be categorized under "Complex cases." *See* Claiming costs in the Tribunal (at https://www.levyandlevy.co.the UK/claiming-costs-tribunal-worth/).

81. Whereas, the Tribunal Procedure Rule 10(5) provides that the Tribunal may not make an order under para. (1) against a person (the "paying person") if the paying person is an individual, considering that person's financial means.

In the above Sussex case, the First-tier Tribunal, in light of the three criteria set forth in the above Shahjahan case, observed the followings: the reason for withdrawal referred to in the above (i) was HMRC's delayed awareness of the fact that there would be no revenue increase from this case because, under VATA §33 (Refunds of VAT in certain cases), even if VAT is imposed on the claimant, the third party who is the business partner can claim the VAT refund; as for the above criterion (ii) on the possibility of withdrawal at an earlier stage, the HMRC's earlier withdrawal from the proceedings was possible now that the claimant made a reference to the above result under VATA §33 at the ADR stage but it was not taken into consideration by the HMRC at that time because the personnel in charge of the ADR was a lay advocate; regarding the above (iii) criterion of whether the delayed withdrawal was reasonable, the HMRC's withdrawal was after the case was considered by a qualified member of staff and the HMRC's inaction at an earlier stage in seeking for a legal advice from him was not reasonable. Based on these observations, the Tribunal decided that the HMRC should bear the claimant's costs incurred in connection with the ADR and the dispute at the Tribunal.

As mentioned above, the First-tier Tribunal also orders costs shifting in a case where a claimant lost in the "Complex cases" pursuant to the FTT rule 10(1)(c), just as he lost at the Upper Tribunal.[82] The validity of such orders was confirmed by the Upper Tribunal decision on Julian Massey and Beryl Massey T/A Hilden Part Partnership, Hilden Park LLP and The Commissioners for HMRC ([2015] UKUT 0405 TCC). In this case, the claimant/partnership that owned the golf course and used to collect VAT at the standard rate from the users of the golf course entered into a contract with a nonprofit organization and rented the golf course and received rents, claimed that both these rents and the services provided by the organization were exempt from VAT under Schedule 9 (Exemptions) of VATA.[83] This claim was dismissed by the preceding First-tier Tribunal's decision ([2013] UKFTT 391 (TC)) that found this contract to be the abusive practice of intending to obtain a tax advantage contrary to the purpose of the VAT Directives so that they are not VAT exempt, and the First-tier Tribunal ordered the claimant to pay the HMRC's costs of the appeals.

In the above decision, the Upper Tribunal held that this scheme in question was an abuse of law within the Halifax principle, so the HMRC was correct to re-characterize the transactions and treat the supplies made by the organization as having been made by the partnership for the relevant years. As for the question of whether this case was substantial and complex, the Upper Tribunal answered in the affirmative by confirming that, in addition to the fact that the appeal is related to several accounting

82. The Tribunal Procedure (Upper Tribunal) Rules 2008 states in 10(Order for costs)(a)(4), "The Upper Tribunal may make an order for costs (or, in Scotland, expenses) on an application or on its own initiative." As for the definition of "costs," *see* Guide §2.1 (The meaning of "costs") of the Senior Courts Costs Office (SCCO) referred to in 1 of Section 4.

83. Schedule 9 of the Act provides that, as for Group 1 (Land) Item No. 1, "The grant of any interest in or right over land or of any license to occupy land ..." is exempt from VAT, and as for Group 10 (Sport, sports competitions and physical education) Item No. 3, VAT is exempted for "the supply by an eligible body to an individual...of services closely linked with and essential to sport or physical education in which the individual is taking part."

periods over a number of years and the appeals involved large sums, this decision required a hearing of two and a half days and this was not a run-of-the-mill case. As for the validity of the First-tier Tribunal's costs order, the Upper Tribunal noted that in a written ministerial statement made on March 10, 2009, the then Financial Secretary to the Treasury confirmed that the Sheldon practice would continue to apply on a transitional basis and the HMRC would not seek costs from appellants in most cases[84] but agreed on the First-tier Tribunal's determination that it was a reasonable exercise of HMRC's discretion to add tax avoidance as another category of exceptions to the Sheldon practice.

In the above Massey case, the HMRC claimed that tax avoidance constitutes a case, apart from "Complex cases," which is outside the scope of "Sheldon practice," and such a claim was upheld by the Tribunals. This HMRC's claim seems to be consistent with its stance of construing narrowly the application scope of the "Sheldon practice" under the current Tribunals system. Such a current stance is also expressed in the Ministry of Justice's 2008 report ("Transforming Tribunals: Implementing Part 1 of the Tribunals, Courts and Enforcement Act 2007 – The Government's Response"). It mentions on page 34 as follows, "the Government considers that the basic principle should be that any power of the tribunal to award costs should apply equally to both parties and intends not to operate the Sheldon practice in the new Tax Chamber ... the Government intends to take forward the proposition in the consultation document that costs should be available for some large, substantial or complex tax cases." Likewise, the Costs Review Group, which was established at the request of the Senior President of Tribunals, confirms in its 2011 Report("Costs in Tribunals: Report by the Costs Review Group to the Senior President of Tribunals")that the HMRC holds the above view and stance on how it applies the "Sheldon practice."[85]

"Rees practice" is another exception to the rule of seeking the payment of the HMRC's appeals costs from the taxpayers who lost in the disputes. The "Rees practice" was expressed by Minister of State at the Treasury, Peter Reeds, on March 12, 1980,[86] and it has generally been followed by the HMRC ever since. Under the "Rees practice," in a case where the HMRC challenges the adequacy of an adverse Tribunal decision in court and the court overturns the decision, the HMRC does not seek the taxpayer to

84. As for "Sheldon practice," *see* 1 of Section 1.

85. Paragraph 50 of the Report states, "The VAT Tribunal had a general power to make costs orders, but HMRC did not normally seek costs against an unsuccessful appellant and normally paid the costs of a successful appellant. This was known as the Sheldon practice. HMRC refused to extend this practice into the Tax Chamber."

86. To be precise, Minister Rees mentioned, "Revenue departments ... are willing in appropriate circumstances, and in particular where it is they who are appealing against an adverse decision, to waiver their claims to costs .... Influential factors include the risk of financial hardship to the other party and whether the case is one of significant interest to taxpayers as a whole, turning on a point of law in need of clarification."

bear the HMRC's appeals costs. The HMRC shows its stance of adhering to this practice in its 2021 Report ("Evaluation of HMRC's Implementation of Powers, Obligations and Safeguards").[87] Such stance of the HMRC is also confirmed in paragraph 75 of the above 2011 Report of the Costs Review Group, while the above 2011 Report proposes in paragraph 194 that the "Rees practice" in the Tax Chamber should be formalized in the Rules now that there are cases like *Jones (Respondent) v. Garrett (Her Majesty's Inspector of Taxes)* ([2007] HL 78 TC 597) in which the HMRC declined to invoke the Rees practice where it should have even if the ground for the HMRC appealing against the adverse judgment in the Court of Appeal on this case was that a point of law of general public importance was involved in this case.[88]

SECTION 4 MAIN POINTS OF ISSUES ON TAX LITIGATION

1 History and Rationale of "English Rule" on Costs

If an aggrieved taxpayer is unsatisfied with the Tribunals' rulings and is willing to dispute them further, the next step is to file, with a Tribunal's permission, a lawsuit in court. As is clear from a comparison of Figures 3.6 and 3.8, there is generally little significant difference between the tribunal and the court in the percentage of the HMRC's assessment being sustained (including those in which the HMRC won on major points),[89] but the recent number of court judgments on tax cases is very small.[90] For example, there were fifty-seven cases (twenty-six direct tax cases and thirty-one indirect tax cases) in 2005, and they were thirty-three High Court judgments, fifteen Court of Appeal judgments and Scottish Court of Civil Appeal judgments, nine House of Lords judgments, while the average number of tax appeals received by the Upper Tribunal and by the courts for 2016-2017 to 2020-2021 was 4.4% and 2.6% respectively of those received by the First-tier Tribunal. The main cause for this should be monetary and time costs associated with appeals at the Tribunals and courts. In particular, a taxpayer's financial risks associated with appeals (especially those related to "costs" or attorney's fees) at the Upper Tribunal and courts are significant compared with those associated with appeals at the First-tier Tribunal, provided that they are not categorized into "Complex cases."

87. At pp. 56-57 of the Report states, "HMRC will normally apply for costs in cases where the tribunal or court has ruled in the Department's favor. However, HMRC will sometimes agree in advance not to seek the costs of an appeal, particularly if it is appealing against an adverse decision at the Upper Tribunal or the appeal courts."

88. In this case, the House of Lords ruled in favor of the taxpayers but they had to make an appeal for recovering their costs.

89. Exceptions are 2019-2020 at the Court of Appeal and the Supreme Court. Similarly, in 1990 and 1991, more than 30% of the decisions of the Value-Added Customs Tribunal were overturned by the courts. *See* Oliver, *supra*, "The Role of the Tax Tribunals," p. 190.

90. For more information, *see* Jones, *supra* "Tax Treaties" p. 35.

Figure 3.8 Number of Tax Dispute Decisions/Judgments and HMRC's Winning Ratio

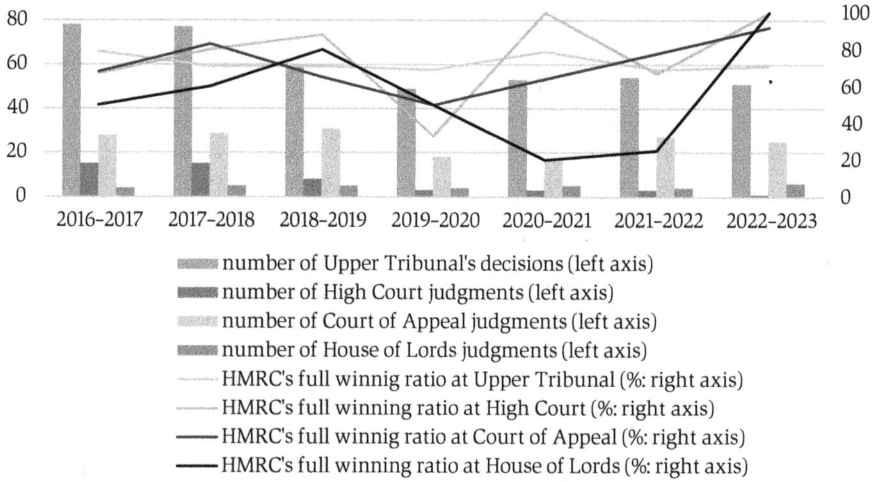

Source: HMRC TAC Reports for 2017-2023, Table: Data relating to decided appeals.

Civil Procedure Rules (CPR) Part 44 (General rules about costs) provides for the payment rules for attorney's fees, etc. In particular, CPR §44.2 (Court's discretion as to costs) states in paragraph (1) that a court has discretion as to whether costs are payable by one party to another, and if the court decides to make an order about costs, the general rule is that the unsuccessful party will be ordered to pay the costs of the successful party. This is the so-called English rule on costs ("Costs follow the event rule"). It is pointed out that the origin of the "English rule" is the law ("An Act that the Defendant shall recover costs against the plaintiff if the plaintiff is nonsuited or if the verdict passed against him.") which was enacted by Parliament in 1531 during the reign of Henry VIII (the second king of the Tudor dynasty).[91] As mentioned above, under paragraph 10 (Order for costs) (1)(c) of the FTT rule, in a case where an appealed case is categorized under the "Complex cases" and the claimant does not make a written request for it to be excluded from the potential liability of costs, costs of the "winning party" ("receiving party") are to be shifted to the "paying person" and this is a *mutatis mutandis* application of the "English rule" to the administrative adjudication stage.

According to the Senior Courts Costs Office (SCCO, which belongs to the High Court) Guide §2.1 (The meaning of "costs"), the costs referred to in the above CPR Part 44 include: (i) disbursements (often incurred by a legal representative acting on his client and comprise counsel's fees, court fees, and witness expenses), and (ii) the fees which a legal representative charges to his client ("profit costs"). As for attorney's fees

91. *See* Judge Mostyn in the High Court (Administrative Court) judgment on the *Kuznetsov* case (2019) to be described later in 2 in this Section.

payable to a barrister, they come under the above (i), and profit costs payable to a solicitor come under the above (ii). What decides how much of the costs of the receiving party is allowed to be recovered is the order of the courts and the Tribunals or the agreement of the parties. In a case where an agreement is not reached, the receiving party could ask for detailed assessments of the costs by submitting a form (N258: Request for provisional/general detailed assessments), and a bill of costs, etc., to SCCO and a costs judge may determine the amount of recoverable costs after hearings from the parties. If the parties are dissatisfied with the SCCO's decision, they can, if permission is granted, bring an appeal to a High Court judge with a further appeal to the Court of Appeal.[92]

Regarding the essence of the "English rule," the Court of Exchequer explained in *Harold v. Smith* ([1860] 5 Hand N 381) as follows, "Costs as between party and party are given by the law as an indemnity to the person entitled to them: they are not imposed as a punishment on the party who pays them, nor given as a bonus to the party who receives them. Therefore, if the extent of the indemnification can be found out, the extent to which costs ought to be allowed is also ascertained....as a general rule, costs are an indemnity." This explanation of the nature of cost recovery under the "English rule" by the receiving party in the litigation has been relied upon in subsequent court judgments as the "indemnity principle'' under which recoverable costs should be less than the actual costs incurred by the receiving party. The 1974 Solicitors Act Part 3 (Remuneration of solicitors)§60 (Effect of contentious business agreement) (3) also provides, "A client shall not be entitled to recover from any other person under an order for the payment of any costs to which a contentious business agreement relates more than the amount payable by him to his solicitor in respect of those costs under the agreement."

As for the calculation methods of the recoverable costs by the receiving party in accordance with the "indemnity principle," CPR §44.3 stipulates that, where the court is to assess the amount of costs, it will assess those costs on the standard basis or on the indemnity basis, but the court will not, in either case, allow costs which have been unreasonably incurred or are unreasonable in amount. Where the amount of costs is to be assessed on a standard basis, the court will only allow costs that are proportionate to the matters in issue, while in the case of costs assessed on the indemnity basis, there is no such proportionality.[93] Furthermore, the standard basis and the indemnity basis differ not only in their way of calculating the amount of recoverable costs but also in the burden of proof regarding the reasonableness of the costs. When the standard basis is employed in calculating the recoverable costs, the receiving party bears the burden of proof on the reasonableness of its costs, while the paying person bears the burden of proof when the indemnity basis is relied on. Therefore, the indemnity basis is

92. For details, *see* SCCO Guide and http://www.gov.the UK/assess-approve-court-costs/get-a-detailed assessment.
93. It is pointed out that the amount of attorney's fees, etc. that the winning party can usually recover is less than 60% of the actual amount (*see supra* "Claiming costs in the Tribunal"), but some say that it is about 65% to 85% (https://www.gdlaw.co.the UK/site/blog/our-services/dispute-resolution/recovery-of-legal-costs-in-the-courts-of-england-and-wales).

preferable for the receiving party, but it is not so common for it to be employed by the court in calculating the receiving party's recoverable amount of costs.

As for the factors to be taken into consideration in calculating the recoverable costs, CPR §44.2 (Court's discretion as to costs) states that the court will have regard to all the circumstances, including – (i) the conduct of all the parties; (ii) whether a party has succeeded on the part of its case; (iii) any admissible offer to settle made by a party, and CPR §44.4 (Factors to be taken into account in deciding the amount of costs) (3) prescribes that the court will also have regard to the amount or value of any money or property involved; the importance of the matter to all the parties; the particular complexity of the matter or the difficulty or novelty of the questions raised; the skill, effort, specialized knowledge, and responsibility involved; the time spent on the case; the place where and the circumstances in which work or any part of it was done; and the receiving party's last approved or agreed budget. Despite these specifications, as the Court of Appeal noted in *Excelsior Commercial & Industrial Holdings Ltd v. Salisbury Hammer Aspden & Johnson* ([2002] EWCA Civ 879), for costs order on an indemnity basis to be made, there must be some conduct or some circumstance which takes the case out of the norm, and there are such circumstances in this case.[94]

2 Transformation of the "English Rule"

As mentioned above, there seem to be uncertainties in some cases about the actual amount of recoverable costs by the receiving party under the "English rule,"[95] and these uncertainties are compounded by the width of discretion a trial judge has, as it was emphasized by the above Court of Appeal judgment on the *Excelsior Commercial* case (2002). Moreover, there are various exceptions to the "English rule," and some of them have metamorphosed over the years. In particular, under the traditional "English rule," a winning litigant in person who should have no attorney fees to pay in connection with his litigation used to be out of the scope of costs order by court, but there were arguments over whether exceptions should be allowed in the following cases: (i) the winning party is a litigant in person but he is a lawyer himself ("lawyer in person" exception), (ii) the attorney of the winning party is not an attorney outside but an in-house lawyer ("employed attorney" exception). Thenceforth, the "English rule" in the UK has metamorphosed in such a way that it incorporates those exceptions, and courts make costs order for them, making it digress from the so-called primary rule, which is observed in such countries as NZ that do not allow these exceptions under the rule of "costs follow the event."[96]

94. In this case, the Court of Appeal also pointed out that, on the issue of costs order based on the indemnity basis, it is dangerous for the court to try and add to the requirements of the CPR which are not spelt out in the relevant parts of the CPR, and this court can do no more than draw attention to the width of the discretion of the trial judge.
95. In this connection, it is notable that CPR §27.14 (Costs on the small claims track) states, "(1) This rule applies to any case which has been allocated to the small claims track (...). (2) The court may not order a party to pay a sum to another party ..., except (a) the fixed costs attributable to issuing the claim."
96. *See* 4 in Section 2 of Chapter 4 for the "primary rule" in NZ.

The above (i) ("lawyer in person" exception) was first recognized in the Court of Appeal judgment on *The London Scottish Benefit Society v. Chorley, Crawford and Chester* ([1884] 13 QBD 872). The Court affirmed the judgment of the Queen's Bench Division ([1884] 12, Q.B.D. 452) and dismissed the action against the solicitor who was successful in the litigation by concluding that he is entitled to the recovery of full costs subject to certain deductions because there is no difference as regards the right to costs between a solicitor and an ordinary person. Particularly, the Court specified the following: (i) private expenditure of labor and trouble by a layman cannot be measured because it depends on the zeal, the assiduity, or the nervousness of the individual while professional skill and labor are recognized, and can be measured by the law; (ii) it would be absurd to permit a solicitor to charge for the same work when it is done by another solicitor, and not to permit him to charge for it when it is done by his own clerk because otherwise, he would always employ another solicitor to avoid unrecoverable loss of time and money; (iii) as Lord Justice Lush mentioned, an attorney regularly qualified is allowed to make the same charges for business done when he sues or defends in person, as when he acts as attorney for another.

The first case that allowed the above (ii) ("employed attorney" exception) was the Exchequer Court judgment on *Attorney-General v. Shillibeer* ([1894] 4 Ex 606, 154 ER 1356). In this judgment, the Court allowed the winning party, with the in-house attorney who was employed as a salary income earner, the recovery of the attorney fee, which was calculated in accordance with the standard applicable to a case where the representative of a taxpayer is not a taxpayer's in-house attorney. The subsequent court judgments followed suit for the reason that the difficulty in calculating the recoverable costs in the case of the in-house attorney is no excuse for denying the recovery. In particular, in *Lloyds Bank Ltd v. Eastwood* ([1975] Ch, 112), the Court of Appeal showed two guiding principles by mentioning that the appropriate method of taxation of a bill of costs where the party was represented by a salaried solicitor was: (i) to treat it as though it were the bill of an independent solicitor assessing the reasonable and fair amount of a discretionary item, having regard to all the circumstances of the case, and (ii) the principle that the tax costs should not be more than an indemnity to the party against the expense he had incurred in litigation.

The validity of the above two principles was also confirmed by the High Court judgment on *Kuznetsov v. London Borough of Camden* ([2019] EWHC 3910 (Admin)). In this case, the claimant, who lost at the Upper Tribunal and was ordered to pay the in-house attorney's fees (GBP 317 per hour) of the winning party (an administrative agency), asserted that this amount violated the indemnity principle in comparison with the maximum hourly wage (found to be GBP 41.75 by the claimant's request for disclosure made to the administrative agency) of an in-house attorney of the winning party. But the Court pointed out that the Court of Appeal judgment on *Cole v. British Telecoms PLC* ([2000] 2 Costs LR. 310) confirmed that the principle set out in the Court of Appeal judgment on the aforementioned *Lloyds Bank* case (1975) was alive even after it was incorporated in CPR,[97] and it dismissed the claimant's assertion by ruling

97. *See* CPR §48.6 mentioned below. In para. 9 of the Court of Appeal judgment on the *Cole* case, Judge Buxton held, "The judgment of this court in In Re Eastwood establishes that the

that GBP 317 encompasses a great deal more than just the costs, the payroll costs, of the people sitting in the offices of the London Borough of Camden, and it extends to a contribution to the infrastructural costs of the borough itself, so this case is not a special case which demands an exception to the general rule on costs.

In particular, the above conclusion of the Court of Appeal on the *Chorley* case (1884) has basically been followed by the subsequent court rulings as the "Chorley exception," which falls out of the principle that costs are not recoverable in the case of "litigants in person" in the UK and some of the Commonwealth Countries.[98] Moreover, in the case of the UK, the Litigants in Person (Costs and Expenses) Act 1975§1(1) (Costs or expenses recoverable) was introduced to allow an unrepresented lay plaintiff who is a receiving party to recover the amount equivalent to attorney's fees.[99] CPR §48.6 (Litigants in person) also provides in paragraph (1) that the rules set forth in this section apply to orders relating to costs awarded to unrepresented prevailing parties and paragraph (2) that the costs allowed under this rule must not exceed, except in the case of a disbursement, two-thirds of the amount which would have been allowed if the litigant in person had been represented by a legal representative,[100] and in paragraph (6) that a litigant in person includes—(a) a company or other corporation which is acting without a legal representative; and (b) a barrister, solicitor, solicitor's employee or other authorized litigator who is acting for himself.

3 Mitigation and Avoidance of Litigation Risk

Paragraph 15 of the aforementioned Costs Review Group 2011 Report points out that legal assistance related to many civil cases has become a thing of the past due to repeated restrictions by the former government, but, as mentioned above, the "English rule" has metamorphosed in such a way that mitigates the costs problem of a litigant in person. As for the court procedure that confronts a litigant in person, there is a problem that he is generally unfamiliar with, and it may also hinder the realization of a speedy trial. Moreover, this problem is compounded by the fact that defense activities in court are, in principle, limited to a lawyer or "an authorized person." But this problem is also mitigated by the 2007 Legal Services Act which stipulates in paragraph

conventional method appropriate to taxing the bill of a solicitor in private practice is also appropriate for the bill of an in-house solicitor in all but special cases where it is reasonably plain that that method will infringe the indemnity principle."

98. While, in the *Pentelow* case (2019), the Australian High Court stated that the "Chorley exception" should not be followed as a judicial precedent in Australia. *See* 4(1) in Section 1 of Chapter 4.
99. The first part of this paragraph prescribes, "Where, in any proceedings to which this subsection applies, any costs of a litigant in person are ordered to be paid by any other party to the proceedings or in any other way, there may, subject to the rules of the court, be allowed on the taxation or other determination of those costs sums in respect of any work done, and any expenses and losses incurred, by the litigant in or in connection with the proceedings to which the order relates," and the second part states that such treatment applies to court judgments and most of the Tribunals' decisions on disputes on civil matters.
100. Practice Direction 46 (Costs-Special cases) §3.4 pertaining to CPR states that the amount which may be allowed to a self-represented litigant is GBP 19 per hour. However, in reality, depending on the circumstances, other amounts may be possible.

1 of Schedule 3 that it also authorizes the court to allow, as an exception, "an exempt person" to act like "an authorized person." Also, there is an option, with the permission of the court, of fighting the case with the help of an unqualified person (known as a "McKenzie friend") in and out of court. This option has become available since the *McKenzie v. McKenzie* case ([1971] P33), in which the Court of Appeal allowed the Australian lawyer who was unable to defend a litigant in English court to assist the unrepresented litigant in court.

Now that there has been an increase in the number of litigants without representatives as well as the potential usefulness of a "McKenzie friend," "Master of Rolls" made public the 2010 Guideline (Practice Guidance—McKenzie Friends: Civilian and Family Courts) that clarifies issues on a "McKenzie friend." In particular, paragraph 23 of the Guideline states that "McKenzie friends" are basically allowed only when there are "special or exceptional circumstances,"[101] but a "McKenzie friend" is in line with the purpose of Article 6 (Right to a fair trial) of the ECHR, and it has become a practice of the court to allow a "McKenzie friend" in court when it determines that it contributes to the implementation of a fair and just trial. Even so, a "McKenzie friend" differs from an attorney in that he cannot act as an agent of a taxpayer to manage cases, defend him in court, or interrogate witnesses. Furthermore, even if the court's judgment is in favor of the taxpayer, any expenses incurred by the "McKenzie friend" cannot be recovered by shifting their burden to the other party.[102] Despite these limitations inherent in a "McKenzie friend," he is a support for the taxpayer, and his advice may help the taxpayer sort out his claims so that he might receive a more favorable court judgment.

Whereas, as pointed out in the above 2010 Guideline issued by "Master of Rolls," lately, there is an increase in the number of those who have not been trained appropriately but take up as profession of serving as a "McKenzie friend" for a fee lower than the standard, with the result that they sometimes do more harm than good to a litigant. In light of such limit and risk inherent in the case of a "McKenzie friend," some may prefer to utilize such arrangements as "conditional fee agreement" and " after-the-fact insurance premiums," which are often offered by insurance companies. In a case where a taxpayer could utilize them, the costs shifted to him on account of the unfavorable court judgment on him are to be borne practically by the insurance company, so he could avoid the risk of paying the other party's attorney's fees regardless of whether the court judgment is favorable to him or not. But, as paragraph 16 of the 2011 Report of the Costs Review Group mentions that it is unclear what kind of risks there are in the use of "conditional fee agreement" and "after-the-event insurance premiums," the implications of utilizing these arrangements vary.[103] Moreover, it is not that every disputing taxpayer can utilize these arrangements.

101. As for examples of cases that come under "special or exceptional circumstances," *see* para. 21 (Terminology for Litigants in Person) of the 2013 Practice Guideline.
102. The recovery of expenses is possible in the case of an "exempt person" (under para. 1 in Schedule 3 of 2007 Legal Service Act) who is in most cases a "solicitor's agent" whose activity at court is more restrictive than an attorney.
103. As for other views of the Costs Review Group on costs, *see* footnote 85 and first paragraph of 3 in this Section.

Therefore, some litigants (including litigants in persons) may prefer other options for reducing the risk of paying the other party's costs. One of such options has come from the Court of Appeal judgment on *Calderbank v. Calderbank* ([1975] 3 All ER 333 EWCA). In this judgment, the court showed a principle that if the amount won by the winning party turned out to be less than the amount of the dispute resolution proposed by the losing party but not accepted by the winning party, the amount of costs that the court orders the losing party to pay to the winning party would become less. Moreover, in *Cutts v. Head* ([1984] 2 WLR 349), the Court of Appeal held that this "Calderbank offer" (or "Without prejudice save as to costs offer") shall be applicable to all civil litigations.[104] Also, the idea of the "Calderbank offer" is incorporated in CPR §44.2 (Courts discretion as to costs) (4), under which a court considers all circumstances in making costs order, and they include whether or not there was an offer made to end the lawsuit, the validity of the allegations, and the need to continue the lawsuit. Therefore, although there are not many examples of its utilization in tax lawsuits, the "Calderbank offer" could function, in conjunction with CPR §44.2, as a measure that may reduce the risk of paying the attorney's fees of the other party.

CPR has some other rules as well that practically revise the "English rule" to the benefit of taxpayers. For example, CPR §3.19 (Costs capping orders— General) and CPR §52.9A (Orders to limit the recoverable costs of an appeal) allow a court to cap the amount of costs order by taking account of the taxpayer's financial resources and the public interest nature of the litigation.[105] In particular, the above CPR §52.9A is adopted practically in response to Lord Jackson's 2009 Report (Review of Civil Litigation Costs: Final Report), which was prepared to address the concern of high-ranking officials of the Ministry of Justice that civil litigation costs could become substantial. In particular, in light of the current rule under which appeals on small claims that reach the Court of Appeal from the High Court are subject to full costs shifting and appeals from the Tribunals to the courts commonly move from a no-costs regime to a costs-shifting regime,[106] this Final Report makes a proposal in paragraph 4.1 of Chapter 34 (Appeals) in Part 5 that appellate courts should have a discretionary power, upon granting permission to appeal or receiving an appeal from a no-costs jurisdiction, to order: (a) that each side should bear its own costs of the appeal, or (b) that the recoverable costs should be capped at a specified sum.

4 Further Changes to the "English Rule"

The "English rule" has metamorphosed further lately. The main causes for such metamorphosis include the Aarhus Convention, which was adopted in 1998 by the UN

104. To be precise, in the *Cutts* case, the Court of Appeal stated, "the practice of making offers in the Calderbank form is by no means limited to the Family Division . ... It seems to me that, if the practice is valid, ... it should then be of universal application."
105. CPR §3.19(1) stipulates, "(a) 'costs capping order' means an order limiting the amount of future costs (including disbursements) which a party may recover pursuant to an order for costs subsequently made; and (b) 'future costs' means costs incurred in respect of work done after the date of the costs capping order."
106. *See* para. 3.3 in Chapter 34 (Appeals) of Part 5 of the Final Report.

Economic Commission for Europe (UNECE) and which many European countries, including the UK, have signed.[107] In particular, the Aarhus Convention Compliance Committee concluded in several Recommendations dated 24 September 2010 that the UK government has not fulfilled its obligation to prevent violations of Article 9 (Access to justice) of the Convention.[108] Specifically, the Committee found that the "English rule" on costs could violate the Convention particularly because: (i) in making costs order, a court has considerable discretion, and there is a significant lack of transparency and risk regarding the amount of costs to be ordered;[109] (ii) the applicable scope of the protective costs order shown by the Court of Appeal judgment on *Corner House Research v. Secretary of State for Trade and Industry* ([2005] EWCA Civ 192) is narrow;[110] (iii) there is a judgment which regarded the principles in the Convention as nothing but one of the factors to be considered in exercising a court's discretion;[111] (iv) there is also a judgment ordering the losing party to bear "prohibitively expensive" costs which are referred to in Article 9 of the Convention.

The judgment referred to in the above (iv) is, according to paragraph 36 of the Aarhus Convention Compliance Committee's 24/9/2010 Recommendation (Findings and recommendations with regard to communication ACCC/C/2008/27 concerning compliance by the United Kingdom of Great Britain and Northern Ireland), the Court of Appeal (Queen's Seat of Northern Ireland) judgment on Kinnegar Residents' Action Group & Ors, Re Judicial Review ([2007] NIQB 90 (7 November 2007) Ref: GIRC 5962). In this judgment, the Court ordered the losing plaintiff to pay GBP 39,454 to the Environment Agency. Whereas, paragraph 49 of the Aarhus Convention Compliance Committee's 24/9/2010 Recommendation (Findings and recommendations with regard to communication ACCC/C/2008/23 concerning compliance by the United Kingdom of Great Britain and Northern Ireland) confirms that the amount (interim costs of GBP 5,132) ordered to be paid by the plaintiff to the Environment Agency, etc., by Judge Seymour in the High Court (Queen's Bench) judgment on *Morgan v. Hilton Organics (Wessex) Ltd.* ([2009] EWCA Civ 107) was not "prohibitively high." There is certainly a fairly large difference between the amount of money ordered to be paid by the paying person in those two judgments.

107. The official title of the Aarhus Convention is Convention on Access to Information, Public Participation in Decision-Making and Access to Justice in Environmental Matters.
108. In particular, Article 9(5) of the Aarhus Convention states, "In order to further the effectiveness of the provisions of this article, each party shall ensure that information is provided to the public on access to administrative and judicial review procedures and shall consider the establishment of appropriate assistance mechanisms to remove or reduce financial and other barriers to access to justice."
109. *See* paras. 135 and 136 of the Recommendation of 24 Sep. 2010 (Findings and Recommendations of the Aarhus Convention Compliance Committee with regard to Communication ACCC/C/2008/33 concerning Compliance by the United Kingdom).
110. *See* para. 99 on ACCC/C/2008/33 above. In this judgment, in accordance with the concept of a "protective costs order," the court, etc., could decide not to order the losing party/the citizen to bear the costs of the winning administrative agency, especially in cases of lawsuits of high public interest.
111. As is acknowledged by para. 62 of ACCC/C/2008/33 above, the Court of Appeal opined in the environmental litigation case (the *Morgan* case (2009) mentioned below) that even lawsuits containing significant personal interests do not necessarily render them to be low in terms of public interest.

As mentioned above, the Aarhus Convention calls for a further review of the "English rule," but environmental lawsuits are not the only cases where litigation costs or costs ordered to be borne by the paying person can be "prohibitively high." In fact, amid calls made from various fields of law for the need for reform, Lord Justice Jackson, appointed by the "Master of Rolls," made public in 2009 the Report (Review of Civil Litigation Costs: Final Report) in which it is pointed out that, now that the "after-the-event insurance" system was introduced by the adoption of the 1999 Access to Justice Act and the applicable scope of the "conditional fee agreements" system has been expanded, the problem associated with the "English rule" has become more serious. Indeed, practically, the users of these systems do not have to bear the success fee regardless of the outcome of the lawsuit, so they accelerate the rise in civil litigation costs. Moreover, the paying party could end up paying a large amount of costs because he might have to bear the expenses associated with the "conditional fee agreements" entered into by the winning party as well as the premiums of the "after-the-event insurance" paid by the winning party to hedge the risk of losing in court.

In view of the abovementioned problems, the above 2009 Final Report made various reform proposals. In particular, it proposes to introduce the "qualified one-way costs-shifting rule" in certain types of litigations (where the power of the parties is not equal). The Report cites as the main reasons for such proposal the following: (i) it is the simplest and clearest way to implement the UK's obligations under the Aarhus Convention; (ii) as stated in the Court of Appeal judgment on the abovementioned *Morgan* case (2009),[112] it is undesirable to have different costs transfer rules for environment-related lawsuits and other lawsuits; (iii) a two-way cost rule is not usually necessary to deter frivolous litigation because a permit system works as an effective filter to weed out worthless litigations; (iv) it is against the public interest for the potential litigant to be deterred from filing sufficiently controversial lawsuits because of substantial financial risks; (v) unilateral cost-shifting has attained some success in Canada; (vi) the "protective costs order" is not effective in protecting plaintiffs against excessive costs due to the lack of transparency regarding the amount of costs and timing.[113]

In response to the above 2009 Final Report, various legal amendments have been made. Those amendments include measures applicable to lawsuits related to the Aarhus Convention and those applicable to lawsuits in general.[114] The latter amendments

112. The Court states in para. 33, "All in all questions to do with costs, the fundamental rule is that there are no rules. Costs are always in the discretion of the courts."; and in para. 42, "Mr. Tromans sought to draw a distinction between actions to vindicate general public rights to a clean environment from actions for private nuisance designed to protect private property rights .... We doubt in any event whether it is helpful in practice to draw such a clear distinction."
113. For details, *see* Chapter 30 (Judicial Review) §4 (Assessment)(i)(One-way costs-shifting) of the Final Report. Lord Sullivan Justice also made public in 2008 the Report (Ensuring Access to Environmental Justice in England and Wales) in which a proposal is made to reform the "English rule" in relation to environmental lawsuits (mainly reforms on the "protective costs order").
114. In the case of a lawsuit relating to the Aarhus Convention, under CPR §45.43 (Limit on costs recoverable from a party in an Aarhus Convention claim) which has been applied since April 2013, the amount of costs to be ordered is, in principle, limited to GBP 5,000 for the plaintiff (GBP 10,000 for non-individuals) and GBP 35,000 for the defendant while this is not so in a case where a plaintiff with a considerable amount of assets does not seek for its application.

include the introduction of Part 44 (General rules about costs) of Chapter II (Qualified one-way costs shifting), and it is intended to limit the recovery of expenses for "conditional fee arrangements" and "after-the-event insurance premiums" and has been applied since April 2013. Specifically, CPR 44.13-44.17 provides for the application of the "qualified one-way costs shifting" rule for personal injury lawsuits in which defendants are ordered to pay the costs of the plaintiffs when they lose while they cannot, in principle, recover their costs even if they win.[115] However, under CPR Part 36 (Offers to settle), if a plaintiff does not accept an offer for a resolution presented by the defendant and the result of the judgment is less favorable for the plaintiff than the amount presented in the offer, the above CPR Part 44 Chapter II shall not apply, so that the court is to order the plaintiff to pay the costs to the extent that they do not exceed the amount determined by the judgment and interest unless the court finds it unjust to do so.[116]

In addition, the 1990 Courts and Legal Services Act was amended by the LAPSO Act (Legal Aid, Sentencing and Punishment of Offenders Act 2012). In particular, due to the introduction of LAPSO Act §44 (Conditional fee agreements: success fees), from April 2013 onwards, it is no longer allowed, except for some cases, to pass "conditional success fees" and "after-the-event insurance premiums" to the losing party. Furthermore, in response to the European Court of Human Rights judgment in *MGN v. United Kingdom* ([2001] 39401/04) that the UK's system at that time allowing 100% recovery of the cost of success fees in privacy-related litigation violated Article 10 (Freedom of expression) of the ECHR, the UK government issued an order on the LPASO Act (Order 2018 SI/2018/1287), and the above LAPSO Act §44 now applies to litigations which are related to publications and privacy. As a result of these revisions, the attractiveness of "conditional success fee" and "after-the-event insurance premiums" has decreased in relation to tax litigation as well, and the associated problems have been alleviated while the importance of what kind of support measures should be taken for plaintiffs with limited means who had a strong need to rely on them has increased.[117]

SECTION 5 CHARACTERISTICS OF HIGHLY DISPUTED ISSUES

1 Disputes over Penalties

(1) Overview

As can be seen from the comparison of Figures 3.3 and 3.9, penalty cases account for a very large proportion of the HMRC's statutory reviews. In terms of the number of cases handled, the proportion of penalty cases to the total was 82% to 88% from FY2011-2012 to FY2015-2016, and in particular, the proportion of automatically

115. The winning defendant can recover their costs only when the plaintiff's allegations are dishonest, as stipulated in Rule 44.16 (Exceptions to qualified one-way costs-shifting where permission required).
116. *See* in particular Rule 36.17 (Costs consequences following judgment).
117. For details, *see* https://panopticonblog.com/2019/04/08/cfa-success-fees-abolished-in-privacy-defamation-cases/.

imposed penalties to the total was high for FY2021-2022 and FY2022-2023. Among the penalty cases, the number of penalty cases related to VAT is particularly high, accounting for 57% to 67% of the statutory review cases from FY2010-2011 to FY2019-2020. Moreover, as shown in Figure 3.9, revocation rate is much higher in the case of penalties: from 2011-2012 to 2019-2020, the ratio of re/assessments, etc., canceled by the statutory reviews was 22% to 36% in cases other than penalty cases while it was 49% to 81% in the case of penalty cases related to VAT.[118] Penalties are stipulated in TMA Chapter 10 (Penalties, etc., §93 to §107), and it was revised considerably by 2007 Finance Act Schedule 24 (Penalties for errors) and 2007 Finance Act Schedule 55 (Penalty for failure to make returns, etc.), but Table 3.1 confirms that even before this revision, penalty cases accounted for a large proportion of the total number of appeals. However, in the Tribunals, penalty cases account for about one-third of the total number of tax appeals.[119]

Figure 3.9 Number of Appeals Against VAT Penalty Cases, Automatically Imposed Penalty Cases, etc. and the Ratio of Their Revocation at Statutory Review

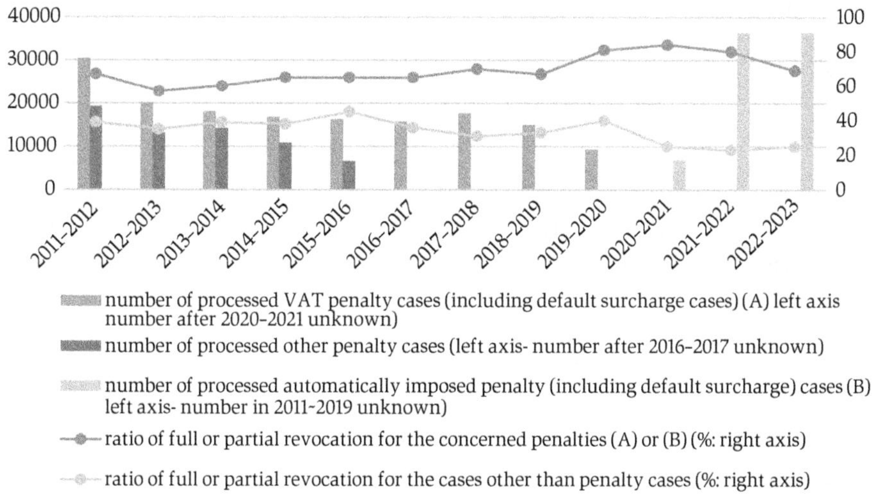

Source: TAC Reports in HMRC Annual Reports for 2012-2023, Table: Overview of dispute outcomes at review and appeal; Annex: Review outcome.

118. For example, in the first nine months of 2009,; (i) 20,778 cases came to "statutory reviews"; (ii) 18,526 cases were reviewed, and approximately 81% of the reviewed cases were those of unrepresented taxpayers; (iii) 15,083 cases (approximately 82%) of the cases reviewed were related to penalties for delayed filing of returns but in more than half of those cases, the penalties were revoked; (iv) the ratio of revocation is about 25% in the case of the other cases subjected to the statutory reviews. *See* Gammie, *supra* "Tax Appeals and Review" p. 667.

119. Between 2009 and 2016, there were approximately 4,500 tax decisions made public by Tribunals, of which about one-third were penalty cases and only about 13% of them were in favor of the taxpayers. For details, *see* Andrew Hubbard, Penalty Appeals, *Tax Journal,* October 20 (2017) p. 6.

Penalties can be broadly categorized into two. One is "automated civil penalties," which are imposed at a fixed amount automatically by the HMRC's computer. The other is "discretionary penalties," which consist of "tax-geared penalties," whose amount is determined in proportion to the unpaid tax amount and "behavioral penalties," whose rates vary depending on the taxpayers' behavior and the HMRC's discretion.[120] Among the number of VAT penalty cases shown in Figure 3.9, there are cases where a "default surcharge," which is one of those automatically imposed penalties, is a point of contention.[121] The exact annual number of "statutory reviews" of "default surcharge" cases is not clear, but automatically imposed penalty cases, including "default surcharges" cases, account for more than half (64% in 2019-2020 and 69% in 2020-2021) of the number of appeals processed by the statutory reviews every year.[122] Penalty cases are highly disputed cases in the Tribunals as well, but in the case of Tribunals and courts, the number and the ratio of automatically imposed penalty cases decreases significantly,[123] while the decrease in those of "behavioral penalties" is not so remarkable. Such a difference should be attributable partially to the fact that "behavioral penalty" cases are generally more complex and involve larger amounts.

Penalty percentages for the failure to file returns and the inaccuracy in returns vary depending on various factors such as categories of income, days of nonpayment, taxpayers' behaviors, etc. As for income sourced in the UK under the Category I prescribed in paragraph 21A in Schedule 24 of the 2007 Finance Act,[124] a failure to file a return for it incurs, pursuant to paragraphs 3 to 5 in Schedule 55 of the Finance Act 2009, an automated civil penalty/a fixed penalty of GBP 100 plus daily GBP 10 penalty in a case where the failure continues during 90 days. If the failure continues after that period, the HMRC issues a penalty notice, and the total amount of penalty increases up to the greater of 5% of the unreported tax amount or GBP 300,[125] provided that the

120. FA2009 Schedule 55 (Penalty for failure to make returns, etc.) §17(3) and (4) are examples of "tax-geared penalties." "Behavioral penalties" have the purpose of not only imposing sanctions but also enhancing taxpayers' compliance by providing a range of penalty rates.
121. The "default surcharge" for failure to comply with the obligation to declare and pay VAT on time is stipulated in VATA §59, and it is to be imposed when no payment is made within the period specified in the first "notice of default charge." For more information, *see* HMRC Notice 700/50.
122. *See* HMRC 2020/2021 Annual Report Table 13.
123. The ratio of the number of automatically imposed penalty cases against the total cases received by the First-tier Tribunal is 23% in 2018/2019, 8% in 2019/2020 and 13% in 2020/2021. *See* Appeals in 2019-2021 HMRC Annual Reports.
124. For the failure of filing a return on PAYE, CIS (Construction Industry Scheme) return, offshore income, etc., the applicable penalties could be higher. As for the failure to file a CIS return, *see* the *Ireton* case below in 1(3) and footnote 156. As for the failure to report an offshore income, the applicable penalty rate becomes higher if it is sourced in foreign countries falling under Category II or Category III with which the UK does not make automatic exchange of information. *See* HMRC's Publication (Compliance checks series—CC/FS7a and Offshore penalties) for details.
125. Once the failure to file a return continues more than six months, it incurs a "tax geared penalty" or a "behavioral penalty." The issue of a penalty notice is not a precondition for "automated civil penalties" while it is for "discretionary penalties." *See* para. 13 (Assessment) of Part 3 (Procedure) in Schedule 24 of the 2007 Finance Act.

failure does not involve deliberate withholding of information and concealment.[126] As for penalties on filing an inaccurate return stipulated under Schedule 24 (Penalties for errors) of the Finance Act 2007, the applicable penalties for Category I (domestic source of income, etc.) vary depending on three types of behavior: (i) careless, (ii) deliberate, (iii) deliberate and concealed. The penalty rate for inaccuracy is zero to 30% of the "potentially lost revenue" in the case of the above (i) behavior,[127] 20% to 70% of that in the case of the above (ii) behavior, and 30% to 100% of that in the case of the above (iii) behavior.[128]

As is clear from the above, in particular, there is a wide range in percentages of penalties possibly applicable in the case of an inaccuracy in the return. TMA §100 (Determination of penalties by the officer of Board), which was amended by the Finance Act 1989 §167 (Determination of penalties), provides for the authorized officers of the tax authority to impose a penalty amount that they consider correct or appropriate, but, in addition to the difference among the above (i), (ii) and (iii), the question of which percentage of inaccuracy penalty is applicable is to be decided mainly by weighing two criteria; ① a taxpayer's disclosure and ② a quality of disclosure (so-called telling, helping and giving). As for ①, the lower percentages of penalties among the respective ranges of the above (i), (ii) and (iii) apply when a taxpayer discloses an inaccuracy in the return, and they become particularly low if such disclosure is an "unprompted disclosure."[129] As for ②, a lower percentage of penalties apply if a taxpayer cooperates with the HMRC in conducting its audit by telling reasons for the inaccuracy (maximum 30% reduction), helping the amount of inaccuracy to be determined (maximum 40% reduction), and giving access to relevant records, etc. (maximum 30% reduction).[130]

Now that the percentages of an inaccuracy penalty vary much and the above three types of taxpayers' behaviors are taken into consideration in determining which percentage of penalty is applicable, it is quite likely that not a few taxpayers wonder

126. In a case where the withholding of information is deliberate and concealed, the penalty amount is the greater of 100% of the unreported income or GBP 300.
127. "Potentially lost revenue" is usually the amount of undeclared tax, but if there is a denial of deductible loss, etc., it can be larger than the actual amount of tax that should be paid. *See* CH82161 for a calculation example. The zero penalty might be applicable in the case of a taxpayer who was careless but made unprompted disclosure.
128. These rules on penalties generally apply to many other taxes such as corporation tax, inheritance tax, etc. and also apply under Schedule 41(Penalties: Failure to notify and certain VAT and excise wrongdoings) of the Finance Act 2008. Moreover, inaccuracies in offshore income falling under Category II and Category III also incur higher percentages of penalties under paras. 4(3) and 4(4) in Schedule 24 of the 2007 Finance Act.
129. A taxpayer's disclosure of the inaccuracy in the return is "unprompted disclosure" if the taxpayer has any reason to believe that it is made before HMRC has discovered or is about to discover the inaccuracy. *See* the above HMRC's Compliance checks series—CC/FS7a for details. This treatment is similar to that in Japan while in the UK penalty percentages could be reduced even if disclosure is "prompted disclosure" (i.e., disclosure not initiated by a taxpayer). Compare it with Ireland's "qualified disclosure" in footnote 51/Figure 5.7 in Chapter 5.
130. As for details on the question of how those "telling," "helping" and "giving" affect the determination of a penalty percentage, *see* CH82430, H82440, CH82450, CH82460 and the above CC/FS7a.

whether the determined penalty percentage is the most appropriate one and make some of them dispute its legitimacy. In particular, the standard percentage of penalty applicable to a taxpayer with inaccuracy in his return is 30% in a case where he was careless and 70% in a case where he was deliberate, so the question of which penalty rate becomes applicable would become a big issue for the taxpayer while it seems that the difference between careless and deliberate could be in some cases so subtle and it must often be difficult to determine which of these two types of behaviors the inaccuracy in a taxpayer's return should fall into.[131] The 2014 Final Report ("Tax penalties") submitted in 2014 by the Office of Simplification, which was established to make recommendations to the government on the simplification of the tax system, also referred to on page 17 the fact that there is a tax representative body expressing its opinion/impression that, unlike the old tax penalty system, it is hard to see how, under the new tax penalty system, the HMRC comes to its decision about penalties and it cannot predict the amount of penalty.

(2) Criteria for Imposing Accuracy Penalties and Suspension of Penalties

(2-1) Criterion of "Careless or Deliberate"

It is not that a penalty shall be imposed wherever there is an inaccuracy in the return. Finance Act 2007 Schedule 24 paragraph 1 (Error in taxpayer's document) dictates that an inaccuracy penalty is not imposed, just like a negligence penalty under IRC §1662(b)(1) in the U.S.[132], if a taxpayer was neither careless nor deliberate (or having taken reasonable care), and the onus of proof on the reasonable care falls on the HMRC, which is to be fulfilled not on the standard of "reasonable doubt" (as in the case of criminal offense) but on the standard of "more likely than not" (or "balance of probabilities").[133] But the reality is that a penalty notice is usually issued automatically without deliberating on whether or not this standard is cleared and without attaching concrete reasons for the penalty.[134] Consequently, there have been a large number of penalties (*see* Figure 3.10 for the large number of "behavioral penalties") and disputes over them. Some of those disputes are over whether or not penalties should be imposed, and others are over which penalty rates are applicable. As for the former disputes, a critical point is how high the hurdle set by the standard of being careless or deliberate is for the HMRC to clear to apply an accuracy penalty or a penalty for the understatement of a liability to tax.

131. In Ireland, some pointed out that the boundary between gross carelessness and insufficient care which attracts different penalty rates is not so clear. *See* 4 in Section 1 of Chapter 5.
132. *See* 2(1) in Section 4/footnote 150 of Chapter 2.
133. *See* HMRC Manual CH54300 (Assessing time limits: Onus of proof and level of proof).
134. *See* Tax penalties at https://www.litrg.org.the UK/tax-guides/tax-basics/enquiries-penalties-appeals-complaints-and-debt/tax-penalties and John Cassidy, Taxpayer Wins Penalty Shoot-out, *Taxation*, September 15 (2016) p. 1. For similar treatment on accuracy-related penalties by the IRS, *see* 2(1) in Section 4 of Chapter 2.

Figure 3.10 Breakdown of the Number of "Behavioral Penalties"

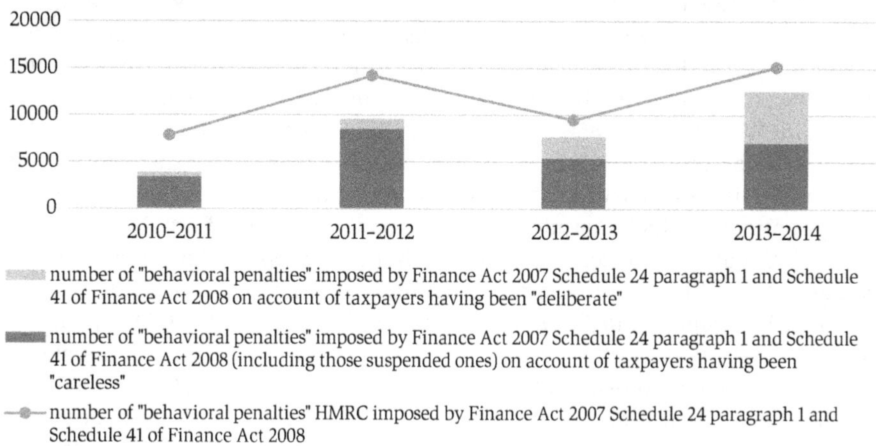

Source: Excerpted and aggregated from data on pages 19 and 27 of the Office of Tax Simplification 2014 Report.

As in the case of the US, the hurdle set by the standard of being careless or lacking reasonable care is not so high. For example, in *David Wald v. Revenue and Customs* ([2011] UKFT 183 (TC)), at issue was the application of a penalty under the old penalty system (to be exact, TMA §95 (incorrect return or account for income tax or capital gains tax). This provision stated, "(1) Where a person fraudulently or negligently—(a) delivers any incorrect return..., he shall be liable to a penalty." In this case, the First-tier Tribunal held, "the mere fact that the appellant has failed to include in a return a payment that was within the appellant's knowledge can amount to prima facie evidence of negligence. Such prima facie evidence, in the absence of any further evidence to show that there was a reason other than negligence, might be sufficient to support a conclusion that negligence has been proved." Also, in *Andersen (deceased) v. Revenue and Customs* ([2009] UKFTT(TC)), the First-tier Tribunal held that to be negligent, the taxpayer's conduct must involve culpability beyond a mere mistake while the error in the Appellant's return was an innocent one, but it was attributable to negligent conduct on the part of the Appellant or a person acting on her behalf and constitutes negligence under TMA §29 (Assessment where loss of tax discovered).[135]

As the above TMA §25 and TMA §29 show, under the old tax penalty system, one criterion for applying a penalty on the inaccuracy in a tax return was a taxpayer's negligence or fraudulence rather than his lack of reasonable care or deliberate inaccuracy adopted under Part 1 of Schedule 24 in the Finance Act 2007. Despite such a difference in phrases, it seems that it does not make any material change to the height

135. TMA §29 stipulated, "... (3) he shall not be assessed under subsection (1) above—... unless one of the two conditions mentioned below is fulfilled. (4) the first condition is that the situation mentioned in subsection (1) above is attributable to fraudulent or negligent conduct on the part of the taxpayer or a person acting on his behalf."

of the hurdle to be cleared for imposing an inaccuracy penalty because the 2007 Finance Act Schedule 24 Part 1 paragraph 3 (Degree of culpabilities) provides that a taxpayer is careless if the inaccuracy is due to failure by him to take reasonable care and HMRC's CH53400 (Assessing Time Limits: Extended time limit. What is careless behavior) confirms that carelessness can be likened to the longstanding concept in the general law of "negligence" by citing the Court of Exchequer judgment on *Blyth v. Birmingham Waterworks* ([1856] EWHC Exch J65) in which Baron Alderson stated that negligence is the omission to do something which a reasonable man, guided upon those considerations which ordinarily regulate the conduct of human affairs, would do, or doing something which a prudent and reasonable man would not do.[136]

Thus, the above phrases imply that the hurdle for the application of inaccuracy penalties is not so high, but inaccuracy penalties were often revoked by the Tribunals and courts. For example, in *Cairns v. Revenue and Customs* ([2009] UKFTT 67), the claimant/representative of the deceased delivered to the HMRC an account showing the value of the inherited real estate at the time of inheritance to be GBP 40,000,[137] but the HMRC determined it to be underestimated and imposed a penalty in accordance with the Inheritance Tax Act §247 (Provision of incorrect information).[138] In this case, the First-tier Tribunal pointed out the following: (i) the claimant/representative finally agreed that the value of the real estate at the time of the inheritance for inheritance tax purposes was its sold price of £60,000 but it does not mean that a prudent representative could have expected such price and filed a return based on that price, (ii) the HMRC have not provided any evidence showing what a prudent representative would have done in this case, (iii) the mere failure to obtain another valuation does not constitute negligence and in this case, the claimant is a solicitor with much experience in the field of real estate. Then, it held that it is simply not possible to conclude that the account was negligently delivered to justify the application of this penalty.

While, in *Herefordshire Property Company and Revenue and Customs* ([2015] UKFTT 79), at issue was whether the penalty imposed pursuant to the 2007 Finance Act Schedule 24 paragraph 3A(Errors related to avoidance arrangements)at the percentage of 25% on the inaccuracy in the claimant's 2005 IT return was lawful or not.[139] This inaccuracy was attributable to the claimant's belief in the tax reduction effect of the tax

136. While in *Verma v. Revenue and Customs* ([2011] UKFTT 737), the First-tier Tribunal held, "reliance on a 19th century authority on negligence in a civil claim can hardly be regarded as authoritative in the context of the interpretation of a statutory provision for tax penalties enacted by the Finance Act 2007. The *Birmingham Waterworks* case is not binding on us ... the standard by which reasonable care fell to be judged is that of a prudent and reasonable taxpayer in the position of the taxpayer in question."
137. The 1984 Inheritance Tax Act §216 states; "(1) the personal representatives of a deceased person ... shall deliver to the Board an account specifying to the best of his knowledge ... the value of that property . ... 3(A) their account shall be in the first instance be sufficient as regards that property if it contains...a provisional estimate of the value of the property."
138. Inheritance Tax Act §247 provides, "(1) If any person liable for any tax on the value transferred by a chargeable transfer fraudulently or negligently delivers, furnishes or produces to the Board any incorrect account, information or document, he shall be liable, ... to a penalty."
139. This paragraph states, "(1) If any person liable for any tax on the value transferred by a chargeable transfer fraudulently or negligently delivers, furnishes or produces to the Board any incorrect account, information or document, he shall be liable ... to a penalty."

avoidance scheme, which was offered by the accounting firm but was negated by the HMRC. In an attempt to resolve the dispute, the disputing parties offered the alternative penalty rate (10% rate by the claimant and 15% rate by the HMRC) in the course of the negotiation, but these offers were not accepted by the other party. In this case, the First-tier Tribunal pointed out the following: (i) the claimant utilized this scheme after having confirmed that it was widely offered by the other major accounting firms as well, (ii) the claimant relied on the accounting firm in the filing of his returns in the past, and he was more than entitled to think, as he did, that this scheme would operate as all expected and its success would depend on the judgment of the courts. Given those points, the First-tier Tribunal concluded that the claimant was not negligent in submitting his tax return.[140]

In some cases, a taxpayer utilizing a tax avoidance scheme offered by a tax agent could be negligent/careless, especially because the onus of proof on reasonable care falls, pursuant to the 2007 Finance Act Schedule 24 Part 4 (Miscellaneous) paragraph 18 (Agency) (3) on a taxpayer who has filed an inaccurate return following a tax agent.[141] In fact, in cases where taxpayers utilized a tax avoidance scheme offered by tax agents, the Special Commissioners in *Rowland v. HMRC* ([2006] Spc 00548) dismissed the HMRC's claim of the negligence of the taxpayer while the First-tier Tribunal in Litman & Anor ([2014] TC 03229) decided in favor of the HMRC that asserted the claimant's negligence. As for the HMRC's general stance on this issue, the 2018 Publication (Reasonable care: tax returns and other documents) explains that if a taxpayer has used tax avoidance arrangements that HMRC later defeats, it is presumed that the taxpayer has not taken reasonable care for any inaccuracy in return, while he has used a tax adviser with the appropriate expertise, the HMRC normally considers him having taken reasonable care unless it comes under a disqualified advice which includes advice given by an interested person or one given without properly taking account of the taxpayer's personal circumstances.[142]

(2-2) Criteria for Suspension of Penalties

One of the other causes for a large number of disputes over inaccuracy penalties can be found in the fact that they could be suspended in some cases. The most relevant provision is the 2007 Finance Act Schedule 24 paragraph 14 (Suspension), which

140. Also, the Tribunal mentioned that, even if this judgment is wrong in relation to the negligence issue, 30% mitigation should have been given, leading to an overall penalty of 10%. This case, the above *Cairns* case (2009), and the following *Rowland* case (2006) are good illustrations of the difference in height of the hurdle for imposing an inaccuracy penalty in UK and that of an underreporting penalty in Japan that does not require a taxpayer's negligence for its imposition.
141. This paragraph prescribes, "P is not liable to a penalty ... in respect of anything done or omitted by P's agent where P satisfies HMRC that P took reasonable care to avoid inaccuracy (...) or unreasonable failure." The First-tier Tribunal also mentioned in *JR Hanson v. HMRC* ([2012] UKFTT 314(TC)) that in circumstances where the liability to a penalty is in respect of anything done by a taxpayer's agent, it is for the taxpayer to satisfy HMRC that he took reasonable care as in the case of a plea of reasonable excuse.
142. As for what constitutes a "disqualified advice," *see* CH81123.

stipulates, "(1) HMRC may suspend all or part of a penalty for a careless inaccuracy under paragraph 1 by notice in writing to P. (2) A notice must specify—(a) what part of the penalty is to be suspended, (b) a period of suspension not exceeding two years, and (c) conditions of suspension to be complied with by P. (3) HMRC may suspend all or part of a penalty only if compliance with a condition of suspension would help P to avoid becoming liable to further penalties under paragraph 1 for careless inaccuracy." About 10% to 30% of the penalties the HMRC imposed on account of the taxpayers' failure to take reasonable care were later decided to be postponed, and by tax category, the average percentage of penalties postponed during the four years of 2010/2011 to 2013/2014 was about 7% for IT, about 11% for CIT, about 19% for VAT, and about 47% for taxes on goods and customs duties.[143] In this connection, the 2007 Finance Act Schedule 24 paragraph 17(4) dictates that the Tribunal may order the HMRC to suspend the penalty only if it thinks that the HMRC's decision not to suspend was flawed.

Eastman v. Revenue and Customs ([2016] THE UKFTT 0527) is one of those cases where the claimant disputed the HMRC's legitimacy of not allowing the penalty suspension. In this case, the HMRC relied on the First-tier Tribunal decision on *Fane v. Revenue and Customs* ([2011] THE UKFTT 210 (TC)), etc., to take a stance that a penalty suspension is not to be allowed in cases where the penalty resulting from an inaccuracy on an issue that will not arise in the future (so-called "one-off error") because there is no point in setting a condition for its suspension,[144] and asserted that this case is one of those cases. But the First-tier Tribunal pointed out that the acid test in determining whether a penalty suspension is appropriate or not is to ascertain what the taxpayer could reasonably have done differently that would have avoided the original inaccuracy and noted that in this case, the claimant could have kept more thorough records to double-check the return prepared by the accountant. Now that the claimant, with the help of the regularly employed accountants, showed concrete ways to do this for the future, the Tribunal held that the HMRC's decision was flawed[145] and should, instead of placing too much emphasis on the nature of the original inaccuracy, take due account of this and suspend the penalty while the conditions for the suspension is for the HMRC to decide.[146]

143. For details, *see* the Office of Tax Simplification 2014 Report, pp. 19 and 27.
144. A similar criterion is also shown in the First-tier Tribunal decision on *Havercroft v. Revenue and Customs* ([2015] UKFTT 0389 (TC)).
145. Similarly, in *David Test v. Revenue and Customs* ([2013] UKFTT 151 (TC)) and *Boughey v. Revenue and Customs* ([2012] UKFTT 398), the First-tier Tribunal held that the penalties should be suspended in response to the claimants' claim that their tax returns will be prepared by a well-qualified accountant in the future.
146. The Office of Tax Simplification Report 2014 points out in pp. 17 to 27 the lack of consistency in the application of the "behavioral penalties" and the difficulty in setting appropriate conditions for the suspension of penalties.

(3) *Criteria for Abating/Suspending Penalties on Failure to File Returns, Etc.*

Penalties on taxpayers' failure to file the return, etc., timely could also be abated if certain conditions are met. The 2009 Finance Act Schedule 55 paragraph 23 (Reasonable excuse) provides, "Liability to a penalty under any paragraph of this Schedule does not arise in relation to a failure to make a return if P satisfies...that there is a reasonable excuse for the failure." While it is to be noted that paragraph 23(2)(c) of this Schedule dictates, "Where P had a reasonable excuse for the failure but the excuse has ceased, P is to be treated as having continued to have the excuse if the failure is remedied without unreasonable delay after the excuse ceased."[147] This penalty for the failure to file a return, etc., can be imposed when a return is prima facie a belated return and the onus of proof on the balance of probabilities regarding a "reasonable excuse" is on the taxpayer,[148] so the hurdle for the imposition of this penalty should be lower than that of an inaccuracy penalty. Such being the case, there were years when the number of belated returns was quite large, and there must also have been years when there were large numbers of disputes over whether those penalties should be abated on account of a "reasonable excuse."[149]

Figure 3.11 displays the number of late filing penalties charged and the number of them successfully appealed among each income decile in 2020-2021. The Tax Policy Associates informs that the number of them is more or less the same for the years 2018-2019 and 2019-2020 as well, while it is not clear how many of those successful appeals are due to a "reasonable excuse" on the part of taxpayers. Until 2011, a late filing penalty used to be canceled in a case where a belated tax return was filed, and there was no tax to pay, but the law was changed in such a way that a late filing penalty is to be imposed on a taxpayer even if he has no taxable income because his income is under the personal allowance of GBP 12,570.[150] The Tax Policy Associates considers that every penalty issued to taxpayers whose income is under this personal allowance amount, which is about 184,000 taxpayers in 2020/2021, is a policy failure.[151] Now that the HMRC has shown its intention to change the penalty system so that, from April 6, 2025, a one-off failure to file a return will not incur a penalty, while a second-time failure will incur GBP 200 fines. So, the current situation for first-time non-filers will

147. Penalties waived on the basis of "reasonable excuse" include those under the aforementioned Schedule 41 of the 2008 Finance Act, Schedule 56(Penalty for failure to make payments on time) of 2009 Finance Act, TMA §8(Personal return)(1)D, etc. *See* HMRC Manual CH401050 (Charging penalties: introduction: overview) for details.
148. *See* para. 15 of the First-tier Tribunal decision on *John Arnfield v. The Commissioners* for HMRC ([2014] UKFTT 52 (TC)).
149. Paragraph 3.1.13 of the Report released in 1983 by the Keith Committee on Enforcement Powers of the Revenue Departments which was appointed by the Chancellor of the Exchequer points out that, in the first half of 1980, about 90% of VAT returns were submitted after the deadline.
150. As for others against this penalty on taxpayers with zero tax liability, *see* Keith Gordon, Do Not Pass Go, *Taxation*, May 3 (2018) p. 8.
151. *See* http://www.taxpolicy.org.uk/2023/06/26/penalties2023/.

improve, but it might get worse for those who are not first-time non-filers, and the latter might increase the number of their appeals on the penalties imposed on them.

Figure 3.11 Number of Late Filing Penalties Charged and Number of Them Successfully Appealed in Each Income Decile in 2020-2021

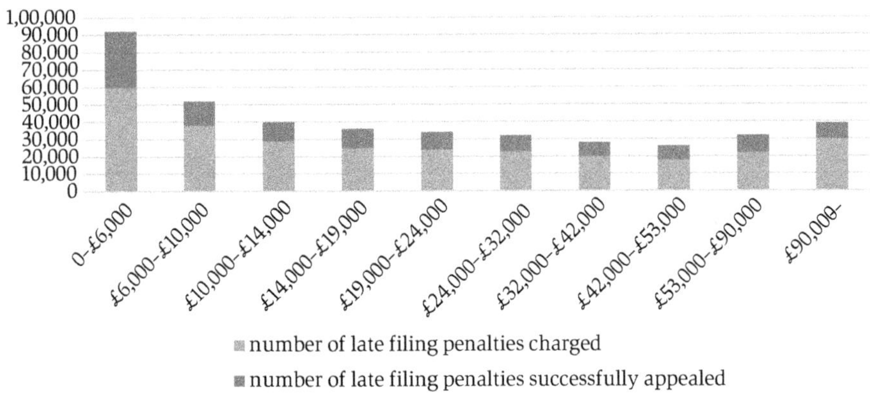

Source: Penalising the poor: 420,000 HMRC penalties charged to people who earned too little to pay tax. That's 40% of all HMRC late filing penalties.—Tax Policy Associates Ltd.

HMRC Manual (SAM10090) explains that a reasonable excuse is normally something that stops taxpayers from meeting a tax obligation on time that they took reasonable care to meet, and it might be due to circumstances outside their control or a combination of events. As typical examples of a "reasonable excuse," the Manual cites: (i) natural disasters, (ii) mental/physical illness, (iii) bereavement, (iv) postal delays, (v) computer failures, (vi) HMRC's inappropriate action, (vii) ignorance of the law, (viii) reliance on another person, (ix) insufficiency of funds caused by external uncontrollable reasons. Even so, the question of whether a certain event or reason constitutes a "reasonable excuse" is to be answered by taking into all the facts and circumstances of the specific case so that there might be cases that formally come under either one of the above (i) ~ (ix) examples but do not constitute a "reasonable excuse" in practice depending on a specific circumstance of a taxpayer. Even so, now that it is not possible to list all the cases that constitute a "reasonable excuse," there might also be cases that do not formally come under either one of the above (i) ~ (ix) examples but constitute a "reasonable excuse" in practice.

Matthew Roper v. The Commissioners for HMRC ([2014] UKFTT 736) is one example that might come under the above (ii) (mental/physical illness) and (ix) (insufficiency of funds). In this case, the First-tier Tribunal held that even if the claimant could not work because of his illness, he filed his return electronically on time, and there appeared to be no reason why either he or his appointed representative could not have contacted the HMRC to arrange a method of paying the outstanding tax over a suitable period, so there is no "reasonable excuse" on the part of the claimant. Whereas, *Farrell and HMRC* ([2019] UKFTT 192) is an example that should come under the above (vi) (HMRC's inappropriate action).[152] In this case, the First-tier Tribunal noted that the main reason for the claimant's failure to file his VAT return in time was his use of a wrong ID for the Government Gateway, but this problem could have been mitigated if the helpline advisor had helped him identify or change his ID before the filing deadline comes and the claimant made reasonable efforts to file the return within the deadline, and it concluded that the default surcharge charged at the rate of 5% by 1994 VATA §59A (Default surcharge: Payments on account) on the claimant should be exempted on account of the "reasonable excuse."[153]

There are other cases intimating that the hurdle for a "reasonable excuse" is not so high. Such cases include the Upper Tribunal's decision on *Perrin v. Revenue and Customs* ([2018] UKUT 0156). In this case, the claimant failed to complete the final stage of his online filing timely for the 2010/2011 return, and this time, differently from the treatment the HMRC gave to the practically identical mistake made for his 2009/2010 return, the fixed penalty was not exempted, and daily penalties were also imposed. The Upper Tribunal sustained the imposition of these penalties by dismissing the claimant's assertion of a "reasonable excuse," but, at the same time, it pointed out that the HMRC's argument of any reasonable excuse to be based on some unforeseeable or inescapable event by echoing Scot LJ's dissenting opinion in *Steptoe v. Commissioners of Customs and Excise* ([1992] STC 757) is regrettable because the concept of reasonable excuse is far wider than that. The Tribunal also stated that it does not see any basis for the frequently cited argument that ignorance of the law is no excuse and does not constitute a reasonable excuse because some requirements of the law are well-known, simple, and straightforward, but others are much less so.[154]

The First-tier Tribunal decision on *Wickenden v. Revenue and Customs* ([2018] UKFT 465) should be one of those taking a view on the "reasonable cause" similar to that shown in the above Perrin case. In this case, at issue was whether or not the nonresident claimant filed an IT return for capital gains from the transfer of the real estate in the UK but failed to file timely the NRCGT form and had a "reasonable excuse" for the penalty of GBP 700 imposed on him by paragraph 5 of the 2009 Finance Act Schedule 55.[155] The First-tier Tribunal pointed out that ignorance of legislation that is

152. *Kirsopp v. HMRC* ([2018] TC 07064) is also a case coming under this example/category. In this case, the First-tier Tribunal held that the claimant residing abroad filed a capital gains tax return on the sale of the UK property on his IT return instead of the NRCGT (Non Residents Capital Gains Tax) Form which has an earlier deadline, but it was, in view of the HMRC's response, understandable and constitutes a "reasonable excuse."

153. 1994 VATA §59A stipulates, "(4) ... if—(a) a taxable person on whom a surcharge liability notice has been served is in default in respect of a prescribed accounting period, (b) ... (c) ... that person shall be liable to a surcharge equal to whichever is the greater of £30 and the specified percentage of the aggregate value of his defaults in respect of that prescribed accounting period. (5)...(b) in relation to the second such period, the specified percentage is 5 per cent."

154. This decision as well as the following *Wickenden* case (2018) are good illustrations of the fact that the hurdle for a reasonable excuse is lower than that of a "justifiable reason" for exempting a penalty for a non-filing/belated filing of a return in Japan.

155. This paragraph states, "(1) P is liable to a penalty under this paragraph if (and only if) P's failure continues after the end of the period of 6 months beginning with the penalty date. (2) The penalty under this paragraph is the greater of—(a) 5% of any liability to tax which would have been shown in the return in question, and (b) £300." As for NRCGT, *see* footnote 152.

complex or uncertain may be a "reasonable excuse in some cases and may not be in other cases, and what matters on this point is what a reasonable person who was cognizant of her obligations about relation to tax and intended to comply with those obligations might very well have acted in the way as the claimant. Then it held that there was no capital gain from this transfer of the real estate, so there was no reason why she should have sought the advice of a tax expert on it, and given the relative obscurity of the NRCGT filing obligation, which was not as widely known as it would ideally have been the case, the claimant had a reasonable excuse for her failure to file her NRCGT form until she did so.

However, some judicial precedents indicate that the hurdle for a "reasonable excuse" is not as low as some might expect. In *Ireton v. Revenue and Customs* ([2011] UKFTT 639), at issue was whether or not the claimant, who was in the construction industry business and had payments to his subcontractors, had a "reasonable cause" for the penalty laid down under TMA §98A (Special penalties in the case of certain returns) which was imposed on his failure to file a CIS (Construction Industry Scheme) return by IT rule (SI 1993/743 Regulation 40A).[156] In this case, the First-tier Tribunal referred to the *Rowland* case (2006) referred to in the above (2-1), etc. in which it was confirmed that reliance on outside experts for direct tax issues may, contrary to VAT issues which are excluded from the scope of a "reasonable excuse" by VATA §71 (Construction for sections 59 to 70),[157] constitute a "reasonable excuse" in cases involving difficult and complex areas of tax law, but held that this case does not come under such cases and, even if the claimant's accountant had a contractual obligation to advise him on his obligation to file the CIS return but failed to do so, it would not give him a "reasonable excuse" for the failure as it could be confirmed by the *Research and Development Partnership Ltd v. Revenue and Customs* ([2009] UKFTT 328).[158]

Barrett v. Revenue and Customs ([2015] UKFTT 329) may intimate a lower hurdle for the application of a "reasonable excuse" than the above *Ireton* case. At issue, in this case, was also whether or not the penalties imposed by TMA §98A for the claimant's failure to register for CIS purposes and failures for the tax years 2006-2007 to 2010-2011 to deduct tax from the payments made to the subcontractors for the timely payment of them. The First-tier Tribunal specified that the concerned filing obligation cannot be described as particularly complex or arcane, but it is inappropriate to seek to rely solely on the formulation shown by the dissenting opinion of Scott LJ in the *Steptoe* case because the fact of whether tax provisions are complex or commonplace is nothing

156. CIS was introduced to make businesses engaged in the construction industry collect income tax and social security tax from their subcontractors, which is outside the scope of the PAYE (Pay As You Earn) system.
157. VATA §71 states, "(1) For the purpose of any provision of sections 59 to 70 which refers to a reasonable excuse for any conduct—(a)... and (b) where reliance is placed on any other person to perform any task, neither the fact of that reliance nor any dilatoriness or inaccuracy on the part of the person relied upon is a reasonable excuse."
158. In addition to this case, the Tribunal also referred to *Richfield and Fashion Co. Ltd v. Revenue and Customs* ([2010] TC 00957) in which the First-tier Tribunal decided that, now that the claimant did not make a claim that the late filing of the return caused by the claimant's agent's error was something other than a simple procedural error, the penalty on the late filing return must be sustained.

more than one of the circumstances to be taken into account in determining the application of a "reasonable excuse." In conclusion, the Tribunal held that it is not unreasonable for a reasonable person or a small trader like the claimant, who was inexperienced on CIS-related obligations and received from the accountant no indication about the obligations despite his submission of relevant documents to him, not to seek from him or the HMRC relevant information on the obligations, so the claimant had a reasonable excuse for the non-filing of the CIS returns.[159]

The above cases and judicial precedents should give some idea of where the hurdles for a penalty to be abated or suspended are set.[160] There are some more provisions that authorize a penalty abatement/suspension and lower the hurdle further. One example of them is the tax authority's discretion in imposing penalties under TMA §102.[161] Furthermore, the 2009 Finance Act Schedule 55 paragraph 16 (Special reduction) stipulates, "(1) If HMRC thinks it right because of special circumstances, they may reduce a penalty under any paragraph of this Schedule... (3) In sub-paragraph (1) the reference to reducing a penalty includes a reference to—(a) staying a penalty."[162] For instance, in *Rosie Arnfield v. Revenue & Customs* ([2015] UKFTT 53 (TC)), at issue was whether the penalty of GBP 100 on the claimant for the delayed filing of the return could be abated, the First-tier Tribunal held that the claimant had no "reasonable excuse," but the penalty should be reduced to GBP 60 because the inappropriate HMRC's action on Form 64-8 (Authoring your agent)and SA1 (Register for self-assessment and get a tax return: fill in and send) sent by the claimant's agent was out of the ordinary run of events and constitutes a special circumstance. This decision confirms that a penalty abatement may be possible even in a case where there is no "reasonable excuse."

(4) Relationship Between Penalties and EU Law, Etc.

Many domestic UK laws incorporate the purport of EU law, and domestic court judgments are handed down in line with it. For example, the ECHR has several provisions that relate to the handling of tax disputes, and the 1998 Human Rights Act has incorporated the purport of those provisions in domestic acts. In particular, (i) the

159. Also, in *B & J Shopfitting Services v. Revenue and* Customs ([2010] UKFTT 78), the First-tier Tribunal specified that reliance on a third party will not normally be a reasonable excuse because a taxpayer should not be able to avoid his liabilities by passing them on to someone else, but the penalty for delay in filing a return due to an agent following incorrect advice from the HMRC help desk is a "reasonable excuse."
160. The hurdle for the application of a "reasonable excuse" which pivots on the nature of a concerned tax provision as well as how a prudent taxpayer would have acted, etc., is similar to that for the application of "reasonable cause" in the U.S., but the former might be lower in light of such cases as the Court of Appeal judgment on the *Knappe* case (2013) analyzed in 2(2) in Section 4 of Chapter 2. Also, the latter's hurdle seems to be going up with respect to FBAR penalties. *See* Matsuda, *supra* "Tax Strategies VS. Countermeasures" pp. 98-102.
161. See footnote 30 for TMA§102. This discretion is exercised in exceptional cases by the HMRC's senior officers. For details, *see* the HMRC Manual EM5310-Penalties: Mitigation.
162. A similar treatment is also provided in para. 11 (Special reduction) of Part 2 of Schedule 24 of the Finance Act 2007, etc. For details, *see* CH170100 (Special reduction: Overview) and CH170000 (Special reduction: contents).

ECHR stipulates, under Article 1 (Protection of property) of the First Protocol, "No one shall be deprived of his possessions except in the public interest and subject to the conditions provided for by law," while this shall not impair the right of a State to control the use of property in accordance with the general interest or to secure the payment of taxes or penalties. Also, (ii) the ECHR dictates, under Article 6 (Right to a fair trial), "In the determination of his civil rights and obligations or of any criminal charge against him, everyone is entitled to a fair and public hearing within a reasonable time by an independent and impartial tribunal established by law." Now that the 1998 Human Rights Act prescribes in Article 6 (Acts of public authorities) that it is unlawful for a public authority to act in a way that is incompatible with a Convention right, the influence exerted by the Articles of the ECHR on the UK's tax system and tax disputes has by no means been negligible.

However, there are some ambiguities with the interpretation and applicable scope of some Articles of the ECHR. They manifested in the ECHR judgment on *Gasus Dosier und Fordertechnik v. Netherlands* ([1995] 20 EHHR 403) in which the above (i) (Article 1 of the ECHR) was a point of focus. In this case, the delinquent taxpayer in the Netherlands purchased goods from a German company/claimant and went bankrupt without paying for the goods, then the Netherlands' tax authority seized the goods and sold them on public auction. At issue was whether this Netherlands' action violates Article 1 of Protocol 1 of the ECHR. In its judgment, the Court specified that the interpretation of this article requires the achievement of a fair balance between the demands of the general interest of the community and the requirements of the protection of the individual's fundamental rights, and to achieve this balance, there must be a reasonable relationship of proportionality between the means employed and the aim pursued. The Court's judgment was in favor of the government of the Netherlands for it having followed the long-established body of case law and the stated policy of the Minister of Finance, but the two judges found its action to have been a violation of the Article because it went beyond the limit of what it may do in this regard by seizing the goods which unquestionably belong to an innocent third party to recover a tax debt owed by another person.

The above (ii) (the right to a fair trial) also has latitude in its interpretation and application. It seems that this provision does not apply to tax matters.[163] For example, in *Vidacar SA and opergrup. SL v. Spain* ([1999] application nos. 41601/98 and 41775/98), the claimant who was dissatisfied with the tax reassessment argued that his right to a fair trial was violated, but the ECHR reiterated, "under the settled case-law of the Convention institutions, Article 6 §1 of the Convention does not apply to "disputes" (*contestations*) relating to public law and, in particular, tax proceedings as such since they do not concern disputes over rights and obligations that are "civil" in character." There are some who question or object to the interpretation of excluding tax matters

163. Paragraph 37 of the Guideline D (Excluded matters) of the European Human Rights Committee also states, "Matters outside the scope of Article 6 include tax proceedings: tax matters still form part of the hard core of public-authority prerogatives, with the public nature of the relationship between the taxpayer and the community remaining predominant."

from the sphere of Article 6 of the ECHR.[164] In fact, in *Melgarejo Martinez de Abellanos v. Spain* ([2021] A application no. 11200/19), the ECHR held that the Spanish Tribunal (Audiencia Nacional) violated Article 6(1) of the ECHR because it found the tax reassessment on the claimant to be null and void but did not void the penalties and interest arose in connection with the reassessment and failed to show the claimant sufficient reasons for such decision, preventing him from ascertaining whether the Tribunal examined his submissions at all.

There is more ambiguity on the interpretation and applicable scope of Article 6(1) of ECHR because the term "criminal charge" in this provision is not limited to criminal penalties for the purpose of the ECHR. For example, in *Bendenoun v. France* ([1994] Application no. 12547/86), the ECHR held that no rights provided for in Article 6 of the ECHR were found to have been violated in this case. But the Court specified that the penalties applied to the claimant were due to acts that amount to "deception" not to "evasion," and the Conseil d'Éat regarded the former offense as a tax offense and the latter as a criminal offense, while both of these penalties are criminal penalties/charges for the purpose of the Article 6 of the ECHR when they are viewed in light of the following criteria: (i) they potentially covers all taxpayers, (ii) they are not intended as pecuniary compensation, (iii) their purpose is both deterrent and punitive, (iv) they are substantial in amount. In response to this judgment and other relevant ones, even in the UK, it is pointed out that the penalty for the underreporting due to taxpayers' "deliberate behavior" is a "civil penalty" under domestic law but a "criminal penalty" for the purpose of the ECHR.[165]

Indeed, the above judgments' influence in the UK at the time when it was an EU member is well observable in such judgments as *King v. Walden* (HM Inspector of Taxes) ([2001] STC 822). In this case, at issue was whether or not the penalty imposed on the claimant under TMA §95 for the submission of any incorrect return made fraudulently or negligently, which could amount to 100% of the "potentially lost revenue" (which could be mitigated maximally by 100%) is a criminal charge for the purpose of Article 6(2) of the ECHR.[166] In this High Court judgment, Judge Jacob specified that the claimant was charged with a criminal offense within the meaning of Article 6 of the ECHR mainly because: (i) the penalty is punitive and deterrent, (ii) its amount is potentially substantial, (iii) it is not related to any administrative matter or costs, (iv) it depends on the culpability of the taxpayer, (v) the onus of proving its unlawfulness is not on the taxpayer. However, as for the question of whether there was a shift of the burden of proof on the imposition of the penalty to the claimant and the question of whether there was an unreasonable delay of hearings for the claimant, the High Court's answers were in the negative, so it concluded that there were no violations of Article 6 of the ECHR with respect to the penalty imposed on the applicant.

---

164. Also, *see* Philip Baker, Taxation and the European Convention on Human Rights, *British Tax Review*, Vol. 40, No. 8 (2000) p. 213.
165. *See* https://gov.wales/tax-collection-and-management-wales-act-2016-penalties-technical-guidance. In view of the large number of inaccuracy penalties imposed on account of a taxpayer being "deliberate" shown in Figure 3.10, the significance and impact of such an interpretation are not small.
166. As for TMA §95, *see* the paragraph just below Figure 3.10 in (2-1).

In the above King case, the High Court also highlighted the following points: ① Mr. Philip Baker's analysis of the Strasbourg case law in "Taxation and the ECHR" mentions, "It now seems clearly established, therefore, that a tax-geared penalty can entail a criminal charge, and the issue of liability to penalties of 25% or higher has been regarded as involving the determination of a criminal charge"; ② in *Georgiou v. UK* ([2001] STC 822), the ECHR held that the UK's 1985 Finance Act §13 (Tax evasion: conduct involving dishonesty) (1) is a civil penalty but it could apply the penalty amounting up to 100% of the evaded VAT amount (which could be mitigated maximally by 50%) and constitutes a criminal charge for the purpose of Article 6 of the ECHR;[167] ③ In *AP, MP, and TP v. Switzerland* ([1998] 26 EHRR 541), the ECHR specified, "In earlier case law the Court has established that there are three criteria to be taken into account when it is being decided whether a person was 'charged with a criminal offence' for the purposes of Article 6. These are the classification of the offense under national law, the nature of the offense, and the nature and degree of severity of the penalty that the person concerned risks incurring."

There is another question of whether the Tribunals, just like courts, could abate penalties in cases where they violate Article 6 of the ECHR. For example, in *Anthony Bosher v. The Commissioners for HMRC* ([2012) UKTFT 631), the claimant appealed against the amount of the penalty (in total GBP 54,100, of which the fixed amount was GBP 26,600)imposed by TMA §98A for his delayed submission of monthly returns for the years 2004-2005 and 2006-2007 on "Construction Industry Scheme" set forth in the ITA Regulations §9. In this case, the First-tier Tribunal noted that the HMRC proposed to reduce penalties other than the fixed amount of penalties under TMA §102[168] but held that the term "incorrect" in TMA §100B(2)(b)(iii) is, in light of Article 3 of the Human Rights Act 1998, to be construed to include those penalties that lack proportionality,[169] so the fixed amount of penalties that lack proportionality should also be abated. But this decision was overturned by the Upper Tribunal decision ([2013] UKUT 0579(TCC)) holding that contrary to the case under TMA §100B, the First-tier Tribunal differs from the Upper Tribunal in that the former has no authority to review HMRC's powers of mitigation under TMA §102.[170]

However, in *Barry Edwards and the Commissioners for HMRC* ([2019] UKUT 0131 (TCC)), a different angle was shown. In this case, the claimant with no taxable income in the relevant years appealed against the penalties imposed on him by the 2009 Finance Act Schedule 55 for his failure to file returns. In the preceding First-tier

167. In the King case, the High Court also stated that the higher percentage of mitigation possible under TMA §95 than that under the 1985 Finance Act §13 also constitutes a reason for the former coming under the "criminal charge" for the purpose of Article 6 of the ECHR.

168. *See* 1(3) in this Section and footnote 30 for TMA §102.

169. TMA §100B (Appeals against penalty determinations)(2)(b) states, "First-tier Tribunal may—(iii) if the amount determined appears ... to be incorrect, increase or reduce it to the correct amount."

170. *See* footnote 30. The question of whether or not the HMRC should exercise its discretionary power is not subject to review by the First-tier Tribunal. *See* footnote 34. While, in this *Bosher* case, the Upper Tribunal stated that the HMRC's discretion on the penalty prescribed under TMA §102 could be subject to the review of courts (and the Upper Tribunal in some cases), so that it does not give rise to a problem of possible violation of Article 6 of the ECHR.

Tribunal decision on this case (2017), the Tribunal dismissed the appeal in light of the Upper Tribunal's decision on the above *Bosher* case. The Upper Tribunal also dismissed the appeal on the ground that there are no special circumstances in this case that call for reduction of the penalties pursuant to paragraph 16 of the above Schedule 55, but it held that the Frist-tier Tribunal had been given the power to consider whether there are special circumstances to justify a reduction in the amount of the penalty under this provision. It was also confirmed in the Upper Tribunal decision on *Tahir Iqbal Khawaja and the Commissioners of HMRC* ([2013] UKUT 0353(TCC))that the First-tier Tribunal's power under TMA §100(B) could be exercised to give relief following Article 13 (Right to an effective remedy) of the ECHR to the breach of the appellant's rights to a hearing within a reasonable time which is guaranteed under Article 6 of the ECHR,[171] so that the penalties at issue, in this case, should be reduced from GBP 13,719 to GBP 12,347.

2 Disputes over Business Expenses

There are also a fairly large number of disputes over business expenses, as could be deduced from the cases in Japan and the U.S.[172] However, there is a striking difference between the standard for business expense deduction adopted in the UK and that in Japan and the U.S. The relevant provisions in the UK include, in particular, the 2005 Income Tax (Trading and Other Income) Act (ITTOIA) §34 (Expense not wholly and exclusively for trade and unconnected losses) (1) and 2009 CITA §54 (Expenses not wholly and exclusively for trade and unconnected losses) (1). These provisions state, "In calculating the profits of a trade, no deduction is allowed for—(a) expenses not incurred wholly and exclusively for the purposes of the trade, or (b) losses not connected with or arising out of the trade." This "wholly and exclusively" standard employs the "dual purpose test" which treats, in principle, those expenses with nonbusiness purposes as nondeductible ones for tax purposes.[173] Despite such differences, a similarity is found in the difficulty in some cases in determining whether or not certain expenses of taxpayers engaged in business are deductible, and such difficulty is a main cause for them to be disputed frequently.[174]

171. Article 13 of the ECHR stipulates, "Everyone whose rights and freedoms as set forth in this Convention are violated shall have an effective remedy before a national authority notwithstanding that the violation has been committed by persons acting in an official capacity."
172. For the fact of this theme frequently disputed, *see* Peter Vaines, Expenses: The Wholly and Exclusively Test, *Tax Journal*, Issue 1577 (25 May 2022).
173. Whereas, 2005 ITA §34(2) and 2009 CITA §54(2) provide, "If an expense is incurred for more than one purpose, this section does not prohibit a deduction for any identifiable part or identifiable proportion of the expense which is incurred wholly and exclusively for the purposes of the trade."
174. Moreover, the fact that, especially in relation to CIT, the dual purpose test plays an important role in preventing erosion of the tax base in the same way as transfer pricing taxation, etc. is also a cause for the large number of disputes over business expenses. For details and court cases other than those mentioned in this book on the dual purpose test, *see* Matsuda, *supra* "Tax Strategies VS. Countermeasures" pp. 161-164.

The "dual purpose test" under the "wholly and exclusively" standard sets a high hurdle for a business expense to be deducted as it is intimated by the House of Lords judgment on *Mallalieu v. Drummond* ([1983] 57 TC 330). In this case, at issue was whether the appellee/barrister could deduct, based on the 1970 Income and Corporation Taxes Act (ICTA) §130(a), which employed the "wholly and exclusively" standard, as business expenses, those black clothes the appellee/barrister bought for the purpose of her profession as well as other related expenses (cleaning costs, etc.). In this case, the House of Lords acknowledged that none of those clothes were of the sort that she would wear for going out in the evening or for other social occasions, and the appellee purchased those clothes because the other clothes she had were not appropriate to wear for work at court. However, Lord Brightman stated, "one object, though not a conscious motive, was the provision of the clothing that she needed as a human being. I reject the notion that the object of a taxpayer is inevitably limited to the particular conscious motive in mind at the moment of expenditure" and concluded that the expenses are not deductible because they were laid out in part for the advantage and benefit of the taxpayer as a living human.[175]

Subsequent court judgments generally followed the view shown in the above *Mallalieu* case with respect to the application of the "dual purpose test" under the "wholly and exclusively" standard. For example, in *Newsom v. Robertson* ([1952] 33 TC 452), at issue was whether the appellant/barrister could deduct traveling expenses between his chambers in London and his home in the suburb because he frequently engaged in his professional work at home as well. The High Court held that they are not deductible under 2005 ITA §34 because the travel between those two locations had a mixed purpose of work and life with his family, so it failed the "wholly and exclusively" test. Likewise, his appeal was dismissed at the Court of Appeal ([1952] 1 Ch. 7). In particular, Sommervell LJ pointed out that the appellant's chamber in London was his professional base, and the traveling expenses to and from home are for private purposes while they may have a subsidiary professional purpose. Romer LJ also held as follows, "Mr. Newsom...conceded that a man's profession is not exercised until he arrives at the place at which it is carried on. In my judgment, this proposition is, in general, true....the object of the journeys, both morning and evening, is not to enable a man to do his work but to live away from it," and also dismissed the appellant's claim that he might have had two places of business.

The High Court judgment on *Sargent v. Burnes* ([1978] 52 TC 335) might serve as a more appropriate indicator of the high hurdle of the "wholly and exclusively" standard. In this case, the appellee dentist, when commuting between home and work, made it a rule to alter the commuting route to visit the laboratory for manufacturing dentures, and he deducted the expenses incurred by traveling among those places. It was not disputed that the laboratory was a proper adjunct of his practice, and the work there was exclusively referable to the practice. In this judgment, Judge Oliver doubted that a taxpayer could convert what was an essentially private journey, travel from

175. Lord Brightman specified that those clothes were not of a special character dictated by the occupation as in the case of a uniform, but, nevertheless pointed out that the existence of a private advantage does not necessarily preclude the exclusivity of the business purpose.

home to place of work into a trade journey by the device of stopping off en route, and he overturned the Commissioner's decision on this case by mentioning that the interruption of a journey does not alter the quality of the journey and it merely furnishes an additional purpose, so the traveling expenses are not deductible under 2005 ITA §34. Likewise, the Upper Tribunal decision on *Samadian v. HMRC* ([2014] BTC 504) denied for IT purposes the deduction of those expenses incurred by traveling among the hospital where the appellant was employed, his rented facilities for work, and his home because the appellant was found to have a mixed object in this pattern of traveling.[176]

As mentioned above, the hurdle intimated by the *Mallalieu* case is quite high, but for expenses other than transportation expenses, there are some cases where the tax authority's reassessment of denying their deductions based on the "dual purpose test" was revoked. For example, in *Osborne v. Revenue & Customs* ([2020] UKFTT 373 (TC)), at issue was the lawfulness of the tax authority's denial of the saturation diver's expenses for training in a fitness gym (including the related traveling expenses and membership fees) whose deduction for IT purpose was claimed under 2005 ITA §34. In this case, the HMRC asserted that the claimant's fitness training also provides a personal benefit for the claimant as a living human being and therefore has a duality of purpose. But the First-tier Tribunal referred to Lord Brightman's statement in the *Mallalieu* case that an expenditure made exclusively to serve the purpose of the business may have a private advantage, and such private advantage does not necessarily preclude the exclusivity of the business purpose[177] and held that the claimant's fitness training regime is far removed from his personal physical needs because of its effects and is extreme by any measure so that there is no duality of purpose in the claimant's expenditure on fitness training and any possible improvement in his fitness is incidental.

However, in *Parsons v. Revenue & Customs* ([2010] UKFTT 110 (TC)), the First-tier Tribunal did not allow the claimant/self-employed stunt performer's deduction of the health and fitness expenditures for the relevant years based on the 1988 ICTA §74 (General rules as to deductions not allowable) while it allowed the claimant's deduction of the chiropractor expenses and the masseur expenses for the relevant years. As the main reason for not allowing the deduction of the health and fitness expenditures, the Tribunal cited the *Mallalieu* case and mentioned, "It follows from Mallalieu, for instance, that expenditure incurred in maintaining a particular standard of dress may not satisfy the 'exclusively' test in s. 74 of ICTA, if the clothing is not of a special character dictated by the occupation and this is so even if clothing of that standard would not have been purchased by the taxpayer but for the need to wear clothes of such a standard at work." Then, the Tribunal concluded that the health and fitness expenditures are incurred by the claimant to meet a particular standard of

176. In this decision on the *Samadian* case, the Upper Tribunal pointed out that the only case in which traveling expenses were allowed to be deducted by clearing the high hurdle set by the *Mallalieu* case was the Court of Appeal judgment *Horton v. Young* ([1971] EWCA Civ J0506-1) in which the taxpayer had no workplace other than his home from which he traveled to visit his customers.

177. *See* footnote 175 on this point.

fitness, but maintaining health and fitness is a general human need, even if it also serves the purposes of the trade or profession, so the claimant's expenditures on health and fitness served a dual purpose.

SECTION 6 SUMMARY AND ANALYSIS

Under the old tax appeal system, there was a large number of tax disputes (*see* Table 3.1). In some years, the number of tax disputes General Commissioners had to process was more than 100,000. Consequently, in many cases, disputing taxpayers could not expect speedy resolution of their cases and taxpayers, in general, were left in the dark because their decisions on them were not made open. Furthermore, the independence and neutrality of various tribunals, including General Commissioners, were not sufficient because there was the tax authority's intervention in the process of taxpayers' filing of appeals to them, posing a problem in relation to Article 6 of the ECHR. However, some of these problems were mitigated by the current tax dispute system introduced by the 2007 TCE Act. In particular, they have made it possible for aggrieved taxpayers: (i) to utilize the HMRC's statutory reviews (similar to internal reviews which were available under the old tax appeal system only to the taxpayers aggrieved over the re/assessments of indirect taxes on them) conducted by a review officer within the Solicitor's Office and Legal Services part of the HMRC, (ii) to opt for direct appeals to the First-tier Tribunal, and so forth. These reforms have contributed to the reduction of taxpayers' time and costs as well as the enhancement of their convenience.

However, the number of tax disputes did not decrease much, even under the current tax appeal system (see Figures 3.3 and 3.6). One of the reasons for the large number of tax disputes being filed with the First-tier Tribunals could be found in the relatively high ratio of its revocations of the disputed re/assessments, etc. (*see* Figure 3.6) because it should work as an incentive for many aggrieved taxpayers to dispute their cases at the First-tier Tribunal. The HMRC and the First-tier Tribunal deal with the challenge of a large number of tax disputes being filed by aggrieved taxpayers, in particular, by actively engaging in flexible settlement of them. The HMRC is empowered with collection and management authority to settle disputes with taxpayers, and ADR, which is considered to give rise to an agreement consistent with law, has been utilized actively. Indeed, flexible resolution of disputes has an aspect of raising an issue of equity and fairness, and there were actually a few cases of flexible tax dispute settlements that caused some concerns and were scrutinized by the National Audit Office. However, such concerns led the HMRC to take a more cautious stance on extra-statutory concessions and to strengthen its internal control over flexible settlements of tax disputes by establishing various management committees under TDRB and appointing the HMRC TAC.

There are also other reasons that may account for the large number of tax disputes at the First-tier Tribunal. They include: (i) HMRC's statutory reviews were not utilized much by taxpayers; (ii) the First-tier Tribunal is highly independent and neutral; (iii) if a disputed case falls under the "Default Paper case" or "Basic case," dispute resolution following the relatively quick and less burdensome procedures is possible; (iv) if a disputed case does not fall under "Complex cases," the "Sheldon practice" excludes the unsuccessful claimants' risk of paying the HMRC's costs; (v) the claimant may request for the reclassification of his case (from the "Standard case" to "Complex case and vice versa) to reduce/increase possible risk/chance on shifting of costs. It is not that there are not any facts about the First-tier Tribunal that should work toward deterring an increase in the number of appeals. They include: ① The ratio of revocation of the re/assessments by the First-tier Tribunal has generally been lower than that at the statutory reviews; ② The recent declining trend in the number of statutory reviews was reversed in FY2021-2022 and FY2022-2023, ③ "Wednesbury unreasonableness" excludes from the review of the First-tier Tribunal those cases on which the HMRC's exercise of discretion is not ultra vires,[178] ④ Unprocessed appeal cases have lately accumulated at the First-tier Tribunal..

As for the number of tax disputes at the Upper Tribunal and courts, it is relatively small. The main reason for that should lie in the fact that at those dispute stages, the taxpayers' costs in terms of time and money could become considerable. Especially, the risk that the "English rule" on costs poses, against the background of not much public support lately given to the litigating citizens, should work toward decreasing the number of appeals at those stages except for those taxpayers considering their chances of winning to be high.[179] While it is true that this risk has lately been mitigated by the following: (i) the "English rule" has metamorphosed in such a way that it is now more favorable to the taxpayers, and the "Chorley's exception" and Litigants in Person (Costs and Expenses) Act 1975 §1 enable the unrepresented winning taxpayers to recover some litigation-related expenses; (ii) "Rees Practice" has been followed so that there may be no-costs shifting to taxpayers who lost by the appeal made by the HMRC, (iii) the utilization of "conditional fee arrangements" or "after-the-event insurance premiums" could wipe out or mitigate the taxpayers' risk of bearing the other party's costs; (iv) "McKenzie friend" and "Calderbank offer" may be utilized; (v) some CPR provisions limit the application of the "English rule" on costs to the benefit of some disputing taxpayers.[180]

As for the cases that are highly disputed, penalty cases stand out from the rest. The main reasons for that should include the following: (i) the number of penalty impositions is large; in particular, penalties are imposed even on those non-filers of returns who do not have taxable income; (ii) some penalty rates are quite high, and the amount of penalties could be quite large; (iii) the penalty system is quite complex. In

178. *See* footnote 34. While the analysis at 2(4) in Section 5 reveals that the First-tier Tribunal may review the HMRC's exercise or lack of exercise of its discretion on the abatement of some penalties.

179. Whereas, 2011 Report of the Costs Review Group points out in para. 62 that the inability to recover costs will have a deterrent effect where the costs of the appeal would exceed the tax in dispute.

180. The relevant provisions include CPR §27.14 (in footnote 95), CPR §3.19 (in footnote 105) and CPR §52.9A (*see* last paragraph in 3 of Section 4). Moves in the same direction include the Aarhus Convention Compliance Committee's 9/24/2010 recommendation to the UK government and a series of revisions (*see* 4 in Section 4) reflecting the 2009 publication of the "Civil Litigation Costs Review (final report)" by Lord Jackson Justice which emphasized the merits of the "qualified one-way costs-shifting."

particular, the applicable percentage of "behavioral penalties" could vary depending on the modes of taxpayers' behaviors and the HMRC's discretion on their abatement is also wide, so many taxpayers wonder if the applied penalty rates are appropriate and there might be some chances of their abatement; (iv) actually, the ratio of revocation is higher in the case of penalty impositions than others; (v) The hurdle for the exemption of penalties on account of reasonable care and "reasonable excuse" is not so high; (vi) the HMRC has wide discretion on suspension of penalties and their abatement by the existence of "special circumstances" may also be possible; (vi) EU Law has added further ambiguity to the appropriate amount of penalties to be imposed because those penalties could be abated if they are so severe as to lack proportionality to the level of noncompliance or contain some procedural deficiencies on the part of the government.

Business expense cases are also highly disputed in the UK. However, in the UK, a business expense is deductible provided that it clears the "double purpose test" under the "wholly and exclusively" standard. A series of judicial precedents have confirmed the high hurdle set by this standard. To be includable in them is the *Lomax v. Newton* case ([1953] 34 TC 558) in which Judge Vaisey of the High Court stated on Rule 9 of Schedule E of ITA of 1918, which adopts the same standard as follows, "The provisions of this rule are notoriously rigid, narrow and restricted in their operation." Such limitation in the application scope could work toward restricting the number of disputes in this case,[181] but the lack of clarity about its scope has been at work in pushing taxpayers to dispute this case. In the High Court judgment on *HMRC v. Banerjee* ([2010] EWHC 62 (Ch)), Judge Henderson also mentioned, in paragraph 28 of the judgment, on ICTA §198 (Relief for necessary expense) as follows, "The requirements of section 198 are notoriously difficult to satisfy, but that is not to say they can never be satisfied." Then, he allowed the deduction of the expenses incurred by the claimant/doctor's attendance in the training courses, even if her attendance at such courses may be a relatively unusual state of affairs. The judgment was sustained by the subsequent Court of Appeal case ([2010] STI 2347).

181. While, in Ireland, the number of disputes on Tax Consolidation Act §114 which incorporates the "wholly and exclusively" standard is relatively small. *See* footnote 126 in Chapter 5.

CHAPTER 4

Status of Commonwealth Countries (Australia and NZ)

SECTION 1 TAX DISPUTE IN AUSTRALIA

1 Background and Effects of Reform of Tax Appeal System

The basic procedures for tax objections are stipulated in Part 4C (Taxation Objections, Reviews and Appeals, 14ZL to 14ZZS) in the Taxation Administration Act (TAA) of 1953.[1] Taxpayers who are dissatisfied with the "notice of assessment" or "taxation decision" issued by the tax authority (ATO) file an appeal ("taxation objection") with the ATO.[2] Under the old appeal system before the organizational reform of the ATO, which was carried out from 2013 to 2014, reviews of the objections were basically conducted by the same line of departments as the examiners, but there were problems with this system. In fact, from the 1990s to the 2010s, government agencies and expert committees published reports calling for reform of the system one after another. Those reports include the 1999 Report (Review of Business Taxation) by John Ralph, who was the appointed chairman of the Board of Business Taxation by the government, the 2015 Report (Management of Tax Disputes) by the Inspector-General of Taxation(IGT), and the 2014 Report (Managing Compliance of High Weight Individuals) by the National Audit Office (NAO).

1. TAA §14ZL (Part applies to taxation objection) states: "(1) This Part applies if a provision of an Act or a legislative instrument (...) provides that a person who is dissatisfied with an assessment, determination, notice or decision, or with a failure to make a private ruling, may object against it in the manner set out in this Part. (2) Such an objection is in this Part called a taxation objection." Likewise, the Income Tax Assessment Act of 1936 §175A (Objections against assessments) states: "A taxpayer who is dissatisfied with an assessment made in relation to the taxpayer may object against it in the manner set out in Part IVC of the Taxation Administration Act 1953."
2. As for details on ATO dispositions (such as decisions not to exempt various interest) that are not subject to objections to ATO, *see* https://www.ato.gov.au/General/dispute-or-object-to-an-ato-decision/object-to-an-ato-decision/decisions-you-can-t-dispute-via-an-objection/.

The basic directions of institutional reforms commonly proposed in the above Reports were: (i) to realize faster dispute resolution, (ii) to increase the independence of those departments in charge of the review of the objections, and (iii) to prevent the occurrence of unnecessary tax disputes. In particular, in relation to the above (i) and (ii), it was pointed out that, against the background of being no particular internal rule prohibiting communication between the person in charge of the examination and the person in charge of reviewing the objections, some taxpayers did not give a high mark to the ATO's review of the objections they filed. For example, in *Binetter v. Commissioner of Taxation* (No. 3) ([2012] FCA 704), the Federal Court referred to the note of correspondence passing between the ATO officers, which was tendered by the taxpayer and implied the ATO's use of the objection process to collect evidence in preparation for litigation to cope with a taxpayer's strategy of flooding the Commissioner with materials at later stages of the dispute. The above IGT's 2015 Report specifies in paragraph 3.63 that this correspondence gives a wrong idea to taxpayers about the lack of independence and objectivity in the objection process.

As for the above (iii) (need for preventing tax disputes), it should make much sense because, as Figure 4.1 discloses, there has lately been an increasing trend of the number of objections to the ATO and its decisions on them, and the average ratio of the decisions revoking (fully or partially)the re/assessments against the total number of decisions (or total number of objections) between the periods of FY2004-2005 to FY2007-2008 was about 58% (or about 47%). In particular, between FY2004-2005 and FY2007-2008, the average ratio of the number of decisions revoking the re/assessments against the total number of decisions (or the total number of objections) on "large business taxpayers" (those with an annual turnover of over AUD 2.5 billion) was about 35% (or 22%),[3] but, between FY2004-2005 and FY2007-2008, the average ratio of the number of decisions revoking the re/assessments against the total number of decisions (977 cases) on the total number of objections (1,548 cases) filed by "large business" increased to about 69%.[4] The average ratio of the number of decisions revoking the re/assessments on "high wealth individuals" against the total number of their objections between FY2007/2008 to FY2013-2014 was also as high as 65% approximately.[5]

3. However, if the data in Table 1 of the IGT's 2015 Report is relied on, rather than the data in Table 4.2 of the IGT's 2009 Report, the average ratio of the number of decisions revoking the re/assessments against the total number of decisions (or total number of objections filed with ATO) for FY2007-FY2008 by "large business taxpayers" is about 43% (or about 24%) instead of about 35% (or 22%).
4. *See* Table 4.2 in the IGT's 2009 Report ("Review into the Underlying Causes and the Management of Objections to Tax Office Decisions") and Table 1 in IGT 2015 Report.
5. "High wealth individuals" are defined as those individuals who are Australian residents, together with their "associates" have effective control over AUD 30 million (now AUD 50 million) in assets. For details, *see* p. 13 of the IGT 2014 Report ("Managing Compliance of High Wealth Individuals").

Figure 4.1 Number of Objections Received/Processed by ATO and Ratio of Revocation of the Re/assessments on "Large Business Taxpayers"

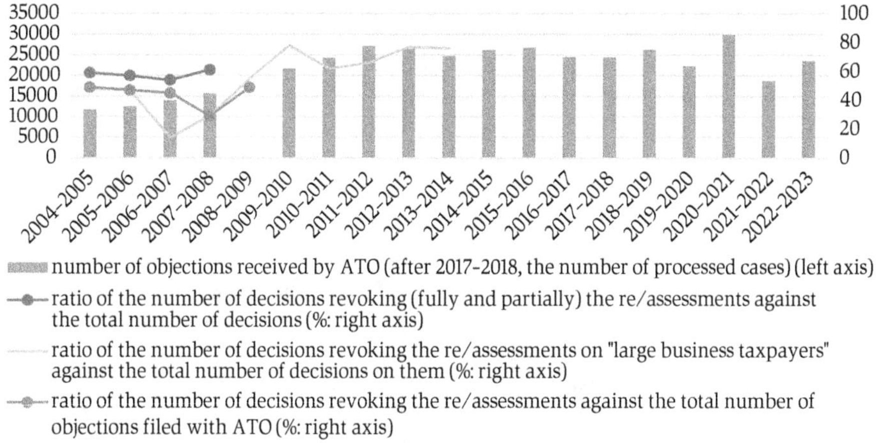

Source: Figure on Tax Disputes in ATO Annual Reports for 2011/2012 to 2022-2023, Tables 1 and 3 in IGT 2015 Report, and Table 4.2 in IGT 2009 Report.

While it is also true that, among those objections to the ATO, there are quite a few that are not "genuine disputes" that pivot on the content of the reassessments. For example, the total number of objections filed with the ATO in 2007/2008 was 18,667, of which approximately 32% were about tax procedures that were not "genuine disputes." In addition, in 2007-2008, the number of "genuine disputes" objections regarding TAA §14ZX (Commissioner to consider application for extension of time), which provides for the Commissioner's authority to grant an "extension of time" for objections and requests for correction,[6] represented about 20% of the total number of objections.[7] Moreover, the hurdles for the grant of the "extension of time" are not so high. For example, in 2007-2008, the number of objections filed by Micro Enterprise and Individuals business line to the decisions on "extension of time" was 2,934, and the ratio of granting it was as high as 78%,[8] while it was true that such a high ratio of granting is partially attributable to the fairly large number of cases where the evidence which had not been submitted at the examination stage was turned in to the ATO at the objection stage.[9]

6. TAA §14ZX states, "(1) After considering the request, the Commissioner must decide whether to agree to it or refuse it. ... (4) If the Commissioner decides to refuse the request, the person may apply to the Tribunal for review of the decision."
7. *See* Table 2.1 in IGT 2009 Report.
8. *See* IGT 2009 Report, para. 27 and Table 2.1.
9. *See* para. 3.62 of IGT 2015 Report.

There are various facts, as described above, behind the high ratio of revocation of the re/assessments at the objection stage, and among them, there were some that need to be corrected. In particular, the NAO specified in paragraph 4.63 to paragraph 5.4 of the above 2014 Report that, as for the examination of "high wealth individuals" and reviews of their objections, there were such facts as: (i) about 40% of the examinations and reviews on them during 2009-2010 to 2012-2013 were not completed within the targeted timeframe;[10] (ii) objections were filed with the ATO at about 65% ratio (approximately 120 cases) of the approximately 200 examinations completed in 2011-2012 and 2012-2013, and about half of the ATO decisions on them were favorable to the taxpayers. These facts led the NAO to conclude that there was room for improvement in the ATO's examination and review of objections filed by "high wealth individuals."[11] In addition, in paragraph 5.2.2 of the IGT 2011 Report (Tax Forum—Next Step for Australia), it is noted that tax officials who review objections belong to the same line of work as tax examiners and taxpayers cannot help feeling that the former receive some kind of input or influence from the latter and such feeling is particularly strong when a dispute is complicated, so it was proposed to establish a more independent review mechanism.

In response to the recommendations of the above reports, etc., the ATO, since around 2013, has been promoting organizational and administrative reforms, including the objection review system. As a result, since 2015, under the tax objection system as shown in Figure 4.2, objections to ATO are basically filed on taxation decisions or tax re/assessments, but in the case of a "large business taxpayer," if he is dissatisfied with the "Statement of Audit Position" presented before the end of the examination, he could sit for an "independent review" comprising a "case conference" to be conducted by a senior independent reviewer who is on a "Review and Dispute Resolution" business line,[12] and if necessary make an objection to the taxation decision to be made in accordance with the result of the independent review. In addition, from July 2018, pilot programs have been implemented to enable "independent reviews" to be utilized as well by those "small businesses (taxpayers)" with an aggregated turnover of less than AUD 10 million who meet certain requirements. It seems that the introduction of the "independent review" and the subsequent expansion of its scope seems to have worked in settling a larger number of disputes at the pre-court stage.[13]

10. For example, in the case of objections filed by "high wealth individuals" with ATO during 2011-2013, it took ATO an average of 352 days from the date of the acceptance to the date of decision. As for details, *see* para. 5.23 and Figure 5.2 of NAO 2014 Report above.
11. *See* paras. 14 and 15 of the Summary of NAO 2014 Report.
12. ATO has set the goal of completing an "independent review" within fifty-six days.
13. Individuals and small businesses have the highest rate of settlement by agreement at the objection stage and the number of agreements reached after going through the "independent review" increased from 64 to 165 between 2014/2015 and 2016/2017. *See* Figure 6 and Tables 2.1 and 2.2 of the NAO 2017 Report (The Australian Taxation Office's Use of Settlements) for details.

Figure 4.2 Tax Objection Procedures after 2015

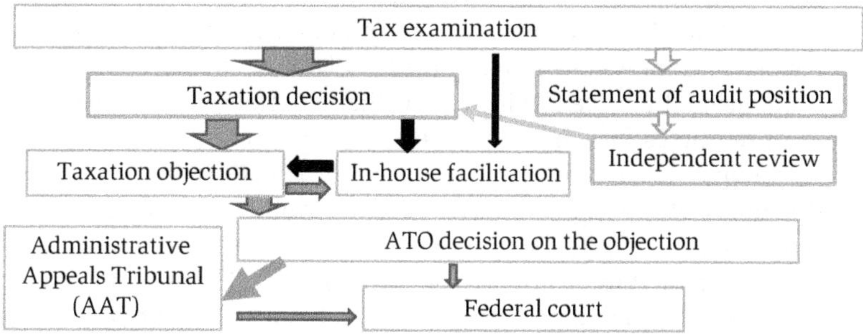

As mentioned above, the tax objection system has changed in recent years to alleviate the problems some taxpayers had found in the old tax objection system. But there has been no major change in the number of objections filed with the ATO. Around the beginning of the 2010s, more than 15 million tax returns were submitted each year, of which less than 5% (750,000) were subjected to re/assessments, and objections were filed on 5% (35,000) of those re/assessments.[14] Also, around the mid-2010s, a total of more than 35 million tax returns and "activity statements" were submitted annually,[15] but the number of objections received and processed by the ATO remained at around 20,000 to 30,000. For instance, in 2011-2012, IT revenue accounted for about 60% of the total tax revenue,[16] and about 80% of the objections to the ATO were on IT/CIT (60 ~ 65% of them were filed by individuals and more than 30% were filed by small enterprises). There has hardly been any recent significant change with those ratios either. Moreover, the introduction of the "independent review" system, despite its significance, has not impacted much on the number of objections because those taxpayers that lately went through "independent reviews" remained 200 or less annually.[17]

14. ATO processes objections in an average of two to three months (e.g., 74 days on average in 2010-2011 and 73 days in 2011-2012), so there is not much difference in the number of objections received and processed each year.
15. Australia's population is about 26 million in 2021. An "activity statement" is a form for registered businesses to submit information related to the payment of goods and services tax, payroll tax, etc. to the ATO. For details, *see* https://business.gov.au/finance/taxation/what-is-an-ctivity-statement.
16. In 2019-2020, taxes on income, profits and capital gains accounted for 59.5%, goods and services tax accounted for 25.8%, and taxes on property is 6.1%, and payroll taxes is 4.5% of the total tax revenue. *See* https://www.abs.gov.au/statistics/economy/government/taxation-revenue-australia/latest-release for details.
17. The ATO reports that from 2018 to March 2021, the number of small businesses that took up the "independent review" is 180 or more. For details, *see* https://www.ato.gov.au/Media-centre/Media-releases/ATO-affirms-importance-of-independent-review-service-for-small-businesses-to-help-resolve-disputes/.

2 Flexible Dispute Resolution

Administrative agencies in Australia have extensive discretion over their affairs. For example, the Financial Management and Accountability Act 1997 §44 (Promoting proper use, etc., of Commonwealth resources) dictates, "A Chief Executive must manage the affairs of the Agency in a way that promotes the proper use of the Commonwealth resources for which the Chief Executive is responsible. Note: A Chief Executive has the power to enter into contracts on behalf of the Commonwealth in relation to the affairs of the Agency." Likewise, the Public Governance, Performance and Accountability Act of 2013 §15 (Duty to govern the Commonwealth entity) provides, "(1) The accountable authority of a Commonwealth entity must govern the entity in a way that: (a) promotes the proper use and management of public resources for which the authority is responsible; ... (2) In making decisions for the purposes of subsection (1), the accountable authority must take into account the effect of those decisions on public resources generally." As for the power of ATO's Commissioner, the Income Tax Assessment Act (ITAA) of 1936 §8 (Commissioner) stipulates, "The Commissioner shall have the general administration of this Act."[18]

The above power of the ATO's Commissioner naturally extends over the affairs of settling tax disputes. For example, in *Precision Pools v. Commissioner of Taxation* ((1992) 37 FCR 554), at issue was whether the ATO Commissioner had the power to agree to receive sales tax paid by the applicants on the basis that if it were to be held subsequently that he had no right to be paid that tax, the Commissioner would repay them. The Federal Court specified that the legal ground for the refunds of taxes based on this agreement cannot be found in the Sales Tax Assessment Act (STAA) (No. 1) §26 (Refunds of tax), which provides for refund of any tax overpaid, but found in §4 of this Act because this is not a case of a refund of overpaid tax.[19] Then, after having confirmed that STAA (No. 1) §4 grants the Commissioner a wide power and it would encompass the power to compromise proceedings in which he was a party or to make agreements concerning the efficient management of a dispute in which he was involved, the Court concluded that this agreement is evidenced by the submitted materials to be a sensible one falling within the power of the Commissioner, and the applicants are entitled to the claims for payments pursuant to the agreement.

The ATO's agreements with taxpayers are also possible in disputes over penalties as Schedule 1 §298-20 (Remission of penalty) of TAA prescribes, "(1) The Commissioner may remit all or a part of the penalty." Indeed, Taxation Ruling (TR) 94/7

18. ITAA of 1997 §1-7 (Administration of this Act) provides likewise. Sales Tax Assessment Act (STAA) (No. 1) §4 of 1930 provides likewise with respect to sales tax.
19. STAA §26 stipulates, "where the Commissioner finds in any case that tax has been overpaid by a person, the Commissioner shall—(a) refund the amount of any tax overpaid."

(Income tax: tax shortfall penalties: guidelines for the exercise of the Commissioner's discretion to remit penalty otherwise attracted) explains, "The discretion to remit penalty otherwise attracted under a shortfall section should be exercised in only those exceptional cases where, having regard to all of the circumstances, the application of a particular shortfall section and/or the rate of the penalty prescribed under that section would provide a clearly unreasonable or unjust result." But, the AAT decision on *Dixon v. FCT* ([2008] AATA 825) and the Full Federal Court judgment on it ([2008] 167 FCR 287) imply that "those exceptional cases" might not be so rare. In the former, the AAT accepted that a taxpayer's inability to recover a penalty from a tax agent whose acts or omissions were responsible for it may be a relevant factor for Schedule 1 §298-20 of TAA,[20] and in the latter, the Court held, "It is not necessary that there be special circumstances before the discretion to remit in s 298-20 can be exercised."

The ATO's guideline (Practical Guide to the ATO code of settlement) 8 (Background) also explains that the basic duty of the Commissioner is the "good management" of the tax system. The good management rule is to make sensible decisions having regard to the best use of limited resources available, and those decisions may, in some cases, be agreements with taxpayers. Nevertheless, as Figure 4.3 shows, until around the first half of 2010, the number of dispute resolutions by agreement was very small, and it was, for example, less than 1 % of the number of objections filed with the ATO between 2004 and 2008.[21] Moreover, at that time, many agreements were reached at a relatively late stage of disputes.[22] The IGT saw this situation as a problem, and in Recommendation 5 of the 2008 Report (Review of the Potential Revenue Bias in Private Binding Rulings involving Large Complex Matters), it stressed the need for efforts to resolve disputes at an earlier stage.[23] Since around 2014, when the ATO also opined that the disputing parties should disclose all the relevant facts on the table at an early stage, the number of agreements has increased significantly and higher ratios of agreements reached at earlier stages of disputes have resulted.

20. Moreover, Schedule 1 §284-75(6)(d) of TAA provides that a penalty may not be imposed on a taxpayer in a case where the false or misleading nature of the statement does not result from his registered tax agent's intentional disregard of law or recklessness. While, in Japan, a taxpayer's prospect of compensation recovery from his tax agent and the agent's level of care do not affect whether or not a penalty is to be imposed on him.
21. *See* Table 4.2 of IGT 2009 Report.
22. Agreements are usually entered into with the drawing up of a stylized "Model Settlement Deeds" by the parties. Model agreement deed can be retrieved from http://www.ato.gov.au/general/dispute-or-object-to-an-ATO-decision/lndetail/avoiding-and-resolving-dispute/settlement/model-settlement-deeds/.
23. *See* IGT 2015 Report, p. 41. The same need in NZ also pushed the 1996 reform of its tax objection review procedure. *See* 1(1) in Section 2.

Figure 4.3 Number of Agreements and Their Breakdown at the Stage of the Conclusion

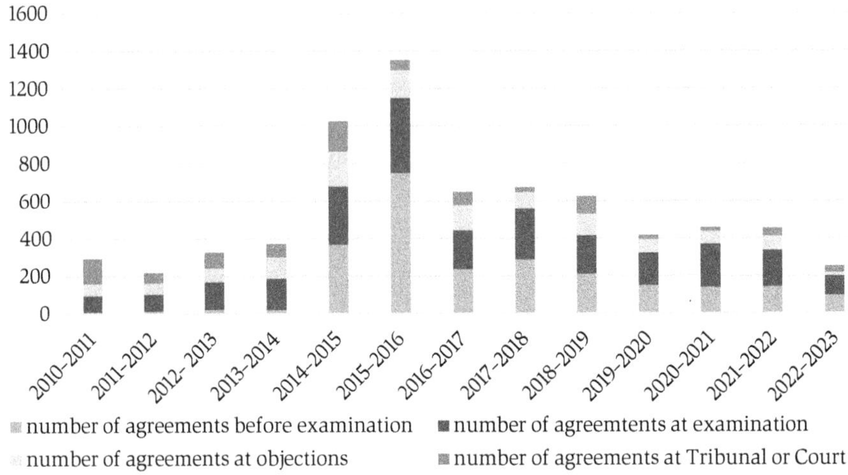

Sources: IGT 2014 Report Tables 5-7, Inquiry into 2016-2023 ATO Report Table 4.1, Dispute Management in 2017-2018 to 2020-2021 ATO Reports, and NAO 2017 Report Figure 1.2.

The main reason for the increase in the number of dispute resolutions through agreements at an early stage is that since 2014, the number of agreements based on the Overseas Income Disclosure Project (referred to as the "Project do it") has increased significantly and the "in-house facilitation" shown in Figure 1 has become available.[24] Unlike the abovementioned "case conference," which does not involve mediation, "in-house facilitation" is a form of ADR. As an independent facilitator, the ATO's staff or its stakeholders provide support in such a way as to narrow down issues and present options for dispute resolution.[25] Such support would enable the taxpayer to reduce his administrative burden in connection with TAA Part IVC (Taxation Objections, Reviews and Appeals). However, it is true that not all tax disputes are suitable for "in-house facilitation,"[26] it is utilized mostly by nonbusiness individuals and small businesses. The number of "in-house facilitation" implemented in 2014-2015 was 93, but it

24. *See* https://www.ato.gov.au/General/Dispute-or-object-to-an-ATO-decision/In-detail/Avoiding-and-resolving-disputes/Settlement/Settlements/. Chapter 3 of the NAO 2015 Report and para. 1.11 of NAO 2017 Report give a positive evaluation of the early dispute resolution effect of the "in-house facilitation." As Figure 4.2 displays, "in-house facilitation" is available at any stage of disputes.
25. Such ATO stakeholders includes, attorneys, staff of the National Mediation Service or the Tax Counsel Network.
26. GST refund cases, appraisal cases, exemption from interest, and cancellation of seizure notices are listed to be particularly suitable for "in-house facilitation." For details, *see* Chris Wallis, In Facilitation Preparation, Scoping and Agility Are Essential, *Taxation in Australia*, Vol. 53, No. 4 (October 2018) pp. 197-198.

increased to 247 in 2017-2018, and the ratio of it leading to a dispute resolution is as high as 90% or above in multiple years.[27]

Indeed, lately, there have been some increases in the number of tax dispute resolutions by agreements, but its number is still relatively small, and this might deter the reform of the objection system from becoming a drastic one.[28] For example, according to Figure 4.1, the number of objections processed by the ATO in 2020-2021 was 29,877, but Figure 4.3 reveals that agreements were reached only on seventy cases (about 0.2%). For the same year, 668 tax appeals were brought to the AAT or courts, but agreements were reached only on thirty-six cases (about 5%). Even in 2013-2014, when the number of agreements reached after taxation decisions were given was comparatively high, the ATO received approximately 24,700 objections, but only 114 cases (about 0.5%) were resolved through agreements. Moreover, every year, the number of agreements reached and their breakdown are more or less the same as shown in the following data for FY2017-2018: business proprietors (287 cases and about 43%), small corporations (173 cases and about 26%), large corporations (95 cases and about 14%), nonbusiness individuals (59 cases and about 9%), others (59 cases and about 9%).[29] Thus, there are more agreements among relatively small-value cases.

The reason for the relatively low ratio of the ATO reaching agreements with the aggrieved taxpayers may lie in the ATO's attitude toward settlement by agreements. Certainly, agreements between the ATO and taxpayers are reached basically in line with the ATO's "Code of Settlement" and "Pre-settlement Assurance Mechanism,"[30] and the ATO, on page 93 of its 2011-2012 Annual Report, notes that there is plenty of room for agreement, particularly where disputes are on facts, or they contain "litigation hazards" or Commissioner's discretion. Moreover, the ATO's Code of Settlement Practice mentions in paragraph 26 that it is appropriate to reach an agreement if: (i) the amount of tax ATO can collect by winning a case is not proportional to its litigation-related costs; (ii) there is uncertainty about the precise application of the law to the disputed cases, or they have special characteristics, so that resolution of those cases by AAT or a court might lead to questionable results. Despite such ATO's positive stance on settlement by agreements, some point out that the Commissioner appears to have reservations on it in some cases owing to the risk of perceived favoritism, or scrutiny by the NAO or the Parliament.[31]

27. For details, *see* the ATO 2018 publication (Administrative Appeals Tribunal Statutory Review) pp. 6-7.
28. This contrasts sharply with the situation (high ratio of dispute settlements by agreement even after examinations are over) in the U.S. and the UK referred to in Chapters 2 and 3.
29. *See* ATO 2017/2018 Annual Report Table 5.6.
30. Under the "Pre-settlement Assurance Mechanism," in principle, consultations and case referrals are carried out with related departments before an agreement is reached. For details, *see* Table 2.1 of the NAO 2017 Report ("The Australian Taxation Office's Use of Settlements").
31. *See* paras. 5.7 and 5.8 of the IGT 2012 Report (Taxation Office's use of Early and Alternative Dispute Resolution).

Indeed, the IGT audits the ATO's agreements and publishes audit results.[32] Such audit results contain, as Figures 4.3 and 4.4 show, the annual number of the ATO's agreements, the annual total amount of the reassessments subjected to agreements and the annual ratio of the amount reduced by agreements against the amount of the concerned reassessments. Moreover, since 2016, the ATO has implemented the "Independent Assurance of Settlements Program (IASP)," in which four reviewers who used to be federal court judges mainly audit the agreements on large-scale and tax avoidance cases. The agreements which are automatically audited under IASP include: (i) those in which the agreed amount exceeds AUD 20 million; (ii) those in which the pre-agreement correction amount exceeds AUD 50 million; (iii) those in which there is a difference of more than AUD 20 million in tax amounts before and after the correction; (iv) those that are acknowledged to be particularly important by Deputy Commissioner of the ATO. IASP is important, especially because, as shown in Figure 4.4, there are years when the percentage of the tax amount reduced by the agreement against the amount of correction exceeds 50%.

Figure 4.4 Amount of Reassessments Subjected to Agreements and Ratios of the Amount Reduced by Agreements Against the Amount Originally Assessed by ATO

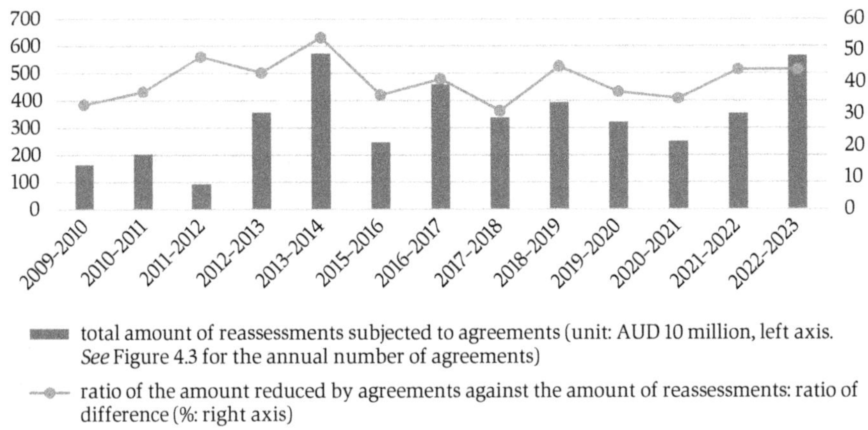

Source: IGT 2015 Report Table 7, NAO 2017 Report Figure 1.2 and Table: Settlements registered by client group in ATO 2016～2023 Annual Reports.

As of October 2019, there were thirty-six agreements subjected to IASP (around ten each year). The average difference in percentage between the agreed amounts and the amounts of the reassessment/correction is about 30% to 40%.[33] The person in charge of IASP said that almost all of the twelve agreements which were subjected to

32. IGT's recent Report includes "Management of Tax Disputes: IGT Report to the Assistant Treasurer 2015."
33. According to Table 6.6 of the ATO 2019-2020 and 2020-2021 Annual Reports, the average "difference" for the fifteen cases subjected to IASP from 2018-2019 to 2019-2020 (or the eighteen cases from 2019/2020 to 2020-2021) was 33% (or 40%).

IASP for FY2017-2018 had no problems while there was one which was difficult to evaluate because of its special nature.[34] It would be difficult to measure the extent of IASP deterring agreements to be reached, and Figure 4.4 indicates that the ratio (or difference) of the total amount reduced by agreements against the total amount of reassessment has not changed much since 2015-2016,[35] but IASP may have some deterrent effect as Figure 4.3 shows the decline in the number of agreements since 2016-2017. Should such a deterrent effect also be at work vis-à-vis cases other than those that fall under (i) to (iv) above, those taxpayers who wish for the ATO's more flexible and proactive stance on dispute settlements by agreements may have mixed feelings on this. The ATO's view is that the above IASP result on the agreements reviewed for FY2017-2018 will not have any particular impact on future agreements.[36]

3 Disputes at AAT and Federal Court

(1) Advantages of Appealing to AAT

Under the tax appeal system that existed until 1986, if a taxpayer is dissatisfied with the ATO's decision on his objection or there was no agreement reached at the objection stage, he could file an appeal to the Taxation Boards of Review consisting of three persons (a legal expert, a tax expert and a senior ATO official who serves as chairperson) appointed by the Governor-General. However, in 1986, with the shift to a self-assessment system, the function of the Taxation Boards of Review was replaced by the Taxation Appeals Division and the Small Taxation Claims of the Administrative Appeals Tribunal (AAT), which had been established based on the 1975 AAT Act. In addition, in 2015, the Taxation Appeals Division and the Small Tax Claims Tribunal were transformed into the Taxation and Commercial Division, which is responsible for hearing appeals related to tax cases as well as nontax commercial cases. Then, in March 2019, the Small Business Taxation Division was newly established in the AAT to deal with small claims cases. As Figure 4.2 depicts, in principle, it is not a requirement for taxpayers aggrieved over the ATO decisions to file appeals with AAT before they file appeals to the Federal Court,[37] but in reality, the majority of them opt not to skip their appeals to the AAT.

34. For details, *see* https://www.ato.gov.au/General/Dispute-or-object-to-an-ATO-decision/In-detail/Avoidng-and-resolving-disputes/Settlement/lndependent-Assurance-of-Settlements-program/. Para. 2.19 of the above NAO 2017 Report also states that there were no problems with the nine agreements that were subjected to IASP by October 2017.
35. As for those agreements reached from 2014-2015 to 2016-2017, the largest in number was those with "high wealth individuals," and the "difference" ranging from 49% to 69%, while the "difference" in the case of "large business taxpayers" and individuals was 31% to 50%. For details, *see* Tables 2.2 and 2.3 of the IGT 2017-2018 Report.
36. *See* https://www.ato.gov.au/misc/downloads/pdf/qc57334.pdf.
37. While in Japan and UK, in principle, an appeal to the Tribunals should precede an appeal to court. Even in Australia, as for disputes over the issue of the Commissioner's discretion on penalties, they should be brought to the AAT. For example, in *Ferguson v. FCT* ([2012] FCA 706), it was held that it was lawful to challenge the legality of the correction in the Federal Court and the appropriateness of the penalties in the AAT.

For example, about 80% of the aggrieved taxpayers preferred to dispute first at the AAT, and in FY2011-2012, 86% of those appeals made to the courts had been filed with the AAT.[38] The reasons and advantages of disputing at the AAT include the following: (i) the judges are highly specialized, impartial, and independent;[39] (ii) the fees are low; (iii) taxpayers can opt for hearings in camera;[40] (iv) there is a Small Business Taxation Division that can resolve cases of a "small business" with the disputed tax amount of less than AUD 5,000 for a small fee (AUD 95) and there are many applicants with those cases who do not appoint their representative;[41] (v) trial procedures and dispute resolution under the Small Business Taxation Division requires less administrative burden because they are simpler, faster and more flexible;[42] (vi) adjudication based on the "merits review" under AAT Act §43 (Tribunal's decision on review) is possible;[43] (vii) even if the applicant loses, the "costs follow the event" rule does not apply, and (viii) if the outcome of the decision or agreement is favorable to the applicant, a partial refund of the fees might be possible.

The advantage of the above (ii) (low fees) is evident from the fact that as of 2020, the fee was AUD 932 (AUD 500 for the Small Business Taxation Division) under 2015 ATT Regulation §20 (Fees)and §27 (Annual increase in fees), whereas under Schedule 1 of the Federal Court and Federal Magistrates Court Regulation 2012, the fee is AUD 4,045 for corporations (AUD 1,390 for the others) and other fees including expenses for hearings are to be charged.[44] The issue of the financial burden is also related to the merits of the above (vii) (disputes without representation). In FY2012-2013, approximately 40% of the applicants whose cases were processed by the Taxation and Commercial Division had no representatives, while the breakdown of the representatives of the applicants (approximately 60% of the total) was lawyers (25%), accountants/tax agents (30%), friends/others (4%), and legal aid (0%).[45] This ratio of

38. *See* the ATO 2011/2012 Annual Report, p. 96 and Tax Dispute Resolution: The AAT Perspective at https://www.aat.gov.au/about-the-aat/engagement/speeches-and-papers/the-honourable-justice-duncan-kerr-chev-lh-preside/tax-dispute-resolution-the-aat-perspective.
39. AAT Judges are also judges appointed by the Governor-General.
40. *See* TAA §14ZZE (Hearings before Tribunal to be held in private if applicant so requests). The AAT strives to realize its goal of publishing all of its decisions on tax cases in accordance with AAT Act §66(B) (Publication of tribunal decisions). *See* https://www.aat.gov.au/resources/aat-decisions.
41. While it is pointed out that the prospect of the applicants without attorneys is particularly dim especially in the case of appeals at AAT. *See* Binh Tran-Nam and Michael Walpole, Effective Access to independent Tax Dispute Resolution in Australia: The Tax Lawyers' Perspective, *Australian Tax Review*, Vol. 47 (2018) p. 13, https:aat.gov.au/about-the-att/engagement/speeches-and-papers/the-honourable-justie-duncan-kerr-chev-Ih-preside/tax-dispute-resolution-the-att-perspective.
42. AAT Act §33 (Procedure of Tribunal) prescribes, "In a proceeding before the tribunal the proceeding shall be conducted with as little formality and technicality, and with as much expedition, as the requirements of this Act."
43. AAT Act §43(1) states, "For the purpose of reviewing a decision, the Tribunal may exercise all the powers and discretions that are conferred by any relevant enactment on the person who made the decision and shall make a decision in writing: ... (c) setting aside the decision under review and: (i) making a decision in substitution for the decision so set aside."
44. *See* Australian Master Tax Guide 2020, Wolters Kluwer, p. 1551.
45. *See* AAT's 2013 document (Submission 65: Submission to the productivity commission's inquiry into access to justice arrangements) p. 4.

applicants with no representative in the case of disputes on tax matters is lower than that of applicants with no representative disputing other administrative matters could be explained much by the fact that more than 70% of individuals entrust to accountants/tax agents the filing of their IT returns.[46]

The above (iv) (the existence of the "Small Business Taxation Division") can also be of great benefit to small taxpayers. The cases falling under the Small Business Taxation Division are those tax disputes brought by "small businesses" with an aggregated turnover of less than AUD 10 million as defined by the ITAA 1997, and those "small businesses" could take advantage of various merits. The abovementioned fee to ATT is, as of 2020, AUD 92 instead of AUD 500 for those cases whose disputed tax amount is less than AUD 5,000, and further reduction of the fee is possible if the applicant's financial situation is severe.[47] In addition, the AAT has been pursuing actions to support "small businesses" for the smooth implementation of the legal proceedings, etc. (so-called Outreach activities), and those "small businesses" without representatives could receive administrative, professional and financial support ("concierge service") from the ombudsman (Australian Small Business and Family Enterprise Ombudsman).[48] Those ATT activities and the Ombudsman's support should enhance the access to the AAT of those "small businesses" that could utilize them.

The above (v) (simpler trial procedures, etc.) is also one of the merits the ATT could provide to the "small business" applicants. But there were times when this merit did not give them as much benefit as it could. Certainly, about 70% to 85% of cases filed with the Taxation and Commercial Division are tax cases, and they are comparatively more complex than other cases, so they usually take longer time to be processed, and the Division (and its predecessor Taxation Appeals Division) set a goal of processing more than 75% of the cases within a year. But the reality was that, as Figure 4.5 shows, the level of attainment of the goal was far from satisfactory from 2000 to 2010.[49] On the other hand, as for the "small business" cases with a disputed amount of less than AUD 5,000 to be dealt with by the Small Taxation Claims Tribunal,[50] they only represented less than 10% of the tax cases during this period, and the goal for processing a case was set to be within twelve weeks. However, it turned out that the level of attainment of that goal was also not so high that it resulted in higher costs for some "small business" applicants.[51]

46. For details, *see* Binh Tran-Nam and Michael Walpole, Independent Tax Dispute Resolution and Social. *See* Justice in Australia, *UNSW Law Journal*, Vol. 35, No. 2, (2012) p. 488.
47. For details, *see* Guide to the Small Business Taxation Division, AAT (2020) p. 5.
48. *See* https://www.icb.org.au/s/news/aat-small-business-tax-concierge-service-MCJE7BJCFOV5A2RK7SDFHXLTVEWI.
49. *See* Tran-Nam and Walpole, *supra* "Independent Tax Dispute" p. 491 and the AAT 2010-2011 Report, p. 24. While, as shown in Figure 1.5 in Chapter 1, the rate of processing the objections within one year by the Tax Tribunal in Japan has been about 95% lately.
50. "Tax dispute cases" accepted by the AAT in Figure 4.5 are the total number of cases received by the "Tax Appeals Division" and the "Small Taxation Claims Tribunal" before 2015, while, between 2015 and 2017, it is the number of cases received by the "Taxation and Commercial Division" and after March 2019 it is the total number of cases received by the "Taxation and Commercial Division" and "Small Business Taxation Division."
51. The AAT 2018-2019 to 2020-2021 Reports show the ratio (90%-100%) of processing the appeals to the "Small Business Taxation Division" in one year instead of twelve weeks. As for the

Figure 4.5 Number of Tax Appeals Received by AAT and Level of Attainment of Goals Set for Processing Days

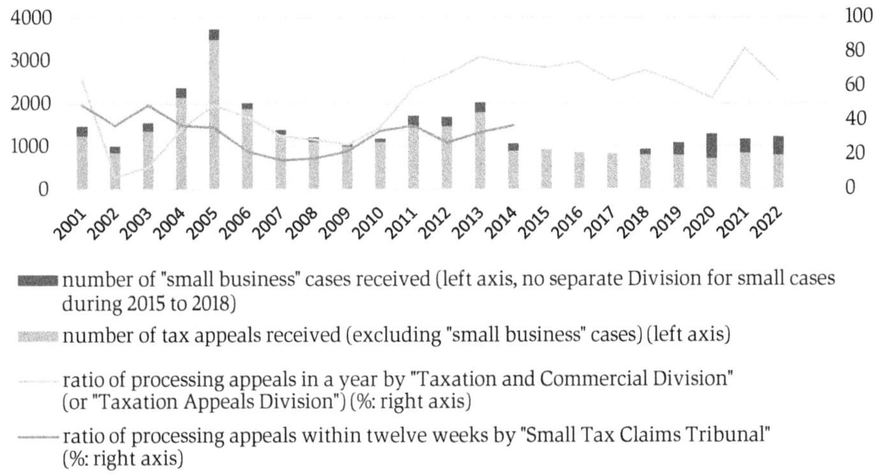

Source: IGT 2006 Report Chapter 3 (Nature and circumstances of tax litigation) Table 3.1, AAT 2000-2023 Annual Reports Chapter 3: Our performance.

However, as shown in Figure 4.5, the number of appeals filed with the AAT peaked in 2005-2006 and then started to show a declining trend.[52] As a result, the facts supporting the merits of the above (v) (simpler trial proceedings, etc.) have become conspicuous lately. Behind the recent decrease in the number of appeals is the fact that, as shown in Figure 4.3, the number and ratio of dispute resolutions through early agreements at the stage of tax audits or tax objections have increased.[53] The average number of processing days has also decreased, and it is partly due to the increase in the ratio of "small business" cases to the total number of appeal cases and the AAT's greater use of ADR, which is consistent with the intent of §34D (Agreement about the terms of a decision, etc.) and §42C (Power of Tribunal if parties reach agreement) of AAT Act.[54] While more than 90% of ADR conducted by the AAT is not official ADR

---

average number of processing days, it was five weeks for FY2018-FY2019 and thirteen weeks for FY2019 (*see* 2018-2019 Report Table 3.7).

52. According to Table 6.5 of the 2020/2021 ATO Annual Report, from 2018-2019 to 2020-2021, 37 million to 39 million returns were filed each year, of which about 1.1% to 1.4% were subjected to reassessments. 4.8% to 6.8% (approximately 26,000 on average over three years) of those reassessments were appealed to the ATO, of which 1.6% to 2.2% (average 520 cases over three years) were filed against the AAT or the courts.
53. In addition to the data in Figure 4.5, ATO data shows that tax cases received by the Taxation and Commercial Division stood at 533 in 2014-2015, 396 in 2015-2016, and 357 in 2016-2017, indicating that the ratio of the number of nontax cases against tax cases in the Division has been increasing recently.
54. The use of ADR or "Conference" by the AAT is particularly high in tax appeal cases. *See* Table A 4.2 in the above AAT's Submission 65.

such as mediation, but is facilitated by skilled persons registered in the Conference Registry, and it is an informal ADR called a "Conference."[55]

Indeed, the comparison of Figures 4.1 and 4.3 reveals that the number of settlements of tax disputes by agreement has not been so large yet, and this may have to do with the relatively high ratio of the AAT decisions revoking the disputed re/assessments. For example, the ATO's 2011-2012 Report Table 2.32 and 2014-2015 Report Figure 2.11 show that the ratio of revocation of the disputed re/assessments at the AAT was about 30% for the years 2011-2012 and 2014-2015. In particular, Figure 4.6 reveals that the ratio of the AAT's revocation of the disputed reassessments on "large business" is high, just like the high ratio of their revocation at the stage of objections to the ATO (*see* Figure 4.1).[56] But such figures do not necessarily mean that most disputants and the AAT are not so eager for flexible and speedy resolutions. On the contrary, from 2010-2011 to 2012/2013, more than 80% of tax cases were finalized without the AAT hearings and, as Figure 4.6 reveals, at least during the late 1990s and early 2000s, the ratios of the AAT finalized reviews setting aside or varying the disputed re/assessments by consent without hearings were much higher than those of setting aside or varying them after the hearings.

Figure 4.6 Ratio of Revocation of Disputed Reassessments Before/After AAT's Hearings, AAT's Ratio of Revocation of Reassessments on "Large Business," Etc.

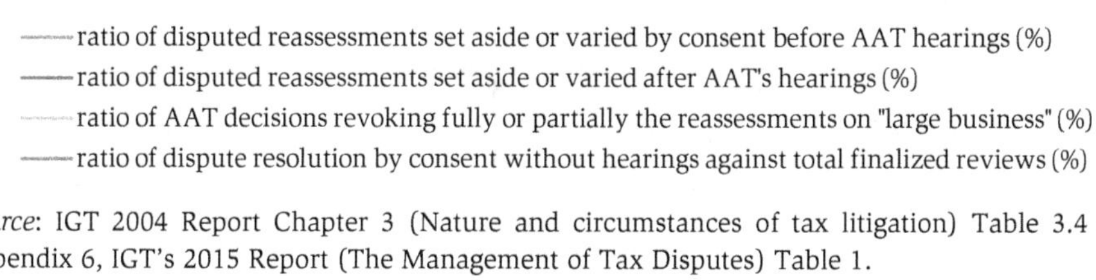

Source: IGT 2004 Report Chapter 3 (Nature and circumstances of tax litigation) Table 3.4 and Appendix 6, IGT's 2015 Report (The Management of Tax Disputes) Table 1.

In fact, it is quite likely that the above AAT's authority to set aside the disputed re/assessments constitutes another reason for taxpayers' choice of the AAT over the

55. AAT Act §42C(2) states, "If the agreement is reached as an agreement as to the terms of a decision of the Tribunal in the proceeding, the Tribunal may make a decision in accordance with those terms without holding a hearing of the proceeding."
56. Similarly, during the period from 2007/2008 to 2013/2014, there were 344 cases in which the re/assessments were revoked in whole or in part by AAT decisions related to the appeals of the "high wealth individuals," with an average revocation rate of 65%. *See* Table 3 of the IGT 2015 Report for details. On the other hand, Table 2.32 of the 2011/2012 ATO Report found that about 26% of all AAT decisions in that year reversed all or part of the re/assessments.

courts. The AAT can not only ① affirm the re/assessment, ② cancel all or part of it ("vary" a decision), ③ remand it to the ATO, but also ④ put aside the re/assessment and set it aside with the new decision. This ④ function of the AAT exercised by the above (vi) (Decisions based on merit reviews) is contrasted with a court's judicial review, which is possible in limited cases on the ATO's discretionary decisions.[57] The merit review enables the AAT to stand in the shoes of the Commissioner and decide what is, in light of the relevant facts and policies, the best exercise of discretion, and, when necessary, set aside the re/assessment under review.[58] Now that there were years when the number of the AAT decisions coming under the above ④ was more than double that of coming under the above ②,[59] there must be many taxpayers who wish for the AAT's active use of merit review vis-à-vis the way of exercise of the Commissioner's discretion on their cases.

It is not that the power and function of a court are quite limited,[60] but there is a significant limitation on its power to substitute the ATO Commissioner's discretion by exercising its judicial review. Just as the UK Court of Appeals ruled in the *Wednesbury* case (1948),[61] such substitution by a court is only possible when an administrative agency acts or decides beyond its powers. In other words, it is only when the decision is absurd and so unreasonable that a reasonable person would not consider it an act within her powers.[62] Such unreasonableness is unreasonableness in a stricter sense (so-called Wednesbury unreasonableness). For example, in *Binetter v. Commissioner of Taxation* ([2016] FCAFC), the Federal Court confirmed that the AAT can reconsider the evidence and substitute its own decision for the re/assessment by merits review, while courts can only intervene with the Commissioner's exercise of the power if the Commissioner did not form the requisite opinion or its power is vitiated by some error of law, and sustained the AAT's decision on the ATO's re/assessment because it found

57. *See* AAT Act §43 (in footnote 43). *See* AAT decision on Apted and FC of T (2020) referred to in 4(2) of this Section for an example of the AAT setting aside ATO Commissioner's decisions.
58. In the case of UK, the function of the First-tier Tribunal is more similar to that of courts on this point. For example, UK's Enterprise Act §120(Review of decisions under Part 3)(4) stipulates, "the Competition Appeal Tribunal shall apply the same principles as would be applied by a court on an application for judicial review." *See* Peter Cane, Judicial Review and Merits Review: Comparing Administrative Adjudication by Courts and Tribunals, Chapter 25, *Comparative Administrative Law*, Rose-Ackerman, Susan; Lindseth, L. Peter (eds.), Edward Elgar Publishing (2010).
59. For example, among the decisions handed down from 1997-1998 to 2004-2005 by the Tax Appeals Division in AAT which went through hearings, those setting aside the re/assessments were 252 and those revoking fully or partially the re/assessments were 130. *See* Appendix 6 of the IGT 2004 Report. This fact also implies that in contrast to the NTA in Japan, the ATO has a wide discretion and it has been exercised frequently.
60. TAA §14ZZP (Order of court on objection decision) states, "Where a court hears an appeal against an objection decision under section 14ZZ, the court may make such order in relation to the decision as it thinks fit, including an order confirming or varying the decision."
61. *See* 1 in Section 2 of Chapter 3.
62. It has been pointed out that "judicial creep" has lately occurred to expand the scope of the court's substitution of the administrative agencies' decisions. *See* NSW Ombudsman 2016 Report (Judicial Review of Administrative Action: An Administrative Decision-Maker's Perspective).

that the plaintiff failed to fulfill, by TAA §14ZZK (Grounds of objection and burden of proof) (b), the onus of proof that the re/assessment is excessive or incorrect.[63]

As described above, there are various advantages for aggrieved taxpayers not to skip appeals to the AAT, but if appeals to the AAT fail to produce satisfactory results, the financial and time costs can be greater for those taxpayers who dispute their cases all the way to courts. Moreover, under the AAT Act §44 (Appeals to Federal Court of Australia from decisions of the Tribunal) (1), an appeal to the court can only be filed on a "question of law."[64] While there are uncertainties as to what constitutes a "question of law."[65] In *Birdseye v. Australian Securities and Investments Commission* ([2003] FCAFC 232), the Federal Court held that "a question of law" is limited to pure legal matters. On the other hand, in *Collins v. AAT* ([2007] FCAFC 111), the Full Court rejected the view that only a question of pure law could be a question of law for that purpose. The view expressed in *Haritos v. FCT* ([2015] FCAFC 92) was supportive of the interpretation taken by the above Collins case because the Full Court held, "Not all so-called mixed questions of fact and law stand outside an appeal on a question of law."[66]

(2) *Advantages of Filing Lawsuits with Federal Court*

It is pointed out that the ratio of appeals to courts by taxpayers who are dissatisfied with the AAT's decisions on their cases has been around 10%.[67] It is positive that the cost-shifting rule in court affects the decision of some taxpayers on whether they should dispute their cases in court.[68] As shown in Figure 4.7, the Federal Courts received about two hundred tax appeals annually around the 1990s and in the first half of the 2000s, and the number of their judgments on tax appeals from 2001 to 2010 was 288 (IT cases about 58%, Procedural/Administrative cases about 24%, Goods & Services Tax cases about 9%, and others about 10%), and the ratio of upholding the disputed re/assessments was 67%.[69] During the same years, the number of judgments (and the ratio of upholding the re/assessments) of the Full Federal Court and the High

63. TAA §14ZZK prescribes, "On an application for review of a reviewable objection; ... (b) the applicant has the burden of proof: ...—that the assessment is excessive or otherwise incorrect and what the assessment should have been; or (ii) in any other case—that the taxation decision concerned should not have been made or should have been made differently." TAA §14ZZO(b) practically stipulates the same.
64. Federal Court generally do not rehear the facts when the issue involves both facts and interpretation of law.
65. *See* Stephen Gageler, What Is a Question of Law?, *Australian Tax Review*, Vol. 43 (2014) pp. 68-74.
66. In this *Haritos* case, the point of dispute was whether the economic benefits obtained by the plaintiff corresponded to deemed dividends or borrowings for tax purposes.
67. *See supra* "ATO 2018 Publication," p. 5. While, according to the abovementioned "IGT 2006 Report," Table 3.2, the ratio was, in most cases, about 2% to 7%.
68. Moreover, as of 2018, the fee for filing a case in the Federal Court was AUD 4,675 (AUD 10,100 for a corporation) if the case had been reviewed by the AAT, and otherwise (AUD 1,390 and AUD 4,045 for corporations).
69. *See* Jeremy Hirschhorn and Alison Chen, Tossing the Coin: A Quantitative Analysis of Tax Decisions 2001 to 2010, 41, *Australian Tax Review*, 154 (2012) pp. 159-160.

Court was 136(59%) and 48(66%), respectively.[70] Therefore, the taxpayers' chance of recovering their costs is not so low. Even so, with the recent ATO's efforts to resolve disputes before litigation, the number of tax disputes appealed, as well as the number of unprocessed tax cases at the Federal Courts, has, as Figure 4.7 shows, been on the decline.[71]

Figure 4.7 Number of Tax Appeals Received and the Cumulative Number of Unprocessed Tax Appeals at Federal Courts

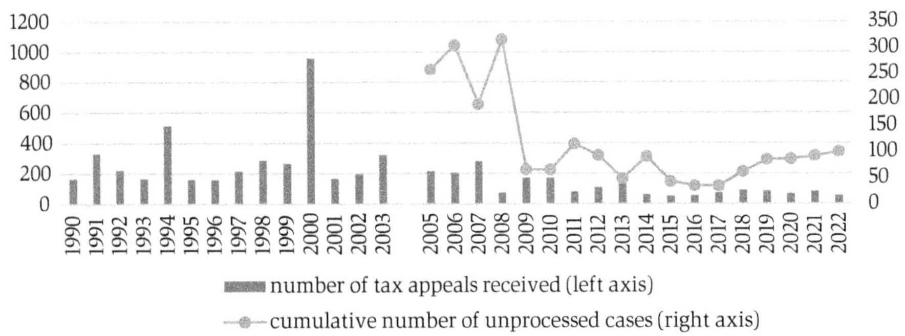

Source: IGT 2006 Report Chapter 3: Nature and circumstances of tax litigation Table 3.2 and Federal Court Annual Reports 2005-2006 to 2022-2023 Table 3.1.

Some taxpayers may prefer appeals to courts because they want to suspend the ATO's action to recover the tax in dispute. Concerning this, TAA §14ZZR (Pending appeal not to affect implementation of taxation decisions) prescribes, "(1) The fact that an appeal is pending in relation to a taxation decision does not in the meantime interference with, or affect, the decision and any tax, additional tax or other amount may be recovered as if no appeals were pending."[72] It is true that the ATO Commissioner could either exercise its power to suspend the recovery of tax, etc., in such cases where taxpayers' appeals have substance and there is little risk of nonpayment or make an offer of a 50:50 arrangement as a condition for deferring the recovery action until the dispute is over.[73] Whereas, if the ATO Commissioner does not approve the suspension of the collection procedure, courts have wider power to suspend it as the Administrative Decision (Judicial Review) Act (AD(JR)Act) §15 (Stay of proceedings) stipulates, "(1) The making of an application to the Federal Court... does not affect the operation of the decision... but: (a) the Court or a judge may, by order, ... a stay of all or any

70. For details, *see* Hirschhorn and Chen, *supra*, "Tossing the Coin," pp. 160-162.
71. The number of tax appeals received after 2004-2005 in Figure 4.7 is based on that outstanding for less than twelve months in the Federal Courts Annual Reports for those years.
72. TAA §14ZZM (Pending Review not to affect implementation of taxation decision) stipulates the same treatment.
73. *See* ATO's PS LA 2011/4 (Recovering disputed debts). If the offer of the 50:50 arrangement is accepted, the taxpayer should pay at least 50% of the disputed primary tax amount plus any other outstanding undisputed tax debts and provide any information that is needed to resolve the dispute in a timely fashion.

proceedings under the decision."[74] Appeals to the AAT may not serve those taxpayers' purposes except for "small business" cases.[75]

There are certainly some cases in which courts overturned the ATO Commissioner's decision of not suspending recovery actions. For example, in *Denlay v. FCT* case ([2013] FCA 307), the ATO Commissioner issued a garnishee notice to the financial institution that held the plaintiff's accounts by Schedule 1 §260-5 (Commissioner may collect amounts from third party) (2) of TAA which prescribes, "The Commissioner may give a written notice to an entity (the third party) under this section if the third party owes or may later owe money to the debtor."[76] But, in this case, the Federal Court specified that the ATO Commissioner should, in determining whether or not the notice is to be issued, take into account various criteria or factors (a possibility of the issue of the notice causing a plaintiff a financial difficulty, chance of a plaintiff's winning in court, and so forth) spelled out in *Snow v. OCT* ((1987) 14 FCR 119),[77] but the Commissioner failed to take account of the plaintiff's chance of winning the case as well as the fact that the issue of the notice would be likely to deprive the plaintiff of the chance of disputing the relevant re/assessment, so it was inappropriate exercise of its power and should be voided.

Other than the points mentioned above, few court-specific powers could work particularly in favor of aggrieved taxpayers, while there are a few other noteworthy points for them. For example, in principle, taxpayers who bear the burden of proof in litigation may find it necessary to change or add grounds for appeals or grounds for claiming illegality of the re/assessments, but the rule dictated by TAA §14ZZK(a) and TAA §14ZZO (Grounds of objection and burden of proof) (a) is that grounds other than those indicated in the taxpayer's "taxation objection" cannot be relied on,[78] so it is basically not permitted to bring up new matters or claim new grounds in the litigation stage after the submission of the "taxation objection." On the other hand, no similar restrictions are imposed on the ATO.[79] Therefore, as a taxpayer, even if changing or adding grounds for appeals and limiting the ATO's change or addition of grounds for the re/assessments can be a critical point, it usually hardly affects their choice of a

74. The courts' power to suspend the ATO's recovery action is also set out in the Federal Court of Australia Act 1976 §23 (Making of orders and issue of writs).
75. TAA §14ZZM(2) provides for the exception to TAA §14ZZM(1) (*see* footnote 72) for "small business" taxpayers in accordance with §41(Stay of action implementing decision) (2) of AAT Act. For this recently adopted exception, *see* the Treasury 2022 document (Extend the power of the AAT to pause or modify ATO debt recovery action) at https://treasury.gov.au/consultation/c2022-238915.
76. ITAA §218, a predecessor of Schedule 1§260-5(2) of TAA, and TAA 1999 §54 (Collection of tax from third parties) stipulates the same.
77. In the *Snow* case, the Federal Court held that, in light of these criteria, the suspension of the ATO's recovery action claimed by the plaintiff that utilized a tax avoidance scheme should be accepted.
78. TAA §14ZZK prescribes, "On an application for review of a reviewable objection decision: (a) the applicant is, unless the Tribunal orders otherwise, limited to the grounds stated in the taxation objection to which the decision relates," TAA §14ZZO(a) provides for the same at the court level.
79. These rules contrast with those in Japan where burden of proof on a re/assessment falls in principle on the assessor and there is a strict application of the rule of showing reasons in writing in the notice of re/assessment. *See* 2(4) in Section 3 of Chapter 1.

forum for his appeal. But, in reality, some courts observed the above rules rigidly while others digressed from them and ruled favorably for the taxpayers on this point.

The former court cases observing the above rules include *FCT v. Reynolds* ([1981] 11 ATR 629). In this case, the ATO claimed to change, at the trial stage, the legal ground for taxing the respondent's gains from the sale of automobiles, which the taxpayer argued was a gift whose payment and receipt were voluntary, from the 1936 ITAA §26 AAA (Assessable income from property purchased and sold within twelve months) to ITAA §25 (Gross income from certain sources) (1)(a).[80] The Supreme Court determined that the gains were not a mere gift but taxable income and allowed such change of the legal ground for taxing it by holding that the application of both of these provisions would result in the same amount of tax, and no injustice has been done to the respondent by this change because he has not been misled into acting to his detriment. Also, in DTMP and Commissioner of Taxation ([2016] AATA 684), the AAT did not accept the applicant's belated "grounds expansion request" made following TAA §14ZZK(a) after it had filed the first objection, and it ruled that no explanation is offered for why the applicant's tax agent did not include at least some of the expanded grounds in the original objection.[81]

The latter court cases not observing the above rules rigidly include *McLean & Anor v. FCT* ([1996] 66 FCR). In this case, at issue was whether or not the "retention payment" made to the plaintiffs with the condition that they would stay with the employer after its subsidiaries were restructured constitutes taxable income. The plaintiffs, at the stage of their appeal to the AAT, newly brought up and claimed ITAA §25(1) and ITAA §23L (Certain benefits in the nature of income not assessable) that treat some fringe benefits as exempt income as grounds for the "retention payment" not being assessable for IT purposes,[82] and the Federal Court allowed this plaintiffs' claim and overturned the AAT decision of not allowing such claim or action of the plaintiffs/applicants. *Danmark Pty Ltd v. FCT* ([1944] 7 ATD 333) is another example of the above rules not strictly followed. In this case, the High Court (Federal Supreme Court) held that the ATO's substitution later at the stage of contestation of the ground for the re/assessment should not be allowed because it would not be fair to do so because the taxpayer's ground for the appeal is confined to that shown in the "taxation objection."

Also, it should be a notable point for some aggrieved taxpayers that the scope of the "reviewable objection decision" stipulated in TAA Part IVC (Taxation, Objections, Reviews and Appeals) §14ZQ (General interpretation provisions) is not unlimited,[83]

80. ITAA §25(1) provided, "The assessable income of a taxpayer shall include—(a) where the taxpayer is a resident—the gross income derived directly or indirectly from all sources whether in or out of Australia; and ... (b) ... which is not exempt income."
81. In this case, the AAT acknowledged that TAA §14ZZK(a) (*see* footnote 78) is a piece of remedial legislation while the onus of proof is upon the applicant.
82. ITAA §23L(1A) dictates, "Income derived by a taxpayer by way of the provision of a benefit (other than ...) that ..., would be a fringe benefit is exempt income of the taxpayer."
83. TAA §14ZQ stipulates, "'*reviewable objection decision*' means an objection decision that is not an ineligible income tax remission decision." So, the ATO Commissioner's decision on taxpayers' objections concerning the exemption of a penalty or interests on unpaid tax, etc., are not subject to review by AAT. Also, The ATO ruling (TR 2011/15) states in para. 145 that objections

but the 1903 Judiciary Act §39B (Original jurisdiction of Federal Court of Australia) allows those ATO decisions which do not fall under TAA Part IVC to be appealed to courts, provided that they fall under the listed items enumerated in the Administrative Decisions (Judicial Review) Act 1977 (ADJRA) §5 (Applications for review of decisions) which include the improper exercise of the ATO Commissioner's power conferred by the enactment.[84] For example, in the *Hell's Angels Ltd v. DFCT* ([1984] 6 ALD 420), the Federal Court specified that, given the convincing claims and the lack of its possibility of dissipating the assets, the ATO Commissioner's decision to dismiss the plaintiff's request for extension of tax payment deadline which was made by ITAA §206 (Extension of time and payment by installments) without showing specific reasons, is subject to judicial review under ADJRA §5(1)(e), and it held that the decision should be revoked.[85]

Another positive note for some aggrieved taxpayers came from *Futuris Corporation Ltd. v. Commissioner* ([2008] HCA 32). ITAA §175 (Validity of assessment) prescribes, "The validity of any assessment shall not be affected by reason that any of the provisions of this Act have not been complied with,"[86] but this High Court judgment confirmed that there is an exception to this. In this case, the respondent/taxpayer disputed the assessment on him based on the Judiciary Act 1903 §39B (Original jurisdiction of Federal Court of Australia) (1A), which dictates, "The original jurisdiction of the Federal Court of Australia includes jurisdiction in any matter: in which a writ of mandamus or prohibition or an injunction is sought against an officer or officers of the Commonwealth," and the High Court specified that an assessment falls out of the scope of ITAA §175 if it is due to the Commissioner's "conscious maladministration" because it becomes akin to being none. Nevertheless, the High Court overturned the Federal Court judgment ([2007] FCAFC) that found the assessment not a be bona fide exercise of the power of assessment and held in favor of the ATO, implying that the hurdle set by the concept of "conscious maladministration"

to the application of the ATO Commissioner's administrative policies including the exercise of his general administrative powers fall outside the scope of Part IVC of TAA.

84. ADJRA §5(1) states, "A person who is aggrieved by a decision to which this Act applies ... may apply to the Federal Court or the Federal Circuit Court for an order of review in respect of the decision on any one or more of the following grounds: ... (b) that procedures that were required by law to be observed in connection with the making of the decision were not observed; (e) that the making of the decision was an improper exercise of the power conferred by the enactment in pursuance of which it was purported to be made." So, some cases falling outside the scope of the TAA Part IVC (such as cases on the application of TAA Div. 286 (Penalties for failing to lodge documents on time) could be subject to the review under ADJRA.
85. This judgment, on the question of whether the request for the extension of the payment deadline is to be accepted, has adopted an approach of making a decision by weighing the level of damage and convenience on the part of the disputing parties, which is in line with the standard of "balance of convenience" relied on in deciding whether interlocutory injunction is to be ordered.
86. This is similar to the U.S. Tax Court's "rule of not looking behind a notice of deficiency." See 2 in Section 2 of Chapter 2. Also, compare it with 2(4) in Section 3 of Chapter 1. There have been arguments over whether ITAA §175 is an "ouster (or 'privative') provisions" which excludes judicial review of administrative agencies' acts and decisions. For details, *see* Sue Milne, The Bottom Line for Review of an Assessment—A Case Note on *Commissioner v. Futuris Corporation Ltd, Monash University Law Review* (2010) pp. 181-206 DOI: 10.2139/ssrn.2363778. As for the Supreme Court decision (2011) on the *Tennadyce* case in NZ which considers this provision not to be an "ouster provision," *see* 3(2) in Section 2.

is rather high.[87] In actuality, there have been few subsequent cases where this hurdle was cleared in favor of the taxpayers.[88]

4 Rules on costs

(1) General Rules

As mentioned in 3(1) above, regardless of the outcome of the AAT's judgments, in principle, the parties to the dispute are responsible for their own attorney's fees.[89] The reasons and grounds for adopting this principle are as follows: (i) the AAT differs from the court in that the essential nature of its function is administrative, and it examines the legality of the re/assessment from the standpoint of an administrative organ;[90] (ii) the "loser pays rule" usually puts applicants at greater risk, unduly restricts access to litigation; (iii) the administrative agency might be obliged to increase unreasonably its financial burden for justifying the legality of the concerned re/assessment.[91] Even in the case of disputes at the AAR to which the "loser pays rule" does not apply, it was estimated around 2012 that legal fees, etc., generally to be borne by an applicant whose case comes under the "Taxation and Commercial Division" (or "Small Taxation Claims Division"), was approximately AUD 6,700 (or AUD 2,500) on average if he asks for the support of an attorney, while it was approximately AUD 4,800 (or AUD 2,000) on average if he does not ask for it.[92]

On the other hand, courts have broad discretionary powers on ordering the payment of litigation-related costs,[93] and they generally apply, irrespective of whether litigations are civil or criminal, the "loser pays rule" unless the disputes are on the application of legislation such as family law under which the disputing parties

87. The height of this hurdle practically implies the high hurdle in Australia of "Wednesbury unreasonableness" (*see* footnote 34 and 1 in Section 2 of Chapter 3).
88. For example, in *Donoghue v. Commissioner of Taxation* ([2015] FCA 235), the Federal Court ruled that the concerned assessment was based on information obtained by the ATO from a third party in violation of the "legal professional privilege" and constituted conscious maladministration, but this ruling was overturned by the Full Federal Court's judgment ([2015] FCAFC 183).
89. Exceptions are cases where the transfer of costs is clearly stipulated by law or cases of disputes that are strongly in the nature of compensation for damages. For example, Safety Rehabilitation and Compensation Act 1988 §67(9) dictates, "Where the Administrative Appeals Tribunal gives a decision setting aside a reviewable decision ..., the Tribunal shall, ... order that the costs of the proceedings before it incurred by the claimant shall be paid by the responsible authority."
90. In this regard, AAT and the Tribunals in UK differs in that the UK's First-tier Tribunal applies "English rule" with respect to "Complex Cases". *See* 2 in Section 3 and 1 in Section 4 of Chapter 3.
91. *See* Costs Shifting—who pays for litigation, ALRC 75 (1995) paras. 5.6-5.10.
92. It is also pointed out that if efforts made by an applicant for the case is converted to a monetary value of USD 25 an hour, then they would amount in total approximately AUD 1,800. *See* Tran-Nam and Walpole, *supra* "Independent Tax Dispute" pp. 490-492.
93. Federal Court of Australia Act 1976 §43 (Costs) states, "(1) The Court of a Judge has jurisdiction to award costs in all proceedings before the court (...) other than proceedings in respect of which this or any other Act provides that cost must not be awarded." Judiciary Act 1903 §26 provides similarly.

generally pay their costs.[94] For example, in the *Latoudi v. Casey* case ([1990] HCA 59), at issue was whether or not the defendant who won the criminal case should be allowed to recover costs, and the High Court ordered the recovery of the costs by the defendant. In particular, Judge McHugh confirmed that, despite the differences between civil and criminal proceedings, there is no difficulty in applying in such proceedings akin to those applicable to the making or refusing of orders for costs in civil cases. Judge Toohey also noted that what arose from many judgments was the recognition that costs were awarded to the winning party as damages, not as a penalty to the losing party, and the stance of these judgments is against the view that defendants should not be awarded costs because it would discourage police officers from bringing prosecutions.

Uniform Civil Procedure Rules 2005 (UCPR) Rule 42.1 (General rule that costs follow the event) also states, "If the court makes any order as to costs, the court is to order that the costs follow the event unless it appears to the court that some other order should be made as to the whole or any part of the costs." Moreover, the courts have applied the "English rule" rather rigidly. For example, *Northern Territory v. Sangare* ([2018] NT CA 10) was a defamation lawsuit, and the Court of Appeal (Supreme Court) of the Northern Territory pointed out that courts are given unfettered discretion over costs orders and ruled that it was appropriate not to grant recovery of costs by the respondent/government because the defendant was financially incapable and the recovery of the plaintiff's costs could not be anticipated. But the ruling was overturned by the High Court judgment ([2019] HCA 25) in which the Court stated, "the courts have consistently rejected the suggestion that a costs order should not be made against an impecunious party because it would be futile to do so. The circumstance that a person may not presently, or even foreseeably, be able to meet an order for costs has not been regarded as a reason to regard the creation of the debt as an exercise in futility."[95]

As for the essence of the "English rule," which is also adopted in Australia, in *Cachia v. Hanes* ([1994] 179 CLR 403), the High Court explains in paragraph 11, "Since 1278, when the Statute of Gloucester ((4) 6 Edw. I c.i.) introduced the notion of costs to the common law, that costs are awarded by way of indemnity (or, more accurately, partial indemnity) for professional legal costs incurred in the conduct of litigation. They were never intended to be comprehensive compensation for any loss suffered by a litigant." In Australia, the method of calculating the amount of attorney's fees, etc., that can be recovered as partial compensation by a person who wins a case in a court is based on "standard basis" and "indemnity basis" (in most cases, the former) just like that under 44.3 of the CPR of the UK. It is pointed out that the calculation based on the "standard basis" usually enables the winning party to recover about 50% to 75% of the

94. For example, Family Law Act 1975 §117 (Costs) stipulates, "(1) Subject to subsection (2), ... each party to proceedings under this Act shall bear his or her own costs."
95. Similar judgments/views can be found in the Supreme Court of Victoria judgment on the *Board of Examiners v. XY* case ([2006] VSCA 190) and Judge McHugh's dissenting opinion in the 1998 High Court decision on the *Oshlack* case (1998), which will be described later in 4(3) of this Section.

actual amount of attorney's fees, etc.,[96] while it is about 65% to 85% of them when the calculation is based on the "indemnity basis."[97]

A case in which an order to pay attorney's fees, etc., is issued on an "indemnity basis," which imposes a heavier burden on the losing party, rather than on the "standard basis," is when the losing party: (i) rejected offers for settlement by agreement;[98] (ii) delayed legal proceedings without reasonable grounds; (iii) filing lawsuits with little substance; or (iv) ignoring facts and laws.[99] An example of the losing party being responsible practically for all of the above (ii) to (iv) was *J-Corp Pty Ltd v. Australia Builders Laborers Federation Union of Workers* ([1992] FCA 42). In this judgment, the Federal Court cited Judge Wilcox in the Federal Court judgment on *Commissioner of Australian Federal Police v. Razzi* ([1991] FCA 267) who stated, "In these days of extensive court delays and high legal costs the courts should use all proper means to encourage parties to consider carefully what matters they will put in issue in their litigation," and pointed out that not only the trial was unnecessarily lengthened by issues on which the applicant/J-Corp insisted and ultimately failed but also the case against one of the respondents was paper thin before it concluded that the order sought by the respondent which moved for indemnity costs should be made.

As for the costs recoverable by a litigant in person successful in court, the "Chorley exception" has been judicially developed in the UK.[100] In Australia, in the above High Court judgment on the *Cachia* case (1994), in which the appellant/litigant in person claimed the compensation for the loss of his time spent in the preparation and conduct of his case, etc., Judge Toohey and Judge Gaudron did mention that, in light of Part 52 Rule 23(2) of the NSW Supreme Court Rules allowing the recovery of necessary or proper costs,[101] and the 1970 NSW Supreme Court Act §19 (Definitions generally) defining costs to include fees, charges, disbursement, expenses, and remunerations, it is hard to see the justification for a rule that an unrepresented litigant may recover no more than out of pocket expenses, and the majority regarded the "Chorley exception" as a somewhat anomalous exception before concluding that costs within the meaning of the Rule are reimbursement for work done or expenses incurred by a

96. *See* Litigation and enforcement in Australia: overview (at https://uk.practicallaw.thomsonreuters.com/4-502-1038?transitionType=Default&contextData=(sc.Default)&firstPage=true.
97. UCPR Regulations 42.5(Indemnity costs) dictates, "If the court determines that costs are to be paid on an indemnity basis—(a) in the case of costs payable out of property held or controlled by a person who is a party to the proceedings—(i) ..., (ii)..., all costs (...) are to be allowed, and (b) in any other case, all costs (other than those that appear to have been unreasonably incurred or appear to be of an unreasonable amount) are to be allowed." As for the view that the recovery rate is 60% to 75% for the "standard basis" and 90% to 95% for the "indemnity basis," refer to Standard Costs and Indemnity Costs (QLD) (at https:// www.armstronglegal.com.au/commercial-law/qld/court-processes/standard-costs-and-indemnity-costs/.
98. Examples of this (i) case includes the Federal Appeals Court decision in the *Clark* (No. 2) case to be described in 4(2).
99. *See supra* "Standard Costs and Indemnity Costs (QLD)."
100. *See* 2 in Section 4 of Chapter 3.
101. This definition of costs differs from that adopted in the UK. *See* SCCO Guide §2.1 in 1 in Section 4 of Chapter 3.

practitioner or his employee, so compensating the loss of time of the applicant cannot constitute costs within the meaning of the Rule.[102]

Moreover, in *Pentelow v. Bell Lawyers Pty Ltd* ([2019] HCA 29), the High Court overruled the NSW Court of Appeal judgment ([2018] NSW CA150) which applied the "Chorley exception" to the respondent/barrister represented by the solicitor for the respondent's work in litigation by pointing out: (i) the "Chorley exception" results in inequality before the law by privileging solicitors over laypersons; (ii) when the "Chorley exception" is applied, a solicitor could benefit from litigation, contrary to the principle of a cost order which is not intended to realize full recovery of the costs; (iii) the "Chorley exception" has been justified on the basis that in the case of a solicitor, it is possible to quantify his amount of work undertaken for his litigation, but, even in the case of a layman who is not a lawyer, it is possible to calculate a reasonable value of his work for his litigation; (iv) the "Chorley exception" is, as pointed out in the High Court judgment in *Cachia* case (1994), an anomalous, non-useful departure from the principle, so its application should not be extended to benefit barristers as well; (v) the "Chorley exception" might as well be abrogated under the Australian jurisprudence,[103] while the Court's conclusion was that the decision as to whether it is wholly or partially abrogated is appropriate to be left to the Parliament, the Rules Committees or the Law Society Committees.[104]

As shown above, a successful litigant in person in Australia is, in terms of cost recovery, in a less favorable position than that in the UK,[105] but the "pro bono referral scheme" stipulated under the Federal Court Rules Division 4.2 (Court referral for legal assistance) could improve such a position.[106] In particular, in *Manieri v. Cirillo* ([2014] VSCA 227), the respondent was represented under a pro bono scheme and entered into a "conditional fee agreement" where he is liable to pay costs if a costs award is made in his favor, so the appellant claimed that there should be no costs order because it would be against the indemnity principle which requires the losing party to pay only those costs which the winning party is legally obliged to pay to the solicitor. But the Victorian Court of Appeal dismissed the appeal by citing Judge Santow's opinion in the NSW Court of Appeal in *Wentworth v. Rogers* ([2006] 66 NSWLR 474), which was, "The general law governing the indemnity principle with its emphasis on flexibility is,

102. A decision to a similar effect was also handed down in the Australian Capital Territory Supreme Court judgment in *Dp v. The Law Society of the Australian Capital Territory* ([2006] ACTSC 61). Also, in *McCullum v. Ifield* ([1962] 2 NZWR 329), the NSW Supreme Court stated, "It is established that if a party to an action has an agreement with his solicitor that he will not have to pay any costs then he cannot recover party and party costs against the adversary."

103. There are also pros and cons arguments on the "Chorley exception" in NZ (*see* 4 in Section 2) while Canada has moved to adopt it (*see* footnote 212).

104. The Court also pointed out that the "Chorley exception" was inconsistent with the definition provided in section 3 (Definitions) of CPA (same as that in above section 19(1) of the 1970 NSW Supreme Court Act).

105. Moreover, in UK, the recent legislative reforms led to Litigants in Person (Costs and Expenses) Act 1975 §1(1) and 1998 CPR §48.6(1) which do not limit the recovery of costs by the successful litigants in person to the "out of pocket expenses." *See* 2 in Section 4 of Chapter 3.

106. In particular, Federal Court Regulation Div. 4.12 (Referral for legal assistance) provides that "(1) The Court may refer a party to a lawyer for legal assistance by issuing a referral certificate, in accordance with Form 9."

in my opinion, quite capable of accommodating conditional fee agreements of this kind. It should do so by recognizing the importance of such agreements in promoting access to justice which may otherwise be unaffordable."

In fact, there are not many cases that are subject to the "pro bono referral scheme,"[107] and even under this scheme, there are also cases where lawyers entrusted by the court and litigants in person do not enter into "conditional fee agreements."[108] While, for some of those who do not qualify for the scheme, there may remain a possibility to receive legal aid through the Legal Aid Commission Act 1979. Just as paragraph 1.2.2 (Means Test) and paragraph 1.2.3 (Merit Test) of the NSW Legal Aid's Policies indicate, the question of whether a litigant in person/applicant could receive intellectual, administrative/legal, and financial support by the Legal Aid Commission Act 1979 is to be determined by taking into consideration the followings: (i) financial situation of the applicant; (ii) the prospect of winning by the applicant; (iii) the benefit the applicant could get by receiving the legal aid; and so forth. Once their application for legal aid is accepted, costs order on them in case of becoming the losing party in court is, in principle, to be shouldered wholly or partially by the Legal Aid Commission in pursuance with the Legal Aid Commission Act 1979 §47 (Payment of costs awarded against legally assisted persons).[109]

(2) Rules on Costs in Tax Disputes

The rules on costs that apply to tax lawsuits are basically the same as the general rules on costs shown in (1) above, but there are some differences. For example, when the ATO, given the complexity and importance of some cases pending in the AAT's "Small Business Tax Division" and similar cases before courts, seeks the assistance of an external legal expert, the ATO may, based on the 2011 Federal Court Rule Schedule 3 (Costs Allowable for Work Done & Services Performed), make an arrangement to provide financial support to the concerned "small businesses" so that they can obtain roughly the same service.[110] In addition, when the ATO considers, at the request of the taxpayer or at its own discretion, that some cases are particularly important, unclear in terms of how the relevant legislation is to be applied, or contain significant public interest, etc., it may pay the whole or a part of the taxpayers' litigation costs to bring them to a court following the "test case litigation program."[111] In particular, those cases in which the ATO lost at the AAT but is eager to contest its decision on them at court

107. Whether or not the court's "pro bono referral scheme" is applicable is to be determined by taking into consideration the financial resources of the unrepresented litigants and the complexity of the case, etc., as stipulated in Federal Court Rule Div. 4.12(2).
108. In light of this, the Australian Pro Bono Center has been calling for legislative action to demand the court to make costs order even in cases where there is no conditional fee agreement between the winning party and the attorney entrusted by court. *See* https://www.probonocentre.org.au/information-on-pro-bono/case-law/.
109. By contrast, in UK, the Cost Review Commission 2011 Report noted that legal aid in relation to many civil cases was a thing of the past. *See* 3 in Section 4 of Chapter 3.
110. *See* https://www.ato.gov.au/General/Dispute-or-object-to-an-ATO-decision/In-detail/Small-business-litigation-funding/ for more information.
111. *See* for details, https://www.ato.gov.au/Tax-professionals/TP/Test-case-litigation-program/.

generally contain important points, so taxpayers with cases on the "test case litigation program" could have them reviewed by courts without paying some or all of their litigation-related costs.

The number of cases subjected to the "test case litigation program" counted at the time of the disputes being resolved was 5 in FY2017-2018, 7 in FY2018-2019, and 10 in FY2019-2020.[112] One notable example of the cases that were subject to the "test case litigation program" was the Full Federal Court judgment on the *Commissioner of Taxation v. Apted* ([2021] FCAFC 45). In this case, the respondent/taxpayer, who had been considering winding up the business, returned the Australian Business Number (ABN) in 2018, which he mistakenly thought was necessary only for GST registration purposes. Then, he restarted his business in September 2019 without reacquiring it but reacquired it in March 2020 again to fulfill the condition (being a holder of ABN by the date of 1/7/2019) for receiving "JobKeeper payment" to be paid under the Corona Economic Response Package (Payments and Benefits) Rules 2020, hereinafter referred to as the "Corona Economic Support Rules"). However, the ATO refused to provide the respondent with "JobKeeper payment" because his reacquisition of ABN was backdated by the Australian Business Register to make him eligible for receiving it.

It was held in the AAT's decision on the above case ([2020] AATA 5139) that the ATO's refusal of the "JobKeeper payment" based on the view that the Australian Business Registry backdated the applicant/taxpayer's acquisition of ABN, was unlawful and set it aside by its decision in favor of the "Jobkeeper payment" to the applicant because, even if it is not unlawful, the ATO should not, based on its belief in the need for maintaining the integrity of ABN, interpret narrowly the "Corona Economic Support Rules" §11 (Entity's entitlement to JobKeeper payment for a business participant) (6) (Integrity rule) which provides for the ATO Commissioner's power to grant the payment even if the application for it is made after the deadline is passed.[113] On the other hand, the Federal Full Court ruled that the respondent's backdated acquisition of ABN does not entitle him to receive the "JobKeeper payment," but the AAT should, in a case like this, exercise its discretionary power under the AAT Act §43(1) so that the respondent can receive the "JobKeeper payment."[114] Now that the ATO has given up on contesting the legality of this Full Court judgment at the High Court, it had to start reviewing again those in similar cases to which it had refused the "JobKeeper payment" to see if they are eligible for it.[115]

Other systems and rules that help reduce litigation risks and burdens of taxpayers include the UK common law principle "Calderbank offer."[116] This principle is also relied upon in Australian litigations. For example, in *FCT v. Clark* (No. 2) ([2011] FCAFC 140), the Federal Full Court specified that now that 1903 Judiciary Act §67

112. *See* Table 6.5 in ATO Annual Report 2019-2020.
113. This provision states, "An entity is not entitled to a JobKeeper payment under this section unless the entity had an ABN on 12 March 2020 (or a later time allowed by the Commissioner)."
114. As for AAT Act §43(1) which authorizes the AAT's merit review, *see* footnote 43.
115. *See* http://www.smartcompany.com.au/business-advice/legal/ato-reviews-rejected-jobkeeper-applications/.
116. *See* footnote 104 and 3 in Section 4 of Chapter 3 for the Court of Appeal judgment on the *Calderbank* case (1975) that gave rise to this principle.

(Execution by Commonwealth or State) dictates, "In any suit to which the Commonwealth or a State is a party, the rights of parties shall as nearly as possible be the same, and judgment may be given and costs awarded on either side, as in a suit between subject and subject," so the "Calderbank offer" is also applicable in the context of tax litigation. The Court also pointed out that this case contains a problem with the factual credibility of the testimony of the witness, so it is presumed that the outcome of this case will be more unfavorable to the ATO than the set of resolutions offered by the taxpayers, but the ATO refused them without showing reasonable grounds. Then, the Court held that the ATO should bear the costs of the taxpayer based on the indemnity basis under the Federal Court Rules §25.14 (Offers to settle and indemnity costs) that practically provides for a "Calderbank offer."[117]

(3) *Modification of the "Loser Pays Rule"*

As mentioned above, there are similarities and differences in the "loser pays rule" as it is applied in the UK and Australia and, as in the case of the UK,[118] recently, some proposals and recommendations have also been made in Australia to amend the "loser pays rule" further. For example, the Office of Regulation Review, which belongs to the Industry Commission (the Government's Advisory body),[119] submitted a report ("The use of cost litigation rules to improve the efficiency of the legal system") in 1995 to the ALRC (Australian Law Reform Commission), and this report pointed out in particular that it is not clear which of the "American rule" and the "English rule" is better but rules on costs should not only help save time and costs of the disputants by encouraging settlement out of court but also not limit access to justice. Based on this view, the report makes various proposals, which include the following proposed exceptions to the current rules on costs: (i) the AAT makes costs order in favor of the applicant in cases where it believes that such order is necessary to permit him to present his case properly or to negotiate a fair settlement taking account his resources and the likely costs of the proceedings; (ii) a party with no legal representation should be able to recover his own costs for work reasonably necessary to prepare and conduct his case.

The ALRC also issued in 1995 a report (Cost-Shifting—Who Pays for Litigation, ALRC 75). It puts forward the following main proposals: (i) Courts' wide discretionary power on costs should be replaced by clearer rules (Proposal 1); (ii) The amount of cost shifting should be reasonable and be capped (Proposals 2 and 39); (iii) In principle, court order on costs should not be appealable (Proposal 33); (iv) If litigation-related

117. The principle of the "Calderbank offer" is now recognized in the 2011 Federal Court Rules 25.14 (Costs where offer not accepted) which stipulates, "(1) ... (3) If an offer is made by an applicant and not accepted by a respondent, and the applicant obtains a judgment that is more favorable than the terms of the offer, the applicant is entitled to an order that the respondent pay the applicant's costs: (a) ... (b) after the time mentioned in paragraph (a)—on an indemnity basis."
118. *See* 4 of Section 4 in Chapter 3.
119. The Industry Commission was reorganized in 1998 into the Productivity Commission.

costs impede the progress of litigation due to lack of financial resources, the "loser pays rule" should not be applied (Proposals 41 to 44); (v) Such rules on costs that do not impede the filing of public-interest litigations should be adopted (Proposal 47); (vi) Recovery of a reasonable amount of litigation-related costs of unrepresented litigants should be allowed (Proposals 57 and 58). Subsequently, in 2003, the Attorney-General's Department issued a Paper ("Federal Civil Justice System Strategy Paper") that supports the implementation of some of the above ALRC 75 proposals, while the National Pro Bono Resource Center submitted in the "Comments on the Federal Civil Justice System Strategy Paper—December 2003 And Its Recommendations " that this Paper should stress further the function of attorneys to extend assistance to those litigants in need.

The above Reports, etc., may have affected some recent courts' judgments that could lead to the further transformation of the "loser pays rule" in Australia. For example, in *Oshlack v. Richmond River Council* ([1998] HCA 11), the High Court reversed the NSW Court of Appeal judgment on the case ([1996] 91 LGERA 99)[120] and affirmed the judgment of the Land and Environment Court of NSW on the case ([1994] 82 LGERA).[121] This High Court judgment stressed the importance and utility of Judge Stein's opinions expressed in the above judgment of the Land and Environment Court of NSW. These opinions included, among other things, the following: (i) the "English rule" or the "loser pays rule" was developed in individual commercial litigation and differs from that under NSW Environmental Planning and Assessment Act 1979 §9.45 (Restraint, etc., of breaches of this Act, previously §123);[122] (ii) being a public interest lawsuit is not a sufficient reason for becoming an exception to the "loser pays rule" and more is needed for it; (iii) the plaintiffs have nothing to gain from this litigation other than upholding environmental law and protecting endangered species; (iv) many in public take a position similar to that of the plaintiffs, and public interests are involved in the outcome of this lawsuit.

It is true that in the above High Court judgment in the *Oshlack* case, Justice McHugh, who gave a dissenting opinion, expressed his concern that large-scale disregard of the principle of the usual order as to costs would inevitably lead to an increase in litigation with an increased, and often unnecessary, burden on the courts. Then, he showed a view in paragraph 69 that a departure from the "loser pays rule" is, in principle, unless it is prescribed so in legislation or regulations, to be limited to cases where the winning party: ① effectively invites the litigation by its lax conduct; ② unnecessarily protracts the proceedings; ③ succeeds on a point not argued before a

120. A "protective costs order" which is consistent with the ALRC Proposals 41-44 and 47 above was denied in the NSW Court of Appeal judgment. As for its application in UK, *see* footnote 110 of Chapter 3.
121. The judgment of the Land and Environment Court of NSW was not to order costs on the unsuccessful litigant.
122. This provision dictates, "(1) Any person may bring proceedings in the Court for an order to remedy or restrain a breach of this Act, whenever or not any right of that person has been or may be infringed by or as a consequency of that breach."

lower court; ④ prosecutes the matter solely to increase the costs recoverable; or ⑤ obtains relief which the unsuccessful party had already offered in settlement of the dispute so that a public interest factor is irrelevant to the question of costs. But, even after such opinion was expressed by Justice McHugh, at least in environmental litigations, many rulings of the courts have generally followed, in determining whether or not a departure from the "loser pays rule" is appropriate, the above (i) to (iv) criteria Judge Stein expressed in the above judgment of the Land and Environment Court of NSW.[123]

5 Highly Disputed Themes

(1) Penalty Cases

Some factors (the ATO's flexible settlements of disputes, relatively high ratio of revoking the re/assessments by AAT and courts, etc.) should incentivize some taxpayers to dispute the re/assessments while some others (the "loser pays rule" applicable in principle in court, the courts' negative view on the "Chorley exception," etc.) may discourage some taxpayers from disputing them. Generally, the influence of the former factors seems to be more conspicuous in the case of highly disputed tax issues/cases. One of the most highly disputed issues is penalty cases, and the ratio of reduction by reviews should be higher in the case of penalties than the others, as in the case of the UK (*see* Figure 3.9 in Chapter 3).[124] Moreover, Figure 4.8 indicates that, for FY2010-2011 to FY2012-2013, the total amount of re/assessments that resulted in disputes (objections, appeals, and agreements) was about AUD 6.8 billion, but it was reduced from that amount to AUD 3.9 billion (a reduction of about 43%) eventually while, in the case of the amount of penalties, their total amount that resulted in disputes was about AUD 2.9 billion before it was reduced through objections, appeals and agreements to AUD 1.4 billion (approximately 52% reduction).[125]

123. Such rulings include NSW Land and Environment Court judgment on *Coal Action Group Inc. v. Coal Mines Australia Pty Ltd* (No. 3) ([2010]) NSWLEC 59) and NSW Land and Environment Court judgment on *Millers Point Fund Inc. v. Lendlease* (Millers Point) Pty Ltd (No. 2) ([2017] NSWLEC 29). Also, the Court of Appeal judgment in *Maori Council v. Attorney-General* ([1994] 1 AC 466) in NZ also did not make costs order on the unsuccessful plaintiff/appellant mainly because the litigation was not initiated by its own personal interests and the litigation let to the clarification of interpretation of the relevant legislation.
124. Table 4 in 2014 IGT Report shows that for FY2010 to FY2012, the average ratio of reduction by ATO reviews for primary tax and penalties was 42% and 51%, respectively. While, in principle, the imposition of penalties is notified to the taxpayers in advance and are given an opportunity to present counterarguments on it. *See* TAA Schedule 1 §298-10 (Notification of liability) as well as paras. 1.82 and 1.146 of the IGT 2014 Report.
125. *See* Table 19 of the IGT 2014 Report.

Figure 4.8 Amounts of Re/assessments and Penalties Resulted in Disputes and Reduction Ratios after Disputes

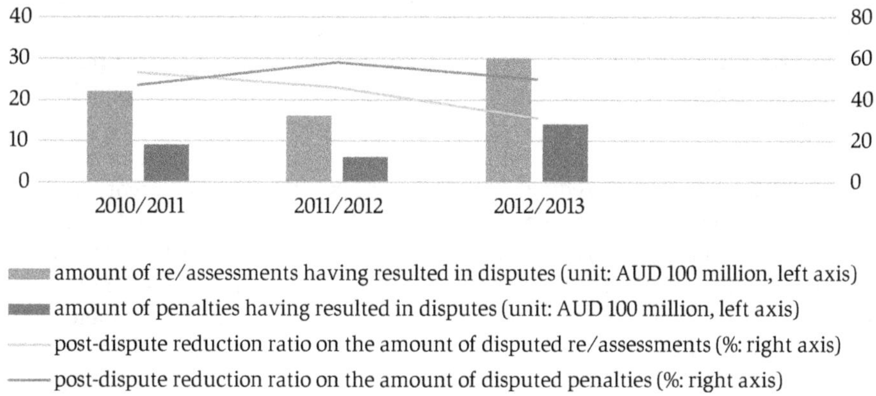

Source: IGT 2014 Report ("Review into the Australian Taxation Office's Administration of Penalties") Table 19.

There are various types of penalties stipulated in TAA Schedule 1 Part 4-25 (Charges and penalties:§§280-1 to 298-110). Many penalties are automatically canceled when the relevant re/assessments are canceled because the majority of disputes over penalties are incidental to the disputes over the re/assessments. Even so, according to the data extracted from the ATO's Integrated Core Process system, between July 2012 and March 2013, the number of re/assessments involving the imposition of penalties to which objections to ATO were made was 2,138, and among those objections, the number of those disputing only the penalties was as many as 407.[126] This may be partially explained by Figure 8 showing the post-dispute reduction ratio on the amount of disputed penalties is generally higher than that of disputed re/assessments. For instance, from July 2012 to March 2013, there were 213 re/assessments accompanying the imposition of penalties that were settled by agreements, and the average ratio of the reduced amount in the case of those re/assessments was 35%, while it was 83% in the case of those penalties.[127]

As the above data and facts indicate, there is a higher inclination for penalties to be abated more significantly than re/assessments through agreements. Such an inclination has raised a concern that the imposition of penalties and their abatements might serve as a basis for maintaining the re/assessments.[128] Indeed, it is explained that the ATO's policy is to reach an agreement on substantial matters as much as

126. IGT 2014 Report, Tables 23-25.
127. IGT 2014 Report, para. A13.76 and Table 27.
128. A similar concern is also voiced in the U.S., but IRM 8.6.4.2(5) mentions that penalty issues are not traded in Appeals. *See* footnote 32 in Chapter 2.

possible before considering whether to agree on penalties, and the team leader checks the appropriateness of the decisions on penalties. Also, while it is true that there are no legal restrictions on the ATO Commissioner's authority to abate penalties which are stipulated in TAA Schedule 1 §298-20 (Remission of penalty),[129] it is to be exercised in line with the ATO's Code of Settlement Practice Statement published in September 2013. Nevertheless, the IGT 2014 Report specifies in paragraph 4.78 that paragraphs 50-51 of the above ATO's Statement imply that there are cases where penalties and interest are taken into consideration as parts of the agreement.[130]

Naturally, there are various kinds of penalties, and there must be variations among them in terms of the frequency and the amount of their abatement. As for the number of penalties imposed, Figure 4.9 indicates that in 2011-2012, the largest was a penalty on the non-filing of a small business, followed by shortfall penalties (in particular, the number of shortfall penalties imposed when the taxpayer fails to take reasonable care; X). As stated in paragraph 16C in the ATO's Practice Statement (PS LA 2012/5), the issue of whether or not a penalty is to be abated is weighed on its merits, taking into consideration all relevant facts and circumstances,[131] so disputes on penalties should tend to arise quite often, particularly in cases where there are such attributes as the relevant facts and circumstances being complicated or the ambiguity/latitude in the criteria in applying penalties. Such being the case, a type of penalty with much of such attribute is, as suggested by the case in the UK, an underreporting/shortfall penalty that does not come first in the number of impositions[132] but constitutes a "behavioral penalty" whose applicable rates vary depending on various factors and usually costs taxpayers more.[133]

129. TAA Schedule 1 §298-20 provides, " (1) The Commissioner may remit all or a part of the penalty." While, for example, in *Sanctuary Lakes Pty Ltd v. FCT* ([2013] FCAFC), the Federal Full Court sustained the AAT decision ([2012] AATA 404) that, contrary to the ATO Commissioner's decision, exempted the underreporting penalty because it found the concerned return stood on the reasonably arguable position.

130. It is explained that included in such cases are: (i) where the cost of litigation becomes too high, (ii) where the facts are complicated, (iii) where there are particularities that are not amenable to litigation (for example, where the valuation of a unique asset is the point of dispute), and so forth.

131. For example, the AAT decision in *Kizquart Pty Ltd v. FCT* ([2005] AATA 582) implies that non-filing penalties could be exempted in cases where returns in the past were filed in time and there are other extenuating circumstances (such as ignorance of a newly introduced tax provision).

132. *See* Section 5 in Chapter 3. Table 9 of 2014 IGT Report reveals that for FY2010 to FY2011, the type of penalty imposed in the largest number was a failure to lodge penalty while any one of the shortfall penalties imposed on account of (X), (Y), or (Z) in Figure 4.9 was larger in amount.

133. A former tax adviser to the ATO also said, "Administrative penalties for statements are set in the legislation at levels that are largely determined by behaviors: the more flawed the behavior, the heavier the penalty. In deciding whether to remit shortfall penalties, we consider a range of factors," and cites fairness among taxpayers, past and future compliance status of taxpayers, etc. as the main factors for determining whether a penalty should be abated or not. *See* John Smith, Administrative Tax Penalties, *Australian Tax Review*, Vol. 30 (2001) pp. 186-187.

Figure 4.9 Ratio and Breakdown of Penalties Imposed in 2011-2012 (%)

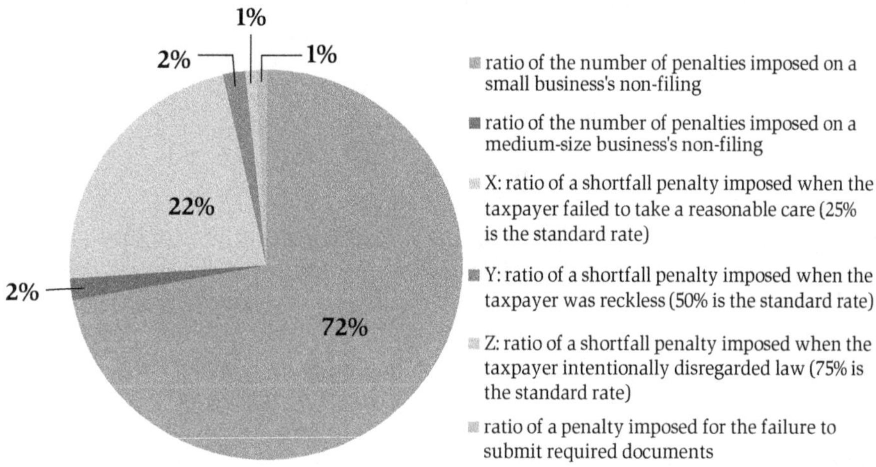

Source: IGT 2014 Report, Table 17.

Shortfall penalties are imposed in accordance with TAA Schedule 1 §284B (Penalty relating to statements), which dictates, "(1) You are liable to an administrative penalty if: (a) you make a statement to the Commissioner …; and (b) the statement is false or misleading in a material particular, whether because of things in it or omitted from it." While a shortfall penalty shall not be imposed where a taxpayer exercised reasonable care.[134] As for the applicable rate of a shortfall penalty, it depends not only on the cause (i.e., X, Y, or Z in Figure 4.9) for the underreporting[135] but also on the degree of cooperation in investigations, the timing of voluntary disclosure of relevant facts, etc. Therefore, if the fact of underreporting is disclosed voluntarily, the base penalty amount (25% (X), 50% (Y), and 75% (Z)) could be reduced up to 80%, while the base penalty amount is increased up to 20% of it if the underreporting is not

134. Moreover, due to TAA Schedule 1 §284-75(6), para. 1.48 of the IGT 2014 Report confirms, "a taxpayer will not be liable to a penalty where a false or misleading statement was made by a registered tax agent due to the agent's lack of reasonable care, so long as the taxpayer provided all the relevant taxation information to the agent." This treatment suggests that the threshold for a penalty waiver is lower in Australia than that in countries covered in the preceding Chapters (*see* 2(2) in Section 3 of Chapter 1, 2(2) in Section 4 of Chapter 2, and 1(2) and 1(3) in Section 5 of Chapter 3).
135. ATO reports that in FY2021- FY2022 (FY2022- FY2023), 12,547 (13,528) behavioral penalties (largest in number is GST followed by IT) were imposed and for FY2022- FY2023 its breakdown was Y (6,151), Z (5,695), X (1,422), others (260) while it reduced about 6% to 7% of the penalty amount by discretion at the time of their impositions. *See* https://www.ato.gov.au/about-ato/research-and-statistics/in-detail/general-research/overview-of-behavioural-penalties. The applicable rates of non-filing penalties also vary depending on its cause as TAA Schedule 1(1A) stipulates, "you are not liable to an administrative penalty … if: … (d) the failure to give the return, notice, statement or other document to the Commissioner did not result from: (i) intentional disregard by the or (ii) recklessness by the agent as to the operation of a taxation law."

disclosed within a reasonable time or the taxpayer obstructed its detection.[136] These facts strongly imply that, even if the breakdown of abated penalties is not clear, the attributes of shortfall penalties, in conjunction with their relatively heavier burden, constitute a major cause for penalty cases to be a very highly disputed issue.[137]

(2) "Deadline Extension" Cases

As mentioned in Section 1, there are also many disputes over "deadline extension" cases. Reasons for this include the ATO Commissioner's broad discretionary power (authorized in particular by TAA §14ZX in footnote 6), high approval ratio of applications for it (*see* footnote 8), the large number of applicable provisions, the AAT's merit review function, etc. Disputes over deadline extension arise in relation to numerous tax provisions stipulating deadlines.[138] The Federal Court judgment on *Hunter Valley Developments Pty Ltd v. Cohen* ([1984] FCA 176) set forth criteria for determining whether a request for a deadline extension should be allowed.[139] The criteria were: (i) reasons for the failure to file an appeal before the deadline; (ii) whether or not the taxpayer's agent or the ATO had been informed of his intention to file an appeal; (iii) whether there would be any disadvantages to the ATO or the general public in permitting the deadline extension; (iv) the issue of equality vis-à-vis other taxpayers in the identical situation, (v) significance and rationality of the plaintiff's allegations on the substantive issue. Judging from these (i) ~ (v) criteria,[140] the Court allowed the extension of the deadline requested by the plaintiff.[141]

However, in the AAT 5/2/1994 decision on Case 18/94, at issue was whether the ATO Commissioner's rejection of the applicant's delayed filing of the objection, which relied on TAA §14ZW (When taxation objections are to be made) (2) that authorizes the ATO Commissioner's discretion to treat it as if it were filed within the deadline was

136. *See* TAA Schedule 1 §284-220 (Increase in base penalty amount) and §284-225 (Reduction of base penalty amount if you voluntarily tell the Commissioner).

137. *See* footnote 132. Also notable is he ATO Ruling (TR 94/78) which states, "The case for remission is strongest ... for example where an amount of assessable income is included by a taxpayer in a year later than the year in which it was correctly assessable. Partial remission of the prescribed penalty may be warranted in these kinds of cases depending on the circumstances." It contrasts with the standard treatment in Japan where no remission of a penalty in such a case is likely because it does not in principle constitute a justifiable reason. *See* 2(4) in Section 2 and 1(2) in Section 4 of Chapter 1.

138. For example, the *Hell's Angel* case (1984) discussed in 3(2) of this section was a litigation in which the ATO lost because it refused without showing reasons the application for the extension of the payment deadline made by the plaintiff that utilized a tax avoidance scheme.

139. The relevant provision of AD(JR)Act §11 (Manner of making applications) states, "(1) An application to the Federal Court ... (c) shall be lodged with a Registry of the court concerned and ... shall be so lodged within the prescribed period or within such further time as the court concerned (whether before or after the expiration of the prescribed period) allows."

140. The substantive issue in this case was that the film made by the plaintiff falls under the category of a "qualifying Australian film" to be eligible for the preferential treatment and deductions under section 10BA (Division) of the ITAA at the time.

141. The ATO's guidance (PS LA 2003/7) is also not so restrictive because it mentions that an application for extension of the deadline for objections to the ATO would be appropriate if: (i) a case involves significant legal matters, (ii) the deadline was missed due to the negligence of the taxpayer's agent, etc.

legitimate.[142] The AAT reviewed this case from the perspective of the criteria shown in the above *Hunter Valley* case as well, and it held in favor of the ATO mainly because on criterion (iv), the applicant's assertion has certain reasonableness, but on the criterion (ii), the AAT concluded that the applicant had not ever made clear to his agent his intention of challenging the substance of the re/assessment on him and the notification to the Commissioner of his wish for contesting the re/assessment was out of time, and on the criterion (iii), the acceptance of the delayed filing of the applicant's taxation objection would not only give rise to problems with both evidentially and procedural matters at the ATO but also incur the problem of inequality with those taxpayers in the identical situation as the applicant.

In this connection, *Brown v. FCT* ([1999] 99 ATC 4516) is also noteworthy because it suggests that different weights should be given to the criteria shown in the *Hunter* case. In this *Brown* case, the Federal Court confirmed that, in deciding whether or not the extension of the deadline should be granted, it needs to weigh various points, including not only the reason for the delay in filing an appeal and other related circumstances but also whether or not an appeal has enough substance. Then, it stressed that if there is merit in the latter point, it is appropriate to allow the extension of the deadline even if there is not much merit in the former point. The Court also specified that the ATO Commissioner and the AAT should not approach the issue of extension of the deadline on the premise that it should be granted only in exceptional cases. Based on these views, the Court concluded that, although the plaintiff's failure to file an appeal within the deadline was his deliberate choice in light of the possibility of bankruptcy, the outcome of the dispute on the substance of this case requires further consideration,[143] so the appeal, in this case, should be deemed to have been filed within the time limit pursuant to TAA §14ZW(2).[144]

The AAT's 5/9/1997 decision on Case 27/97 was one of those cases where an application for an extension of the deadline for the taxation objection was made because of a mistake attributable to the applicant's tax agent. The AAT observed that the substance of this case is arguable because it contained a possibility that the sales price of the applicant's asset conveyed by his agent to the ATO officer and the tax assessment based on that price might be incorrect. It also referred to *Lighthouse Philatelics Pty Ltd. v. FCT* ([1991] FCA 667), in which the Federal Court stated in paragraph 38, "To refuse to allow the amendment on the grounds of objection on the

142. TAA §14ZW(2) dictates, " If the period within which an objection by a person is required to be lodged has passed, the person may nevertheless lodge the objection with the Commissioner together with a written request asking the Commissioner to deal with the objection as if it had been lodged within that period." As for the possible extension of the application deadline for an appeal to the AAT, AAT Act §29 (Manner of applying for review) (7) prescribes, "The Tribunal may, upon application in writing by a person, extend the time for the making by that person of an application to the Tribunal for a review of a decision (including a decision made before the commencement of this section) if the Tribunal is satisfied that it is reasonable in all the circumstances to do so."

143. The substance of this case was whether or not the re/assessment of not regarding the economic benefits obtained by the plaintiff as gifts but compensation for his service was legitimate for the reason that it is taxable income under ITAA §26 (Certain items of assessable income) (e) which encompasses economic benefits accrued in direct or indirect relation to the provision of service.

144. *See* footnote 142 for TAA §14ZW(2).

basis that the failure to claim deductions otherwise properly allowable was a mistake of the taxpayer's accountant, would involve an error of law." Then, the AAT concluded that not granting the extension of the deadline for taxation objection in this case on the basis that the applicant had placed his affairs in the hands of his tax agent and his recourse for any errors was against that person would also be an error of law. It seems that this case, as well as those cases mentioned above, provide good explanations of why there has been a large number of disputes over "deadline extension" cases.[145]

SECTION 2 TAX DISPUTE IN NZ

1 Tax Objection Procedures and Their Characteristics

(1) New Tax Objection System and Background for Its Introduction

The procedures for objections to the Inland Revenue (IR) are set out in Part IVA(Disputes procedures: §89A-§89P) of the Tax Administration Act (TAA) of 1994.[146] This procedure was, as mentioned in paragraphs 11 to 20 of the IR's Standard Practice Statement (SPS) 11/05 (Disputes resolution process commenced by the Commissioner of Inland Revenue),[147] adopted in 1996 following the recommendations of the 1994 Report of the Organizational Review of the Inland Revenue Department by the Richardson Committee (hereinafter referred to as "1994 Richardson Report"). Appendix E(Tax Disputes resolution) to the 1994 Richardson Report pointed out such problems with the older tax objection system as: (i) during the tax objection stage, there was room for the IR to rethink grounds for re/assessments, which discouraged correct re/assessments before that; (ii) too much time and money was needed to resolve tax disputes; (iii) independence, neutrality, and expertise of those in charge of reviews of the re/assessments in dispute were insufficient; (iv) taxpayers sometimes refrained from disclosing information at the tax objection stage, which could lead to the delay of the resolution of the disputes.

In particular, the 1994 Richardson Report Appendix E mentioned on the above (i) (IR's rethinking of grounds for re/assessments) and (iv) (taxpayers belated disclosure of information) that the 1993 IRD Report of the Dispute Resolution Evaluation refers to the fact of 48% of the re/assessment being canceled (29% of them were fully canceled) after objections were filed and explains that many of those cancellations were due to new information obtained after the examination. It also mentioned, regarding the above (ii) (much time and money required for resolution of disputes), that survey results and unofficial reports indicate that 80% of cases brought to the Court of Appeal

145. There are also cases such as the AAT 3/17/1993 decision on Case 8/93 which suggest that extension of the time limit is not automatically granted just because the agent committed an error.
146. NZ's population in 2022 is about 5.1 million. Of the approximately NZD 94.5 billion in revenue received by IR in 2021, about 48% of is from personal IT, about 20% is from CIT, about 28% is from GST, and about 4% is from the others. *See* 2021 IR Annual Report, p. 14 for details.
147. This SPS is now withdrawn but the same is written in Tax Information Bulletin Vol. 22, No. 11 (December 2010).

over the past five years needed five years or more (25% of them needed ten years or more) before its judgments were handed down and the average amount of disputed taxes was about NZD 20,115 at the litigation stage (NZD 4,863 at the objection stage), so there are more cases of aggrieved taxpayers either giving up from the beginning disputing the re/assessments or withdrawing them in the middle of the objection or litigation stage on the belief that their cases do not match the time and costs needed for their resolution.[148]

TAA §89A (Purpose of This Part) confirms that TAA Part 4A emphasizes the dispute resolution at the "pre-reassessment stage" with an aim to coping with the problems referred to in the 1994 Richardson Report because it prescribes, " (1) The purpose of this Part is to establish procedures that will—... (b) reduce the likelihood of disputes arising between the Commissioner and taxpayers by encouraging open and full communication...;and (c) promote the early identification of the basis for any dispute...(d) promote the prompt and efficient resolution of any dispute."[149] In particular, TAA §89A(1)(d) requires that the disputing parties disclose all relevant facts, evidence and interpretations of law or disclose "all the cards on the table" at the stage of objection to the IR and this requires, save for exceptional cases, an aggrieved taxpayer and the IR to go through the steps or procedures stipulated under TAA Part 4A before he brings his case to the Taxation Review Authority (TRA) or the High Court and it should make it possible to clarify at an early stage of the dispute, points of disputes and sort out claims of the disputing parties.[150]

The objection and review process under TAA Part 4A, as shown in Figure 4.10, differs slightly depending on whether it is initiated by the IR or by the taxpayer.[151] It proceeds as follows: ① Either the IR Commissioner or the taxpayer issues to the other party a "Notice of Proposed Adjustment" (NOPA) indicating the amount of correction or tax to be payable, the amount of the penalty and the grounds for the correction, etc.,[152] and the other party objecting to NOPA returns a "Notice of Response" (NOR) indicating the reason for the objection,[153] then, the disputing parties, in principle,

148. In 2017, the average number of days to complete the tax objection reviews (not including those for the initial examination and litigation) was 651 days. *See* https://assets.kpmg.com/content/dam/kpmg/nz/pdf/Aug/The-secret-to-winning-tax-disputes-TAX-CHAT.pdf.

149. However, in such exceptional cases as those stipulated in §89C (Notices of proposed adjustments required to be issued by Commissioner) (e) of TAA (e.g., when there is a risk of taxpayers leaving the country), IR Commissioner may issue corrections without going through dispute resolution procedures.

150. This is similar to the rule in Australia where attempts to resolve (potential) disputes at the stage of objections to the tax authority are required (*see* Figure 4.2) and contrasts with such countries as Japan where they are optional (*see* Figure 1.1 in Chapter 1).

151. There are also statutory appeal procedures that are not set out in TAA Part 4A. *See* the IR's SPS 16/05 (Disputes resolution process commenced by the Commissioner) and SPS 16/06 (Disputes resolution process commenced by a taxpayer).

152. TAA §89B (Commissioner may issue notices of proposed adjustments) applies in the case of the IR Commissioner submitting a NOPA, while TAA §89DA (Taxpayer may issue notice of proposed adjustments for taxpayer assessment) applies in the case of a taxpayer submitting a NOPA.

153. As TAA §89C (Notices of proposed adjustment required to be issued by Commissioner) dictates, the IR Commissioner, in principle, presents a NOPA before the reassessment. While a taxpayer initiates the objection process in such cases where he objects to the "default

participate in a "conference"; ②If no agreement is reached yet, save for exceptional cases where the following objection steps are skipped, the IR Commissioner issues a "Disclosure Notice" and "Statement of Position" (SOP) that sets out the facts, allegations, evidence, and grounds, etc., pertaining to the matter at issue,[154] and the taxpayer who has received it also submits the SOP to the IR; ③ These Disclosure Notice and SOPs are sent for review to the Adjudication Unit (after 2012, Disputes Review Unit, DRU) which constitutes a part of the Office of the Chief Tax Counsel.

Figure 4.10 Tax Appeal Procedure

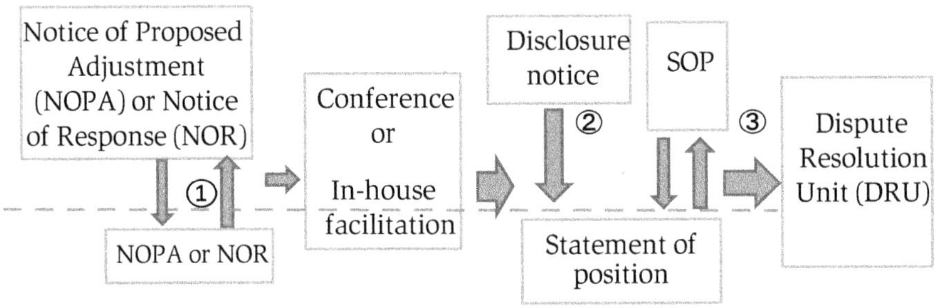

There are some cases where it is possible or appropriate to skip, at the above ② stage, the subsequent objection process. In particular, TAA §89N (Completing the disputes process), which was added in December 2004, states in paragraph (1) that such cases include the following: (i) the taxpayer's action delayed the review process; (ii) the Commissioner has reasonable grounds to believe that the taxpayer will take steps to make it difficult to collect the tax in dispute; (iii) the taxpayers and the IR agree that the dispute would be resolved more efficiently by sending it to the court or the TRA,[155] or they should suspend disputes process until a similar case is decided by the court. Also, SPS 16/06 (now replaced by SPS 23/01) specified in paragraph 196, "If the taxpayer has participated meaningfully during the conference phase and signed a declaration that all material information has been provided, the Commissioner will agree to the taxpayer's preference to opt out of the disputes process in circumstances where one of the following applies: (a) the total amount of tax in dispute is NZD 75,000 or less except where the dispute is part of a wider dispute; (b) the dispute turns on issues of fact (e.g., facts that are to be determined by reference to expert opinions or

assessment" on his non-filing of returns. *See supra* SPS 16/6 and SPS 08/01 (Disputes resolution process commenced by the Commissioner of Inland Revenue) for further details.

154. *See* TAA §89M (Disclosure notices) for more information on what to be included in a Disclosure Notice and SOPs.

155. While TAA §138B (When disputant entitled to challenge assessment) assures that "(2) A disputant is entitled to challenge an assessment by commencing proceedings in a hearing authority if—... (b) the disputant is subsequently issued with an amended assessment."

valuation) only," and in paragraph 198 that this opt-out leads to the Commissioner's issue of a "challenge notice."[156]

As for those objections that have gone through the above ①~③ steps, the head of the DRU, which consists of three examiners with legal or accounting qualifications, decides on them. DRU decides without utilizing flexible dispute resolution such as ADR, additional investigations,[157] and direct communication with the taxpayer and the Examination Division while there are some uncertainties about the binding nature of the DRU's decision.[158] Under such objection procedures, (i) the disputing parties should, as mentioned above, follow all of the procedures in ① to ③ above in principle, and if the taxpayer fails to complete these procedures within the prescribed timeframe, further stages for dispute resolution would not be available in principle; (ii) TAA §138G (Effect of disclosure notice) dictated, before its revision in 2011, after the Disclosure Notice is issued, the "evidence exclusion rule," which guarantees the principle of "disclose all the cards on the table" at the stage of objection to the IR, limits what the disputing parties could claim to those facts, evidence, propositions of law, etc. stated in the SOPs submitted by the disputing parties to the other party in stage ② and ③.[159]

(2) *Dispute Resolution under TAA Part IVA*

The procedure for dispute resolution under TAA Part IVA is, as it is called, a "ritual dance,"[160] a series of rules requiring the taxpayer and the IR to complete each step of the procedures within the prescribed timeframe. If no conference is held between step ① and step ②, the dispute is to be sent to the DRU in a week or so. From June 2006 to March 2007, the average days needed for the DRU to process the disputes was 6 weeks in the case of simple disputes, thirteen weeks in the case of standard cases, and 25

156. While some propose that, since the IR is not always willing to skip the objection process, even in a case where its process is initiated by the IR Commissioner, a disputing taxpayer should be allowed to opt out of the process. *See* Developments in Tax Disputes Procedure—Another Step Backwards at http://www.mikelennard.com/?t=49.
157. The one who has a direct communication with the taxpayer and the Examination Division is the Senior Technical and Liaison Advisor of the Office of the Chief Tax Counsel. *See* IR's Publication (The Disputes Review Unit—its role in the dispute resolution process) for details.
158. *See* https://www.taxtechnical.ird.govt.nz/general-articles/the-disputes-review-unit-its-role-in-the-dispute-resolution-process. Regarding the nature of the decision of IR's "Adjudication Unit" which was the predecessor of the DRU, *in Ch'elle Properties (NZ) Ltd v. CIR* ([2008] Vol.14:4 NZJTLP 425,445), the High Court held that the claims of the disputants were limited to the facts and "propositions of law" set forth in the NOPA, but otherwise were not bound by its decision and reasoning in the adjudication report. Indeed, para. 264 of SPS 11/05 (Disputes resolution process commenced by the Commissioner of Inland Revenue) states that the IR is not necessarily bound by the DRU decisions, whereas para. 304 of SPS 11/06 (Disputes resolution process commenced by a taxpayer) states that the IR is bound by them.
159. TAA §138G(1) originally stipulated, "if the Commissioner, issues a disclosure notice to a disputant, and the disputant challenges the disputable decision, the Commissioner and the disputant may raise in the challenge only—(a) the facts and evidence, and the issues arising from them; and (b) the propositions of law,—that are disclosed in the Commissioner's and disputant's statements of position."
160. *See* Geoffrey Clews, "Chapter 20," p. 220 in "*The Disputes and Litigation Review (7th Edition)*" ed. Simon Whitehead (2014) Law Business Research Ltd.

weeks in the case of complex cases.[161] But, lately, more than 90% of cases have been processed within three months, and the IR subsequently reset a goal and now it aims to make decisions on more than 90% of the disputes within ten weeks.[162] As shown in Figure 4.11, about fifty to eighty cases are decided annually by the DRU, and about 70% to 90% of the decisions generally sustain the IR's NOPAs and claims. The DRU's decisions are to be made solely based on its review of the submitted documents, etc., and the "adjudication report" describing in considerable detail the laws and reasons that served as the basis for the decision as well as a summary of them is to be sent to the disputing parties.[163]

Figure 4.11 Number and Results of the DRU (or "Adjudication Unit" Before 2012) decisions

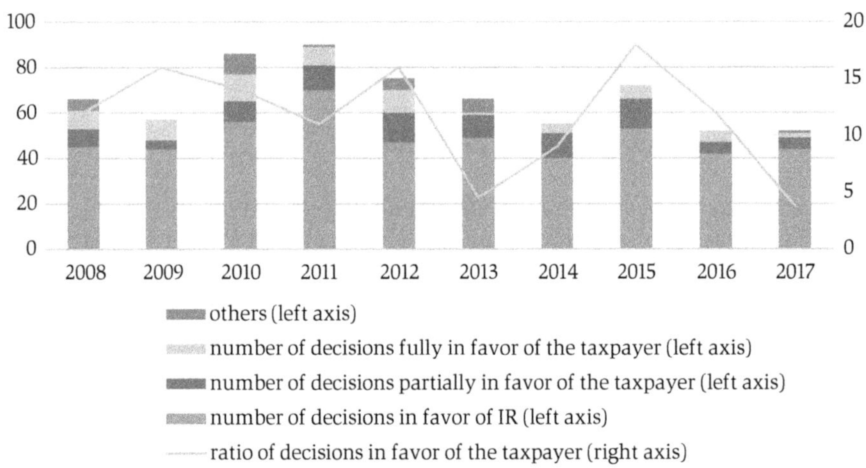

Source: IR document "Outcome of cases decided by Disputes Review Unit 2008 to 2017."

Ever since the introduction in 1996 of TAA Part IVA, as shown in Figure 4.12, the number of TRA decisions and court judgments on tax cases has shown a declining trend. The IR regarded this trend as the realization of the objective of the introduction of TAA Part IVA and its success.[164] However, there is a view that this trend and relevant facts imply that there is a heavier administrative burden on the disputing taxpayers (especially those with a small amount of disputed tax) at the objection stage and heavier financial costs on them at the litigation stage.[165] Likewise, the Report (The

161. *See supra* "Tax Information Bulletin," Vol. 19, No. 16 (November 2007).
162. *See* IR 2017-2020 Annual Report, Output 5.2 Litigation Management. In particular, in 2017, the DRU has basically sustained as much as more than 90% of the claims of the IR.
163. For details, *see* IR, *supra* "Tax Information Bulletin" Vol. 19, No. 16 (November 2007).
164. *See* para. 1.7 in the 2003 Report (Resolving tax disputes: a legislative review) by Michael Cullen (Finance Minister at that time). This Report also points out that in 1997 about 2% of the cases investigated resulted in tax disputes, but in 2002 the percentage decreased to about 0.9%.
165. *See supra* "Developments in Tax Disputes Procedure."

Disputes Resolution Procedures in Part IVA of the Tax Administration Act 1994 and the Challenge Procedures in Part VIIIA of the Tax Administration Act 1994, hereinafter referred to as the "2008 Joint Proposal") published in 2008 by the Tax Committees of the NZ Law Society and the NZ Institute of Chartered Accountants Act points out that the declining trend in the number of tax disputes does not necessarily mean that the current tax dispute settlement system is functioning well and that the problems specified by the 1994 Richardson Report still exist in different forms.

Figure 4.12 Number of TRA Decisions and Court Judgments on Tax Cases

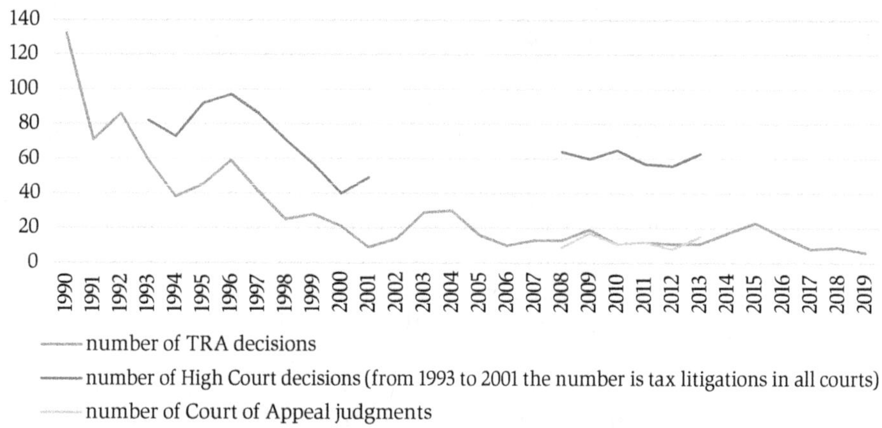

Source: Sarah Miles, "The price we pay for specialized society" Appendix 1 and 5, New Zealand Taxation Review Decisions 1984-NZLII, "2008 Joint Proposal" Appendix A and Finance Minister's "2003 Report" Figure 1.

For example, in paragraph 2.1 of the 2008 Joint Proposal mentions the followings vis-à-vis some of the problems pointed out in the 1994 Richardson Report: as for the problem (i) (IR's rethinking of grounds for re/assessments), as confirmed by the Court of Appeal in *Zentrum Holdings Limited v. CIR* case ([2006] 22 NZTC 19912), in a case where the IR had not issued a Disclosure Notice, its claim is not limited to the facts and propositions of law, so it still remains room for change of the claim; as for the problem (ii) (High administrative, financial and time costs), there is not only an overlap between the materials that the taxpayer should prepare at the objection stage and those at the litigation stage but also high administrative costs at the objection stage which do not guarantee disputes resolution in the face of such limitations as the "evidence exclusion rule" under TAA §138G,[166] with the result that many taxpayers are reluctant to file an objection and litigate; As for the problem (iii) (Independence, neutrality, and

166. The "2008 Joint Proposal" points out in para. 2.1 that the taxpayer would need more than NZD 25,000 to challenge the IR position in court, so the IR may issue questionable matters below NZD 25,000 with impunity.

expertise of the reviewers), the IR has, under TAA §89N(3), a broad discretion of whether or not it utilizes the DRU's review.[167]

It might be true that the problems specified in the 1994 Richardson Report have not been completely resolved even under the current system, but after the publication of the 2008 Joint Proposal, measures were taken, and court rulings were handed down that could work towards mitigating those problems further. They include the following: (1)① the Taxation (Tax Administration and Remedial Matters) Act 2011 (2011 No. 63, hereinafter called "T(TARM) Act 2011") introduced TAA §89P (Challenge notice for taxpayer-initiated disputes), which enables the IR to skip the objection stage without making re/assessments if it issues a "challenge notice" (*see* footnote 156) in response to the NOPA submitted by the taxpayer in the taxpayer-initiated objection procedure; ② the optional conference in the Figure 4.10 was, since April 2010, supplemented by the "in-house facilitation" in which a trained senior IR staff outside the Examination Division takes part; ③T(TARM) Act 2011 amended TAA §138G in such a way that the evidence exclusion rule applies only to the issues mentioned in the SOPs and the propositions of law.[168]

In particular, the above ② ("in-house facilitation") may be defined as a form of ADR. As for ADR, the 2008 High Court Regulations Subpart 8 (Negotiations for settlement) stipulates that a judge will conduct ADR, including mediation in certain cases,[169] but in practice, there were not many cases of tax disputes being resolved by ADR at any stage of dispute resolution.[170] However, with the introduction of the abovementioned "in-house facilitation," the usage rate increased to about 50%, and approximately its ratio of resolution on more than five hundred cases of disputes involving individuals and small businesses over the five years after its introduction was about 55%.[171] Therefore, the "in-house facilitation" should be one of the main reasons for the recent decrease evidenced in Figure 4.11 in the number of DRU decisions. When the "in-house facilitation" does not lead to the resolution of the dispute, the objection process tends to take much time. Moreover, the rate of dispute resolution by the

167. TAA §89N has para. (1) (*see* 1(1) of Section 2) as well as para. (3) which states, "the Commissioner may apply to the High Court for an order that allows more time for the completion of the disputes process, or for an order that completion of the disputes process is not required." While, in *ANZ National Bank Ltd v. CIR* (No. 2) ([2006] 22 NZTC 19,835), the High Court noted that this provision would give broader discretion to the IR in deviating from the normal appeal procedure, regardless of whether or not the requirements for TAA §89N(1) are met.
168. TRA Act §17 (Evidence in proceedings before an Authority) 2A provides for the same effect. Compare it with TAA §138G(1) in its original version (*see* footnote 159).
169. For example, High Court Regulation §7.79(5) states, "A judge may, with the consent of the parties, make an order at any time directing the parties to attempt to settle their dispute by the form of mediation or other alternative dispute resolution (...) agreed to by the parties."
170. Melinda Jone, Evaluating New Zealand's Tax Dispute Resolution System: A Dispute Systems Design Perspective, (2016)22, NZJTLP, p. 13.
171. IR Tax Information Bulletin Vol. 27, No. 10 (November 2015) p. 69 and Andrew Maples, Melinda Jone and Alistair Hodoson, Inland Revenue Facilitated Conferences: Better Than Settling Disputes with 'Clubs and Spears'?," *eJournal of Tax Research*, Vol. 18, No. 2 (2020) p. 474. "In-house facilitation" is also implemented even after the objection stage. This differs from with Japan where no ADR is used for tax disputes while they are similar in that the ratio of review authorities sustaining the disputed re/assessments is rather high.

decisions of the DRU is not so high because 20% to 40% of the taxpayers dissatisfied with them take their cases to the TRA or the High Court.[172]

2 Objections Filing with TRA and Its Processing

The TRA (Taxation Review Authority) is composed of a judge with no less than seven years of service experience in a district court or the High Court, a reviewer appointed by the Governor-General based on the recommendation of the Ministry of Justice, and their support staff. Just as the TRA Act §13 (Functions of an Authority), the 1998 TRA Regulations §13A (General jurisdiction of Authorities) provides, "The functions of an Authority are to sit as a judicial authority for hearing and determining objections and challenges." The Act also stipulates in §20A(Hearings on papers) that, with the consent of the disputing parties, a decision may be made based only on papers without hearings in camera. The TRA could order the IR to pay taxpayer fees,[173] and some of its decisions are made public, subject to necessary masking.[174] In the past, the TRA also had the "Small claims jurisdiction," but this division had a narrow entrance to applicable cases, and its decisions could not be disputed in court.[175] Due to these rules and restrictions, the number of cases coming under the "Small claims jurisdiction" was not many,[176] and eventually, it was abolished by the T(TARM) Act 2011.[177]

The procedures for filing objections with the TRA and filing tax lawsuits with the High Court are stipulated in TAA Part 8 (Objections: §125A to §138) and Part 8A (Challenges: §138A to §138S). In particular, TAA §138P (Power of hearing authority) stipulates, "a hearing authority may—(a) confirm or cancel or vary an assessment, or reduce the amount of an assessment, or increase the amount of an assessment to the extent to which the Commissioner was able to assess an increased amount at the time the Commissioner made the assessment to which the challenge relates."[178] In *Legarth v. CIR* ([1969] NZLR 137), the Court of Appeal ruled that contrary to the view held by the Board of Review (predecessor of the TRA), it is empowered to review the entire

172. Some consider that, although the tax dispute settlement system is administratively complex, formal, and burdensome, it provides early resolution of tax disputes that should not be litigated in court. *See* Clews, *supra* "Chapter 20," p. 237.
173. *See* TRA Act §22B (Power to order costs for filing fees) and §30 (Regulations)(2)(e).
174. *See* TRA Rules §36 (Reports of decisions).
175. But the impact of the abolition of the "Small claims jurisdiction" may not be so grave due to the TRA Act §26 (*see* footnote 184) and the reason mentioned in footnote 177.
176. The 1994 Richardson Report, Appendix E, para. 24, noted that about half of the tax disputes involved less than NZD 5,000 in disputed tax amount.
177. For details, *see* IR's Tax Information Bulletin Vol. 23, No. 8 (October 2011) p. 20. Even after the abolishment of this division, it is customary for objections with disputed tax amount of NZD 75,000 or less to be processed expeditiously by the simplified procedures. *See* SPS 10/04.
178. TRA Act §16 (Hearing of proceedings) (2) also prescribes, "an Authority shall have all the powers, duties, functions, and discretions of the Commissioner in making the determination." So, the power of the TRA on this point seems to be similar to the merit review function of the Australia's AAT. *See* the next footnote below and the footnote 43 in Section 1.

process of assessing additional tax, and for that purpose may exercise the Commissioner's function.[179] The 1994 ITA §136 (When objection may be referred directly to the High Court) (17) also provides that "the High Court may—(a)...(b) make any assessment which the Commissioner was empowered to make at the time the Commissioner made the assessment to which the objection relates, or direct the Commissioner to make such an assessment, in which case an assessment shall be made by the Commissioner to conform to that direction."[180]

Whereas, TAA §109 (Disputable decisions deemed correct except in proceedings), referred to as the "ouster (or privative) provision," provides, "Except in objection proceedings under Part 8 or a challenge under Part 8A—(a) no disputable decision may be disputed in a court or in any proceedings on any ground whatsoever; and (b) every disputable decision and, where relevant, all of its particulars are deemed to be, and are to be taken as being, correct in all respects." Also, some other rules might work unfavorably for the taxpayers. For example, TAA §114 (Validity of assessments) dictates, "An assessment made by the Commissioner is not invalidated—(a) through a failure to comply with a provision of this Act or another Inland Revenue Act."[181] Moreover, TRA Act §17(2B) stipulates that disputants may bring up new matters or new propositions of law if certain requirements are met, and there are actually cases such as the above Zentrum case (2006) in which a "disclosure notice" was not issued but by loosely interpreting the "evidence exclusion rule" stipulated in the TAA §138G, the Court allowed the IR to bring up a new ground for the re/assessment even after hearings were completed.

Certainly, it is good for a taxpayer that TAA §128 (Payment of disputed tax where competent objection lodged) (2) provides that except for those cases where there is a substantial risk of him not paying the disputed tax in spite of him losing his case at the objection or litigation stage, there is no obligation on him to pay the disputed tax amount, the shortfall penalty and interest in advance,[182] but the success rate of taxpayers at the objection/litigation stage does not seem to be so high. Although the details of the rate of revocation by the TRA of the re/assessments are unavailable, at least recently, there seems not to be much difference in the rate of revocation (about 10 to 20%) of the re/assessments by the court shown in Figure 4.13 and that by the TRA.[183] Moreover, as provided in TRA Act §26 (Appeals to High Court) and §26A

179. Also, in *Edwards v. Commissioner* ([2016] NZHC 1795) in which at issue was the IR's delayed re/assessment on a fictitious return made in accordance with TAA §108(Time bar for amendment of income tax assessment)(2), the High Court followed the ruling on this *Legarth* case (1969) by holding that the TRA could review the re/assessment by standing in the commissioner's shoes.

180. This illustrates NZ's departure, in the case of a direct appeal to the High Court, from the "Wednesbury unreasonableness" principle observed in UK and Australia. *See* 1 in Section 2 of Chapter 3 and 3(1) in Section 1/footnote 62 of Chapter 4.

181. This also contrasts with a standard treatment in Japan where disputed re/assessments are canceled when they are not accompanied by the written notice explaining correctly and sufficiently the reasons for them. *See* 2(4) in Section 3 of Chapter 1.

182. TAA §138I (Payment of disputed tax) provides for the identical rule.

183. Between November 2011 and August 2012, 86.7% of the tax disputes heard by the TRA or the High Court upheld the re/assessments. For details, *see* Brendan Brown, "New Zealand Case Law Development" (2012) quoted in Sarah Miles, The Price We Pay for a Specialized Society:

(Challenges appealed to High Court), the taxpayer or the IR may appeal the decision of the TRA to the High Court only on issues concerning propositions of law cases or cases where the disputed tax amount is relatively large, so those disputes that do not come under those cases cannot be contested in the High Court.[184]

Figure 4.13 Changes in the Number of Court Judgments on Tax Cases and the Rate of Upholding Re/assessments

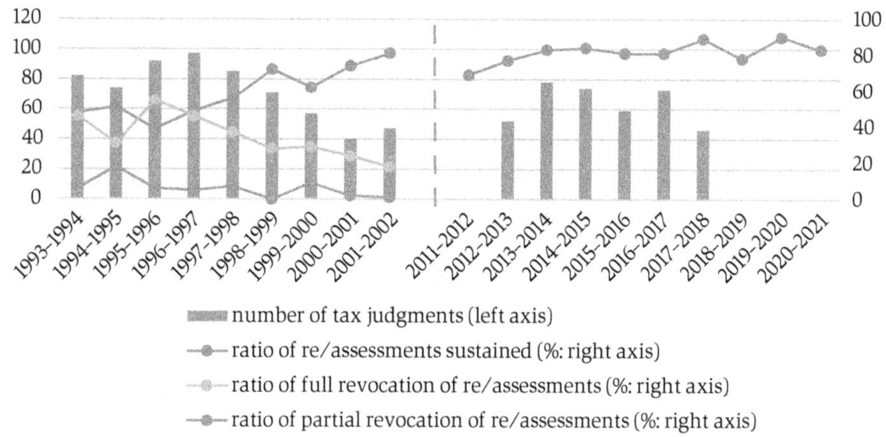

Source: Prepared from IR 2012-2021 Annual Reports, Output 5.2 Litigation Management, and Figure 1 in 2003 Publication (Resolving tax disputes: a legislative review) by the Minister of Finance.

Figures 4.12 and 4.13, even if they are not comprehensive, give a rough estimate of the recent annual number of tax cases brought to the TRA and the courts (High Court, Court of Appeal, Supreme Court), and there seem to have been more taxpayers who prefer appeals to the High Court to objections to the TRA even though at the TRA, the fee is only NZD 410; hearings in camera could be possible; and there is no application of the "loser pays rule" while at the High Court, the fee is NZD 1,350 in principle and hearings are held in public.[185] Some point out that the reasons for such taxpayers' preference might include the following: (i) since tax experts have conducted sufficient reviews at the stage of objections to the IR, some believe that it would be more meaningful to have a judge who is not a tax expert examine the case from a

Do Tax Disputes Require Greater Judicial Specialization?, *Victoria University of Wellington Law Review*, Vol. 46 (2015) DOI: 10.26686/vuwlr.v46i2.4922. *See* pp. 376-377.

184. TRA Act §26 states, "(1) The determination of an Authority on any objection shall be subject to appeal to the High Court in any case where, ... (a) the amount of tax involved in the appeal to the High Court is NZ$2,000 or more; or ... (c) the amount of loss involved in the appeal to the High Court is $4,000 or more; or (d) the appeal relates to questions of law only,—but shall be final and conclusive in all other cases."

185. The population of NZ was 5 million in 2020 (approximately 5% of Japan's population), but the annual number of tax litigations at court is 50-90 (while the ratio of disputes against the number of examinations is not so high as footnote 164 suggests), compared to Japan's 150-350 (*see* Figure 1.8 in Chapter 1).

different perspective in the High Court; (ii) the days needed for the judgment at the High Court are generally shorter than at the TRA;[186] (iii) the High Court has a wide range of authority on the taxpayer's recovery of costs.[187]

3 Commissioner's Discretionary Powers

(1) Changes in Her Stance

As mentioned above, recently "in-house facilitation" has been actively utilized as a form of ADR in resolving tax disputes. Whereas, in the past, there was some debate as to whether or not the IR Commissioner could settle disputes by agreements with taxpayers. For example, in *Brierley Investments Ltd v. CIR* ([1993] 18 TRNZ 1), the Court of Appeal dismissed the appellant's claim that the IR's 1989 notification of its intention of examining the taxpayer's capital/income and interest deductibility in years before 1990 should violate the formulae agreed by the IR and relied upon by the appellant. In particular, Judge Richardson stated, "there is nothing in the NZ legislation to justify the conclusion that the commissioner may elect not to assess taxpayers or may elect to charge them with less tax." Judge Casey also did agree with the judgment of dismissing the appeal but mentioned that the Commissioner's decision to act inconsistently with a taxpayer's legitimate expectation could amount to an abuse of power and also intimated that there is no essential distinction between his obligations and those of the UK's Tax Commissioners that are specifically charged with the care and management of the taxes.

As mentioned above, there used to be different views on whether the IR Commissioner could settle disputes flexibly. But lately, Judge Casey's view expressed in the above *Brierley Investments* case (1993) has gradually become dominant. In particular, a report released in 1993 by the Valabh Committee took a position to assert that obliging the IR Commissioner to assess and recover all taxes that are due is unrealistic and stressed in section 9.4.2 of the report that there should be legislative recognition of the Commissioner's managerial discretion. Also, a report released in 1994 by the Organizational Review Committee (ORC) recommended that, now that a general expectation is that the IR will collect the most revenue that it can within certain limitations, there should be an explicit recognition of its managerial discretion. In light of such assertion, recommendation, etc., TAA §6A (Commissioner's duty of care and management) (2), which was newly introduced in 1995, dictates, "The commissioner is charged with the care and management of the taxes covered by the Inland Revenue Acts and with such other functions as may be conferred on the Commissioner."

186. *See* Miles, *supra* "The Price We Pay for a Specialized Society?" pp. 373-379. The abovementioned 1994 IT Act §136 (17) which provides for courts' substitution of the Commissioner's discretion in the case of direct appeals to the courts may also be one of the incentives for skipping the objection filing with the TRA.
187. The TRA's orders on recovery of expenses which could be given in accordance with the TRA Act §22 (Power to order costs in certain cases) and TRA Act §22B (Power to order costs for filing fees) are only limited to the fees, etc.

Moreover, TAA §6A(3) prescribes, "In collecting the taxes committed to the Commissioner's charge, and despite anything in the Inland Revenue Acts, it is the duty of the Commissioner to collect over time the highest net revenue that is practicable within the law having regard to—(a) the resources available to the Commissioner; and (b) the importance of promoting compliance, especially voluntary compliance, by all persons with the Inland Revenue Acts; and (c) the compliance costs incurred by persons." However, even after these legislative actions were taken, the IR did not seem to believe for some time that it had the authority to agree with taxpayers to settle tax disputes. It is pointed out that one of the reasons for this is that the wide discretionary powers of the Commissioner under TAA §6A might give rise to taxation outside the framework of the law.[188] For example, the IR SPS (INV-350 Finalizing Agreements in Tax Investigations Standard Practice Statement), which was published in August 1998, acknowledged that there are cases where the IR could negotiate with the taxpayers on such matters as the valuation of assets and the determination of arm's length prices, etc., but they are exceptions rather than the rule.

Indeed, the above SPS cautioned as follows, "As the Commissioner is under a statutory obligation to assess and collect the correct amount of tax, it is inappropriate that the risks of litigation be factored into the final agreement. While litigation risk is an appropriate consideration in terms of commercial agreements, it is not appropriate in the context of finalizing an agreement of taxation disputes. If the law is uncertain and there is only a 50/50 chance of the Courts taking one view or the other, it is not possible to simply give a taxpayer one-half of the advantage or disadvantage in recognition of the uncertainty. Agreements are based on the same statutory criteria as those for making other assessments. ... There are circumstances or situations where Inland Revenue will not enter into negotiations. These are: not assessing a clearly assessable amount, or allowing a deduction, rebate, or credit that is clearly not allowable where Inland Revenue's view of the law on a particular issue is firm (e.g., as stated through the Courts or Inland Revenue's legal opinion is in agreement with the treatment of the issue) and this view is supported by the evidence; penalties and/or prosecution action; where an adjustment can be made only on an all or nothing basis."

Recent judgments of the courts have come to show more positive views on the Commissioner's discretionary power in dispute settlements. For example, in *Auckland Gas Co Ltd v. CIR* ([1999] 2 NZLR 409), the Court of Appeal held, "Both the taxpayer and the Commissioner operating under the care and management responsibilities imposed by ss 6 and 6A are entitled to make sensible litigation, including settlement, decisions. We do not endorse the restricted view of the Commissioner's ability to settle a taxation dispute." Also, in *Attorney-General v. Steelfort Engineering Co Ltd* ([1999] 1 NZCC 61030), the Court of Appeal stated, "in exercise of a managerial discretion, the Commissioner now has a broad power to enter into a compromise where that course is consistent with his duty under ss 6 and 6A (TAA 1994)." Furthermore, in Accent

188. http://www.mikelennard.com/?t=48.

Management Ltd v. CIR ([2005] 22 NZTC 19027), the High Court referred to the above two judgments and ruled in paragraph 73;" "In light of the strong dicta of the Court of Appeal in both of those cases I accept...that in tax litigation,...the Commissioner is entitled, during the course of litigation, to take account of factors including litigation risk and cost to reach a settlement with one or more taxpayers." These rulings must have worked towards making more proactive the IR Commissioner's stance on the settlement of disputes by agreements.[189]

In fact, in recent years, there has been a larger number of settlements of tax disputes by agreements. This is evident even from the above *Accent Management* case (2005), in which it was revealed that when Mr. Lennard was head of the Litigation Division of the IR, following the above *Auckland Gas* case, less than one-third of those cases commenced in the TRA or the High Court has been resolved by its decisions or judgments while, of the remaining two-thirds, the majority involved settlement on a compromise basis rather than either the taxpayer or the Commissioner conceding the case entirely. In addition, the IR's 2010 Interpretation Statement (IS) 10/07 (Care and management of the taxes covered by the Inland Revenue Acts) also states in paragraph 157 that the Commissioner would decide to settle disputes by agreements by taking account of the following: (i) litigation risks; (ii) resources required to undertake litigation; (iii) the amount the taxpayer would pay if the Commissioner were to settle; (vi) relationships with other similar cases and similarly situated taxpayers; (v) likely effects on taxpayer perceptions of the integrity of the tax system of settling or litigating, etc.

As noted above, recently, the IR Commissioner has taken a more proactive stance toward exercising its discretionary powers to settle disputes by agreements. Quite obviously, there are certain restrictions on such flexible settlements. In this connection, the IR guideline (SPS 15/01: Finalizing agreements in tax investigations) published in 2015 spells out in paragraph 23 cases where they would not be utilized. They include: (i) a case where the IR fails to assess an amount that is clearly assessable; (ii) a case where the agreement would result in treatment contrary to a settled view of the law; (iii) a case where the only consideration is the taxpayer's ability to pay; (iv) all-or-nothing cases. Furthermore, the above SPS 15/01 confirms in paragraph 25, "staff may not impose shortfall penalties of a less culpable category (for example, reducing a penalty for "gross carelessness" to "not taking reasonable care") to persuade a taxpayer to agree to a proposed adjustment on a substantive tax issue. Conversely, staff may not use the potential of increasing the category of shortfall penalty or the likelihood of prosecution action being taken by the Commissioner, as leverage for finalizing tax investigations."

189. Mark Keating and Kirsty Maclaren, The Settlement of Tax Disputes: The Commissioner is Able But Not Willing, *New Zealand Journal of Taxation Law and Policy* Vol. 15, No. 4 (2009), p. 323. As for TAA§6, see the first para of 3(2).

Agreements involving penalties have the above restrictions.[190] Moreover, as shown in Figure 4.14,[191] the breakdown of the shortfall penalties imposed recently reveals that the ratio of them imposed at the standard rate of 20% by TAA §141A (Not taking reasonable care) is less than that imposed at the rate of 40% by TA §141C (Gross carelessness) or that imposed at the rate of 150% by TAA §141E (Evasion or similar act) which shifts the relevant burden of proof to the Commissioner.[192] Even so, the requirements for abatement of penalties are not so strict,[193] and due to the adoption of TAA §141FB (Reduction of penalties for previous behavior),[194] from April 2000 onwards, a shortfall penalty on a taxpayer with a good compliance record, etc., can be reduced by 50%, and it has been applied to many taxpayers.[195] It is quite likely that the variability and uncertainty of penalties whose applicability and applicable rates could

190. However, now that in 2013, there were 5,245 cases that could be subject to the "shortfall penalties," but only 1,736 cases (33%) were actually applied, some pointed out that a penalty is still used as a bargaining tool for reaching an agreement. *See* https://www2.deloitte.com/content/dam/Deloitte/nz/Documents/tax/Tax-alert/2014/tax-alert-december-final-1-2014.pdf. TAA §156 (Mode of recovery of unpaid tax) (1) may have some relevance in this respect because it stipulates, "All unpaid tax shall be recoverable by the Commissioner on behalf of the Crown by suit in the Commissioner's official name." This treatment in the case of unpaid penalties also holds true in Ireland (*see* TCA §1061 in footnote 60 of Chapter 5) while it differs from Japan where both tax arrears and uncollected administrative penalties are subject to the regular collection procedures that could be completed without the intervention of courts (*see* Figure 1.18 in Chapter 1).
191. Lately, as in the case of Australia's behavioral penalties (*see* footnote 135), the largest number of shortfall penalties is GST-related penalties (2,500 to 3,000 each year), followed by penalties related to IT (including withholding tax (Pay-as-you-earn, PAYE) which are 500 to 1,500 in number each year. *See* the 2014 IR Annual Report and Deloitte Tax Alert November 2015 at https://www2.deloitte.com/nz/en/pages/tax-alerts/articles/tax-shortfall-penalties-understanding-the-trends.html.
192. This is similar to the situation in Australia (*see* footnote 135) while it contrasts with Japan's situation. So does TAA §149A (Standard of proof and onus of proof) which states, "(2) The onus of proof in civil proceedings—(a) relating to evasion or similar act to which section 141E applies or to obstruction rests with the Commissioner: (b) relating to any other matter or thing rests with the taxpayer." Although imposed less frequently, shortfall penalties include those imposed at the standard rate of 20% by TAA §41B (Unacceptable tax position) and those imposed at the rate of 100% by TAA §141D (Abusive tax position).
193. Contrary to Japan, exemption from the shortfall penalties is often granted when it is caused by an arithmetical error or mistakes attributable to a tax expert. *See* IR 240 (Taxpayer Obligations, Interest and Penalties, April 2013) pp. 28-29.
194. TAA §141FB dictates, "(1) A shortfall penalty (called the current penalty) for which a taxpayer is liable under section 141E ... (2) ... under any of sections 141A to 141D is reduced, to 50% of the amount that would be payable by the taxpayer in the absence of this section, if the taxpayer is not—(a) convicted of an offence that is a disqualifying offence: (b) liable for another shortfall penalty that is a disqualifying penalty for the purpose of this subsection." IR 240 also states that if the taxpayer has not been subject to the same penalty for four years (the past two years in the case of taxes related to GST), he shall be eligible for a 50% reduction. *See* INV295 and SPS (ED0086: Reduction of shortfall penalties for previous behavior). This treatment is asymmetrical in terms of a taxpayer's burden to that under Articles 66(4) and 68(4) of AGRNT in Japan (*see* 2(3) in Section 3 of Chapter 1).
195. The number of cases to which the TAA §141FB was applied to reduce the shortfall penalties by 50% was 97.4% in FY2020 and 97.3% in FY2021. *See* the IR Publication (Application of shortfall penalties under the Tax Administration Act 1994 for the year ended 30 June 2021 Table 5).

differ due to various factors have a strong effect on increasing the number of disputes over penalties.

Figure 4.14 Number of Shortfall Penalties Imposed, Etc.

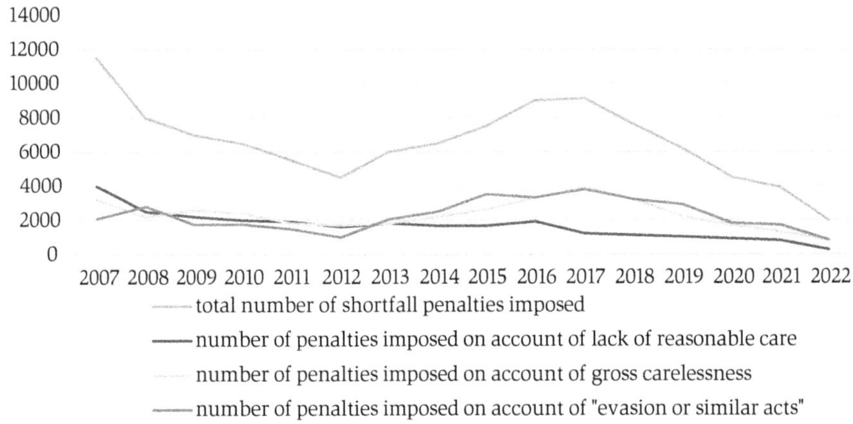

Source: IR publication ("Shortfall penalty impositions 2007 to 2016"), IR publication ("Application of shortfall penalties under the Tax Administration Act 1994 for the year ended 30 June 2021"), https://www2.deloitte.com/nz/en/pages/tax-alerts/articles/trends-in-shortfall-penalties.html, and https://www.deloitte.com/nz/en/services/tax/research/november-2023-reductions-in-shortfall-penalties.html.

(2) Its Nature and Current Status

TAA §6 (Responsibility of Ministers and officials to protect the integrity of the tax system) stipulates, "(1) Every Minister and every officer of any government agency having responsibilities under this Act...must at all times use their best endeavors to protect the integrity of the tax system." (2)...the integrity of the tax system includes—...(b) the rights of persons to have their liability determined fairly, impartially, and according to law." TAA §176 (Recovery of tax by Commissioner) (1) states, "The Commissioner must maximize the recovery of outstanding tax from a taxpayer." In *Raynel & Anor v. CIR* ([2004] 21 NZTC 18583), the High Court clarified the interrelationship of these provisions. In this case, the plaintiff claimed that it went bankrupt and could not pay the tax because of the Commissioner's rejection of the installment payment proposal, and it violated TAA §176. But the Court dismissed his claim and held that TAA §6A(3), which provides for the Commissioner's duty to collect the highest net value of the tax,[196] is not absolute and TAA §6 and §6A can override the obligation to maximize the recovery of outstanding tax prescribed under TAA §176

196. As for TAA §6A(3), *see* 3(1) of this section.

which differs from TAA §6A(3) which contains the phrase "despite anything in the Inland Revenue Acts."

In *Michael Hill Finance (NZ) Ltd. v. CIR* ([2016] NZCA 276), the Court of Appeal explained more in detail the nature and supremacy of TAA §6, which was confirmed by the above *Raynel* case (2004).[197] In this case, the appellant asserted that the ruling issued by the Commissioner on it was inconsistent with his earlier assessment of not taxing another taxpayer that entered into a similar transaction, and such inconsistency breached his duty under TAA §6 and TAA §6A. But the Court of Appeal specified that the Commissioner's responsibility under TAA §6(1) to protect the integrity of the tax system is not of an absolute nature, and the aspirational nature of this provision reflects Parliament's recognition of the limitations imposed on the commissioner and those limitations may well result in a degree of inconsistency among taxpayers, viewed at any point in time. Then, the Court confirmed that TAA §6 and TAA §6A do not grant taxpayers specific rights to seek remedies by stating, "a duty of consistency of taxation treatment or interpretation, if it exists, is owed to the public at large....An individual taxpayer does not acquire a correlative right of action for breach," and it dismissed the appellant's assertion.[198]

As is evident from the above, there is some opacity in the Commissioner's discretionary powers under TAA §6 and TAA §6A, while there are many other provisions that also impress the width of these discretionary powers.[199] TAA §113 (Commissioner may at any time amend assessments) is one of those provisions. This provision is relevant in such a case where a taxpayer has to make a "TAA §113 request" because he either overstated his tax due and the overstatement could not be adjusted in the next tax period owing to its amount exceeding NZD 500 or the requirement for filing an objection to the IR would not be met owing to the taxpayer's delayed discovery of the overstatement.[200] The Commissioner's response to such request is based on its care and management function, and it is to be constrained by the available resources. Such being the case, there are cases where no investigation needed to ascertain the validity of the request might be made because they are not such simple cases as the overstatement being attributable to miscalculations of tax amount but complex cases

197. Some point out that, when there are multiple correct answers in terms of taxation, the highest priority should be given to fairness and equity rather than maximizing revenue, and, as for the relationship between TAA §6 and TAA §6A, legislative action should be taken to spell out that the former takes precedence over the latter. *See* Adele Issacs, "Making Dollars, Not Sense: The Tax Administration Act's Requirement for Impartial Partiality" (2018) at https://www.otago.ac.nz/law/otago710989.pdf.
198. For main points of this judgment, *see* IR's Tax Information Bulletin, Vol. 28, No. 7 (August 2016) pp. 48-50.
199. For example, 1976 ITA, which was repealed by 1994 ITA, contained more than 500 provisions allowing the Commissioner to exercise discretionary powers, increasing the complexity and uncertainty of tax treatment. *See* PL Reddy, Objecting to Discretionary Determinations by the Commissioner of Inland Revenue, *Victoria University of Wellington Law Review* (1981) pp. 126-127.
200. *See* IR's SPS 20/03 and https://www2.deloitte.com/nz/en/pages/tax-alerts/articles/amending-return-errors-taxpayer-friendly-high-court-ruling.html. This roughly corresponds to Japan's procedures on the refund request and the adjustment in the ongoing year on items to be corrected for tax purposes. *See* 2(1) in Section 3 of Chapter 1.

where costs and resources involved in determining the validity of the request would become excessive even with the taxpayer's submission of relevant materials.[201]

The width of the discretionary power of the Commissioner under TAA §6A is further implied by TAA §109, which is, as mentioned in 2 of this section, an "ouster provision" precluding dispute resolution procedures other than those prescribed under TAA Part IVA, Part VIII and Part VIIIA.[202] This point is well illustrated by *Westpac Banking Corp. v. CIR* ([2009] NZCA 24). In this case, the appellant/taxpayer asserted that the tax re/assessment applying the anti-avoidance rule on the structured finance transaction utilized by the appellant should be revoked because it is inconsistent with the binding ruling the appellant had received from IR and against the "legitimate expectation" of the appellant. But the Court of Appeal held that breach of "legitimate expectation" does not provide a basis for judicial review[203] and that the correct interpretation of TAA §109 and TAA §114 (Validity of assessments) leads it to the conclusion that the judicial review is not available because this case does not come under those cases where there is practically no assessment or the re/assessment is conscious maladministration referred to in Australia's *Futuris* case (2008).[204]

Moreover, in *Tannadyce Investments Ltd. v. CIR* ([2011] NZSC 158), the Supreme Court presented a view that further narrows down the scope of judicial review of the Commissioner's exercise of discretion. In this case, the appellant filed a lawsuit for judicial review without resorting to the legal proceedings stipulated in TAA Part VIIIA, but the Court held that the appellant's assertion of the IR not returning back to it a part of the documents related to its filing of the return does not justify its inability or failure to comply with the proceedings under TAA Part VIIIA. Also, the Court pointed out that, despite the similarity of Australia's ITAA §175 and NZ's TAA §109,[205] they are different in that the latter is clearly designed to oust the jurisprudence of courts generally other than in proceedings brought under Part VIIIA so that the *Futuris* case (2008) which was confirmed by the above *Westpac Banking* case (2009) is not a sound basis on which to determine the correct construction and application of NZ's TAA §109 because allowing for an unwritten "exceptional circumstances" or "proper grounds" escape from s 109

201. The Commissioner's refusal of a "TAA §113 request" is, under TAA §138E (Certain rights of challenge not conferred) (1)(e)(iv), not subject to the objection by the taxpayer but may be subject to review in court. In *Westpac Securities NZ Ltd v. CIR* ([2014] NZHC 3377), the High Court implied that the Commissioner, in response to the "TAA §113 request," could exercise his discretion in granting relief to the taxpayer with a "regretted choice" over its failure to apply for foreign tax credits in its original return. A "regretted choice" is hardly allowed in Japan. *See* footnote 88 of Chapter 1.

202. *See* 2 in Section 2 of this chapter for TAA §109.

203. While, in EU countries, a taxpayer's "legitimate expectation" is strongly protected. *See* 1(1) in Section 2 of Chapter 5.

204. As for TAA §114 stipulating that the Commissioner's assessment shall not be nullified by its failure to comply with other provisions, *see* third paragraph in 2 of Section 2. This provision was repealed by the Taxation (Venture Capital and Miscellaneous Provisions) Act 2004 §119 which prescribes similarly. As for the status of judicial review in Australia and the High Court judgment in the *Futuris* case (2008), *see* 3(2) in Section 1.

205. *See* 4 in Section 1 for Australia's ITAA §175.

would not be consistent with the purpose which Parliament was trying to achieve in what it enacted.[206]

Now that the scope of judicial review on the Commissioner's discretionary power is quite limited,[207] it becomes more important for taxpayers to resolve disputes through the standard procedures without expecting much out of judicial reviews on nonsubstantive issues. As for the taxpayers in the above *Westpac Banking* case (2009) and three other financial institutions that utilized the tax avoidance scheme, they litigated respectively at the High Court (*BNZ v. CIR* ([2000] 19 NZTC 15.732), *ASB Bank Ltd v. CIR* ([2014] 26 NZTC 21,106), *ANZ National Bank and Ors v. CIR* ([2008] 23 NZTC 21,918)), and moved to reach an agreement with the IR. The agreement set the total tax payment (including interest but not penalties) at approximately NZD 2.2 billion (of which, in the case of Westpac, which lost the case in the High Court judgment above, the agreed amount of payment was approximately NZD 900 million, or about 80% of the disputed tax amount).[208] The related costs incurred by the IR in connection with the lawsuits against these four taxpayers were about NZD 40 million.[209] It seems that TAA §109 has the effect of reducing the number of disputes as well as increasing the number of dispute resolutions by agreement.

4 Rules on Costs

It is obvious from the High Court Rules §47 (Costs to follow event) that NZ courts, prior to its amendment in 2000, in principle, have adopted the "English rule" as a rule for the payment of attorney's fees, etc. Nevertheless, the High Court Rules §46 (Court's overriding discretion), before it was amended, provided that, in subsection (1), all matters relating to the payment of litigation-related costs shall be determined by the court's discretion, unless expressly provided for by statute; in paragraph (2), the court shall exercise its discretionary power and not order the losing party to bear attorney's fees (referred to "Costs lie where they fall"), or that the winning party's attorney's fees, etc., could be ordered to be split between the litigant parties, and such an order was actually issued on and off. Now that Figure 4.6 indicates the taxpayers' success rates in tax litigation have been on the decline from 1993 to 2001, such flexible application of

206. Before the enactment of the TAA §109, there was 1976 ITA §36 as the ouster provision under which the scope of judicial review was wider but the number of disputes over its application was small compared with that in Australia. *See* Reddy, *supra* "Objecting to Discretionary Determinations," pp. 150-151.
207. In light of these court cases on the issue of judicial review, some point out that there is no possibility of success for taxpayers seeking judicial review of the procedures as an incidental point of dispute over the re/assessment. *See* https://mikelennard.com/2009/07/28/judicial-review-no-thanks-july-2009/.
208. https://www.scoop.co.nzlstories/BU0912/S00597/resolution-to-nz-structured-finance litigat ion.htm.
209. *See* Adrian Sawyer, New Zealand Settles Disputes with Australian Banks, *Tax Notes International*, Vol. No. (2010) pp. 311-314 and Adrian Sawyer, A Further Bank Tax Dispute Is Settled: A Recurrent Alternative to Litigation, *Journal of International Banking Law & Regulation*, Vol. 31, No. 3 (2016), pp. 136-138.

the "English rule" must have reduced the financial burden of some taxpayers who lost their tax cases in courts.

As mentioned above, although there has been some uncertainty in NZ in the application of the "English rule" in lawsuits, after the 2000 revision, the High Court Rules §14.2 (Principles applying to determination of costs) (1) stipulates, "The following general principles apply to the determination of costs: (a) the party who fails concerning a proceeding or an interlocutory application should pay the cost to the party who succeeds: So, there is no question about which cost rule is adopted. More specifically, the High Court Rule 14.2(1) prescribes further that: (b) an award of costs should reflect the complexity and significance of the proceeding: (c) costs should be assessed by applying the appropriate daily recovery rate to the time considered reasonable for each step reasonably required in relation to the proceeding or interlocutory application: (d) an appropriate daily recovery rate should normally be two-thirds of the daily rate considered reasonable in relation to the proceeding or interlocutory application: (e) what is an appropriate recovery rate...should not depend on ...the time actually spent by the solicitor....: (g) so far as possible the determination of costs should be predictable and expeditious."

Even so, there were some differences in the actual application of the "English rule" under the post-2000 High Court Rules §14.2 and the abovementioned pre-2000 High Court Rules §46. These differences are well illustrated by the High Court judgment in *Nonomi Holdings Ltd v. Elders Pastoral Holdings Ltd* ([2001] 15 PRNZ 155 (HC)). In this judgment, Judge Chambers stated that under the old costs rule, it was customary for the winning party to notify the court of the actual costs for their recovery. However, under the High Court Rule §14.2, as amended in 2000, consideration of litigants' actual costs is contrary to the principle set out in paragraph (e), and the costs to be recoverable should be predictable and expeditious as paragraph (g) dictates so that such notification is no longer necessary and it is rather inappropriate for lawyers to continue to provide information that is irrelevant to determining the amount of recoverable costs. Paragraph 3.43 of the NZ Law Society's 2020 Submissions to Rules Committee Consultation Paper also states that, compared with the costs rule of other countries, the correlation between the amount of costs incurred by the winning party and its recoverable amount of costs is weak in the case of the costs rule in NZ.[210]

The fact that there is little correlation between the amount of costs that the winning party can recover and the amount of the actual costs suggests that the former is likely to be considerably less than the latter. Actually, there are cases where the amount of costs recovered by the winning party turned out to be quite small. It is pointed out that the substance of such NZ's rule on costs is the "reasonable contribution" rule or the "notional model" rule and is positioned in between the UK's "full cost" rule and the US's "no cost" rule.[211] Also, the "loser pays rule" applicable in the case of

210. *See* https://www.lawsociety.org.nz/news/legal-news/modernising-costs-regime/. This Submissions was made in response to the document issued in May 2020 by the Rules Committee referred to in footnote 211. The statutes governing the establishment of the "Rules Committee" are the Judicature Act 1908 §51B and the Senior Courts Act 2016 §155 (Rules Committee).

211. *See* para. 3.2 of NZ Law Society's 2020 Submissions to Rules Committee Consultation Paper above.

a successful litigant in person in NZ and in the UK where the 1975 Act (Litigants in Person (Costs and Expenses) Act 1975) has been adopted is also different because in NZ, in principle, the "primary rule" is applicable so that a litigant in person winning in court can recover the relevant disbursements but not costs or attorney's fees. In this sense, the rule on costs applicable in the case of a successful litigant in NZ is similar to that in Australia, referred to in 4(1) in Section 1.[212]

Indeed, in *Joint Action Funding Limited v. John Revans Eichelbaum* ([2017] NZCA 249), the Court of Appeal stated in paragraphs 56 to 58: "if the Chorley exception is to be observed...the advantage of the new regime will be lost ... In each case involving a lawyer-litigant an inquiry would need to be undertaken either as to the extent of the litigant conduct for which the lawyer should be compensated or in the assessment of the time expended as a measure of the lawyer's opportunity cost ... The fact that such an exercise must be undertaken dilutes the predictability and expedition in the costs determination and hence tends to undermine the objective in r.14.2(g) ... Consequently we conclude that the lawyer-litigant exception should no longer apply in New Zealand." Whereas in *Jeremy James McGuire v. Secretary for Justice* ([2018] NZSC 116), the Supreme Court ruled that the *Joint Action Funding* case (2017) was wrongly decided, but if there is to be reform to the law, it could be done by the legislature.[213] In response to this Supreme Court's ruling, the Rules Committee issued in May 2020 a consultation document ("Costs for Litigants in Person") to ask whether exceptions to the "primary rule" should be allowed in the future.[214]

As mentioned above, changes in the "English rule" have also occurred in NZ, but they are more pronounced in the UK. In addition, in the case of NZ, if an objection or an appeal is filed, the collection procedure is, in principle, suspended until a decision or judgment is made,[215] while the high interest rate (8.22 % per annum) on the unpaid amount continues to arise. Therefore, the problem remains that taxpayers who dispute their cases without paying (or without the means to pay) the full amount of the disputed tax could end up bearing a considerable burden. As a response to this problem, in 2018, the IR introduced the tax pool intermediaries system. Under this system, an authorized private body (Tax Management NZ, etc.) can pool and use the interest on refunds from overpaid taxpayers in order to make low-interest loans to

212. While Canada has departed from the "primary rule" as it was ruled by the British Columbia District Court of Appeal judgment in *Skidmore v. Blackmore* ([1995] 122 DLR (4th) 330) as follows, "There are good reasons for allowing self-represented lay litigants to receive the benefit of recent developments in the law of costs. There is no logical reason for allowing a self-represented solicitor to claim costs under Appendix B of the Supreme Court Rules, while denying the same to a self-represented lay litigant."
213. Negative views on the "Chorley exception" and its extended application to litigants in person are also shown in the *Cachia* case (1994) and the *Pentelow* case (2019) in Australia, but there are moves lately for its extended application. *See* 4(3) in Section 1.
214. On this document, the NZ Law Society issued a document (*see* footnote 211) with opinions which either abandon the "primary rule" or keep a part of it (i.e., not allowing the recovery of costs in the case of a lawyer litigant in person).
215. This differs from the treatment under Japan's AGRNT §105 (*see* second paragraph in 3(1) in Section 3 in Chapter 1) and UK's TMA §55 (*see* footnote 61 in Chapter 3) but is more or less the same as US's IRC §6330(e) (*see* footnotes 6 and 165 in Chapter 2) and that in Ireland (*see* 1(1) in Section 1 of Chapter 5).

underpaid taxpayers. Although the use of this system may alleviate the financial burden on some taxpayers, which becomes heavier with the protraction of dispute resolution, it is a far cry from being a panacea for all.

SECTION 3 SUMMARY AND ANALYSIS

1 Summary and Analysis of Section 1

In Australia, the 2012 IGT Report pointed out that the objections to the ATO had problems in terms of the review organ's independence, neutrality and flexibility. However, such problems were mitigated because (i) since 2013, senior officials in the Review and Dispute Resolution Business Line have conducted "independent reviews" of large business taxpayers prior to the conclusion of the ATO's examinations, and its scope has lately been expanded to cover some "small business taxpayers"; (ii) since 2014, "in-house facilitation" in which a trained ATO official mediates for dispute resolution has become available to nonbusiness individuals and small businesses; (iii) the ATO's recent placement of emphasis on disputes resolution at an earlier stage of disputes has attained some success. At the same time, the ratio of re/assessments canceled at the objection stage has gone up lately. It remains true that the level of independence and neutrality of the review organ in the ATO and the ratio of settlements by agreements are not as high as those of the Independent Office of Appeals in the IRS, and the number of agreed settlements has shown a declining trend since 2010-2011.

Certainly, the ATO's Code of Settlement Practice gives the impression that the scope of tax dispute resolution by agreement is not narrow, but the ATO's stance on the resolution of tax disputes by agreement may not, as pointed out in paragraphs 5.7 and 5.8 of the IGT 2012 Report, be so proactive as it could be. Behind this, there lies a fact that not only the number of agreements as well as the amount/percentage reduced by the agreements against the concerned re/assessments is made public, but also large-scale agreements are subject to audits under an "Independent Assurance of Settlements Program" from 2016 onwards. While it is true that publicizing such information is a useful measure to dispel public suspicions about the fairness of taxation and secure trust in tax administration and paragraph 3.51 of the 2018 IGT Report also stresses that the transparency of tax dispute resolution by agreement in Australia is higher than that in any country. However, this high level of transparency might make the ATO hesitate in settling disputes by agreements in some cases, with the result that some taxpayers might incur larger amounts of costs in money, time, and compliance with objections/appeals procedures.

Nonetheless, the burden of those taxpayers who have not received favorable decisions or have not reached a settlement by an agreement at the objection stage may not become too heavy mainly by the following rules and practices at the AAT. In particular, (i) the AAT judges' expertise, neutrality, and independence are high; (ii) cases involving disputed tax amounts of less than AUD 5,000 can be quickly resolved by the AAT's Small Business Taxation Division with a small fee (AUD 95); (iii) it is not uncommon for an aggrieved taxpayer not to have an agent in the AAT's proceedings; (iv) decisions based on the Commissioner's wide discretionary power could be substituted by the AAT's merit review conducted by the reviewers standing in the shoes of the Commissioner, and there are actually many cases of such substitution of the decisions; (v) there is no application of the "loser pays rule," but the fee to the ATT could be repaid when the AAT's decision or the result of the settlement is favorable to the taxpayer. Furthermore, the ratio of the disputed reassessments canceled in whole or in part by the AAT's decisions has been quite high.

Indeed, the ATO can dispute the validity of the AAT decisions in court, and if the taxpayer loses his case in court, he will be ordered to pay the litigation costs of the ATO in principle. However, a taxpayer's risk and burden of payment of the ATO's litigation costs can be reduced in such cases: (i) if a disputed case is subject to the "test case litigation program" due to its importance, etc., the ATO will bear some or all of the litigation-related costs of the taxpayer; (ii) when the ATO seeks the assistance of outside legal experts due to the importance or complexity of a disputed case, the ATO will take a step to ensure that the "small business" disputant can obtain similar assistance. (iii) there are cases where legal aid is provided by the "Legal Aid Commission"; (iv) a "Calderbank offer" is also available in Australia, so that, in a case where the ATO does not accept the dispute resolution offer proposed by the taxpayer without reasonable grounds and the court's judgment is more favorable to the taxpayer than the offer, the court will order the ATO to pay the taxpayer's costs in accordance with the indemnity basis.

Among various types of tax disputes, penalty cases are a highly disputed theme in Australia as well. The reason for this is that, as in the case of the UK, Australia has tax systems containing "behavioral penalties" which have not a little uncertainty and variability in their application and the number of their applications and full or partial revocations, especially at the objections stage, are quite large. There are also a large number of disputes over the Commissioner's rejection of taxpayers' requests for deadline extensions because there are not only many tax provisions setting deadlines that are subject to the extension by the Commissioner's discretionary power but also many Commissioner's decisions on them that are substituted or revoked by the AAT and courts. Above all, in the *Hunter* case (1984), the Federal Court held that various factors have to be taken into consideration in determining whether or not a request for a deadline extension should be allowed, but it is essential to attach greater importance to the substance (rationality of a taxpayer's allegations on the substantive issues) of the requests rather than their formalities.

2 Summary and Analysis of Section 2

Some of the problems related to the independence and efficiency of tax proceedings that existed in the NZ tax objection system before the 1996 revision were mitigated by the IR's recent moves and the new measures adopted under the revised system. They include: (i) the rule of "disclose all the cards on the table" and the evidence exclusion rule at the objection stage has been adopted and it has reduced the number of disputes brought to the TRA and courts; (ii) the IR's stance on disputes settlement by agreements has become more proactive, (iii) since April 2010, the "in-house facilitation" has become available as a form of ADR. But there are some who stress the need for further reform by pointing out remaining problems including: ① The limited publication of TRA decisions aggravates the problem of lack of predictability on taxation; ② Taxpayers' time costs and clerical costs related to the procedures at the objection stage have actually become heavier as a whole despite the adoption of the 2011 Taxation Act which limits the scope of the evidence exclusion rule; ③ Most of the DRU's decisions are in favor of the IR, and taxpayers' time and money costs involved in continuing their disputes tend to become considerable.

Indeed, it still remains true that, compared with US, UK, and Australia, the ratio of settlements of disputes by agreement and the ratio of the tax authority's decisions on the objections in favor of the taxpayers is much lower in NZ. In particular, the view expressed in IR SPS is quite restrained in utilizing settlement by agreement. As for those aggrieved taxpayers who could not receive favorable results at the stage of objections to the IR, they may have to consider the next dispute stage, and many of them prefer courts to the TRA in spite of the fact that the application fee is higher in court. This is in contrast to the case in Australia, where the AAT is preferred over the courts more often. This is partially because, at the stage of objections to the IR, under the rule of disclosing all the cards on the table and the evidence exclusion rule, generally, a thorough review is to be made, and this may prompt those taxpayers who place a priority on the reduction of costs by skipping additional time and expenses that might otherwise arise in the case of them going through the review at the TRA where no ADR is employed, and it is presumed that the ratio of its decision favorable to them is not particularly high compared to that in courts.[216]

Filing objections with the TRA does have some merits. For example, if the parties to the dispute agree, they can have the TRA decisions which are based solely on the review of the written submissions with no hearings. Furthermore, there must have been cases where the fact that the TRA decisions on cases disputing no more than NZD 2,000 (or those cases disputed at the "Small claims jurisdiction" of the TRA before it was abolished by the 2011 Taxation Act) or not hinging on a matter of law were not appealable to the High Court under TRA Act §26 is/was a merit for some taxpayers. On the other hand, in the case of the High Court, in addition to the merit of being able to expect flexible and early resolution of disputes, it has the authority, which is not granted to the TRA, to order the IR Commissioner to submit detailed grounds and evidence for the re/assessment in question. Such authority of the court could be a very important point for some disputing taxpayers in formulating their litigation strategies. It is pointed out that these could also constitute the main reasons for some taxpayers to prefer disputes at court as a form for resolving their tax disputes.[217]

Nevertheless, the number of cases brought to courts has not been so large. This is partly because attorney's fees and interest rates on unpaid disputed tax are high, and

216. *See* https://home.kpmg/nz/en/home/insights/2018/08/the-secret-to-winning-tax-disputes-.html.

217. *See* Reddy, *supra* "Objecting to discretionary determinations" pp. 128-129.

the NZ courts have limited power to review the appropriateness of the IR Commissioner's exercise of discretion (even if ITA §136 provides for an exception to the review of objections referred directly to the High Court).[218] The latter point has a lot to do with the fact that TAA §109 is a more powerful ouster provision than Australia's ITAA §175, as it is confirmed by the *Westpac Banking* case (2009) in which the Court of Appeal held that contrary to the *Futuris* case (2008) in Australia, such an exceptional case as the Commissioner's conscious maladministration does not come under judicial review. Another major reason for the relative scarcity in the number of tax cases at court should be found in the fact that the "loser pays rule" adopted in NZ is the "primary rule" under which a successful litigant in person could recover his disbursements but not costs because the "Chorley exception" available in the UK may not be applicable to a lawyer in NZ.[219] Those reasons should work towards deterring some aggrieved taxpayers from bringing their cases to court.

NZ is similar to Australia and the UK in that a penalty case stands out as a very highly disputed theme partially because it contains a "behavioral penalty." Moreover, in NZ, as in the case of Australia, the larger number of shortfall penalties has lately been applied to the more serious category of underreporting resulting from "gross carelessness" and "fraud or similar acts" than that resulting from "lack of reasonable care" (*see* footnote 135 and Figure 4.14), while the majority of them are subject to a 50% reduction since 2000. As for NZ's comprehensive expense deduction requirement (relevance to business) stipulated in the 1994 ITA BD2 (Allowable deductions), it even allows a partial deduction for expenses that are related to both business and private purposes,[220] as it was confirmed by the Court of Appeal judgment in *CIR v. Banks* ([1978] 3 NZTC 671, 236).[221] Therefore, the threshold for an expense deduction under this provision seems to be conceptually and practically lower than that ("wholly and exclusively" standard) in the UK. Despite such a difference, they are similar in that they contain some opacity in their application standards, so there must be not a few disputes over the deductibility of expenses under the standard adopted in the above 1994 ITA BD2, etc.

218. While the 1994 ITA §136(17) authorizes the High Court to make any assessment which the Commissioner was empowered to make at the time the Commissioner made the assessment. *See* footnote 180.
219. *See* the Court of Appeal judgment in *Joint Action Funding* case (2017) at 4 in Section 2.
220. 1994 ITA BD2(1) (Definition) provides, "An amount is an allowable deduction of a taxpayer (a) ... (b) to the extent that it is an expenditure or loss (i) incurred by the taxpayer in deriving the taxpayer's gross income, or (ii) necessarily incurred by the taxpayer in the course of carrying on a business for the purpose of deriving the taxpayer's gross income." Australia's general expense deduction provision is basically the same now that the 1977 ITAA §8-1 (General deductions) stipulates: "(1) You can deduct from your assessable income any loss or outgoing to the extent that: (a) it is incurred in gaining or producing your assessable income; or (b) it is necessarily incurred in carrying on a business for the purpose of gaining or producing your assessable income."
221. In this judgment, the deduction is allowed for the expenses which are related to parts of the home that are also used for business purposes. The Court of Appeal ruled likewise in *Buckley & Young Ltd. v. CIR* ([1978] 3 NZTC 61,271). The IR's publication (Tax Information Bulletin, Vol. 21, No. 3, 2009) gives a guidance on expense deductions for "mixed-use assets."

CHAPTER 5

Status of EU Member States (Ireland and Netherlands)

SECTION 1 TAX DISPUTE IN IRELAND

1 Tax Objection Procedures Before 2016 Revision

Generally, under the old tax appeal system, which existed until March 2016, a taxpayer aggrieved over the notice of assessment or penalty impositions issued to him by the Revenue (Irish Tax and Customs) on IT, CIT, capital gains tax, capital acquisitions tax (including inheritance and gift tax), stamp tax, residential property tax, vehicle registration tax, VAT, etc. should,[1] as Figure 5.1(A) shows, on condition of paying the undisputed amount of tax,[2] file an objection or a complaint to the Revenue in accordance with the "Taxes Consolidation Act (TCA)," and a Local Review is conducted on it. Whereas, if (i) a taxpayer does not apply for a Local Review,[3] (ii) he is aggrieved over a notice of opinion issued by an auditor on the penalty imposition on him before the conclusion of the audit, or (iii) he is aggrieved over the result of the

1. In 2022, Ireland's population was about 5 million, and it is reported that the Revenue conducted about 17,000 tax examinations (about 5% of the number of tax returns) annually. *See* The Law Reform Commission (LRC), "Consultation on a Fiscal Prosecutor and a Revenue Court": LRC CP 24-2003, at https www.lawreform.ie/publications/consultation-paper-published.134.html) p. 37.
2. *See* The Irish Appeals System—The Rules and Procedures Governing Irish Tax Appeals, Irish Taxation Institute (March 2008) p. 56. Also, TCA §957(2)(a) prescribes, "No appeal shall lie against that assessment until such time as—(I) ..., and (II) ... the chargeable person pays or has paid an amount of tax on foot of the assessment which is not less than the tax which would be payable on foot of the assessment if the assessment were made in all respects by reference to the statements and particulars contained in the return delivered by the chargeable person."
3. *See* 4.10.1 (Review Procedures) in 2010 Code of Practice for Revenue Audit. Now CS4 (Revenue Complaint and Revenue Procedures Leaflet) which replaced in 2013 the Statement of Practice (SP-GEN-/2/99) on the Revenue's complaint and review procedures mentions in Appendix A that, as (B) in Figure 5.1 shows, a Local Review must be completed before a request for an Internal/External Review is initiated.

Local Review, he should, within thirty days from the date of the notice, etc., could apply for an "Internal Review" to be conducted by a Revenue official who was not involved in the audit. Moreover, since 1999, it has become possible for him to apply for an "External Review" or a "Joint Review" in which an external tax expert appointed by the Revenue also participates.

Figure 5.1 Tax Objection Procedures

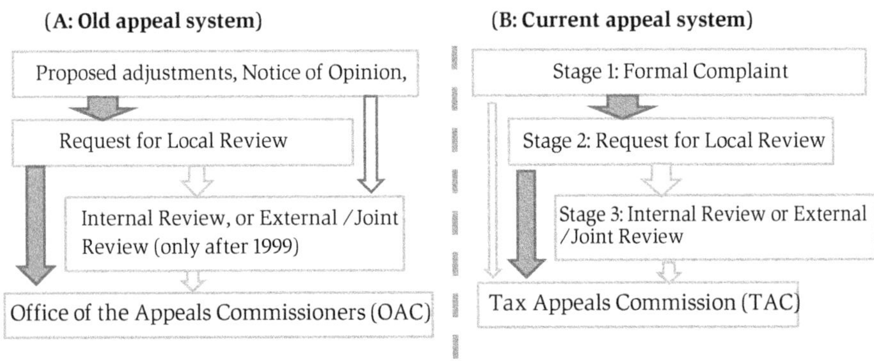

Source: Revenue Complaint and Review Procedures Leaflet-CS4, Revenue Operational Manual 0.0.0 (Tax and Duty Appeals Manual), Appendix I of The Irish Appeals System (2008) by Irish Taxation Institute, etc.

The Revenue's 2015 Tax Complaint and Revenue Procedures Leaflet (CS4) 6. 2 (Decision of Reviewers) spells out that an Internal/External Review is recommended to be conducted within thirty days after receipt of the objection. If the objection cannot be processed within that timeframe, explaining the review status to the taxpayer is customary. As shown in Figure 5.2, the percentage of revision of all or part of the assessments, etc., by Internal/Joint Review has been about 20%, and the majority of aggrieved taxpayers chose Local Reviews rather than Internal/External (Joint) Reviews. In particular, since 2013, Internal/External (Joint) Reviews have been utilized less frequently, and their number was fewer than the number of complaints on tax examinations filed with the Ombudsman, whose function is to report their examination results on those cases requested by taxpayers and make correction requests to the Revenue.[4] Moreover, the majority of applications for Internal/External (Joint) Reviews were not on the substance of the assessment, etc., but on the issue of audit procedures and interest.[5]

4. Moreover, the number of tax complaints received by the Ombudsman, shown in Table 6 of the Ombudsman's annual report, has been somewhat higher than those shown in Figure 5.2 (e.g., 83 in 2021, 99 in 2020, 106 in 2019, and 65 in 2017). Between 1998 and 2001, 80 to 140 complaints were received annually. *See* p. 52 of the 2003 Consultation Document of the Law Reform Commission.
5. For example, about half of forty external reviews conducted in 2006 were on the issue of audit procedures or interest. *See* Irish Tax Review 2008 January by Irish Tax Institute (also at

Figure 5.2 Number of Objections/Complaints Processed by Revenue/Ombudsman and the Ratio of Re/assessments Upheld by Internal/External (Joint) Reviews

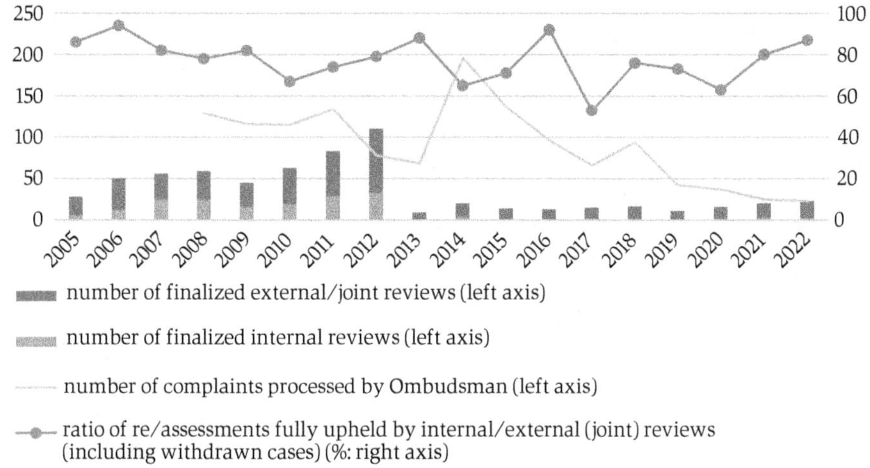

Source: Revenue Annual Reports 2007-2022 Table: Internal & External Reviews, Table: Complaints relating to Revenue completed by the Ombudsman, and Irish Tax Review 2008 January.

When an objection to the Revenue does not resolve the dispute on IT, CIT, etc., basically, the aggrieved taxpayer should, by TCA §933 (Appeals against assessment) or TAC §945 (Appeals against assessments),[6] submit a notice of appeal to the Revenue to appeal to the Office of the Appeal Commissioners (OAC).[7] When the Revenue received the notice of appeal, it sent it and AH1, which explained relevant points on the disputed case to the OAC, and the OAC conveyed to the appellant through the Revenue relevant information on the appeal procedures. The reason for the Revenue receiving the notice of appeal before it goes to the OAC was originally for the Revenue to suspend the collection action on the disputed tax.[8] While, by any chance, if the Revenue refused to accept a notice of appeal,[9] the aggrieved taxpayer could, under TCA §933(1)(c), make an appeal to the OAC within fifteen days from the date of the refusal disputing the

https://www.taxfind.ie/document/ITR_2008_01_XML-c10-3306198725). As for summaries of 2018 internal reviews and external reviews, *see* https://www.revenue.ie/en/corporate/documents/customer-service/summary-of-sample-internal-external-reviews-2018.pdf.

6. TCA §933(1)(a) dictates, "A person aggrieved by any assessment to income tax or corporation tax made on that person by the inspector or such other officer as the Revenue Commissioner appoint in that behalf (...) shall be entitled to appeal to the Appeal Commissioners on giving, within 30 days after the date of the notice of assessment, notice in writing to the inspector or other officer."
7. As for appeals to the OAC on cases on tax items other than IT, CIT, etc., the relevant provisions were the 1972 VATA §25 (Appeals), the 2003 Capital Acquisitions Tax Act §66 (Appeals regarding value of real property) and §67 (Appeals in other cases), etc.
8. *See* Law Reform Commission, 2004 Report, paras. 7.40 and 7.45.
9. A notice of appeal is refused mostly in such cases where it is submitted after the deadline is passed, or the grounds for the appeal are not reasonable. *See* https://www.lexology.com/library/detail.aspx?g=2d595176-87ad-4462-9efa-517e42a1681c.

appropriateness of the Revenue's refusal of accepting the notice of appeal and requesting the listing of the appeal at the OAC.

The OAC members were two accountants from the private sector (Before 1993, members were the Revenue Commissioner, a tax expert, and a lawyer). When their decisions differ, the chairman, who was decided in advance by their agreement, had the final say.[10] The Treasurer appointed them in accordance with TCA §850 (Appeals Commissioners), and they were independent of the Revenue. Indeed, TCA Schedule 27 Volume 1 (Form of declaration to be made by Appeal Commissioners acting in respect of tax under Schedule D) confirmed that the OAC members had a statement of oath declaring their decisions to be fair and neutral.[11] But no legislation spelled out the independence of the OAC and its members. The lack of a high level of independence was implied, as mentioned above, by a notice of appeal being submitted to the OAC through the Revenue. Moreover, basically, only the conclusion of the OAC's decisions made following the result of the hearing in camera was on the form AS1 (which was prepared by the Revenue) and was sent to the appellant. The Revenue also intervened in the listing of the taxpayer's appeal to the Circuit Court.[12]

Taxpayers' concerns about appeals under the OAC were not limited to their lack of independence. For example, when the legality of a notice of assessment is contested in OAC, the primary burden of proof is on the taxpayer under TCA §934 (Procedure on Appeals) (3),[13] and the OAC could even make a decision to increase the assessment amount under TCA §934(5),[14] so an appeal to the OAC had a risk of increasing the taxpayer's tax burden. Also, most taxpayers appointed tax experts as their agents (10%-15% of them were those with legal qualifications, and more than 80% of them were (tax) accountants),[15] so even if the assessment was revoked by the OAC's decision, the cost of the taxpayer for paying the agent could become quite high. Furthermore, reasons for the decisions were given orally to the taxpayer but were neither written in AS1 nor publicized to the public, giving little clue to taxpayers and tax agents in general when they decide whether or not their cases should be appealed to the OAC and how they should dispute them if they decide to do so.[16]

10. Joint review by two members is limited to large-scale cases. *See* the Law Reform Commission, 2003 Consultation Document, p. 98.
11. Taxes stipulated in Schedule D are IT and CIT.
12. For details, *see* LRC's "2003 Consultation Document" pp. 92-93 and the 2004 Report, para. 7.107.
13. TCA §934(3) stipulates, "Where on an appeal it appears to the Appeal Commissioners ... that the appellant is overcharged by any assessment, the Appeal Commissioners shall abate or reduce the assessment accordingly, but otherwise the Appeal Commissioners shall determine the appeal by ordering that the assessment shall stand." The High Court ruled in para. 22 of its judgment in *Menolly Homes Ltd. v. Appeal Commissioners & Revenue Commissioners* ([2010] IEHC 49): "The burden of proof in this appeal process, is as in all taxation appeals, on the taxpayer."
14. TCA §934(5) dictates, "where on an appeal against an assessment appears to the Appeal Commissioners—... (c) that the appellant ought to be charged in an amount exceeding the amount contained in the assessment, they may charge the excess by increasing only the amount which is chargeable to income tax or corporation tax."
15. LRC's "2003 Consultation Document" reports that those appellants with no agents were about 3%, which is very low compared to the ratio at the pre-litigation stage in the U.S. Australia, etc.
16. *See* 2003 Consultation Document of the Law Reform Commission, pp. 100 and 121-125.

The facts mentioned above should discourage taxpayers from filing appeals to the OAC, but in actuality, more than 10,000 appeals (counted on a cumulative basis) were annually filed to the OAC from the 1970s to 1980s, and there was a large backlog of appeals in the OAC,[17] obliging many appellants to wait for their turn of hearings and decisions. But the backlog of appeals gradually became less and it was about 350 at the end of 2001 (about 330 at the end of 2002).[18] The reasons for the decrease in the backlog of appeals included: (i) about 90 % of the listed cases in the OAC were resolved by agreement of the disputing parties before the hearings;[19] (ii) the conditions for appeals to the OAC became stricter due to the 1983 amendment and the introduction of a self-assessment system by the 1988 Finance Act.[20] Even so, the backlog of appeals remained, and it was about 3,000 in 2016. This backlog was particularly problematic when the OAC's decision turned out to be unfavorable to the appellants because advance payment of the disputed tax amount was not a precondition for filing an appeal to the OAC and interest accrual (1 % monthly until 2002, recently 8 % ~ 10 % per annum) fell heavily on the shoulders of some taxpayers.[21]

There were also some rules and facts that were not so favorable to the Revenue. As mentioned above, the Revenue should suspend the collection action on the receipt of the AH1. Also, when the Revenue wants to dispute the OAC's decision, it has, just like the disputing taxpayer,[22] an option of whether it is to be appealed to the High Court or the Circuit Court, which does a full hearing in camera of those cases whose disputed tax amount was less than EUR 75,000 (before it was revised by the 2015 Finance (Tax Appeals) Act) and makes decisions which are not appealable to higher courts.[23] But in the case of the Revenue, there was a limitation on that option now that its appeal to the Circuit Court could be made, under the 2003 Capital Acquisitions Tax Consolidation Act §67 (Appeals in other cases), only when the disputed issue was on capital

---

17. For example, in 1983/1984, the OAC received 16,552 appeals (cumulatively or representing the number of assessments appealed) on IT and CIT alone and the 1985 Fifth Report of the Commission on Taxation mentioned that the system of assessments and appeals at that time was virtually broken down. *See* p. 86 and para. 4.16. The number of tax objections received by TAC which succeeded OAC is also counted on a cumulative basis, *see* footnote 32.
18. *See* the 1985 Fifth Report of the Commission on Taxation, p. 87 and LRC's "2003 Consultation Document" pp. 91-94.
19. The OAC held about 300 hearings annually (*see* data in footnote 18).
20. Due to this amendment, it became necessary for an appellant to pay the disputed tax before the OAC accepted his appeal filed after twelve months had passed since the issuance of the notice of assessment. For details, *see supra* the Fifth Report 1985, pp. 87-89.
21. *See* Mary Healy, Tax Appeals: Institute Response to TAC Consultation—September 2017, *Irish Tax Review,* November 4 (2017), *see* p. 95. While TCA §958 (Date for payment of tax) (9)(b) provides that, if 90% or more of the amount determined by the OAC has been paid in advance and the rest is paid within one month after the determination, no interest will accrue.
22. TCA §942 (Appeals to Circuit Court) (1) prescribed, "Any person aggrieved by the determination of the Appeal Commissioners in any appeal against an assessment made on that person may, on giving notice in writing to the inspector or such officer as the Revenue Commissioners shall authorize in that behalf (...) within 10 days after such determination, require that the appeal shall be heard by the judge of the Circuit Court."
23. Section 949AP (Appeals against determinations) of the Finance (Tax Appeals) Act of 2015 (2) states, "A party who is dissatisfied with a determination as being erroneous on a point of law may by notice in writing require the Appeal Commissioners to state and sign a case (in this Chapter referred to as a 'case stated') for the opinion of the High Court."

acquisitions tax.[24] Therefore, in the case of the Revenue, if an OAC decision was on taxes other than capital acquisitions tax, that decision could be appealed only to the High Court, and it had to be on the point of law or statutory construction of law.[25]

2 Current Tax Objection Procedures and Their Status

As mentioned in 1 above, most tax disputes were resolved through agreements between the Revenue and taxpayers, but, as for those disputes which were not resolved by them, the ratio of their revocation by the reviews of the Revenue was by no means high, as Figure 5.2 shows. Such being the case, among taxpayers and tax experts, especially those who have gone through the dispute resolution procedures but could not obtain favorable results, there were some who did not consider that the level of independence of their reviews was sufficient. Some others also saw as problems those elevating costs on the part of the taxpayers as the backlog of appeals increased in the OAC. Moreover, as the Law Reform Committee's 2004 Report (Report on a Fiscal Prosecutor and a Revenue Court: LRC 72-2004) pointed out on p. 98, the appeal system under which an appeal to the OAC was submitted via the Revenue and the Revenue could even refuse to accept it in some cases, some claimed that it might violate the right to an independent and fair trial stipulated under Article 6(1) of ECHR.[26]

The 2015 Public Finance (Tax Appeals) Act, which came into effect in March 2016, was implemented from the perspective of the need to address the abovementioned issues, and it built the foundation of the current tax objection/appeal system. Quite noteworthy is that, under the Finance (Tax Appeals) Act 2015, the Tax Appeals Commission (TAC) was created to replace the OAC as the reviewing authority. Like the OAC, the TAC is an organization of the Ministry of Finance, and although it consists of three commissioners (one of whom is an accountant) and support staff (about twelve at the time of its establishment), the independence of its systems and functions is higher than those of OAC, partly due to changes made to the relevant tax law provisions following the 2015 Finance (Tax Appeals) Act.[27] In particular, in relation to appeals relating to IT, CIT, and capital gains tax, the new addition of Part 40A (Appeals to Commissioners. 949A-949AV) to TCA has mitigated some of the problems that

24. Capital Acquisitions TCA §67(b) states, "The Commissioners shall, subject to their giving notice in writing in that behalf to the appellant within 10 days after the determination of an appeal by the Appeals Commissioners, have the same right as the appellant to have the appeal reheard by a judge of the Circuit Court."
25. https://www.irishtimes.com/new/who-are-the-appeal-commissioners-1.226321.
26. As for Article 6(1) of ECHR, *see* 1(4) in Section 5 of Chapter 3.
27. While the TAC published in 2018 a Report ("Review of the Workload and Operations of the Tax Appeals Commission") in which there were also discussions over whether the TAC should become an organization separate from the Ministry of Finance in order to further increase its independence. *See* p. 34 (also at http://www.budget.gov.ie/Budgets/2019/Documents/18.%2 0Independent%20review%20of%20the%20workload %20and%20operations%20of%20the% 20Tax%20Appeals%20Commission.pdf).

existed under the old appeals system. Surely, those measures have also enhanced the level of convenience on the part of aggrieved taxpayers.[28]

In particular, under the new appeal system, as shown in Figure 5.1 (B), a taxpayer dissatisfied with taxation notices, etc., is not required, under TCA §959AF (Appeals in relation to assessments), to go through a review by the Revenue so he can choose, pursuant to TCA §949I (Notice of Appeal), directly submit to the TAC a written notice of appeal stating the reasons for the incorrectness of the notice of assessment, etc.[29] When the TAC receives a notice of appeal, etc., a copy of it is to be sent to the Revenue. If the Revenue determines that they have not fulfilled the necessary procedural requirements or there is no valid reason for the appeal, it can submit, according to TCA §949L (Objection by Revenue Commissioners), a notice of objection, which shows reasons for such determination, to the TAC within 30 days from the date of the receipt of the copy. The TAC also has the authority to request a face-to-face discussion (a "case management conference") with the disputing parties if it deems it difficult to resolve the dispute without doing so.

Indeed, the TAC's hearings are, in contrast to hearings at the OAC, open to the public in principle, but in a case where the applicant expresses an intention to keep them in camera, the TAC can render a decision based solely on a notice of appeal filed by the applicant without a hearing. Also, in cases where there are decisions, etc., that could serve as precedents for the disputed cases, the TAC, as stipulated in TCA §949AN (Appeals raising common or related issues), can render decisions on them without hearings regardless of the applicant's intention. Moreover, the TAC differs from the OAC in that the TAC, under TCA §949AO (Publication of determinations),[30] gives all of its decisions in writing, and they are also posted on the TAC website, subject to necessary masking. However, no change is made on the following points: (i) the applicant/taxpayer bears the burden of proof in principle; (ii) the TAC and the OAC can not only request the submission of documentary evidence and summon witnesses but also have the authority of increasing or decreasing the tax amount determined in the re/assessment; (iii) the TAC and the OAC do not have the authority to make further investigation of the appealed case or make costs order on the party that received the decision unfavorable to it.[31]

The Finance (Tax Appeals) Act 2015 also made changes to the litigation proceedings. It is worth noting that the Circuit Court was abolished, and taxpayers no longer have the option to file an appeal with it. This means in particular that: (i) another

28. Recently the Revenue has also published on its website a Summary of Internal & External Reviews decisions each year pursuant to 9 (Publication of Statistics on Reviews and Cases Studies) in CS4.
29. TCA §949A (Interpretation) (i) provides, "'Appeal Commissioner' has the same meaning as it has in the Finance (Tax Appeals) Act 2015." As for an appeal regarding property valuation, it must be made to the Land Values Reference Committee.
30. TAC §949OA stipulates, "(1) subject to subsection (2), the Appeal Commissioners shall publish a report of each of their determinations on the internet not later than 90 days after notifying the parties in accordance with section 949AJ."
31. The review by the TAC is confined to those stipulated in laws and regulations, as it is confirmed in the TAC decision (06TACD2016), so that those matters not stipulated in laws and regulations (e.g., principle of good faith, legitimate expectations, etc.) are not subject to its review.

opportunity for a hearing is no longer available; (ii) a review of relevant facts on the appeals from a new perspective is not to be made; (iii) speedy dispute resolution on small cases due to the judgments on them not being appealable to higher courts may not be possible. So, now, the only option for the party wishing to dispute the TAC decision is to appeal to the High Court on the interpretation of the law, and some wonder if it is sufficient for protecting the taxpayers' rights. Moreover, now that the number of cases received by the OAC exceeded the number of cases processed for a long time, it resulted in the TAC succeeding in March 2016 with about 3,000 accumulated unprocessed cases (about 10% of them settled by agreements around the time of succession, and they are not included in the number of agreements shown in Figure 5.3 for 2016). So, as Figure 5.3 shows, the number of accumulated unprocessed cases in the TAC did not decrease so easily.

Figure 5.3 Number of Cases Accepted and Processed by TAC, Cumulative Number of Pending Cases and Number of Agreements Reached in TAC

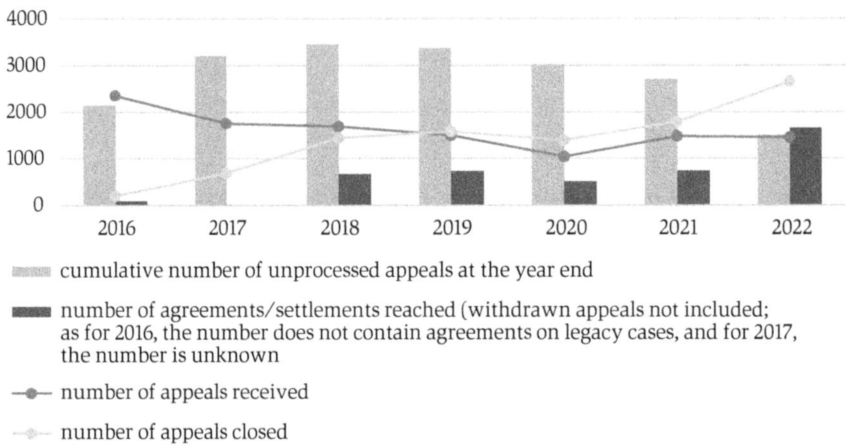

Source: Statistics "Overview of appeals" and "Key outputs" in TAC Annual Reports 2016 to 2022.

But the appellants' burden was lessened by the 2018 Finance Act which did away with the appellant's obligation to respond to the review organ's request at an early stage of the appeal for the provision of detailed information and documents required under the older system. As for the problem of a large number of unprocessed cases in the TAC, the Parliament took up this problem, and the Finance Minister subsequently announced that: (i) the TAC's budget would be increased significantly, (ii) information technology would be pursued further to speed up processing appeals, (iii) the number of the TAC staff would be increased, and so forth. Also, the recent number of appeals to the TAC has decreased, and there has been an increase in the number of agreements by the disputants.[32] Owing to them, the number of processed cases has lately come to outnumber the receipt of appeals in the TAC.[33] What was particularly notable in connection with the recent decline in the number of unprocessed cases in the TAC is that, as Figure 5.4 shows,[34] the number of appeals on IT, which generally represent more than half of the appeals to the TAC, has declined remarkably since 2016.[35]

Figure 5.4 Number of Appeals Received Annually by TAC by Tax Category

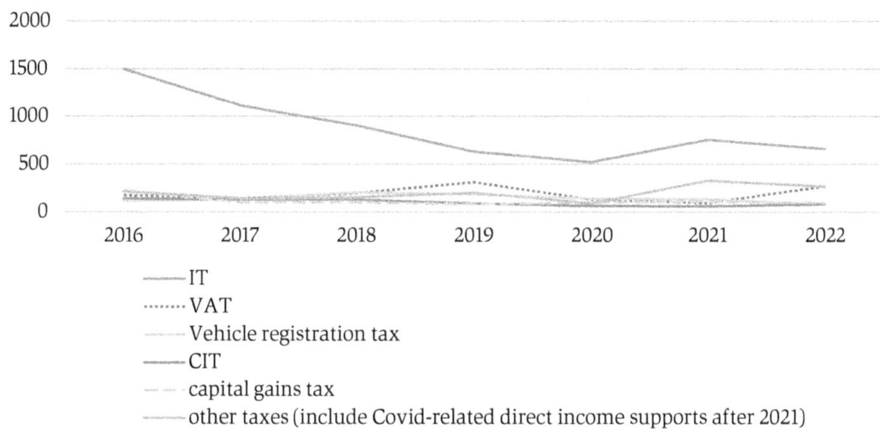

Source: Created from "Appeals closed" in 2022 TAC Annual Report.

The reasons for the declining trend of IT-related appeals brought to the TAC, especially since 2016, must be various and complex, and it may not be easy to list the main causes.[36] However, Figure 5.5 strongly suggests that the recent downward trend in the effective tax rate of IT should be one of the main reasons.[37] Ireland's IT rate is two-tiered (the standard tax rate is 20%, and a rate of 40% is applied over a certain

32. About one-third of all appeals span multiple years, and these appeals are counted as multiple rather than one. *See* the 2017 TAC Annual Report, p. 37.
33. Whereas, the number of appeals against multiple tax items has lately been on the rise, and the number of such appeals processed was 74 in 2016, 209 in 2017, 122 in 2018, 91 in 2019, and 120 in 2020, 318 cases in 2021. *See* the 2021 TAC Annual Report, p. 32.
34. A comparison of footnote 1 and Figure 5.4 shows that the number of appeals filed against CIT cases is particularly small compared to the proportion of its tax revenue, while the number of appeals against the proportion of tax revenue is large for vehicle registration tax and capital gains tax.
35. *See* Q&A on the Tax Appeals Regime at https://taxinstitute.ie/tax-insight/tax-administration/tax-appeals-regime/. About half of the appeal cases pending with TAC are cases where the disputed tax amount is less than EUR 10,000.
36. Also, the breakdown of the number of complaints to the Ombudsman reveals that the percentage of those related to IT exceeded 50% in 2008 and 2009, but gradually decreased thereafter, reaching 23% to 42% in 2017-2019. *See* Table: Complaints relating to Revenue made to the Ombudsman in the Revenue's 2008-2009 Reports, and Table 6 in the Ombudsman Annual Reports 2018-2019.
37. On the other hand, the ratio of IT revenue to total tax revenue from 2016 to 2021 was stable at around 40% each year.

amount), and Figure 5.5 shows changes in the effective tax rate (e.g., if a person with an annual income of EUR 50,000 has an income tax burden of EUR 10,000 after applying deductions, the effective tax rate is 20%) on the following categories of income earners: (i) a single person with an annual income of EUR 25,000; (ii) only one of the spouses earns income, and the annual income is EUR 40,000; (iii) both spouses earn income, and the total annual income is EUR 60,000. If it is not wrong to assume that the effective tax rate of IT is related or proportional to the number of appeals related to IT, one of the main reasons for the large number of appeals and accumulated unprocessed cases during the OAC era may be found in the fact that the effective tax rate of IT was quite high around the 1990s.

Figure 5.5 Changes in the Effective Income Tax Rate

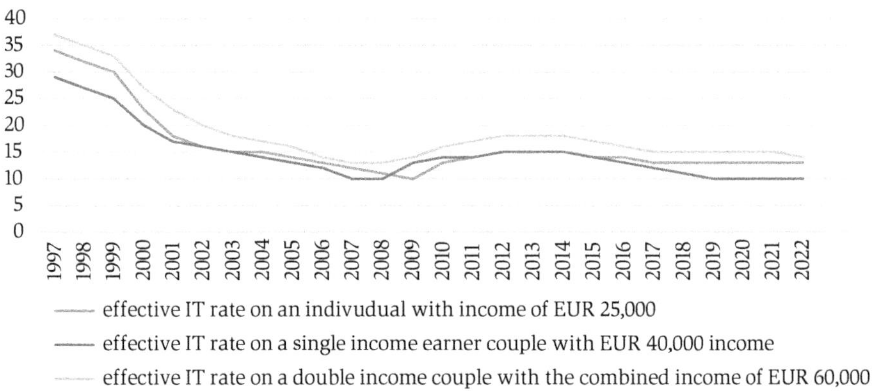

Source: https://www.socialjustice.ie/article/effective-tax-rates-after-budget-2022-and-why-ireland-remains-low-tax-country.

3 Flexible Settlements of Disputes

After the 2015 Finance (Tax Appeal) Act came into effect, the number of appeals filed with the TAC has been on a downward trend mainly as a result of the decrease in the number of appeals (IT appeals in particular), but, as Figure 5.3 shows, the TAC still has a large number of outstanding cases. The important tool in reducing them is the scope of the Commissioner's discretionary powers and his stance on exercising them. Under the old appeals system, as noted above, the Commissioner's discretion was exercised fairly proactively, and in practice, most tax disputes were resolved by agreements between the Revenue and the taxpayers. As for the Commissioner's discretionary powers, TCA §849 (Taxes under care and management) (3) states, "The Revenue Commissioner may do all such acts as may be deemed necessary and expedient for raising, collecting, receiving and accounting for tax in the like and in as full ample a manner, as they are authorized to do in relation to any other duties under their care and management." Also, TCA §1065 (Mitigation and application of fines and penalties) (1) dictates, "(a) The Revenue Commissioners may in their discretion mitigate any fine or penalty, or stay or compound any proceedings for the recovery of any fine or penalty."[38]

The 2019 version of the Revenue's Code of Practice for Revenue Audit and other Compliance Interventions (hereinafter referred to as the "Code of Practice") 5.1 (Monetary settlement) also states that the monetary settlement plays an important role in the Revenue's compliance program, and the use of appropriate financial settlement procedures by the Revenue is consistent with the efficient administration of the tax system, optimal use of the Revenue resources and the minimization of taxpayers' compliance costs. Nevertheless, the scope of management and control powers of the Revenue Commissioner has long been viewed to be narrower than those in the UK, as they must be subject to fairly strict statutory constraints. The grounds for this view may be found in paragraph 3.16 of the 1985 Fifth Report of the Commission on Taxation, which refers to the Revenue Commissioner's statement to the effect that the Revenue is allowed to fail to collect tax under the care and management provisions, but those provisions neither allow the Commissioner to do "extra-statutory tax concessions" nor give an exemption.[39]

Whereas, paragraphs 3.17 and 3.18 of the above "Fifth Report of the Fiscal Commission" state that the tax code is practically unworkable without the flexibility of some tax concessions and the way certain legislation is interpreted in a given situation may amount in practice to an extra-statutory concession. Thus, there is some degree of uncertainty about the scope of the Revenue Commissioner's management and control powers, but, as shown by the TAC's 2018 data in Figure 5.3, the number of agreements (668 cases, 891 cases when cases withdrawn are included) accounts for about 46% (about 62% when cases withdrawn are included) of the processed cases (1440 cases). Therefore, many appeals received by the TAC are settled by agreements of the disputing parties without its decisions. The OAC decisions were indeed made on only about 10% of the listed cases, so the percentage of cases where agreements were reached under the TAC has declined,[40] but the Revenue Commissioner's powers of management and control have been actively exercised at any stage of disputes when it is deemed desirable to do so.

Even at the litigation stage, many tax disputes are resolved through the agreements of the disputing parties. Some of those agreements are briefed in the Reports on the Accounts of the Public Services (hereinafter called "Account Reports") published by the Office of the Comptroller and Auditor General (C&AG). One example reported in

38. While TCA §1065(2) stipulates, "Notwithstanding subsection (1)-(a) where a fine or penalty is mitigated or further mitigated, as the case may be, after judgment, the amount or amounts so mitigated shall, subject to *paragraph (b)*, not be greater than 50 per cent of the amount of the fine or penalty."
39. As for the practice of "extra-statutory tax concessions" in the UK, *see* 1 in Section 2 and footnote 39 of Chapter 3.
40. According to the TAC's 2020 Annual Report, the breakdown of the 1,392 cases handled by the TAC in 2002 was as follows: 607 were withdrawn, 509 were settled (36.5%), 191 were decided, and 85 were others (dismissed, etc.).

the C&AG's 2012 Account Report is the case of Subsidiary A,[41] which was established in Ireland by the foreign parent company, and received an investment from it and used that investment to provide a loan to it but received no interest and did not file CIT returns for the business years of 2001-2002 and 2002-2003. The Revenue made an assessment of Subsidiary A's corporate income for those years. In this case, the OAC revoked the assessment for 2001-2002 but sustained the assessment for 2002-2003, so Subsidiary A contested the legality of the latter at the Circuit Court. However, before its judgment is made, the Revenue agreed to settle the dispute with Subsidiary A on the term that Subsidiary A should pay the amount of EUR 800 (including interest but no penalty imposed) while the Revenue estimated that the amount should have been EUR 1,400 if the Circuit Court's judgment in favor of the Revenue were handed down.

Certainly, as stated in 5.2 (Basis of Compliance Intervention Settlement)of the Revenue's Code of Practice 2019, to reach an agreement with the taxpayer, a written dispute resolution proposal (including a proposal on penalties) must be approved by the Commissioner or Senior Management of the Revenue,[42] so there are certain conditions and restrictions on it. In addition, a broad interpretation of the Commissioner's power to manage and control may, in some cases, give rise to issues of fairness among taxpayers and issues of legislative action by the Revenue, so there are, naturally, restrictions on how such authority is exercised. For example, the Ombudsman, in a Special Report ("Redress for Taxpayers") submitted to Congress in 2012, pointed out that, in *Lawrence O'Rourke v. The Revenue Commissioner* ([1996] ITR p. 81), the High Court ruled that despite the lack of legal grounds for the refund to the taxpayer to carry interest, the Revenue allowed it by the doctrine of "unjust enrichment," so it should be unjust not to apply the same treatment to some other taxpayers in similar situations.

Some cases with flexible dispute resolution are also subject to audit by the C&AG. Based on the audit results, the C&AG issues warnings and recommendations to the Revenue, and the audit results and the Revenue's response to them are shown in its Accounts Reports. Although the scope of the audit by the C&AG is limited, the C&AG Account Reports had some statements pointing out that there were some settlements whose appropriateness was hard to confirm from the submitted files, etc.[43] That may not be surprising now that the Commissioner's power to settle disputes flexibly is exercised in various ways, and so is its effect. For example, the primary function of TCA §1086 (Publication of names of tax defaulters) (2) is to name and shame those tax defaulters,[44] and it may also encourage some taxpayers to take corrective action and make "qualified disclosure" in an attempt to avoid their names being on the published

41. *See* 27.31-27.63 of this Report (also at https://www.auditgov.ie/en/ Find-eport/Publications/ Report%20on%20the%20Acounts%20of%20the%Public%20Services/Report-on-the-Accou nts-of.the-Public-Services-2012.pdf).
42. If the amount (including penalty and interest) of a settlement offer is less than EUR 50,000, the approval of the "Audit Manager" is required, and if it is less than EUR 100,000, the approval of the "Assistant Secretary" is required. If the amount is EUR 100,000 or more, the approval of the "Revenue Commissioner" is required. *See* Law Reform Commission, *supra* "2003 Advisory Document" p. 39.
43. *See* para. 22.77 in the C&AG 2012 Account Report.
44. For details, *see* the Revenue's Code of Practice Chapter 6 (Publication in List of Tax Defaulters).

list of tax defaulters.[45] Whereas, the published lists include some tax defaulters who made agreements with the Revenue in exchange for the Revenue refraining from initiating proceedings for the recovery of penalties on them, and so forth.[46]

As for ADR for flexible settlement of tax disputes, it has been utilized much less frequently. This has a lot to do with the fact that the 2012 General Scheme of Mediation Bill states in Head 3 (Scope and application) that the Act does not apply to any dispute relating to any tax or customs charge and that the Mediation Act 2017 also dictates, "This Act shall not apply to:...(c) a matter that may be determined by—(i) an Appeal Commissioner..., (ii) the High Court...(d) an application under section 901,...or 1077B of the Taxes Consolidation Act 1997." Even so, now that the EU Commission has issued the 2008 Mediation Order, the 2013 ADR Directive, and the EU Directive (2017/1852 of 10 October 2017 on tax dispute resolution mechanisms in the EU), which provides in the Preamble (5): "It is crucial to introduce an effective and efficient framework for the resolution of tax disputes which ensures legal certainty and a business-friendly environment for investments in order to achieve fair and efficient tax systems in the Union,"[47] more active use of ADR in the context of Ireland's tax disputes has been called for. The TAC also proposes in its 2018 Report (Review of the Workload and Operations of the Tax Appeals Commission) that the possibility of using ADR should be explored.

4 Characteristics of Disputes over Penalties

As shown in Figure 5.4, the number of appeals on IT received by the TAC has been on the decline recently, but it is nevertheless large in number compared to its revenue ratio, which is 40% for IT, compared to 27% for CIT, 23% for VAT, and 10% for others (including 2.4% for capital gains tax and 0.9% for property acquisitions tax) against the total. In contrast, the number of CIT disputes is small compared to its ratio of revenue against the total. This should be related much to the difference in the level of their tax burden. As for IT, its tax rate is currently 20% and 40%, while the CIT rate is much lower (12.5% since 2003). Also, in the case of civil penalties on the non-filing of tax returns, the number and amount of the "P35 penalty" applied in the case of an employer's non-filing of Pay As You Earn (PAYE) is, as Figure 5.6 shows, much larger than those applied in the case of non-filing of VAT,[48] and it is pointed out that an

45. As for qualified disclosures, *see* 4 of this section, Figure 5.7, and footnote 51.
46. On this point, *see* 4 for details. TCA §1086(2) stipulates, "The Revenue Commissioners shall, ... compile a list of the names and addresses and the occupations or descriptions of every person—(a) on whom a fine or other penalty was imposed by a court under any of the Acts... (*c*) in whose case the Revenue Commissioners, pursuant to an agreement made with the person in that relevant period, refrained from initiating proceedings for the recovery of any fine or penalty of the kind mentioned in *paragraphs (a)* and *(b)* and, in place of initiating such proceedings, accepted or undertook to accept a specified sum of money in settlement of any claim by the Revenue Commissioners in respect of any specified liability of the person under any of the Acts."
47. As for the European Commission's 2008 Mediation Order and 2013 ADR Directive, *see* 2 in Section 2 of Chapter 3.
48. PAYE-related appeals to the TAC in 2017 are the second largest in number next to IT and represented more than 10% of the total but decreased in the following years. *See* TAC 2017

employer's failure to file PAYE is incurred quite often by the errors in the Personal Public Service Number of his employees. So, even in the case of penalties, those related to IT are very large in number and amount, and it should give rise to many disputes on them.

Figure 5.6 Number of Summary Criminal Convictions on Non-filing of Returns and Number/Amount of Civil Penalties on Non-filing of PAYE or VAT

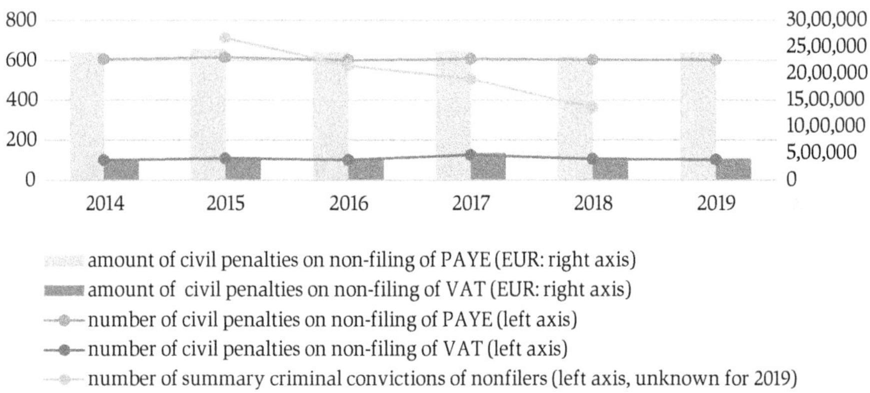

Source: Prepared from the Revenue Annual Reports 2014-2019, Table: Summary Criminal Convictions and Table: Civil Penalties for Not Filing Returns.

Also, the annual number of summary criminal prosecutions on the non-filing of tax returns is also quite large (e.g., 361 in 2018) because it usually represents more than half of all the summary criminal convictions (e.g., 695 in 2018) while the number of summary criminal convictions by means of VAT/P35 prosecution programs represents a small portion (e.g., 3% in 2018).[49] So, it seems that the majority of penalties on the non-filing of VAT/P35 returns are not so serious in nature and the structure of penalties on non-filers of returns are not so complex.[50] There are greater variations in the applicable rates of behavioral penalties, as in the case of the UK (*see* 1 in Section 5 of Chapter 3). In concrete, rates of behavioral penalties vary, as presented in Table 5.1, depending on the level of care taken by a taxpayer, the status of "qualified disclosures," the level of a taxpayer's cooperation with the examination, etc. Such uncertainty should often give rise to differences in views among the concerned taxpayer, the tax auditor, and the concerned staff in the Revenue on what amount of penalty should be paid by the taxpayer, resulting in many disputes over penalties.

Annual Report, p. 42 and 2019 Report, p. 52. While the number of disputes over vehicle registration tax (mostly on valuation of imported used cars) received by the TAC is, as Figure 5.4 shows, quite large compared to its revenue.

49. A large number of summary criminal convictions are filed against evaders of indirect taxes on cigarettes and marketed mineral oil, etc. *See* Table 23 of the 2018 Revenue Annual Report.

50. For instance, penalties for non-reporting include one stipulated under the TAC §1084 (Surcharge for late returns) and the amount and the rate of this penalty vary depending on the period of non-reporting, the cause of non-reporting, etc.

Table 5.1 Civil Penalties for Underreporting after December 24, 2008

Disclosures	*Category of Behavior*	*Full Cooperation Is Not Given by the Taxpayer (%)*	*Prompted Qualifying Disclosure and Full Cooperation—Penalty Reduced To (%)*	*Unprompted Qualifying Disclosure and Full Cooperation—Penalty Reduced To (%)*
All qualifying disclosures in this category[51]	Careless behavior without significant consequences	20	10	3
1st qualified disclosure	Careless behavior with significant consequences[52]	40	20	5
	deliberate behavior	100	50	10
2nd time[53] qualified disclosure	Careless behavior with serious consequences	40	30	20
	deliberate behavior	100	75	55
3rd time onwards qualified disclosure	Careless behavior with significant consequences	40	40 (no reduction)	40 (no reduction)
	deliberate behavior	100	100 (no reduction)	100 (no reduction)
Disclosure, etc.	Category of behavior	Full cooperation is not given by taxpayer	No disclosure made — full cooperation penalty reduced to	

51. A "qualified disclosure" requires disclosure of all information on the underreported portion, which must be accompanied by payment of such portion, penalties and interest. *See* para. 3.7 of the 2019 Code of Practice. Depending on whether "qualified disclosures" are prompted and unprompted, the applicable penalty rate differs. Unprompted "qualified disclosures" should be made in writing before the notification of a Revenue audit is issued while prompted "qualified disclosures" are usually made sometime between the notification of a Revenue audit and the commencement of the audit. Japan's underreporting penalty rate (basically 10%) is also reduced to nil (5%) if an amended return is filed before (after) an audit notification is made to a taxpayer provided that the amended return is filed without anticipating the reassessment. *See* footnote 129 in Chapter 3 for comparison with the UK.
52. "Careless" is defined in TCA §177 as a lack of reasonable care. As for the definition of "significant consequences," it is not defined in the Acts but para. 5.6.1 of the 2019 Code of Practice informs that it is a case where the tax underpaid exceeds 15% of the tax correctly payable.
53. When there are multiple "qualifying disclosures" for the same tax item within a five-year period, the reduction of the penalty rate becomes less. *See* 3.11 of the 2019 Code of Practice. Impositions of penalties and taxpayers' compliance in the past affect the current penalty rates in some countries (e.g., 2(3) in Section 3 of Chapter 1 and pp. 34-5 of IR240, footnote 194 in Chapter 4).

Disclosures	*Category of Behavior*	*Full Cooperation Is Not Given by the Taxpayer (%)*	*Prompted Qualifying Disclosure and Full Cooperation—Penalty Reduced To (%)*	*Unprompted Qualifying Disclosure and Full Cooperation—Penalty Reduced To (%)*
No disclosure	Careless behavior without significant consequences	20	15	
	Careless behavior with significant consequences	40	30	
	deliberate behavior	100	75	

Source: Revenue's 2019 Code of Practice, paragraph 5.6.2.

For instance, under the penalty system applied before December 24, 2008 (hereinafter referred to as the "old penalty system"), the rate of a penalty applicable to the underreporting caused by a taxpayer's "gross carelessness" and the rate applicable to that caused by his "insufficient care" was different,[54] but it was indicated that the line between them was not clear-cut and the Commissioner had wide discretion on their application.[55] The penalty system for underreporting was indeed reformed by the Finance Act 2008 (No. 2) on December 24, 2008, but the reform was, as Table 5.1 divulges, not drastic enough to make a change to the fundamental fact that the underreporting penalties are behavioral. Also, now that TCA §1065 (Mitigation and application of fines and penalties) expressly allows the Commissioner to reduce the amount of penalties by no more than 50%,[56] undoubtedly, the Revenue can exercise broad discretion over penalties. Such being the case, the abovementioned indication of the lack of clarity on the applicable penalty rates under the old penalty system could also be directed to those under the current penalty system.

Under the current penalty system, as paragraph 5.5 of the Revenue 2019 Code of Practice mentions, if the amount of tax underreported is less than EUR 6,000, and it is not due to deliberate behavior, a penalty is exempted, but penalties are imposed on the underreporting of more than EUR 6,000 which is caused by "careless behavior" as well as any underreporting caused by "deliberate behavior."[57] If a penalty is imposed, the degree of its reduction is the highest in a case where: (i) the unprompted qualifying

54. While, under the old penalty system, the Revenue 2002 Code of Practice, stated in Introduction that, if a shortfall is exclusively within the Insufficient Care Category and the shortfall does not exceed EUR 3,000, no penalty will be imposed. Also, *see* Revenue Tax Briefing Issue 49 (August 2002) p. 7 (at https://www.charteredaccountants.ie/taxsource/1997/en/act/pub/0039/tb/sec0902-1-tb.html).
55. *See supra* LRC's "2003 Consultative Document" p. 43.
56. *See* footnote 38 and 3 in Section 1 for TCA §1065.
57. Compare this with footnote 54.

disclosure is made, (ii) the underreported amount does not exceed 15% of the tax payable, and (iii) the taxpayer is cooperative with the examination, while the degree of its reduction goes down as the number of facts coming under the above (i) to (iii) becomes less.[58] Behavioral penalties whose applicable rates vary depending on such various factors tend to induce disputes, but such inducement is reduced not only by the treatment under the above paragraph 5.5 of the Revenue 2019 Code of Practice but also by the fact mentioned in its paragraph 5.5.3 (Penalties determined by a relevant court) that taxpayers can dispute them at the Revenue and courts but not at the TAC.[59]

Moreover, TCA §1061 (Recovery of penalties) requires the Revenue to file a lawsuit to collect unpaid penalties, including those resulting from failure to reach an agreement with the taxpayer,[60] so unpaid penalties increase the Revenue's administrative burden significantly. Such being the case, there must be an incentive for the Revenue to attempt to resolve penalty cases before they go to court, and it should often result in their resolution by agreement at the stage of objections to the Revenue.[61] In fact, as shown in Figure 5.6, even the recent number of civil and criminal penalties on nonfilers of returns has by no means been small, but it used to be pointed out that the Revenue's lawsuits filed by the TCA §1061 were not many.[62] In other words, the number of disputes over penalties is likely to be large up to the stage of appeals to the Revenue, but the next stage for them is, as mentioned above, not the TAC but the High Court,[63] so it is quite likely that relatively small number of penalty cases brought to courts are generally limited to those that are quite ill-natured and large in amount.

In addition, TAC §1086(2), which, as mentioned in the above 3, provides for the Commissioner's duty to publish a list of "tax defaulters," also exerts an effect similar to the above TCA §1061.[64] This is because the exclusion from the naming and shaming list is possible for potential "tax defaulters" if they come under the following cases: (i)

58. The applicable penalty rates vary further in cases where an underreported tax amount or "qualifying disclosures" are related to tax avoidance. *See* para. 8.13 of the Revenue 2019 Code of Practice. Under the old penalty system, this (ii) served as a general guidance to tell whether the shortfall comes under the Gross Carelessness Category or the Insufficient Care Category. *See* http://docplayer.net/7215362-Revenue-audits-article-by-eamon-staunton-mba-anti-cpa-examiner-formation-2-taxation.html.
59. Paragraph 5.5.3 in the Revenue 2019 "Code of Practice" states, "Where a person does not agree liability to a penalty or does not pay a penalty which that person has agreed liability to, then it is a matter for a relevant court to determine whether that person is liable to a penalty." This point is also referred to in LRC's "2003 Consultative Document" pp. 44-127.
60. The TCA §1061 stipulates, "An officer of the Commissioners authorized by them for the purposes of this subsection may sue in his or her own name by civil proceedings for the recovery of the penalty in any court of competent jurisdiction as a liquidated sum."
61. As mentioned in footnote 38, the TCA §1065 grants the Revenue Commissioners discretion to mitigate the penalty.
62. *See supra* LRC's "2003 Consultative Document" para. 2.35.
63. The Ombudsman Act 1980 §5 (Exclusions)(1)(a) dictates, "The Ombudsman shall not investigate any action taken by or on behalf of a person—(a) if the action is one in relation to which—... the person affected by the action has a right of appeal, reference or review to or before a person other than a person specified in Part I of the First Schedule to this Act," and TAC is not included in this "a person specified in Part 1." So, cases disputable in the TAC is outside of the Ombudsman's jurisdiction, while penalty cases that are outside of the TAC's review are within its jurisdiction.
64. As for TCA §1086(2), *see* footnote 46 and 3 in this section.

cases where a "qualifying disclosure" is accepted by the Revenue (TCA §1086(4)(a)); (ii) cases where "the specified sum" prescribed under TAC§1086(2) does not exceed EUR 35,000 (TCA §1086(4)(c)); (iii) cases where the penalty (agreed with a taxpayer or determined by a court) does not exceed 15% of the amount of the tax ultimately due (TCA §1086(4)(d)). Therefore, if potential "tax defaulters" want to avoid being on the list, they are likely to be incentivized to do a "qualifying disclosure" or settle their disputes with the Revenue, especially if it would enable their cases to come under those mentioned in the above (i), (ii) or (iii). The Revenue 2010 Code of Practice and the Revenue publication (Tax Defaulters under Section 1086 TCA 1997) show examples of how a calculation is made to determine whether or not a taxpayer is to be on the list.

5 Litigation in Courts and the Impact of EU Law, Etc.

(1) Impact of Article 6 of ECHR

The next stage of contestation for those disputes that were not resolved at the stage of objections to the Revenue or at the stage of appeals to the TAC in ways that provide relief to aggrieved taxpayers is a court. Approximately ten to fifteen tax cases were brought annually to the Circuit Court, and only about ten cases were annually appealed to the High Court.[65] In the three years from 2016 to 2018, after the appeals to the Circuit were no longer available, only twelve cases appealing against the TAC decisions were made to the High Court, and about half of them were either agreed or withdrawn.[66] Even so, the resolution of disputes which were not resolved by agreements in court was not always prompt. In particular, the High Court decisions in *O'Connell v. Kelegham* ([2001] 2 IR 490), in which capital gains taxation was at issue, and in *Neenan v. O'Siochain* (Inspector of Taxes) ([1999] IR 533), in which at issue was the attribution of income, took more than four years to process. It is pointed out that they are in contrast to the *Barclays Mercantile* case in the UK, which took less than two years to be resolved since the decision of the Special Commissioner was appealed to the High Court ([2002] STC 1065) and subsequently to the Court of Appeal ([2003] STC 66).[67]

It was not that time and money costs were the only reasons why the number of tax disputes filed in the courts was relatively small. For example, by TCA §934 (Procedure on appeals) (7), the OAC was required to state its decision on appeals on Form AS1 prepared by the Revenue, but, as mentioned 1 above, the reasons for the decisions, etc., were only presented orally to the appellants and they were not shown in Form AS1. Moreover, even after TCA §944A (Publication of determination of Appeal Commissioners) was introduced by the 1998 Finance Act §134 (Appeals) to make the OAC publish its decisions with necessary masking on it when it finds it appropriate,

65. *See supra* LRC's "2003 Consultative Document" p. 110. Taxpayers' appeals to the Circuit Court also had to be made through the Revenue.
66. *See* https://www.oireachtas.ie/en/debates/question/2019-07-04/110/.
67. *See supra* LRC's "2003 Consultative Document" p. 142.

only thirty-four decisions were published.[68] As a result, taxpayers, their agents, tax experts, etc., unlike the Revenue, could often not have sufficient knowledge of the OAC decisions, which might contain some useful views and insights regarding their cases and were placed in a more disadvantageous position in their disputes. These facts, together with the time and money costs, may have worked among some aggrieved taxpayers to give up litigation.

Whereas, in the case of disputes over penalties, as mentioned above, taxpayers aggrieved over the Revenue's decisions on their objections to penalties can file appeals with the High Court but not with TAC, and the Revenue should, under the TCA §1061, file a lawsuit to the High Court to collect unpaid penalties.[69] There were pros and cons arguments on such procedures,[70] and those arguments were greatly affected by the idea of penalties underlying the European Convention on Human Rights (ECHR). In particular, Article 6 (Right to fair trial) of ECHR provides for citizens' rights to fair and public hearings within a reasonable time by an independent and impartial tribunal in the determination of their civil rights and obligations of any criminal charge against him,[71] but there is a problem that the scope of "civil rights and obligations of any criminal charge against him" is not clear. This problem gave rise to arguments in Ireland, just as in some other countries like the UK,[72] over whether paragraph 1 of ECHR could also be applicable to some noncriminal tax cases in Ireland, and if it could, on what kind of tax cases it would apply to.

On the above arguments, the ECHR judgment in *Ferrazzini v. Italy* ([2001] ECHR 4 4759/98) provides one useful insight. In this case, the applicant, who faced the Italian tax authority's assessment on his capital gains tax, etc., and the imposition of civil penalties, alleged that his claim is pecuniary in nature and there was a delay in the domestic legal proceedings, which should constitute a violation of Article 6(1) of ECHR. However, the ECHR explained that the dispute being pecuniary in nature is not in itself sufficient to attract the application of Article 6 of ECHR because there may exist pecuniary obligations vis-à-vis the State which, for the purpose of Article 6§1, are to be considered as belonging exclusively to the realm of public law and are accordingly not covered by the notion of "civil rights and obligations." The ECHR also mentioned in paragraph 26, "the scope of Article 6§1 should not be extended to cover disputes between citizens and public authorities as to the lawfulness under domestic law of the tax authorities' decisions." In conclusion, the ECHR stated that tax disputes fall outside the scope of civil rights and obligations, despite the pecuniary effects that they necessarily produce for the taxpayer, so Article 6§1 of the Convention does not apply to this case.

68. Submission to the Consultation on the Reform of the Appeal System for Tax Matters by the Office of the Revenue Commissioners (2014) 6.1-6.3 at p. 12.
69. *See* footnote 60 for TCA §1061.
70. This OAC's function contrasts with Australia's AAT's merit review function (*see* 3(1) in Section 1 and footnote 43 in Chapter 4). Paras. 3.79 and 3.80 of LRC's "2003 Consultative Document" states: "It is arguable that the current system of appeals strikes a balance between the Revenue Commissioner's right to enforce penalties, utilizing their discretion under the 'care and management' provisions and, on the other hand, a taxpayer's right to be treated fairly."
71. *See* 1(4) in Section 5 of Chapter 3 for Article 6(1) of ECHR.
72. *See* 1(4) in Section 5 of Chapter 3.

As for the question of what a "criminal charge" in this Article means, the ECHR judgment in *Adolf v. Austria* ([1982] ECHR 2) gives a guideline. In this case, the applicant was charged with the offense of inflicting bodily harm on another person, but the Austrian district court ruled that no offense could be established on facts or existed in law. Nevertheless, the applicant alleged that the district court took its decision without holding a trial hearing and without proper inquiry into the evidence, so it violates Article 6(1) of ECHR. In this judgment, the ECHR confirmed that the expressions of "criminal charge" and "charged with a criminal offense" are to be interpreted as having an autonomous meaning in the context of the Convention and not on the basis of their meaning in domestic law. The ECHR also dismissed the Austrian government's allegation that, due to the district court's ruling of finding the applicant innocent, there was no "charge" or "offense" in this case by stating that the ruling does not alter the fact that the applicant was subjected to the criminal proceeding. However, the ECHR concluded that there was no need for the district court to do hearings, etc., on him, who had already been found innocent, and so there was no violation of Article 6 of ECHR.[73]

The definition of "criminal charge" is clarified further by the ECHR judgment in *Engel and Others v. The Netherlands* ([1979] 1 ECHR 706). In this case, the Netherlands Army applied various penalties on the applicants for their offenses against the military disciplines, and they alleged that these disciplinary punishments violated Article 6, etc., of ECHR because no hearings by an independent and impartial tribunal were given to them and they did not have legal assistance, etc. The ECHR specified that the question of whether the concerned charge counts as "criminal" within the meaning of Article 6 of ECHR is to be answered by mainly taking into consideration three criteria: ((i) the treatment under domestic law; (ii) the very nature of the offense; (iii) the degree of severity of the penalty. The ECHR considered these criteria and ruled that the penalties imposed on the applicants and disciplinary proceedings applied to them vary, but the "charge" against some applicants came within the "criminal" sphere since their aim was the imposition of serious punishments involving deprivation of liberty, so the proceedings against them that involve hearings in camera before the Supreme Military Court violate Article 6(1) of ECHR.

The above criterion (iii) (the degree of severity of the penalty) shown in the above *Engel* case intimates that now that TMA §95, which was a focal point in the UK's High Court judgment in the *King* case (2001) analyzed in 1(4) in Section 5 of Chapter 3, is very much similar to TCA §1053 (Penalty for fraudulently or negligently making incorrect returns, etc.),[74] the penalty stipulated in the latter might also fall under "criminal charge" in the context of Article 6 of ECHR. This raises the question of whether the current dispute resolution system over tax-related penalties guarantees the

73. While three judges out of seven expressed their dissenting opinions holding this case to violate Article 6 of ECHR.
74. The TCA §1053 dictates, "(1) Where any person fraudulently or negligently—(a) delivers any incorrect return ..., (b) makes any incorrect return, ... that person shall, ... be liable to a penalty of—(i) £100, and (ii) the amount or, in the case of fraud, twice the amount of the difference specified in subsection (5)," and "the difference" is the amount of income tax payable and that payable if the return had been correct.

rights granted to taxpayers by Article 6 of ECHR. On this point, the Law Reform Commission expressed, in paragraphs 2.90 and 128 of the "2003 Consultative Document," a view that, although changes to the current system may not be necessary, it would be more in line with Article 6 of ECHR to incorporate the OAC's review of penalties into the current system. Indeed, some penalties are large in amount, and if a dispute over a penalty remains unresolved after appealing to the Revenue, taxpayers usually have to hire attorneys to litigate in the High Court, often incurring heavy costs on their part.

(2) Impact of the Aarhus Convention

International spotlights have also been cast lately on the abovementioned issue of taxpayers' high litigation costs in Ireland. There are also supranational rules other than EU Law that exert an influence on litigation-related systems in Ireland. Ireland is one of the signatories to the Aarhus Convention, which sets standards on environmental matters to be observed by the signatories to secure: (i) their citizens' access to information, (ii) their participation in the decision-making process, and (iii) their access to justice. Just as in the case of the UK, these standards could oblige Ireland to amend the "loser pays rule" because it might pose a problem, particularly concerning the above standard (iii). Furthermore, unlike the UK, which exited from the EU on February 1, 2020, Ireland, as an EU Member State, is under the direct influence of the revised EU Aarhus Regulations (Regulation (EC) No. 136 7/2006) and the Environmental Impact Assessment (EIA) Directive (85/337/EEC, hereinafter referred to as "EIA Directive"). Therefore, the impact of the Aarhus Convention on Ireland's "loser pays rule" could be more profound.

On the relation of the "loser pays rule" with the above standard (iii) (access to justice), it is to be noted that Article 10A of the EIA Directive, as amended by the Council Directive (2003/35/EC), prescribes, "Member States shall ensure that ... members of the public concerned: (a) ... (b) ... have access to a review procedure before a court of law ... to challenge the substantive or procedural legality of decisions, acts or omissions subject to the public participation provisions of this Directive ... Any such procedure shall be fair, equitable, timely and not prohibitively expensive," and Council Directive 85/337/EEC of June 27, 1985 on the assessment of the effects of certain public and private projects on the environment also has Article 15A with similar purport. The relationship of Ireland's law with this provision became an issue in the 2009 ECJ judgment in the *European Commission v. Ireland* (C-427/07), in which the Commission made an allegation that Ireland failed to comply with the rules of EIA Directive in permitting the concerned development plan and Ireland's relevant law, which sets no cap on costs that might be borne by a loser in a lawsuit, fails to incorporate the requirements under Article 10A of EIA Directive.

In the above case, the ECJ confirmed that the development construction project in question would have a considerable impact on the environment due to its nature, scale, and location as defined in Article 2 of the EIA Directive, and this project falls under the category of projects listed in Annex II (Projects subject to Article 4(2)) of EIA

Directive, so it is subject to assessment by Article 4 of the Directive. Now that this assessment requires member countries to take all possible measures to make them subject to this Directive before authorizing their development,[75] it follows that the cost of relevant legal proceedings should not be prohibitively expensive. Then, the ECJ ruled that, although it is common ground that the Irish courts may decline to order an unsuccessful party to pay the costs and can, in addition, order expenditure incurred by the unsuccessful party to be borne by the other party, that is merely a discretionary practice on the part of the courts and the mere practice cannot be regarded as a valid implementation of the obligations arising from Article 10A of the Directive 85/337, so Ireland has failed to fulfill its obligations under this Directive.

Although the above ECJ case (C-427/07) was an environment-related one, the ECJ did rule that the "loser pays rule" in Ireland violates EU law. Therefore, its impact will not be limited to Ireland's environment-related context, and it is expected that there will be discussions and moves among some member states toward reforms of the relevant systems and rules.[76] Such discussions and moves shall be facilitated further now that Article 260(2) of TFEU prescribes, "If the Commission considers that the Member State concerned has not taken the necessary measures to comply with the judgment of the Court, it may bring the case before the Court after allowing that State to submit its observations. It shall specify the amount of the lump sum or penalty payment to be paid by the Member State concerned which it considers appropriate in the circumstances." In fact, in the *European Commission v. Ireland* (C-261/18), the ECJ ordered Ireland to pay a daily penalty of EUR 15,000 until it takes a remedial measure because it had not taken one ever since the ECJ ruled in *the European Commission v. Ireland* (C-215/06) that Ireland violated the EIA Directive.

SECTION 2 TAX DISPUTE IN THE NETHERLANDS

1 Tax Dispute Resolution Procedures and Current Status

(1) Objections and Flexible Dispute Resolutions

Tax filing procedures of IT, CIT, Social Security Tax, etc., are different from those of Wage Tax, VAT, Dividend Tax, etc. As for the former, those taxpayers who paid those taxes in the preceding years usually receive "official assessments" (ambtshalve aanslag) or "provisional assessments" (voorlopige aanslang) prepared by the tax authority (Belastingdienst) based on information and data they possess, and they either pay the amount of tax shown on them or they send them back to the tax authority by correcting the amount and pay the amount of tax shown in the final assessments

75. Article 2(1) of EIA Directive, as amended by the Council Directive (2003/35/EC), states, "Member States shall adopt all measures necessary to ensure that, before consent is given, projects likely to have significant effects on environment by virtue, inter alia, of their nature, size or location are made subject to a requirement for development consent and an assessment with regard to their effects."
76. As for such discussions and moves in UK, *see* 4 in Section 4 of Chapter 3.

which are usually sent to them within three months after those corrected assessments were received by the tax authority. When a taxpayer is dissatisfied with the amount of tax shown in the final assessment or the penalty shown in the determination of the auditor, he should, in principle, pursuant to the "General Tax Act"(Algemene wet inzake rijksbelastingen, hereinafter called "GTA"),[77] file an objection with the tax authority within six weeks from the issue date of the final assessment, etc.,[78] and the tax authority,[79] on the receipt of the objection, defers the payment deadline of the disputed tax amount unless there is a special circumstance.[80]

The tax authority's review of the applicants' objections shall be conducted by its staff other than those who audited them. The applicants could make requests for oral explanations of their objections and have access to the tax authority's documents on their cases. The tax authority usually renders a decision on the objection within six to ten weeks after its receipt unless it gains the applicant's consent and extends its review period (up to one year under Article 25 of GTA).[81] Article 104 of the Constitution sets out the principles of taxation under the law,[82] but the tax authority may reach an agreement with taxpayers on the disputed tax, penalties (including criminal penalties),[83] and interest in accordance with the Civil Code (Burgerlijk Wetboek) 7:900 which sets out the definition of the "settlement agreement" ("Vaststellingsovereenkomst"), Article 7:902 of the Act which establishes the relationship between the "settlement agreement" and mandatory statute, and the "principle of (protection of) legitimate expectations" ("reformatio in peius").[84] Also, the tax authority may, based on

77. An English version of the main articles of GTA is available at https://download.belastingdienst.nl/itd/beleid/awr0503.pdf.
78. But, if the taxpayer and the tax authority agrees, the dispute could be brought directly to the district court.
79. Final assessments can be issued before the statute of limitation on a re/assessment (in principle, three years) has passed. While Articles 13 and 14 of GTA stipulate that, when it takes some time for the amount of tax due to be finally determined, an auditor can issue a "provisional assessment" showing the tax amount up to the amount that will be shown in the final assessment. New filers and nonresidents can apply for the issue of "provisional assessments" which might enable some to spread the payment of taxes over multiple years. *See* https://www.kvk.nl/english/starting-a-business-in-the-netherlands/receiving-your-first-provisional-tax-assessment/.
80. Such a special circumstance includes a case where the tax authority believes that the disputed tax amount may be misused by the disputant.
81. If a decision is not made within this period, it could be deemed that the objection is dismissed, and a lawsuit can be filed with the district court, and compensation might be paid if the delay is unreasonable. *See* Tax Controversy in Netherlands at https://www.lexology.com/library/detail.aspx?g=11d4fadc-5951-4708-8632-b2a7c661d94d.
82. English translation of Article 104 of the Constitution is "Taxes imposed by the State shall be levied pursuant to Act of Parliament. Other levies imposed by the State shall be regulated by Act of Parliament." *See* www.government.nl/ for this translation.
83. Since July 2011, the tax authority can impose penalties on criminal tax cases through fiscal punishment orders while settlement and mediation procedures are available in tax cases where a criminal investigation is pending. When a taxpayer objects to a fiscal punishment order, the public prosecutor takes over the case. *See* Tax Litigation in the Netherlands: Overview at https://uk.practicallaw.thomsonreuters.com/6-623-1826?transitionType=Default&contextData=(sc.Default)&firstPage=true.
84. The English translation of Article 7:902 (Establishment in conflict with mandatory law) of the Civil Code is "The establishment of a new legal status in order to end any uncertainty or dispute on the field of law on property is also valid if it would appear to be in conflict with mandatory

Chapter 8, Part 5 of the GTA, abate them.[85] In fact, more than 90% of the objections are resolved without going to court,[86] and a large number of them are resolved by agreements.

The "principle of legitimate expectations" originated from the German principle of "protection of trust, etc." (Vertrauensshutz) and now it has established its status of being applicable under the EU jurisprudence through a series of ECJ judgments.[87] This principle serves as the basis for claiming the invalidity of Member State law and EU law, which run counter to it.[88] Although the definition and scope of the "principle of legitimate expectations" are not univocally clear, in the field of taxation, it becomes likely that the tax authority's re/assessments or treatments are void if they are against the legitimate expectation of the taxpayers because they are not in line with its agreements with them.[89] It is explained that this shall also apply in the Netherlands, and the agreements with the taxpayers bind the tax authority because Article 7:900(1) of the Civil Code prescribes that, under a settlement agreement for ending or avoiding any uncertainty or dispute about what applies to them legally, parties bind themselves toward each other to the establishment of a new legal status between them which are intended to apply as well as far as it differs from their previously existing legal status.[90]

Thus, much regard is to be given to the "principle of legitimate expectations," but not all agreements between taxpayers and tax authorities are protected by this principle. The Supreme Court (Hoge Raad) judgment (HCLI: NL:HR:2017:19) may serve as a guideline for its scope of protection. In this judgment, at issue was the validity of the contract on salaries entered into between the taxi drivers and their employers against the background of the lack of transparency in the amount of salaries that the taxi drivers could receive. The Taxi Association (Sociaal Fond Taxi) alleged

law, unless its content or necessary implications are in conflict as well with public morals or public order." As for English translation of this and Article 7:900(1) of the Civil Code, *see* http://www.dutchcivillaw.com/legislation/dcctitle771515.htm.

85. Under Article 63 of GTA, the Minister of Finance could give a lenient treatment under such circumstances where unfairness arises due to the application of tax laws, and abates penalties indicated in the final assessments pursuant to Article 66 of GTA. While, as a policy of the tax authority, there are restrictions on abating penalties for the sake of changing the amount of tax. *See* Diana van Hout, Chapter 19 in *Netherlands in EATLP International Tax Series*, Vol. 18 (2021) 19.3.2. Interest on unpaid tax is 4% per annum (8% for CIT) for 2019.
86. *See* Anna De Ambrosis Vigna and Dsariusz R. Kijowski, The Principle of Legitimate Expectations and the Protection of Trust in the Polish Administrative Law, *Bialostockie Studia Prawnicze*, Vol. 23, No. 2 (2018) p. 40 DOI: 10.15290/bsp.2018.23.02.03 and Hout, *supra* "Chapter 19 in Netherlands" 19.1.2.
87. For example, in *Gemeete Leusden and Holin Groep BV cs v. Stattssecretaris van Financiën* (C-487/01 and C-7/02, 2004), the ECJ stated, "The principle of the protection of legitimate expectations and legal certainty form part of the Community legal order. They must be accordingly observed by the Community Institutions (case 74/74 CNTA v. Commission [1975] ECR 533)."
88. *See* Esther Drabkin-Reiter, the Europeanization of the English and European Union Courts on the Protection of Legitimate Expectations in Administrative Law (2015), European University Institute, pp. 18-19.
89. Supreme Court of Italy judgment on May 11, 2021 (no. 12372/2021) is one example that invalidated such treatments. As for its summary, *see* https://blog.pwc-tls.it/en/2021/05/25/tax-settlement-procedure-italian-revenue-agency-is-bound-by-the-minutes-signed-within-a-settlement-agreement-in-compliance-with-the-principle-of-protection-of-legitimate-expectations/.
90. Hout, *supra* "Chapter 19 in Netherlands" 19.3.2.

that the contract is contrary to the mandatory Collective Labour Agreement. The Supreme Court confirmed that an agreement in breach of a mandatory law is valid under Article 7:902 of the Civil Code provided that its objective is to terminate existing disputes or uncertainties because the legislator only meant to exclude from the scope of this article those agreements that seek to prevent future uncertainties or future disputes and unacceptably undermine mandatory law. Then, the Court ruled that the contract in question, which does not have such an objective and falls out of the scope of the protection of this article, is void.[91]

As is evident from the above, the legal ground for settlements of tax disputes by agreement in the Netherlands is essentially different from those in Ireland (and other Commonwealth countries), but there is little difference in that they are actively utilized in both countries. There is no independent administrative appeals body for tax disputes in the Netherlands, but ADR (mostly mediation) has also been actively utilized since 2005 as a means of resolving tax disputes. An offer for mediation could be made by the taxpayers, the tax authority, and the courts at any stage of tax disputes. Once an agreement is reached for the use of mediation, mediation is commenced by an internal mediator appointed by the tax authority or an external mediator selected by the taxpayer or the court. The mediators are usually the members of the Netherlands Tax Mediation Association (Vereninging voor Fiscale Mediation) who abide by the rules of the Association, which includes their obligation to keep the content of the mediation confidential. The taxpayer shares the burden/cost of the mediator only when the mediator is not the one appointed by the tax authority or the mediator is chosen by the court.

Various types of cases are subject to mediation, but the tax authority explains that types of cases appropriate for mediation fall under more than one of the following cases: (i) cases that are not settled by agreement and expected to take a long time to be resolved; (ii) the disputing parties prioritize speedy and effective resolution of their cases; (iii) it can be expected that mediation can resolve cases rationally; (iv) one of the disputing parties lend no ear to the opinions of the other; (v) one or both of the disputing parties seeks for a resolution peculiar to the case; (vi) mediation is expected to cut costs to be incurred for the resolution of the case; (vii) it is highly recommendable that further deterioration of the relationship between the disputing parties is avoided.[92] The effectiveness of mediation in tax disputes is evidenced by the fact that more than 80 % of the cases subjected to mediation (many of them should fall under more than one of the above (i) to (vii) cases)are resolved. As for those cases that are not resolved despite the mediation efforts, one of the parties to the dispute cannot use the statements, etc., of the other party presented in the mediation process in the subsequent dispute stages.

91. As for a summary of this Supreme Court judgment in English, *see* http://www.stibbeblog.nl/all-blog-posts/commercial-litigation/dutch-supreme-court-elaborates-on-the-validity-of-a-settlement-agreement-that-is-contrary-to-mandatory-law/.

92. *See* Roelof Vos, Mediating Tax Disputes in the Netherlands, *Dutch-Flemish Magazine for Mediation and Conflict Management Journal*, Vol. 18, No. 3 (2014), p. 2.

Now that disputes on penalties may not only be settled by agreements but also be incorporated in the issues to be mediated, there are a large number of objections filed by aggrieved taxpayers on penalty cases. Some other reasons for the large number of penalty cases disputed at the objection stage should include the following: (i) the number of penalties imposed is large; (ii) there are some ambiguities in their application standards; (iii) some of them could be quite high in amount.[93] As for the above (ii), it is to be noted that a penalty is abated in the following cases: ① the taxpayer's non-reporting or underreporting is based on a justifiable tax law interpretation based on judicial precedents or relevant documents; ② the taxpayer's non-reporting or underreporting resulted despite the taxpayer's action which would be rationally required to avoid it; ③ there are excusable circumstances; ④ the taxpayer has made a voluntary disclosure of it.[94] The hurdle set by these for abating the penalty seems not to be so high for some taxpayers and it may also be one of the reasons why penalty cases are disputed frequently.

(2) Tax Litigation and Its Current Status

Taxpayers who are not satisfied with the tax authority's decisions on their objections or did not realize flexible resolutions can, in principle, within six weeks from the date of issuance of the decision (or the extended review period), file appeals with a district court (Arrondissementsechtbank).[95] About 25,000 tax disputes are filed with nineteen district courts annually.[96] The burden of proof is, in principle, on the tax authority concerning facts that increase the amount of tax paid and on the taxpayer concerning facts that reduce the amount of tax paid. Court hearings on tax disputes are, in principle, in camera unless they involve administrative penalties.[97] The judgments of the district court can be challenged in an appellate court (Gerechtshof), which exists in five locations,[98] but if there is an agreement between the disputing parties or a referral request from the district court, an appellate court can be skipped to seek for a judgment

93. Article 67C of GTA provides for penalties (maximally EUR 5,278 as of 2019) on non-reporting and underreporting of tax while Article 67e and 67F provide for penalties (maximally 100% of the unreported tax amount) in the case of a taxpayer's intentional or gross negligence (standard rate is 50% and 25%, respectively).
94. *See supra* "Tax Controversy in Netherlands" for details. As for interest on unpaid tax, it accrues at an annual rate of 4% (as of 2019, 8% for CIT) after six months have passed since the payment deadline.
95. *See* Snapshot: tax litigation in Netherlands at https://www.lexology.com/library/detail.aspx?g=c6f16f14-80ba-4e25-abf0-bsd95ba4be99 for details.
96. In 2019, the fee for filing a tax lawsuit to a district court was, depending on the type of tax, EUR 47 or EUR 174 for individuals, EUR 345 for corporations, and in the case of an appellate court, EUR 128 or EUR 259 for individuals and EUR 519 for corporations. *See* Tax Controversy 2019 Netherlands (at https://www.stibbe.com/en/news/2019/june/tax-controversy-in-the-netherlands-2019) 9.2 for further details.
97. *See supra* "Snapshot: tax litigation in Netherlands."
98. An appellate court, like a district court, hears and decides on facts and interpretation of law. For more information, *see* Paul Kraan, Chapter 19 in The Tax Disputes and Litigation Review (7th ed.), ed. Simon Whitehead, *Law Business Research* 2019.

of the Supreme Court.[99] Approximately 4,000 tax disputes are pending in appellate courts each year (approximately 3,800 in 2017 and 4,000 in 2018).[100] The appellate courts' judgments can be challenged in the Tax Department of the Supreme Court as stipulated in Chapter 5, Part 3 of GTA.[101]

The following data may be useful in having a rough idea of tax lawsuits in the Netherlands. The population of the Netherlands in 2022 is about 17 million, and the tax revenue breakdown in 2018 reveals that IT revenue is about 21%, CIT revenue about 9%, social security tax revenue about 36%, VAT revenue about 18%, GST revenue about 12%, and other tax revenues 5%.[102] The breakdown of national tax cases appealed to the Supreme Court in 2014 (776 cases) shows that about 59% of them were on IT, about 11% on VAT, about 8% on payroll tax and social security tax, about 5% on automobile tax, about 4% on CIT, about 3% on collection action, about 25% on inheritance and gift taxes, about 8% on other national taxes.[103] In 2014, the Supreme Court handed down about 1,000 judgments on tax lawsuits (about 76% of them on national tax-related cases, about 17% on local tax-related cases, and 9% on others). About 32% (144 cases of them voided the preceding court judgments) of these approximate 1,000 judgments followed regular litigation procedures, while the other cases were processed by summary proceedings due to their insufficient grounds for appeals, etc.[104] The Supreme Court only considers matters related to legal interpretation.[105]

As mentioned above, the number of tax lawsuits is relatively large. However, the number of lawsuits on CIT-related cases in the Supreme Court is relatively small, even though the CIT standard rate is 25.8% for the year 2022.[106] In this connection, quite noteworthy is the "horizontal monitoring" ("horizontaal toezicht") program. This program has been implemented since 2005 to reach agreements between the tax authority and some big corporations on main points where their views differ in advance of the corporations' filing of returns. The fact that "horizontal monitoring" possesses a high potential in terms of effectiveness and usefulness is implied by its

99. Likewise, according to Article 5a of GTA, when there are many similar litigations, the Minister of Finance shall designate a representative case and courts do not rule on other similar cases until the final court judgment is rendered on that case. *See* Peter J. Wattle, Tax Litigation in Last Instance in the Netherlands: The Tax Chamber of the Supreme Court, Bulletin for International Taxation, January/February 2016, pp. 48-49 DOI: 10.59403/1fce5ws.
100. *See* above "Tax Controversy 2019 Netherlands" 10.1.
101. *See* https://iatj.net/content/congresses/rome2010/Netherlands.pdf.
102. For details, *see* 2020 OECD Revenue Statistics: Key findings for the Netherlands.
103. Such data discloses that in the Netherlands, like in Ireland, the number of lawsuits on VAT and CIT is small compared to their ratios of revenue, while the number of lawsuits on automobile tax is large compared to its ratio of revenue. In particular, there was a significant increase in 2019 in the number of litigations over the 1992 Tax Act on privately-owned cars and two-wheel drives. For details, *see* above "Tax Controversy 2019 Netherlands" 10.1.
104. *See* Wattle, *supra* "Tax Litigation in Last Instance in the Netherlands," pp. 46-47 for further details.
105. While in some cases, the Supreme Court may decide on grounds not asserted by the disputing parties (e.g., relevant provisions of EU law, etc.).
106. The number of CIT-related disputes is relatively small in the case of Ireland as well, but Ireland differs from the Netherlands in that its CIT rate is low and its CIT structure is not so complex. On this latter point, *see* 5 in Section 1 and Figure 6.1 in Chapter 6.

influence on the OECD,[107] as well as many OECD countries that followed suit in their own ways.[108] Moreover, it is expected that the positive effects of the "horizontal monitoring," including the prevention of differences in the views of the taxpayers and those of the tax authority from escalating into tax disputes, would become stronger[109] now that the number of big corporations to which it is extended has become larger lately in the Netherlands.[110]

The number of litigations is also affected by the rules on costs in court, and in many EU member states, the "loser pays rule" is adopted as a general rule. The expenses to be borne by the losing party usually include the winning party's fees to courts, a reasonable amount of the winning party's attorney's fees, and other litigation-related disbursements.[111] Basically, the Netherlands is no exception in this sense, but in tax disputes, it may be possible for taxpayers to get reimbursed for a part or a reasonable amount of objection/litigation expenses (including traveling and lodging expenses for hearings, opportunity costs for leave from work, attorney's fees, expenses for expert supports, etc.) when the organ in charge of the review changes or revokes the disputed re/assessments in favor of the taxpayers at the objection/litigation stage, provided that the taxpayers requested in advance for their reimbursements when the reviewer's decision/judgment was favorable to them.[112] If the taxpayers lose in court, the only case that obliges them to bear the litigation-related expenses of the tax authority is basically where they obviously irrationally utilized the court procedures.[113]

107. The OECD published a book ("Co-operative Compliance: A Framework from Enhanced Relationship to Co-operative Compliance") in 2013, which describes "enhanced relations" between taxpayers and tax authorities. and the introduction of the concept of "cooperative compliance." For details, *see* Francesco Cannas and Kristof Wauters, The Rise of Cooperative Compliance Programs and the Rule of Law: A Comparison Between Belgium and Italy, *European Taxation*, December 2019, pp. 561-571 DOI: 10.59403/37xjpkn, and Florian Fiala and Lisa Ramharter, Cooperative Compliance in Austria, *European Taxation*, August 2019, pp. 385-390 DOI; 10.59403/40ckwf.
108. *See* Hugo Vollebregt, From Red Tape to Red Carpet: How the Netherlands Has Changed the Traditional Dispute Landscape for Tax Issues, *International Transfer Pricing Journal*, Vol. 16, No. 3 (2009) pp. 161-165 DOI: 10.59403/x78rbd, Lisette van der Hel-van Dijk and Theo Poolen, Netherlands/International—Horizontal Monitoring in the Netherlands: At the Crossroads, *Bulletin for International Taxation*, November 12 (2013) pp. 673-678 DOI: 10.59403/12tshpy.
109. *See* Figures 6.2 and 6.5 in Section 5 in the Chapter 6 for further analysis on this point.
110. *See* Job van del Pol, How to Manage Tax Disputes in the Netherlands, *International Tax Review*, November 1 (2012) (also at https://www.internationaltaxreview.com/article/2a69l7rce9dqie47v4lc0/how-to-manage-tax-disputes-in-the-netherlands) and Wattle, *supra* "Tax Litigation in Last Instance in the Netherlands" p. 48.
111. For details, *see* Werner Penningstorf, The European Experience with Attorney Fee Shifting, Law and Contemporary Problems, *Duke University School of Law*, Vol. 47, No. 1 (1984) pp. 44-49 DOI: 10.2307/1191436.
112. For details, *see* Otto Marres, Chapter 13 of Courts and Tax Treaty Law, ed. Gulielmo Maisto, *EC and International Tax Law Series*, Vol. 3, IBFD (2007) p. 313 and https://langendorff-tax.com/about-your-assessment-and-how-to-file-an-objection/. Also refer to "Tax Controversy 2019 Netherlands" with a reference that the recoverable expense related to a tax objection varies depending on the complexity of a disputed tax case, but is normally be around EUR 254 in 2019.
113. *See* Wim Wijnen and Paul Bongaarts, The Judicial System of the Netherlands in Tax Matters at https://iatj.net/content/congresses/rome2010/Netherlands.pdf, and *supra* "Tax Controversy in Netherlands."

2 Relationship with EU Law

(1) Powers of the European Commission and the ECJ

Now that the Netherlands is also an EU Member State, it also needs to ensure the consistency of its tax system and tax dispute system with EU law. Sometimes, taxpayers dispute re/assessments on them mainly from the perspective that tax provisions serving as grounds for the re/assessments conflict with EU law or domestic rules that incorporate it. Also, a court of the Member States can, where there might be cases of a possible violation of EU law, apply for the preliminary rulings of the ECJ under Article 267 of the Treaty on the Functioning of the European Union (TFEU) on how the relevant EU law applies to such cases.[114] This court's application for the preliminary rulings of the ECJ, as Article 267(3) of TFEU prescribes,[115] becomes obligatory in a case where the court that could apply for it is the final court in a Member State. A "preliminary judgment" handed down by the ECJ has res judicata and binding force, so it serves in principle as a decisive settlement method for domestic tax disputes in Member States that have implications with EU law.

Disputes over domestic provisions' possible violation of EU law could also arise from the initiative of the Commission now that Article 258 TFEU provides, "If the Commission considers that a Member State has failed to fulfill an obligation under the Treaties, it shall deliver a reasoned opinion on the matter after giving the State concerned the opportunity to submit its observations. If the State concerned does not comply with the opinion within the period laid down by the Commission, the latter may bring the matter before the Court of Justice of the European Union."[116] Disputes could also be brought up by the other Member States as well as the European Parliament and the European Council, as Article 259 of TFEU prescribes, "A Member State which considers that another Member State has failed to fulfill an obligation under the Treaties may bring the matter before the Court of Justice of the European Union," and Article 263 of TFEU states that the ECJ "shall for this purpose have jurisdiction in actions brought by a Member State, the European Parliament, the Council or the Commission on grounds of lack of competence, infringement of an

114. Article 267(1) of TFEU dictates, "The Court of Justice of the European Union shall have jurisdiction to give preliminary rulings concerning: (a) the interpretation of the Treaties; (b) the validity and interpretation of acts of the institutions, bodies, offices or agencies of the Union; Where such a question is raised before any court or tribunal of a Member State, that court or tribunal may, if it considers that a decision on the question is necessary to enable it to give judgment, request the Court to give a ruling thereon."

115. Article 267(3) of TFEU states, "Where such question is raised in a case pending before a court or tribunal of a Member State against whose decisions there is no judicial remedy under national law, that court or tribunal shall bring the matter before the court."

116. As for the cumulative number of applications for preliminary rulings on direct taxes as of 2013, those filed by Member States in accordance with Article 267 of TFEU is 215 cases, while those filed by the European Commission in accordance with Article 258 of TFEU is 52 cases. The number of those filed after 2000 was particularly large. *See* Marcel G.H. Schaper, 30 Years of Direct Tax Litigation Before the Court of Justice of the European Union: An Empirical Survey, *Bulletin for International Taxation*, April/May 2014, p. 237 DOI: 10.59403/1a0h8c3.

essential procedural requirement, infringement of the Treaties or of any rule of law relating to their application, or misuse of powers."

Irrespective of which of the above procedures are followed to bring to the ECJ a matter of a Member State's possible violation of EU Law, if such violation is confirmed by the ECJ's judgment, the concerned Member State shall, as Article 260 of TFEU stipulates, be required to take the necessary measures to comply with the judgment. If the Commission considers that the Member State concerned has not taken the necessary measures to comply with the judgment of the Court, it may bring the case before the Court after allowing that State to submit its observations. It shall specify the amount of penalty to be paid by the Member State concerned which it considers appropriate in the circumstances. If the ECJ finds that there is an infringement, it may also impose a penalty payment on the Member State concerned not exceeding the amount specified by the Commission. Moreover, Article 261 of TFEU provides, "Regulations adopted jointly by the European Parliament and the Council, ... may give the Court of Justice of the European Union unlimited jurisdiction about the penalties provided for in such regulations."

In the context of taxation, there has recently been an increase in the number of cases in which Member States and their taxpayers bring their tax matters to the ECJ in response to the European Commission's determination that those matters contain issues that violate EU law. Behind the increase in the number of such cases is the Commission's stance that has recently gotten stricter against taxpayers' tax-motivated actions and Member States' grant of preferential tax treatments. In particular, the Commission has proactively applied its authority under Article 108 of TFEU to review Member States' tax systems and practices that might constitute "state aids."[117] "State aids" violate EU law because Article 107 of TFEU provides, "Save as otherwise provided in the Treaties, any aid granted by a Member State or through State resources in any form whatsoever which distorts or threatens to distort competition by favouring certain undertakings or the production of certain goods shall, in so far as it affects trade between Member States, be incompatible with the internal market."[118]

One example of cases where the Commission found a system of a Member State to constitute a "state aid" was its 11/1/2016 letter (SA 37667) issued against the Belgium government on the "excess profit exemption system" under Article 185(2)(b) of the 1992 ITA. In this letter, the Commission raised various arguments, which included an observation that this system allows entities resident or operating through a permanent establishment in Belgium that are part of a multinational group to reduce their corporate tax liability in Belgium by deducting from their profit actually recorded so-called excess profit which is determined by estimating the hypothetical average profit that a standalone company carrying out comparable activities could be expected to make in comparable circumstances while such treatment is not available to all

117. Article 108 of TFEU stipulates, "The Commission shall, in cooperation with Member States, keep under constant review all systems of aid existing in those States. It shall propose to the latter any appropriate measures required by the progressive development or by the functioning of the internal market."
118. Article 92 of ECC provides for the same purport.

corporate entities that are in similar legal and factual situation. In conclusion, the Commission decided that the "excess profit exemption system" constitutes a "state aid" because it leads to taxation which is not in line with the arm's length principle, and Belgium should amend the regime and collect additional taxes from thirty-five multinational companies that benefited from this system.

Belgium v. Commission (T-131/16 and T-263/16) is a case (2019) in which the Belgian government and one of the corporations to which the "excess profit exemption" system was applied filed a lawsuit with the ECJ on the above Commission's decision. In this case, the ECJ specified that the Belgian tax authorities, in issuing advance rulings on excess profit, carried out a qualitative and quantitative assessment of each request on a "case-by-case" basis because the beneficiaries of the alleged aid scheme are not defined in a general and distinct manner, so it does require a further implementing measure within the meaning of Article 1(d) of the Council Regulation 2015/1589 that defines an aid scheme to be deficient of such measure.[119] In conclusion, the ECJ ruled that, under the "excess profit exemption" system, the Belgian tax administration had a genuine margin of discretion in deciding whether it was appropriate to grant such downward adjustments to the corporations, so the reliance on the Commission's assertion on Article 1(d) of the Council Regulation is not sustainable and its concerned decision should be void. The ECJ also ordered, under Article 138 (General rules as to allocation of costs), etc., of the Rules of Procedure,[120] the Commission to pay the costs of the other parties.

(2) Relationship Between Article 107 of TFEU and Dispute Settlement by Agreement

As mentioned above, there are some European Commission's decisions on "state aids" that were canceled by the ECJ, while preferential measures that the European Commission considers to be "state aids" include not only legal provisions but also agreements between tax authorities and taxpayers. For example, the European Commission, in its decisions dated 21/10/2015 (SA.38374 and SA.38375), determined that the Advance Pricing Agreement (APA) concluded in 2012 between the Netherlands tax authority and the Dutch-based Starbucks Manufacturing Emea BV (SMBV) as well as the APA concluded in 2012 between the tax authority of Luxembourg and Fiat Chrysler Finance Europe resulted in lowering the tax burden of those corporations in those Member States through income shifting to their foreign-affiliated companies by means of excessive royalty payments to them, so that they constitute "state aids" that distort competition in the EU market and are incompatible with the Article 107(1) of the TFEU,

119. Article 1(d) of the Council Regulation 2015/1589 dictates, "'aid scheme' means any act on the basis of which, without further implementing measures being required, individual aid awards may be made to undertakings defined within the act in a general and abstract manner."
120. Article 138(1) of the Rules of Procedure provides, "The unsuccessful party shall be ordered to pay the costs if they have been applied for in the successful party's pleadings." Article 184 (Costs in appeals) prescribes, "(1) Subject to the following provisions, Articles 137 to 146 of these Rules shall apply, mutatis mutandis, to the procedure before the Court of Justice on an appeal against a decision of the General Court."

obliging those Member States to recover from those corporations the amounts equivalent of those "state aid" amounts.

The above Commission's decisions were also appealed by the Member States and the taxpayers, respectively, to the ECJ. In *Netherlands v. Commission* (T-760/15 and T-636/16), the ECJ's 24/9/2019 ruling was in favor of the appellants mainly for the reason that the Commission has not demonstrated that the concerned APA derogated from the transfer pricing rule stipulated under Article 8b of CIT and from the transfer pricing decree and that it had thus conferred an advantage on SMBV within the meaning of Article 107(1) TFEU. While *in Grand Duchy of Luxembourg and Fiat Chrysler Finance Europe (FCFE) v. European Commission* (T-755/15 and T-759/15), the ECJ's 24/9/2019 ruling was that the Transactional Net Margin Method (TNMM) relied on in the concerned APA as an arm's length price calculation method for the amount of the royalty payments to be received by the FCFE in Luxembourg led to the underestimation of the capital necessary to carry out FCFE's activities and bear the associated risks, so the FCFE's remuneration under the concerned APA was not a reliable approximation based on market conditions and thus resulted in a reduction of its tax burden and an advantage within the meaning of Article 107 of TFEU.[121]

As mentioned above, in recent years, the tax authorities of EU Member States have generally been steering toward flexible tax dispute resolution and active use of ADR. While the European Commission's 2016 publication ("Notice on the notion of State aid as referred to in Article 107(1) of the Treaty on the Functioning of the European Union, 2016/C 262/01) specifies that Member States' tax statutes, APA, rulings, agreements with taxpayers, tax amnesties, etc. could be subject to the Commission's review from the perspective of whether they constitute "state aids." Thus, EU law is, on the one hand, acting towards fostering flexible resolution of tax disputes, but on the other hand, working as a deterrent to it. On the latter point, depending on which tax treatment in a Member State is questioned by the Commission from the perspective of the "state aid," it could also affect non-Member States and their taxpayers, so there are some among them that are critical of the Commission's approach and its legal grounds which became particularly clear in the abovementioned ECJ rulings.[122]

In particular, the US Treasury showed its critical view in its 2016 publication ("White Paper on the European Commission's Recent State Aid Investigations of Transfer Pricing Rules") on the Commission's approach to how the arm's length principle is applicable to transfer pricing issues. The main assertions in this White Paper include: (i) this Commission's approach is new and departs from prior EU case

121. While, the ECJ's 15/7/2020 ruling in *Commission v. Ireland* (T-778/16) and in *Apple Sales International and Apple Operations Europe v. Commission* (T-892/16) on TP issues were against the Commission's decisions that "state aids" were granted specifically to those taxpayers.

122. Some consider that adopting the arm's length principle, which is unique to EU law, in determining whether there is a "state aid" would violate the constitutional obligations of Member States to collect taxes that are not explicitly stated in domestic law. *See* Stephen Daly, The Constitutional Implications of an EU Arm's Length Principle, *European Taxation*, February/March (2020) pp. 70-75 DOI: 10.59403/1k885s0.

laws and Commission decisions; (ii) the Commission should not seek retroactive recoveries under its new approach; (iii) the Commission's new approach is inconsistent with international norms and undermines the international tax system. On the above (iii), the White Paper expounds on page 20, "the Commission has suggested that it 'may have regard' for the OECD TP Guidelines and that a ruling in compliance with the OECD TP Guidelines is 'unlikely' to give rise to State aid, but the Commission has indicated neither the circumstances that will cause a 'breach' of the arm's length principle nor when such a breach will be considered 'manifest,' leaving Member States and companies without meaningful guidance on how the Commission intends to apply its version of the arm's length principle."

Indeed, the Dutch government asserted in paragraph 133 of the above Netherlands case (T-760/15 and T-636/16) that the Commission should not review the APA in question based on an arm's length principle particular to EU law, and SMBV also argued that the Commission's approach is a departure from the Dutch transfer pricing rules. In response to this, the European Commission argued that the examination of whether or not the concerned APA had a selective advantage was not based on the arm's length principle but on the reference to a framework derived from domestic law. In conclusion, the ECJ reversed the Commission's decision of this APA constituting a "state aid" because the Commission did not fulfill its burden of proof that it granted a selective advantage, but it is to be noted that the ECJ confirmed in paragraphs 154 to 155 as follows: "the Commission cannot be criticized for having used a methodology for determining transfer pricing that it considers appropriate in this instance ... the Commission correctly observed that it cannot be formally bound by the OECD Guidelines."

Moreover, when the Commission decides that there exists a "state aid," in some cases, the concerned Member State might find it difficult to recover the aid. For example, in *Commission v. Germany* (C5/89), the Commission was the applicant because the German government did not comply with the Commission's decision (88/174/EEC of 17 Nov. 1987) that confirmed the government's permission of the domestic corporation's undertaking producing semi-finished and finished aluminum products to constitute a "state aid." The German government's reason for failing to recover the aid from the corporation was its obligation to protect the taxpayer's legitimate expectations. In this case, the ECJ ruled in 1990 in paragraph 18, "the German Government may not rely, as making it absolutely impossible to implement the Commission's decision, on the obligations to which the competent administrative authority is subject under the particular rules governing the protection of legitimate expectations in Paragraph 48 of the Verwaltungsverfahrensgesetz ... As the Court has consistently held, a Member State may not plead provisions, practices or circumstances existing in its internal legal system to justify a failure to comply with its obligations under Community law."[123]

123. There are some who are critical of this ruling. For example, *see* A. Winckler and F.-C. Laprévote, Reconciling Legal Certainty, Legitimate Expectations, Equal Treatment and the Prohibition of State Aids, *European State Aid Law Quarterly*, Vol. 10, No. 2 (June 2011), pp. 321-326 DOI: 10.21552/estal/2011/2/232.

As mentioned above, EU law contains some treaties and rules that place certain restrictions on flexible tax dispute resolutions in Member States, but most of them work towards fostering flexible tax dispute resolutions. Actually, in the Netherlands, the number of tax disputes resolved flexibly has been on the increase recently. This increase has been facilitated much by the foundation of the Dutch Tax Mediation Association (Vereniging voor Fiscale Mediation) in 2007, the notice issued in 2011 by the EU Council seeking the Dutch government to take remedial measures for the delay in implementing the 2008 Mediation Directive, and a law (official gazette (Staatblad) 2012, 570) adopted in the Netherlands to implement the Directive in 2012.[124] As for arbitration, there are Articles 1022 to 1077 of the Dutch Civil Procedure Law, but the active use of arbitration in the context of tax disputes was after the Tax Arbitration Act (Wet Fiscale Arbitrage) in 2019, which was enacted particularly in the wake of the 2016 EU Arbitration Order and the Council Directive (EU) 2017/1852 of 10 October 2017 on tax dispute resolution mechanisms in the European Union.[125]

SECTION 3 SUMMARY AND ANALYSIS

1 Summary and Analysis of Section 1

The Irish old tax objection/appeals system had such problems as: ① the Revenue's involvement at the entrance and exit of the taxpayer's appeal procedure to the OAC might have a problem with Article 6 of ECHR, and its independence was not sufficient; ② the reasons for the OAC's decisions were only presented orally to the appellants; ③ the OAC's decisions were not made public until the 1998 Finance Act was enacted; ④ time and money costs of the appeals to the OAC tended to be high due to the accumulation of unprocessed appeals. However, since 1999, aggrieved taxpayers could use an "external review." Moreover, under the current tax appeals regime created by the Finance (Tax Appeals) Act 2015, (i) the TAC, which is more independent than the OAC, has been established; (ii) taxpayers can opt to skip objections to the Revenue and file appeals with the TAC directly; (iii) reasons for the TAC decisions are communicated to the appellants in writing; (iv) the TAC decisions are publicly available; (v) increased budget and personnel as well as a recent decrease in the number of appeals filed with the TAC have resulted in a decrease in the backlog of unprocessed appeals. They have improved the taxpayers' convenience and reduced their time and financial burden.

The average rate of cancellation of the re/assessments at the stage of objection to the Revenue is about 20%, which is not that high, but the reason why the number of

124. *See* Nederlandse Vereniging Voor Rechtsvergelijking, Mediation in the Netherlands: Past-Present-Future, Vol. 6.4 (also at https://www.ejcl.org/64/art64-8.html).

125. The European Parliament's Resolution of September 12, 2017 on the implementation of the Mediation Directive, states in the Main conclusions 4 that "many Member States provide financial incentives for parties to use mediation, either in the form of cost reductions, legal aid, or sanctions for unjustified refusal to consider mediation; observes that the results achieved in these countries prove that mediation can provide a cost-effective and quick extra-judicial resolution of disputes through processes tailored to the needs of the parties."

objections to the Revenue is by no means small in number should be attributable considerably to the fact that a large number of them are settled by agreements between the Revenue and the taxpayers by the care and management power of the Revenue Commissioner under TCA §849. The scope of this Commissioner's discretionary power is indeed more limited than in the UK, and the use of ADR in tax matters is quite limited, but such power can also be exercised in relation to penalties. This Commissioner's power can be beneficial not only to the Revenue but also to the taxpayers, particularly concerning disputes on penalties, which are quite large in number due partly to their complexities and ambiguities in their applicable scope, as in the case of the UK.[126] In cases where disputes over penalties are not resolved at the stage of objection to the Revenue, (A) aggrieved taxpayers could dispute them at court (not at TAC), and (B) the Revenue must file suits with the court if they are not paid.

The above (A) and (B) procedures could cause considerable clerical, time, and financial burden on taxpayers and the Revenue, so they should often work toward settling disputes over penalties by agreements before they end up in courts. Those procedures may also have issues with Article 6 of ECHR,[127] particularly because Ireland has some severe penalties, and they might come under "criminal charge" in the context of ECHR in light of the criteria shown in the ECJ ruling in the *Georgiou* case (2001).[128] If some of Ireland's severe penalties come under "criminal charge," the ECHR would oblige Ireland to ensure those taxpayers who dispute them access to a fair and public hearing within a reasonable time by an independent and impartial tribunal established by law by Article 6 of ECHR. Actually, the High Court judgment in the UK *King case* (2001) held that the penalty prescribed in the UK's TAA §95 falls under the category of "criminal charge" in the ECHR,[129] and, in this connection, it should be noted that there was much similarity between the UK's TAA §95 and Ireland's TCA §1053.

In addition to Article 6 of ECHR, some other supranational conventions and rules affect the way how tax disputes in Ireland are to be handled. In particular, they include Article 10A of the EIA Directive which rendered Ireland's "loser pays rule" to be incompatible with EU law because the costs of a litigant taxpayer could be prohibitively expensive. The EU Charter of Fundamental Rights is also influential in this respect now that it has Article 47 (Right to an effective remedy and to a fair trial), which provides, "Everyone is entitled to a fair and public hearing within a reasonable time by an independent and impartial tribunal previously established by law. Everyone shall have the possibility of being advised, defended, and represented. Legal aid shall be made available to those who lack sufficient resources in so far as such aid is necessary to ensure effective access to justice." In this connection, it is also notable that the EU

126. As for disputes over expense deduction, Ireland also relies on the "wholly and exclusively" standard under TCA §114 (General rule as to deductions), but, unlike UK, the Revenue's manual ("General rule as to deduction of expenses in employment: Part 05-02-20") states that the number of lawsuits on them is small.
127. *See* footnote 70. Para. 7.10 of LRC 72-2004 also states, "Assuming that the Appeal Commissioners is restructured in a manner that is consistent with the recommendations made by the Commission in the Report, ... then an appeal to the Appeal Commissioners in relation to the impositions of penalties would comply with Article 6 requirements."
128. For the *Georgiou* case, *see* Section 5(4) of Chapter 3.
129. For the *King* case, *see* Section 5(4) of Chapter 3.

Council Directive on tax dispute resolution mechanisms declares in the preamble (9) that this Directive respects the fundamental rights and observes the principles recognized in particular by the Charter of Fundamental Rights of the European Union.

2 Summary and Analysis of Section 2

The Netherlands, unlike some other civil law countries such as Germany,[130] utilizes actively flexible settlement of tax disputes at the administrative objection stage as well and has resulted in a significant reduction in time and financial costs of the aggrieved taxpayers as well as the tax authority's burden associated with disputes. Many such flexible settlements of tax disputes are realized by settlements by agreement between the tax authority and the taxpayers, but recently, there has been an increase in the number of cases that are resolved by utilizing ADR. Behind this active utilization of ADR, there is ADR-related legislation that was introduced in the wake of various EU laws that foster flexible settlements of tax disputes. Moreover, now that the Netherlands has adopted the conditional unilateral costs shifting rule favorable to the taxpayers,[131] it helps reduce the taxpayers' financial risk associated with disputing re/assessments which could otherwise be quite high. These facts have resulted in increasing the number of tax disputes not only at the administrative objection stage but also in court.

In the Netherlands, some other systems and practices could further reduce taxpayers' time and financial costs associated with tax disputes. In particular, they include the following: (i) "horizontal monitoring" programs, which served as a model for the OECD's "cooperative compliance," have been implemented vis-à-vis top-ranking big corporations since 2005, and they have expanded their coverage of big corporations since 2008;[132] (ii) as for a dispute whose point of contention is limited to the issue of interpretation of the law, it can be agreed by the tax authority and the taxpayer to bring the dispute directly to the Supreme Court without going through the appellate courts; (iii) since 2003, there has been a statute that suspends decisions and judgments on those cases which are designated by the Ministry of Finance and have similar cases that are already litigated; (iv) since 2016, it has become possible for district courts to refer to the Supreme Court a preliminary question of law which is also

130. Germany is similar to Japan in that in principle flexible settlement of tax disputes is not possible but is different from Japan in that the number of tax disputes is so large. For example, in 2015, the number of tax litigations on IT and VAT of individuals, corporations, and partnerships in the Fiscal Courts was over 130,000. In principle, the German tax authority bears the costs of the litigant taxpayers when they win at court. *See* https://uk.practicallaw.thomsonreuters.com/9-623-5696?transitionType=Default&contextData=(sc.Default)&firstPage=true.

131. In the judgment (2004, NJ2005, 361, BNB 2005/239), the Supreme Court stated that the Netherlands current cost-sharing rule in tax disputes does not violate Article 47 of the Charter of Fundamental Rights of the European Union. *See* Marres, *supra* "Chapter 13 in Courts and Tax Treaty Law" p. 314.

132. Ireland and the Netherlands are similar in that the number of disputes on CIT is small compared to its ratio of revenue. In the case of Ireland, one of the causes for that should lie in the low CIT rate, while in the case of the Netherlands where the standard CIT rate is 25% (as of 2021), it should be found primarily in the efforts toward building cooperative relationships with taxpayers, as represented by "horizontal monitoring" programs.

at issue in many other cases, just as the courts of the Member States apply for a preliminary ruling of the ECJ.

Indeed, the above (i) ~ (iv) possess an effect of reducing the burden of either or both taxpayers and the tax authority, but they (excluding the above (i) (function of "horizontal monitoring" programs) do not seem to possess a significant effect on the number of tax disputes. EU law does possess such effect markedly now that EU law complicates the issue of how domestic tax law and tax treatments of the Member States stand in terms of their relation to EU law. To clarify this complicated issue, Member States, their taxpayers, and courts, as well as the EU Commission, could either file suits with domestic courts or apply for preliminary rulings of the ECJ, and particularly the EU Commission has lately become more active in applying for preliminary rulings of the ECJ on Member States' possible violation of the rule prohibiting "state aids." Moreover, EU law has many rules and Council Directives that function in a way to foster taxpayers' rights/interests and active use of ADR. So, it is positive that EU law has generally been at work in adding fuel to the increase in the number of tax disputes not only in Ireland and the Netherlands but also in other Member States.

It is also true that the rule prohibiting "state aids" has an aspect of deterring Member States from resolving tax disputes by agreement with some taxpayers because if the EU Commission determines that they constitute "state aids," or the ECJ judgments sustain such determinations, they cannot be justified even by the principle of legitimate expectations and they become obliged to recover such tax amounts that constitute "state aids." Moreover, the effect of EU law is not necessarily limited to the Member States. This is manifested particularly in the fact that among tax treatments that are determined to constitute "state aids," there are APAs, etc., which are concluded by Member States and multinational enterprises of various countries because they are not in line with "the arm's length principle particular to EU law." Another example of the EU law's extraterritorial effect is found in the revision of Article 25 (Mutual Agreement Procedure) of the OECD Model Tax Convention as well as a subsequent increase in the number of tax treaties that have lately been amended, in the wake of the EU Law fostering the use of ADR for tax disputes resolution, to incorporate an arbitration clause to settle international double taxation issues.[133]

133. Those treaties incorporating an arbitration clause include Article 11 of the 2013 Revised Protocol of Japan-U.S. Tax Treaty and Article 24, para. 5(b) of the Japan-Netherlands Tax Treaty. Now, over 150 tax treaties have such a clause.

CHAPTER 6

International Comparison and Options for Reform

SECTION 1 *KEY FACTORS* AFFECTING THE NUMBER OF TAX DISPUTES ABROAD

1 Components of Key *Factors* and Their Status

Various facts and factors influence the number of tax disputes, and what constitutes them may vary from one country to another. Therefore, there is a certain degree of limitation in generalizing about them. Despite such a limitation, the analyzes in Chapters 1 to 5 reveal some facts on them and they intimate that generally those influential or key factors could mainly be; *Factor 1 (tax structure*: level of tax burden, complexity of tax system, nature/attributes of taxes, number of taxpayers subjected to taxes, scope of tax authority's discretionary power, etc.); *Factor 2 (tax audit:* audit ratio, ratio/volume of re/assessments, etc.);[1] *Factor 3 (compliance*: taxpayers' nature and attitudes, etc.); *Factor 4 (dispute resolution methods:* availability/frequency of flexible dispute resolution, etc.); *Factor 5 (level of disputing taxpayers' burden); Factor 6 (structure and performance of the reviewing bodies*: level of their independence, ratio of revocation of disputed re/assessments, etc.), *Factor 7 (complementary administrative/legal measures favorable for taxpayers:* level/extent of measures for mitigating the problems related in many cases to the above *Factor 1* and the power

1. As for the relation of audit ratio/amount of re/assessments, etc., with the number of tax disputes, *see* 4 in Section 1 of Chapter 1.

imbalance between taxpayers and tax authority, etc.);[2] *Factor 8 (requirement for and effect of filing tax objections/litigations)*.[3]

The key *Factors 1 to 8* above generally work to increase the number of tax disputes in such cases: as for *Factor 1 (tax structure)*, (i) tax burden is heavy, (ii) tax system is complex with many provisions lacking transparency on their applicable scope, (iii) there are many taxpayers subjected to taxes, (iv) tax authority's discretionary power is wide, etc.; as for *Factor 2 (tax audit)*, audit ratio and ratio/amount of re/assessments are high and the accuracy of the re/assessments is not sufficient; as for *Factor 3 (compliance)*, neither taxpayers' trust in tax administration nor their compliance level is high; as for *Factor 4 (dispute resolution methods)*, flexible dispute resolution is possible and actively utilized; as for *Factor 5 (level of disputing taxpayers' burden)*, time, money, and clerical burden on the disputing taxpayers is relatively low; as for *Factor 6 (structure and performance of the reviewing bodies)*, their independence and their ratio of revocation of re/assessments are high; as for *Factor 7 (complementary (administrative/legal) measures favorable for taxpayers)*, the level of administrative/legal support for disputing taxpayers is high; as for *Factor 8 (requirement for and effect of filing tax objections/litigations)*, the payment of the disputed tax amount is not a precondition for appeals, and the appeals suspend tax collection action in principle.

Answers to the question of which of the above key *Factors 1* to *8* strongly affect the number of tax disputes may also vary depending on a country, but it could be said that *Factors 1* to *6*, which are more fundamental and wide-ranging, should generally be more influential than *Factors 7* and *8*. For example, the analysis in Chapter 1 confirms that *Factor 1* is very influential because, in addition to the level of tax burden and the number of taxpayers subject to taxes, the complexity and structure of tax provisions make a big difference in the number of tax disputes resting on their applications. The highly disputed issues in many of the countries covered in Chapters 2 to 5 also pivot on tax provisions with ① ambiguity in the scope of application, ② preferential treatments, ③ wide room for discretion, or ④ exceptions. For example, in the case of Australia, as mentioned in Chapter 4, not only the scope of the ATO Commissioner's discretionary power is wide, but also the AAT can render a decision to substitute it with its own, so many disputes have arisen on tax provisions that have such attributes as the above ③ (wide room for discretion) and ④(exceptions).

It still holds that even *Factors 7* and *8* could, in some cases and in some countries, incentivize or disincentivize taxpayers strongly enough to affect the number of tax disputes significantly. However, as for *Factor 7 (complementary measures favorable for taxpayers)*, in particular, its relationship with the number of tax disputes is manifold

2. The power imbalance between the taxpayers and the tax authority or their "inequality of arms" at the objection/litigation stage is particularly pronounced when the taxpayers are unrepresented. *See* the U.S. TAS 2017 Report, pp. 298-301 and the UK Tax Law Review Commission 2021 Report, p. 85.
3. Includable in this *Factor 8* is a risk in some countries of the disputed re/assessment amount increased by disputing them at the objection stage.

and is not definitive enough.[4] Therefore, the correlation between the above key *Factors 1* to *8* with the number of tax disputes may not be so simple in some cases, but it should at least be clear that if there exist facts that are in sharp contrast to those mentioned above (in the second paragraph of 1 of this section), those facts should generally work towards decreasing the number of tax disputes. So, it could be said that the way the main facts relevant to these eight key *Factors* impact the number of tax disputes is generally predictable, and, in the following parts (2 ~ 5) of this section, attempts are to be made to confirm and sort out what kind of facts on *Factors 1* to *8* are observable conspicuously in the countries covered in the preceding chapters and how they are affecting the number of tax disputes respectively. Such attempts are also expected to shed more light on how Japan stands internationally with respect to her main rules and practices relevant to *Factors 1* to 8.

2 U.S. Aspects of Key *Factors*

In the case of the U.S., litigations are rampant as it is often referred to as a litigious society. Therefore, in the U.S., there must be various facts suggesting that *Factor 1 (tax system structure)* and *Factor 3 (compliance)* mentioned in 1 above should be working strongly in the direction of increasing the number of tax disputes. In concrete, as for *Factor 1*, there are particular facts such as: (i) the tax system is complex;[5] (ii) there are various types of information returns to be submitted, and failures to file them shall incur penalties;[6] (iii) "Citizenship-based taxation" system is adopted; (iv) There are various countermeasures against actively utilized tax strategies. Typical examples of cases that reflect many of those facts are the penalty system and the obligation to report foreign assets.[7] In particular, in the case of FBAR (Report of Foreign Bank and Financial Accounts), it was strengthened after the UBS scandal in which many wealthy U.S. citizens' unreported incomes were unveiled between 2000 and 2007 by imposing heavier penalties on the failure to file FBARs and lower hurdles for their applications on the non-filers of FBARs as it can be confirmed by the Utah State District Court judgment in *McBride v. United States* (2010 U.S. Dist. LEXIS 161206) and the Fourth Circuit Court of Appeals judgment in *Williams v. United States (489* Fed. App. 655; 2012), etc.[8]

4. As for *Factor 7*, for instance, if the level of information disclosure to taxpayers increases, transparency on the tax authority's tax treatments and decisions of the reviewing bodies increase, and they could work toward decreasing the number of tax disputes by enlightening taxpayers. While enlightening taxpayers might in some cases deepen their doubts and prompt them to dispute their cases.
5. *See* Figure 6.3.
6. Various penalties on failures to file information returns are prescribed under IRC§6721 (Failure to file correct information returns), IRC§6725 (Failure to report information under section 4101), etc.
7. As for the fact that there are more than 150 provisions on various penalties, *see* 2(1) in Section 4 of Chapter 3. IRM 20.1.1.1.1 (11-25 2011) also states that in 1955 IRC had provisions for roughly fourteen penalties, but now has more than ten times that number. Section 10-Penalties and Interest Provisions (at https://irs.gov > pub > 6209-section10-2016) shows what those penalties are.
8. For details, *see* Matsuda, *supra* "Tax Strategies VS. Countermeasures" pp. 125 ~ 136.

Moreover, many of those "most litigated issues" in the U.S. Tax Court, which were analyzed in Section 4 of Chapter 2, contain some of the attributes (①~④) mentioned in the above 1 in such a way that they strongly work towards increasing the number of tax disputes. Particularly, in the case of penalties, those attributes (① (ambiguity in the scope of application), ③ (wide scope for discretion), and ④ (exceptions)) are conspicuous. The large number of penalties being imposed and abated later showcases this fact of penalty cases possessing these attributes markedly,[9] and the main reasons for a large number of penalty abatements include: (i) as Figure 2.10 in Chapter 2 shows, in the case of "negligent penalties" under IRC§6662(c), many of them are canceled after the issue of "90-day letters";[10] (ii) "First Time Abate" is available for non-filers, etc., since 2001 on request provided that the requirements are met; (iii) the Office of Appeals can abate penalties while in principle they cannot use penalties as bargaining chips for sustaining the re/assessments or reaching settlements by agreement; (iv) an "accuracy-related penalty" is exempted where there is a "reasonable cause" which might include a taxpayer's ignorance of law and an underreporting stemming from the agent's misunderstanding on technical points.[11]

Cases on "innocent spouse" relief stipulated in IRC §6015 and "collection cases" are also "most litigated issues," and, as for "innocent spouse" cases, just like "penalty cases," the abovementioned attributes of ①, ③ and ④ must be at work significantly. In particular, the strong effect of the attribute ①(ambiguity in the scope of application) is obvious because determining whether or not IRC §6015 is applicable could be very difficult in some cases because the determination is to be made from the perspective of equitability by taking into account of various issues including: (i) whether the taxpayer had no reason to know the causes of the other spouse that are attributable to the underreporting of income; (ii) whether the taxpayer benefited from this underreporting of income. In the case of "collection cases," the attribute most strongly at work should rather be ③ (wide scope of discretion). Even so, for such disputes as "offers-in-compromise" cases, which also come under among "collection cases," not only *Factor 4 (dispute resolution methods)* but also *Factor 8 (requirement for and effect of filing tax objections/litigations)* must be at work as strong influencers as well because the objections/litigations filed on them not only suspend the collection action in principle but also could often lead to more flexible resolutions.

In the case of the U.S., just like *Factor 1 (tax structure), Factor 4 (dispute resolution methods),* and *Factor 6 (structure and performance of the reviewing bodies)* are strong triggers for tax disputes. The Office of Appeals, in addition to the prohibition of the "ex parte communications" rule, can neither make nuisance value settlements nor use penalties as bargaining chips for disputed re/assessments, but, despite such limitations, more than 90% of the appeals are resolved at the stage of the Office of Appeals. Moreover, there are increasing numbers of resolutions of potential disputes

9. *See* 2 in Section 4 of Chapter 2.
10. Some also point out that, although IRC §6751 was adopted to regulate the IRS's process of imposing penalties, it has not been observed strictly enough. *See* 2 in Section 1 of Chapter 2.
11. On the other hand, under IRC §6662(d)(2)(C) (Reduction not to apply to tax shelters), there is no waiver of the penalty based on the opinion of tax experts involved in tax shelters.

because the Appeals officers attempt to resolve some of them in the examination stage as well. The high dispute resolution ratio by the Office of Appeals intimates that many appellants could obtain some concessions from the IRS, and it should incentivize many taxpayers to file appeals with the Office of Appeals. Moreover, now that the 2019 Taxpayer First Act adopted measures that transformed the Office of Appeals into the Independent Office of Appeals, which has a higher level of independence, it should enhance further aggrieved taxpayers' expectation that they might be able to gain some concessions from the Office of Appeals.

As for *Factor 6 (structure and performance of the reviewing bodies)*, its influence at the litigation stage is also strong, particularly in the Tax Court.[12] Indeed, the ratio of revocation of the disputed re/assessments in the Tax Court is not high compared with that in other courts, and the "rule of not looking behind a notice of deficiency" is adopted,[13] but the majority of taxpayers prefer to litigate their cases at the Tax Court mainly for the following reasons: (i) many disputed re/assessments are resolved by agreements; (ii) it differs from the other courts in that the payment of the disputed tax amount is not a precondition for filing a suit, (iii) there are many litigants in persons, (iv) cases coming to the "Small Claims Division" can be expected to be processed and finalized more speedily. These reasons suggest the importance of convenience and low costs on the part of taxpayers in choosing a forum for tax disputes, so they lend support to the idea that *Factor 5 (level of disputing taxpayers' burden)* and *Factor 8 (requirement for and effect of filing tax objections/litigations)* should also be considerably at work in incentivizing taxpayers to file tax litigation with the Tax Court.[14]

As for *Factor 5 (level of disputing taxpayers' burden)*, taxpayers' burden is heavier in terms of the onus of proof at court (*see* footnotes 66 and 149 in Chapter 2) than that in such civil law countries as Japan and the Netherlands (*see* footnote 74 in this Chapter and footnote 97 in Chapter 5), but is generally less so in terms of costs rule compared to those countries with the "loser pays rule." Moreover, the "American rule" has changed recently to become more favorable to the taxpayers. Such changes include: (i) IRC §7430 adopted in 1982 enables the prevailing taxpayers that clear the net worth requirement to recover reasonable administrative/litigation costs unless the government/IRS can establish that its position in the proceeding is substantially

12. The number of tax disputes is also affected by the stance of the courts. The "Chevron deference" is derived from *Chevron USA Inc. v. Natural Resources* (467 U.S. 837; 1984) and it was relied upon for example by the Ninth Circuit Court of Appeals decisions in *Altera Corporation and Subsidiaries v. CIR* (No. 16-70496 and No. 16-70497 (2018)) to sustain the re/assessment of applying the commensurate with income standard while there is ambiguity on this principle and there are also many Treasury regulations and some IRCs that were struck down by courts.
13. While differences in rulings of the Circuit Courts among States (e.g., the "conjunctive test" versus the "disjunctive test" on the interpretation of the "two-prong test" on economic substance test) may incentivize taxpayers' forum shopping and increase the number of cases at the Circuit Courts.
14. While, if the fact of the "90-day letter" referring specifically to the Tax Court as the forum for litigation is, as some point out, one of the main reasons for many taxpayers filing suits to the Tax Court, it implies a strong effect that *Factor 7* could exert. Such strong effect is also implied in UK where many taxpayers did not utilize the HMRC's statutory review because they did not know it. *See* 1 in Section 3 and footnote 65 in Chapter 3.

justified; (ii) "qualified offer" under IRC §7430(e) could enable the prevailing taxpayers that clear the net worth requirement to recover costs regardless of whether the government/IRS can establish the above if the amount of tax payable determined by the court is less than the amount of the qualified offer unaccepted by the government. As for *Factor 7 (complementary measures favorable for taxpayers)*, it can be pointed out that courts and groups of attorneys lend helping hands to those taxpayers with difficulties through Calendar Call programs and so forth.

As for *Factor 2 (tax audit)*, the declining trend between 2012 and 2020 in the number of "90-day letters" issued annually is shown in Figure 2.5 in Chapter 2, and the number of appeals to the Office of Appeals is shown in Figure 2.3 in Chapter 2, and they intimate the recent declining trend in the number of tax audits. Indeed, as Figure 6.1 shows, the number of field and correspondence tax audits has been on a declining trend during this period.[15] Certainly, among facts and rules relevant to *Factor 2*, some work toward increasing the number of tax disputes, as in the case of the "90-day letter," whose correctness in content is not strictly required. However, the above facts suggest the existence of a strong positive correlation between the number of tax audits (or tax audit ratio) and the number of tax disputes. This positive correlative relation could be presumed to be so powerful that, in the case of the U.S., almost all the *Factors* other than *Factor 2* have general effects of increasing the number of tax disputes, but the recent declining trend of the number of tax audits under *Factor 2* countervail those effects so much so that the number of tax disputes has lately been on the decline. If this presumption is not mistaken, particularly in the case of the U.S., *Factor 2* containing this versatile element has been exerting a very strong influence on the number of tax disputes.

Figure 6.1 Number of Field Audits and "Correspondence" Audits of Federal Tax Returns

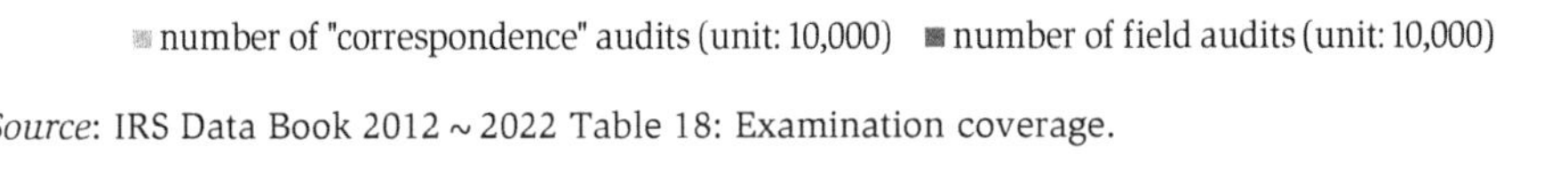

Source: IRS Data Book 2012 ~ 2022 Table 18: Examination coverage.

15. Among the total number of audits (e.g., it was 738,959 for 2021), those on individuals usually represent more than 90%. In the case of tax audits on IT returns, they were 659,012 for the year 2021. The recent ratio of audits against IT returns of individuals has been around 0.3%. For instance, in the case of individuals with annual income less than USD 100,000, the average ratio of audits was 0.9% in 2011 but kept declining since then to 0.5% in 2017. *See* IRS Data Book 2021 Table 18 and pp. 34 ~ 36. Compare it with footnote 201 in Chapter 2.

3 UK Aspects of Key *Factors*

Among the major *Factors* that affect the number of tax disputes in the UK discussed in Chapter 3, one notable fact on *Factor 1 (tax structure)* could be confirmed by the establishment of the Office of Tax Simplification following the recommendation by the Tax Reform Commission in the 2006 Report ("Tax Matters: Reforming the Tax System") which pointed out the need for reform of the UK tax system which became untenably complex while Australia, NZ, Ireland, and the Netherlands recently implemented tax reforms that led to the simplification of their tax systems, resulting in improved financial conditions and economic growth. The Office of Tax Simplification also made various recommendations which include those shown in the 2014 Report (Tax Penalties: Final Report). Certainly, as shown in Diagram 1, Figures 3.7, 3.8, and 3.11 in Chapter 3, there are facts showing a large number of penalty impositions, disputes over penalties, and their abatements.[16] There are various causes giving rise to these facts,[17] and in the case of late filing penalties, the primary cause is found in the rule adopted in 2012 that imposes them even on taxpayers whose income is under the personal allowance of GBP 12,750 while the HMRC has shown its intention of addressing this issue soon.

As for the primary cause for a large number of disputes over "behavioral penalties," the analysis in Chapter 3 reveals that they have the following aspects: (i) there is a lack of transparency regarding their application, and there is a lack of consistency in their application by examiners;[18] (ii) the scope of their abatement based on a "reasonable excuse" is not so clear-cut but not so narrow; (iii) the number of cases where their executions are suspended in the case of taxpayers meeting certain conditions is not small; and (iv) the recent increase in the number of cases where higher rates of behavioral penalties are applied should enhance further taxpayers' willingness to dispute their validity and they could be compounded by their relation with EU law.[19] The above 2014 Report of the Office of Tax Simplification not only acknowledges those difficulties surrounding "behavioral penalties" while its view was that the problem was not so much their complexity as the lack of transparency and consistency in their application.[20] Such being the case, the Report is uncertain about the degree of attainment of their purpose of effecting a change on the taxpayers'

16. Penalties related to the recently-introduced tax avoidance disclosure schemes (DOTAS in TMA §98C(3), etc.) and the follower notice penalty are recent additions to the complexity of the penalty system. The follower notice penalty is imposed when a dispute on a tax avoidance scheme is pursued even after the effect of the similar tax avoidance scheme has already denied in court. *See* HMRC's document (Follower notices and penalties) for details on this penalty.
17. For example, among VAT-related penalties, there are many that come under default charges which are imposed automatically for delayed filing and payment but the reasons for disputing them should differ to some extent from those for disputing "behavioral penalties." *See* 1(2) in Section 5 of Chapter 3.
18. *See* the 2014 Report 3.2 and 3.3 by the Office of Tax Simplification.
19. The Tax Reform Commission's 2006 Report 1.1.2 pointed out that one of the reasons for the complexity of the UK tax system is the UK's failure to anticipate the rulings of the ECJ that has been expanding the scope of its function.
20. It might be true that, even if tax provisions are complex, they may not induce many tax disputes on them provided that they are clear on their scope of application. Conversely, 2005 ITA §34 on

compliance level, but it anticipates that those difficulties will be mitigated as the HMRC's examiners have become more used to the ways of how they are to be applied.[21]

Ambiguity on the scope of application (which may be partly due to the HMRC's practice) is not the only reason for a particular theme to be disputed frequently. Flexible tax dispute resolution vis-à-vis *Factor 4 (dispute resolution methods)* is another major reason for the increase in the number of tax disputes. As in the case of the U.S., many taxpayers in the UK file their objections to the tax authority with some expectation that the HMRC actively exercises its discretion based on the care and management power in resolving disputes on taxes, penalties, and interest flexibly and such discretion is also exercised with respect to the use of ADR. The HMRC's statutory reviews do not utilize ADR, and that might also be one of the reasons for the relatively low ratio of its usage while ADR is actively used in other dispute resolution stages. The usefulness and importance of flexible settlements of disputes through ADR include: (i) it is provided free of charge by a trained Revenue staff; (ii) it offers various merits such as possible win-win outcomes for both of the disputing parties; (iii) the ratio of resolving disputes subjected to ADR is very high; (v) the disputing party's refusal to utilize ADR without rational reasons might work unfavorably to it at the Tribunals and courts.

As for the main features of *Factor 6 (structure and performance of the reviewing bodies)*, it can be pointed out that the statutory reviews conducted by the Solicitor's Office and Legal Services of the HMRC have not been utilized so actively yet, but the ratio of cancellation of the disputed re/assessments has been as high as 40% to 60% while in the case of reviews by the Tribunals, the ratio of cancellation of the disputed re/assessments is generally 20% to 40% but its level of independence is higher than the General/Special Commissioners and many disputes are resolved flexibly. As for *Factor 7 (complementary measures favorable for taxpayers), it* is to be noted that the decisions of the Tribunals are, unlike those of the General Commissioners, made public in principle.[22] Also, the option of relying on the practice of a "McKenzie friend" who can give support to taxpayers in their litigations without much financial cost may be available. Thus, many notable and significant facts mentioned above in *Factors 6 and 7* should work toward increasing the number of tax disputes, even if their degree of influence may be less comprehensive and profound than the facts mentioned above in relation to *Factors 1 and 4.*

However, some rules and facts are effective in putting a brake on the increase in the number of tax disputes. One such example of *Factor 4 (dispute resolution methods)* is the strengthened internal control over flexible settlements of some complex and high-volume cases by the establishment of the Tax Dispute Resolution Board, the

expense deduction, as mentioned in 2 in Section 5 of Chapter 3, is simple in its structure but gives rise to many disputes on it because of the ambiguity on its scope of application.

21. *See* the Office of Tax Simplification 2014 Report 1.10 and 3.21.
22. While some view that Tribunals' hearings conducted in public and the disclosure of the disputing taxpayers' private information in their decisions which were not adopted nor observed by the Commissioners under the old appeal system constitute one of the reasons for discouraging tax disputes. *See* the above "2012 Report of the Tax Law Review Commission" p. 85.

revised Code of Governance for Resolving Tax Disputes, etc.[23] While, on *Factor 5 (level of disputing taxpayers' burden)*, it can be pointed out that: (i) the volume of backlog of unprocessed cases at the First-tier Tribunal has lately been on the increase:[24] (ii) taxpayers' actions which unreasonably delay the proceedings at the First-Tier Tribunal could incur costs orders against them;[25] (iv) the burden of proof is on taxpayers and the HMRC can appeal the validity of the Tribunal's decisions.[26] As for *Factor 7 (complementary measures favorable for taxpayers)*, it is to be noted that the 2011 Report of the Costs Review Group states in paragraph 15 that public legal support for litigants has become history because of the former government's restriction on it. As *for Factor 8 (requirement for and effect of filing objections/litigations)*, a reference can be made to TMA §55, providing for the principle of non-suspension of tax recovery contingent on a taxpayer's filing of objection with the First-tier Tribunal.

The examples in the preceding paragraph could be cited as representative facts or rules that should have an effect of deterring the increase in the number of tax disputes, but the "English rule" on costs coming under *Factor 5 (level of disputing taxpayers' burden)* may exert such an effect more strongly. It is true that the "English rule" may work in some cases as an incentive for taxpayers' objections and litigations, but it should work as a disincentive for a larger number of cases. Now that there has been an increase in the backlog of unprocessed cases at the First-tier Tribunal, the deterrent effect of the "English rule" must have become more conspicuous.[27] As mentioned in 1 Section 4 of Chapter 3, the 2011 Report of the Costs Review Group states in paragraph 62 that not allowing the taxpayers successful in court to recover their costs disincentivizes them to file appeals, but, at least at the point of deciding whether or not they file appeals, it is pointed out that most taxpayers including big corporations find more demerits than merits in the "English rule" and prefer their cases not to come under "Complex cases" at the First-tier Tribunal.[28] The Tax Law Review Commission's 2012 Report also reveals that even in cases where there is not a little chance of winning, many people give up fighting in the Upper Tribunal because of the risk of financial burden.[29]

As mentioned above, the increasing backlog of unprocessed cases at the First-tier Tribunal and the "English rule" work as deterrents to the increase in the number of tax

23. There are some who show concerns and point out some facts on the HMRC becoming less proactive in settling disputes flexibly vis-à-vis the strengthened control of them. *See* footnote 49 in Chapter 3.
24. *See* Section 3 in Chapter 3 and Figure 3.7.
25. In U.S., IRC §6673 which works similarly has exerted an effect in suppressing the increase in collection cases. *See* Section 4.3 in Chapter 2.
26. *See* TMA §50 and footnote 79 in Chapter 3. Whereas, if a tax authority cannot dispute the decision of a Tribunal as in the case of Japan, it would generally increase the number of disputes than otherwise. At the same time, if the tax authority can dispute the decision of a Tribunal, it would increase the number of cases at court, but it would also discourage some taxpayers to initiate the dispute. This is another example of opacity about the dispute-inducing effect of some *Factors (Factor 6* in this case).
27. On the other hand, the "English rule" also has the aspect and effect of giving rise to disputes over whether the amount of costs ordered is appropriate.
28. *See* https://www.levyandlevy.co.uk/claiming-costs-tribunal-worth/.
29. *See* 42-48 of this Report.

disputes, but, at least at the stage of objections to the HMRC, the relevant facts on the *Factors* generally point toward the direction of increasing tax disputes. Moreover, the "English rule" has lately been applied in a way that is less unfavorable to taxpayers in some cases because: (i) the HMRC's "Sheldon practice" of not claiming the recovery of its costs against the unsuccessful taxpayers applies at the First-Tribunal unless their appeals come under the "Complex cases"; (ii) HMRC's "Rees practice" of not claiming the recovery of its costs against the unsuccessful taxpayers applies in principle when courts void the Tribunals' decisions that revoked the disputed re/assessments; (iii) the Litigants in Person (Costs and Expenses) Act 1975 that enables the successful taxpayers with no agents to recover more than "out of pocket fees" was adopted.[30] Also, the problem of the lack of legal support, which is a conspicuous fact related to *Factor 7 (complementary measures favorable for taxpayers)*, has been mitigated by the availability of the "conditional fee arrangement" and "after-the-event insurance premiums" to some taxpayers.

As for *Factor 2 (tax audit)*, Figure 6.2 shows that the "compliance yields" have lately been on the increase, intimating strengthened tax audits and the resulting increase in the number of tax disputes. The "compliance yields" are composed of the following: (i) "cash expected"—which is the estimate of the additional revenue due when the HMRC identifies past noncompliance; (ii) "revenue losses prevented"—the estimate of the tax revenue the HMRC has prevented from being lost to the Exchequer; (iii) "future revenue benefit"—an estimate of the effect of the HMRC's compliance work on taxpayers' future behavior; (iv) "upstream product and process yield" —an estimate of net tax receipts from legislative and administrative changes to reduce tax avoidance and evasion; (v) "accelerated payments"—an estimate of the impact of the HMRC's activities to promote compliance.[31] Some of those components are not directly related to tax audits, but the major "compliance yields" raisers are. So, they should indicate the recent general rising trend of the additional revenue earned by tax audits and their effectiveness. It is also pointed out that the HMRC's stance on corporations underpaying tax has hardened significantly lately, and it is only likely to get tougher as it uses big data, artificial intelligence, and more compliance workers to help it pursue unpaid tax.[32]

30. But the degree of transformation of the "English rule" is not so clear. For example, in the judgments on nontax disputes, there are such cases as *Baxendale-Waler v. Law Society* ([2007] EWCA Civ. 233) in which the Court of Appeal voided the Tribunal's costs order against the administrative agency because it would have a deterrent effect on the agency's power for the public good.
31. HMRC defines "compliance yield" to be revenue collected and protected that otherwise have been lost to the Exchequer through error or deliberate noncompliance. As for details on its constituents, *see* p. 28 of HMRC Reports and Accounts 2022 to 2023.
32. *See* HMRC's tax investigation yield increases to GBP 30.8 billion, *Tax Journal*, Issue 1566, March 2 (2022). HMRC's 2022 publication ("Managing tax compliance following the pandemic") states in p. 45 that HMRC expects to have around 2,500 (10%) more compliance staff in 2022-2023 than in 2021-2022 to raise the average additional tax revenue generated (about GBP 1.3 million) by a compliance staff which dropped to about GBP 1.1 million during the pandemic.

Figure 6.2 HMRC's Annual "Compliance Yields"

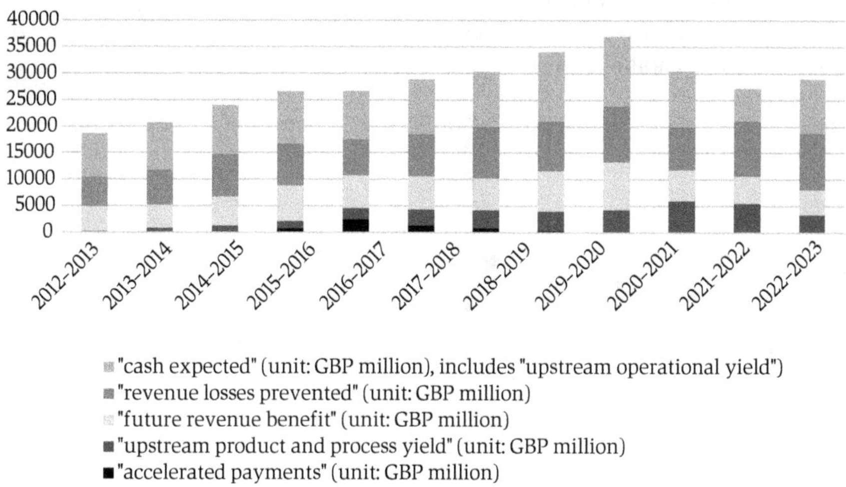

Source: HMRC Annual Reports and Accounts, 2022-2023 Figure 6, 2018-2019 Figure 4 and 2015-2016 Figure 3.

4 Aspects of Key *Factors* in Australia and NZ

In the case of Australia highlighted in Chapter 4, as for *Factor 1 (tax structure)*, the simplification of the tax system has long been an important issue, just like in the UK. In 2010, the Henry Tax Review Panel appointed by the government published the Final Report ("Australia's Future Tax System"), outlining proposals that would simplify the tax system.[33] However, even after the publication of this Report, little progress has been made in simplifying the tax system, and it has been pointed out that the current tax system is more complex than the tax system at that time.[34] For example, the survey results based on a large-scale and wide-ranging questionnaire conducted in 2016 and compiled by Mr. Hoppe et al. on "tax code complexity" related to multinational corporations in OECD countries show that the level of complexity of Australia's CIT system is quite high,[35] as shown in Figure 6.3 where the level of complexity of the CIT

33. This final report is available at https://treasury.gov.au/review/the-australias-future-tax-system-review/final-report.
34. B. Tran-Nam, Tax Reform and Tax Simplification: Conceptual and Measurement Issues and Australian Experiences in James/Sawyer/Budak (eds.): *The Complexity of Tax Simplification*, Palgrave Macmillan: Basingstoke, pp. 11-44. This differs from the view expressed in the 2006 Report of the Tax Reform Commission mentioned in above 3.
35. This survey was conducted with over twenty large-scale accounting firms from around the world. *See* Thomas Hoppe, Tax Complexity in Australia: A Survey-Based Comparison to the OECD Average, Discussion Paper No. 251 (2020) pp. 1-27 for details.

system is determined by five elements (ambiguity, uncertainty related to interpretation, frequency of amendments, details of related regulations, and severity of bookkeeping obligations) for fifteen main corporate tax regulations.[36] In Australia, the complexity is particularly evident in TP rules, GAAR, CFC rules, consolidated group taxation rules, and capital gains taxation rules.[37]

Figure 6.3 "Tax Code Complexity" Index for Corporations in OECD Countries

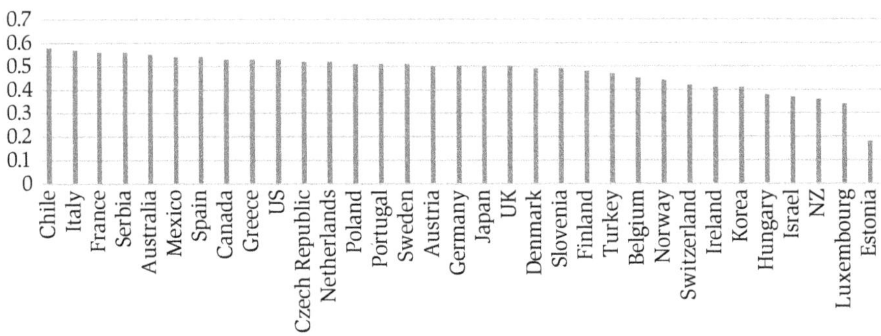

Source: Thomas Hoppe, Tax Complexity in Australia—A Survey-Based Comparison to the OECD Average, Discussion Paper No. 251(2020) Figure 1.

Naturally, there is a limit to comparing the complexity of tax systems by country. Nor does the level of complexity in the CIT system of the OECD countries, as indicated in Figure 6.3, represent the order of the complexity of the overall tax system of the respective OECD member countries. Even so, in the case of Australia, it seems that the complexity of its tax system is not limited to CIT because it is pointed out that the tax system on capital gains/loss is also quite complicated.[38] Furthermore, this complexity of the tax system is compounded, as discussed in 2 in Section 1 of Chapter 4, by the lack of clarity of many provisions (particularly those on penalties and deadline extension) that grant discretion to the ATO Commissioner and the merit review function of the AAT which is a conspicuous feature relating to *Factor 6 (structure and performance of the reviewing bodies)*. Indeed, there is a relatively larger number of disputes over those provisions, and many of them have resulted in the full or partial cancellation of the Commissioner's decisions. These facts stand out and indicate that major facts and rules in Australia relating to *Factors 1* and *6* strongly point toward inducing tax disputes.

There are also some facts, other than those mentioned above, that should work toward increasing the number of tax disputes. Particularly, in connection with *Factor 4 (dispute resolution method)*, *Factor 5 (level of disputing taxpayers' burden)* and *Factor 6 (structure and performance of the reviewing bodies)*, it can be pointed out that; the

36. *See* Hoppe, *supra* "Tax Complexity in Australia" pp. 4 and 11.
37. The survey reveals that among those, TP rule is generally the most complex in Australia and the other OECD countries. *See* Hoppe, *supra* "Tax Complexity in Australia" p. 8.
38. For example, the 1977 ITAA Part 3-1 and Part 3-3 contain more than 400 pages of provisions on capital gains and losses. For details, *see* Hoppe, *supra* "Tax Complexity in Australia" p. 11.

ratio of revocation of objections by the reviewing bodies have been fairly high as Figures 1 and 6 in Chapter 4 show;[39] (ii) hearings in camera could be requested at the AAT; (iv) the AAT has a "small business taxation division" with low fees and simple trial procedures; (v) the number of settlements of tax disputes by agreement at the stage of objections to the ATO is, as Figure 4.3 in Chapter 4 shows, not as large as that in U.S. and UK,[40] but, since 2014, ADR in the form of "in-house facilitation" that could be utilized in any stage of dispute has become available, (vi) as shown in Figure 4.5 in Chapter 4, the average number of days needed for the AAT to process disputes has become less lately; (vii) unlike courts, there is no application of "loser pays rule," and the recovery of fees paid to the AAT could be possible if its decisions or agreements are favorable to the taxpayers.

Moreover, as for *Factor 4 (dispute resolution method) and Factor 5 (level of disputing taxpayers' burden)*, it can be pointed out that: ① the Federal Rules of Court Div. 4.2 provides for a "pro bono referral scheme," and a conditional fee agreement may also be available; ② intellectual and financial support for lawsuits by taxpayers with limited means is provided based on the "Legal Aid Committee Act"; ③ in the case of litigations that have important issues in terms of public interest, interpretation of the law, etc., a "test case litigation program" has been implemented in which the ATO bears all or part of the litigation burden of the taxpayer; ④ as in the case of UK, "Calderbank offer" could work against the successful party in court if it refuses to accept it without reasonable grounds by restricting the costs it could recover.[41] While the dispute-inducing effect of the above (i) to (vii) and ① to disputes ③ should be dampened by the following facts: (I) Since 2016, an "Independent Assurance of Settlements Program" has been implemented for agreements on complex cases, etc.; (II) The amount of reduction by agreement against the amount of re/assessments is made public;[42] (III) TAA §14ZZK provides for the burden of proof on taxpayers in appealing against the Commissioner's decisions, and recoverable costs by a litigant in person are more limited than those in UK.[43]

The survey result shown in Figure 6.4 may give more clues to Australia's status on *Factors* other than *Factor 1*. This survey is on the "tax framework complexity" of OECD countries. The "tax framework complexity" is measured on the following five

39. As shown in Figure 4.6 in Chapter 4, the rate of cancellation of the re/assessments by courts is also fairly high, so it can be pointed out that the possibility of recovering attorney's fees is not so low.
40. While, from 2011/2012 to 2019/2020, only 1.5%-3.5% of the tax disputes pending before AAT or the Australian courts were resolved by their decisions or judgments. *See* Figure 4.3 in Chapter 4.
41. As mentioned in 3(2) in Section 1 of Chapter 4, TAA §14ZZR (which provides for the principle of non-suspension of collection action by the filing of objections and appeals) and TAA §14ZZK (which restricts only the taxpayers from bringing up new issues and legal grounds for the disputes) basically work toward decreasing the number of tax disputes while there are also some administrative decisions and court judgments that do not follow strictly the rules under those provisions.
42. Such disclosure may not only act to deter agreements but also increase the number of disputes in relation *to Factor 7 (complementary measures favorable for taxpayers)* because the relatively high ratio/amount of reduction may encourage aggrieved taxpayers.
43. *See* footnote 63 and 4(1) in Section 1 in Chapter 4.

elements: (a) tax guidance, (b) tax law enactment, (c) tax filing and payments, (d) tax audits, and (e) tax appeals. Therefore, if the index or the level of complexity related to these elements (a) to (e) is low, it generally follows that the level of convenience that taxpayers can enjoy is high, and the problem posed by the "tax code complexity" is mitigated and becomes less. Even so, the effect of the "tax framework complexity" on the number of tax disputes is not clear enough because it could have multiple effects on the taxpayers' willingness to dispute their cases.[44] In the case of Australia, as shown in Figure 6.3, the level of "complexity of the tax system" is ranked high. While, as Figure 6.4 shows, primary facts, particularly on the above (a) and (e), are fairly positive for taxpayers and rank Australia somewhere in the middle on the index of the "tax framework complexity."[45] This must result in mitigating the problems caused by the high index of the "tax code complexity" in Australia, while Figure 6.4 shows that the degree of its mitigation is not so strong as that in Japan and the Netherlands.

Figure 6.4 Index of "Tax Framework Complexity" in OECD Countries

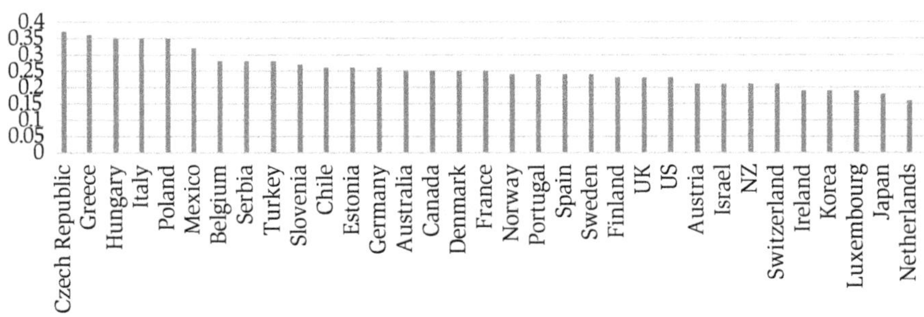

Source: Hoppe, *supra* "Tax Complexity in Australia" Figure 3.

In NZ, as discussed in 1 in Section 2 of Chapter 4, the 1994 Richardson Report, states in Appendix E that the old tax appeal system had problems including the following: (i) there is room for reexamining the grounds for re/assessments, and this hindered incentives to conduct accurate taxation at the time of the audit; (ii) tax dispute resolution takes much time and money; (iii) there is insufficient independence, neutrality, and expertise of those in charge of the review of objections; (iv) disputing parties (especially taxpayers) often refrain from disclosing information at the objection stage, resulting in the delay of the dispute resolution. The effects of the above facts (i) to (iv) on the number of tax disputes are multifaceted, but in relation to *Factor 2 (tax*

44. For example, the element (e)(tax appeals) is determined by such facts: (i) unpredictable time period between the filing of an appeal and its resolution; (ii) inconsistent decisions; (iii) lack of specialized agents/staff; (iv) influence of third parties. Lack of problems with them results in a low index/ranking, and it should mitigate the problem of "tax code complexity," but it could also work in some cases toward increasing the number of tax disputes. *See* footnote 4.

45. This survey shows that in the case of Australia, among various elements constituting the "tax framework complexity," the element (b)(tax reform process) and element (d)(tax audit) has a relatively higher level of complexity, while the element (e)(tax appeals) has a relatively low level of complexity. For details, *see* Hoppe, *supra* "Tax Complexity in Australia" pp. 11-21.

audit), Factor 5 (level of disputing taxpayers' burden), Factor 6 (structure and performance of the reviewing bodies), and *Factor 7 (complementary measures favorable for taxpayers)*, at least the above (ii) and (iii) must have worked in putting a brake on the number of tax disputes. Moreover, around that time, the Revenue's interpretation of its authority and stance on settlements by agreement was rather negative, and the ratio of revocation of the disputed re/assessments by court judgments was, as Figure 4.13 in Chapter 4 shows, not so high.

The current objection procedures, which were introduced in 1996 in response to the 1994 Richardson Report, etc., intended to mitigate the above problems (i) to (iv) mentioned in the Report by adopting not only the "evidence exclusion rule," which encourages the disputing parties to disclose their cards on the table at the objection stage but also setting up the Disputes Review Unit (DRU) to replace the Adjudication Unit inside the IR. In addition, the adoption of "in-house facilitation," which could be defined as a form of ADR, as well as the increase in the number of disputes resolved through agreements by actively exercising the discretionary powers of the IR Commissioner, must have led to the alleviation of the above (ii) (time and money costs) problem. However, despite those reforms, the number of tax disputes showed a declining trend, as Figures 4.11 and 4.12 in Section 2 of Chapter 4 indicate. This trend suggests that those reforms may contain some that could lead to the increase in tax disputes, but they also have others that come especially under *Factor 5 (level of disputing taxpayers' burden)*, and the latter were more influential, particularly in working towards increasing aggrieved taxpayers' clerical, monetary and time costs so that they discouraged not a few taxpayers to file objections and appeals.[46]

In addition to the above, Figure 6.3 on "tax code complexity" shows that NZ's ranking among the OECD countries is among the lowest. So, it could be said that, in NZ, as far as the rules and facts on *Factor 1 (tax structure)* are concerned, they do not generally work strongly toward increasing tax disputes. Likewise, in connection with *Factor 4 (dispute resolution method), Factor 5 (level of disputing taxpayers' burden),* and *Factor 6 (structure and performance of the reviewing bodies)*, there are some facts that are likely to disincentivize taxpayers to file objections and appeals. They include: (i) The ratio of flexible dispute resolution is not as high as that in the U.S. and UK,[47] and ADR is not utilized at the TRA; (ii) Clerical and financial costs for tax objections and appeals could be quite high;[48] (iii) TRA's "Small claims jurisdiction" whose decisions

46. In fact, it is pointed out that there are some who give up the idea of disputing the re/assessments on them because of the heavy burden the current objection procedure imposes. *See* 1(2) in Section 2 and footnote 166 of Chapter 4.
47. Unlike UK and Australia, NZ has the IR guidance (para. 25 of SPS 15/01) that states that penalties cannot be used as bargaining chips to reach an agreement on the disputed tax. *See* 1 in Section 2 of Chapter 3, 2 in Section 1 of Chapter 4, and 3(1) in Section 2 of Chapter 4.
48. As mentioned in 4 in Section 2 of Chapter 4, the interest rate on tax arrears is so high (8.22% per annum) and it is heavy burden when the facility of the "Tax Pool Intermediaries" is not available. *See* footnote 166 in Chapter 4 as well for high litigation costs. Moreover, TAA §14ZZO(Grounds of objection and burden of proof) prescribes, "(b) the appellant has the burden of proving: (i) if the taxation decision concerned is an assessment—that the assessment is excessive or otherwise incorrect..."

were not appealable was abolished in 2011;[49] (iv) as Figures 4.11 and 4.13 of Chapter 4 indicate, the ratio of revocation of the disputed re/assessments by the DRU and courts is not high; (v) TAA §109, an ouster provision, limits the judicial scope of review on the discretion of the IR Commissioner.[50] Therefore, even if NZ is ranked low in Figure 6.4 on "tax framework complexity," it may not increase the number of tax disputes as much as the majority of countries ranked high in Figure 6.3 on "tax code complexity."

Nevertheless, some notable facts and rules should work toward increasing the number of tax disputes. For example, in connection with *Factor 4 (dispute resolution methods)*, it can be pointed out that the IR has recently come to change its former passive stance on the flexible resolution of disputes.[51] On *Factor 5 (Level of disputing taxpayers' burden)*, 1994 TRAA §22B provides for the TRA's power to order the IR to bear the taxpayer's filing fee in a case where its decision is in favor of the taxpayer. As for *Factor 8 (requirement for and effect of filing tax objections/litigations)*, TAA §128 stipulates that, in principle, the filing of an objection does not require the taxpayer to pay the disputed tax, penalties, and interest.[52] Furthermore, as displayed in Figure 4.5 in Section 2 of Chapter 4, recently, there has been a larger number of shortfall penalties applied to more serious types of cases as in the case of Australia while, differently from Australia, since 2000, shortfall penalties of a large number of taxpayers with good past compliance record are halved by TAA §141FB. Thus, some rules and facts counteract those more conspicuous effects of applying a brake on the increase in the number of tax disputes, but such counteraction is not so strong and is weakened further by the recent declining ratio of tax disputes against the number of audits (*see* footnote 164 in Chapter 4) that relates to *Factor 2 (tax audit)*.

5 Aspects of Key *Factors* in Ireland and the Netherlands

In the case of Ireland, Figure 6.3 on "tax code complexity" shows that it is ranked low among the OECD countries, and its CIT rate has been as low as 12.5% since 2003. They suggest that primary facts in Ireland on *Factor 1 (tax structure)* do not work as strongly as those in the UK and Australia toward increasing the number of tax disputes, while they have many similarities (e.g., "behavioral penalties," etc.) in their tax systems. In addition, under the old Irish tax objection procedures, some facts and rules that are particularly relevant to *Factor 5 (level of disputing taxpayers' burden)*, *Factor 6 (structure and performance of the reviewing bodies)*, and *Factor 7 (complementary measures favorable for taxpayers)* must have worked toward putting on a brake on the increase in the number of tax disputes. They include: ① The independence of the OAC was not sufficient; ② Most taxpayers at the OAC were represented by tax experts, while the OAC had a considerable number of accumulated backlogs and it took a long time to

49. *See* 2 in Section 2 and footnote 177 of Chapter 4.
50. *See* 3(2) in Section 2 of Chapter 4.
51. It is pointed out that, since 2000, TRA and High Court render their decisions/judgments only about one-third of all the tax disputes that were brought to them. *See* 3 in Section 2 of Chapter 4.
52. *See* 2 in Section 2 and footnote 182 in Chapter 4.

receive a hearing even though the interest on unpaid tax was high; ③ Only the conclusion of the OAC decisions was given in writing to the disputing taxpayers; ④ TCA § 934(5) allowed the OAC to decide to increase the amount of the re/assessment.

However, in reality, the number of cases brought to the OAC was quite large (for example, in 1983/1984, the aggregate number of tax objections on IT and CIT cases reached 16,552 by counting the number of assessments appealed). Therefore, it should be that there were also facts and rules that worked toward increasing the number of tax disputes and probably they included the following: (i) in connection with *Factor 4 (dispute resolution methods)*, about 90% of the cases received by the OAC were settled by agreements before the hearings were held in spite of the fact that the Commissioner's power of management and control was more limited than that in UK and ADR was hardly utilized; (ii) in relation with *Factor 5 (level of disputing taxpayers' burden)*, the burden of proof is on taxpayers in all taxation appeals (*see* footnote 13 in Chapter 5), but "loser pays rule" does not apply at the OAC; (iii) on *Factor 7 (complementary measures favorable for taxpayers)*, there was a fact that the OAC's decisions were hardly made public; (iv) in connection with *Factor 8 (requirement for and effect of filing tax objections/litigations)*, collection action of the disputed tax was suspended contingent on the filing of objections with the OAC, and the payment of the disputed tax amount was not a precondition for filing objections with the OAC before 1988.

Under the current tax objection system in operation since March 2016, there are, in addition to the above (ii), (iii), and (iv), the following rules and facts: (I) Various measures were taken to enhance the level of independence of the TAC which replaced the OAC; (II) It has become possible for taxpayers to make direct objections to the TAC and it has removed the Revenue's intervention in the objection procedure; (III) the TAC's decisions must be fully documented, and they are shown on the TAC website; (IV) The TAC can make a decision based only on the "Notice of Appeal" without a hearing if there is a taxpayer's agreement or similar cases; (V) The TAC's resources were strengthened, and the number of unprocessed cases has recently decreased significantly. These rules and facts should work further toward increasing the number of disputes. But the reality was that, as Figure 5.3 in Chapter 5 shows, the total number of cases received by the TAC has declined considerably since 2016. Behind this, there exist the following facts: (a) As Figure 5.3 in Chapter 5 exposes, there were a large number of unprocessed cases in TAC, and it increased from 2016 to 2019;[53] (b) In 2015, the Circuit Court whose decisions are not appealable was abolished.

Obviously, the above facts of (a) and (b) should not be enough to account for the reasons for the decline in the recent number of appeals to the TAC now that there are facts and rules mentioned above in relation to (ii) to (iv) and (I) to (V) that should exert a stronger impact on the number of tax appeals. Therefore, there should be other reasons that explain the recent declining trend of tax disputes in the TAC. Such reasons could be found in the fact that there has lately been a significant decline in the number of tax disputes on IT received by the TAC, as Figure 5.4 in Chapter 5 indicates, and it

53. From 2018 to 2020, the number of objections received by the TAC was around 1,500 to 2,000, while it was not uncommon for the OAC to receive more than 10,000 objections annually. *See* 1 in Section 1 and Figure 3 in Chapter 5.

could be assumed that this declining trend is attributable to the recent declining effective IT tax rates evidenced in Figure 5.5 in Chapter 5. If this assumption is not mistaken, the validity of the idea that the level of the tax burden, which is one of the attributes of *Factor 1 (tax structure)*, has a considerable impact on the number of tax disputes is proven not only by the relationship between the CIT burden and the number of CIT-related disputes but also by the relationship between the IT burden and the number of IT-related disputes in Ireland.

In the case of the Netherlands, as Figure 6.3 exhibits, among OECD member countries, the "tax code complexity" for CIT is ranked high, whereas Figure 6.2 indicates that the ranking of "tax framework complexity" is the lowest. As mentioned above, the impact of the "tax framework complexity" on the number of tax disputes is complex and multifaceted, but in the case of the Netherlands, it seems that the impact of its high ranking on the "tax code complexity" that should increase the number of tax disputes is offset much by the low ranking of the "tax framework complexity" because the latter contains some facts and rules with strong offsetting effect.[54] Included in them, above all, must be the Netherlands' traditional approach of the "polder model," under which the parties with different opinions make cooperative efforts to reach agreements amicably. This approach related primarily to *Factor 4 (dispute resolution methods)* should also be adopted in the context of tax administration and the tax authority's relationship with taxpayers particularly in the form of the "horizontal monitoring" for big corporations. This model/approach must have a lot to do with the fact that the ratio of disputes over CIT represents only about 4% of the total number of lawsuits at the Supreme Court in 2015 despite its relatively high tax rate.

However, the number of disputes on taxes other than CIT is large in the Netherlands. So, there should be, in addition to those issues related to *Factor 1 (tax structure)*, some facts and rules that work toward increasing the number of tax disputes in this country. In fact, in connection with *Factor 4 (dispute resolution methods)*, it is to be noted that the Netherlands is a civil law country but, on account of Articles 7:900 and 7:902 of the civil law as well as the "principle of legitimate expectations," it is possible to settle tax disputes by agreement beyond the principle of legality and mandatory provisions. Moreover, the Fiscal Mediation Association (VFM) was established in 2007, and there are many trained mediators in the Netherlands. Indeed, the tax authority is indeed restricted in using penalties as bargaining chips for settling the disputed tax amount,[55] but the availability of flexible tax dispute resolution and its active use has a lot to do with the fact that there are a large number of disputes over taxes other than CIT and more than 90% of the tax disputes are resolved without going to court. As for *Factor 6 (structure and performance of the reviewing bodies)*, it is to be pointed out that the ratio of the disputed re/assessments revoked by courts is fairly high.

There are also other facts and rules that are favorable for taxpayers in the Netherlands to become inclined to dispute the re/assessments on them. As for *Factor 5 (level of disputing taxpayers' burden)*, it can be pointed out that: (i) unlike a mediator

54. *See* footnote 44.
55. *See* Kraan, *supra* "Chapter 19: Netherlands" pp. 207-208.

prepared by courts, a mediator prepared by the tax authority enables a disputing taxpayer to avail himself of it free of charge; (ii) not only the tax authority but also a disputing taxpayer can bring in a mediator to participate in the mediation; (iii) a unilateral costs shifting rule favorable to a disputing taxpayer is adopted, so that, even if the taxpayer loses at court, he would not be ordered to pay the costs of the tax authority, unless he has abused the court procedures without rational reasons; (iv) if the tax authority cancels the re/assessments in response to the objections filed by the taxpayers, some of their expenses incurred in connection with the objections could be borne by the tax authority. In connection with *Factor 8 (requirement for and effect of filing tax objections/litigations)*, it can be pointed out that, in principle, the payment of the disputed amount of tax is not a precondition for filing objections/appeals.

Now that the Netherlands is an EU member country, it is influenced greatly by EU law and some other supranational laws. Now that they have many provisions that solidify the rights of taxpayers vis-à-vis tax disputes, they affect facts and rules relating in particular to *Factor 4 (dispute resolution methods) and Factor 5 (level of disputing taxpayers' burden)*.[56] However, their effect/influence in the case of the Netherlands and other EU Member Countries is much stronger with respect to *Factor 1 (tax structure)* because EU law, in particular, adds further complication to tax issues and works toward increasing the number of tax disputes in Member countries. Complications of tax issues also lead to an increase in the number of requests for the ECJ's preliminary rulings, which are often made not only by taxpayers but also by other Member Countries and the EU Commission. Moreover, recently, the EU Commission has actively been pursuing a possible case of "state aid," which is prohibited by Article 107 of TFEU, but "state aid" issues also contain ambiguity as in such cases where the question of constituting a "state aid" must be determined based on the "arm's length principle particular to EU law" whose difference from the conventional arm's length principle is not so clear-cut.[57]

SECTION 2 STATUS OF *KEY FACTORS* AFFECTING THE NUMBER OF TAX DISPUTES IN JAPAN

1 On *Factor 1 (Tax Structure)*

In the case of Japan, as for *Factor 1 (tax structure)*, as Figure 6.3 reveals, it can be pointed out that the "tax code complexity" for multinational corporations ranks

56. As one example of such effect on tax dispute procedures, it can be pointed out that, after the 2005 reform, the reviews of facts are now conducted by district courts and appellate courts (*see* footnote 98 of Chapter 5) and such reform has a lot to with Article 14(5) of the International Covenant on Civil and Political Rights which states, "Everyone convicted of a crime shall have the right to his conviction and sentence being reviewed by a higher tribunal according to law." *See* Hout, *supra* "Chapter 19: Netherlands," 19.2.2.

57. For instance, for EU member countries, the impact of the "principle of legitimate expectations" on *Factor 4* is also significant but the ambiguity of the principle also has an impact on *Factor 1*. On the issue of the ECJ's interpretation of it in various rulings being ambiguous, *see* Esther Drabkin-Reiter, The Europeanization of the Law on Legitimate Expectations at https://cadmus.eui.eu/bitstream/handle/1814/40324/2015_Drabkin-Reiter_LLM.pdf?sequence = 1.

roughly around the middle among OECD countries. Certainly, in fiscal 2020, CITA has reached about 730 pages, while, in the case of ITA and CTA, they are about 700 pages and 240 pages, respectively, and IGTA is about 100 pages.[58] So, even from the point of view of the "tax code complexity" related to major taxes, it may sit somewhere around the middle of the OECD countries. While *Factor 1* comprises, other than the complexity of tax structure, major elements such as the nature of tax (number of taxpayers subjected to tax, etc.), tax rates, opaqueness in the application of tax provisions, the number of provisions stipulating exceptional treatment, the nature and extent of the discretionary powers of the tax authority, etc. that should exert not a little influence on the number of tax disputes.[59] Therefore, it is quite difficult to position Japan's situation internationally from the perspective of *Factor 1*, but it may be useful to point out some of its distinctive features and points.

In particular, the mere fact that Japan differs from some countries in that it has IGT works toward increasing the number of tax disputes. Moreover, as exhibited in Figures 3 and 7 in Chapter 1, IT-related disputes are the largest in number, but in terms of the ratio of the number of objections to the Tax Tribunal against the number of field audits, there is little difference between IT and IGT, and they are higher than CIT as Figure 1.13 in Chapter 1 exposes. This must be partly because the tax rates of IT and IGT are highly progressive (in 2022, the maximum tax rate for IT is 45%, and the maximum tax rate for IGT is 55%), and their tax burden could be considerable. Also, IT and IGT have, as analyzed in Section 2 in Chapter 1, many provisions with attributes that induce tax disputes. While Japan is not an exception in that there are many disputes over penalties. In light of these facts, the following will focus on a few representative themes related to IT, GIT, and penalties from the perspective of *Factor 1 (tax structure)* and highlight their distinguishing features. Although the scope of this analysis is quite limited, it is expected to shed more light on an answer to the question of how Japan stands internationally with respect to *Factor 1*.

(1) Income Tax (Taxable Unit, Necessary Expenses, and Blue Return System)

IT has a large number of taxpayers, so the number of tax disputes can greatly increase or decrease depending on how its system is designed. Therefore, its system design affects the number of tax disputes significantly. For example, the U.S. Federal IT has adopted a system that allows married couples to opt to file jointly, which incurs complexities in taxation and enforcement, particularly with respect to the applicability of the "innocent spouse" relief.[60] However, Japan's ITA does not allow such an option

58. The number of pages for these Acts include Enforcement Ordinances but not Enforcement Regulations. When relevant provisions stipulated in STMA (including Enforcement Ordinances but not Enforcement Regulations) are added respectively to their numbers, it is about 820 pages for CIT, about 670 pages for IT, about 100 pages for CT, and about 260 pages for IGT.
59. While, CT is unique in that, although the number of taxpayers is quite large, the number of disputes related to the system specific to CT is small mostly because its system design is relatively simple.
60. *See* 4 in Section 4 of Chapter 2.

for married couples.[61] Nevertheless, under Article 56 of ITA, which makes an exception to the individual unit taxation system, a business proprietor cannot deduct for IT purposes as necessary expenses those salaries/compensations paid to his family members who share the same livelihood with him unless they are fully engaged in his business.[62] As for salaries paid by a business proprietor to his family members who work full time for his business, they are deductible for IT purposes as necessary expenses of his business, while they are not fully deductible if they are not reasonable in amount or he is not a blue return filer. These tax treatments of intra-family transactions not only help deter the occurrence of income shifting motivated by tax avoidance but also prevent disputes from arising.

On the other hand, in many foreign countries, although there are cases where certain restrictions are imposed,[63] compensations paid by a business proprietor to his family employees are deductible for IT purposes so long as certain requirements ((a) payment of compensation is limited to business purposes, and (b) the amount paid is a reasonable amount as compensation for labor, etc.) are met.[64] However, such treatments often give rise to disputes over whether or not those requirements are met. For example, in *Earlspring Properties Ltd v. Guest* ([1993] STC 473), the UK High Court specified that a decision of whether a business operator's compensation to his family worker is deductible for IT purposes is not necessarily made based solely on objective data collected by the tax authority on the amount of compensation among independent parties because some other issues such as a business operator's motive for the compensation should also be taken into consideration.[65] In the *William McAdam v. HMRC* case ([2016] UKFTT 838 TC), the UK's First-tier Tribunal denied the tax deduction of the applicant's compensation paid to his family employee because it did not find it being paid wholly and exclusively for his business purpose.

61. Even in Japan, until it was abolished by the 1987 tax reform, certain property-related incomes of a family member were aggregated and taxed for IT purposes.
62. In this case, if there are expenses incurred by such family members in fulfilling the engagement with the business proprietor, they can be included in the necessary expenses of the business proprietor while no income and necessary expenses are deemed to have arisen on those family members for IT purposes.
63. For example, in India, under ITA §37 (General deductions allowed for business and profession), expenses incurred wholly and exclusively for business purposes are basically deductible. But, pursuant to ITA §40A(2) (Transaction with related parties) and 44AB (Audit of accounts of certain persons carrying on business or profession), a tax audit report of a business operator whose gross income exceeding INR 1 crore per year (INR 5 crore after the enactment of the Finance Act 2020) which is submitted to the tax authority should contain information about transactions between family members, and limits are set on the amount of such transactions.
64. For example, Ireland's 1997 TCA §81(2) states: "no sum shall be deducted in respect of—(a) any disbursements or expenses, not being money wholly and exclusively laid out or expended for the purposes of (b) any disbursements or expenses of maintenance of the parties, their families or establishments, or any sums expended for any other domestic or private purposes distinct from the purposes of such trade or profession"; UK also has a similar provision based on the "wholly and exclusively" standard (e.g., 1988 Income and Corporation Tax Act §74 (General rules as to deduction not allowable). *See* 2 in Section 5 of Chapter 3 as well.
65. For this case, *see* https://www.markmclaughlin.co.uk/spouses-wages-legitimate-expense-or-tax-dodge/.

(2) *Inheritance Tax (Interaction with IT)*

IGT is a nonrecurring tax with a relatively fewer number of taxpayers, but it contains an issue of valuation of property that is peculiar to it. Also, just like IT, IGT's tax burden, due to its high top marginal rate, can be quite heavy, and there are not a few IGT provisions that have some problem of uncertainty about their application scope, as mentioned in 3 in Section 2 of Chapter 1. This problem is compounded further by the insufficiency of clarity on inheritance tax's interaction with IT. Certainly, Article 9(1)6 of ITA stipulates that IT is not imposed on items acquired through inheritance, bequest, or gift from an individual. However, this provision does not completely solve the problem of possible double taxation of IT and IGT because there is a question of what constitutes double taxation of IT and inheritance tax, as well as a question of which double taxation should be relieved. Such questions arose in the well-known Supreme Court 7/6/2010 judgment (2008 (GyoHi) No. 16) in which the Court voided a part of the disputed reassessment of the beneficiary/appellant' inherited right to receive pension annually in the subsequent years because the disputed reassessment of deeming it to be inherited property gave rise to double taxation of the right by IT and inheritance tax.

The possible double taxation problem of IT and inheritance tax mentioned above can also arise in relation to Article 60 of ITA, which provides for carrying over the acquisition price of inherited property at the time of inheritance for IGT purposes. Certainly, under Article 39 of STMA, when applying Article 33 on capital gains, a part of inheritance tax imposed on the transferred property is added to the acquisition price by the calculation formula stipulated under the relevant Enforcement Ordinance, and its application alleviates the problem of double taxation to some extent. But Article 39 of STMA requires that, in principle, for such treatment to be applicable, the inherited property was transferred within three years from the time of inheritance, and detailed statements are attached to the IT return of the concerned year. Also, it is to be noted that, in the 7/5/2019 decision, the Tax Tribunal specified that the treatment under Article 39(1) of STMA is not a rule but an exception allowed from the standpoint of administrative policy. Thus, there are indeed some rules and measures that protect taxpayers from the possible double taxation of IT and inheritance tax, but it is not so comprehensive as to give full or some relief to all possible cases of double taxation of IT and inheritance tax because the "exceptions" are limited.

In contrast, in the U.S., the UK, Ireland, etc., the acquisition price of an inherited property is not carried over, so the market price at the time of inheritance becomes the acquisition price of the inherited property for IT purposes, reducing, in almost all cases, the amount of capital gains from its future sale.[66] For example, in the U.S., specifically, IRC §1014 (Basis of property acquired from a decedent) stipulates, "the basis of property in the hands of a person acquiring the property from a decedent or to whom

66. For example, the UK Taxation of Chargeable Gains Act 1992 §62 (Death: general provisions)(4) states, "On a person acquiring any asset as legatee(...)—(a) no chargeable gain shall accrue to the personal representatives, and (b) the legatee shall be treated as if the personal representatives' acquisition of the asset had been his acquisition of it."

the property passed from a decedent shall, if not sold, exchanged, or otherwise disposed of before the decedent's death by such person, be—(1) the fair market value of the property at the date of the decedent's death." It is true that recently, in the U.S. and the UK, reforms have been proposed to adopt the rule of carrying over the acquisition price of inherited property, but there is little prospect for their adoption.[67] Moreover, the minimum taxable threshold of the U.S. federal estate tax is quite high at USD 5.3 million (about JPY 700 million), and various measures are taken to avoid it. Consequently, the ratio of estate tax payment is said to be 0.1% (roughly 1 in 700 decedents) of inheritance cases, so it is irrelevant to most people.[68] As for Canada and Australia, capital gains of inherited property are deemed to arise and taxed at the time of inheritance in principle,[69] but these countries do not have taxes equivalent to inheritance tax or estate tax.

(3) Penalties

As for penalties, although their burden in Japan is relatively low compared to that in other countries, the standards for their abatement are stricter. For example, in Japan, a taxpayer's ignorance of the law and mistakes/misunderstandings of his agents are almost always not "justifiable reasons" for abatement of his non-reporting/underreporting penalty. Whereas, some countries covered in the preceding chapters abate penalties in such cases and have the following features: (i) the degree of care exercised by taxpayers for the filing of their returns, etc., are relevant in determining whether penalties should be abated; (ii) the degree of penalty abatements could vary, and there is a lack of transparency regarding that degree;[70] (iii) violations of disclosure obligations incur civil penalties,[71] (iv) tax authorities are legally authorized to mitigate penalties,[72] and, even if there is a legal restriction on using penalties as bargaining chips for sustaining re/assessments, the availability of flexible settlements does increase taxpayers' chance of penalty abatement. These differences

67. *See* the American Families Plan proposed by the U.S. President Biden in April 2021 and the July 2020 report of the UK's Office of Tax Simplification (Capital Gains Tax—second report: Simplifying practical, technical and administrative issues). It has been pointed out, however, that if such a reform bill is adopted in the U.S. without abolishing the estate tax, the tax burden and the difficulty of tax administration will increase markedly due to the worsening problem of asset valuation. *See* https://www.fb.org/files/FBETC_Stepped-Up_Basis_Report_2021.
68. In contrast, in Japan, as shown in Figure 1.12 in Chapter 1, the ratio of taxable inheritance (number of taxable inheritees divided by number of inheritors) is about 10% in 2022. In the UK, the nontaxable threshold is GBP 325,000 (about USD 440,000), and about 4% (1 in 20 estates) is subject to Inheritance Tax. *See* https://www.bbc.com/news/business-36014533.
69. *See* Canada's ITA (RSC, 1985, c. 1 (5th Supp.)) §70(5) (Capital property of a deceased taxpayer) and Australia's 1997 ITAA § 128-15(Effect on the legal personal representative or beneficiary).
70. *See*, for example, the First-tier Tribunal decision on the Cairns case (2009) in the UK referred to in 1(2) in Section 5 in Chapter 3.
71. Examples of such penalties include penalties for failure to file U.S. Form 5472 as set forth in Chapter 2 and the UK's TAA §102 (see footnote 30) of Chapter 3.
72. *See* paras. 50-51 of the 2013 ATO's Code of Settlement Practice Statement, footnote 129 in Chapter 4, and Ireland's TCA §1065 (see footnote 38 of Chapter 5).

between Japan and those foreign countries explain why the number of disputes over penalties in Japan is quite small compared to that in those countries.

As mentioned above, the dispute-inducing effect of penalties is stronger in the foreign countries covered in the preceding chapters than in Japan. Moreover, this effect has become more conspicuous in some of those foreign countries owing to the recent adoption and strengthening of countermeasures against tax avoidance and evasion. Examples of these countermeasures in the U.S. include: (i) "No fault penalty" imposed by IRC §6707 (Failure to furnish information regarding reportable transactions) for breach of the obligation to disclose "reportable transactions" prescribed under IRC §6111 (Disclosure of reportable transactions); (ii) revised IRC §6662 (Imposition of accuracy-related penalty on underpayments) which leaves no room for the abatement of accuracy-related penalty in a case where the disclosure obligation of "reportable transactions" is not fulfilled; (iii) IRC §6708 (Failure to maintain lists of advisees with respect to reportable transactions) against promoters who fail to maintain lists of clients using "reportable transactions"; (iv) penalties imposed by IRC §5321 (Civil penalties) (5) (Foreign financial agency transactions) on violations of the reporting obligations under IRC §5314 (Records and reports on foreign financial agency).

Some other major countries are following suit and have adopted countermeasures like those in the U.S. For example, since 2004, the UK has imposed disclosure obligations on users of certain tax avoidance schemes and imposed penalties for violations of these obligations. In addition, in Schedule 10 (Penalties: Offshore income etc.) of the Finance Act 2010, heavier penalties are adopted for the failure to report IT and capital gains tax related to overseas assets, and their applicable rates vary depending on the cause for the failure and the location of assets (a penalty rate is higher in a country with which the UK does not have exchange of information provisions in the tax treaty). Also, in Ireland, heavier penalties are adopted under TCA §1077E (Penalty for deliberately or carelessly making incorrect returns, etc.) that was amended by §56 of the 2016 Finance Act, and they are imposed on those who failed to disclose voluntarily non-reported income or foreign assets by April 2017. In Australia, since 2006, promoter penalties have been imposed on those who promote certain tax avoidance schemes based on Division 290 (Promotion and implementation of schemes) of Schedule 1 to the AAT.[73] Japan's recent moves have not gone far enough to make its penalty regime strict enough to be comparable to those in the above countries.

2 On the Other *Factors* (② to ⑨)

The analysis in the above 1 is sketchy and deals only with some representative tax rules in Japan, but it may lend support to the view that Japan's ranking among the OECD countries on the complexity of tax structure is not among the top group and main facts on *Factor 1 (tax structure)* do not stand out in particular. While main rules and facts on

73. Schedule 1 § 290-50 (Civil penalties)(3) states, "If the Federal Court of Australia is satisfied, on application by the Commissioner, that an entity has contravened subsection (1) or (2), the Court may order the entity to pay a civil penalty to the Commonwealth."

Factor 2 (tax audit) in Japan include: (i) differences in views between taxpayers and auditors are usually ironed out flexibly at the stage of tax audits; (ii) the requirement of writing reasons for re/assessments clearly and sufficiently in a notice of reassessment acts in the direction of making them solid.; (iii) on-site audit rates have lately been on the decline. Similarly, in relation to *Factor 3 (compliance)*, it can be pointed out that taxpayers' overall compliance level is high, and they are generally less prone to settling disputes through litigation. Moreover, in relation to *Factor 4 (dispute resolution method)*, it is to be noted that flexible tax dispute resolution is not possible after re/assessments are made. Generally, these facts should not only support the observation that Japan's index of "tax framework complexity," shown in Figure 6.4, is the second lowest but also such low ranking should, in the majority of cases, be working toward suppressing the increase in the number of tax disputes.

Now that the above main rules and facts relevant to *Factors 1* to *4* should have a fairly strong impact on the number of tax disputes, it should follow that, even if the main rules and facts in Japan on F*actor 5 (disputing taxpayers' burden), Factor 6 (structure and performance of the reviewing bodies), Factor 7 (complementary measures favorable for taxpayers), Factor 8 (requirement for and effect of filing tax objections/litigations)* act in the direction of inducing tax disputes, their effect should be limited and be countervailed by those main rules and facts on *Factor 1* to *4*. Indeed, the main facts and rules on *Factors 5 to 8* do contain some that have not a little effect of inducing disputes and they include: particularly, in relation to *Factors* 5 *and 6*, (i) since 2014, all taxpayers can opt for filing an objection directly to the Tax Tribunal, (ii) the Tax Tribunal's decision cannot change the disputed re/assessment unfavorably for the claimant, and it is binding on the NTA; (iii) the Tax Tribunal's ratio of processing tax objections within 1 year is very high. However, the dispute-inducing effect of these rules and facts on the Tax Tribunal is more than counteracted by the above main rules and facts relevant to *Factors 1* to *4*, as well as the fact that the Tax Tribunal's ratio of revoking the disputed re/assessments is not so high.[74]

The abovementioned facts and rules on the main constituents under *Factors 1* to *8* should shed light on some of the major reasons for the relatively small number of tax disputes in Japan. If this situation, vis-à-vis the global trend of strengthening taxpayers' rights and enhancing their access to justice in particular, calls for measures to be taken in the same direction in Japan, Japan has more leeway for them while it is highly recommended that those measures should be helpful especially for those worthwhile tax cases to come to the Tax Tribunal and courts. It is by no means easy to find out what could become such measures, mainly because Japan's situation is rather exceptional, and there could be various opinions on what they could be. Even so, in the following Sections 3 to 5, an analysis is to be made of the major reform proposals shown in 2 and 3 in Section 4 of Chapter 1 and weigh their merits and demerits. Then, drawing out

74. The fact that Tax Tribunal reviews disputed re/assessments in terms of their appropriateness should have an effect of inducing tax disputes, but such effect must be not so strong now that the number of tax provisions granting discretion to NTA is relatively small in number and such discretion is bound by law and allows little room for its administrative volition. While such effect may be stronger when it comes to the burden of proof at court because it is in principle on NTA regarding its re/assessments as it was confirmed by the Supreme Court 3/3/1963 judgment.

some inputs from such analysis, an attempt is to be made to present some other possible reform options to address the challenges the current rules and facts relevant to tax dispute resolution in Japan pose.

SECTION 3 PROS AND CONS OF REFORM PROPOSALS FOR TAX APPEALS REVIEW ORGANS

1 Merits and Demerits of "Proposal of Transferring Tax Tribunal to Cabinet Office"

The "Proposal of transferring Tax Tribunal to Cabinet Office" referred to in 2 in Section 4 of Chapter 1 has a primary purpose of enhancing the level of independence and neutrality of the Tax Tribunal in Japan. Indeed, in many countries, there are strong calls for enhancing the independence of organs in charge of reviewing tax objections and the neutrality of proceedings. For instance, in the U.S., the TAS often pointed out that the rule of prohibition of ex parte communication is not strictly followed by the Office of Appeals, and in 2019, it was renamed the Independent Office of Appeals. In the UK, the 2007 TCE Act established the Tribunals with a higher level of independence than General/Special Commissioners. The 2016 replacement of the OAC by the TAC in Ireland has a similar effect because it is realized in such a way that it excludes the IR's intervention in the procedures of appeals to the TAC. It is also to be noted that, in the case of EU Member States, Article 6 of ECHR provides for the citizens' rights to hearings by an independent and fair tribunal, and this has facilitated the reform of the reviewing organs in the Member States in the direction of enhancing their independence and neutrality.

Thus, the idea underlying the "Proposal of transferring Tax Tribunal to Cabinet Office" is basically in line with the idea behind the above recent global trend and has a point. But, it should be noted that, as Article 102 of AGRNT ordains, the Tax Tribunal's decision binds the NTA while the tax authorities in the UK, Australia, Ireland, etc., can dispute at court the decisions of the administrative reviewing organs. In other words, the tax authorities in those foreign countries are not obliged to give up their authority to dispute the validity of decisions/judgments revoking the disputed re/assessments unless they are those of the Supreme Court. In other words, any measures to enhance the independence and neutrality of the tax reviewing bodies in those countries are based on the premise that they would not oblige the tax authority to give up such authority. For example, in Australia, the ATO's re/assessment made by exercising its Commissioner's discretion is reviewed and could be set aside or substituted by the decision of the AAT standing in the shoes of the Commissioner, but the ATO is not totally precluded from disputing such decision at court.

Except for the binding nature of decisions/judgments on small tax claims cases in some countries,[75] quite rare in the world are the countries that have the decision of an

75. For such cases, *see* 1 in Section 2 of Chapter 2 and IRC §7463 which provides for the non-appealable nature of the summary judgment of a special trial judge of Tax Court (see

independent reviewing body other than the Supreme Court bind the tax authority. For example, in India, ITA §245S (Applicability of advance ruling) provides that the ruling of the Authority of Advance Ruling (AAR) binds the disputing parties,[76] but in *Columbia Sportswear Company v. DIT* (Special Leave Petition (c) No. 31543 of 2011), the Supreme Court ruled that the AAR is a Tribunal and its ruling does not affect the authority of the High Court and the Supreme Court to accept the application for disputing the AAR's rulings, and the Court explained that such authority of the courts is based on Article 227 (Power of superintendence over all courts by the High Court) of the Constitution and such authority is not vitiated by the law providing for the binding nature of the AAR's rulings. In fact, there are cases of the Indian tax authority disputing in court the validity of the AAR's rulings, and the Supreme Court judgment in DIT (International Taxation), *Mumbai v. Morgan Stanley & Co.* (Civil Appeal No. 2914 of 2007) is just one of them.

Certainly, the "Proposal of transferring Tax Tribunal to Cabinet Office" would enhance the independence and neutrality of the Tribunal, but if this proposal is premised on maintaining the purport of the abovementioned Article 102 of the AGRNT, it would follow that the authority other than the NTA nor courts has a final say in the determination of the validity of a disputed re/assessment and it would become quite different from the cases in the other countries and be quite unrealistic. However, if the above proposal is based on the premise that the NTA could dispute at court the validity of the Tribunal's decision, then the function of the Tax Tribunal under this proposal would become similar to the Tax Court under the "Proposal of establishing Tax Court." Then, some may prefer the "Proposal of establishing Tax Court" to the "Proposal of transferring Tax Tribunal to Cabinet Office" because the level of independence and neutrality of the reviewing body should be higher in the former, in which the reviewers are mainly judges and tax experts than the latter in which the reviewers are mainly ex tax officials transferred to the Cabinet Office.

2 Merits and Demerits of "Proposal of Establishing Tax Court"

As mentioned above, for the "Proposal of establishing Tax Court" and the "Proposal of transferring Tax Tribunal to Cabinet Office" to be realistic options, they should be based on the premise that its decision/judgment allows the NTA to dispute it at court/higher court if it chooses so. Then, it follows that the "Proposal of establishing Tax Court" is preferable in terms of the level of independence while the time and financial cost for an aggrieved taxpayer would become generally higher than those incurred under the "Proposal of transferring Tax Tribunal to Cabinet Office." Inevitably, those two proposals should give rise to a demerit of incurring higher time and

footnote 63), footnote 175 of Chapter 4 for "small claims jurisdiction" of TRA in NZ abolished by T (TARM) Act 2011, and 2 in Section 1 of Chapter 5 for Ireland's Circuit Court abolished by the 2015 Finance (Tax Appeals) Act.

76. ITA §245S stipulates; "(1) The advance ruling pronounced by the Authority under section 245R shall be binding only—(*a*) on the applicant who had sought it; (b) ...and (c) on the Principal Commissioner or Commissioner, and the income-tax authorities subordinate to him, in respect of the applicant and the said transaction."

money costs on the part of aggrieved taxpayers, especially in cases where their decisions/judgments in favor of them are disputed at a higher level by the NTA. Such being the case, it is quite likely that this demerit becomes grave enough for some aggrieved taxpayers to prefer the status quo of the Tax Tribunal, which could realize the speedier and less costly resolution of disputes when there is sufficient rationality in the disputing taxpayers' claims.[77]

As mentioned in Section 2 in Chapter 2, the U.S. Tax Court's decision on small claim cases is binding on the disputants, and they are restricted from filing appeals to the Court of Appeal. The Supreme Court confirmed in *Luckenback S.S. Co. v. United States* ([1926] 272 U.S. 533) that the Parliament affirmed such restriction, and it does not violate the due process clause under the Fifth Amendment to the US Constitution.[78] Following this example, the "Proposal of establishing Tax Court" could incorporate such a system design that prohibits appeals to the higher court by the disputing parties for its judgments on "small tax cases" (hereinafter called "Proposal of establishing Tax Court with the small claim case department." This should speed up the resolution of "small tax cases." While it should be noted that in the U.S., the Tax Court Rules §173 and the IRS manual (IRM 35.1.3.2 (Small tax case procedure: 07-24-2012)) (4) stipulate that the Tax Court can exclude some cases from "small tax cases" if it determines that there are reasonable grounds for it, making it possible to prevent, if necessary, those cases that contain new issues and important points from being resolved once and for all without going to the Court of Appeal.

Naturally, even among "small tax cases," there are some that contain important legal issues. Therefore, even if it might not violate the due process clause of the Japanese Constitution to restrict the disputing parties or only the NTA from disputing "small tax cases" in the High Court, it would be necessary to incorporate an exception to the "Proposal of establishing Tax Court with the small claim case department." In reality, in the case of the U.S. Tax Court, there are not many cases that fell out of the regular treatment under "small tax cases" on account of the above Tax Court Rules §173 and IRM 35.1.3.2,[79] but behind this, there exist in the U.S. such facts and circumstances: (i) the need for a speedy resolution of disputes is particularly high against the background of a large number of disputes (especially "small tax cases"), (ii) flexible settlements of tax disputes are possible; (iii) the Tax Court judgments on "small tax cases" are not publicized nor serve as precedents. The facts and circumstances in Japan are different, so that under the "Proposal of establishing Tax Court with the small claim case department," there would be more cases that should be excluded from the

77. Even under the current system, as mentioned in footnote 9 in Chapter 1, Article 115 (1)1 of AGRNT dictates that a taxpayer can choose to file an appeal with a district court once he has filed a request for review at the Tribunal and three months have passed since then without its decision.
78. In this judgment, the Supreme Court stated, "the well-settled rule applies that an appellate review is not essential to due process of law, but is a matter of grace ... The Constitutional requirements are all satisfied if one opportunity is had for the trial of all parts of a case. Everything beyond that is a matter of legislative discretion, not of constitutional right."
79. *See* Badum, *supra* "The Small Tax Case Procedure" p. 394.

"small tax cases" because of their importance in terms of the need for clarity of interpretation, potential impact on other similar cases, etc.

Aside from those problems mentioned above on the "Proposal of establishing Tax Court (with the "small claim cases" department)," there are also negative opinions on it from different perspectives. For example, it is opined that the adoption of the adversarial system of a Tax Court would mean the loss of the Tax Tribunal's semi-guardianship function of covering the insufficiency of legal capacity of some taxpayers in pursuing their cases and would not be beneficial to the taxpayers.[80] There is also an opinion that the replacement of the Tax Tribunal should be complemented by measures to strengthen the administrative relief system for the taxpayers from the perspective of protecting their rights.[81] Indeed, the Tax Tribunal functions in assisting the applicants in such ways that it sorts out points of contention of the disputing parties by drafting a list of their claims and enables the applicants to understand the NTA's views by allowing them to see the documents and evidence relied on by the NTA, and so forth. If such function of the Tax Tribunal is not maintained under the "Proposal of establishing Tax Court (with the "small claim cases" department)," the situation of many disputing taxpayers under this proposal might become worse.[82]

Truly, in the U.S., the usefulness of the Tax Court is very high, but there are significant differences between it and the Tax Court contemplated under the "Proposal of Establishing Tax Court (with the "small claim cases" department)" in terms of the premises on which they are based. In the U.S., aggrieved taxpayers, in principle, before they dispute their cases at the Tax Court, dispute them at the Office of Appeals, whose level of independence and granted authority are much greater than that of the NTA's local tax offices. The Office of Appeals can settle disputes flexibly, and even if they are not resolved, its settlement process should usually enable the disputing parties' claims to be sorted out sufficiently. However, if the Tax Tribunal is abolished by the adoption of the "Proposal of establishing Tax Court (with the "small claim cases" department)," a large number of disputes whose points of contention are not sorted out well enough would come to a Tax Court and hang heavily on it. Moreover, now that this Proposal is based on the abolition of the Tax Tribunal, a Tax Court should face the difficult task of taking over the Tribunal's function of determining whether or not the disputed re/assessment is appropriate and, whenever necessary, sets it aside or substitutes it by its decision while this is not usually done by the court.[83]

80. Hiromasa Minami, Bibliography (15), p. 30.
81. Fujimagari, *supra* Bibliography (3) on Chapter 1, p. 261.
82. While the situation may be less worse under "Proposal of Establishing Tax Court with the 'small claim cases' department" because the procedures for "small claim cases" in the Tax Court are not so burdensome even for pro se litigants, as the U.S. Tax Court Rules 174 (Trial) states, "(b) Conduct of Trial and Evidence: Trials of small tax cases will be conducted as informally as possible consistent with orderly procedure, and any evidence deemed by the Court to have probative value shall be admissible. (c) Briefs: Neither briefs nor oral arguments will be required in small tax cases unless the Court otherwise directs."
83. The courts' stance in this regard has manifested typically in re/assessment by estimation cases analyzed in 1(3) of Section 2 in Chapter 1. Courts' limited function in this regard is also observable in many countries as the "Wednesbury unreasonableness" principle is generally followed in many Commonwealth countries.

Indeed, the establishment of a Tax Court by doing away with the Tax Tribunal following the "Proposal of establishing Tax Court (with the "small claim cases" department)" should enhance the taxpayers' trust in the independence and neutrality of the reviewing body and the ratio of revocation of the disputed re/assessment at a Tax Court might become higher because of the nonbinding nature of its judgments on the disputants. But, in light of the abovementioned problems, the demerits of this Proposal, which include higher costs on the part of the taxpayers, might outweigh its merits for the majority of the taxpayers. However, if the number of tax disputes increases in the future against the background of further globalization of economic activities and their complications and it works toward increasing the need for resolving tax disputes flexibly and effectively, the potential usefulness of the flexible settlement of tax disputes recommended under this Proposal would become greater. So, how arguments on flexible settlements of tax disputes will evolve in the future should also affect the pros and cons arguments on this Proposal, but as the next Section 4 shows, arguments on flexible settlements of tax disputes are not necessarily predicated on the existence of a Tax Court.

SECTION 4 PROS AND CONS OF REFORM PROPOSALS FOR RESOLVING TAX DISPUTES FLEXIBLY

1 Merits and Demerits of "Proposal of Flexible Dispute Resolution"

As discussed in Chapters 2 to 5, in many foreign countries, it is almost impossible to imagine tax dispute resolution without flexible settlements. For example, in France, which is a civil law country just like the Netherlands, it is possible to resolve tax disputes by agreement under certain conditions, even if the dispute is already at the objection/litigation stages. Its legal basis is the Tax Procedures Law (Livre des Procedures Fiscales) L. 247, etc., which provides for "tax transaction." According to this provision, if the parties to the dispute agree, even after the re/assessments are made, the penalty will be reduced on the condition that the disputed tax amount and penalty are to be paid and no lawsuit is to be filed against them.[84] Also, in a case where there is an ambiguity on how relevant laws apply to a case in question, a "global settlement" might be available, and it would allow a reduction of penalties or the disputed amount of tax on the condition that a lawsuit is not to be filed. As for a criminal defendant for tax evasion, he may be eligible for the convention judiciaire d'intérê public (Public Interest Judicial Convention (CJIP)), in which courts allow a criminal prosecution to be dropped on the condition that he agrees to pay the criminal penalties and abide by the legal compliance program, etc.[85]

84. *See* https://news.bloombergtax.com/daily-tax-report-international/how-to-negotiate-a-tax-adjustment-in-france/ for more information.
85. Law No. 2018-898 can be cited as a basis for CJIP. For a notable example of a "global settlement" or CJIP, *see* https://tpcases.com/mcdonalds-has-agreed-to-pay-e1-25bn-to-settle-a-dispute-with-french-authorities-over-excessive-royalty-payments/

Thus, even among civil law countries, flexible settlement of tax disputes is utilized in some cases, so the situation in Japan may rather be an exception. While, nowadays, even in Japan, there seems to be more now in support of the idea of flexible settlement of tax disputes. For example, Article 52 of "Administrative Litigation Law Draft" released in 2003 by Japan's Federation of Bar Association provides that compromised settlement at the litigation stage by the disputing parties is possible to settle fully or partially the dispute on the administrative decision, provided that it is not against the law,[86] and it does not explicitly exclude cases of disputes on taxation. There is also a view that much greater relief would become possible to citizens aggrieved over administrative decisions, including those on taxation if a system of dispute settlement by compromise and agreement at every stage of contestation is introduced. One who holds such a view points out that there is no law explicitly denying such a settlement method even in the case of litigation on administrative dispositions, and a tax lawsuit is, just like a reparation lawsuit against the government, on debts and credits against it, so a settlement by agreement should be possible and it should be consistent with flexible tax treatment at the audit stage.[87]

However, the view and the proposal mentioned above have not gained much support from those other than taxpayers and their agents despite some possible merits and benefits that flexible settlement of tax disputes could bring to the NTA, the Tax Tribunal, and courts. The principal reason for the lack of support lies in Article 84 of the Constitution, which ordains taxation under law, and other reasons include: (i) the discretion of a local tax office's director is not the discretion of carte blanche but legal discretion;[88] (ii) the number of tax disputes is not so large, and there is not much backlog of unprocessed cases at the Tax Tribunal and the courts, so the need for flexible settlement is not so high, (iii) the need for flexible settlement is particularly low for the NTA now that the ratio of the Tax Tribunal's decisions and court judgments revoking the disputed re/assessments are relatively low. Because of these reasons, there seems not to be much need for flexible settlements, even on the part of the Tax Tribunal and the courts. Moreover, as is evident from the analysis in Chapters 2 to 5, flexible tax dispute resolution would give rise to various problems and challenges that include the issue of the appropriateness of settlements, equity among taxpayers, and the need for monitoring and checking them by third parties.

Moreover, once a flexible settlement of a tax dispute is made possible, it would induce some taxpayers to initiate tax objections primarily for seeking concessions from the NTA, while some of their cases might have little ground to stand on and lack merits. The increase in the number of such meritless tax disputes would increase not only the burden of the NTA and the Tax Tribunal but also that of those disputing taxpayers with

86. *See* https://www.nichibenren.or.jp/library/ja.../data/2003_18.pdf.
87. Yamashita Seibei, Bibliography (16), p. 205.
88. *See* 2 in Section 1 of Chapter 1 for the difference between legal discretion and carte blanche discretion. While in Australia, as referred to in 5(2) in Section 1/footnote 43/57 of Chapter 4, there are many provisions that grant discretion to ATO and AAT often substitutes its decisions by the "merit review" function. So, the scope of discretion of ATO and AAT on the application of some types of provisions is not narrow and it may sit somewhere between legal discretion and carte blanche discretion.

meritorious cases. Therefore, if a flexible tax dispute settlement method is to be adopted in Japan, it would be advisable for some mechanism to be adopted to lessen its negative aspects. Courts/Tribunals in such countries as the U.S. and the UK apply penalties on taxpayers who make frivolous claims or delay review proceedings,[89] while it might be more effective in the case of Japan to limit the scope of tax disputes that could be subject to a flexible settlement.[90] The most likely candidates for a flexible settlement should be those disputes that contain possible margins on the amount of re/assessments (e.g., TP issues, issues on taxation by estimation, necessary expenses, etc.). Whereas, if there is no way to make the "Proposal of flexible dispute resolution" acceptable vis-à-vis Article 84 of the Constitution, the one shown in the following 2 might be an option.

2 Merits and Demerits of "Proposal of Review at Pre-Assessment Stage"

The "Proposal of Review at Pre-Assessment Stage," which was briefly shown in 2(2) of Section 4 in Chapter 1, is based on Korea's "Pre-Assessment Review System" that allows, in some cases, third parties to participate in the review of the proposed re/assessment before it is finalized by the tax examiner. Actually, in Korea's Pre-Assessment Review System," the proposed re/assessment that meets some conditions is to be reviewed by a review committee composed of 4 senior tax officials (including a chairman of the Committee) who are not in the examination department and the same number of tax experts from the public sector) and its review decision, which determines the tax authority' re/assessment to be made, is finalized by a majority vote. Now that the chairman does not have a right to vote, there could arise cases where the votes of the reviewers from the tax authority are not enough to sustain the proposed re/assessments. This is unique because it could practically be an abdication in advance of the tax authority's inherent right to determine re/assessments. Even in the case of the U.S., only the Office of Appeals could intervene in limited cases in the process of the IRS's right to determine re/assessments and make a change to the proposed re/assessments.

It is to be noted that behind the innovative nature of Korea's "Pre-Assessment Review System," there are such facts and reasons: (i) Article 8 of the Charter of Taxpayer's Rights provides for taxpayers' right to prompt relief prior to the re/assessment; (ii) the cases covered by this system are limited to those that meet certain requirements;[91] (iii) the members of the review committee are senior tax

89. *See* footnote 167 in Chapter 2 and footnote 81 in Chapter 3.

90. Types of tax disputes unsuitable for flexible settlements vary among countries but typical ones are shown in 3 in Section 2 of Chapter 3 and 1(1) in Section 2 of Chapter 5.

91. In South Korea, from 2003 to 2005, the number of requests for the "pre-assessment review" was 2,671 to 4,431 and the ratio of decisions favorable to the taxpayers was 35.7% to 37.6%. In the case of objections to the tax offices, their numbers were 7,138 to 8,806 cases and the ratio of decisions favorable to the taxpayers were 32.6% to 41.2%. In the case of objections to the Tax Bureau, their numbers were 1,421 to 1,539 and the ratio of decisions favorable to the taxpayers were 30.2% to 42.7%. In the case of objections to the Tax Tribunal, their numbers were 3,890

officials and outside tax experts appointed by the tax authority. In the case of Japan, even if a provision such as Article 8 of the Charter of Taxpayers' Rights is introduced, it would not be realistic for the "Proposal of Review at Pre-Assessment Stage" to be adopted because it would require the NTA to abdicate its inherent right to determine re/assessments. So, it would be better for the Proposal to be amended in such a way that the members of the review committee should be composed of senior NTA officials (one of them is the chairperson) as well as lawyers and tax experts appointed by the NTA, but also the review organ under the Proposal is allowed to substitute the proposed re/assessments with their own provided that they are approved by the chairman (hereinafter called "Revised Proposal of Review at Pre-Assessment Stage").

Indeed, there has lately been an increase in the potential usefulness of the option of having a third party intervene at the stage before re/assessments are made. However, the most common way of intervention by a third party at the pre-assessment stage is, as the analysis in the preceding chapters shows, mediation. In the U.S., such intervention is realized in the form of FTS, FTM, Early Referral, etc., but the one in charge of them is the trained staff in the Office of Appeals. Similarly, in NZ, such intervention is realized in the form of "in-house facilitation," and the one in charge of it is a senior Revenue officer.[92] While it is also conceivable that one who mediates at the pre-assessment stage should be an expert trained in mediation from outside (hereinafter called a "Proposal of Pre-Assessment Mediation") as in the case of the UK and the Netherlands (*see* 1(1) in Section 2 of Chapter 5).[93] At least, the hurdle for the adoption of this Proposal should be lower than that for the adoption of the above "Proposal of Review at Pre-Assessment Stage," which would require the NTA's abdication of its inherent right to make re/assessments or that for the adoption of the above "Revised Proposal of Review at Pre-Assessment Stage" which would entail heavier administrative costs.

In addition, the above "Proposal of Pre-Assessment Mediation" may have the following merits: (i) the opinion of a mediator or a facilitator is not binding to the parties who do not disagree with it; (ii) a flexible tax dispute settlement mediated/facilitated by a third party might be neither unconstitutional nor unlawful even under the present system in Japan so long as it is realized before the re/assessment is made; (iii) the intervention of a third party such as a tax expert, etc., could help correct the power imbalance between the NTA and the taxpayers which may otherwise arise due to differences in tax knowledge, experience, fiscal resources, etc.; (iv) especially in a case where a point of contention between a taxpayer and an auditor primarily concerns a matter of fact and evidence, a third party experienced in

to 4,746 and the ratio of decisions favorable to the applicants was 31.6% to 38.7%. Thus, there were not significant differences among them in terms of the ratio of decisions to the taxpayers. For details, *see* Hasegawa, *supra* Bibliography (14)p. 77.

92. *See* 1(1) in Section 2 of Chapter 4. In Australia, an "in-house facilitator utilizable at any stage of dispute is an ATO staff or its stakeholder." *See* footnote 25 in Chapter 4.

93. An outside mediator could be brought in for disputes with HMRC (*see* second paragraph in 3 of Section 2 of Chapter 3) and HMRC's Guidance (Use alternative dispute resolution to settle a tax dispute) mentions that, if HMRC have opened an enquiry into a taxpayer's tax affairs, he can apply for ADR at any stage of the enquiry.

mediation/facilitation and taxation could evaluate their claims and relevant pieces of evidence independently and explain the risk and potential burden if it escalates into a tax dispute once the re/assessment is made on it, and then he could propose a modified re/assessment which might be acceptable to both of them without incurring the problem of unlawfulness and the contestation at the Tax Tribunal or the courts.

Even so, even under the above "Proposal of Pre-Assessment Mediation," its application should be better limited to those cases where both the taxpayer and the auditor agree to have a third party's intervention in their case. There should be arguments over the types and scope of potential tax disputes, which could be subject to the pre-assessment mediation/facilitation, but it could be particularly useful and effective in such cases as mentioned above that is most suitable for a flexible settlement (i.e., transfer pricing cases, issues of estimated taxation, cases on necessary expenses, etc.). In other words, the "Proposal of Pre-Assessment Mediation" could be a relief for a taxpayer as well as the NTA, especially in such cases where there are problems of insufficient evidence or uncertain facts surrounding proposed re/assessments and the black or white decisions on them may neither be appropriate nor efficient because they have to be handed down despite those problems. As for a mediator/facilitator, he could affect the NTA's reassessments and some similar cases in the future, so he should be someone trained in mediation and, to lower the hurdle for the adoption of this Proposal and minimize possible costs on taxpayers,[94] it might be better for him be approved or appointed in advance by the NTA.[95]

The "Proposal of Pre-Assessment Mediation" would not undermine the NTA's right to make re/assessments because its use and the acceptance of the mediator's opinion is optional, and it could prevent some potential disputes with insufficient evidence and uncertain facts from escalating into objections/litigations. Therefore, in some cases, this Proposal could be beneficial and efficient for both taxpayers and the auditor, as the experiences of some countries imply. Even so, mediation incurs administrative, time, and financial costs that should be designed to fall basically on the NTA, so there is a question of whether its adoption is worthwhile in terms of cost-effectiveness. The answer could be in the negative if it would not produce sufficient results. It could be suspected reasonably that such sufficient results would be hard to attain in Japan now that even in cases where flexible settlements might be suitable, a tax auditor in charge might not become so willing to let a mediator join because flexible settlement of potential tax disputes is practically possible during tax audit if he opts for it and there are very few mediators with such capacity and skill who could meet the expectation of the parties.[96]

94. Bringing in an external mediator/facilitator usually incurs costs on taxpayers. *See* 1(1) in Section 2 of Chapter 5. While an external reviewer is brought in by the IR in Ireland. *See* 1(1) in Section 1 of Chapter 5. In the Netherlands, an external mediator could be brought in by a taxpayer. *See* 1(1) in Section 2 of Chapter 5.
95. If NTA bears the costs for an external mediator/facilitator in a case where a taxpayer's fiscal means are limited, and it would at least require NTA's prior appointment of him.
96. This also illustrates the difficulty of employing ADR as a method of resolving administrative disputes in Japan while there are a good number of trained mediators in such countries as the Netherlands (*see* footnote 124 in Chapter 5).

SECTION 5 PROS AND CONS OF "LOSER PAYS RULE"

1 Trends in Rules on Costs

If flexible tax settlement is against the Constitution and the "Proposal of Pre-Assessment Mediation" is not likely to produce sufficient results in Japan, the next proposal referred to in 3 in Section 4 of Chapter 1 is the "Proposal of adopting Costs Shifting Rule." Indeed, there have been arguments over which cost rule is the best, and there are variations of it among countries. On the two ends of the spectrum of such variations, there is the "American rule" (or "Party/party rule") and the "English rule" (or "Loser pays rule"). The rationale and merits of the "American rule" include: (i) it is in line with the idea that the right to assert a position that one believes correct without being deterred by the possibility of having to pay the other party's costs is a tradition of democracy and a defense of impartiality;[97] (ii) if the "U.S. rule" were to be abandoned and the other party's costs were to be borne by the unsuccessful party, the hurdle for filing a lawsuit would become higher, and access to justice would be practically restricted especially for those who lack financial means.[98] Japan's rule on costs in litigation is basically based on the "American rule," but the "American rule" is rather an exception in the world. Moreover, as shown in Section 3 of Chapter 2, the "American rule" has lately undergone considerable transformation in the U.S.

In contrast, the rationale and merits of the "English rule" that have long been adopted in UK and many other European countries include: (a) if a creditor successful in litigation cannot recover costs from a debtor who does not pay his debt, the creditor cannot be whole and unharmed;[99] in other words, a creditor who is obliged to file a lawsuit in order to secure its credit against the debtor who is not willing to pay its debt has a right to recover the full amount of the credit and it would be unjust if he could recover less than that for the reason that he filed the lawsuit; (b) if it is a principle that a loser pays the other party's cost, it can be expected that people with good reasons and justification will become more active in filing a lawsuit, and conversely, a person who only has weak grounds will become more reluctant to file a lawsuit; (c) it deters and penalizes groundless and frivolous actions which abuse judicial systems; (d) providing an economic incentive to a beneficial litigation is desirable in order to correct power imbalance between the disputing parties; (e) providing incentives for litigation that are

97. In *Newman v. Piggie Park Enterprises, Inc.*, the Court of Appeals for the Fourth Circuit ([1967] 377 F 2d 433, 437) also held, "No litigant ought to be punished under the guise of an award of counsel fees (or in any other manner) from taking a position in court in which he honestly believes—however lacking in merit that position may be."

98. For an actual example of such a case, *see* Albert Ehrenzweig, Reimbursement of Counsel Fees and the Great Society, *California Law Review*, Vol. 54 (1996) pp. 792-800 DOI: 10.2307/3479426. For other arguments in favor of the "American rule," *see* Richard Falcon, Award of Attorneys' Fees in Civil Rights and Constitutional Litigation, *Maryland Law Review*, Vol. 33, No. 4 (1973) pp. 379-419.

99. The 1925 report of the Massachusetts Judicial Council (First Report, 11 Mass. LQ 1, 63-64) also argued against the traditional "American rule" by stating, "On what principle of justice can a plaintiff wrongfully run down on a public highway recover doctor's bill but not his lawyer's bill?"

desirable and beneficial to the public interest is recommendable ("Private attorney general theory").[100]

Generally, the merits/demerits of the "American rule" are the demerits/merits of the "English rule" and vice versa. While their demerits or negative effects become conspicuous, particularly in the context of administrative litigations in which the issue of access to justice could become more important. For instance, under the "English rule," the financial burden of the losing party could become heavy, so it has the effect of inclining the disputing citizen to seek for settlement by agreement. Such an effect is desirable from the perspective of speedy resolution of the dispute, but it is a demerit from the perspective of enhancing access to justice.[101] Also, there is a view that the "English rule" is the worst rule with many problems, and its negative aspect becomes particularly conspicuous in disputes that have a strong public interest aspect.[102] On the other hand, under the "American rule," there is a merit of avoiding a large financial burden in the case of not becoming the "prevailing party" in litigation, so it would generally be less restrictive on access to justice while, in disputes against administrative bodies, citizens who are the "prevailing party" cannot recover the litigation costs, regardless of the degree of public interest in the dispute, so this could also hinder access to justice in some cases.

As mentioned above, the demerits of both the "American rule" and the "English rule" could manifest concerning the issue of enhancing access to justice under different circumstances. Therefore, in the countries covered in Chapters 2 to 5, some changes have been made to those rules to alleviate those demerits, and it seems to have become a global trend. As discussed in Chapter 2, in the case of the U.S., the "American rule" is modified by the adoption in some cases of the "unilateral loser pays rule" by the "Civil Rights Attorney Fees Act" and the "Equal Access to Justice Act," etc. For example, under IRC §7430, which falls under the category of the "Equal Access to Justice Act," reasonable administrative/litigation costs could be recoverable in a case where the "prevailing party" is the taxpayer who clears the net worth requirements and the IRS/government cannot substantially justify its position in the proceeding. Indeed, the number of cases where it has become possible for taxpayers to recover reasonable costs is not so large, but the taxpayer's utilization of the "qualified offer" could increase further his chance of the recovery of costs.

Even in the UK and major Commonwealth countries that have adopted the "English rule," there have lately been moves to modify it in such a way that its demerits

100. For details, *see* Thomas D. Rowe Jr., The Legal Theory of Attorney Fee Shifting: A Critical Overview, *Duke Law Journal*, Vol. 1982:651, p. 653 DOI: 10.2307/1372495 and Penningstorf, *supra* "The European Experience" pp. 65-67.

101. It is pointed out that it is unclear which of the "American rule" and the "English rule" is better, but, under the "English rule," the number of suits filed on unreasonable grounds should decrease while those on reasonable grounds could also decrease because attorney fees tend to increase in an attempt to decrease the risk of becoming the losing party. *See* 1995 Report ("The use of cost litigation rules to improve the efficiency of the legal system") of the Office of Regulation Review") 3.1 (at https://www.pc.gov.au/research/supporting/cost-litigation-rules/costliti.pdf).

102. *See* John E. Bonine, Best Practices—Access to Justice (Agenda for Public Interest Law Reform), p. 22 (also available at accessinitiative.org/resources/best-practices-access-justice).

are mitigated. In concrete, such modification is primarily realized by the application in some cases of the "unilateral costs shifting rule" or rules with a similar effect. In the case of the UK, the "English rule" does not apply to the cases disputed at the stage of administrative objections unless they come under "Complex cases" in the First-tier Tribunal or they are disputed at the Upper Tribunal. In addition, even if a taxpayer loses in court, the "English rule" may not apply on account of the "Rees practice" if its judgment is sought by the HMRC being the appellant. Furthermore, even at the litigation stage, a "protective costs order" rendered by courts on cases with the public interest and the "Calderbank offer" utilized by some taxpayers could provide a possibility of excluding the application of the "English rule" or limiting the amount of costs payment in a case where the tax authority becomes the successful party in the litigation.[103] In Australia, the "English rule" does not apply to disputes in the AAT, while the taxpayer's fee to the AAT could be recovered if the taxpayer wins at the AAT. "Calderbank offer" could also be utilized in Australia as well.

Nevertheless, it remains true that, in the case of the UK, as pointed out by the 2010 recommendations of the Aarhus Convention, the litigation-related costs could be prohibitively expensive. Such high costs could result basically because of the application of the "English rule," and it is aggravated by the "after the event insurance," "conditional fee arrangement," etc., that make it possible for their users who have won the litigations to shift the costs on those contracts to the losers, and not to pay fees to their attorneys when they lose the litigations. However, the merit of these mechanisms for their users dissipated much by the adoption of the LASPO Act §44, which does not allow the costs on those contracts to be shifted to the losers in litigation except for some cases, including those coming under CPR §44.13 to §44.17 which apply the qualified one-way costs shifting favorably to the plaintiffs in the cases on claim for damages for personal injuries, etc. Now that the LPASO Act §44 has some implications in the context of tax disputes as well, it may work toward mitigating the risk and the problem associated with the possibility of paying high costs in the case of tax litigation that could arise under the "English rule."[104]

Of course, the countries considered in Chapters 3 to 5 are not the only ones where the "English rule" has gone through a change. For example, as mentioned in Section 4 of Chapter 3, progress in discussions and movements toward a unilateral attorney's fee-shifting rule in Canada can be confirmed by the "Review of Civil Litigation Costs (Final Report)." In particular, since around the 1970s, the appropriateness and necessity of such change have been pointed out by some government-appointed expert committees and courts, especially in relation to public interest lawsuits. For instance, the 1989 "Report on the Law of Standing" of the Ontario Law Reform Commission, which was created under the State law, proposed in its Draft Act ("An Act respecting Access to Courts") legislative reforms to improve access to courts. Included in them are proposed reforms to restrict costs order on the plaintiffs in the following cases: (i) the litigated cases involve issues whose importance extends beyond the immediate interests of the parties; (ii) the plaintiffs do not have a personal, proprietary or

103. *See* 3/4 of Section 4 in Chapter 3 and 4 in Section 1 of Chapter 4.
104. *See* 4 in Section 4 of Chapter 3 for details.

pecuniary interest in the outcome of the litigation; (iii) the issues have not previously been determined by a court in a proceeding against the same defendant; and (iv) the defendant has a superior capacity to bear the costs of the proceeding.[105]

Also, Canada has a noteworthy judgment of the Supreme Court of British Columbia in *BC v. Okanagan Indian Band* ([2003] 3 SCR 371) that denotes the transformation of the "English rule." Its judgment upheld the Court of Appeal judgment ([2001] 95 BCLR (3d) 273), which ordered the state government to pay the interim costs of the lawsuit filed by an indigenous defendant who was accused of having logged trees without a statutory permit. There were dissenting judges who warned that the awarding of interim costs in this appeal might appear as a form of judicially imposed legal aid that should not lie with the judiciary. While the majority of the BC Supreme Court ruled that courts could decide not to apply the "English rule" at its discretion,[106] and this case meets the following three conditions: (i) the litigation would be unable to proceed unless interim costs were not made; (ii) the litigant's claim to be adjudicated is prima facie meritorious; (iii) the issues raised transcend the individual interests of the particular litigants and has not been resolved in earlier litigation. Those conditions or criteria shown in this judgment have also exerted not a little influence on administrative litigations in various fields of the other Provinces.[107]

Moreover, the transformation of the "English rule" in Canada has progressed in the form of amending some relevant provisions. The Federal Court rules (SOR/98-106)that were revised in 1998 state in Part 11 (Costs)§400 (Discretionary powers of Court) that it shall have full discretionary power over the amount and allocation of costs and the determination of by whom they are to be paid, and in exercising its discretion, it may consider: (i) the result of the proceeding; (ii) the amounts claimed and the amounts recovered; (iii) the importance and complexity of the issues; (iv) the apportionment of liability; (v) the amount of work; (vi) whether the public interest in having the proceeding litigated justifies a particular award of costs; and (vii) any other matter that it considers relevant. It also specifies in Chapter 5 §334.39 (No costs) that no costs may be awarded against any party to a motion for certification of a proceeding as a class proceeding. Likewise, in principle, courts do not order costs in litigations on the issues of citizenship, immigration, and refugee protection by the Federal Courts Citizenship, Immigration and Refugee Protection Rules (SOR/93-22) §22 (Costs).

In particular, in the French-speaking Province of Quebec, digression from the "English rule" is pronounced. For instance, under the new Civil Procedure Act (C-25.01) adopted in 2016 in the Province of Quebec, the successful party's litigation-related expenses that are to be shifted to the losing party do not contain its attorney's

105. *See* pp. 183-185 of the Report.

106. BC Supreme Court Regulations (Reg. 221/90) §57(9) provides, "costs of and incidental to a proceeding shall follow the event unless the court otherwise orders."

107. *See* Brian McLaughlin, Cheryl Tobias, and Craig Cameron, Interim Costs: The Impact of Okanagan Indian Band, UNB Law Journal, Revenue de Droit de L'un-B Vol/Tome 54(2005)p. 129. "Review of the Rules on Costs Discussion Paper" published in 2015 by the Federal Court of Appeal and Federal Court Committee points out a growing awareness of the need to address the issue of opacity on cases where the "English rule" is not to be applied.

fees in principle, so the amount of litigation-related expenses recoverable by the successful party is generally less than that recoverable by it in other Provinces. It is explained that such rule in the Province of Quebec basically derives from the traditional treatment in France, where the recoverable expenses ("depens") of the successful litigant under Article 695 of the Civil Procedure Law (Code de procedure civile) are court fees, fees for experts, translation fees, etc., while attorney's fees, travel expenses, etc., are unrecoverable expenses ("frais irrepetibles") as stipulated in Article 700 of the same law.[108] However, in fact, in France, under Article 700 of the Civil Procedure Law,[109] an order of partial recovery of the successful party's attorney's fees is often made on the losing party based on the judge's discretion and judgment based on the parties' economic situation, fairness and so forth.[110]

2 Review of Costs Rules in Japan's Tax Litigation

As mentioned above, the transformation of the "American rule" and the "English rule" has become a global trend. Various factors are driving this transformation, but in many cases, administrative lawsuits and public interest lawsuits are the major driving forces. In fact, in Japan as well, environmental lawsuits have changed the environment surrounding administrative lawsuits. For instance, as mentioned in 3(2) in Section 3 of Chapter 1, in the Supreme Court 3/14/1978 judgment, the Court ruled that the person with the benefit of appeal is the one whose personal rights or legally protected benefits are infringed or are likely to be inevitably damaged, so the benefits for the consumers in general by the provisions of the Act against Unjustifiable Premiums and Misleading Representations are only reflective benefits that arise as a result of the protection of the public interest, which is the purpose of the provisions, but not legally protected benefits. But, in the 2/17/1989 judgment (1982(Gyo-Tsu) No. 46) and 9/22/1992 judgment (1989(Gyo-Tsu) No. 131) of the Supreme Court, the scope of the persons with the benefit of appeal has practically been expanded, and the standing to sue of the neighboring residents of the concerned facilities in construction was recognized.

In the above Supreme Court 2/17/1989 judgment, the Court confirmed that a person who has a legal interest means a person whose own rights or legally protected interests are infringed or necessarily infringed by the disposition concerned. Even so,

108. H. Patrick Glenn, Costs and Fees in Common Law Canada and Quebec, at http://www-personal.umich.edu/~purzel/national_reports/Canada.pdf.
109. Article 700 of the Civil Procedure Law is translated as; "in all proceedings, the judge will order the party obliged to pay for legal costs or, in default, the losing party, to pay to the other party the amount which he will fix on the basis of the sums outlayed but not included in the legal costs. The judge will take into consideration the rules of equity and the financial condition of the party ordered to pay. He may, even sua sponte, for reasons based on the same considerations, decide that there is no need for such order." *See* https://allowb.org/acts_pdfs/CPC.pdf.
110. Philippe Cavalieros, Litigation & Dispute Resolution (2nd Edition) Global Legal Group (2003) p. 95, at https://www.roedl.com/insights/litigation-arbitration/france-jurisdiction-system-structure-costs-duration-protection reference. While, if the losing party in the administrative litigation is the taxpayer, he is rarely ordered to pay the successful party's attorney's fees. *See* https://uk.practicallaw.thomsonreuters.com/5-624-3429?transitionType=Default&contextData=(sc.Default)&firstPage=true.

the Court explained that the administrative law on the disposition does not stop at absorbing and dissolving the specific interests of the unspecified majority into the general public interest but rather has a purport of protecting them as individual benefits of those to whom they belong, then such benefits also come under legally protected interests. Likewise, in the above Supreme Court 9/22/1992 judgment, the Court clarified that the question of whether the administrative law has a purport of protecting the specified interests of the unspecified majority as individual benefits of those to whom they belong should be answered by taking into consideration the purport of the administrative law in question as well as the content and nature of the benefits intended to be protected by those provisions. These Supreme Court's views exerted an influence on the wording of Article 9(2) of the Administrative Case Litigation Act.[111] But they are not public interest litigations (including residents' lawsuits) and have hardly led to the activation of discussions on the review of rules on costs.[112]

Naturally, the number of litigations and circumstances surrounding litigations vary from country to country, and an answer to the question of which rule on costs is desirable depends not only on its rationality but also on the expected effect of the rule.[113] Even so, it generally follows that those countries where the large number of lawsuits causes various problems should find great merit in the "English rule" that works toward suppressing the increase in the number of lawsuits. However, many countries with a large number of administrative disputes have lately transformed the "English rule" by partially incorporating the unilateral attorney's fee-shifting rule or by taking measures to prevent the rules on costs from deterring meritorious litigations.[114] Behind these moves, there must be recognition of the importance of today's viewpoint that it is vital to promote "access to justice" as outlined in Goal 16 of the UN's "Sustainable Development Goals." From such a viewpoint, in Japan, where the number of administrative disputes is relatively small, there should be wider room for incorporating a unilateral attorney's fee-shifting rule under certain conditions or introducing a mechanism that mitigates the effect of deterring administrative disputes.

The opinion of the Japan Bar Association expressed on August 22, 2003, on the handling of attorney's fees for the unsuccessful party mentions that administrative

111. For details, *see* Kaoru Inaba, Bibliography (17) p. 63 onwards. Article 9(2) of this Act provides that, in determining whether a person other than those against which the administrative disposition/decision is directed has relevant legal interest, courts should take into consideration not only words of the relevant Act but also their purport and objective as well as the nature of such legal interest.
112. While residents' lawsuits are those that are not restricted by the limitations on the plaintiffs applicable to the revocation suits of administrative dispositions, and are filed through a resident audit request to the audit committee prescribed in Article 242 of the Local Autonomy Act by local residents for the purpose of environmental protection, prevention of pollution, and so forth.
113. It should follow that the main criteria for determining the desirable rule on costs include the degree of effectiveness in inducing or suppressing lawsuits, promoting settlements, increasing or decreasing litigation-related costs, correcting the power imbalance between the disputing parties, etc.
114. Such measures include "after-the-event insurance premiums" introduced in UK by the 1999 Access to Justice Act, protective costs order by UK courts, legal aids, the U.S.'s low income taxpayer clinic prescribed under IRC §7526, NZ's Tax pool intermediaries, and so forth.

litigation is the litigation type in which the unilateral costs shifting rule should be adopted because it would lead to the promotion of the use of trials by citizens, and it stresses that the scope of lawsuits where the unilateral costs shifting rule could be introduced should be examined promptly and concretely. However, the Association finds that the discussion on the above has been quite insufficient so far. Also, the Judicial System Reform Deliberation Committee recommends in its 2001 Memorandum that there should be discussions in the direction of introducing the system of shifting a part of the attorney's fee to the losing party as the costs necessary for litigation under certain conditions. These opinions strongly suggest that the adoption of the unilateral shifting of costs to the losing party in some types of administrative litigations is appropriate. While it would be difficult to determine in which types of administrative litigations the introduction of the unilateral shifting of costs to the losing party would be most appropriate and whether tax litigation could be included in them.

The following analysis is based on the premise that tax litigations are included in such types of administrative litigations (hereinafter called "qualified administrative litigation types") where the unilateral shifting of costs to the losing party (government agencies) could be appropriate under certain conditions. Those conditions could vary, as the relevant rules in those countries covered in the preceding chapters show.[115] Such being the case, it would be an option to let the court have the discretion to decide in what cases a certain amount of the successful litigant's attorney's fee could be recovered and how much it should be (Option A). Option A has the merit of applying the unilateral shifting of costs to the losing party possibly in any cases coming under the "qualified administrative litigation types." On the other hand, Option A has a demerit of the lack of transparency on when and how much costs are recoverable, as well as the possible demerit of instigating litigations falling under "qualified administrative litigation types" unnecessarily.[116] Therefore, there could also be an option to limit the recovery of the successful litigant's costs in the "qualified administrative litigation types" to such cases where he clears certain legally prescribed conditions (Option B).

As for the above legally prescribed conditions under Option B, those adopted in the U.S. may provide some insights. 28 U.S.C. §2412(d) provides that the successful litigant may not pass its attorney's fees if: (i) it does not meet the net worth requirements; (ii) the other party/government can substantially justify its position; (iii) there are special circumstances that make it unjust. As for IRC §7430, the above (iii) is not included in the criteria for not passing the attorney's fees of the successful party on to the losing party. In fact, the number of cases where the attorney's fee of the taxpayer successful in litigation is passed on is quite small, but the possibility of recovery of the taxpayer's attorney's fee could be increased by utilizing a qualified offer under IRC

115. Moreover, there might be an option that the successful litigant in the "qualified administrative litigation types" could also recover some expenses incurred at the stage of objection to the administrative review organs such as the Tax Tribunal under certain conditions, as it is possible in some countries such as the U.S.

116. While, in a country like Japan, where there is much restriction on the settlement of administrative disputes by agreements and the ratio of revocation of the disputed re/assessments is relatively low, such demerit would not likely to become conspicuous.

§7430(g)(2). In the case of Japan, where flexible resolution of a tax dispute is not basically possible, there should be a legal limit in incorporating a mechanism like a qualified offer as in the above Option B. While the above (i) to (ii) or (i) to (iii) might be adopted as the legally prescribed conditions of the above Option B (hereinafter called "Option B-1") that function as the standard that limits the shifting of the successful taxpayer's attorney's fee to the government.

There should be arguments over which of the above Option A and Option B-1 is preferable, but there should be a significant meaning in introducing the unilateral costs shifting rule in one way or another in light of the following facts: (a) the strict application of the "American rule" under which each party of the dispute bears its own attorney's fee digresses from the global standard on the rule on costs; (b) in the majority of EU countries, rules on costs similar to the "English rule" has been established but recently they have been transformed in such a way that they become more advantageous to their citizens and taxpayers; (c) the 2001 recommendation of the Judicial System Reform Committee to enhance people's access to justice in Japan should be based on the idea identical or similar to the one on which the Equal Access to Justice Act in U.S. is based, and the fact that in the process of it being legislated, the attorney's fees were seen as the factor constraining people's act of vindicating their rights is observable more or less in Japan as well. Therefore, the introduction of either Option A or Option B-1 should be fine, while the higher predictability and the level of clarity in terms of the scope of application might make Option B-1 preferable.

However, as implied by the application of IRC §7430, B-1 would often give rise to difficulty in determining whether the government succeeds in proving that its position in the proceeding is substantially justifiable. In the U.S., there used to be arguments over whether the phrase "substantially justifiable" in the Equal Access to Justice Act is synonymous with "not unreasonable,"[117] but, as suggested by the fact that the wording of IRC §7430 changed in 1986,[118] now it is clear that the current hurdle for the government to clear to justify its position is higher. Even if the hurdle for the government to clear to prevent cost shifting has become higher now, the hurdle with comparable height would not pose in almost all cases a serious problem on the part of the NTA/government under Option B-1 because it would be quite likely that the number of those cases where the NTA cannot clear this hurdle should be less than that in the case of IRS. The main reason for this could be found in the facts: (i) the number of tax disputes is much smaller in Japan, (ii) sufficient and justifiable reasons are required to be shown in notices of reassessments, (iii) disputed re/assessments on which the NTA cannot justify its position substantially are quite likely to have been revoked by the Tax Tribunal's decisions.

As is clear from the above, Option B-1, despite its merit of clarity and predictability, has a demerit of its narrow scope of application. Therefore, it might be a good idea to draw some insight from "Rees practice" in the UK and come up with an option (hereinafter called "Option C") in which unilateral shifting of costs is possible in a case

117. For details, *see* Awards of Attorneys' Fees by Federal Courts and Federal Agencies at https:www.everycrsreport.com/reports/94-970.html.

118. *See* 3 in Section 3 and footnote 123 of Chapter 2.

where the NTA disputes the validity of a decision of the court at the higher court, and the higher court upheld it provided that the disputing taxpayer meets the net worth requirements and the disputed case is not a tax avoidance case.[119] In other words, under Option C, a court judgment revoking the disputed re/assessment for the taxpayer being the plaintiff or the appellant does not entitle him to the recovery of his attorney's fee, while a higher court judgment sustaining the lower court judgment that revokes the disputed re/assessment entitles him the recovery of the reasonable amount of his attorney's fees so long as the above requirements are met, irrespective of whether the NTA/government can substantially justify its position on the re/assessment, etc. It is also conceivable not to incorporate the net worth requirements in Option C (Option C-1) to give more effect to the significance of introducing the unilateral shifting of costs to the losing party.[120]

Irrespective of which of the above Option A, Option B, and Option C is adopted, the one which decides the recoverable amount of attorney's fees by the successful taxpayers in litigation should be the court clerk of the district court by following Article 71(1) of the Civil Procedure Act. As for the method of determining the amount to be recovered, the Supreme Court stated in the 2/24/2012 judgment (2011(Gyu)1039) that the recoverable expense should have relevance to the case and be within the amount that should be deemed reasonable by taking into consideration the difficulty of the case, the amount claimed, the amount allowed, and other various circumstances, so this statement could be used as a reference. When the disputing parties are dissatisfied with the amount to be borne by the losing party, Article 71(6) and Article 121 of the Civil Procedure Act stipulate that those who are dissatisfied with the amount of recoverable expenses determined by the court clerk could file a request of review with the court.[121] But, from the perspective of relieving the burden on courts and increasing transparency and predictability, it might be preferable to make the method of calculating the amount of recoverable attorney's fee simpler by fixing it as a certain percentage of the disputed tax amount/the actual amount of the attorney's fee, and so forth.[122]

119. There is a fundamental difference between "Rees practice" and Option C because "Rees practice" is an exception to the "English rule" and the exception applies when HMRC wins at a (higher) court while under Option C, it is an exception to the "American rule" and the exception applies when NTA loses at a higher court.
120. As for Option C-1, it might as well be modified to limit its application solely to a case where the tax authority loses in the Supreme Court judgment (Option C-2).
121. Article 122 of the Civil Procedure Act stipulates that the provisions relating to judgments shall apply *mutatis mutandis* to decisions and orders unless they are of a different nature.
122. This might be a good idea to prevent disputes over the costs order. The proposal 33 made in the Australia's Law Reform Committee's 1994 Report (ALRC 75) is also in favor of the idea of not allowing an appeal to the determined amount of the recoverable costs.

Epilogue

Compared with the situations, especially in those countries ranked high in Figure 6.3, the impact of *Factor 1 (tax structure)* and *Factor 3 (dispute resolution method)* on the number of tax disputes seem not to be so strong in Japan, mainly for the following reasons: (i) such impact is by no means negligible in the case of IGT which often entails an issue of property valuation, but, it is not so strong in the case of the other taxes which do not have provisions granting wide discretion to the NTA; (ii) flexible settlement of disputes after re/assessments is not possible. Moreover, the fact that the Tax Tribunal's decisions bind the NTA and the number of objections, as well as the number of unprocessed cases at the Tax Tribunal, is relatively small, has also contributed to the speedy resolution of tax disputes. This situation contrasts with the situation of many other major countries where there has been a growing need for utilizing flexible dispute resolution methods at the early stages of disputes to cope with a large number of tax disputes, and it is also indicative of the fact that there should exist in Japan wider breathing room or leeway for taking measures on other challenges possibly in such a way that would decrease disputing taxpayers' burden and correct the power imbalance between the taxpayers and the tax authority.[1]

Moreover, the fact that the number of tax disputes in Japan is considerably smaller than that in other major countries does not necessarily mean that it is free from demerits or negative elements. Included typically among those negative elements is the possible existence of deterrents on aggrieved taxpayers' access to justice. If such deterrents exist among *Factors 1* to *8* mentioned in Sections 1 and 2, questions arise as to which *Factors* have them and which of them are particularly in need of correction or

1. In 2021, the Netherlands, which has a population of 17.41 million, has about 30,000 tax lawsuits received by the courts (about 100 cases received by the Supreme Court alone). *See* 1 in Section 2 of Chapter 4. In Australia, which has a population of 25.78 million in 2021, the total number of tax disputes recently received by the AAT and courts is annually 20,000 to 25,000 (*see* Figure 3.2 in Section 1 of Chapter 3). In the UK with a population of 68 million in 2021, the total number of tax disputes received by the Tribunals and courts is 7,500 in 2017-2018 (*see* Chapter 2, Table 2.2). In contrast, the number of tax disputes received by courts in Japan, which has a population of 125,000, is about 200 (or about 1,000 even if it is combined with the estimated number of annual cases received by Tax Tribunal). *See* Figures 1.6 and 1.7 as well as 3 in Section 1 of Chapter 1.

improvement. The unilateral costs-shifting rule based on Options A to C is intended to address the problems associated with *Factor 5 (level of disputing taxpayers' burden)*. As for the "(Revised) Proposal of Review at Pre-Assessment Stage" and "Proposal of Pre-Assessment Mediation," they are options for addressing the problems in Japan that are associated with *Factor 4 (dispute resolution method)*, but they also have an aspect of addressing some problems associated with *Factor 5*. Therefore, those latter two options are more comprehensive and drastic, and they could contribute to reducing taxpayers' costs quite considerably in some cases.

Even among those countries covered in Chapters 2 to 5, various measures that exert an influence on the status of *Factor 5 (level of disputing taxpayers' burden)* have been lately taken. Those measures include: (i) reform of costs-shifting rule in the direction of making it more favorable to taxpayers; (ii) taxpayers could recover some costs incurred at the stage of the administrative objection; (iii) more active use of flexible tax dispute resolution methods including ADR; (iv) flexible tax dispute resolution at the pre-re/assessment stage; (v) greater support for litigant taxpayers in difficulties. If some of those measures are also adopted in Japan, the degree of the issues relevant to *Factor 5* limiting access to justice will become less. While, in the case of Japan, the need and usefulness of taking the above (ii) measures would be relatively small, and the above (iii) measures could conflict with the Constitutional principle of taxation by law. As for the above (iv) measures, the above "(Revised) Proposal of Review at Pre-Assessment Stage" and "Proposal of Pre-Assessment Mediation" might be possible options for it, but they may not clear the costs/benefits test. Therefore, the above (i) and (v) measures (in particular (i)) might be the most promising candidate for Japan's reform option for aggrieved taxpayers.[2]

As for the above (i) (Reform of costs-shifting rule) measure, a unilateral costs-shifting rule (with net worth requirement), which is also in line with the global reform trend, might be a realistic option. It is to be noted that, depending on the structure of the adopted unilateral costs-shifting rule, it might give rise to recognizable changes in tax administration and tax disputes. Those changes might appear in the ratio of re/assessments, the Tax Tribunal/court's ratio of revocation of the disputed/reassessments, the time needed for reviewing them, etc. Also, the hurdle for its adoption would become higher if the arguments against the adoption of a similar rule in administrative fields other than tax fields are strong, and it cannot be adopted unless a similar rule is adopted simultaneously or in advance, at least in some other administrative fields. Thus, the hurdle for adopting the unilateral costs-shifting rule might not be low, but the above Options A to C should help lower the hurdle because, under these Options, (a) the number of cases to which the unilateral costs-shifting rule becomes applicable would be small in number, and it should make its negative impact on the NTA and courts to be small; (b) they would not lead to the significant increase in the number of meritless tax litigations.

2. Even in Japan, with the widening gap between the rich and poor as well as the increase in the workers from abroad, in the future there will be more taxpayers with financial or communication difficulties who might have meritorious cases but give up disputing them due to those difficulties.

In practice, the adoption of the unilateral costs-shifting rule might not be enough for some aggrieved taxpayers because not all meritorious tax cases are filed by taxpayers with attorneys. Moreover, not all meritorious tax cases are those in which the taxpayers are successful in litigation. For example, in the famous Supreme Court 3/27/1985 judgment in *Oshima* case (1080(GyoTsu)No. 15), the appellant who claimed the ITA's failure to treat salary-income earners and business income earners equally did not win, but Judge Kido added that the sense of inequality on taxation felt by salary-income earners at that time was strong enough to demand urgent actions for correction, and it led to the subsequent year's amendment of ITA which increased the deductible amount in calculating the taxable salary income. Some other meritorious cases are not disputed because the re/assessed amount does not match costs in time, money, physical/mental stress, etc., even if they may bring favorable consequences for taxpayers. The failure of those meritorious cases to be reviewed by the Tax Tribunal or courts could mean a delay in clarifying what the right tax treatment is and could, in some cases, be a loss to taxpayers in general as well as the NTA.[3]

The above suggests that it might also be an option to adopt a measure to encourage some meritorious cases to come to the Tax Tribunal/courts. In this sense, Australia's test case litigation program may provide useful insight, and it might be an option to financially support the litigation-related costs of the taxpayer with a meritorious case.[4] Or, it might be that a mechanism is established or strengthened to enable an Ombudsman or a group of tax experts and lawyers to receive relevant information on their cases or requests for consultations from taxpayers and their agents more easily and systematically so that there would be a fewer number of potentially meritorious tax cases that, due to the inability of taxpayers/agents to assess them well, do not come out in the Tax Tribunal and courts. The perspectives on which those options stand basically overlap with those underlying the above (v) (greater support for litigant taxpayers in difficulties), the "(Revised) Proposal of Review at Pre-Assessment Stage," and "Proposal of Pre-Assessment Mediation." Indeed, they all have problems in terms of cost-effectiveness and so forth, but they might contain useful insights in seeking measures to complement the functional limit of the above Options A to C on the unilateral costs-shifting rule in tax litigations.

As Figure 1.10 in Chapter 1, Figure 2.2 in Chapter 2, and the comparison of Figure 3.6 in Chapter 3 with Figure 6.2 in this chapter suggest, there is a strong positive correlation between the ratio of on-site audits and the number of tax disputes. Therefore, in the case of Japan, the declining trend in the ratio of on-site audits is likely to accelerate the declining trend of the number of tax disputes. But this declining trend of tax disputes will be counteracted by the increasing need for more resources of the

3. In this sense, Tokyo District Court's 28/5/2015 (2012(GyoU)152) is particularly striking now that it should affect many taxpayers by ruling that tax reliefs under tax treaties are available to the plaintiff who submitted a written notice for their application after having failed to attach it to its return at the time of its filing while Article 9-2 of the Special Enforcement Act on Tax Treaties requires its attachment when a return is filed.
4. If this option is adopted, the most appropriate agency to determine whether a case is meritorious enough to be reviewed by courts might be the Tax Tribunal. But it might require the Tax Tribunal to go through some structural and functional changes.

NTA vis-à-vis the inevitable rise in the number and complexity of globalized transactions and tax strategies. Such an expected future situation should also increase the importance of reviewing and reforming some systems and rules relevant to tax dispute resolution by giving due consideration to the perspectives contained in the reform options proposed above. Even so, eventually, it should follow that the question of what kind of reform is to be implemented would be answered by taking into consideration such factors as the balance among measures to realize efficient/effective tax administration, fair taxation among taxpayers, protection of taxpayers' rights, and so forth. Also, the answer would be dependent on which reform will be adopted in other administrative fields.

Such being the case, even if it would be limited in the scope of applicable taxpayers, it might be more realistic, and the hurdle for reform could be lower if a measure is taken so that taxpayers engaged in business are allowed to deduct for IT purposes expenses incurred in connection with tax objections/litigations over the re/assessments of income of their business. It was disputed in the Tax Tribunal's 5/29/2013 decision whether the NTA's reassessment/denial of the deduction for IT purposes of the expenses the applicant/blue return filer incurred in connection with the litigation at court over the alleged excess amount of the salary paid to the family employee of his business. The applicant claimed that these litigation-related expenses should be deductible because they are expenses necessary for carrying out his income-producing business as a certified tax accountant. However, the Tax Tribunal dismissed his claim by explaining that these expenses are neither directly related to his business nor objectively necessary in carrying out his business. It also mentioned that, now that the concerned litigation that incurred these expenses was over the reassessments previously made on his IT, the above explanation is in line with the purport of Article 45 of IT, which does not allow IT to be deducted in calculating business income.

The interpretation shown in the above Tax Tribunal's 5/29/2013 decision is in line with the AR 37-23(3) on IT and may not be erred, but it is not necessarily a universally accepted interpretation of what constitutes deductible expenses of a business proprietor for IT purposes. For example, in *Trust of Bingham v. Commissioner* ([1945] 325 U.S. 365), at issue was whether expenses incurred by trustees in contesting an income tax deficiency assessment are deductible under 1939 IRC §23 (Deduction from gross income), which stated, "In computing net income there shall be allowed as deductions: (a) Expenses." The Supreme Court ruled, "To the extent that Treasury Regulations 103, §19.23(a)-15 purports to deny deduction of litigation expense unless it is to produce income, ... it conflicts with the meaning and purpose of s §23(a)(2), and is unauthorized." Then, it concluded that the trust may deduct litigation expenses when they are directly connected with or proximately result from the enterprise—the management of property held for production of income.[5] Following this judgment, the above Treasury Regulation was amended by T.D. 5513 (1946-1), which expressly allowed the deductibility of legal expenses incurred in the determination of IT and

5. A similar conclusion is handed down in the *Tellier* case (1996) mentioned in 5(2) in Section 4 in Chapter 2.

property tax liability while it did not allow the deduction of them incurred in the determination of liability for other taxes.[6]

Now that Japan's ITA §37, differently from IRC §162, does not specifically require deductible necessary expenses to be ordinary as well (*see* footnote 37 in Chapter 1), it would be all the more theoretically possible to treat business proprietors' expenses incurred in connection with tax objections/litigations as necessary expenses for their business. While it might be apprehended that if business proprietors can deduct for IT purposes expenses associated with tax objections/litigations, it would unnecessarily incline them to dispute re/assessments on them because, even if they do not win favorable decisions/judgments, they can at least reduce income tax liability by deducting these expenses for IT purposes. Therefore, a possible reform option might be that a measure is taken so that a reasonable amount of expenses incurred by business proprietors in connection with tax objections/litigations over their business income tax liability is deductible as necessary expenses provided that the disputed re/assessments are revoked fully or partially by the Tax Tribunal or courts. There might be arguments over whether such a measure has to be a legal or administrative one, but if an administrative measure is sufficient (and probably is so), it would become a more realistic option with the relatively low hurdle for its adoption.

6. For details, *see* William S. Stinnette, Income Tax – Deductibility of Legal Expenses, Washington Law Review, Vol. 28, No. 1, (1953) p. 66. The amended Regulation prescribes, "Expenses paid or incurred by an individual in the determination of liability for taxes upon his income are deductible." Then, 1954 IRC §212 (Expenses for production of income) states, "In the case of an individual, there shall be allowed as a deduction all the ordinary and necessary expenses paid or incurred during the taxable year—...(3) In connection with the determination, collection or refund of any tax." While the Tax Cuts and Jobs Act of 2017 introduced IRC §67 (2% floor on miscellaneous itemized deductions)(g) that narrowed down the scope of deductible legal fees for tax purposes.

Appendix Attachment: Tax Tribunal's Decisions Published on Its HP (2,594 as of 8/9/2022) as Summarized and Translated in English by the Author*

Number of Published Decisions on AGRNT (Act of General Rules on National Taxes): 433

(1) 【General rules】; 16 decisions
(2) 【Finalized payment obligation】; 87 decisions

Breakdown: 『Refund request』: 57
Others: 30

(3) 【Payment and collection】: 9 decisions
(4) 【Refund】: 11 cases
(5) 【Suspension of payment and security】: 21 decisions
(6) 【Penalties】: 234 decisions

Breakdown: 『Under-reporting penalty』: 42 ([Justifiable reason]: 24)
『Non-reporting penalty』: 27([Justifiable reason]: 18)
『penalty for failure to withhold』: 6([Justifiable reason]: 4)
『strict penalty』: 144
Others: 15

(7) 【Time limit for correction, collection, etc.】: 19 decisions
(8) 【Investigation】: 3 decisions

* The Attachment lists all items in 【 】shown in the list on the Tax Tribunal's HP while its breakdown (items in『 』, [ ], etc.) lists only major items of disputes.

(9) 【Requests for review】: 33 decisions

Breakdown: 『Benefit of appeals/Standing to sue』: 16
『Procedures for filing objections』: 6
Others: 11

(10) Others: 1 decision

Number of Published Decisions on ITA (Income Tax Act): 681

(1) 【General rules】; 50 decisions
(2) 【Income categories】; 128 decisions

Breakdown: 『Interest income』: 2
『Dividend income』: 4
『Real estate income』: 10
『Business income』: 18
『Salary income and retirement income』: 22
『Capital gains』: 21
『Temporal income』: 23
『Miscellaneous income』: 26

(3) 【Amount of revenue】; 94 decisions
(4) 【Necessary expenses】; 167 decisions

Breakdown: 『Business income』: 64
『Capital gains』: 49
『Real estate income』: 40
Others: 14

(5) 【Foreign-currency denominated transactions】; 1 decision
(6) 【Special rules on income calculation】; 44 decisions
(7) 【Set-off of profit and loss and carry-over of loss】; 15 decisions
(8) 【Income deduction】; 43 decisions
(9) 【Calculation of tax amount】; 13 decisions
(10) 【Payment, refund, etc.】; 7 decisions
(11) 【Denial of a family company's actions or calculations】; 15 decisions

Breakdown: 『Denial of a family company's actions or calculations』: 15

(12) 【Tax obligation of nonresidents and corporations】; 17 decisions

Breakdown: 『Income sourced in Japan』: 16
Others: 1

(13) 【Withholding tax】; 51 decisions

Breakdown: 『Salary, etc.』: 34
『Remunerations, fees』: 7
Others: 10

(14) 【Approval and revocation of blue return status】; 10 decisions
(15) 【Investigation procedures】; 1 decision
(16) 【Estimated taxation】; 22 decisions

Breakdown: 『Re/assessment by estimation』: 22

Number of Published Decisions on CITA (Corporate Income Tax Act): 442

(1) 【General rules】; 34 decisions
(2) 【Calculation of amount of income】; 323 decisions

Breakdown: 『Attributable business years of taxable profits』: 46
『Scope and calculation of taxable revenue』: 41
『Attributable business years of deductible expenses』: 28
『Scope and calculation of deductible expenses』: 180
Breakdown: 『Director's remunerations, bonus, and retirement money』: 58
『Corporate contribution』: 29 (Breakdown: [Gratuitous transfer of economic benefits]: 15, others: 14)
『Depreciation』: 22
Others: 28

(3) 【Calculation of tax amount】; 14 decisions
(4) 【Payment, refund, etc.】; 9 decisions
(5) 【Blue return】; 14 decisions

Breakdown: 『Revocation of blue return status』: 14

(6) 【Consolidated payment】; 1 decision
(7) 【Correction and determination】; 16 decisions

Breakdown: 『Denial of a family company's actions or calculations』: 7
『Estimated taxation』:4
『Reasons for reassessments』: 4
Others: 1

(8) 【Tax obligation of foreign corporations】; 8 decisions
(9) 【Taxation of income at liquidation】; 3 decisions

Number of Published Decisions on IGTA (Inheritance and Gift Tax Act): 381

(1) 【Taxpayers】; 2 decisions
(2) 【Time of assets acquisition】; 9 decisions
(3) 【Scope of property subject to Inheritance Tax】; 55 decisions

Breakdown: 『Cash and deposits in financial institutions』: 16
『Land and contracts on land』: 15
『Securities』: 10
『Loans』: 5
Others: 9

(4) 【Scope of property subject to Gift Tax】; 37 cases
(5) 【Calculation of taxable amount of inherited property】; 53 decisions

Breakdown: 『Deductible debt』: 29
『Gift made within 3 years before inheritance』: 5
Others: 19

(6) 【Calculation of taxable value of gifted property】; 1 decision
(7) 【Calculation of tax amount】; 8 decisions
(8) 【Property appraisal】; 167 decisions

Breakdown: 『Principles of appraisal』: 27
『Rights and surface rights on land』: 140
(Breakdown: [Adjustments based on various influential factors]:27, [unlisted stocks]: 25, [Leasehold right]:11, [loaned residential lot]:11, others: 66)

(9) 【Filing and payment】; 26 decisions

Breakdown: 『Special rules for requests for revision/refund』: 12
『Joint payment obligation』: 10
Others: 2

(10) 【Payment deferral and payment in kind】; 22 decisions
(11) 【Special rules for correction and determination】; 2 decisions

Number of Published Decisions on CTA (Consumption Tax Act): 140

(1) 【Taxpayers】; 13 decisions
(2) 【Taxable scope】; 13 decisions

Breakdown: 『Taxable transactions』: 15
『Nontaxable transactions』: 11
『Tax-exempt transactions』: 13

(3) 【Time of property transfer 】; 2 decisions
(4) 【Tax base】; 13 decisions
(5) 【Tax credit, etc.】; 70 decisions

Breakdown: 『Input tax credit』: 69 (Breakdown:『Simplified taxation method』: 26, others: 43)
『Tax credit in the case of bad debt』: 1

(6) 【Special rules for Government agencies】; 2 decisions
(7) 【Special rules for filing and request for correction】; 1 decision

Number of Published Decisions on Collection Act: 173

(1) 【General rules】; 10 decisions
(2) 【Adjustment with other claims】; 20 decisions
(3) 【Secondary tax payment obligation】; 66 decisions

Breakdown:『Secondary tax payment obligation for receiving a defaulter's property with no/low costs』: 46 ([cases of gratis transfer of property]: 15, [cases denying gratis transfer of property]: 14, [Calculation of transferred benefit]: 6, [others]:11), 『Others』: 20

(4) 【Seizure】; 47 decisions

Breakdown: 『Rules on seizure』: 36 (Breakdown: 21 ([Attribution of seized property]), 15 (others))
『Seizure of various properties』: 11 (Breakdown: 3 [real estate], 2 [claims], 6 [Others])

(5) 【Request for shared distribution】; 5 decisions
(6) 【Procedures for cashing seized property】; 17 decisions

Breakdown: 『Estimated price of public auction property』: 6
『Public notice of public auction of seized property』: 5
Others: 6

(7) 【Distribution of cash conversed from seized property】; 3 decisions
(8) 【Suspension of collection action】; 2 decisions
(9) 【Special rules for requests for review and appeals】; 3 decisions

Number of Published Decisions on STMA (Special Taxation Measures Act):282

(1) 【Special rules on ITA】; 168 decisions

Breakdown: 『Special rules on capital gains』: 126 (Breakdown:[Special credit for capital gains from the transfer of a resided property]: 46, [Special credit for capital gains from the transfer of a business property]: 30, others: 50)
『Special credit for housing loans』: 24

(2) 【Special rules on CITA】; 86 decisions

Breakdown: 『Entertainment expenses, etc.』: 19, 『Special tax rates for specific transfer of land 』:19, 『Anti-tax haven rules』: 8, 『Transfer pricing rule』: 6, 『Special depreciation for specific equipment』: 6, others: 28)

(3) 【Special rules on IGTA】; 23 decisions

Breakdown: 『Special rules on calculation of taxable price of small resided property』: 16, 『Deferral of Gift Tax payment on agricultural land』: 3, others: 4)

(4) Others (【Special rules on Registration and License Tax Act】): 6 decisions

Bibliography (in Order of Citation)

Introduction/Chapter 1

(1) Yasutaka Abe, "*Gyousei soshou no arubeki seido,arubeki unnyou ni tuite*" (Regarding the Ideal System for Administrative Litigation and Its Operation), Houritsubunnka (2004)

Andrian Zuckerman, "Justice in Crisis: Comparative Dimensions of Civil Procedure," *Civil Justice in Crisis: Comparative Perspectives of Civil Procedure,* Oxford University Press (1999)

(2) Rie Nagata, "*Kokuzei Fufuku Shinpansho no sonzai igi to shinri tetsuzuki jyou no kadai*" (Significance of the National Tax Tribunal and Problems in Trial Procedures), *Sozei Soushou* (Tax Disputes) No. 6, Zaikei Shouhosha (2012)

(3) Takemi Fujimagari, "*Saiketsujirei nimiru saiketsu no mondaiten tou*" (Problems of Decisions Found in Actual Cases), *Sozei Soushou* (Tax Litigation) No. 6, Zaikei Shouhosha (2012)

(4) Hiroshi Kaneko, "*Sozeihou*" (Tax Law) 18th ed., Koubundou (2013)

(5) Satoshi Matsuzawa, "*Shinpan Sozei Jittaiho—Houjinzeiho Kaishaku no Kihongenri*" (New Edition of Tax Law Essentials—Basic Principles of CITA Interpretation), Chuou Keizaisha (1999)

(6) Suetada Ito, "*Oyako kaisha kan torihiki ni taisuru kifukin kazei nituite no ichikousatsu*" (Thought on Corporate Contribution on Parent-Subsidiary Transactions), *Kyushu Kokuisai Daigaku Law Review,* Vol. 11 (2009)

(7) Minoru Nakazato, "*Koramu ③Kougin jiken*" (Column 3: Industrial Bank of Japan Incident), *Jurist Supplement* No. 178 (2005)

(8) Sadao Kishida, "Souzoku chokuzen ni shutoku sareta souzoku zaisan no hyoukagaku nituki hyouka tsuutatsu ni yorazuni sono shutoku kagaku ni motozuite sareta shobun wo tekihou to shita jirei" (A Case Where the Appraisal Value of an Inherited Property Acquired Immediately Before the Inheritance Was Sustained While It Was Based on Its Acquisition Price Rather Than That in AR on Property Valuation), *Jurist* No. 1059 (1995)

(9) Masahiro Midorikawa, *"Zaisan hyouka niokeru 'tokubetsu no jijyou' to sono koushi"* (Special Circumstances in the Case of Property Appraisal and Their Application), *Zeiri* Vol. 39 No. 9 (1996)

(10) Keiko Iizawa, *"Koudaichi hyouka wo meguru tsutatsu to saibanrei no mondaiten"* (Problems with AR on Property Appraisal and Judicial Precedents Concerning The Specific Spacious Land), *Zeiken* No. 178 (2014)
Naoki Matsuda, Tax Strategies VS. Countermeasures, XLibris (2015)

(11) Tadatsune Mizuno, "Gaikoku zeigaku koujyo ni kansuru saikin no saibanrei to sono mondaiten" (Recent Judicial Precedents and Issues Concerning Foreign Tax Credits), *Kokusai Zeimu* Vol. 23, No. 3 (2018)

(12) Fumihiro Komamiya, "Sozei soushou seido kaikakuan" (Tax Dispute System Reform Proposal), *Jurist* No. 1238 (2005)

(13) Hiroshi Hasegawa, "Kankoku no nouzeisha hogotantoukan seido" (Korea's System of Protecting Taxpayers' Rights), Soze Soushou, No. 4, Zaikei Shouhousha (2010)

(14) Hiroshi Hasegawa, "Kokuzei fufukuseido no kokusai hikaku " (International Comparison of Tax Objection System), *Zeiseikenkyu*, No. 52 (2007)

Chapter 2

Gerald A. Kafka, Rita A. Cavanagh, and Sean M. Akins, Do IRS Appeals' Office Ex Parte Prohibitions Need Strengthening?, *Tax Notes*, March 30 (2009)

Andrew Strelka and Sean Morrison, The IRS and America's Longest Running ADR Program, *The Federal Lawyer* (October/November 2016)

Thomas Carter Louthan and Steven C. Wrappe, Building a Better Resolution: Adapting IRS Procedures to Fit the Dispute, *Tax Notes International* (1996)

John Klotsche, Jousting with the Tax Man: ADR at the IRS, Part II, *Tax Notes*, July 27 (2009)

David Parsly, The Internal Revenue Service and Alternative Dispute Resolution: Moving from Infancy to Legitimacy, *Cardozo Journal of Conflict Resolution*, Vol. 8:677 (2007)

Amy Elliott, ADR Options for IRS Debated at Tax Analysts Conference, *Tax Notes*, June 29 (2009)

Carolyn Miller Parr, Why Postappeal Mediation Isn't Working and How to Fix It, *TAX.COM* (September 16, 2009)

Stephen Folan, Even ADR Must Pay Its Dues: An Analysis of the Evolution of the Internal Revenue Service's ADR Programs and Where They Still Need to Grow, *Pepperdine Dispute Resolution Law Journal*, Article 3 (2013)

Marie Sapirie, The Increase in Cases Designated for Litigation, *Tax Notes*, March 14 (2016)

Peter J. Panuthos, Procedural Issues of Human Rights and Taxation, Access to Justice, *Bulletin for International Taxation* (July 2017)

Sheila A. Murphy, *Reports of the United States Tax Court*, Vol. 41, U.S. Government Printing Office (2013)

Christopher J. Badum, The Small Tax Case Procedure: How It Works—Does It Work?, *Fordham Urban Law Journal*, Vol. 44, No. 2 (1976)

Keith Fogg, The United States Tax Court: A Court for All Parties, *Bulletin for International Taxation*, January/February (2016)

Howard Matthew, *Judicial Decision Making, IRS Policy and Taxpayer Litigation, Interdependence and Democratic Control*, UMI Dissertation Services (1998)

Peter N. Cubita, Jeffrey S. Lichtman and Daniel D. Rubino, Awards of Attorney's Fees in the Federal Courts, *St. John's Law Review*, Vol. 56. No. 2 (1982

H.A. Zionts, *the Civil Rights Attorney's Fees Awards Act of 1976: A View from the Second Circuit*, *Buffalo Law Review*, Vol. 29, No. 3 (1980)

Kyle A. Loring, The Catalyst Theory Meets the Supreme Court—Common Sense Takes a Vacation, *Boston College Law Review*, Vol. 43, No. 4 (2002)

Lionel M. Lavenue and Forrest A. Jones, Rule 68 Offer of Judgment: A Neglected Tool for Patent Infringement Defendants, *Westlaw Journal Intellectual Property*, March 1 (2017)

Harris Bonnette, The IRS Absolutely, Positively Not Pay Your Attorneys' Fees (Or will They ?), *Florida Bar Journal*, Vol. 84, No. 5 (2010)

Carlton Smith, Tax Court Orders: The Unpublished Litigation, *Tax Notes*, August 22 (2016)

Richard Stark, A Principled Approach to Collection and Accuracy Related Penalties, *Tax Notes*, April 2 (2001)

Michael F. Lax, The Innocent Spouse Provision under Section 6013 (e) of the Internal Revenue Code: Relief or Refuse, *University of Arkansas at Little Rock Law Review*, Vol. 12, No. 1 (1989)

Richard Beck, The Innocent Spouse Problem: Joint and Several Liability for Income Taxes Should Be Repealed, *Vanderbilt Law Review*, Vol. 43:317 (1990)

Chapter 3

Stephen Oliver, The Role of the Tax Tribunal, Striking the Balance: Tax Administration, Enforcement and Compliance in 1990, *the Institute for Fiscal Studies Sixth Residential Conference 16-17* (April 1993)

Lord Nolan, Some Historical Recollections of Tax Practice and of the Special Commissioners, *British Tax Review*, No. 1 (2005)

Stephen Oliver, Twenty-five Years of the VAT tribunals: A View from the President, *British Tax Review*, No. 6 (1998)

John F. Avery Jones, The Reform of the Tax Tribunals: A Story of Uncompleted Business, *British Tax Review*, No. 3 (2006)

John F. Avery Jones, Tax Treaties: The Perspectives of Common Law Countries, *Courts and Tax Treaty Law*, IBFD (2007)

Guglielmo Maisto, Courts and Tax Treaty Law, *EC and International Tax Law Series*, Vol. 3, IBFD (2007)

Judith Freedman and Johan Vella, HMRC's Management of the UK. Tax System: The Boundaries of Legitimate Discretion, *Legal Research Paper Series* (Paper No. 73/2012)

Judith Freeman, UK Institution for Tax Governance: Reviewing Tax Settlements, *British Tax Review*, Issue 1 (2016)

Chris Davidson, Examining the tax Assurance Commissioner's Latest Report, *Tax Journal*, August 5 (2016)

Malcolm Gammie, Tax Appeals and Reviews: the New Landscape, *British Tax Review*, Vol. 6 (2010)

Andrew Hubbard, Penalty Appeals, *Tax Journal,* October 20 (2017)

John Cassidy, Taxpayer Wins Penalty Shootout, *Taxation*, September 15 (2016)

Keith Gordon, Do Not Pass Go, *Taxation*, May 3 (2018)

Naoki Matsuda, Tax Strategies VS. Countermeaures, Xlibris (2015)

Philip Baker, Taxation and the European Convention on Human Rights, *British Tax Review,* Vol. 40, No. 8 (2000)

Peter Vaines, Expenses: The Wholly and Exclusively Test, *Tax Journal,* Issue 1577 (May 25, 2022)

Chapter 4

Chris Wallis, In Facilitation Preparation, Scoping and Agility Are Essential, *Taxation in Australia,* Vol. 53, No. 4 (October 2018)

Binh Tran-Nam and Michael Walpole, Effective Access to Independent Tax Dispute Resolution in Australia: The Tax Lawyers' Perspective, *Australian Tax Review*, Vol. 47 (2018)

Binh Tran-Nam and Michael Walpole, Independent Tax Dispute Resolution and Social Justice in Australia, *UNSW Law Journal*, Vol. 35, No. 2 (2012)

Peter Cane, Judicial Review and Merits Review: Comparing Administrative Adjudication by Courts and Tribunals, Chapter 25, *Comparative Administrative Law*, ed. Rose-Ackerman, Susan; Lindseth, L. Peter, Edward Elgar Publishing (2010)

Stephen Gageler, What Is a Question of Law?, *Australian Tax Review*, Vol. 43 (2014)

Jeremy Hirschhorn and Alison Chen, Tossing the Coin: A Quantitative Analysis of Tax Decisions 2001 to 2010, *Australian Tax Review*, Vol. 41 (2012), 154

Sue Milne, The Bottom Line for Review of an Assessment—A Case Note on Commissioner v Futuris Corporation Ltd, *Monash University Law Review* (2010)

John Smith, Administrative Tax Penalties, *Australian Tax Review*, Vol. 30 (2001)

Geoffrey Clews, Chapter 20 in "*The Disputes and Litigation Review (7th Edition)*" ed. Simon Whitehead, Law Business Research Ltd. (2014)

Melinda Jone, Evaluating New Zealand's Tax Dispute Resolution System: A Dispute Systems Design Perspective, (2016)22, NZJTLP

Andrew Maples, Melinda Jone and Alistair Hodoson, Inland Revenue Facilitated Conferences: Better Than Settling Disputes with 'Clubs and Spears'?", *eJournal of Tax Research,* Vol. 18, No. 2 (2020)

Sarah Miles, The Price We Pay for a Specialized Society: Do Tax Disputes Require Greater Judicial Specialisation?, *Victoria University of Wellington Law Review*, Vol. 46 (2015)

Mark Keating and Kirsty Maclaren, The Settlement of Tax Disputes: The Commissioner is Able But Not Willing, *New Zealand Journal of Taxation Law and Policy* Vol. 15, No. 4 (2009) 323

P.L. Reddy, Objecting to Discretionary Determinations by the Commissioner of Inland Revenue, *Victoria University of Wellington Law Review*, Vol. 11 (1981)

Adrian Sawyer, New Zealand Settles Disputes with Australian Banks, *Tax Notes International*, (2010)

Adrian Sawyer, A Further Bank Tax Dispute is Settled: A Recurrent Alternative to Litigation, *Journal of International Banking Law & Regulation*, Issue 3 (2016)31

Chapter 5

Mary Healy, Tax Appeals: Institute Response to TAC Consultation—September 2017, *Irish Tax Review*, November 4 (2017)

Diana van Hout, Chapter 19 in *Netherlands in EATLP International Tax Series*, Vol. 18 (2021)

Anna De Ambrosis Virgna and Dsariusz R. Kijowski, The Principle of Legitimate Expectations and the Protection of Trust in the Polish Administrative Law, *Bialostockie Studia Prawnicze*, Vol. 23, No. 2 (2018)

Esther Drabkin-Reiter, the Europeanization of the English and European Union Courts on the Protection of Legitimate Expectations in Administrative Law (2015), European University Institute

Roelof Vos, Mediating Tax Disputes in the Netherlands, Dutch-Flemish Magazine for Mediation and Conflict Management Journal, 2014 (18)

Paul Kraan, Chapter 19: Netherlands in The Tax Disputes and Litigation Review (7th edition), ed. by Simon Whitehead, *Law Business Research* 2019

Peter J. Wattle, Tax Litigation in Last Instance in the Netherlands: The Tax Chamber of the Supreme Court, Bulletin for International Taxation, January/February 2016

Francesco Cannas and Kristof Wauters, The Rise of Cooperative Compliance Programmes and the Rule of Law: A Comparison Between Belgium and Italy, *European Taxation*, December 2019

Florian Fiala and Lisa Ramharter, Cooperative Compliance in Austria, *European Taxation*, August 2019

Hugo Vollebregt, From Red Tape to Red Carpet: How the Netherlands Has Changed the Traditional Dispute Landscape for Tax Issues, *International Transfer Pricing Journal*, Vol. 16, No. 3 (2009)

Lisette van der Hel-van Dijk and Theo Poolen, Netherlands/International—Horizontal Monitoring in the Netherlands: At the Crossroads, *Bulletin for International Taxation*, November 12 (2013)

Job van del Pol, How to manage tax disputes in the Netherlands, *International Tax Review*, November 1 (2012)

Werner Penningstorf, The European Experience With Attorney Fee Shifting, Law And Contemporary Problems, *Duke University School of Law*, Vol. 47, No. 1 (1984)

Otto Marres, Chapter 13 in Courts and Tax Treaty Law, ed. Gulielmo Maisto, *EC and International Tax Law Series*, Vol. 3, IBFD (2007)

Marcel G.H. Schaper, 30 Years of Direct Tax Litigation Before the Court of Justice of the European Union: An Empirical Survey, *Bulletin for International Taxation*, April/May 2014

Stephen Daly, The Constitutional Implications of an EU Arm's Length Principle, *European Taxation*, February/March (2020)

A. Winckler; F.-C. Laprévote. Reconciling Legal Certainty, Legitimate Expectations, Equal Treatment and the Prohibition of State Aids. *European State Aid Law Quarterly*, June 2011 (10)/2

Chapter 6

B. Tran-Nam, Tax Reform and Tax Simplification: Conceptual and Measurement Issues and Australian Experiences in James/Sawyer/Budak (eds.): *The Complexity of Tax Simplification*, Palgrave Macmillan: Basingstoke

Thomas Hoppe, Tax Complexity in Australia—A Survey-Based Comparison to the OECD Average, Discussion Paper No. 251 (2020)

(15) Hirokata Minami, "*Kokuzei fufuku shinpansho no sousetsuki no kaiko*" (Reflection of the establishment of the National Tax Tribunal), *Jurist* No. 954 (1990)

(16) Seibei Yamashita, "*Keisoubi no sennmonteki funnsou kaiketsu shisutemu no yuuisei tokyougi wakai seido no hituyousei*" (Advantages of a lightly armed professional dispute resolution system and the need for a system of consultation and settlement), *Sozei Soushou* No. 6, Zaikei Shohosha (2012)

Albert Ehrenzweig, Reimbursement of Counsel Fees and the Great Society, *California Law Review*, Vol. 54 (1966)

Richard Falcon, Award of Attorneys' Fees in Civil Rights and Constitutional Litigation, *Maryland Law Review*, Vol. 33, No. 4 (1973)

Thomas D. Rowe, Jr., The Legal Theory of Attorney Fee Shifting: A Critical Overview, *Duke Law Journal*, Vol. 1982:651

Brian McLaughlin, Cheryl Tobias, and Craig Cameron, Interim Costs: The Impact of Okanagan Indian Band, UNB Law Journal, Revenue de Droit de L'un-B Vol/Tome 54 (2005)

Philippe Cavalieros, Litigation & Dispute Resolution (2nd Edition) Global Legal Group (2003)

(17) Kaoru Inaba, "T*orikeshi soshou no genkoku tekikaku*" (Standing to sue), ed. by Itsuo Sonobe, Gyousei (2006)

William S. Stinnette, Income Tax—Deductibility of Legal Expenses, *Washington Law Review*, Vol. 28, No. 1 (1953)

Table of List of Decisions/Rulings (in Chronological Order)

Chapter 1

Chapter 2

Chapter 3

Section 1 of Chapter 4

Section 2 of Chapter 4

Chapter 5

Chapter 6

Index

T

U

W